Stadtentwicklung zur Moderne – Die Entstehung großstädtischer Hafen- und Bürohausquartiere
Urban Development towards Modernism – The Birth of the Metropolitan Harbour and Commercial Districts

INTERNATIONAL COUNCIL ON MONUMENTS AND SITES
CONSEIL INTERNATIONAL DES MONUMENTS ET DES SITES
CONSEJO INTERNACIONAL DE MONUMENTOS Y SITIOS
МЕЖДУНАРОДНЫЙ СОВЕТ ПО ВОПРОСАМ ПАМЯТНИКОВ И ДОСТОПРИМЕЧАТЕЛЬНЫХ МЕСТ

Frank Pieter Hesse (Hrsg.)

Stadtentwicklung zur Moderne
Die Entstehung großstädtischer Hafen- und Bürohausquartiere

Urban Development towards Modernism
The Birth of the Metropolitan Harbour and Commercial Districts

Internationale Fachtagung, veranstaltet von ICOMOS Deutschland und der Kulturbehörde Hamburg/Denkmalschutzamt in Zusammenarbeit mit der HafenCity Universität Hamburg und der Sutor-Stiftung

International Conference organized by ICOMOS Germany and the Hamburg Ministry of Culture/Department for Heritage Preservation in Cooperation with the HafenCity University and the Sutor Foundation

Hamburg, 13./14. Oktober 2011

ICOMOS · HEFTE DES DEUTSCHEN NATIONALKOMITEES LIV
ICOMOS · JOURNALS OF THE GERMAN NATIONAL COMMITTEE LIV
ICOMOS · CAHIERS DU COMITÉ NATIONAL ALLEMAND LIV

ICOMOS Hefte des Deutschen Nationalkomitees
Herausgegeben vom Nationalkomitee der Bundesrepublik Deutschland
Präsident: Prof. Dr. Michael Petzet, München
Vizepräsident: Prof. Dr. Jörg Haspel, Berlin
Generalsekretär: Dr. Werner von Trützschler, Erfurt
Geschäftsstelle: Maximilianstraße 6, D-80539 München, Postanschrift: Postfach 100 517, 80079 München
Tel.: +49 (0)89 242 237 84, Fax: +49 (0)89 242 198 53, E-mail: icomos@icomos.de

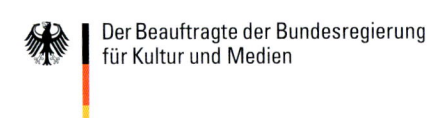

Der Beauftragte der Bundesregierung für Kultur und Medien

Gefördert vom Beauftragten der Bundesregierung für Kultur und Medien aufgrund eines Beschlusses des Deutschen Bundestages

Funded by the Federal Government Commissioner for Culture and the Media upon a Decision of the German Bundestag

Hamburg | Kulturbehörde   HCU HafenCity Universität Hamburg   Sutor-Stiftung

Gefördert von der Kulturbehörde Hamburg/Denkmalschutzamt in Zusammenarbeit mit der HafenCity Universität Hamburg und der Sutor-Stiftung

1. Auflage 2012
© 2012 ICOMOS, Nationalkomitee der Bundesrepublik Deutschland

Redaktionelle Arbeit/Editorial work: Romaine Becker und Dr. Agnes Seemann, Kulturbehörde Hamburg/Denkmalschutzamt

Abbildungsnachweis: Wenn nicht anders angegeben, wurden die Bilder von den Autoren und dem Bildarchiv des Denkmalschutzamtes bereitgestellt.

Die Deutsche Nationalbibliothek verzeichnet diese Publikation in der Deutschen Nationalbibliografie; detaillierte bibliografische Daten sind im Internet unter http://dnb.d-nb.de abrufbar.

Alle Rechte vorbehalten. Nachdruck, auch auszugsweise, sowie Verbreitung durch Film, Funk und Fernsehen, durch fotomechanische Wiedergabe, Tonträger und Datenverarbeitungssysteme jeglicher Art, nur mit schriftlicher Genehmigung des Verlages.

2012 Gesamtherstellung und Vertrieb:
hendrik **Bäßler** verlag · berlin
Fon: +49 (0)30.240 858 56 · Fax: +49 (0)30.249 26 53
E-Mail: info@baesslerverlag.de · Internet: www.baesslerverlag.de

ISBN 978-3-930388-17-2

Inhalt

Vorwort / Foreword 7

Grußwort der Kultursenatorin
der Freien und Hansestadt Hamburg 8

Welcome Address by the Ministry of Culture,
Free and Hanseatic City of Hamburg 10

Grußwort des Präsidenten von
ICOMOS Deutschland 12

Welcome Address by the
President of ICOMOS Germany 13

Grußwort des Präsidenten
der HafenCity Universität Hamburg 14

Welcome Address by the President
of the HafenCity University Hamburg 15

Grußwort der Sutor-Stiftung Hamburg 16

Welcome Address by the Sutor Foundation 17

Einführung / Introduction:
**Stadt und Hafen – Hafen und Stadt/
City and Harbour – Harbour and City**

Frank P. Hesse
Hamburg auf dem Weg zum Welterbe 20

Carola Hein
Port Cityspaces: Town and Harbour Development
in the Global Context 24

Robert Lee
The Social Life of Port Architecture: History,
Politics, Commerce and Culture 33

Dirk Schubert
Hamburg – Amphibische Stadt im
(inter-)nationalen Kontext 53

Speicherbauten / Warehouse Buildings:
**Deutsche Seehäfen und Speichergebäude/
German Seaports and Warehouse Buildings**

Ralf Lange
Die Hamburger Speicherstadt 64

Georg Skalecki
Speicherbauten in Bremen 79

**Speichergebäude und -komplexe in europäischen
Seehäfen / Warehouse Buildings and Districts
in European Seaports**

Antonella Caroli Palladini
The Old Port of Trieste: Characteristics and
Specificities of the Hydrodynamic Power Station
and the Warehouse District 88

John Hinchliffe
Liverpool Maritime Mercantile City World Heritage
Site: Lessons for the conservation and management
of port cities 95

Axel Föhl
Der Hafen von Antwerpen 101

Paul Meurs
Rotterdam: from Port City to Harbor Landscape ... 109

Axel Priebs
Der Südliche Freihafen in Kopenhagen 113

**Speicher- und Lagerkomplexe außerhalb Europas/
Warehouse and Storage Districts Beyond Europe**

Sara E. Wermiel
Shaped by Function: Boston's Historic Warehouses . 124

Alfredo Conti
Puerto Madero, Buenos Aires,
Evolution of a Warehouse Area 134

Bürohausbauten / Office Buildings:
**Das Hamburger Kontorhaus im (inter-)nationalen
Vergleich / The Hamburg Office Building in
(Inter-)national Comparison**

Carol Herselle Krinsky
The Office Building Architecture
of the Early 20th Century in New York 142

Kristen Schaffer
The Early Chicago Tall Office Building:
Artistically and Functionally Considered 148

Christopher Woodward
The Office Building Architecture
of the Early 20th Century in London 157

Herman van Bergeijk
Dutch Office Building 1900–1940:
A Question of Style or Mentality? 163

Vladimir Slapeta
Prag, die Entstehung der neuen Metropole 170

**Deutsche Bürohausarchitektur /
German Office Building Architecture**

Wolfgang Pehnt
Sehnsucht nach dem Anderen – Bürohäuser in den
Jahren des Expressionismus 178

Wolfgang Voigt
Deutsche Bürohausarchitektur 1924–1940 186

Robert Habel
Berliner City-Architektur (1871–1933) 195

**Das Hamburger Kontorhaus /
The Hamburg Office Buildings**

Jan Lubitz
Von der Kaufmannsstadt zur Handelsmetropole –
Entwicklung des Hamburger Kontorhauses
von 1886–1914 206

Ralf Lange
„Steigerung zum Monumentalen":
Das Kontorhausviertel mit Chilehaus,
Meßberghof, Sprinkenhof und Mohlenhof 215

Hartmut Frank
Die Hamburger Schule in der Architektur.
Höger, Schumacher, Schneider und andere 227

Redner / Speakers 236

Architektenregister 237

ICOMOS · Hefte des
Deutschen Nationalkomitees 238

Vorwort/Foreword

Die Freie und Hansestadt Hamburg beabsichtigt, sich 2014 mit dem Ensemble „Speicherstadt und Chilehaus mit Kontorhausviertel" um die Anerkennung als Weltkulturerbe zu bewerben.

Die zwischen 1883 und 1928 auf der Grundlage des Zollanschlusses Hamburgs an das Deutsche Reich entstandene Hamburger Speicherstadt bildet mit ihren 17 sieben- bis achtstöckigen Lagerhäusern in Backsteinbauweise, ihrer spezifischen funktionalen, baulichen und städtebaulichen Struktur mit Straßen, Wasserstraße, Eisenbahnanschlüssen und zwischengeschalteten Bauten das größte zusammenhängende, einheitlich geprägte Speicherensemble der Welt. Das 1922–24 von Fritz Höger errichtete Chilehaus gehört zu den bedeutendsten Leistungen des deutschen Backstein-Expressionismus und der Baugattung „Kontorhaus". Das Hamburger Kontorhausviertel, geprägt durch Chilehaus, Meßberg-, Sprinken- und Mohlenhof, ist eines der eindrucksvollsten Stadtbilder der 1920er Jahre in Deutschland und das erste reine Büroviertel auf dem europäischen Kontinent. Beide Ensembles von bedeutendem Umfang – im Überlieferungszustand und in einmaliger Konzentration eindrucksvolle Beiträge zur Entwicklung der europäischen Architektur des ausgehenden 19. und der ersten Hälfte des 20. Jahrhunderts sowie der zeitgenössischen Idealvorstellungen funktionaler Stadtplanung – befinden sich topografisch in enger Nachbarschaft und ergänzen sich in den wirtschaftlichen Funktionen.

Um die Bedeutung der Hamburger Ensembles in einen internationalen Kontext zu stellen, haben ICOMOS Deutschland und die Kulturbehörde Hamburg/Denkmalschutzamt in Zusammenarbeit mit der HafenCity Universität Hamburg und der Sutor-Stiftung 2011 eine internationale Tagung mit dem Thema „Stadtentwicklung zur Moderne – Zur Entstehung großstädtischer Hafen- und Kontorhausquartiere" veranstaltet, in der internationale Vergleichsbeispiele für beide Themenbereiche, d. h. sowohl für die Architektur von Speicherhaus-Komplexen um 1900 als auch für die moderne Bürohaus-Architektur der 1920er/30er Jahre präsentiert und diskutiert wurden. Über die Fragestellung hinaus, welche vergleichbaren Objekte es in anderen Ländern gibt, war dabei auch deren Überlieferungszustand von besonderem Interesse.

The Free and Hanseatic City of Hamburg is going to file a submission for recognition of the ensemble *Speicherstadt und Chilehaus mit Kontorhausviertel* (warehouses and complex of office buildings including Chilehaus) as world cultural heritage in 2014.

The *Hamburger Speicherstadt* (district of warehouses), built between 1883 and 1928, was the result of Hamburg's integration into the Customs Union of the German Empire. It consists of 17 brick warehouses with seven to eight storeys. This ensemble of warehouses is unique in terms of its specific functional and design features, because of the construction techniques employed and because of its contribution to the cityscape of Hamburg. The ensemble is structured by a network of streets, canals, railway lines and interspersed buildings. This makes it the largest integrated complex of uniformly designed warehouse buildings in the world. The *Chilehaus*, built by Fritz Höger between 1922 and 1924, is one of the most prominent achievements of German Brickwork Expressionism and a fine example of the *Kontorhaus* type of building (office block). Together, *Chilehaus*, *Meßberghof*, *Sprinkenhof* and *Mohlenhof* form the characteristic part of the *Hamburger Kontorhausviertel* which is one of the most impressive cityscapes dating from the 1920's in Germany. At the same time, it constitutes the first dedicated complex of office buildings on the European continent. Topographically, the two ensembles of *Kontorhausviertel* and *Speicherstadt* are close neighbours and complement each other in their functionalities. They are both of considerable size, have been preserved well and largely in their original shape, and, in their concentrated density, represent impressive contributions to the development of European architecture in the late 19th and the first half of the 20th century. Also, they have significantly contributed to the formation of the ideals of functional town planning at the time.

To put the Hamburg ensembles in an international context and give them the prominence they deserve, ICOMOS Germany and the Department for Heritage Preservation of the Hamburg Ministry of Cultural Affairs, in cooperation with the HafenCity University and the Sutor Foundation, in 2011 organised an international conference with the title "Urban Development towards Modernism – The Birth of the Metropolitan Harbour and Commercial Districts". During the conference, comparative international examples of both the architecture of warehouse complexes from around 1900 and of modern office buildings from the 1920's and 1930's were presented and discussed. The conference addressed not only the question of similar objects that exist elsewhere in the world, but also their respective state of preservation and repair.

Prof. Barbara Kisseler,
Kultursenatorin der Freien und Hansestadt Hamburg

Grußwort der Kultursenatorin der Freien und Hansestadt Hamburg

Sehr geehrte Abgeordnete der Hamburger Bürgerschaft, sehr geehrter Herr Lahr, sehr geehrter Herr Prof. Dr. Petzet, sehr geehrter Herr Dr. Pelka, sehr geehrter Herr Schoch, lieber Herr Hesse, sehr geehrte Damen und Herren,

ich begrüße Sie ganz herzlich im Namen des Senates der Freien und Hansestadt zum Internationalen Symposium: „Stadtentwicklung zur Moderne – Zur Entstehung großstädtischer Hafen- und Bürohausquartiere". Insbesondere unseren Referenten und Gästen aus Übersee gilt ein herzliches Willkommen in unserer Stadt. Wir freuen uns sehr, dass Sie unserer Einladung gefolgt sind und die Mühen der Reise auf sich genommen haben, um uns auf dieser Tagung zu unterstützen. Insbesondere freuen wir uns darauf, dass Sie uns mit Kenntnissen und Erkenntnissen anzureichern, die uns helfen, unserem Ziel näher zu kommen: Der Bewerbung der Speicherstadt und des Kontorhausviertels mit dem berühmten Chilehaus für die UNESCO-Liste des Welterbes.

Das Chilehaus und die Speicherstadt gehören neben unserem Hamburger Michel – der Hauptkirche St. Michaelis – bis heute zu den bekanntesten Wahrzeichen unserer Stadt. Kommen Touristen in unsere Stadt – und das sind nicht wenige – kommen sie auch ihretwegen. Viele Hamburger führen ihre Gäste gern dorthin – erst recht, seit die Speicherstadt aus dem Freihafengebiet entlassen und sie ein Bindeglied zur neuen HafenCity geworden ist. Dass wir an einem weiteren Wahrzeichen bauen, der Elbphilharmonie, wird die Attraktivität der bestehenden nicht schmälern – im Gegenteil: Schon durch ihre nachbarschaftliche Lage wird sich ihre Attraktivität steigern, da bin ich mir sehr sicher.

Über ihre Strahlkraft als Wahrzeichen hinaus tragen diese historischen Bauten und Quartiere vielfache Bedeutungen. Es sind Zeugnisse unserer Baugeschichte, der Stilgeschichte des Bauens in Deutschland, und auch des Städtebaus, dem letzten Endes wirtschaftliche Entwicklungen – um nicht zu sagen Umwälzungen – und entsprechende einschneidende historische politische Entscheidungen zugrundelagen, die weit über Hamburg hinaus Bedeutung hatten.

In den kommenden zwei Tagen werden Sie sich intensiv damit auseinandersetzen, in welchem geschichtlichen Kontext die Speicherstadt, das Chilehaus und sein umgebendes Kontorhausviertel auch im internationalen Vergleich stehen. Unser und vielleicht auch Ihr emotionaler Bezug zum Bild unserer Stadt, das wir schätzen und mit dem wir uns identifizieren, erlangt so noch einmal eine spannende, wissenschaftliche Fundierung.

Das Chilehaus war seit seinem Bau weltbekannt und ist einer der bedeutendsten Hamburger Welterbe-Kandidaten. Es wurde bis 1924 von dem Architekten Fritz Höger errichtet und gilt heute als die größte baukünstlerische Leistung des deutschen Backstein-Expressionismus. Es ist nicht nur eines der ersten Hochhäuser in Deutschland, sondern gehört auch zu den bedeutendsten „Kontorhäusern" der Welt. Dieser Bautyp dokumentiert in vielen Großstädten, wie sich deren Innenstadt-Bereiche von ihrer ursprünglichen Mischnutzung von Wohnen und Arbeiten zu einer rein kommerziellen Nutzung gewandelt haben. Das Kontorhausviertel um den Meßberg herum ist eines der eindrucksvollsten Stadtbilder der 1920er Jahre in Deutschland und das erste gewissermaßen monofunktionale Büroviertel auf dem europäischen Kontinent. Und die Hamburger Speicherstadt bildet das größte zusammenhängende, in städtischer Verantwortung geplante und einheitlich geprägte Lagerhausensemble der Welt aus der Zeit vom späten 19. bis in das erste Drittel des 20. Jahrhunderts.

Die beiden Ensembles vermitteln bis heute den historischen und funktionalen Zusammenhang von Warenlager, Warenumschlag und Handel, dessen papiergebundene und kommunikative Vorgänge mit dem Verlust der alten Kaufmannshäuser in die Kontore der Innenstadt zogen und sie so zur City machten. Hier wurde die wirtschaftliche Grundlage für den heutigen Wohlstand der Stadt gebildet und damit vieles, was Hamburg bis heute ausmacht – insbesondere sein verantwortungsbewusstes Bürgertum, das sich bis heute dadurch auszeichnet, dass es sich mit seinem Wohlstand kulturell und sozial für die Gesellschaft engagiert.

Solch einheitliche und mit vielen Details hervorragend erhaltenen Gebäudeensembles sind ein einmaliger Schatz, den es zu bewahren gilt. Dieses Erbe ist eine große Verantwortung, und daher möchte ich auch an dieser Stelle betonen: Hamburg steht in aller Konsequenz hinter der Welterbe-Bewerbung! Wir alle wissen, dass ein Bundesland und eine Stadt mit dem Welterbe eine besonders große Verpflichtung übernimmt – vor den Augen der Welt gewissermaßen. Jede neue städtebauliche Entwicklung, die in Bezug zum Chilehaus, zum Kontorhausviertel oder der Speicherstadt steht, jede neue Architektur innerhalb dieser Quartiere oder in ihrer Nachbarschaft werden sich an ihrer Verträglichkeit mit dem historischen Erbe messen lassen müssen. Dieser Verpflichtung muss und will Hamburg gerecht werden. Unter Denkmalschutz stehen die beiden Quartiere schon lange, die Verpflichtung auf die Einhaltung der Welterbekonvention werden wir in unserem Denkmalschutzgesetz verankern!

Wir freuen uns sehr, dass wir heute unsere große Fachtagung beginnen und dafür so viele internationale Fachreferenten haben gewinnen können – sei es aus den Niederlanden, Italien, Dänemark, der Tschechischen Republik oder Großbritannien, oder sogar aus den USA und Argentinien.

Sie, sehr verehrte Referenten, vermitteln uns historische Zusammenhänge über andere Hafenquartiere und Speicherstädte ebenso wie über Bürohausarchitektur des frühen 20. Jahrhunderts in aller Welt und sorgen dafür, dass wir über unseren hanseatischen Tellerrand weit hinausschauen können. Mit diesen internationalen Perspektiven können wir einen neuen, differenzierteren Blick auf unser Hamburger Erbe gewinnen und die Qualität unserer kommenden Bewerbung bei der UNESCO steigern, um sie letztlich zum Erfolg zu führen.

Weil wir gerade den Faust von Goethe in unserem Thalia-Theater spielen – beide Teile übrigens im 7-stündigen Marathon: Lassen Sie mich abschließend ihn zitieren:

„Was du ererbt von deinen Vätern hast,
erwirb es, um es zu besitzen!
Was man nicht nützt, ist eine schwere Last
Nur was der Augenblick erschafft, das kann er nützen."

Daran halten wir uns und die Eigentümer der Denkmäler sich gern: Das Chilehaus ist vor einigen Jahren restauriert und vollvermietet in guten Händen, ebenso wie die großen Kontorhäuser um es herum. Die Speicherstadt wird als Warenlager immer weniger gebraucht, aber umso mehr für die Kultur und die Kreativen – wie wir das hier sehen können, auch als Büros und für die Gastronomie. So wird das Erbe von Kontorhausviertel und Speicherstadt weiterhin gebraucht und genutzt und das hält die beiden am Leben und sichert ihnen die Zukunft. Das ist – so meine ich – eine der besten Voraussetzungen für die Anerkennung als Welterbe.

Zum Schluss sage ich meinen herzlichen Dank an die HafenCity-Universität für ihre große Unterstützung, sowohl bei der inhaltlichen Konzeption als auch bei der Ansprache der Referenten und durch eigene fachliche Beteiligung an dieser Tagung. Besonders danke ich Prof. Dr. Schubert, der mit seinen guten Kontakten in alle Welt maßgeblich dazu beigetragen hat, dass die heutige Tagung wissenschaftlich so hochkarätig besetzt ist. Ebenso tatkräftig bei der Vorbereitung unterstützt hat uns Herr Dr. Lange, der im Rahmen der Tagung selber zwei Beiträge vorstellt und Sie durch das Kontorhausviertel und die Speicherstadt führen wird.

Mein Dank geht ebenfalls an Sie, Herr Petzet, und das Deutsche Nationalkomitee von ICOMOS, für Ihre Bereitschaft, diese Tagung mit uns gemeinsam zu veranstalten und ihre Ergebnisse zu veröffentlichen. Und ich danke der Sutor-Stiftung, die mit ihrer finanziellen Unterstützung unser Zusammenkommen erst ermöglicht und die gesamte Vorbereitung kontinuierlich begleitet hat.

Eine solche Tagung mit mehreren Veranstaltern bringt es mit sich, dass – ehe Sie in die wissenschaftlichen Beiträge eintauchen – zunächst noch einige Grußworte erdulden müssen. Ich danke Ihnen hierzu für Ihre Aufmerksamkeit und wünsche Ihnen für die kommenden zwei Tage eine spannende Veranstaltung, viele Erkenntnisse und gute Anregungen!

Prof. Barbara Kisseler
Kultursenatorin der Freien und Hansestadt Hamburg

Welcome Address by the Ministry of Culture, Free and Hanseatic City of Hamburg

Members of the Hamburg Parliament, Mr. Lahr,
Prof. Dr. Petzet, Dr. Pelka, Mr. Schoch, Mr. Hesse,
Ladies and Gentlemen,

On behalf of the Senate of the Free and Hanseatic City of Hamburg I would like to cordially welcome you to the International UNESCO Expert Conference on „Urbanization to Modernism – Formation of Metropolitan Harbour and Commercial Districts". I would particularly like to welcome speakers and guests from across the Atlantic. We are happy to have you and very much appreciate the fact that you have taken the trouble of travelling this far. It is of great value to us that you should be lending us your support by giving us your knowledgeable input and insights. This will help us in our endeavour to nominate the *Speicherstadt* (warehouse district) and the *Kontorhausviertel* with the famous *Chilehaus* as UNESCO World Heritage.

In addition to our famous *Michel* (St. Michael's Church), *Chilehaus* and the *Speicherstadt* continue to be the best-known tourist sites of our city. A large proportion of those who come and visit our city – and we are indeed talking about a sizeable number of tourists – come here specially to see those sites. Many Hamburg citizens enjoy showing them to their guests, even more so since the *Speicherstadt* is no longer part of a freeport and now acts as a nexus to the *HafenCity*. You may be aware that we are in the process of building yet another landmark in Hamburg, namely the *Elbphilharmonie*. This latest addition to the cityscape of Hamburg will, if anything, further boost the attractiveness of existing tourist sites: I am very confident that, because all of these sites are situated in each other's vicinity, they will attract even more visitors to our city.

But quite apart from their significance as landmarks these buildings and districts carry historical meaning. They bear witness to our architectural history, the history of architectural styles in Germany as a whole and to city development. At the end of the day, these development processes were the result of radical economic changes and the corresponding political watershed decisions all of which had a wider significance far beyond the city of Hamburg.

Over the next two days, you will discuss in some detail the historical context of the *Speicherstadt*, *Chilehaus* and the surrounding office buildings, the *Kontorhausviertel*, and you will compare them to other similar buildings elsewhere in the world. The way we relate to Hamburg and its cityscape and perhaps even your emotional connection with it, too, will thus be given a new and fascinating scientific dimension. We greatly prize Hamburg's looks – the face of the city that is our home.

Right from its erection, the *Chilehaus* became world famous and it is now one of the most important candidates for the World Heritage List. The *Chilehaus* was built by the architect Fritz Höger and is today considered the greatest achievement within German red-brick expressionist building design. Not only is it one of the first high-rise buildings in Germany, but it also ranges among the most important *Kontorhäuser* (office buildings) of the world because it is this type of design and construction that evidences how the inner city areas of many metropolises changed at the time: Whereas before they used to be characterised by a mix of people who lived there and others who came for work, inner cities exclusively became the place for commerce. The *Kontorhausviertel* around *Meßberg* is one of the most impressive cityscapes from the 1920s in Germany. It can rightly claim to be the first multi-functional district of office buildings on the European continent. The *Speicherstadt* is the world's largest integrated complex of warehouses in a definable area and with a uniform appearance, planned and built by municipal authorities dating back to the period between the late 19th and the early 20th centuries.

Both *ensembles* to this day convey the historical and functional connections between warehouses, the handling and transshipment of goods and trade. Written and oral communication which were the organisational backbones of trade and commerce were no longer conducted in the old *Kaufmannshäuser* (merchants' houses), but moved to the central part of town turning it into the city. This is where the economic foundations were laid for the city's later prosperity and for many of the things that make Hamburg special and have characterized it over time. I am thinking particularly of the sense of responsibility among Hamburg's citizens who have consistently contributed both culturally and socially to the well-being of their community.

The buildings and complexes mentioned, with their uniform appearance and their many details, are cultural treasures which need to be preserved and require a great deal of responsibility on the part of the city. So let me underscore here that Hamburg is throwing its full weight behind the nomination of the two ensembles as World Heritage sites and will do justice to the responsibilities connected with that status. We are aware of the serious commitment that any federal state and city in Germany is making vis-à-vis the world when applying. Any new city development in relation to *Chilehaus*, the *Kontorhausviertel* or the *Speicherstadt* and any new piece of architecture within these districts or in their immediate vicinity will have to be checked against their compatibility with the historical heritage. Hamburg has firmly committed itself to respecting this. Both districts have long been listed, but the requirements of the World Heritage Convention still need to be enshrined in our Listed Buildings Act (Denkmalschutzgesetz).

We are both happy and proud to commence our expert conference today in the presence of so many international speakers who have come from the Netherlands, Italy, Denmark, the Czech Republic, Great Britain and even the US and Argentina. It is you, honoured speakers, who will contribute the international perspective to our deliberations at this conference by informing us about other port and warehouse districts as well as office architectures of the early 20th century and their historical contexts elsewhere in the world. You will thus be making sure that we get *outside of the box* of our Hanseatic viewpoints and approaches. Such an international perspective will sharpen our senses and make us view our local heritage even more discerningly. This, in turn, will further heighten the quality of our nominations and thereby contribute to their chances of success.

One of our big theaters, the *Thalia-Theater*, is putting on Goethe's *Faust* right now so let me quote from the seven hour marathon version being put on stage there:

What you have inherited from your fathers
Work on, that you may possess it.
That which you do not use will prove a burden
Only what is created by the moment will be profitable

These are words that we readily adhere to and so do the owners of the listed buildings: A few years ago, the *Chilehaus* was restored. It is in good hands and all of its office space is fully rented – the same is the case with the *Kontorhäuser* around it. The *Speicherstadt* is being used less and less for storing. Instead, by creative people and providers of cultural activities are arriving on the scene. As can be seen right here in this building, offices and catering companies, too, have moved in. In this way we are making sure that the heritage sites of *Kontorhausviertel* and the *Speicherstadt* continue to be in operation and remain alive. This will secure their future existence which I believe is one of the best guarantees for obtaining World Heritage status.

Let me conclude by thanking the HafenCity-University for their support of this conference both in terms of designing its structure and content, but also when it comes to contacting speakers and contributing their own expertise. I would particularly like to express my gratitude to Prof. Dr. Schubert. Through his excellent international contacts he has been instrumental in securing the participation of so many high-ranking scientists and researchers. Similarly, Dr. Lange has given us his full support. He will be making two presentations himself and will act as our guide through the *Speicherstadt*.

Also, I would like to thank Mr.Petzet and the German National Committee of ICOMOS for their willingness to organise this conference together with us and to publish its results. Furthermore, my thanks go to the Sutor Foundation which, through its financial support, has made it possible for us to meet and which has accompanied the entire preparation process for this conference.

As usual in a conference held jointly by several organisers you will have to endure several more introductory statements and greetings before you can delve into the scientific subject matter. I would like to anticipate my thanks for your patience in this regard and for your attention. For the coming two days I wish you a conference full of suspense, insights and good ideas!

Prof. Barbara Kisseler
Ministry of Culture, Free and Hanseatic City of Hamburg

Grußwort des Präsidenten von ICOMOS Deutschland

Die Konferenz „Stadtentwicklung zur Moderne/Zur Entstehung großstädtischer Hafen- und Bürohausquartiere" (Hamburg, 13.–14. Oktober 2011) in Zusammenarbeit mit der HafenCity Universität Hamburg sowie der Sutor-Stiftung, gemeinsam veranstaltet von ICOMOS Deutschland und dem Denkmalschutzamt der Kulturbehörde Hamburg, war eine internationale Fachtagung, bei der ich auch zahlreiche ausländische Experten begrüßen konnte, darunter unser Kollege Alfredo Conti, Vizepräsident von ICOMOS International und Präsident von ICOMOS Argentinien. Die von Frau Senatorin Prof. Barbara Kisseler eröffnete Veranstaltung setzte die bewährte Kooperation von ICOMOS Deutschland mit der Stadt Hamburg fort, die bereits zu einem ersten internationalen ICOMOS Symposium in Hamburg-Bergedorf (14.–17. Oktober 2008) geführt hatte: „Cultural Heritage of Astronomical Observatories/From Classical Astronomy to Modern Astrophysics" (veröffentlicht als Bd. XVIII der Reihe *Monuments and Sites*, Berlin 2009). Die hier als Band LIV der Reihe *Hefte des Deutschen Nationalkomitees* veröffentlichten Ergebnisse sind ebenso wie die Ergebnisse des Symposiums über die Observatorien ein weiterer Beitrag zu den von der UNESCO geforderten globalen thematischen Studien. ICOMOS ist ja im Rahmen der Welterbekonvention von 1972 Berater der UNESCO und hat schon mehrfach auf die globale Strategie für eine repräsentative, ausgewogene und glaubwürdige Welterbeliste mit speziellen Studien reagiert, darunter die Publikation „The World Heritage List/Filling the Gaps – An Action Plan for the Future" (Bd. XII der Serie *Monuments and Sites*, München 2005), der sogenannte Lückenreport, der in einem typologischen, chronologisch-regionalen und thematischen Rahmenwerk mögliche Lücken in der bestehenden Welterbeliste aufzeigt, sowie die Publikation „The World Heritage List/What is OUV?" (Bd. XVI der Reihe *Monuments and Sites*, Berlin 2008).

ICOMOS Deutschland, das sich im Rahmen des Preventive Monitoring schon seit Jahren mit einer Arbeitsgruppe unter der Leitung von Giulio Marano um die deutschen Welterbestätten kümmert, befasst sich mit denkmalpflegerischen Fragen unterschiedlichster Art und ist als Berater auch in dem erfolgreichen Programm des Bundesbauministeriums für die nationalen Welterbestätten tätig. Die Stadt Hamburg ist in der Vorschlagsliste der Bundesrepublik Deutschland für das Weltkulturerbe mit einem bemerkenswerten Vorschlag vertreten: Speicherstadt und Chilehaus mit Kontorhausviertel, ein Vorschlag, dessen Bedeutung sich im Rahmen von globalen Vergleichsstudien erschließt, zu denen unsere Hamburger Konferenz eine Fülle von neuen Aspekten beigetragen hat.

Das Kontorhausviertel zwischen Steinstraße und Meßberg, „eines der eindrucksvollsten Stadtbilder der 20er Jahre in Deutschland" (zit. nach Dehio, Handbuch der deutschen Kulturdenkmäler, Hamburg 1971) hat sich aus einem Sanierungsprojekt an der Stelle eines früheren Gängeviertels der Altstadt als ein geschlossener Komplex von Bürohäusern entwickelt, mit dem wie ein Eisbrecher wirkenden Chilehaus als Gallionsfigur, mit dem ehem. Ballinhaus (Meßberghof), Sprinkenhof und Mohlenhof ein einzigartiges Ensemble in dem für Hamburg charakteristischen „Backsteinstil", der auch in der künstlerischen Ausgestaltung der Fassaden und im Innern der Gebäude expressionistische Motive einsetzt. Während im Kontorhausviertel die ursprüngliche Nutzung als Bürohäuser weiterbesteht, kann die in den 1880er Jahren als Teil des Freihafens entstandene Speicherstadt, ein bedeutendes Dokument der Hamburger Hafen- und Handelsgeschichte, unter den heutigen Rahmenbedingungen nur in Verbindung mit sich anbietenden neuen Nutzungskonzepten in ihrer charakteristischen Struktur erhalten werden. Außerdem wandelt sich das Umfeld der als Ensemble geschützten „Insel" der Speicherstadt, die ihre Ziegelbautraditionen beim Wiederaufbau nach den Zerstörungen des Zweiten Weltkriegs bewahrt hat, durch das neue Akzente setzende Großprojekt HafenCity Hamburg und den noch unvollendeten Bau der Elbphilharmonie.

Unter diesen Voraussetzungen sind neben dem in mancher Hinsicht einzigartigen Kontorhausviertel die in unserer Konferenz vorgestellten Vergleichsstudien zur Hamburger Speicherstadt von besonderem Interesse, der Blick auf „historic urban landscapes" von historischen Hafenstädten mit ihren speziellen Einrichtungen, darunter bereits in der Welterbeliste verzeichnete Städte wie Valparaiso (eingetragen 2003) und Liverpool (eingetragen 2004). Im Namen des Deutschen Nationalkomitees von ICOMOS gilt mein Dank den Autoren für ihre Beiträge sowie den Hamburger Kollegen vom Denkmalschutzamt, Frank Pieter Hesse, Dr. Agnes Seemann und Romaine Becker für die hervorragende Organisation und die Vorbereitung der im hendrik Bäßler verlag · berlin erschienenen Publikation. Besonderer Dank für die Förderung und Finanzierung der Drucklegung gilt schließlich dem Beauftragten der Bundesregierung für Kultur und Medien.

Prof. Dr. Michael Petzet

Welcome Address by the President of ICOMOS Germany

The conference "Urbanization to Modernism / Formation of Metropolitan Harbour and Commercial Districts" (Hamburg, 13–14 October 2011), jointly organized by ICOMOS Germany and the Hamburg Ministry of Culture / Department for Heritage Preservation in cooperation with the HafenCity University and the Sutor Foundation, was an international meeting where I could also welcome a number of foreign experts, among them our colleague Alfredo Conti, Vice President of ICOMOS International and President of ICOMOS Argentina. This conference opened by Senator Prof. Barbara Kisseler was once again a successful cooperation between ICOMOS Germany and the City of Hamburg, the earlier cooperation being the symposium in Hamburg-Bergedorf on "Cultural Heritage of Astronomical Observatories / From Classical Astronomy to Modern Astrophysics" (14–17 October 2008; published as vol. XVIII in the *Monuments and Sites* series, Berlin 2009). Both the conference proceedings in this vol. LIV of the Journals of the German National Committee and the proceedings of the symposium on observatories are contributions to the global thematic studies of ICOMOS as advisory body to UNESCO. ICOMOS has already reacted several times to the global strategy for a representative, balanced and credible World Heritage List through specialized studies, for instance through the publication "The World Heritage List / Filling the Gaps – An Action Plan for the Future" (vol. XII of the *Monuments and Sites* series, Munich 2005), the so-called Gap Report which in a typological, chronological-regional and thematic framework lists possible gaps in the existing World Heritage List; and with the publication "The World Heritage List / What is OUV?" (vol. XVI of the *Monuments and Sites* series, Berlin 2008).

ICOMOS Germany, which as part of Preventive Monitoring has been looking after the German World Heritage sites for years with the help of a working group (chaired by Giulio Marano), concerns itself with a wide variety of conservation matters, and as advisor is also involved in the successful program of the Federal Building Ministry for national World Heritage sites. The City of Hamburg is represented on the German tentative list for the World Heritage with a remarkable proposal: the Chilehaus with office building district and adjoining warehouse district – a proposal whose significance becomes apparent in global comparative studies, to which the Hamburg conference has added many new aspects.

The office building district between Steinstrasse and Meßberg, "one of the most remarkable townscapes of the 1920s in Germany" (Dehio, Handbuch der deutschen Kulturdenkmäler, Hamburg 1971), developed from a rehabilitation project at the site of a former quarter with narrow alleyways in the old town and became an entire complex of office buildings, with the Chilehaus as figurehead looking like an icebreaker, the former Ballinhaus (Meßberghof), the Sprinkenhof and the Mohlenhof. Together they form an outstanding ensemble in the "brick style" characteristic for Hamburg, also using Expressionist motifs on the facades and inside the buildings. While the office building district is still used in the original way, the warehouse district, erected in the 1880s as part of the free-trade zone and an important testimony to the history of Hamburg's port and trade, today can only be preserved in its characteristic structure by allowing new utilization concepts. Furthermore, while the warehouse "isle" itself is protected as an ensemble, also due to the fact that the brick tradition was continued after the war destructions, the surroundings are presently in a process of change, i.e. through the mega project HafenCity Hamburg creating new landmarks and the not yet completed Elbphilharmonie.

Given these preconditions, apart from the office building district outstanding in many respects, the comparative studies for the warehouse district presented at our conference are of particular interest, i.e. studies that look at "historic urban landscapes" of historic harbor cities with their specific infrastructure, among them cities already on the World Heritage List, such as Valparaiso (listed in 2003) and Liverpool (listed in 2004). On behalf of the German National Committee of ICOMOS I would like to thank the authors for their contributions and the colleagues at the Hamburg Department for Heritage Preservation, Frank Pieter Hesse, Dr. Agnes Seemann and Romaine Becker, for the excellent organization and preparation of this publication printed by hendrik Bäßler verlag · berlin. Finally, we would like to thank the Federal Government Commissioner for Culture and the Media for the generous funding of this publication.

Prof. Dr. Michael Petzet

Grußwort des Präsidenten der HafenCity Universität Hamburg

Sehr geehrte Frau Senatorin Prof. Kisseler, sehr geehrter Herr Prof. Petzet, sehr geehrter Herr Schoch, sehr geehrter Herr Hesse, meine Damen und Herren,

als Präsident der HafenCity Universität darf ich mich mit einem Grußwort anschließen. Schon der Name unserer Universität legt es nahe, sich mit Themen an der Schnittstelle von Hafen und Stadt zu beschäftigen. Für die auswärtigen Gäste, die mit unserer Universität nicht vertraut sind, darf ich anschließen, dass die 2006 gegründete HafenCity Universität – Universität für Baukunst und Metropolenentwicklung – eine kleine, fokussierte Universität ist, die (endlich) 2013 ihr neues Gebäude in der HafenCity beziehen wird.

Um die Chancen, die sich aus der Gründung einer so spezialisierten Universität ergeben, auch wirklich nutzbar zu machen, haben wir eine öffentliche Debatte über die drängenden Fragen der Entwicklung, der Gestaltung und der Zukunft unserer gebauten Welt begonnen. Wir wollen die Lehr- und Forschungsschwerpunkte unserer Fachgebiete hinterfragen, eigene Stärken innerhalb dieser Fachgebiete herausarbeiten, innovative Themen und Methoden unserer zukünftigen Ausrichtung an den Schnittstellen der Disziplinen definieren sowie inter- und transdisziplinäre Lern- und Forschungsfelder entwickeln. Gemeinsam wollen wir neue Lösungsansätze für die Probleme unserer Städte im 21. Jahrhundert entwickeln. Die Metropolregion Hamburg bildet einen faszinierenden Experimentierraum für zukunftsfähige Lösungen im Zeitalter der Globalisierung. In der dynamischen Hafenstadt liegen die Zukunftsthemen „vor der Tür" und in besonderem Maße am Wasser.

Hamburg ist nicht nur eine Seehafenstadt „am Fluss", sondern zugleich eine Metropole „im Fluss", um diese beliebte Metapher zu verwenden. Bilder und Szenen von Hamburg sind ohne Hafen kaum vorstellbar. Es gibt ein ganzes Genre von Belletristik über Hamburg als „Tor zur Welt", über hafenstädtisches Milieu, die „Welthafenstadt" und das besondere Ambiente, das die „Warenmarke Hamburg" ausmachen.

Der Umbau der Uferzone und die Revitalisierung der Waterfront bieten mit der HafenCity die Jahrhundertchance, Hafen und Stadt zu einer neuen, zukunftsfähigen Symbiose zu verschmelzen. Der Bewusstseinswandel und die positive Neubewertung von diesen vormals brach gefallenen Hafen- und Uferzonen lässt sich auch am Einstellungswandel der Öffentlichkeit und an einem beifälligen Medienecho festmachen. Noch bis vor gut einem Jahrzehnt waren diese Bereiche noch weitgehend aus dem täglichen Erlebnisbereich der Stadtbevölkerung verdrängt.

Aber diese Gestaltung der Zukunft ist ohne die Gegenwart und Einbeziehung der Vergangenheit nicht leistbar. Mit der Speicherstadt haben wir in unmittelbarer Nähe zur Hafen-City einen einmaligen Bestand an historischen Speichergebäuden und weiter nördlich schließt sich – mit ähnlichen Alleinstellungsmerkmalen – das Kontorhausviertel an. Zwei besondere Ensembles, um die uns Kolleginnen und Kollegen in anderen Seehafenstädten beneiden und die es zu erhalten und weiter – unter Berücksichtigung des Denkmalschutzes – zu nutzen und zu pflegen gilt. Die beiden Quartiere liegen nicht nur räumlich in enger Nachbarschaft sondern ergänzen sich mit ihren spezialisierten Funktionszuweisungen der Güterlagerung und des Warenhandels. Beide Areale sind nicht nur Symbole für Wirtschaftskraft der Hafenstadt sondern zugleich bedeutende Symbole hamburgischer Baukultur.

Ich freue mich, dass Prof. Carola Hein und Prof. Dirk Schubert von der HafenCity Universität an diesem Projekt mitgearbeitet haben und ihre Kontakte genutzt werden konnten, um dieses spannende Tagungsprogramm zusammen zu stellen. Wir hoffen, dass die Bewerbung Hamburgs mit diesen beiden Arealen um den Status als Weltkulturerbe auf den Weg gebracht und dann auch erfolgreich abgeschlossen werden kann.

Ich darf Ihnen für die Tagung interessante Vorträge und spannende Diskussionen wünschen, vor allem aber hoffe ich, dass Sie selbst Speicherstadt und Kontorhausviertel kennen und wertschätzen lernen – und wiederum, dass wir mehr über ähnliche Areale und Baudenkmäler in anderen Seehäfen erfahren.

Dr. Ing. Walter Pelka

Welcome Address by the President of the HafenCity University Hamburg

Senator Prof. Kisseler, Prof. Petzet, Mr. Schoch, Mr. Hesse, Ladies and Gentlemen,

In my capacity as President of HafenCity University it is my privilege to continue the round of introductory statements. The name of our university says it all: It seems natural that we at HafenCity University should dedicate ourselves to the interface between the port and the city. For those of you who have come here from abroad let me tell you that the HCU – its full title is *University of the Built Environment and Metropolitan Development* – was established in 2006. It is a small, highly focused university. At long last, in 2013 we will be able to move into our new building.

In order to fully benefit from the opportunities that such a highly specialised university offers, we have started a general public debate about the most pressing issues concerning the development, the shaping and design as well as the future of our built environment. We would like to question the didactics and focuses of our scientific disciplines. We want to develop our strengths in the various subjects. Also, we strive to define the innovative issues and methods of our future orientation at the interfaces of separate disciplines. And we wish to develop interdisciplinary and transdisciplinary didactic and research approaches. We aim to jointly develop new solutions for the problems of our cities in the 21st century. As a metropolis, Hamburg offers an excellent playground for solutions that need to be compatible with the future requirements of the globalisation age. In this dynamic port city the issues of the future that we must tackle are particularly visible, in fact, you could say they are on our doorstep, more particularly on the waterfront.

Hamburg is not only a city which has a seaport and is situated on a river, but a metropolis that has to *go with the flow* to use a popular local phrase. It is almost inconceivable to take or show photographs or films of Hamburg without the port featuring in them. Poets and literati have been prolific in their *oeuvre* about Hamburg and they describe it as the *Gateway to the World* and a *World Port City*. They speak of the *Hamburg Brand* and the special atmosphere that prevails in this city.

Restructuring and revitalising the water front offers a unique and opportunity to bring together the port and the city the port and the city so they can form a symbiotic whole with a future. Changes in attitude and a positive new appreciation of the formerly derelict port and embankment zones are palpable in the public and in the media. Until fairly recently, these zones played hardly any part in the everyday lives of the people of Hamburg, in fact, that was the case until around a decade ago.

But the future cannot be shaped without recourse to the present and without making reference to the past. Right next to the *HafenCity*, the *Speicherstadt* constitutes a unique example of a series of historical warehouses. Further to the North and adjacent to it is the *Kontorhausviertel* (complex of old store houses buildings). These two ensembles are the envy of many a colleague in other seaport cities. They must be preserved and should continue to be used and well looked-after – due respect being given, of course, to the requirements of heritage preservation. Not only are the two ensembles very close to one another, but their functions of storing goods and conducting trade, respectively, complement each other. They both symbolize the economic might of the port city and at the same time epitomize typical local building traditions.

I am very pleased that Prof. Carola Hein and Prof. Dirk Schubert from the HafenCity University were able to contribute to this exciting agenda of the conference with lectures. We hope, that the launch of the nomination of these two ensembles as World Heritage sites will be crowned by success.

I wish you interesting presentations and thought-provoking discussions during this conference and I hope that you will have the opportunity to get to know for yourselves both *Speicherstadt* and *Kontorhausviertel*; that you will come to appreciate them, and, that we will all learn a great deal about similar cityscapes and heritage buildings in other seaports the world over.

Dr. Ing. Walter Pelka

Grußwort der Sutor-Stiftung Hamburg

Sehr geehrte Frau Senatorin Kisseler,
sehr geehrter Herr Präsident Pelka, sehr geehrte Vertreter des ICOMOS, sehr geehrte Gäste und Teilnehmer,

auch ich möchte Sie herzlich im Herzen von Hamburg begrüßen. Mein Name ist Dirk C. Schoch und ich leite die Sutor-Stiftung. Wir freuen uns über die Zusammenarbeit zum Wohle der Baukultur.

Die Sutor-Stiftung fördert die Wissenschaft der Architektur und der Technik. Werner Sutor gründete seine Stiftung im Jahr 1984. Aufgewachsen in einer hanseatischen Banktradition, gehörte seine Leidenschaft den Details in der Architektur und technischen Konstruktionen.

Aber seine Leidenschaft gehört viel mehr Dingen, der Kunst, Büchern, Städten und Konstruktionen, Schiffen, Eisenbahnen, Flugzeugen und noch viele mehr. Sein Credo könnte lauten: „Die Architektur ist die Mutter aller Künste".

Die Familien-Tradition begann schon viel früher. Werner Sutors Ur-Ur-Großvater, Carl Ludwig Wimmel, war der erste Stadtbaudirektor. Und zwar in der Zeit des grossen Hamburger Brandes 1842, der fast die Hälfte der zentralen Stadt Hamburgs zerstörte.

Wimmel plante in einem Gebiet, dass sich vom westlichen Ende der Speicherstadt bis zum Chilehaus erstreckte. Das Wissen dazu verdankte er seiner guten und breiten Ausbildung. Er war früh gefördert worden und reiste mit Unterstützung der Patriotischen Gesellschaft nach Rom und London. Heutzutage folgt die Sutor-Stiftung dieser Tradition und fördert Auslandsstipendien und Promotionen.

Die Sutor-Stiftung ist sehr froh, dass wir alle heute die Qualität von Hafenstädten, Lagerhäusern und Kontorhäusern untersuchen. In unserem Interesse stehen die Speicherstadt und das Chilehaus. Lassen Sie uns gemeinsam auf die Details schauen und die Qualitäten erkennen.

Ich danke Ihnen für Ihre Teilnahme und wünsche uns eine interessante Arbeit und eine gute Zeit in Hamburg.

Dirk C. Schoch

Welcome Address by the Sutor Foundation

Dear Frau Senatorin Prof. Kisseler, dear Mr. President Pelka, dear representatives of ICOMOS, dear guests and participants,

I would like to welcome you all to Hamburg. My name is Dirk Schoch and I am the manager of the Sutor-Stiftung, which is a foundation for science – in architecture and technology.

Werner Sutor founded the Sutor-Stiftung in 1984. Grown up in a Hanseatic banking tradition, his biggest interests were the knowledge of technical mechanisms and the details in architecture.

But he was interested in much more, nearly everything: arts, construction, ships, airplanes and so on. His credo could have been: "Architecture is the mother of all arts!"

The family tradition started much earlier. Sutor's great-grandfather, Carl Ludwig Wimmel, was the first "Stadtbaudirektor", director of urban planning.

It was the time of the great fire in 1842, which razed nearly half the city centre of Hamburg. So Wimmel planned the area from the west end of the "Speicherstadt", up to the "Chilehaus". He built the stock exchange, which is close to the city hall.

Carl Ludwig Wimmel's knowledge was based on a broad education. He traveled to other countries, sent by the "Patriotische Gesellschaft" to Rome and to London. Nowadays the Sutor-Foundation follows this tradition by sending graduate students to other universities abroad.

Today we are very glad that all of you are here and will discuss the quality of Port Cities and Harbour Buildings, Speicherstadt and Chilehaus. Let us look at the details and the quality of architecture.

Thank you very much for being here. I hope you will have an interesting conference and a good time in Hamburg.

Dirk C. Schoch

HANSESTADT HAMBURG

»DEUTSCHLAND«
ZEITSCHRIFT FÜR INDUSTRIE, HANDEL U. SCHIFFAHRT

THE HANSEATIC TOWN OF HAMBURG · LA CIUDAD HANSEATICA HAMBURGO · LA VILLE HANSÉATIQUE DE HAMBOURG

Einführung / Introduction
Stadt und Hafen – Hafen und Stadt
City and Harbour – Harbour and City

Frank Pieter Hesse

Hamburg auf dem Weg zum Welterbe

Sehr geehrte Frau Senatorin Kisseler, sehr geehrter Herr Lahr, lieber Herr Petzet, lieber Herr Pelka, sehr geehrte Kolleginnen und Kollegen, meine Damen und Herren,

in der Diskussion um die Hamburger Welterbekandidaten wird häufig betont, dass Hamburg das einzige deutsche Bundesland sei, das noch kein Objekt auf der großen UNESCO-Liste des Welterbes habe. Dies sei gleich vorweg gesagt: das ist nicht der Grund, dass wir Anlauf genommen haben, gleich zwei Areale auf den Weg zum Welterbe zu schicken. Die Welterbestätten sind eine nationale Angelegenheit der Staaten, die der Welterbekonvention beigetreten sind, und es ist der föderalen Struktur unseres Staates geschuldet, dass wir uns mit den anderen Bundesländern einigen müssen, wann welche Stätte beim Welterbekomitee zur Nominierung ansteht.

1998 wurde die letzte Tentativliste mit 22 Positionen von der Ständigen Konferenz der Kultusminister der Länder beschlossen, jetzt stehen noch immer 11 Positionen zur Aufnahme an, von denen die eine oder andere schon in Paris vorgelegt worden war, vom Welterbekomitee jedoch nicht zur Aufnahme beschlossen wurde. Ein solches Schicksal wollen wir uns gern ersparen und daher legen wir auf eine sorgfältige Begründung des *outstanding universal value* der Hamburger Stätten äußerst großen Wert. Wir wollen übernächstes Jahr unsere Bewerbung bei der Kultusministerkonferenz einreichen, um sie dann ein Jahr später auf die Reise nach Paris zu schicken.

Es waren damals, 1998, zu Zeiten der Installation der letzten, noch gültigen deutschen Tentativliste, noch vergleichsweise einfache Bedingungen, unter denen die Welterbe-Bewerbungen eingereicht werden konnten. Weder musste der *outstanding universal value* vorab dargelegt werden noch sollte ein Managementplan über die künftigen Bedingungen der Erhaltung des Welterbes Auskunft geben. Umfassten die Operational Guidelines in ihrer ersten Fassung 1977 noch 16 Seiten mit 28 Artikeln, so hätten wir damals immerhin 139 Paragrafen zu beachten gehabt – heute sehen wir einem umfangreichen Dokument mit 290 Paragrafen gegenüber! So sind auch die Anforderungen an die Darstellung des möglichen Welterbes, seiner Geschichte, seines Erhaltungszustandes, die Darlegung seiner Authentizität und Integrität, die Maßstäbe für die internationalen Vergleiche stetig gestiegen. Die Bewerbungsschriften sind zu dicken Büchern geworden.

Zu einem Bestandteil der Bewerbungen sind zwischenzeitlich auch die Konferenzen geworden, in denen der Typus des Kandidaten von fachkundigen Experten einem in der Regel internationalen Vergleich unterzogen wird, um nachzuweisen, dass das in Frage stehende Objekt den Vergleich nicht zu scheuen braucht, ja aus allen ähnlichen mit einer gewissen Einzigartigkeit und globalem Geltungsanspruch als Erbe der Menschheit herausragt.

Die jüngsten Welterbeprojekte in der Bundesrepublik Deutschland, die sich dann wohl 2015 auf der nächsten Tentativliste finden werden, wurden bereits zusammen mit ICOMOS auf entsprechenden Tagungen vorbereitet:

– 2008 in Hamburg die Sternwarten an der Wende vom 19. zum 20. Jahrhundert in der Absicht, die Hamburger Sternwarte im Rahmen einer transnationalen seriellen Bewerbung ebenfalls auf den Weg zur Welterbeliste zu schicken.
– 2010 in Baden-Baden die „Europäischen Kurstädte und Modebäder des 19. Jahrhunderts" ebenfalls im Hinblick auf transnationale serielle Bewerbungen
– 2011 in Berlin Jüdische Friedhöfe des 19. Jahrhunderts und
– ebenfalls dieses Jahr in Hamburg insbesondere jüdische Friedhöfe aus dem 17. Jahrhundert, die der Sefarden, die mit ihrer migrationsbedingten weltumspannenden Sepulkralkultur ein Welterbe im Wortsinne darstellen.

So steht auch diese Konferenz in der Absicht, für unsere beiden Ensembles, die Speicherstadt und das Kontorhausviertel Vergleichbares zu sichten und zu bewerten.

Seit 1998 sind fast 15 Jahre vergangen, als die Freie und Hansestadt Hamburg Fritz Högers Chilehaus über die Ständige Konferenz der Kultusminister der deutschen Bundesländer auf die deutsche Tentativliste setzen ließ – jene legendäre 1922–24 errichtete Inkunabel des deutschen Backstein-Expressionismus. Es steht seitdem auf Position 19 dieser Liste, die insgesamt 22 nationale Nominierungsvorhaben und weitere fünf transnationale serielle Nominierungsprojekte umfasste. Angesichts der hinteren Position des Hamburger Objektes auf dieser Liste gab es zunächst keine größeren Anstrengungen, den Aufnahmeantrag vorzubereiten.

Erst im Juni 2005 startete das Verlagshaus Gruner + Jahr mit der Verlegerin Angelika Jahr an der Spitze und im Verbund mit der Deutschen Umwelthilfe die Initiative „UNESCO Modernes Erbe Hamburg" – eingebettet in das größere Projekt „Lebendige Elbe", das sich der Kulturlandschaft des Flusses von der Quelle bis zur Mündung verschrieben hatte. Das heute am Baumwall residierende Verlagshaus hatte in seiner Gründungszeit Mitte der 1960er Jahre seine Büros im Chilehaus und im Sprinkenhof – daher seine besondere Beziehung und Initiative für das Quartier. Diese Initiative setzte sich für eine Erweiterung des Hamburger Welterbekandidaten Chilehaus auf das Kontorhausviertel und die angrenzende Speicherstadt ein und für eine Vorverlegung des Nominierungsjahres auf 2007. Promoter der Initiative war der Gründungsdirektor des Welterbezentrums, Prof. Bernd von Droste zu Hülshoff, der aufgrund der Hinwendung des Welterbezentrums zum Erbe der Moderne gute Aussichten sah, dass Hamburg mit seinen relativ jungen Kandidaten auf der berühmten Liste Aufnahme findet. Und die 2004 von ICOMOS veröffentlichte Studie „Filling the Gaps" gab ihm Recht, denn das Erbe der Moderne, der Industrialisierungszeit ist auf der Welterbeliste noch immer schwach vertreten.

Die Initiative stieß bei den Eigentümern der Liegenschaften durchaus auf große Zustimmung: So bei der Hamburger Hafen und Logistik Aktiengesellschaft, die man hier HHLA nennt und die seit der Ausgründung des Freihafens 1888 für das Management des Hafens zuständig ist. Der für die Immobilien, also auch die Speicherstadt zuständige Vorstand Roland Lappin sagte damals – und das ist auch heute noch seine Auffassung: *„Wir glauben, dass dieses bauhistorisch wie hafengeschichtlich einzigartige Quartier in ganz besonderer Weise dafür prädestiniert ist, Hamburgs Beitrag zum Weltkulturerbe darzustellen. Wir freuen uns darauf, gemeinsam mit unseren Partnern das Projekt ‚UNESCO Modernes Erbe Hamburg' zum Erfolg zu führen."* Auch die Eigentümerin des Chilehauses, die Union Investment Real Estate GmbH, und die der anderen bedeutenden Kontorhäuser Sprinkenhof und Meßberghof und die sie vereinende Interessengemeinschaft Kontorhausviertel stimmten in den zustimmenden Chor ein. Ein internationales Expertentreffen sollte mit Unterstützung der Kulturbehörde noch 2005 stattfinden. Allerdings sollte es doch noch sechs Jahre dauern, bis es dazu kam: hier und heute.

Auf wenig Gegenliebe stieß damals jedoch in der städtischen Politik und Verwaltung die Absicht der Vorverlegung der Bewerbung, denn seit einigen Jahren war die so genannte HafenCity im Entstehen, deren gedeihliches Wachstum in unmittelbarer Nachbarschaft zur Speicherstadt man nicht durch weitere Reglementierungen gefährdet sehen wollte, schon gar nicht aus supranationaler Perspektive, die Diskussion um das Dresdener Elbtal war ja bereits im vollen Gange. Auch die gerade geborene Idee der Nutzung des vormaligen Kaispeichers A auf der Spitze des Kaiserkais für ein großes, die Speicher um mehr als das Doppelte überragendes Konzerthaus – die Elbphilharmonie – sollte frei bleiben von Mutmaßungen über ihre mögliche Gefährdung durch das Welterbevorhaben. Das Projekt am anderen Ende der Speicherstadt auf der Ericusspitze, das die alten Speicherbauten ebenfalls mächtig überragende neue Verlagsgebäude des SPIEGEL, war damals noch nicht entworfen – heute ist es fertig und in Nutzung.

Dem Gedanken einer Erweiterung der Welterbekandidatur über das Chilehaus hinaus konnte die Kulturbehörde allerdings und hier das Denkmalschutzamt durchaus etwas abgewinnen. Wir bereiteten daher die Texte für die Erweiterung unserer Position auf der deutschen Tentativliste vor und übermittelten noch im Herbst 2005 der Kultusministerkonferenz offiziell den Wunsch, die Hamburger Kandidatur auf „Chilehaus mit Kontorhausviertel und angrenzender Speicherstadt" zu erweitern. Diesem Wunsch wurde entsprochen. Eine Vorverlegung des Nominierungsjahres war ohnehin nicht möglich – zumal einige Kandidaten vor Hamburg auf der Tentativliste standen, es aber auch an einem entsprechenden Auftrag des Senats mangelte, der aufgrund der erwähnten Bauprojekte HafenCity und Elbphilharmonie nicht zu bekommen war. Daher gab es auch zunächst keine Expertentagung.

Um diesen Bedenken nachzugehen, aber auch generell die Welterbefähigkeit vorab sachverständig beurteilen zu lassen, haben wir im November 2006 eine Expertengruppe des Deutschen Nationalkomitees von ICOMOS eingeladen, die Objekte und ihr Umfeld mit der geplanten HafenCity anzusehen. Professor Petzet, der Vorsitzende des deutschen Nationalkomitees von ICOMOS, und Giulio Marano, der Sprecher der Monitoring-Gruppe von ICOMOS Deutschland ließen sich von der hohen Qualität der Instandhaltung der Kontorhäuser, insbesondere des Chilehauses, des Meßberg- und Sprinkenhofs überzeugen, insbesondere auch von der hohen Qualität der vollzogenen Umnutzungsmaßnahmen in der Speicherstadt wie z. B. bei der HHLA und der Hamburg Port Authority – beide nutzen ehemalige Speicherblocks als Büros, in denen noch die ursprüngliche Konstruktion deutlich zu erkennen ist. Auch wurden die bereits vollzogenen bzw. noch bevorstehenden Baumaßnahmen in dem südlich der Speicherstadt neu entstehenden Quartier der HafenCity mit der Elbphilharmonie anhand des Master-Planes kritisch überprüft und für kompatibel mit der Wirkung der Gesamtanlage „Speicherstadt" betrachtet. Die Welterbefähigkeit der beiden Ensembles wurde bejaht, auch die der Speicherstadt – trotz der erlittenen Kriegsverluste und der gegenüber dem historischen Zustand recht radikal geänderten Topografie an ihrem südlichen Rand, wo an Stelle der früheren flachen Lagerschuppen bereits der erste Bauabschnitt der neuen HafenCity am historischen Sandtorhafen mit Neubauten entstanden war, die bis an die Firsthöhe der Speichergebäude reichten. Das Fazit der ICOMOS-Experten lautete: „Keines der vorgestellten Projekte in der HafenCity gefährdet einen Antrag auf Aufnahme oder den späteren Verbleib der Speicherstadt und des Kontorhausviertels als Weltkulturerbe". Sie haben uns dazu geraten, die Abgrenzung des Welterbe-Kernbereichs auf die historischen Bereiche der Speicherstadt und die drei oder vier bedeutendsten Kontorhäuser zu beschränken, ansonsten aber eine angemessene Pufferzone mit den bedeutendsten Sichtbeziehungen auszuweisen. Kritische Anmerkungen fand die Verkehrsführung durch die Speicherstadt, die in Nord-Süd-Richtung historisch nie bestand, nun aber als Durchgangsstation zur HafenCity und über die Elbquerung zu den südlich der Norderelbe gelegenen Hafen- und Stadtbereichen erheblich von Verkehr belastet wird.

Erst im Frühjahr 2010 hatte dann der Senat mit seinem neu beschlossenen „Leitbild Hamburg – Wachsen mit Weitsicht" die Kulturbehörde beauftragt, die für die Anmeldung für die Liste des Welterbes erforderlichen Antragsunterlagen für die beiden Ensembles zu erarbeiten. Es ist uns gelungen, hierfür eine besondere Projektstelle einzurichten, die seit dem 1.5.2010 von Dr. Agnes Seemann wahrgenommen wird und in deren Händen mit tatkräftiger Unterstützung von Romaine Becker die Vorbereitung dieser Tagung lag. Dafür herzlichen Dank!

Die Bearbeitung des eigentlichen Antrages erfolgt seit kurzem in einer Arbeitsgruppe, der der freischaffende Architekturhistoriker und Mitbetreiber des Speicherstadtmuseums Dr. Ralf Lange sowie Professor Dirk Schubert von der HafenCity Universität angehören. Beide werden Sie im Laufe unserer Veranstaltung mit ihren Beiträgen noch kennenlernen.

Nachdem das Welterbekomitee im Juni dieses Jahres beschlossen hat, dass ab 2012 die Vertragsstaaten nur dann zwei Stätten zur Evaluierung anmelden können, wenn eine davon eine Naturerbe oder eine Kulturlandschaft ist – wird, wenn alles gut geht, im August 2013 das Hamburger Antrags-Gutachten in Paris zur ersten Vorprüfung eingereicht sein, dann endgültig im Februar 2014 zur Nominierung. So stehen wir nun am Beginn der Ausarbeitung unserer Bewerbungsschrift und unsere Tagung kommt zur rechten Zeit, um anhand Ihrer Beiträge unsere Maßstäbe an die Erfüllung der Welterbe-Kriterien zu schärfen. Ich möchte der Ständigen Vertretung Deutschlands bei der UNESCO, Frau Nibbeling-Wrießnig, und hier in ihrer Vertretung Herrn Lahr für die dieses Frühjahr ausgesprochene Empfehlung ausdrücklich danken, zeitnah ein solches Symposium durchzuführen, um damit die von der UNESCO geforderte *comparative study* in Gang zu setzen.

Hamburg hat in beiden Arealen, in der Speicherstadt und im Kontorhausviertel, das Glück, mit Eigentümern zu arbeiten, die ihrerseits mit dem Ziel der Welterbenominierung nicht nur einverstanden sind, sondern diese auch befördern wollen, indem sie die Bauten denkmalgerecht nutzen, erhalten und pflegen. Was das Kontorhausviertel angeht, so ist dort ein außerordentlich hohes Maß an Authentizität und Integrität gegeben. Die Nutzung hat sich seit der Errichtung der Bauten praktisch nicht verändert. Die Bauten waren ohne größere Kriegsschäden geblieben, die originalen Ausstattungsteile sind nahezu vollständig erhalten oder entsprechend der ursprünglichen Fassung in teils aufwändigen Restaurierungsmaßnahmen wieder hergestellt worden. Sie werden Gelegenheit haben, sich davon ein Bild zu machen.

Im Falle der Speicherstadt sieht die Situation wesentlich anders aus: nicht nur hat der Krieg rund 50 % der Bausubstanz teils total, teils in Teilen zerstört, sodass der Wiederaufbau unter der Leitung des Architekten Werner Kallmorgen in ganz unterschiedlicher Weise vorgenommen wurde: von der möglichst nahe dem Original nachempfundenen Rekonstruktion über die vereinfachte Wiederherstellung bis zum völligen Neubau, der die Materialkontinuität des charakteristischen Backsteins wahrt. Bis in die 1990er Jahre unterschieden sich Warentransport und -veredelung in den Speicherbauten kaum von den im späten 19. Jahrhundert angewandten Techniken. Dann jedoch hat die Containerisierung des Hafenumschlags den Quartiersleuten und ihren hergebrachten Arbeitsweisen allmählich ein Ende bereitet. So war es durchaus ein schwieriger, am Ende aber sehr weitsichtiger Kraftakt, dieses große Ensemble 1991 unter Denkmalschutz zu stellen, nachdem zuvor ernsthafte Überlegungen angestellt worden waren, die Speicher – vielleicht auch auf Abriss – zu verkaufen. Die stadteigene damalige Hamburgische Hafen- und Lagerhaus Aktiengesellschaft – heute ist das Lagerhaus im Namen bezeichnenderweise durch die Logistik ersetzt – hat sich des Erbes angenommen und gemeinsam mit dem Denkmalschutzamt Zug um Zug die Umnutzung der einzelnen Speicherblöcke geplant und – freilich nicht immer konfliktfrei – durchgeführt. Zu den einfacheren Projekten dieser Art gehören auch die im Sommer 2007 neu geschaffenen Künstler-Ateliers, die schon jetzt als Erfolgsgeschichte bezeichnet werden können. Sie tragen mit dazu bei, ein lebendiges und kreatives Viertel als Bindeglied zwischen City und HafenCity zu schaffen. Darüber hinaus zieht eine Vielzahl von einzigartigen Museen und Veranstaltungsorten wie auch dieser „Dialog im Dunkeln" viele begeisterte Touristen und Hamburger Bürger in die Speicherstadt. Und wo es denkmalpflegerisch vertretbar ist, soll auch Wohnen in der Speicherstadt möglich sein.

Nachhaltige Unterstützung erfährt der UNESCO-Antrag von der planenden Verwaltung, der Behörde für Stadtentwicklung und Umwelt. Die vor einiger Zeit von ihr in Zusammenarbeit mit der Kulturbehörde herausgegebene „Verordnung zur Gestaltung der Speicherstadt" hat zum Ziel, deren vorhandenes Erscheinungsbild vor unkontrollierten Eingriffen und irreparabler Zerstörung zu schützen. Ein vor der Fertigstellung stehendes „Erhaltungskonzept Speicherstadt" zeigt die Perspektiven und Potenziale der Speicherbauten auf und formuliert gestalterische Anforderungen an den historisch geprägten Freiraum, der den absehbar starken fließenden und ruhenden Verkehr der Beschäftigten und Besucher der Speicherstadt aufnehmen muss. Wir haben dieses Konzept kritisch begleitet und es wird ein wesentlicher Bestandteil des Managementplanes sein.

Meine Damen und Herren, wir werden uns nun auch Gedanken machen, wie wir den *outstanding universal value* der Ensembles formulieren und unter welchen Kriterien der Operational Guidelines unsere Kandidaten beim Welterbekomitee antreten sollen. Als gutes Vergleichsbeispiel, das bereits auf der Welterebeliste steht, kann uns die *Maritime Mercantile City of Liverpool* dienen, die 2004 nach folgenden Kriterien in die Welterbeliste eingetragen wurde:

Kriterium II: das Gut sollte einen Zeitraum oder in einem Kulturgebiet der Erde einen bedeutenden Schnittpunkt menschlicher Werte, in Bezug auf die Entwicklungen der Architektur, des Städtebaus oder der Landschaftsgestaltung darstellen;

Kriterium III: es ist ein einzigartiges oder zumindest außergewöhnliches Zeugnis von einer kulturellen Tradition oder einer bestehenden oder untergegangenen Kultur

Und Kriterium IV meint ein herausragendes Beispiel eines Typus von Gebäuden, architektonischen oder technologischen Ensembles oder Landschaften, die einen oder mehrere bedeutsame Abschnitte Geschichte der Menschheit versinnbildlichen. Ich denke, dass auch die Hamburger Kandidaten alle drei genannten Kriterien erfüllen.

Außerdem trifft für das Chilehaus und die Speicherstadt auch sicherlich Kriterium I zu: Meisterwerke menschlicher Schöpfungskraft, die wir der Kreativität des Ingenieurs Franz Andreas Meyer und des Architekten Fritz Höger und anderer bekannter Hamburger Architekten verdanken.

Für die Erörterung dieser entscheidenden Themen mit unseren in Welterbesachen erfahrenen Projektpartnern Prof. Kunibert Wachten, Michael Kloos und Martin Ritscherle – sie bearbeiten den Managementplan – sowie mit Birgitta Ringbeck, der Delegierten der Kultusministerkonferenz beim Welterbekomitee und nicht zuletzt mit den Experten von ICOMOS Deutschland sei an dieser Stelle und zum Schluss ausdrücklich gedankt. Sicherlich werden wir noch Gelegenheit haben, darüber und über vieles mehr hier zu sprechen.

Abstract

Hamburg on its way to World Heritage

Since 1998 the Chile House (Fritz Hoeger 1922–24) is on the German Tentative List for World Heritage; the nomination should be submitted in 2014. In 2005 a private initiative of the publishing house "Gruner+Jahr" in conjunction with the "Deutsche Umwelthilfe" pushed the discussion both to expand this position to the surrounding Kontorhaus (office building) district and the Speicherstadt (warehouse district) and to submit an earlier nomination. However, the proposed date by the Tentative List and the reluctance of the Hamburg senate, which did not want to endanger the ongoing projects of the HafenCity and Elbphilharmonie by a UNESCO-protected status of the warehouse district both spoke against a previous nomination.

However, the Hamburg Ministry of Culture had taken up this debate and in 2006 ICOMOS Germany was invited to make a critical assessment of the two ensembles as well as the related urban planning. ICOMOS Germany did not recognize any contradictory aspects to world heritage, and gave useful recommendations for the nomination. The development of the nomination was set up in 2010 and we followed the recommendation of the Permanent Delegation of Germany to UNESCO and other experts to support it by an international symposium which should discuss similar objects – e. g. port-related warehouse areas and inner-city office building neighbourhoods from a similar time. After this step the application document, including the management plan will be further elaborated and submitted to the World Heritage Centre in 2014.

Carola Hein

Port Cityscapes: Town and Harbour Development in the Global Context

Figure 1: The Chilehaus Hamburg on the cover of the journal "Deutschland", 1941

Figure 2: Traditional warehouses of the Hanseatic period. Lübeck, Hamburg, Amsterdam, Tallinn

Designed to look like a ship's prow, the Chilehaus office building made Hamburg's international maritime connections visible in form and name. It showcased the commitment of local elites to the port, their creation of urban form for maritime business purposes, and their use of architectural imagery to express and even celebrate the global connections of their Hanseatic city. It was built between 1921 and 1924 by Henry Brarens Sloman (1848–1929); he made his fortune from trading in saltpetre from Chile, used particularly in agricultural production. He funded the construction with profits from Chile and named it in gratitude for the business. Marrying local materials and imagery with local maritime and trading history, and giving it the name of another country, the building exemplifies global/local interactions in the built environment. As such, the Chilehaus and Hamburg itself are useful sites in which to discern interactions distinctive to port cities: not only between the global and the local, but in their changing built environments, we can read the relationship between global and local forces, and the effects of economic flows (Fig. 1).

As a result of the various flows between port cities, specific elements of their respective urban environments are related, including funding, technology, style, concept, and building material. No single form, pattern, or dynamic characterizes port cities, yet they show common traits, making them faraway mirrors of each other. In its chronological discussion, this chapter shows that port cities have long been hot spots of exchange and that such interaction continues to be part of sea-trade as well as for the transformation of old waterfronts. The warehouses of the Hanseatic cities in the North and Baltic seas, for example, resemble each other closely and make visible the trade connections of the 13th to 17th century (Fig. 2). The extent of these global interchanges is also visible in the brick warehouse districts of the 19th century in London, Gloucester, Hamburg, Yokohama, Kobe, and Hakodate. Many of them have more recently been parts of preservation and waterfront reconstruction projects, creating another set of connections.

Port functions effectively entered a city's very heart beyond the waterfront. Global shipping and trade not only left their imprint on ports and warehouses, then, but also on headquarters, religious institutions, residences, and leisure facilities. As shipping networks expanded across the globe, they also extended further from the port into the city and its hinterland. Building on Brian Hoyle's investigation of the relationships among ports and cities (Hoyle 1989), I argue that ports, port sector (waterfront), city, and port city support structures (which may be located in other cities) are interconnected (Hein 2011). How any of the shipping

Figure 3: Map of Hamburg showing the integration of trade into the core of the city, 1588

requirements are filled beyond the port, depends on a broad range of local conditions, actors, and institutions as well as on larger networks formed by traders and trade groups, diasporas, religious congregations, or ethnic groups. Historical views of Amsterdam, Venice, and Hamburg, such as those by Georg Braun and Franz Hogenberg (1572 and 1588), show smaller ships and barges bringing goods directly to city buildings (Fig. 3). In these buildings, in contrast to the warehouse districts, we usually see builders' attempts to fit into local contexts historically and today; only flags and signs signal the larger global networks of funding and function. The Hamburg-based shipping company Hapag-Lloyd, for example, has a longstanding and far-flung network of regional headquarters, ranging from a neo-historic building in Tsingtao, China (1867) to a modern company headquarters in Tokyo. The company also had offices at the Bourse in Philadelphia (as of 1912). Erected as the city's commercial exchange in 1895, the structure's function was possibly modelled on the Hamburg exchange, its skyscraper-like appearance, however, was very different from the low-rise original (Taylor and Schoff 1912) (Fig. 4 and 5).

To demonstrate how ports and waterfronts have been literally shaped by the port function and the necessary commonalties of trade and shipping networks and how global and local interaction plays out concretely in the built environment, this contribution examines Philadelphia, London, and Tokyo, three port cities (or ports, waterfronts, and cities) that are very different from each other and that have seen very different development patterns for their harbours and waterfronts. It also weaves in some other examples from around the world. Philadelphia's original design between two rivers reflected colonial interests in connecting the American interior to the east coast and to Europe, but by the mid-20th century, the city had to give up its leading maritime status in favour of the New York/New Jersey port and its waterfront has seen little redevelopment. London is a millenial city transforming in tune with the changing needs of its port. The construction and reconstruction of port facilities along the Thames River has been a major drive of the city's urban development and the tranformation of the Docklands has drawn attention worldwide. Tokyo's history as a global port went hand in hand with the presence of foreigners in Japan; and in the greater metropolitan Tokyo area, we can observe the improvement and development of a modern port in parallel with the redevelopment of old waterfront areas.

Port functions were a key aspect of the design of Philadelphia, but here people created a new city in response to port activities. When Thomas Holme, surveyor general for William Penn, the proprietor and governor of the province of Pennsylvania, arrived in America in June 1682 to lay out a "large town or new city" (1774), he emphasized the importance of rivers and ports for maritime trade in the selection

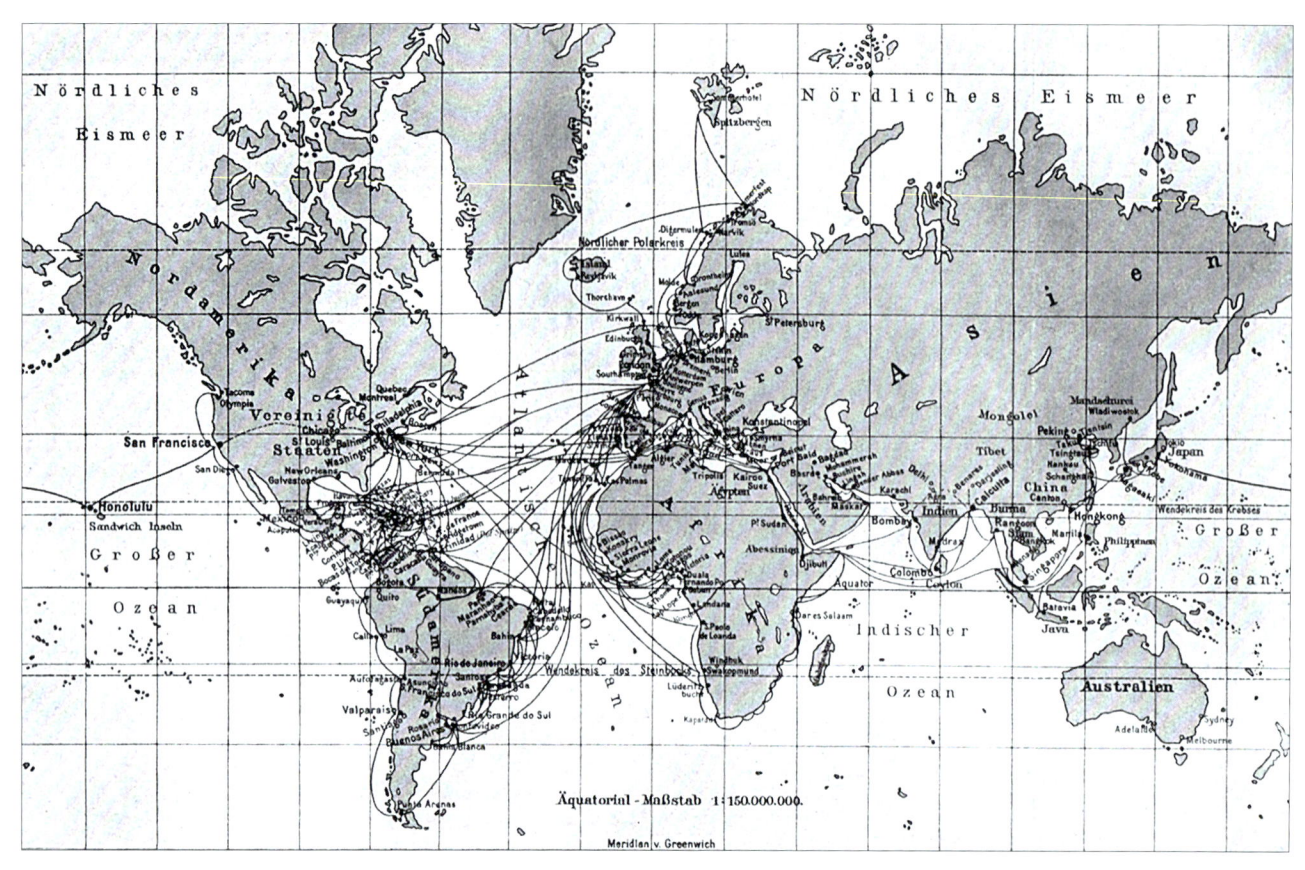

Figure 4: The global network of the shipping lines of Hapag/Hamburg-America Line (1914)

Figure 5: Philadelphia Bourse

of the site and the city plan (Fig. 6). He modelled the city "between two navigable rivers, upon a neck of land," providing access to ocean-going ships on the Delaware River and inland ships on the smaller Schuylkill River. In the city charter, Penn himself emphasized the waterfront as public space. Holme, taking into account the financial means and functional needs of the future proprietors, specified the sizes of the lots near the waterfront, creating a landscape of warehouses, wharves, shops, factories and homes mediating between the sea and the city center. But despite Penn and Holmes' careful design, as people settled in the newly laid-out city, they followed their own needs and interests. Ship-related commerce and craftsmen, through individual actions and investments, created a several-block district of commercial, industrial, wholesale, and financial activities. The western side of Penn's projected city remained largely undeveloped, as documented in the map by A. P. Folie of 1794, until the later nineteenth century (Fig. 7).

The Philadelphia waterfront itself was originally built without a central governing authority. Private interests built the piers and waterfronts and established its reputation and its key role in the region's economic growth. In the 19th and early 20th century, various public entities took control of waterfront organization, building municipally owned piers and warehouses near the private businesses, among them the Municipal Pier at Vine Street (Fig. 8). The port of Philadelphia thrived as part of global networks into the 20th century, with factories, warehouses and other industries proliferating near the waterfront. By 1912, Philadelphia could point to a range of improvements such as new permanent piers

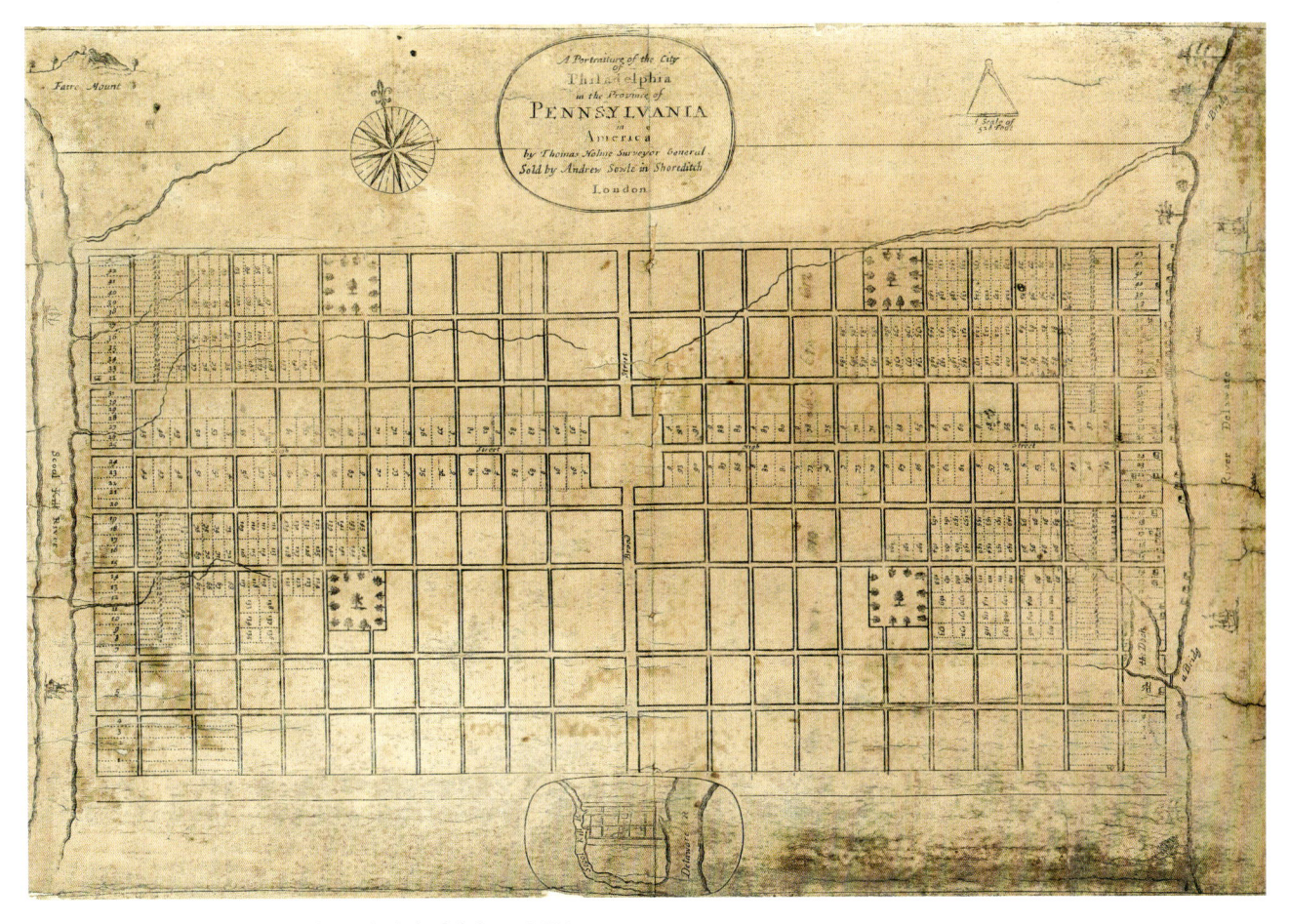

Figure 6: Thomas Holme, Plan of Philadelphia, 1683

(started in 1907) and also to new plans addressing maritime problems particular to her situation. Philadelphia and New Jersey now had thirty-eight miles of shipping frontage, with hundreds of acres still available for the construction of factories along the Delaware and Schuylkill rivers. However, by this time, Philadelphia had already lost its role as a major passenger port to New York, and extensive dredging of the river would become necessary for the port to host bigger ships and rival the ports of Boston, Baltimore or New York.

London is as an example of a city where government and trading companies worked together to build networks and influence the form of port cities around the world. British ships linked the port and city of London with seaports from the Pacific to the Indian Ocean up to the earliest 20th century. Multiple layers of the urban environment in London, as well as in other port cities of the British Empire, register the growth (and decay) of the Empire and its trading connections. The close connection between public interests and private investments appears notably in the workings of the East India Company. Founded in 1600 by a group of merchants, the company had monopoly privileges over British trade with the East Indies. Its impressive neo-classical London headquarters, located on Leadenhall Street in the City of London, seen here in 1817 (Fig. 9), demonstrate the importance of the company in the British capital as well as the office's key function in the larger network of the company. The East India Company developed numer-

Figure 7: A. P. Folie, and R. Scot, Plan of the City and Suburbs of Philadelphia, 1794

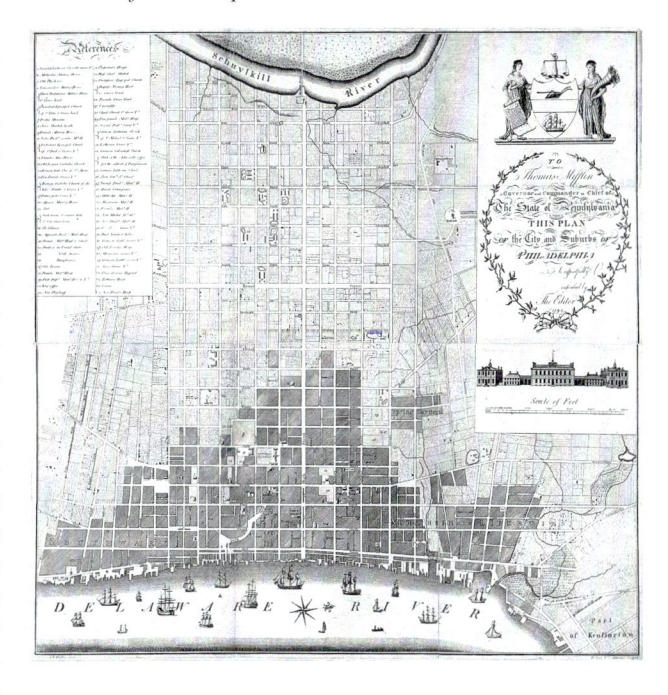

ous trading ports: the three towns of Calcutta, Bombay and Madras, for example, served as military and economic bases for trade with the home country and expansion inland. Calcutta had special connections to the metropolis, as it was

Figure 8: New Municipal Pier at Vine Street, Shore Front

Figure 9: East India House in Leadenhall Street, London as drawn by Thomas Hosmer Shepherd, 1817

Figure 10: Esplanade Row and the Council House, Thomas Daniell, 1788

the administrative seat of the company starting in 1773 as well as the capital of British India (Fig. 10). Its two-square-mile esplanade, known as Maidan, displayed numerous neoclassical buildings such as the government house, the courthouse, and the post office, as well as other administrative, residential, and leisure institutions (Kosambi and Brush 1988).

As early as 1802, British trading companies sailing between London and the West Indies obtained permission to build a new harbour complex on the Isle of Dogs outside London. The new complex was surrounded by warehouses, fences, and canals and enclosed by docks; it provided a secure environment for transferring goods from large ships to land. New steamships also required different facilities, forcing harbours around the world to rebuild wharves (which had to change in both form and size), equipment to load and unload the ships, and service and storage facilities for fuel. The sheer number of steamships brought about yet another round of transformations: by 1830, the new Brunswick Wharf provided a place where they no longer had to wait for the tide to enter the dock, but could cast off un-der their own power (Fig. 11). Other new docks included the Royal Albert Dock (1880), which served steamboat lines trading in the southern hemisphere. London integrated port and city; docks and wharves became the heart of economic development. Their construction was studied and imitated around the world. Glasgow, Edinburgh, Southampton, and other cities around the world adopted docks for their harbours.

Shipping networks have regularly adapted to port facilities as well as trade patterns and the cities within the network show these changes. As Western trade interests helped open numerous Asian ports, their waterfronts registered the foreign presence. This was particularly evident in Canton, where Westerners trading and interacting with and within China (known as *factors*) formed a dense urban neighborhood called Thirteen Factories (residences of the factors). The buildings here, originally of Chinese construction, acquired classical Western facades in the eighteenth century while still featuring Chinese interior spaces. Western influences in these Chinese cities were limited to the vicinity of the port (with the exception of German-planned Tsingtau); local architecture and urban form characterized most of the remaining city (Farris 2011). The opening of Japan to global trade, in the mid 19th century, sparked the construction of port facilities in several Japanese cities (including Yokohama and Kobe), as well as of new headquarters, leisure facilities, and residences for traders throughout their urban areas. The Japanese government set up a new town of shipping and trading facilities for foreigners and its own citizens in Yokohama. Foreigners here numbered only about two hundred in the 1860s (with the biggest contingent being British). Their warehouses and residences were located behind walls in the east, while the smaller buildings in the west housed the Japanese commercial district. (The road between them led to the entertainment quarter) (Fig. 12). The new town had a functional layout and the architectural design was limited to necessities, as Sir Ernest Satow (1843–1929) observed: "Architectural ambition at first was contented with simple wooden bungalows, and in the latter part of 1862 there were not more than a dozen two-storied buildings in the foreign portion of the town." (MIT Visualizing Cultures Image Database 2005) Nonetheless the new foreign influence is visible in details like the stair leading to the second floor, a feature that was not typical for traditional Japanese buildings. The larger architectural networks are equally evident in the later construction of the red brick warehouses by the Japanese architect Yorinaka Tsumaki in 1911 (current Building no. 2) and 1913 (current building no. 1) that were used as custom houses (Fig. 13): in material and design they matched the warehouses of Europe.

The construction of the first railroad in Japan, in 1872, connected the Yokohama waterfront with the heart of Tokyo, the capital and Japan's main port city. Tokyo had been the location of foreign-inspired structures since the Meiji Restoration in 1868 (Fig. 14). After a major fire, also in 1872, the new railroad station at Shimbashi became the starting point for a new thoroughfare. The Tokyo governor had decided that reconstruction in the Ginza area should set an example of fireproof residential construction and demonstrate that Tokyo was a major capital on par with the great metropolises of the west. The result was an avenue with brick buildings, a unified streetscape, and the separation of traffic. Media, including woodprints, showcased the avenue as a symbol of the new Tokyo. Headquarters of trading companies originally located at the Yokohama waterfront, moved to more central locations in Tokyo in the following years. The Mitsubishi company – established in 1870 as a shipping firm and rapidly diversified to include coal-mining, ship-building, marine insurance, etc. – bought a great deal of land that had fallen empty and used it to start Japan's first business district, the Marunouchi district (Hein 2010).

The company quickly sited other buildings across Tokyo as well, from production sites to headquarters and housing. The architect of key public and private Mitsubishi buildings was the British Josiah Conder, who had designed numerous buildings associated with the new Meiji government, such as the Rokumeikan hall, where the Meiji-era elite gathered for grand balls in Western style, and a museum in Ueno affiliated with the Ministry of Works. As advisor to Mitsubishi, Conder notably designed the Mitsubishi headquarters, a complex of three-story red brick buildings with steep roofs that resembled London office buildings, including Mitsubishi No. 1 Building (1894) (Fig. 15). The Mitsubishi chairmen also invited Conder to design their villas. In fact, Conder designed the Fukagawa mansion of the second Mitsubishi chairman, Yanosuke Iwasaki, the first truly European-style home in Japan. He also designed the Kaitokaku, a palatial hilltop villa in Tokyo used for special events. We thus see the creation of a group of buildings that are linked through a company's public and private ventures and architect. We also see that the administration of shipping has moved away from the waterfront into the main business areas.

Ports and port cities have long been military targets, and in World War II ports in Europe and Japan suffered extensive destruction, losing population as well as port infrastructure and experiencing extensive damage to the urban centre. Many of these ports had already suffered greatly from the decline in world trade due to the Great Depression (Clark 2009). The ports of Yokohama and Tokyo, which had just been rebuilt and improved with government support after massive destruction in the 1923 Great Kanto Earthquake, were again largely destroyed. After the war, the American military took over the Japanese ports and it was not until 1951 that the Harbour Law gave control of the ports back to local governments. By 1950, most of the destroyed cities

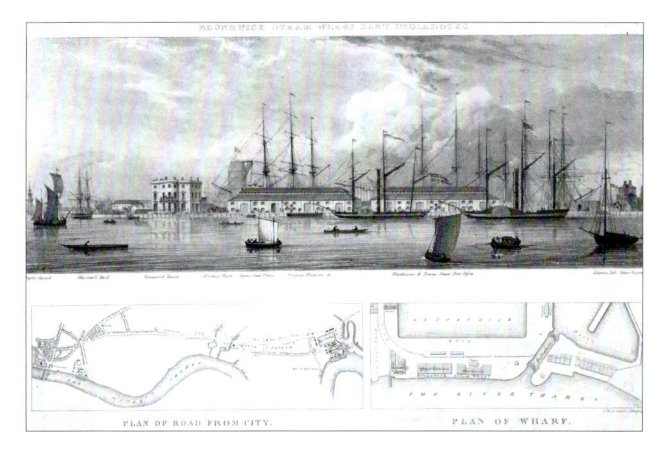

Figure 11: London, Brunswick Steam Wharf, c. 1860. (Brunswick Steam Wharf, c. 1860)

Figure 12: Sadahide, Yokohama Honcho, 1860

Figure 13: Red Brick Warehouses Yokohama

had rebuilt and were growing again. The ports of Tokyo Bay developed rapidly as part of the capital's national post-war growth. Tokyo opened the Shinagawa container terminal in 1967 and continued to expand it.

Throughout the 20th century and particularly in the post-Second World War period, ports worldwide responded quickly to ongoing transformations in manufacturing and shipping. Starting in the 1960s, the port and city began to grow apart physically. From the late 1960s to the late 1970s, ship sizes increased, passing the barrier of 50 000 tons gross (Hayuth 1982). Few ports were able to handle oil and bulk carriers of that size in the existing terminals, so new ones were developed on the outskirts. Ports and cities in all parts

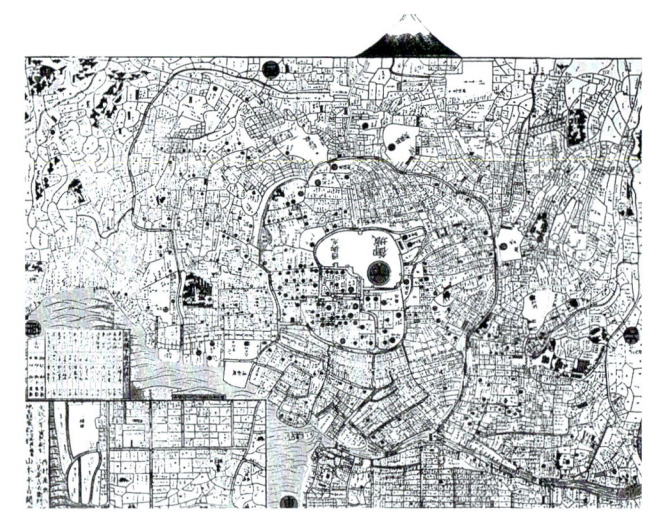

Figure 14: The spatial structure of Edo in 1818

*Figure 15: The Marunouchi brick district
Little London*

of the world faced pressure from changing global systems and new local production patterns. New ports emerged, notably in China as more and more goods began to originate there; indeed, since the 1970s, Chinese leaders have emphasized the growth of ports. In Hong Kong, the quasi-governmental Trade Development Council (TDC) established a global position for its port through aggressive and innovative marketing despite political, economic, and geographic adversities (Yiu 2011).

Most importantly, containerization led to wholesale restructuring of shipping networks, trade patterns, port facilities, port city hierarchies, and urban form. Containerization pushed cities to construct port-specific industrial areas, in the short term shrinking the workforce and in the longer run abandoning warehouses and other structures that no longer met the evolving needs of the port. This period is also characterized by the construction of new port facilities: Dubai, for example, constructed the Jebel Ali port in the 1970s to compete with neighbouring emirates and to secure oil profits; more recently, Shanghai built the Yangshan deep water port, a new container terminal on a man-made area between two islands off the Shanghai shore, and a connected new satellite city of 800 000 people, Lingang New City (designed by Von Gerkan, Marg and Partners). At the same time, this period was also characterized by the redevelopment of old port areas.

Numerous ports lost their former standing and experienced high levels of unemployment. In Europe, port cities in the later 20th century suffered the highest level of economic contraction of all urban centres. However there were some winners and new leaders, such as Rotterdam, in the competition between ports. Perhaps one of the best examples of the effect of the relocation of cargo facilities is the rapid development of the Port of Oakland, which offered wide berthing facilities and good access to transportation, and the concomitant decline of the Port of San Francisco, which was limited by its existing finger piers and topography. In general, as port activities withdrew from the waterfront and the port and city separated (as summarized by Hoyle), large-scale port-related redevelopment continued throughout cities, sometimes hidden and sometimes more evident. For example, companies constructed new large headquarter buildings throughout urban areas, and cities built new rail and road infrastructure to the hinterland. These changes signalled the beginning of a new globalized era in shipping that would take a less clearly identifiable local form.

In the three cities, Philadelphia, London, and Tokyo, that this chapter has concentrated on, we see extensive changes in the built environment as a result of the transformation of shipping. Even though the port was essential to the design of Philadelphia, the city's shipping industry started to decline in the late nineteenth century and the business community moved away from the riverfront; by the mid-1950s, the shipping industry had largely abandoned the city (McGovern 2008). In response, planners and policy-makers introduced a north-south urban highway, Interstate I-95, separating the river from the centre city. On landfill along the Delaware River, they also created a waterfront area called Penn's Landing; it has since been the focus of multiple visions for waterfront revitalization, only small parts of which have been completed. Despite interventions by internationally successful developers such as Rouse & Associates (headed by the Philadelphia-based Willard Rouse III, nephew of James Rouse, Baltimore's waterfront developer), world-famous architects including Robert Venturi and Denise Scott Brown (Venturi 2003), and most recently a civic initiative led by Penn Praxis, Philadelphia has not joined the global movement for waterfront revitalization. Penn's Landing still awaits development.

London has managed to juggle both aspects of current port developments, waterfront redevelopment on the one hand and port development on the other. The London Docklands, inspired by renewal projects in Baltimore and Boston, has since become a model for redevelopment for mostly office use. London is also currently building a new deep-water terminal, London Gateway, in Thurrock, Essex. The new deep-water port will be able to handle large container ships, provide a logistics park and road and rail infrastructure to London and Great Britain as a whole. Construction on the former Shell oil refinery site of 1 500 acres started in 2010 and is done by DP World, a large maritime terminal operator.

In contrast, Tokyo's metropolitan region demonstrates an intriguing pattern of collaboration and competition among its multiple ports and waterfronts. The ports of Tokyo, Yokohama, and Chiba – are part of a single metropolitan area – are among the leading ports, with Tokyo being number 26 in terms of container shipping, whereas Chiba and Yokohama rank numbers 18 and 25 in terms of cargo handling. While the three ports are jointly contributing to the economic predominance of the global metropolis Tokyo, their respective waterfront developments have been designed to highlight the different and local particularities of each place. In the Tokyo Bay, Yokohama developed the first comprehensive plan for redevelopment in 1965. On 186 hectares of former industrial land (including a Mitsubishi site), the 1981 master plan projected Minato Mirai (Port of the Future), a new development including housing and a multitude of business, commerce, and culture functions. The Landmark Tower, the Convention Centre, and the Clock 21 Ferris Wheel, as well as the traditional red-brick restored warehouse district and the nearby Chinatown, have made the district a tourist attraction. The new port district resulted from close collaboration between national and local governments as well as investors. Chiba came to host infrastructures that were too big for the capital, such as Narita International airport, and other large-scale developments, including Tokyo Disneyland. Tokyo developed its waterfront to showcase the global character of Japan's capital through landmark projects by internationally recognized architects, including the influential Modernist Tange Kenzo.

While Philadelphia's port (as well as its waterfront development) could not live up to the competition of the New York/New Jersey port or the Baltimore waterfront redevelopment, the port economy remains essential to the present and future of London and Tokyo. Both cities are constantly striving to improve their harbours, though expansions might destroy environmentally sensitive areas, and to develop other port-related functions. Despite the physical detachment of port and city, the city and port authority in London and in the Tokyo Metropolitan area are eagerly constructing and imagining visible and invisible, tangible and virtual relationships between their working port and the city. Meanwhile new ports are rising in other areas of the world: Dubai, Shanghai, and Singapore all have built new ports in the last several decades.

Throughout history, port and city have been closely interrelated in political, economic, and social structures as well as in the built environment. That relationship between port and city has changed dramatically over time, as these examples illustrate, but as of global cargo ship movements, maritime transport continues to be a major element of globalization.

Abstract

Hafenstadträume: Stadt- und Hafenentwicklung im globalen Kontext

Hafenstädte haben eine lange Geschichte als Orte, über die wirtschaftlicher Austausch erfolgt und Menschen und Güter sowie bauliche und städtische Gestalt transportiert werden. Sie sind zwar nicht durch ein(e) einzelne(s) Form, Muster oder Dynamik charakterisiert, weisen aber gemeinsame Wesenszüge auf, in denen sie einander auch über große Entfernungen hinweg spiegeln. Als Ergebnis des zwischen den Hafenstädten erfolgenden Austauschs sind bestimmte Elemente ihres jeweiligen urbanen Umfelds über eine Reihe von Faktoren verbunden. Zu diesen Faktoren zählen Finanzierung und Technologie sowie Stil, Konzept und Baumaterial. Wenngleich Häfen durch die dem Handel eigenen Gesetzmäßigkeiten in ähnlicher Weise geformt werden, sei, so argumentiert Prof. Dr. Hein, die Art und Weise, wie die verschiedenen Anforderungen im Hafenviertel – der Schnittstelle zwischen dem eigentlichen Hafen und der Stadt – und im Stadtgebiet mit seinen vielfältigen lokalen Bedürfnissen erfüllt werden, jedoch von einem breiten Spektrum lokaler Bedingungen, Akteure und Institutionen abhängig. So unterschiedliche Städte wie London, Philadelphia und Tokio haben sich allesamt in Abhängigkeit von ihrer Hafenfunktion entwickelt. Während in London zu beobachten ist, wie sich weltumspannede Handelsverbindungen in dem Londoner Hafen niederschlagen, wie alte Hafenräume (Docklands) umgestaltet werden, und wie sich die Hafenfunktionen an neue Bedürnisse anpassen, steht Philadelphia beispielhaft für eine Stadt, die praktisch um die Schifffahrt herum erbaut wurde, die sich aber seit Mitte des 20. Jahrhunderts vom Hafen und vom Hafenrand abgewandt hat. Am Großraum Tokio wiederum lässt sich das Vordringen von hafenrelevanten Funktionen in das Stadtzentrum nachvollziehen, sowie die Entstehung drei separater Hafen- und Hafenrandräume in der selben Bucht. Seit Mitte des 19. Jahrhunderts haben die Veränderungen in Transport und Schifffahrt – insbesondere der Einsatz von Containern – auch zu einem Wandel der städtebaulichen Gestalt geführt. Der Bau neuer großer Häfen, z. B. in Dubai oder Shanghai, sowie die Sanierung und Neugestaltung aufgegebener Hafengebiete wie in Baltimore oder Melbourne verdeutlichen beispielhaft die sich stetig verändernde Beziehung zwischen Hafen und Stadt.

Bibliography

(1774). An Abstract of the Concessions of Mr. Penn to the first adventurers and purchasers in Pennsylvania; which the foregoing release recites. *An Explanation of the Map of the City and Liberties of Philadelphia.* J. Reed. Philadelphia, Brooks.

CLARK, P. (2009). *European Cities and Towns. 400-2000.* Oxford University Press.

FARRIS, J. (2011). Treaty Ports of China: Dynamics of Local and Global in the West's Architectural Presence. *Port Cities: Dynamic Landscapes and Global Networks.* C. Hein. London, Routledge.

HAYUTH, Y. (1982). "The port-urban interface: an area in transition." *Area* 14 (3): 219–224.

HEIN, C. (2010). "Shaping Tokyo: Land Development and Planning Practice in the Early Modern Japanese Metropolis." *Journal of Urban History* 36 (4): 447–484.

HEIN, Carola, ed. *Port Cities: Dynamic Landscapes and Global Networks.* London: Routledge, 2011.

HOYLE, B.S. (1989). "The Port-City Interface: Trends, Problems and Examples." *Geoforum* 4: 429–435.

KOSAMBI, M. and BRUSH J. E. (1988). "Three Colonial Port Cities in India." *Geographical Review* 78 (1): 32–47.

McGOVERN, S. (2008). "Evolving Visions of Waterfront Development in Postindustrial Philadelphia: The Formative Role of Elite Ideologies." *Journal of Planning History* 7 (4): 295–326.

MIT Visualizing Cultures Image Database (2005) Sadahide (1807–ca. 1878). Picture of a Salesroom in a Foreign Mercantile Firm in Yokohama. Yokohama ijin shōkan uriba no zu 1861:9.

TAYLOR, F. H. and W. H. Schoff (May 1912). *The Port and City of Philadelphia*. Philadelphia, Local Organizing Commission of the Congress (12.th International Congress of Navigation).

VENTURI, S. B. a. A., Inc. (2003). Penn's Landing Planning Study Philadelphia.

YIU, M. (2011). Hong Kong's global image campaign: port city transformation from British colony to Special Administrative Region of China. *Port Cities: Dynamic Landscapes and Global Networks*. C. Hein. London, Routledge: 214–229.

Sources of illustrations

Fig. 1: Schulze, Adolf. 1941. Hansestadt Hamburg (special issue). Deutschland. Zeitschrift für Industrie, Handel u. Schiffahrt, 9.

Fig. 2: Top Left: Lübeck (Carola Hein), Top right: Amsterdam (© Hartemink | Dreamstime.com) August 2010, Bottom left: Hamburg (Carola Hein), Bottom right: Tallinn (Carola Hein)

Fig. 3: [Hamburgum] Hambvrgvm. – [Agrippina Ubiorum Colonia], [ca. 1588]. Braun, Georg/Hogenberg, Franz: Civitates Orbis Terrarum. Courtesy Staats- und Universitätsbibliothek Hamburg, KS Kt H 202.

Fig. 4: Kurt Himer: Geschichte der Hamburg-Amerika Linie, Vol. 2.: Albert Ballin (Hamburg, 1927), 154.

Fig. 5: 7. Photocopy of early 20th century photo showing the Bourse Building. Photocopied by James L. Dillon and Company, Inc., photographers - Philadelphia Bourse, 11-21 South Fifth Street, Philadelphia, Philadelphia County, PA. Reproduction Number: HABS PA, 51-PHILA,651--7. Repository: Library of Congress Prints and Photographs. http://www.loc.gov/pictures/item/pa1053.photos.139872p/Division Washington, D. C. 20540 USA

Fig. 6 and Fig. 7: The Library Company of Philadelphia.

Fig. 8: Taylor, F. H. and W. H. Schoff (May 1912). The Port and City of Philadelphia. Philadelphia, Local Organizing Commission of the Congress (12.th International Congress of Navigation).

Fig. 9 and Fig. 10: © British Library Board (K.Top 24.10.c and P97).

Fig. 11: © National Maritime Museum, London, H6067

Fig. 12: © Arthur M. Sackler Gallery, Smithsonian Institution: S1998.48a-c, Gift of Ambassador and Mrs. William Leonhart.

Fig. 13: © Chun Kit Ho, Dreamstime.com, 2011.

Fig. 14: Kazumasa Yamashita, Chizu de yomu Edo jidai [Japanese maps of the Edo period] (Tokyo: Kashiwashobo, 1998), 103.

Fig. 15: Kasai, Masaaki (ed,), 1993. Tokyo. The Making of a Metropolis, (Tokyo: Tokyo Metropolitan Government), 23.

* The photo rights have been clarified by the author and she has the responsibility.

Robert Lee

The Social Life of Port Architecture: History, Politics, Commerce and Culture

Introduction

Inevitably, the architecture of port-cities is entangled in the social, political, economic, and cultural histories of these places and their wider role in international trade. Historically, the merchants constituted the dominant political elite in port cities and the major architectural projects which they commissioned, whether relating to dock development, the creation of a civic and commercial infrastructure, or the construction of domestic residences, enabled them to materialize their status in prominent urban spaces. The political and cultural frames of reference into which such buildings were inserted also served to provide a way to embed trade and commerce in a clearly defined set of broader civilizational values. As such, architecture was one of the key sites for referencing the cultures of other places, either through the use of historicist styles and discourses which were designed to civilize the working class, or by the deliberate choice of 'exotic' motifs. More crucially, port-city architecture offered visual representations of local traditions and achievements, whether in the context of major public architecture, commercial buildings, or even residential housing. But port architecture also reflected the social interactions which were crucial for knitting together trading networks both within and beyond the city, while the configuration of internal building spaces reveals both implicit and explicit assumptions about the ordering of social relationships and the structuring of class-specific hierarchies more widely.

This chapter is designed to address a number of interrelated issues relating to the structure, function and perception of port-city architecture. How did the trading function of port cities affect the construction of urban space and the proliferation of architectural styles? To what extent did the social practices and values (whether religious or secular) which were crucial for assembling and maintaining trading networks effectively shape the architecture of port cities? Historically, the demographic growth of port cities was generally characterized by a disproportionate dependency on long-distance immigration, often with a markedly variegated ethnic structure.[1] But how far did ethnic in-migration and the selective consolidation of diasporic networks affect the physical and experiential qualities of port-city architecture? From the early nineteenth century onwards, there was a rapid professionalization of architectural practice, but to what extent did practitioners in port cities draw on international symbols and construction techniques or attempt to particularize them in seeking to create a distinctive, local, urban image? And perhaps most challenging of all in terms of a specific research agenda, what can we conclude about the general perception and interpretation of port city architecture beyond the realms of literary writings and professional critiques? In order to address these issues, this chapter will focus on a number of interrelated themes: the significance of trading empires, whether Venetian or British, in disseminating specific architectural styles in port cities; the impact of trading patterns and commercial relationships on the availability and use of raw materials in building construction; the role of architects in reinforcing the language and materialist imagery of imperial authority; the processes of wealth creation through commerce and trade and their legacy in terms of the business centres of port cities and the domestic residences of individual merchants; and the configuration of sailortown itself, particularly in relation to the establishment and use of seamen's homes. But it will also analyse the significance of in-migration and settlement as a contributing factor in configuring the ethnic and cultural identity of port cities. Finally, it will discuss issues relating to the perception of port-city architecture, its symbolic relationship with political and economic actors, and wider issues relating to redevelopment and the need to preserve the legacy of the past in a way which reflects a better understanding of its social life and significance. In order to take forward this agenda, the paper will draw on a wide range of material, but it will also reflect recent research on Liverpool within the framework of the Mercantile Liverpool Project and by architectural historians, cultural anthropologists and sociologists who have begun to explore the social life of its architectural history and the cultural, economic, and political significance of many of its key buildings.[2]

Establishing a port-city typology

At one level, any attempt to analyze port-cities within a comparative context must recognize that functional differences between various types of ports became more apparent over time. Some ports benefited from their multi-functionality, such as the capital cities of Buenos Aires, Copenhagen, London, Montevideo, and Stockholm; naval ports (including Kiel, Portsmouth and Toulon) had a negligible amount of commercial traffic; the development of Bremen and Hamburg, together with Singapore (following full independence in 1965) was influenced by their distinct political framework as city-states, while *entrepôt*, ferry and free ports have increasingly fulfilled a more specialized function. To this extent, a comparative analysis of port city architecture must take into consideration not only a range of economic criteria, including port function, relative size, principal trades,

Figure 1: Venice, Ca'Loredan or Ca' Farsetti

Figure 2: Istanbul, Tekfur Sarayi

and the extent of local industrialization, but also the political framework of long-run development in terms of different forms of governance, ownership and administration, as well as specific locational factors relating to the quality of both the land and water site, which undoubtedly played a key role in underpinning the success of individual port-cities and influenced both the form and nature of urban building construction, whether in the case of Genoa, New York or Rotterdam.[3]

Irrespective of site-specific differences the process of urban expansion (or decline) has been strongly influenced by the changing pattern of world trade: maritime commerce has been a powerful factor behind urbanization and ports, after capital cities, have often registered the highest rates of population growth. Because of their maritime nexus, the architectural development of port cities has been influenced, to varying degrees, by links with foreign lands, the changing nature of international trade, and by the in-migration and settlement of diverse ethnic communities.[4] Despite their functional diversity, the urban structure of port cities particularly in the nineteenth and early twentieth centuries has also been influenced by a number of generic socio-economic factors. The nature of their local economies was associated with a high dependency on casual employment, a markedly unequal distribution of wealth, and a range of adverse social conditions. Long-distance in-migration, a pronounced degree of ethnic and class-specific residential segregation, together with the ideology of merchant capital, also directly affected the cultural identity of port-city architecture in a context where both public and private buildings were confgure by power and the 'resource of power'.[5]

Trading Empires and the Architecture of Port Cities

Trading empires with port cities as their focal points have often used architecture to reinforce authority or to symbolize their power. In line with the Lacanian theory of signification, the design of specific buildings has therefore reflected the perceived historical relationship between architecture, culture and imperial power.[6] But the ways in which trading empires have sought to use architecture as a means of sustaining world domination have varied considerably, both in the colonial territories themselves, as well as in the metropolitan and port-city centres of commercial power. A great deal has been written about the architectural history of Venice, the important legacy of 'Veneto-Byzantine' houses and palaces, and the development of Venetian Gothic.[7] But the Venetian Republic can serve as an instructive example of how trading empires contributed to the transfer and assimilation of architectural styles based on a significant degree of artistic and intellectual reciprocity.[8] The development of the Piazza San Marco undoubtedly reflected contemporary inspirations from eastern architectural practice, in particular the profusion of mosaics represented a thematic borrowing from the Great Mosque in Damascus; the outer cupolas of the palace itself were an adaptation of the well-known profiles of Islamic mausolea in Egypt; while the *campanile* of San Pietro di Castello was modeled on the Pharos lighthouse of Alexandria.[9] The design of many of the *palazzi*, with semicircular arches opening on to the canal and extended second-storey loggias (Fig. 1), as well as some of the warehouses, demonstrated clear similarities with the domestic architecture of Byzantium, whether in Constantinople or elsewhere (Fig. 2).[10] The mercantile prosperity of Venice was dependent on the exploitation of trading opportunities in the Adriatic, the eastern Mediterranean, and the Middle East, within the framework of a dynamic, if at times problematical, relationship with Islam. But spatial consciousness, like a sense of its historic past, was a crucial ingredient in structuring the Republic's self-identity and the assimilation of key elements of eastern architectural practice helped to convey its collective aspirations, both materially and spiritually.[11] Moreover, there was an important degree of reciprocity in terms of architectural styles between Venice and its overseas colonies with cultural forms exchanged and transferred from and to the metropolitan centre, as the case of Crete and the influence of its Byzantine architectural heritage on the Venetian townscape clearly illustrates.[12]

But not all trading empires were characterized by extensive reciprocity in terms of artistic and intellectual cross-fertilization, the dissemination of architectural styles, or the social structuring of the urban landscape of port cities. If the architecture of Trieste before 1914 reflected the 'language of hybridity' which underpinned the multilingual character of the Austro-Hungarian Empire, the extension of Italian control in East Africa in the interwar period, particularly in coastal towns, was associated with the emergence of the imperial apartheid city, reflecting the fascist belief that Africans were 'a-historical' and incapable of modernization.[13] Both the British in India and the French in Indo-China sought to retain effective control of the semantic context of the styles in which they built. Imperial authority was created and reinforced by the explicit use of classical prototypes, as the example of the Town Hall in Calcutta (1807–13) clearly illustrates, while many of the early Anglican churches simply used the same prototype derived from James Gibbs's St. Martins-in-the Fields, as was the case with St. John's, Calcutta, erected between 1788 and 1787.[14] Moreover, the Gothic revival in England, associated in particular with A.W.N. Pugin, with an implicit belief that it represented a product of a visibly purer society, also influenced colonial building styles in India, particularly in the port cities of Calcutta and Madras.[15] But both public and domestic architectural styles imposed by the colonial power had to be adapted to the exigencies of the Indian climate, in particular the intense heat and blazing light. In the longer term, however, the dominant architectural forms imposed by the British colonial authorities were modified by the assimilation of traditional Indian practices and the use of elements of western architectural vocabularies to create essentially hybrid products. But the narrative of adaptive strategies also reflected the changing policies of colonial rule, particularly after the Indian Mutiny of 1857, and the creation of pseudo-Indian (or Indo-Saracenic) architectural styles with their explicit borrowings from the Islamic architecture of India's previous Mughal and Afghan rulers can be interpreted as a means of strengthening imperial control by incorporating a visible element of continuity with the Indian past.[16] Indeed, this process was also reinforced by the British Orientalist movement which contributed substantially to the Hindu architectural renaissance, as well as by ethnographic research which increasingly posited a direct relationship between architectural styles and race.[17] It is important to note, however, that the flow of architectural forms from the imperial metropolitan centre to India was not reciprocated by any perceptible influence of Indian practices on British design. The relatively brief vogue for the 'Hindoo style' was influenced by the landscape painters Thomas Daniell (1749–1840) and his nephew, William Daniell (1769–1837), with the belief that Indian architecture 'presents an endless variety of forms' and it was reinforced in the late-eighteenth century by travel writers, such as William Hodges, but apart from a few select buildings (including the Pavilion at Brighton), its overall impact on Britain and its port cities was either marginal or non-existent.

Trade and the flow of building materials and architectural ideas

However, the presence of a colonial power was only one factor which influenced the configuration of port-city architecture, as the pattern of international trade by itself often served as a mechanism for facilitating the flow of building materials and architectural designs across oceans and continents. A number of examples will be used to illustrate the impact of trade flows on the configuration of port-city architecture. First, the coastal areas of the Red Sea provide evidence of a sustained cross-cultural continuity in terms of the use of building materials, as well as the spatial organization and functional use of port-city buildings.[18] Maritime trade, with a significant degree of involvement by Indian merchants and Baniyan brokers (both Hindu and Jain), tied the Red Sea to both the Mediterranean and Indian Ocean.[19] In ports such as Mocha and Jidda both the design and structure of urban housing reflected the needs of 'commercially oriented residents' and the availability of building materials made available through established trading patterns. The *rawshan*, the elaborate carved woodwork which was a feature of housing in many Red Sea ports played a 'critical role' in defining an early modern cosmopolitan maritime community', but it was made from Asian hardwood which was imported from abroad, from ports such as Cochin, as a convenient and profitable ballast for Indian Ocean-going vessels.[20]

Secondly, in coastal areas of Ghana (previously the Gold Coast), elite residential architecture between the 1860s and 1920s sought to combine elements of the Akan courtyard house with European Palladian architecture and the Afro-Portuguese *sobrado*.[21] In ports such as Anomabo the hybridity of domestic architecture was a source of cultural authentication and demonstrates how the Fante and other coastal Africans succeeded in appropriating and transforming building designs and technologies which enabled them to communicate visually their status and identity. But if some elements of architectural design were derived indirectly from the British colonial authorities and the Methodist Church, the availability of suitable stones for house construction was a result of existing patterns of trade, while the adoption of the *sobrado* reflected the importance of trade links with Brazil and the employment of Brazilian masons.[22]

Thirdly, international trade often acted as a conduit for the dissemination of innovative architectural practices and the application of new technology. As a key element in the redevelopment of Liverpool's waterfront in the early years of the twentieth century, the construction of the Liver Building (commissioned by the Royal Liver Friendly Society and designed by a local architect, Aubrey Thomas) represented a significant break with traditional design principles which had previously influenced the development of commercial buildings in Liverpool (Fig. 3).[23] When completed in 1911 it was the tallest office building in Britain with an extensive basement area, ten upper floors and six further stories located in the twin towers above the roof level. More importantly, it signified the application of new building techniques, in particular a system patented by François Hennebique using reinforced concrete as a skeletal framework on which was hung grey granite cladding in thin blocks.[24] As such, it reflected key structural developments in America between 1885 and 1895 which fostered the greater efficiency, height and stability of multi-storey buildings, namely the replacement of cast iron by steel, the introduction of sway-rod wind bracing, and the development of portal framing.[25] The fact

Figure 3: The Liver Building, Liverpool

that Liverpool was the first British city to emulate American architectural achievements was almost certainly a result of the interconnectivity of trade and commercial links. The Atlantic trade had underpinned Liverpool's rise to international prominence: in 1850 American cotton accounted for 67 per cent of Britain's imports and Liverpool was 'the chief emporium for cotton in the Empire'.[26] The majority of emigrants who passed through Liverpool in the period prior to 1914 were bound for North America and banking, commercial and trading links between Liverpool and east coast American ports were not only long established but particularly intense.[27] Many Liverpool businessmen and ship owners had a fascination with American technology and there were strong trading links with Chicago and New York in particular where the development of skyscrapers around the turn of the century was most apparent.[28]

Fourthly, commercial and trading links played an important role in the internationalization of architectural practice. In terms of cultural production, it has been argued that architects increasingly operated as 'mediators' between authoritarian power and humanistic aspiration, but their ability to fulfil this function was a result of the professionalization of architectural practice from the mid-nineteenth century onwards.[29] The key elements behind professionalization were similar to those of other professions: they included the creation of institutional structures, including associations, the control of licensing laws, the establishment of schools, and the exclusion of competitors, in particular general builders.[30] It was predicated on the development and dissemination of specialist journals, including *The Builder* (first printed in 1842), which became the most influential weekly journal devoted to the world of building, and national publications such as *The American Architect*, *The Architectural Record*, and *The Inland Architect*.[31] It was also reinforced by architectural competitions which increasingly attracted international submissions: in nineteenth-century Britain there were over 780 separate competitions, many of which were held in port cities such as Liverpool (42), Newcastle-upon-Tyne (32), Bristol (25), Hull (24), Sunderland (23) and Glasgow (20).[32]

The professionalization of architectural practice also facilitated the dissemination of best practice within the framework of a rapidly changing discourse, particularly in terms of the need to establish larger partnerships, to improve office procedures, and to design more cost-effective buildings.[33] The inter-connectedness of commerce and trade was replicated by the international links of architects practicing in major port cities and other metropolitan centres. For example, Charles Herbert Reilly from the Liverpool School of Architecture (1904–1933) was able to utilize his contacts in the USA to place students for office practice on a regular basis, largely in New York, at least until the onset of the interwar depression.[34] Moreover, the establishment of architectural schools in universities, whether in Britain, France or Italy, also reinforced the transfer of design concepts and architectural styles within a framework of cultural imperialism. Again, the case of the Liverpool School of Architecture is instructive in this context: Liverpool graduates took up official positions as government architects in Egypt and Iraq; they also undertook commissions in Baghdad, Cairo and Zanzibar, in some cases combining European Modernism with local architectural traditions.[35] But the School also accepted between five and six overseas students each year and played an important role in training native-born architects and in exporting the Liverpool system of training to both Egypt and Thailand.

But the existence of extensive trading links and business connections did not necessarily imply a rapid adoption of new building styles in individual port cities or the implicit rejection of traditional architectural practices. Despite the fact that Hamburg improved its comparative ranking amongst European ports from fifth in 1879 to second by 1900 and its shipping companies had extended significantly their world-wide links, the early twentieth century witnessed a reassertion of traditional construction methods for commercial buildings.[36] From the early 1900s onwards, the 'common ordinary brick' had become associated with a range of political, social and even spiritual qualities by a number of architects and writers: modernism was increasingly criticized for its disregard of place and location; and, according to Paul Bröcker in the city's planning department, 'the brick skin of an office block should tell us; this is a Hamburg building'.[37] The ten-story Chilehaus, completed in 1924, was symptomatic of a deliberate attempt to provide a local synthesis of modernism and tradition, with the use of 4.8 million bricks representing an explicit symbol of continuity with earlier traditions of office construction.[38] It could of course be argued that the reaffirmation of a traditional brick culture in Hamburg after 1918 reflected a wider sense of middle-class disillusionment with American-inspired modernism resulting from Germany's defeat in the First World War which resulted in the need to revive local (or regional) architectural styles, but it also suggests that embeddedness in international trading networks was not a necessary precondition in major port cities for the direct assimilation of new building concepts and techniques.[39]

In-migration and the structuring of the port-city townscape

As a result of their seaborne links, a significant proportion of port-city in-migrants were of non-national or overseas origins, given that the final destination was often a function of information disseminated through existing communication networks. Because of their international connections, port cities attracted human capital from relatively distant regions; they were focal points for the circulation of peoples, goods and information; and there was a high degree of continuity in the maintenance of family trading networks and diasporic memory.[40] For example, Genoa housed migrants from all over the Mediterranean; Trieste accommodated different Armenian, Greek, Jewish and Serbian 'nations'; and a complex mix of French, Italians, Greeks, Albanians, Bulgarians and Germans exercised a powerful influence in shaping the character of Odessa.[41]

Whether in the case of Baniyan brokers and money-changers in the Red Sea port of Mocha or Tatar merchants in the river port of Kazan, in-migrants often influenced the design and spatial configuration of residential buildings.[42] In other cases, in-migrant communities were responsible for the construction in port cities of communal buildings, including churches, which helped to reinforce their sense of national identity and separateness. In Sweden, for example, the German parish in Gothenburg was founded in 1623 only two years after the city's establishment and its church (the *Christinenkirche*) was consecrated in 1648 as a focal point for in-migrant Protestants from Germany, Holland and Scotland (Fig. 4). But it was not until 1855 that the foundation stone for St Andrew's, a separate church for the increasingly influential English (Scottish) community, was finally laid by Robert Dickson a 'Merchant and Senior of the British Factory of Gothenburg'.[43] In the case of the mission churches established overseas by the Swedish Patriotic Evangelical Society from the early 1860s onwards the intention was to seize every opportunity to proclaim God's word amongst Scandinavian sailors in foreign ports and to offer a welcoming, but clearly recognizable, environment with a range of local newspapers, traditional refreshments, and, when necessary, welfare support.[44] Where new mission churches were built in major port cities, such as Liverpool and Hamburg, they invariably incorporated Swedish or Scandinavian design elements.[45] In Liverpool, in particular, the church designed by W. D. Caröe (1883–1884) incorporated many distinct, Scandinavian features, including stepped gables and a concave-sided, lead-covered spire over the entrance (Fig. 5). It is often argued that architecture, in a reflexive way, can express 'contested and ambiguous national identities'.[46] For Scandinavians nationality itself became an increasingly important issue in the course of the nineteenth

Figure 4: The Christinekirche, Gothenburg (1648)

Figure 5: Gustaf Adolfs Kyrka, Liverpool (1883–84)

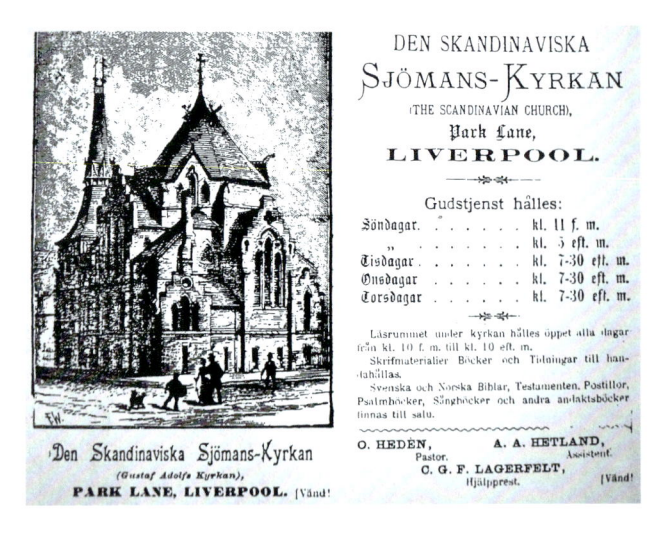

Figure 6: The Scandinavian Church, Liverpool: advertising card from the mid-1890s

Figure 7: Gustaf-Adolfskirche, Hamburg (1906–07)

century, whether within the framework of the personal union between Sweden and Norway, or within Finland where there is evidence of a united attempt to avoid the assimilation of Finnish culture by Russian laws and customs. But although the Seamen's Church in Liverpool catered for all Scandinavians, the local vicars became increasingly involved in defining or determining nationality entitlement, while its overall design (Fig. 6) served to reinforce a sense of 'separateness' and distinctiveness from the indigenous local community.[47] Similarly in Hamburg (Fig. 7), the Swedish Seamen's Church with its network of related associations (including the Swedish School and Lecture Societies, the Swedish Ladies Club, and the Swedish Club, established in 1906) not only served the common interests of Swedish residents but sought directly to 'preserve' the national language.[48]

By the early twentieth century the church authorities and mission societies of many European countries, including Britain, Denmark, Germany and Sweden, had established a dense network of overseas churches in individual port cities, reflecting the needs of in-migrant national communities, transient seafarers and emigrants. In Buenos Aires, for example, an Anglican Church (St. John's Cathedral) was established after the Treaty of 1825, the foundation stone of the Presbyterian Church was laid in 1833, and a separate Protestant Church, with English, Scots, American and German merchants as its principal supporters, was opened in 1862.[49] Frequently, church buildings associated with specific in-migrant groups reflected their continued sense of nationality and the architectural legacy of their countries of origin. This was certainly the case with the Greek Orthodox Church of St. Nicholas in Liverpool (executed by Henry Sumners following a competition won by W & J Hay in 1864) which represented a smaller-scale version of the Church of St. Theodore in Constantinople (Fig. 8).[50] But the wider cultural and social significance of in-migrant church architecture was absent in some port cities because properties were either rented or taken over from other denominations. The church maintained by the *Congregación Sueca* in Buenos Aires in the early 1930s, although it attracted over 9,000 visitors annually to its reading room left 'something of a provisional impression', just as the premises used for the Swedish Seamen's Church in Bremen in the period after the Second World War had simply been rented on a provisional basis.[51] Similarly, despite the relative importance and commercial status of many German in-migrant merchants in Liverpool in the nineteenth century, the congregation of the Deutsche Evangelische Kirche (established in 1846) initially worshipped in Anglican premises, subsequently purchased the Newington Chapel in Renshaw Street, and finally occupied the Presbyterian Church in Canning Street.[52] Although the church, with its extended institutional and welfare network, undoubtedly functioned as a focal point which helped to sustain a sense of Germanness, its visual presence was never made explicit and the difficulty of reinforcing a sense of German separateness without upsetting the local population was highlighted in 1877 when members of the congregation on their summer outing to New Ferry felt it necessary to carry both German and English flags.[53]

Two points need to be emphasized. First, the architectural legacy in port cities of in-migrant communities, whether in relation to church, commercial or residential buildings, was essentially a result of trade patterns and the role of overseas commercial networks: it was not dependent on the extension of colonial power. Secondly, ethnicity became an increasingly dominant factor in constructing the international division of labour from the late-nineteenth century onwards, with the result that larger commercial port cities, such as Hamburg, Liverpool, Marseille, Portland, Rotterdam, witnessed the settlement of increasing numbers of in-migrants from China, West Africa, the Middle East and the Philippines.⁵⁴ These communities were often characterized by spatial concentration; they attracted considerable attention from the indigenous population; and China Town (as a concept) was generally viewed as an 'exotic' place with a close association with drugs, gambling and prostitution.⁵⁵ But although these communities had a perceptible impact on the external appearance of their immediate environment, their initial influence on port-city architecture was marginal and it is only with the passage of time that ethnically distinct features have been developed.⁵⁶

Architecture, Commercial Practices and the Profits of Port City Trade: the case of Liverpool

Port cities, in general, were dominated not only by commerce and trade, but also by the ideology of merchant capital.⁵⁷ The townscape structure (including the docks and warehouse, the commercial centre and residential areas) as well as the social life of individual buildings often reflected the interplay between these two factors.⁵⁸ In order to explore the extent to which the underlying economic and social profile of port cities affected the relationship between architecture, culture and daily life, the social significance of three specific types of buildings from Liverpool in the late-nineteenth and early-twentieth century will be assessed as representative of distinct port-city typologies which provide a basis for understanding the historic organization of urban commercial sectors in the modern period.

Both in a Byzantine and Venetian context, public structures were provided for the facilitation of trade and for guaranteeing a certain degree of transparency over commercial transactions. Despite Liverpool's rapid development during the second half of the eighteenth century, to a great extent directly connected with the slave trade, many of its merchants still preferred to do business in the open street as the earlier Exchange was no longer adequate for coping with the increased volume of business transactions.⁵⁹ At the beginning of the nineteenth century, however, a decision was made to clear away some remaining houses north of the Town Hall and to create commercial buildings which would harmonize with its neo-classical style. Significantly, the venture was taken forward by a share-holding company (valued at £80,000) which was over-subscribed within three hours. The three-sided structure of The Exchange enclosed an open area ('a noble neoclassical quadrangle') for conducting business and consisted of a news-room, counting houses and extensive warehousing facilities. It offered 'dignity and repose' and it was generally agreed that the combination of commercial and municipal buildings has 'never been surpassed'.⁶⁰ But the facilities offered by the New Exchange, completed in 1808, failed to keep pace with the growing commercial needs of Liverpool's merchants and it was replaced in the mid-1860s by a more substantial building in the Flemish (or French) Renaissance style, designed by T. M. Wyatt, with 'numerous storeys and offices': even if it was 'not especially adapted for architectural effect', its news-room was deemed to be 'a noble apartment'.⁶¹ Later

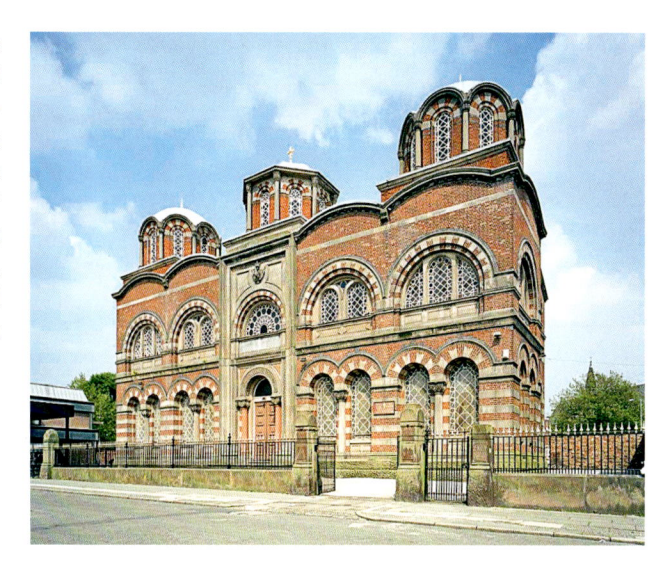

Figure 8: The Greek Orthodox Church in Liverpool (1870)

photographs (Fig. 9), including one by Francis Frith from 1893, provide a clearer indication of the social life of the Exchange and reflects its wider importance in the structuring of commercial relations within the city.⁶²

Commerce and long-distance overseas trade in nineteenth-century Liverpool (as elsewhere) were invariably associated with a high degree of risk and uncertainty. As a major port city, Liverpool attracted a large number of individuals determined to make a fortune as quickly as possible, either as agents, brokers, merchants or ship-owners. In the late nineteenth century over 50 per cent of the subscribers to the Exchange had not been members a decade earlier and it has been estimated that over three-quarters of them would encounter difficulties in meeting their liabilities at some point in time.⁶³ Indeed, the risk of failure was ever present. Of all the business partnerships registered in 1852, approximately 60 per cent had either been dissolved or had ceased trading by 1863 and 83 per cent of the sole traders operating within Liverpool's merchant community in 1873 were never heard of again.⁶⁴ But business uncertainty and transaction costs could be reduced (although never eliminated) by the creation of a common business culture which reflected shared attitudes, aspirations and goodwill. Not only did the establishment and maintenance of personal relations offer a tangible solution to the persistent problems of agency and asymmetrical information, but networks were often of critical importance in determining commercial survival at a time when the business environment, as a whole, continued to be characterized by 'low trust and morality'.⁶⁵ Within such a context, entrepreneurial networks embedded within an increasingly cohesive cultural framework helped to minimize market imperfections by coordinating valuable information and by strengthening trust and reputation. It is within this context that the social life of the Liverpool Exchange needs to be understood. Trading on Change, as it was known, brought together many of the key operators within the local business community within a carefully regulated framework: it promoted physical proximity and personal interaction; while the dress code required for 'trading on the

Figure 9: The Exchange, Liverpool (1864–67)

Figure 10: The Cunard Building, Liverpool (1916)

flags' helped to reinforce reputation and trust. Indeed, Queen Victoria on a visit to Liverpool in 1851 observed that she had 'never seen so many well-dressed gentlemen together', as had been the case on the Exchange.

But external appearances were also important in defining and profiling the trustworthiness of individual companies. By the end of the nineteenth century, Cunard, with its government mail contract and its fleet of large, passenger-carrying steamers, was undoubtedly Liverpool's flagship shipping company.[66] The Company had also outgrown its previous offices and therefore utilized the opportunity created by the development of the waterfront site (following the closure and infilling of George's Dock) to develop a new headquarters designed by the Liverpool practice of Willinck and Thicknesse in conjunction with the Anglo-French architectural practice of Mewès & Davis in a style which represented a mixture of Italian Renaissance and Greek Revival influences.[67] The original architectural competition was intended to produce a design which would harmonize with the new offices of the Mersey Docks and Harbour Company, but neither the winning submission nor the final building completed in 1916 ever fulfilled that purpose. Instead, the six-storey structure constructed by Holland, Hannen & Cubitts using a reinforced concrete frame clad in Portland stone sought to provide an impression of resilience, rugged strength and solidity, with public spaces, in particular the first-class passenger lounge on the first floor, deliberately used to evoke the character of great Cunard ships (Fig. 10).[68] Indeed, the commercial success of the firm had been built on 'convenience and comfort', rather than gratuitous luxury or unproven technology.[69] Unlike many of its rivals, it had avoided the extremes of extravagance and parsimony; it had rejected any improvements which had not been satisfactorily tested; and it had prioritized the construction of strong, reliable and well-manned ships.[70] To this extent, the new Cunard headquarters was explicitly intended to reflect the key, underlying qualities of the shipping company itself.

In a wider context, the ideology of merchant capital which dominated many port cities in the nineteenth century implied a belief in the concept of the 'night-watchman' state, an adherence to liberal economic principles, and an underlying commitment to prevent any serious disruption to commerce and trade.[71] It was also accompanied by a general unwillingness to countenance unnecessary social welfare expenditure and a disproportionate reliance on charity and philanthropy.[72] The motives behind charitable involvement were undoubtedly varied: it often involved an emphasis on moral reform and seldom addressed the underlying socio-economic causes of ill-health, poverty and destitution.[73] The involvement in charitable activity was also a means of developing and consolidating network links within Liverpool's business community; it served to enhance the reputational profile of individual merchants; and endowed them with additional powers of social control.

In individual cases, this was evident in the institutional structures which were established throughout the city as evidence of charitable and philanthropic activity by members of the mercantile community. The Royal Liverpool Seamen's Orphan Institution (Fig. 11) is one example of the architectural legacy of local charity. Seafaring had always involved significant domestic costs in terms of the impact of the prolonged absence of maritime husbands on the allocation of family responsibilities and the high risk of occupational injury through accidents onboard ship and premature death by drowning.[74] In 1866, for example, almost 5,000 British seafarers died at sea (approximately 2.4 per cent of the registered workforce), of whom 2,390 were reported drowned: in 1880 it was reported that 'sorrow on the sea is still very great, almost unabated'.[75] The initiative to establish a charitable institution to support and educate the orphans of seafarers was taken by a group of leading Liverpool ship owners at a meeting in December 1868 at the Mercantile Marine Service Association Rooms. The orphanage opened in August of the following year in temporary accommodation in Duke Street with 60 resident children, but the acquisition of land from the Town Corporation in 1870 led to the construction of a purpose-built orphanage designed by Alfred Waterhouse (1830–1915) which included a school, an infirmary, a chapel, a boy's swimming pool, and shared dining facilities, with the children accommodated in separate boys' and girls' wings. By the end of the century 321 children attended the orphanage, while a further 508 were supported on the basis of outdoor relief. At its formal opening in 1874 Lord Derby emphasized that saving orphaned children 'from the workhouse or the streets is not merely an act of charity; it is an act of duty and of justice'.[76]

Figure 11: The Royal Seamen's Orphan Institution, Liverpool

However, the establishment of the (Royal) Liverpool Seamen's Orphan Institution has a wider significance in terms of understanding the social life of the city, the ideology of merchant capital with its emphasis on charitable giving (rather than improved social welfare provision), and the class- and gender-specific treatment of the asylum's children. Despite Liverpool's increasing dependency on commerce and trade from the mid-eighteenth century onwards, the foundation of a suitable institution for the children of sailors who had been lost at sea took place at a comparatively late date. The (Royal) Merchant Seamen's Orphan Asylum had been established in London's docklands as early as 1827, while the Seamen's and General Orphan Asylum had been opened in Hull in 1866. Although a number of prominent Liverpool merchants played a critical role in developing the Seamen's Orphan Institution, including leading ship owners such as Bryce Allan, James Beazley, and Ralph Brocklebank, many members of the merchant community remained 'deaf to the loud calls which the widows and orphans of sailors continually make': despite the fact that mariners ploughed the ocean and brought home their produce, too many simply made an excuse that the financing of the Institution did not concern them.[77] By 1912, the orphanage only had 507 subscribers, despite the fact that they were entitled to nominate children for admission, and it was disproportionately dependent for annual funding on the contributions to collection boxes on steamers and other ships which were subject to considerable fluctuation. Moreover, charity came at a price. The dining hall was 'cavernous and austere'; the Institution was run on extremely strict rules and regulations; girls were trained to become domestic servants; and many boys were directed into seafaring through an arrangement with the training ship *Indefatigable* and suffered the same fate as their fathers.[78]

Port cities were also generally characterized by extreme wealth inequality. On the one hand, significant wealth could be accumulated through commerce and trade, despite its inherent risks, while, on the other hand, both seafaring and the operation of dock and warehousing systems relied heavily on casual labour in a context where wages were driven down by high rates of in-migration. Even in relatively iso-

Figure 12: Broughton Hall, West Derby

lated coastal communities, such as the trading posts on the Lofoten Islands, merchants deliberately created information for other users of local space by the size and external colour of their housing in a manner which set them apart from other social classes, while in larger commercial ports the design and interior decoration of residential housing was intricately related to status and public standing.[79] This was explicitly the case in Liverpool, where people of wealth and position 'surrounded themselves with certain attributes of power and wealth', as means of providing the populace with 'some indication of their rank and their social status'.[80] Indeed, in the window tax assessment of 1850 (which was based on properties with eight or more windows), Liverpool registered the highest assessment total in Britain (well in excess of Manchester or Bath), but the grandeur of a private residence was not necessarily a reliable indicator of status as references in the contemporary press to 'shams and glitters' suggests that it was widely understood that rapidly acquired wealth could just as easily be lost.[81]

The houses designed and constructed for Liverpool's merchant elite, particularly in the late –nineteenth and early-twentieth century, were intended to reflect the social and business lives of their occupiers. Although there were few residences with dining rooms for more than 30 guests, provision was regularly made for extensive picture galleries, libraries and billiard rooms.[82] The imposing Gothic revival mansion, Broughton Hall (Yew Tree Lane, West Derby), designed by Walter Scott for the in-migrant German merchant Gustavus C. Schwabe (Fig. 12) could only be managed with the assistance of a large residential staff: the dining room was particularly spacious; while it was over a game of billiards here that Schwabe suggested to Thomas Henry Ismay the founding of a new transatlantic shipping line which later became the White Star Line.[83] Indeed, entertaining at home was an integral aspect of interaction and networking for Liverpool's merchant elite, particularly during the winter season: it was arranged in a structured, reciprocal manner which still allowed opportunities for spontaneous celebrations, and its scale was sometimes very substantial. On 15 February 1882, for example, the Holts (one of Liverpool's pre-eminent cotton-trading firms) held a party for 'fully 140, chiefly young dancing people', while the family residence (Sudley) also included 'farming and poultry yards and fields' which led to additional visits from close friends within the business community.[84] To this extent, architecture, artistic taste, as well as an interest in agriculture and horticulture, combined to reinforce the perception of reputation and social status.

Structuring the world of the seafarer ashore

Most ports had a distinct, if not notorious, sailortown which invariably served as a focal point for life ashore: Baltimore's 'The Block' was 'renowned among seafarers'; in Hamburg, St. Pauli (at least until 1939) was 'one great web of predatory spiders' with numerous beer-gardens, dance-halls and taverns; in Liverpool, the area in from the new quay was 'a mass of sailor taverns and low-class drinking houses with gin palaces in every adjacent street'; while the 'watering holes' and bath-houses of Yokohama were well known amongst foreign seamen.[85] Sailortown, with its extended range of attractions, delights and depravities, was an important aspect of the social life of port cities: it was a 'zone of cultural contact' with a well-defined diaspora space where seafarers ashore spent their hard-earned wages on 'beer, women and song'.[86]

But the increasing establishment of sailors' homes from the mid-1830s onwards modified the landscape of sailortown, as civic agencies and mission societies sought to cater for the welfare needs of seafarers.[87] By the early 1850s, the Sailors Home in London catered for approximately 5,000 sailors each year and its bed capacity was doubled in 1865, although many remained dependent on private sector lodging keepers, sometimes of questionable reliability.[88] The Liverpool Sailors' Home catered for 1,822 sailors and 410 apprentices in 1845, its first year of operation, but by 1902 it accommodated 7,245 boarders.[89] It was a massive presence close to the waterfront: it was architecturally 'extravagant externally', while inside the simple and plain bedrooms opened off an impressive galleried atrium with decorative ironwork (Fig. 13, 14).[90] In Bombay, the Royal Alfred Sailors' Home (Fig. 15), designed in the Gothic style by Frederick William Stevens (1847–1900) was a 'rather luxurious hostel' with large airy rooms and bathrooms.[91] Its foundation stone was re-laid in 1872 and the work on the sculptures which were designed to enhance its appearance was supervised by John Lockwood Kipling, as Professor of Architectural Sculpture. In addition, sailors' homes were increasingly provided by individual mission societies, sometimes for specific groups of seafarers, whether defined by nationality, religion or ethnicity. For example, the German Seamen's Mission in Hoboken, New York, regarded as a 'suburb of Bremen' by many seafarers, attracted over 18,000 visitors in its first year of operation in 1907.[92] In the course of the twentieth century individual shipping lines, such as the Blue Funnel Line and the Elder Dempster Line, also created hostels for their crew, particularly if they had been recruited overseas.[93]

But the provision of sailors' homes was designed to achieve wider objectives in changing or even transforming the lives of seafarers, specifically by curbing the excesses normally associated with seamen on shore leave. The ministers at the Finnish Seamen's Mission in London perceived seamen in foreign ports as 'helpless figures, lonely, gullible and carefree to the point of recklessness' and always prone to fall victim to the 'Devil's emissaries'.[94] Similarly, in Liverpool the pastor and his assistant at the Scandinavian Seamen's Church regularly visited Nordic ships with the intention of distributing religious tracts. But there is some evidence to suggest that the provision of accommodation for seafarers, sometimes located in imposing architectural structures, did facilitate a more careful husbandry of financial resources. Or perhaps some sailors never fitted the dominant, stereotypical image. In its first 40 years of operation the London Sailors' Home had taken deposits of over £2m, of which over £700,000 had been remitted to family and friends: in 1902 the Sailors' Home in Liverpool accepted £31,073 on deposit for safekeeping or for remitting home; the Finnish Seamen's Mission in London registered annual deposits of £1,040 between 1889 and 1899; while the Scandinavian Seamen's Church in Liverpool received deposits valued at over £9,491 between 1940 and 1948 from 68 individual seafarers.[95] Sailors' homes, therefore, provide an invaluable insight into the social lives of seafarers while ashore and the extent to which they retained a sense of commitment and responsibility to family and friends, despite a persistent view amongst elite groups in society that they were generally 'dissolute' and 'easily led astray'.[96]

Conclusion: the interpretation and preservation of the social life of port-city architecture

Today, as was the case in the past, architecture plays a key role in terms of how port cities represent themselves to external observers and the wider world.[97] The architectural profile of port cities reflects a changing and symbiotic relationship with economic actors involved in trade and commerce; civic buildings were designed to display the aspirations and influence of the political elite; office buildings reflected a deliberate use of historical styles and building materials to reinforce status and to emphasize their role as a 'visible embodiment of modern commerce'; while places of worship were often structured to justify the manipulation of the social order by the dominant, mercantile classes or to reinforce a sense of confessional, ethnic or national identity.[98] Even within an established port-city typology, architectural styles could sometimes reflect the need to assert a specific local or regional identity (as was the case with Hamburg after the First World War), but the changing pattern of international commerce and trade with port-cities as a focal point also served as a mechanism for the assimilation of historic design features as well as for the dissemination of new architectural forms.

This chapter has attempted to raise some general, theoretical questions relating to the social life of port architecture drawing on a range of historical and site-specific case studies. It has sought to disentangle the factors which have helped to structure the townscape of ports, not only in relation to their commercial operations, but also in the context

Figure 13: The Sailors' Home, Liverpool

Figure 14: The interior of the Sailors' Home, Liverpool

Figure 15: The Royal Alfred Sailors' Home, Bombay

of the provision and significance of charitable, civic, religious and residential buildings. Too often, architectural historians and city planners are concerned primarily with the design and structure of port architecture, rather than its wider social life or the relationship between building design and the articulation of economic and political power, despite the fact that the ground used for building in most cases has been defined by the state or set aside by legislative decrees.[99] There is seldom any attempt to analyse the role of individual buildings within the framework of a social theory of space, to disentangle the wider objectives of commercial, political or religious actors in structuring urban space, or to conceptualize urban landscapes as public history.[100] The waterfront regeneration of many ports in the last few decades has also served to undermine a traditional sense of place identity, as links with the maritime and trading past become weaker, just as recent economic development has sometimes changed the character of commercial areas and led to the demise of sailortown.[101] But the architectural history of port-cities is embedded in a range of cultural, economic and political factors; it reflects the importance of the business community and the ideology of merchant capital; the influence of ethnic in-migrants and alternative sub-cultures; and the mediating role of a rapidly professionalizing architectural profession. All of these issues need to be addressed if we are to provide a more convincing appreciation of the social life of port architecture or to offer a better interpretation for the choice of form and materials in the design of specific port-city buildings and their wider significance both for contemporaries and for wider audiences today.

I would like to express my thanks to my colleague Paul Jones and other participants at the international workshop on the Social Life of Port Architecture, held at the Centre for Port and Maritime History, University of Liverpool, in June this year and supported financially by English Heritage. Without such a lively and productive exchange of ideas, this contribution would never have assumed its final form.

Abstract

Das soziale Leben der Hafen-Architektur: Geschichte, Politik, Wirtschaft und Kultur

Die Architektur von Hafenstädten ist untrennbar verknüpft mit der gesellschaftlichen, politischen, wirtschaftlichen und kulturellen Entwicklung dieser Städte und ihrer Rolle im internationalen Handel. Historisch waren es Kaufleute, die die herrschende politische Elite in den Hafenstädten stellten. Sie waren es, die größere Projekte in Auftrag gaben: Ob beim Bau von Docks, der Schaffung einer Infrastruktur für

Bürger und Wirtschaft oder bei der Errichtung von Wohngebäuden – die Kaufleute konnten auf diese Weise ihren Status an herausragender Stelle im städtischen Raum manifestieren. Der politische und kulturelle Bezugsrahmen, in den diese Bauten und Gebäude hineingesetzt wurden, bot die Möglichkeit, Handel und Gewerbe in klar definierte, breit angelegte zivilisatorische Werte einzubetten. Die Hafenstadt-Architektur wurde so zu einem der Hauptaustragungsorte der Beschäftigung mit anderen Kulturen, indem man sich historisierender Stilmittel bediente und in einen Dialog mit der Arbeiterklasse trat, die es zu zivilisieren galt, oder, indem man bewusst ‚exotische' Motive verwendete, die ein Spiegel der Handelsverbindungen des Hafens in alle Welt waren. Vielleicht noch entscheidender war die Tatsache, dass die Hafenstadt-Architektur eine visuelle Manifestation lokaler Traditionen und Leistungen war, und zwar besonders im Kontext öffentlicher wie gewerblicher Großarchitektur. Sie war jedoch gleichzeitig Spiegel der gesellschaftlichen Interaktionen, die wiederum Voraussetzung waren für das Knüpfen von Handelsnetzwerken sowohl innerhalb der Städte als auch darüber hinaus. Die Baugliederung der inneren Räume macht die impliziten und expliziten Prämissen sozialer Beziehungen der Zeit und ganz allgemein der klassenhierarchischen Strukturen sichtbar.

Der vorliegende Beitrag befasst sich mit Faktoren wie Struktur, Funktion und Wahrnehmung von Hafenstadt-Architektur, die miteinander in enger Beziehung stehen. Wie wirkte sich der Handel auf die Bebauung des öffentlichen Raumes in Hafenstädten und auf die Verbreitung bestimmter Baustile aus? Wie wirkmächtig waren gesellschaftliche Usancen und Werte (religiöse wie weltliche) angesichts ihrer Bedeutung für die Herstellung und Aufrechterhaltung von Handelsnetzwerken bei der architektonischen Ausgestaltung von Hafenstädten? Der Bevölkerungszuwachs der Hafenstädte war durch eine übermäßige Abhängigkeit von der Zuwanderung aus fernen Ländern geprägt, mit dem Ergebnis einer oft deutlich multi-ethnischen Bevölkerungsstruktur. Inwieweit hatte diese Vielvölker-Einwanderung und die selektive Festigung von Netzwerken in der Diaspora Einfluss auf die physischen Eigenschaften der Hafenstadt-Architektur und wie wirkte sie sich auf das Erleben dieser Architektur aus? Seit Beginn des 19. Jahrhunderts professionalisierten sich die in der Architektur praktisch Tätigen zusehends. Aber in wie großem Umfange bedienten sich die Praktiker in den Hafenstädten dabei internationaler Symbolik und moderner Bautechniken? Bemühten sie sich um die Schaffung eines eigenen, lokalen Stadtbildes, das sich von anderen abhob? Und, was für die Forschung von vielleicht größtem Belang ist: Was lässt sich – außerhalb von literarischen Beschreibungen und in der Fachkritik – über die allgemeine Wahrnehmung und Auslegung der Hafenstadt-Architektur sagen?

Um die aufgeworfenen Fragen anzugehen, konzentriert sich der vorliegende Beitrag auf eine Reihe miteinander in Beziehung stehender Aspekte: Die Bedeutung von mächtigen Handelsimperien wie Venedig und Großbritannien für die Verbreitung bestimmter Architekturstile in Hafenstädten sowie der Einfluss von Handelsströmen und -beziehungen auf die Verfügbarkeit und Nutzung von bestimmten Baustoffen; die Rolle der Architekten, die den Sprachduktus und die materialistische Bildsprache imperialer Macht noch verstärkten; ferner die Entstehungsprozesse des durch Handel und Gewerbe wachsenden Reichtums, das architektonische Erbe, das in den Geschäftszentren vieler Hafenstädte sowie an den Wohnhäusern einzelner Kaufmannsfamilien erkennbar wird; und die Herausbildung von Matrosenvierteln, insbesondere in Bezug auf die Schaffung und Nutzung von Seemannsheimen. Der vorliegende Beitrag analysiert darüber hinaus die Bedeutung der Einwanderung sowie Niederlassung von Einwanderern als Beitrag zur ethnisch-kulturellen Identitätsstiftung in Hafenstädten. Schließlich soll diskutiert werden, wie die Hafenstadt-Architektur wahrgenommen wurde, welche symbolische Beziehung zwischen ihr und den politischen und wirtschaftlichen Akteuren bestand und es soll eine Erörterung des Spannungsfeldes zwischen Stadterneuerung und Erhaltung historischer Bausubstanz vorgenommen werden, in der ein vertieftes Verständnis für das gesellschaftliche Leben in Hafenstädten aufscheint, das über sie selbst hinausweist. Um die aufgeworfenen Fragestellungen voranzubringen, stützt sich der vorliegende Beitrag auf eine breite Materialauswahl. Jedoch sollen auch jüngste Forschungsergebnisse aus Liverpool herangezogen werden, die im Rahmen des Mercantile Liverpool Project erzielt wurden, sowie die Arbeiten von Architekturhistorikern, Kulturanthropologen und Soziologen, die damit begonnen haben, das gesellschaftliche Leben von Hafenstädten im Laufe ihrer geschichtlichen Entwicklung zu erkunden sowie die kulturelle, wirtschaftliche und politische Bedeutung vieler maßgeblicher Bauten zu beleuchten.

Bibliography

ALBION, Robert Greenhalgh, The Rise of New York Port (1815–1860), Hamden, Connecticut 1961 (reprint of 1939 edition)

ALEXANDER, Michael, Medievalism: the Middle Ages in modern England, Yale University Press, 1987.

ALOFSIN, Anthony, When Buildings Speak: Architecture as Language in the Habsburg Empire and Its Aftermath, 1867–1933, Chicago and London: University of Chicago Press, 2006.

AMENDA, Lars, Chinese seafarers in European Ports 1880 to 1950, unpublished paper presented at the 10th North Sea History Conference, The Parallel Worlds of the Seafarer Ashore, Afloat and Abroad, Gothenburg, September 2011.

ARSLAN, Eduardo, Gothic Architecture in Venice, 1971, New York: Phaidon.

John R. ASHTON, Lives and livelihoods in Little London The story of the British in Gothenburg 1621–2001, Sävedalen: Warne Förlag, 2003.

BABCOCK, F. Lawrence, Spanning the Atlantic, New York, 1941.

Gülsüm BAYDAR, The Cultural Burden of Architecture, in: Journal of Architectural Education, 2004, Heft 57, Nr. 4, pp. 19–27.

BEAUMONT, E. W., CHRISTOFIDES, G. F. HORSFALL, T. E. HALL, An Historical Survey of the Area between The Exchange Flags and Custom House 1725–1936, The

School of Architecture, University of Liverpool, Liverpool, 1936.

BELCHEM, John, Shock City: Sailortown Liverpool, paper presented at the conference On the Waterfront Culture, Heritage and Regeneration of Port Cities, BT Convention Centre, Kings Waterfront, 19–21 November 2008 (http://www.english-heritage.org.uk/context/publications/docs/waterfront-part2.pdf).

BELCHEM, John and MACRAILD, Donald M., Cosmopolitan Liverpool, in: John Belchem ed.), Liverpool 800 Culture, Character & History, Liverpool: Liverpool University Press, 2006, pp. 311–392.

BOYLE, Bernard Michael, Architectural Practice in America, 1865-1965 – Ideal and Reality, in: Spiro Kostof (ed.), The Architect, Chapters in the History of the Profession, Oxford and New York: Oxford University Press, 1977, pp. 309–344.

BRAIN, David, Practical Knowledge and Occupational Control: The Professionalization of Architecture in the United States, in Sociological Forum, Heft 6, Nr. 2, 1991, pp. 239–268.

BREEN, A. and RIGBY, D., The New Waterfront: a Worldwide Urban Success Story, London: Thames and Hudson, 1996.

BROOKS, Michael, 'The Builder' in the 1840s: The Making of a Magazine, The Shaping of a Profession, in: Victorian Periodicals Review, Heft 14, Nr. 3, 1981, pp. 87–91.

BROWN, Sarah and FIGUEIREDO, Peter de; Religion and Place Liverpool's historic places of worship, Swindon: English Heritage, 2008.

BUSQUETS, Joan; Barcelona: The Urban Evolution of a Compact City, Rovereta and Cambridge, Mass., 2005.

CATTARUZZA, Marina, Population Dynamics and Economic Change in Trieste and its Hinterland, 1850–1914, in: Richard Lawton and Robert Lee (eds.), Population and Society in Western European Port-Cities, c. 1650–1939, Liverpool: Liverpool University Press, 2002, 176–211.

CHAMBERLAIN, Mary; Diasporic Memories: Community, Individuality, and Creativity – A Life Stories Perspective, in: Oral History Review, Heft 36, Nr. 2, 2009, pp. 177–187.

CHOJNACKI, Stanley, Social Identity in Renaissance Venice: The Second Serrata, in: Renaissance Studies, Heft 8, Nr. 4, 1994, pp. 341–358.

COCK, Randolph; DAVIES, John and MÄENPÄÄ, Sari, The Liverpool Merchant Community: a Reconstruction, in: Robert Lee (ed.), Networks of Power and Influence: business, culture and identity in Liverpool's Merchant Community, 1800–1914, Aldershot: Ashgate, 2012 (forthcoming).

COOKSON, Gillian; Family Firms and Business Networks: Textile Engineering in Yorkshire, 1780–1830, in: Business History, Heft 39, Nr. 1, 1997, pp. 1–20.

CRINSON, Mark; Empire Building: Orientalism and Victorian Architecture, London and New York: Routledge, 1996.

'Critical Words from Abroad', in: American Architecture and Building News, Heft 34, 26 December 1891, p. 198.

CROUCH, Christopher; Design Culture in Liverpool 1880-1914 The Origins of the Liverpool School of Architecture, Liverpool: Liverpool University Press, 2002.

CUSACK, Patricia; Architects and the reinforced concrete specialist in Britain, 1905–1908, Journal of the Society of Architectural Historians of Great Britain, Heft 29, 1986, pp. 183–196.

DELANTY; Gerard and JONES, Paul R., European Identity and Architecture, in: European Journal of Social Theory, 2002, Heft 5, Nr. 4, pp. 453–466.

Edward Henry Earl of DERBY, Speeches and Addresses by Edward Henry, Earl of Derby, London, 1894.

DEUTSCHE EVANGELISCHE KIRCHE ZU LIVERPOOL, Neun und Dreißigster Jahres-Bericht über die Deutsche Evangelische Kirche zu Liverpool, Liverpool: Scholl & McGee, 1888.

DOSTOGLU, Sibel Bozdogan; Towards Professional Legitimacy and Power: An Inquiry into the struggle, achievements and dilemmas of the architecture profession through analysis of Chicago 1871–1909, unpublished doctoral dissertation, University of Chicago, 1982.

DUBIN, Lois C.; The port Jews of Habsburg Trieste: absolutist politics and enlightenment culture (Stanford studies in Jewish history and culture), Stanford University Press, 1999.

DUNNE; Jack and RICHMOND, Peter; The World in One School The History and Influence of the Liverpool School of Architecture 1894–2008, Liverpool: Liverpool University Press, 2008.

DURAND, A.; La politique française a l'égard des ports maritimes sous la troisième république, Paris, 1904.

EKELUND, Kristina; Svenska Gustaf-Adolfskyrkan 100-år, Hamburg, 2007.

ELLIS, Aytoun, Heir of Adventure The story of Brown, Shipley & Co. Merchant Bankers 1810-1960, London: Brown, Shipley & Co. Ltd., 1960.

ENGELBERG, Eva von; Die Bautradition der Republik Venedig, in: Weiterbauen (Sutor-Professur für Denkmalpflege und Entwerfen, Band II, 2006–2008), 2009, pp. 88–93.

EVANS, Bob; Mersey Mariners, Birkenhead: Countyvise, 1997 (2002 reprint).

L. FABI, La carita dei ricchi. Povertà e assistenza nella Trieste laica e asburgica del XIX secolo, Milan, 1976.

FALKUS, Malcolm; The Blue Funnel Legend. A History of the Ocean Steam Ship Company, 1865–1973, Basingstoke: MacMillan, 1990.

FELLONI, Giuseppi, The Population Dynamics and Economic Development of Genoa, 1750–1939, in: Richard Lawton and Robert Lee (eds.), Population and Society in Western European Port-Cities, c. 1650–1939, Liverpool: Liverpool University Press, 2002, 74–90.

FENSKE, Gail; The Beaux Arts Architect and the Skyscraper, in: Roberta Moundry (ed.), The American Skyscraper, Cultural Histories, Cambridge and New York: Cambridge University Press, 2005, pp. 19–37.

FEYS, Torsten; Fischer, Lewis R.; Hoste, Stéphanie and Vanfraechem, Stephan (eds.), Maritime Transport and Migration. Connections Between Maritime and Migration Networks (Research in Maritime History, Nr. 33), St. John's Newfoundland, 2007.

FIGUEIREDO, Peter de; Symbols of Empire: The Buildings of Liverpool Waterfront, in: Architectural History, Heft 46, 2003, pp. 229–254.

W. B. FORWOOD, Recollections of a Busy Life, Liverpool: H. Young & Sons, 1910.

FROST; Diane (ed.), Ethnic Labour and British Imperial Trade: A History of Ethnic Seafarers in the UK, London: Frank Cass, 1995.

FROST, Diane; Racism, Work and Unemployment: West African Seamen in Liverpool 1880s–1960s, in: Diane Frost (ed.), Ethnic Labour and British Imperial Trade: A History of Ethnic Seafarers in the UK, London: Frank Cass, 1995, pp. 22–33.

FULLER, Mia; Moderns Abroad: Architecture, Cities, and Italian Imperialism, London and New York: Routledge, 2007.

GEORGOPOULOU, Maria; Mapping Religious and Ethnic Identities in the Venetian Colonial Empire, in: Journal of Medieval and Early Modern Studies, Heft 26, Nr. 3, 1996, pp. 467–496.

GEORGOPOULOU, Maria; Venice's Mediterranean Colonies Architecture and Urbanism, Cambridge: Cambridge University Press, 2001.

GILES, Colum; Building a Better Society Liverpool's historic institutional buildings, Swindon: English Heritage, 2008.

GILES, Colum; The character of port cities: an assessment of the value of surviving buildings, unpublished paper presented at the International Workshop on The Social Life of Port Architecture: History, Politics, Commerce, and Culture (from the early eighteenth century to the present day), Centre for Port and Maritime History, University of Liverpool, June 2011.

GILES; Colum and HAWKINS, Bob; Storehouses of Empire Liverpool's Historic Warehouses, London: English Heritage, 2004.

GOY, Richard J.; The House of Gold: Building a Palace in Medieval Venice, Cambridge, 1992.

GOY, Richard J; Venice The City and its Architecture, London, 1997.

GREGORY, Daniel Platt; Magazine Modern: A Study of the American Architectural Press, 1919–1930, unpublished doctoral dissertation, University of California, Berkeley, 1982.

GRITT, Andrew; Representations of mariners and maritime communities c. 1850–1850 (http://www.history.ac.uk/ihr/Focus/Sea/articles.html).

HAGGERTY, Sheryllynne; The British-Atlantic trading community, 1760–1810: men, women, and the distribution of goods, Leiden: Brill, 2006.

HARPER, Roger H.; Victorian Architectural Competitions An Index to British and Irish Architectural Competitions in The Builder 1843–1900, London: Mansell Publishing Limited, 1983.

HAYDEN, Dolores; The Power of Place: Urban Landscapes as Public History, Cambridge, Mass., and London: The MIT Press, 1995.

HERDMAN; W. and PICTON, J. A.; Views in Modern Liverpool, Liverpool: Marples, 1864.

HERLIHY, Patricia; Greek Merchants in Odessa in the Nineteenth Century, in: Harvard Ukrainian Studies, Hefte III–IV, 1979/80, pp. 399–420.

HERLIHY, Patricia; Odessa: A History, 1794–1914, Cambridge, Massachusetts, 1986.

HERNDON, Ruth Wallis; The Domestic Cost of Seafaring: Town Leaders and Seamen's Families in Eighteenth-Century Rhode Island, in: Margaret Creighton and Lisa Norling (eds.), Iron Men, Wooden Women: Gender and Seafaring in the Atlantic World, 1700–1920, Baltimore: Johns Hopkins Press, 1996, pp.

HERZNER, Volker; Die Baugeschichte von San Marco und der Aufsteig Venedigs zur Großmacht, in: Wiener Jahrbuch für Kunstgeschichte, Heft 38, 1985, pp. 1–58.

HINKKANEN, Merja-Liisa; Expressions of Longing, Sources of Anxiety? The Significance of Contacts with Home for Finnish Sailors in London and Hull in the Late Nineteenth Century, in: Lewis R. Fischer and Walter Minchinton (eds.), People of the Northern Seas (Research in Maritime History, Nr. 3), St. John's, Newfoundland, 1992, pp. 63–79.

HISE, Greg; Architecture as State Building: A Challenge to the Field, in: Journal of the Society of Architectural Historians, Heft 67, Nr. 2, 2008, pp. 173–177.

HOPE; E. W. (ed.), City of Liverpool Handbook compiled for the Congress of the Royal Institute of Public Health, Liverpool: Lee & Nightingale, 1903.

HOPE, Ronald; The Shoregoer's Guide, London: The Maritime Press Limited, 1964.

HIRST, P.; Space and Power: Politics, War and Architecture, Cambridge: Polity Press, 2005.

HOWARD, Deborah; The Architectural History of Venice, London, 1980.

HOWARD, Deborah; Venice and Islam in the Middle Ages: Some Observations on the Question of Architectural Influence, in: Architectural History, Heft XXXIV, 1991, pp. 59–74.

HOWARD, Deborah; Venice and the East. The Impact of the Islamic World on Venetian Architecture 1100–1500, New Haven and London, 2000.

HOYLE, B.S; PINDER; D.A. and HUSAIN, M.S. Revitalising the Waterfront. International dimensions of Dockland redevelopment, London: Belhaven Press, 1988.

HUGILL, Stan; Sailortown, London: Routledge and Kegan Paul, 1967.

HYDE, Francis Edwin, Cunard and the North Atlantic, 1840–1973, Basingstoke: MacMillan, 1975.

ISRAEL, Jonathan; Diasporas Jewish and non-Jewish and the World Maritime Empires, in: Ina Baghdiantz McCabe, Gelina Harlaftis and Ioanna Pepolasis Minoglu (eds.), Diaspora Entrepreneurial Networks Four Centuries of History, Oxford and New York: Oxford University Press, 2001, pp. 3–26.

JAUHIAINEN, J.; Waterfront redevelopment and urban policy: the case of Barcelona, Cardiff and Genoa, in: European Planning Studies, Heft 3, 1995, pp. 3–18.

JEFFERIES, Matthew; Hamburg A cultural & literary history, Oxford: Signal Books, 2011.

JEFFERIES, Matthew; Hamburg: a city held together by brick? Unpublished paper presented at the International Workshop on the Social Life of Port Architecture: History, Politics, Commerce, and Culture (from the early eighteenth century to the present day), Centre for Port and Maritime History, University of Liverpool, 2011.

JENKINS, Jennifer; Provincial Modernity: Local Culture and Liberal Politics in Fin-de-Siècle Hamburg, Ithaca and London, 2003.

JONES, Paul; Putting Architecture in its Social Place: A Cultural Political Economy of Architecture, in: Urban Studies, 2009, Heft 6, Nr. 12, 2519–2536.

JONES, Paul; The Sociology of Architecture, Liverpool: Liverpool University Press, 2011.

JONES, Paul; The Iconic Rebranding of Liverpool (Or: A Cloud on the Horizon), unpublished paper presented at the International Workshop on The Social Life of Port Architecture: History, Politics, Commerce, and Culture (from the early eighteenth century to the present day), Centre for Port and Maritime History, University of Liverpool, June 2011.

KADISH, Sharman; Contrasting Identity: Anglo-Jewry and Synagogue Architecture, in: Architectural History, Heft 45, 2002, pp. 386–408.

KAMIYA, Takeo; James Fergusson and Indian Architecture, in: Discovery of Asia by Architectural Historians, 2001.

KAMIYA, Takeo; The Guide to the Architecture of The Indian Subcontinent, Goa: Architecture Autonomous, 2003.

KARLSSON, Lennart; Ett hem långt hemifrån Svensk sjömanskyrkohistoria, Uppsala: EFS förlaget, 1988.

KELSALL, Dennis and Jan; Francis Frith Lancashire a Second Selection, London, 2003.

KENNERLEY, Alston; Seamen's Missions and Sailors' Homes: Spiritual and Welfare Provision for Seafarers in British Ports in the Nineteenth Century, with some Reference to the South West, in: Stephen Fisher (ed.), Studies in British Privateering, Trade, Enterprise and Seamen's Welfare, 1775–1900, Exeter: Exeter University Press, 1987, pp. 121–165.

KENNERLEY, Alston; The Sailors' Home, London and Seamen's Welfare, 1829–1974, in: Maritime Mission Studies, Heft 1, Spring 1998, pp. 24–56.

KOSAMBI, Meera, Bombay in Transition: The Growth and Social Ecology of a Colonial City, 1880-1980, Estoorlmo: Almqvist & Wicksell International, 1986.

KVERNDAL, Roald, Seamen's Missions Their Origin and Early Growth, South Pasadena, Calif.: William Carey Library, 1986.

LAAR, Paul Th. Van de, Port traffic in Rotterdam: the competitive edge of a Rhine-port (1880–1914), in: Reginald LOYEN, Erik BUYST and Greta Davos (eds.), Struggling for Leadership: Antwerp-Rotterdam Port Competition between 1870–2000, Heidelberg 2003, pp. 63–86.

LEE, Antoinette J., Architects to the Nation, The Rise and Decline of the Supervising Architect's Office, Oxford: Oxford University Press, 2000.

LEE, Robert and LAWTON, Richard, Port Development and the Demographic Dynamics of European Urbanization, in: Richard Lawton and Robert Lee (eds.), Population and Society in Western European Port-Cities, c. 1650–1939, Liverpool: Liverpool University Press, 2002, pp. 1–36.

LEE, Robert, The socio-economic and demographic characteristics of port cities: a typology for comparative analysis, in: Urban History, Heft 25, Nr. 2, 1998, pp. 147–172.

LEE, Robert, History and Heritage: The Scandinavian Seamen's Church in Liverpool, Liverpool: A. Wood & Co., 2009.

LEE, Robert, Architecture, Culture and Identity: The Scandinavian Seamen's Church in Liverpool, unpublished paper presented at the International Workshop on The Social Life of Port Architecture: History, Politics, Commerce, and Culture, Centre for Port and Maritime History, University of Liverpool, June 2011.

LEE, Robert, Einwanderung, wirtschaftliche Netzwerke und Identität Die Integration deutscher Kaufleute in Liverpool im 19. Jahrhundert, in: Dittmar Dahlmann and Margrit Schulte Beerbühl (eds.), Perspektiven in der Fremde? Arbeitsmarkt und Migration von der Frühen Neuzeit bis in die Gegenwart (Migration in Geschichte und Gegenwart, Bd. 6), Essen: Klartext, 2011, pp. 145–170.

LEE, Robert, 'Beer, women and song': a reappraisal of the traditional image of the seafarers' urban world, unpublished paper presented at the 10th North Sea Conference, The Parallel Worlds of the Seafarer Ashore, Afloat and Abroad, Gothenburg, September 2011.

LIVERPOOL RECORD OFFICE, 920 DUR, 1/2, Family Diary maintained by George Holt, 3 March 1851.

LIVERPOOL RECORD OFFICE, 920 DUR, 4/28/3, List of Parties Begun 1867, 15 February 1882.

LOMBARD, Denys and AUBIN, Jean (eds.), Marchands et hommes d'affaires asiatiques dans l'Océan Indien et la Mer de Chine, 13–20e siècles, Paris: EHESS, 1988.

MACAULAY, James, Thomas, The Gothic Revival, 1745–1845, Glasgow: Blackie, 1975.

McCARTHY, J., The Origins of the Gothic Revival, Yale University Press, 1987.

McBRIDE, Elyse Gundersen, The Development of Architectural Office Specialization as Evidenced by Professional Journals, 1890–1920, unpublished M.A. dissertation, Washington University, St. Louis, Missouri, 2009.

MELLER, Helen E., Leisure and the Changing City, 1870-1914, London: Routledge & Kegan Paul, 1976.

MERSEYSIDE MARITIME MUSEUM, Maritime Archive and Library, D/SO/2/1/1, Report of the Seamen's Orphan Institution for the year ending 31st December 1869, Liverpool, 1870.

MERSEYSIDE MARITIME MUSEUM, Maritime Archive and Library, D/SO/2/1/1, Report of the Seamen's Orphan Institution for the year ending 31st December 1873, Liverpool, 1874.

MERSEYSIDE MARITIME MUSEUM, Maritime Archive and Library, D/SO/2/1/1, Report of the Seamen's Orphan Institution for the year ending 31st December 1876, Liverpool, 1877.

METCALF, Thomas R., A Tradition Created: Indo-Saracenic Architecture under the Raj, in: History Today, Heft 32, Nr. 9, September 1982, pp. 40–46.

MICOTS, Courtnay, Art and Architecture of Anomabo, Ghana: A Case Study in Cultural Flow, in: Athanor, Heft XXVII, 2009, pp. 105–111.

MICOTS, Courtnay, African Elite Colonial Architecture: Urban Assemblages Emphasizing Status and the Desire for Global Recognition, paper presented at the Chicago Graduate Student Association Symposium, Chicago, Illinois, 9 October, 2010.

MICOTS, Courtnay, Status and Colonial Mimicry: Port Architecture in Coastal Ghana, unpublished paper presented at the International Workshop of The Social Life of Port Architecture: History, Politics, Commerce, and Culture (from the early eighteenth century to the present day), Centre for Port and Maritime History, University of Liverpool, July 2011.

MILNE, Graeme, Trade and traders in mid-Victorian Liverpool Mercantile business and the making of a world port, Liverpool: Liverpool University Press, 2002.

MINOGLU, Ioanna P., The Greek Merchant House of the Russian Black Sea: A Nineteenth-Century Example of a Traders' Coalition, in: International Journal of Maritime History, Heft X, Nr. 1, 1998, pp. 85–96.

NOVIKOVA, Anna, The regeneration of river ports on the Middle Volga: Ecological, Economic, Political and Social issues, unpublished paper presented to the International Workshop on the Social Life of Port Cities: History, Politics, Commerce, and Culture (from the early eighteenth century to the present day), Centre for Port and Maritime History, University of Liverpool, June 2011.

PADGITT, Clint, German Seamen's Mission of New York, 1907–2001, in: Newsletter of the International Association for the Study of Maritime Mission (IASMM), Spring/Summer 2001 (http://www.gsmny.org/padgitt-history.html).

PALMER, Sarah B., Seamen Ashore in Late Nineteenth Century London, in: Paul Adam (ed.), Seamen in Society, Bucharest, 1980, pp. 54–64.

PICTON, J. A., Memorials of Liverpool Historical and Topographical including A History of the Dock Estate, London: Longmans, Green, and Co., 1873, Vol. II Topographical.

PIELHOFF, Stephen, Paternalismus und Stadtarmut. Armutswahrnehmung und Privatwohltätigkeit im Hamburger Bürgertum 1830–1914 (Beiträge zur Geschichte Hamburgs, Band 56), Hamburg, 1999.

PINDER, D. A., Visitor's Illustrated Guide to Bombay, London, 1904.

POOLE, Braithwaite, Statistics of British Commerce being A Compendium of the Productions, Manufactures, Imports, and Exports of the United Kingdom, in Agriculture, Minerals, Merchandise, etc., London: W. H. Smith and Simpkin, Marshall & Co., 1852.

POWERS, Alan, Architectural Education in Britain 1880-1914, unpublished doctoral dissertation, University of Cambridge, 1982.

REBER, Vera Blinn, British Mercantile Houses in Buenos Aires 1810–1880, Cambridge, Massachusetts: Harvard University Press, 1979.

ROCHE, Thomas William Edgar, Samuel Cunard and the North Atlantic, London: Macdonald & Co., 1971.

ROWE, Richard, Jack Afloat and Jack Ashore, London: Smith Elder & Co., 1875.

SANDGREN, Birger (ed.), 'Så Länge Svenksa Män Färdas På Elbes Vatten Svenska sjömanskyrkan i Hamburg 100 år 1883–1983, Hamburg: Svenska Gustav Adolfs-kyrkan, 1983.

SHARPLES, Joseph, (ed.), Charles Reilly and the Liverpool School of Architecture 1904–33, Liverpool: Liverpool University Press, 1996 (catalogue).

SHARPLES, Joseph, Liverpool (Pevsner Architectural Guides), New Haven and London: Yale University Press, 2004.

SHARPLES, Joseph, Merchant Palaces Liverpool and Wirral Mansions Photographed by Bedford Lemere & Co., Liverpool: The Bluecoat Press, 2007.

SHARPLES, Joseph, Built on Commerce Liverpool's central business district, Swindon: English Heritage, 2008.

SHARPLES, Joseph, 'The Mark of Opulence, Taste and Skill': Liverpool Merchants' Houses, in: Robert Lee (ed.), Networks of Power and Influence: business, culture and identity in Liverpool's Merchant Community, 1800–1914, Aldershot: Ashgate, 2013 (forthcoming).

SKINNER, Frederick W., Odessa and the Problem of Urban Modernization, in: Michael F. Hamm (ed.), The City in Imperial Russia, Bloomington, 1986, pp. 214–XXX.

SMITH, Crosbie, 'A most terrific passage': Putting Faith into Atlantic Steam Navigation, in: Robert Lee (ed.), Commerce and Culture Nineteenth-Century Business Elites, Aldershot: Ashgate, 2011, pp. 285–316.

SMITH, Crosbie, HIGGINSON, Ian and WOLSTENHOLME, Phillip 'Avoiding Equally Extravagance and Parsimony': The Moral Economy of the Ocean Steamship, in: Technology and Culture, Heft 44, Nr. 3, 2003, pp. 443–469.

SOJA, E., Thirdspace: Journeys to Los Angeles and Other Real-and-Imaginary Spaces, Oxford: Blackwell, 1996.

STOREY, Tony, Cunard Liverpool: spiritual home of the world's famous ocean liners, 1840–2010, Liverpool: Trinity Mirror, 2010.

SUYKENS, F., The City and Its Port – An Economic Appraisal, in: Geoforum, 1989, Heft 20, Nr. 4, pp. 437–445.

SVENSKA KYRKANS ARKIV, Uppsala, Gustaf Adolfs Kyrka, Liverpool, Kassabok 1940–48.

SVENSKA KYRKANS ARKIV, Uppsala, A 300, Hamburg, Liverpool ang. Sjömanskyrkan, P. M. angående EFS:s sjömansmission, 1959.

SVENSKA KYRKANS ARKIV, Uppsala, A 300, Hamburg, Liverpool ang. sjömanskyrkan, Svenska Klubben Hamburg, Svenska Klubbens in Hamburg engagement in Svenska Skolan, 1976.

TEKELI, Ilhan, The Social Context of the Development of Architecture in Turkey, in: Renata Holod and Ahmet Evin (eds.), Modern Turkish Architecture, University of Pennsylvania Press, 1984, pp. 9–33.

THISTLEWOOD, David, Liverpool School of Architecture: Centenary Review, in: The Architects' Journal, 11 May 1995, p. 60.

THOMAS, Leslie, Built like Bridges: Iron, Steel and Rivets in the Nineteenth-century Skyscraper, in: Journal of the Society of Architectural Historians, Heft 69, Nr. 2, 2010, pp. 234–261.

THUN, I. R., Werden und Wachstum: der Deutschen Evangelischen Seemannsmission, Hamburg: Deutsches Seemannsmission, 1959.

TSCHUMI, Bernard, Comment made during a discussion forum; in C.C. Davison (ed.), Anyplace, New York, Cambridge, Mass. and London: Anyone Corporation and The MIT Press, 1995, p. 229 (cited in Murray FRASER, The cultural context of critical architecture, in: The Journal of Architecture, Heft 10, Nr. 3, 2005, pp. 317–322.

UM, Nancy, Spatial Negotiations in a Commercial City: The Red Sea Port of Mocha, Yemen, during the First Half of the Eighteenth Century, in: Journal of the South of Asia History, Heft 62, Nr. 2, 2003, pp. 178–193.

UM, Nancy, The Merchant Houses of Mocha: Trade and Architecture in an Indian Ocean Port, Seattle, Wash.: University of Washington Press, 2009.

UM, Nancy, Imported Constructs: Viewing Red Sea Architecture from the Sea, unpublished paper presented to the International Workshop on the Social Life of Port Architecture: History, Politics, Commerce, and Culture (from the early eighteenth century to the present day), Centre for Port and Maritime History, University of Liverpool, June 2011.

UMBACH, Maiken, German Cities and Bourgeois Modernism, 1890–1924, Oxford, 2009.

VASSALLO, Carmel, Maltese Entrepreneurial Networks, in: Ina Baghdiantz McCabe, Gelina Harlaftis and Ioanna Pepolasis Minoglu (eds.), Diaspora Entrepreneurial Networks Four Centuries of History, Oxford and New York: Oxford University Press, 2001, pp. 125–144.

WILSON, Derek, Francis Frith's Travels: A Photographic Journey through Victorian Britian, London: J.M. Dent & Sons, Ltd., 1985.

WIŚNIEWSKA, Olga, The Structure and Functions of Trading Posts in Northern Norway in the Second Half of the Nineteenth Century, unpublished paper presented at the International Workshop on The Social Life of Port Architecture: History, Politics, Commerce, and Culture from the early eighteenth century to the present day, Centre for Port and Maritime History, University of Liverpool, June 2011.

WOODMAN, Richard, Blue Funnel Voyages, Bebington: Avid Publications, 1988.

WOODS, Mary N., From Craft to Profession: The Practise of Architecture in Nineteenth-Century America, Berkeley and Los Angeles: University of California Press, 1999.

WONG, Marie Rose, Sweet Cakes, Long Journey The Chinatowns of Portland, Oregon, Seattle and London: University of Washington Press, 2004.

Sources of illustrations

Fig. 1, 2: Maria Georgopoulou, Venice's Mediterranean Colonies Architecture and Urbanism, Cambridge: Cambridge University Press, p. 80.
Fig. 3; Fig. 4; Fig. 9; Fig. 15: postcard
Fig. 5 to Fig. 6: courtesy of the Trustees of the Nordic Church, Liverpool and Jan Wallin
Fig. 7: Svenska Kyrka, Ett hem långt hemifrån Svensk sjömanskyrkohistoria, Uppsala: EFS-förlaget, 1988, p. 65
Fig. 8; Fig. 10 to Fig. 14: courtesy of English Heritage

* The photo rights have been clarified by the author and he has the responsibility

---

[1] LEE and LAWTON, Port Development, 2002, pp. 12–13.
[2] DELANTY and JONES, European Identity and Architecture, 2002, pp. 453–66; Jones, Putting Architecture in its Social Place, 2009, pp. 2519–36; Jones, The Sociology of Architecture, 2011; Sharples, Liverpool, 2004.
[3] ALBION, The Rise of New York Port, 1961; Suykens, The City and Its Port, 1989, pp. 437–445; Laar, Port Traffic in Rotterdam, 2003, pp. 63–86.
[4] LOMBARD and AUBIN, Marchands et hommes d'affaires, 1988.
[5] HIRST, Space and Power, 2005, p. 3.
[6] BAYDAR, The Cultural Burden of Architecture, 2004, pp. 19–27.
[7] ARSLAN, Gothic Architecture in Venice, 1971; Howard, The Architectural History of Venice, 1980; Goy, The House of Gold, 1992; Goy, Venice, 1997.
[8] HOWARD, Venice and the East, 2000; Georgopoulou, Venice's Mediterranean Colonies, 2001.
[9] HOWARD, Venice and the East, 2000, pp. 83, 98, 100; Engelberg, Die Bautradition der Republic Venedig, 2009, p. 89; Herzner, Die Baugeschichte von San Marco, 1985, pp. 1–58.
[10] GEORGOPOULOU, Venice's Mediterranean Colonies, 2001, p. 78.
[11] HOWARD, Venice and Islam, 1991, pp. 59–74; Howard, Venice and the East, 2000, pp. 4–5; Chojnacki, Social Identity in Renaissance Venice, 1994, pp. 341–358.
[12] GEORGOPOULOU, Venice's Mediterranean Colonies, 200; Georgopoulou, Mapping Religious and Ethnic Identities, 1996, pp. 467–496.
[13] ALOFSIN, When Buildings Speak, 2006; Fuller, Moderns Abroad, 2007.
[14] NILSSON, European Architecture in India, 1968, Figures 40 and 55.
[15] MACAULAY, The Gothic Revival, 1975; Alexander, Medievalism, 1981; McCarthy, The Origins of the Gothic Revival, 1987.
[16] METCALFE, A Tradition Created, 1982, pp. 40–46; Crinson, Empire Building, 1996.
[17] KAMIYA, James Fergusson, 2001; Kamiya, The Guide to The Architecture of The Indian Subcontinent, 2003.
[18] UM, The Merchant Houses of Mocha, 2009.
[19] UM, Spatial Negotiations, 2003, pp. 178–193.
[20] UM, Spatial Negotiations, 2003, p. 184; Um, Imported Constructs, 2011.
[21] MICOTS, Art and Architecture, 2009, pp. 105–109; Micots, Status and Colonial Mimicry.
[22] MICOTS, African Elite Colonial Architecture, 2010.

[23] CUSACK, Architects, 1986, p.183; de Figueiredo, Symbols of Empire, 2003, p.237.
[24] DE FIGUEIREDO, Symbols of Empire, 2003, p.238.
[25] THOMAS, Built like Bridges, 2010, pp.234–261.
[26] POOLE, British Commerce, 1852, pp.107–108; Milne, Trade and traders, 2002, pp.56–57.
[27] HAGGERTY, The British-Atlantic trading community, 2006; Ellis, Heir of Adventure, 1960.
[28] DE FIGUEIREDO, Symbols of Empire, 2003, p.239; Fenske, The Beaux Arts Architect, 2005, pp.19–37.
[29] TSCHUMI, Comment, 1995, p.229; Woods, From Craft to Profession, 1999.
[30] DOSTOGLU, Towards Professional Legitimacy, 1982; Powers, Architectural Education, 1982; Brain, Practical Knowledge, 1991, pp.239–268; Crouch, Design Culture in Liverpool, 2002; Tekeli, The Social Context, 1984, p.17. For example, the Association of Turkish Architects was founded in 1927.
[31] BROOKS, The Builder in the 1840s, 1981, pp.87–91; Gregory, Magazine Modern, 1982; McBride, The Development of Architectural Office Specialization, 2009.
[32] HARPER, Victorian Architectural Competitions, London, 1983.
[33] Critical Words from Abroad, 1891, p.198; Boyle, Architectural Practice in America, 1977, pp.309–344; Lee, Architects to the Nation, 2000; McBride, The Development of Architectural Office Specialization, 2009.
[34] SHARPLES, Charles Reilly, 1996, pp.37–38.
[35] DUNNE and RICHMOND, The World in One School, 2008, p.19; Thistlewood, Liverpool School of Architecture, 1995, p.60.
[36] DURAND, La politique français, 1904, p.287.
[37] JEFFERIES, Hamburg, 2011, p.150; Jefferies, Hamburg: a city held together by brick? 2011, p.4.
[38] JEFFERIES, Hamburg, 2011, p.123.
[39] JENKINS, Provincial Modernity, 2003; Umbach, German Cities, 2009.
[40] Israel, Diasporas Jewish and non-Jewish, 2001, pp.3–26. Vassallo, Maltese Entrepreneurial Networks, 2001, pp.125–144; Chamberlain, Diasporic Memories, 2009, pp.177–187.
[41] FELLONI, The Population Dynamics, 2002, pp.74–90; Cattaruzza, Population Dynamics and Economic Change, 2002, pp.176–211; Dubin, The port Jews of Habsburg Trieste, 1999; Herlihy, Greek Merchants in Odessa, 1979/80, pp.399–420; Herlihy, Odessa, 1986; Minoglu, The Greek Merchant House, 1998, pp.85–96; Skinner, Odessa, 1986,
[42] UM, Spatial Negotiations, 2003, pp.178–193; Novikova, The regeneration of river ports, 2011.
[43] ASHTON, Lives and livelihoods, 2003, pp.113–115.
[44] LEE, History and Heritage: the Scandinavian Seamen's Church, 2009, p.4; Karlsson, Ett hem långt hemifrån, 1988. .
[45] SANDGREN, 'Så Länge Svenska Män Färdas På Elbes Vatten, 1983; Ekelund, Svenska Gustaf-Adolfskyrkan, 2007.
[46] DELANTY and JONES, European Identity, 2002, p.453.
[47] LEE, Architecture, Culture and Identity, 2011.
[48] SVENSKA KYRKANS ARKIV, Uppsala, A300, Svenska Klubbens in Hamburg engagement, 1976.
[49] REBER, British Mercantile Houses, 1979, p.44.
[50] BROWN and DE FIGUEIREDO, Religion and Place, p.27; Kadisch, Contrasting Identity, 2002, pp.386–408.
[51] SVENSKA KYRKANS ARKIV, Uppsala, A300, Hamburg; Svenska Församlingen, Buenos Aires (Congregación Sueca), Brev korrespondens, 15. August 1932; Sjömansmissionen Bremen 1958–1960, Sammandrag av redovisningar, 1958; Liverpool, 1959.
[52] LEE, Einwanderung, wirtschaftliche Netzwerke und Identität, 2011, pp.163–166; Belchem and MacRaild, Cosmopolitan Liverpool, 2006, p.365.
[53] DEUTSCHE EVANGELISCHE KIRCHE zu Liverpool, 39 Jahres-Bericht, 1888, p.12.
[54] LEE, 'Beer, women and song', 2011, p.18; Feys et al., Maritime Transport and Migration, 2007; Frost, Ethnic Labour, 1995; Wong, Sweet Cakes, Long Journey, 2004; Amenda, Chinese Seafarers, 2011.
[55] JEFFERIES, Hamburg, 2011, pp.166–169; Amenda, Chinese Seafarers, 2011.
[56] BELCHEM and MacRaild, Cosmpolitan Liverpool, 2006, pp.370–375; Wong, Sweet Cakes, Long Journey, 2004, pp.204–262.
[57] LEE, The socio-economic and demographic determinants, 1998, pp.167–171.
[58] GILES and HAWKINS, Storehouses of Empire, 2004.
[59] BEAUMONT et al., An Historical Survey, 1936.
[60] PICTON, Memorials of Liverpool, 1873, p.35.
[61] PICTON, Memorials of Liverpool, 1873, p.36.
[62] WILSON, Francis Frith's Travels, 1985; Kelsall, Francis Frith, 2003.
[63] MILNE, Trade and traders, 2000, pp.149–150.
[64] COCK et al., The Liverpool Merchant Community, 2012.
[65] COOKSON, Family Firms and Business Networks, 1997, pp.1–20.
[66] ROCHE, Samuel Cunard, 1971; Hyde, Cunard, 1975; Milne, Trade and traders, 2000, p.14; Storey, Cunard Liverpool, 2010.
[67] SHARPLES, Liverpool, 2004, p.71; de Figueiredo, Symbols of Empire, 2003, p.243.
[68] DE FIGUEIREDO, Symbols of Empire, p.245.
[69] BABCOCK, Spanning the Atlantic, 1941, pp.97–99; Smith, 'A most terrific passage', 2011, p.285.
[70] SMTIH, HIGGINSON, and WOLSTENHOLME, 'Avoiding Equally Extravagance and Parsimony', 2003, pp.443–469.
[71] LEE, The socio-economic and demographic characteristics, 1998, p.168.
[72] MELLER, Leisure and the Changing City, 1976; L. Fabi, La carita dei ricchi, Milan, 1984; Pielhoff, Paternalismus, 1999.
[73] GILES, Building a Better Society, 2008, p.17.
[74] HERNDON, The Domestic Cost of Seafaring, 1996, p.57.
[75] MERSEYSIDE MARITIME MUSEUM, Maritime Archive and Library, D/SO/2/1/1, 1870, pp.5–8.
[76] DERBY, Speeches and Addresses, 1894, p.52; Giles, Building a Better Society, 2008, p.68.

77 MERSEYSIDE MARITIME MUSEUM, Maritime Archive and Library, D/SO/2/1/1, 1873, p. 19; 1877, p. 22.
78 GILES, Building a Better Society, 2008, p.68.
79 WIŚNIEWSKA, The Structure and Functions of Trading Posts, 2011; Sharples, 'The Mark of Opulence, Taste and Skill', 2012.
80 FORWOOD, Recollections, 1910, p. 60.
81 SHARPLES, 'The Mark of Opulence, Taste and Skill', 2012.
82 SHARPLES, Merchant Palaces, 2007, pp. 4–7.
83 SHARPLES, Merchant Palaces, 2007, p. 16.
84 LIVERPOOL Record Office, 920 DUR 4/28/3; DUR 1/2.
85 HUGILL, Sailortown, 1967, pp. 99, 137–140; Hope, The Shoregoer's Guide, 1964, p. 21; Woodman, Blue Funnel Voyages, 1988, p. 137.
86 BELCHEM, Shock City, 2008; Lee, 'Beer, women and song', 2012.
87 KVERNDAL, Seamen's Missions, 1986; Karlsson, Ett hem långt hemifrån, 1988..
88 PALMER, Seamen Ashore, 1980, pp. 57–59; Rowe, Jack Afloat, 1875, p. 8; Kennerley, Seamen's Missions and Sailors' Homes, 1987, pp. 121–165; The Sailors' Home, 1998, pp. 24–56.
89 HOPE, City of Liverpool Handbook, 1903, pp. 84–85.
90 GILES, Building a Better Society, 2008, p. 65.
91 PINDER, Visitor's Illustrated Guide, 1904. For a general study of the development of Bombay, see Kosambi, Bombay in Transition, 1986.
92 PADGITT, German Seamen's Mission, 2001. For a general study of German seamen's missions, see Thun, Werden und Wachstum, 1959.
93 FALKUS, The Blue Funnel Legend, 1990, pp. 114, 310; Frost, Racism, Work and Unemployment, 1995, p. 27; Evans, Mersey Mariners, 2002, p. 84.
94 HINKKANEN, Expressions of Longing, 1992, p. 66.
95 ROWE, Jack Afloat, 1875, p.90; Hope, City of Liverpool Handbook, 1903, p. 85; Hinkkanen, Expressions of longing, 1992, p. 66; Svenska Kyrkans Arkiv, Gustaf Adolfs Kyrka, 1940–48.
96 GRITT, Representations of mariners (accessed 2011).
97 JONES, The Iconic Rebranding of Liverpool, 2011.
98 HERDMAN and PICTON, Views in Modern Liverpool, 1864, p.33; Sharples, Built on Commerce, 2008, p. 39; Jones, Putting Architecture in its Social Place.
99 HISE, Architecture as State Building, 2008, pp. 173–177; Busquets, Barcelona, 2005.
100 SOJA, Thirdspace, 1996; Hayden, The Power of Place, 1995.
101 GILES, The character of port cities, 2011; Hoyle, Pinder and Husain, Revitalising the Waterfront, 1988; Breen and Rigby, The New Waterfront, 1996; Jauhiainen, Waterfront redevelopment, 1995, pp. 3–18.

Dirk Schubert

Hamburg – Amphibische Stadt im (inter-)nationalen Kontext

Zu Beginn des 19. Jahrhunderts fielen in vielen Seehafenstädten Richtung weisende Entscheidungen der Stadtentwicklung und des Hafenausbaus. Vor dem Hintergrund der Industrialisierung und der raschen Zunahme und Internationalisierung des Handels galt es unter erheblichem Zeitdruck Weichenstellungen vorzunehmen, die bis heute für Stadt- und Hafenentwicklung nachwirken. Seehafenstädte wie Hamburg waren dabei Kulminationspunkte von Neuerungen aus Wirtschaft, Gesellschaft und Kultur.[1] Sie können als Orte gelten, wo Phänomene der späteren Globalisierung vorweg genommen wurden.[2] In diesem Beitrag soll nur auf die Stadt- und Hafenentwicklung Hamburgs bis zum Ersten Weltkrieg eingegangen werden.

Kreative Milieus und Netzwerke von Kaufleuten, Unternehmern, Finanzierungs- und Versicherungsinstituten trieben – häufig ausgehend von „Kommandozentralen" in Seehafenstädten – die Austausch- und Verflechtungsbeziehungen international und schließlich global voran. Bremer Kauleute prägten dafür – lange bevor der Begriff Globalisierung verbreitet war – den Slogan: „Buten un binnen – Wagen un Winnen" (Outside and Inside – Venture and Win).

Seehafenstädte wie Hamburg weisen Alleinstellungsmerkmale auf und kein Seehafen der Welt gleicht dem anderen wie Abbildungen u. a. aus Häfen von Dublin, Genua, Marseille und New York zeigen. Alle haben ein eigenes Gesicht, einen besonderen Charakter und eine individuelle Geschichte. Dies trifft auf Hamburg in besonderem Maße zu: Nicht nur die Größe und Dimensionierung der Hafeninfrastrukturen und logistischen Einrichtungen wie sie in Hamburg geschaffen wurden, sondern auch neue Maßstäbe, korrespondierend mit technischen Neuerungen und die bauliche Geschlossenheit und Ensemblewirkung sind überwältigend.

Viele Seehafenstädte weisen Nutzungszonen mit unterschiedlichen Spezialisierungen auf. Fährhafen, Fischerei, Schiffbau, Schiffsreparatur, Güterumschlag, Seehafenindustrien, Marine und Militär haben jeweils besondere Anforderungen an Infrastrukturen und unterschiedliche Bezüge zum städtischen Kontext. Vernetzt mit den sozialen Netzwerken, den Nischen und (Sub-)Kulturen der Hafenarbeiter und Seeleute[3], den Nischen – mit besonderem exotischen Duft und Reiz für die heimischen Kleinbürger – entstanden die bedeutenden technischen Infrastrukturen. Mittels technischer Innovationen ergaben sich im 19. Jahrhundert qualitativ neue Möglichkeiten der Raumüberwindung über kürzere und längere Distanzen. Mit der Erfindung der Telegrafie, der Optimierung der Segelschifffahrt und der Einführung der Dampfschifffahrt auf See sowie der Eisenbahn auf Land konnten Raumdistanzen zeitlich verkürzt und Wirtschaftsabläufe planbarer gestaltet werden.[4]

Seehäfen bildeten die Lokomotiven der Internationalisierung des Güteraustausches. Ca. 50 % des deutschen Außenhandels wurden vor dem Ersten Weltkrieg über Hamburg abgewickelt. Kamen zwischen 1851–1860 knapp 4 700 Schiffe mit 765 000 Nettoregistertonnen (NRT) nach Hamburg, so stieg die Zahl bis 1901–1910 auf über 15.000 Schiffe und 10 610 000 NRT an. Während die Anzahl der Schiffe sich „nur" verdreifachte, verdreizehnfachte sich das Umschlagsvolumen durch die zunehmende Größe der Seeschiffe.[5] Es galt dabei die Schnittstelle zwischen Anforderungen des See- und Landverkehrs, die Kais und Häfen, so zu planen und zu organisieren, dass sie immer neuen Herausforderungen der internationalen und schließlich globalen Verkehre angepasst werden konnten. Entscheidungen zu Beginn des 19. Jahrhunderts über Organisation des Hafenbetriebs, über Art und Weise des Hafenaus- und Umbaus und der Zuordnung von Wohnstätten zum Arbeitsort Hafen erwiesen sich als wirkungsmächtig und häufig später als irreversibel.

Ursprünge des Hamburger Hafens

Der Hafen entstand in Hamburg an der Einmündung der Alster in die Elbe. Der Alsterhafen bot vielen Schiffen Platz und Schutz. Im 13. Jahrhundert entstand um den Hafen am Nicolaifleet das Stadtzentrum mit Rathaus, Gericht, Börse, Zoll und Waage. Wichtigster Exportartikel Hamburgs war zunächst Bier. Im 15. Jahrhundert lagerten viele größere Seeschiffe dann außerhalb der Stadt auf Reede vor Anker. Das Löschen und Laden der Schiffe geschah von Hand und mit dem Ladegeschirr der Schiffe.

Der amphibische Charakter der Stadt, durchzogen von Flüssen und später angelegten Kanälen, wie der des ganzen Stromspaltungsgebietes wird trefflich in dem Plan von Homann um 1600 dokumentiert. Er liefert beeindruckendes Zeugnis dieser Vielfalt von Wasserläufen, von dessen Struktur allerdings wenig erhalten geblieben ist. Natürlich war der Hafen mit den Schiffen und wertvollen Waren, wie u. a. der Plan von 1589 zeigt, in die Befestigungen einbezogen.

Als 1816 das bewunderte erste Dampfschiff (die „Lady of the Lake") die Elbe befuhr, kündigte sich ein neues Zeitalter an.[6] Für die Ausweitung, Verdichtung und Beschleunigung weltweiter Beziehungen eröffneten sich neue Optionen. Eisenbahnverbindungen von Altona nach Kiel wurden 1844 und die Verbindung zwischen Hannover und Harburg 1847 fertig gestellt. Dies wiederum zog eine rasante Zunahme

Abb. 1: Mastenwald von Segelschiffen, im Hintergrund des linken Bildteils der Kaispeicher A

des lokalen Schiffsverkehrs zwischen Harburg und Hamburg nach sich. Der Hafen wurde von einem Besucher als „eine der lebhaftesten Szenen, die man sich denken kann" beschrieben. „Er präsentiert einen Mastenwald aus allen Nationen und allen Erdteilen (…)".[7] Die Segelschifffahrt hatte 1866 ihren Höhepunkt erreicht und ging von da an absolut und relativ zurück. Mit der Ausweitung der Dampfschifffahrt „wurde eine Festlegung nicht nur der Schiffsabfahrten, sondern auch der ungefähren Ankunftszeiten möglich und dadurch alle Kalkulation erleichtert sowie der Spekulation ein neues Feld eröffnet."[8]

Der Güterumschlag erfolgte zu Beginn des 19. Jahrhunderts noch vorwiegend im Strom. Die Schiffe ankerten in der Elbe oder wurden an Pfählen festgemacht, die Waren dann mittels Schuten befördert und zu den Speichern transportiert. Der Stromumschlag erfolgte mit den seeschiffseigenen Geräten und mittels schwerer und gefahrvoller körperlicher Arbeit. Die Waren vom Seeschiff wurden auf ein kleineres Wasserfahrzeug verbracht und dann landseits und zu den Lager- und Kaufmannshäusern befördert. Hier wurden sie gelagert, teilweise veredelt und dann wiederum landseits oder wasserseits weiter befördert. Die Kaufmannshäuser dienten als Wohn- und Kontorraum sowie als Speicher und waren von Wasser- und Landseite aus zugänglich.

Zunächst existierten wenig Möglichkeiten Waren direkt vom Schiff an Land zu verbringen. So gab es spezielle Schwergutkräne an denen die Stadt einen Kranmeister und Kranknechte beschäftigte. Der Umschlag im Strom war das Betätigungsfeld privater Unternehmen. Ein separiertes Hafenareal gab es in Hamburg zunächst nicht. Das gesamte hamburgische Staatsgebiet war Zollausland und bildete einen Freihafen.

Ein Vergleich der Stadtpläne von 1813 und 1942 dokumentiert, dass sich bezogen auf die Hafeninfrastrukturen wenig verändert hatte. Aber mit der Zunahme des Güterumschlags mussten auch in Hamburg Überlegungen für Hafenerweiterungen angestellt werden. Mit den Veränderungen in der Seeschifffahrt bildeten sich arbeitsteilige und Risikomindernde Strukturen heraus. So wurde innerhalb weniger Jahre die Schiffsreederei zu einem neuen selbständigen, rein kapitalistisch organisierten Wirtschaftsbereich. Eine Katastrophe sollte allerdings Prozesse der Veränderung beschleunigen. 1842 brach in einem Speicher in der Deichstraße ein Feuer aus, das in den nächsten Tage große Teile der Innenstadt vernichten sollte.

Der Wiederaufbau wurde als Chance für Modernisierungen genutzt. Neue Eisenbahnlinien wurden eröffnet, vor allem aber galt es sich für die strategische Ausrichtung des Hafens zu entscheiden. Es war naheliegend sich dabei an den Vorhaben im größten Hafen der Welt, an London, zu orientieren. Dies umso mehr als seit Jahren in Hamburg Stadtplanungs-, Hafenbau- und Infrastrukturingenieure aus England tätig waren, deren Expertise genutzt werden konnte. Die ersten Vorschläge zum Hafenausbau zielten daher auf einen Dockhafen nach Londoner Vorbild ab. Es waren vor allem die englischen Ingenieure Charles Vignoles, William Lindley und James Walker, die einen Dockhafen vorschlugen.

Die Beispiele aus England dokumentieren, wie der Typus der Dockhäfen dort perfektioniert wurde, dass auch immer größere Schiffe geschleust werden konnten. Der ganze Osten Londons (Isle of Dogs) wurde mit künstlich angelegten Docks überformt.[9] Private Gesellschafen planten, bauten und betrieben die Docks mit ihren Lagerhäusern und Infrastrukturen – eine übergeordnete Hafenentwicklungsplanung gab es also nicht. Ähnlich stellt sich auch die Struktur des Hafens in Liverpool mit den Schleusen, Fingerpiers und Lagerhäusern dar.

Hatten die englischen Ingenieure zunächst noch mit dem Hamburger Wasserbaudirektor Heinrich Hübbe zusammen einen Plan vorgelegt, distanzierte sich Hübbe bald von dem Projekt. Hübbes Nachfolger als Wasserbaudirektor Johannes Dalmann bezog dann eindeutig Position für einen offenen Tidehafen ohne Schleusen. Das zentrale Argument war der geringere Tidenhub von ca. 2,50 Meter in Hamburg gegenüber fünf oder sechs Metern in London und Liverpool. Höhere Kaimauern ermöglichten hier einen Ausgleich und das zeitaufwendige Schleusen entfiel. Das jahrelange Hinauszögern der Weichenstellung sollte letztlich zu neuen, innovativen Pfadentwicklungen führen.

Der zwischen 1859–1866 entstandene über einen Kilometer lange Sandtorkai bildet die erste moderne Kaianlage nach dieser Grundsatzentscheidung, der eigens für Dampfschiffe gebaut war und der mittels eines neuen künstlichen Hafenbeckens entstand. Fortschritte beim Bau der Kaimauern ermöglichten einen direkten Umschlag vom Schiff an Land und direkte Eisenbahnanschlüsse. Der Sandtorkai machte es auch größten Seeschiffen möglich, am Kai festzumachen. Einstöckige Kaischuppen, wo die Waren kurzfristig gelagert werden konnten, bewegliche Kaikräne mit denen Waren geladen und gelöscht werden konnten und Transportanschlüsse für binnenländische Verkehrsträger waren integraler Bestandteil der Anlage. Schuten und Ewer konnten wasserseits Güter von den Seeschiffen übernehmen.[10] Nach dieser Richtungsentscheidung für den offenen Tidehäfen in Stromrichtung wurden später weitere Hafenbecken angelegt, und damit der Aufbruch in die Moderne durchgesetzt. Hamburg nutzte sozusagen den „late-comer advantage", um gut informiert die maßgeschneiderte, beste Lösung zu finden.

Grundsätzlich wurde entschieden, dass Hafenbaumaßnahmen als Infrastrukturmaßnahmen auf Staatskosten durchzuführen waren. Der Kaiumschlag war zunächst auch ausschließlich kommunal organisiert, später wurde auch die Verpachtung von Kaistrecken zugelassen. Im Lagergeschäft gab es kommunale Speicher, die vermietet und verpachtet wurden, wie auch private Speicher. Bei verpachteten Kaistrecken konnten die Reedereien ihre Schiffe nach eigenem Belieben abfertigen, bei von der Stadt betriebenen Kais gab es eine unparteiische Platzzuweisung, die eine gleichmäßige Ausnutzung gewährleisten sollte. Die staatliche Kaiverwaltung organisierte den Güterumschlag am Kai, die Verladung auf Bahn, Fuhrwerke, Binnenschiffe und Schuten, übernahm die Aufsicht über Kräne, Schuppen und Kais und zog Gebühren für die Kaibenutzung, Lager- und Wägegelder

Abb. 2: Sandtorkai (vor dem Bau der Speicherstadt) 1877

ein. Die Leitungsaufgaben übernahm ein beamtetes Personal. Mit den Liegegebühren wurden neue Logistikeinrichtungen wie Dampfkräne finanziert.

Hamburg rückte damit in die Spitzengruppe der Welthäfen auf. 1872 wurden die Elbbrücken fertig gestellt und Hamburg bekam einen direkten Eisenbahnanschluss an die Strecken des Deutschen Reiches. Mit der Lage der Elbbrücken war bestimmt, dass zukünftig zu erstellende Hafen- und Kaianlagen westlich der Elbbrücken liegen mussten. Die Elbbrücken markierten die Scheide zwischen See- und Flussschifffahrt und wiesen die zukünftige Hafenentwicklung in westliche Richtung.

Die Vorteile des Hamburger Hafens wurden gerühmt, während über die Londoner Docks berichtet wird: „Die vielberühmten Londoner Docks (Dock bedeutet korrekt nur einen mit Schleusen abgeschlossenen Hafen, keinesfalls Trockendock, wofür das Wort im Deutschen meist gebraucht wird) (…), (…) Sieht man sie heute, so kommen sie einem höchst altertümlich, fast kindlich vor. (…) Aber von Zurüstungen für Durchgangsverkehr, für raschen Umschlag, für sofortigen Übergang vom Schiff auf die Eisenbahn keine Spur".[11]

Von der Freihafenstadt zur Stadt mit Freihafenbezirk

Der erste Zeitabschnitt der Hafenerweiterung bis 1880 erfolgte in Hamburg nach der Grundsatzentscheidung für den offenen Tidehafen und der Notwendigkeit neue Einrichtungen für den zunehmenden Güterumschlag zu schaffen. Die folgende Phase stand unter der Notwendigkeit des Zollanschlusses von Hamburg an das Deutsche Reich.[12] Hamburg war seit Jahrhunderten Freihafen gewesen und hatte damit die Möglichkeit Waren zollfrei zu lagern und zu bearbeiten. Erst wenn die Waren aus Hamburg – meist in kleinen Mengen – ausgeführt wurden, musste Zoll entrichtet werden. Diese für Kaufleute und Reeder vorteilhafte Situation, stellte sich für Gewerbebetriebe als erheblicher Nachteil dar. Sie mussten Zoll wie ausländische Unternehmen entrichten, wollten sie ihre Waren außerhalb Hamburgs verkaufen.

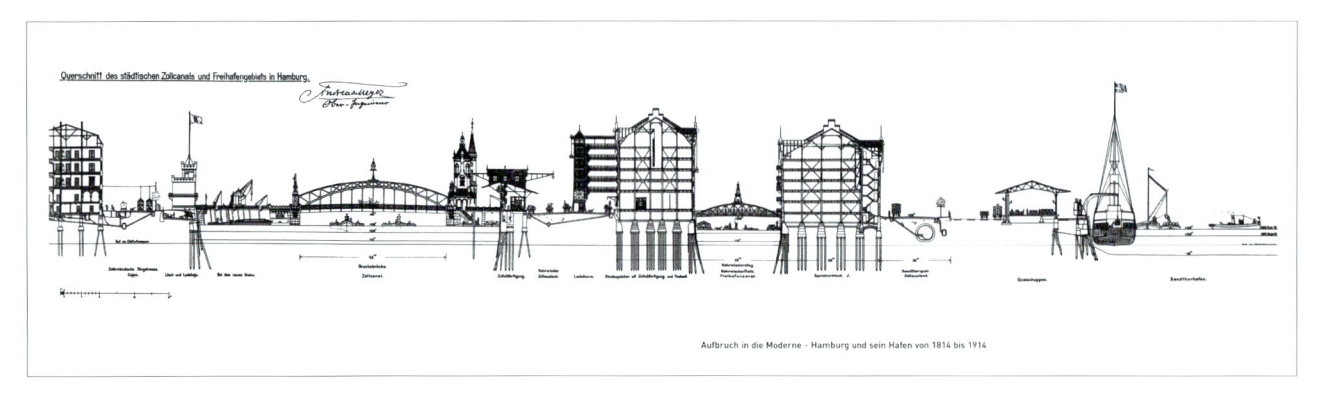

Abb. 3: Querschnitt durch Zollkanal und Freihafen mit Speichern und Transitschuppen

Im deutschen Binnenland waren immer wieder Vorwürfe gegen den hanseatischen Sonderweg und Separatismus laut geworden. Es gab eine Kolonie englischer Kaufleute und vor allem in der Oberschicht gab es eine Affinität zum „English way of life", so dass Hamburger der Anglomanie bezichtigt wurden und Hamburg als die „englischste Stadt des Kontinents" galt.

Über 1 200 Speicher waren, meist an Wasserläufen gelegen, über die Stadt verstreut. Sie ermöglichten die zollfreie Lagerung von Waren. Nun wurden von den Kaufleuten zwischen 40 000 bis 45 000 Quadratmeter für Speicherflächen veranschlagt. Nach ersten informellen Vorgesprächen zur Freihafenfrage zwischen Hamburg und dem Reich kristallisierte sich als Lösung heraus, Hamburg nicht insgesamt als Freihafenstadt beizubehalten, sondern einen kleineren Freihafenbezirk innerhalb des Hafengebietes vorzusehen. Kontrovers war dabei die Finanzierung, Größe und Lage des Freihafenbezirks. Verschiedene Alternativen wurden erwogen. Der Freihafenbezirk sollte möglichst innenstadtnah liegen und durfte nicht bewohnt sein.[13]

Schließlich verständigte man sich auf eine Lösung, die ein Areal nördlich und südlich der Elbe einbezog und als Speicherbezirk die Wandrahminsel vorsah. In dem Vertrag zwischen Hamburg und dem Reich war weiter vorgesehen, dass die Zollverwaltung in hamburgischer Hand blieb, dass die zollfreie Zufahrt über die Unterelbe bis Hamburg gesichert war und dass im Freihafenbezirk Firmen angesiedelt werden sollten, die zollfrei Rohstoffe lagerten oder Halbfertigprodukte herstellten. Das Reich gewährte einen finanziellen Zuschuss in Höhe von 40 Millionen Reichsmark zu den baulichen Umgestaltungsmaßnahmen, die sich insgesamt auf über 100 Millionen Reichsmark beliefen. Die bestehende Bebauung in diesem Bereich wurde abgerissen, um Platz für neue Speicher zu schaffen. Insgesamt mussten ca. 20 000 Menschen weichen und sich nach einer neuen Bleibe umsehen, um den folgenden Bau der Speicherstadt zu ermöglichen. Die baulichen Maßnahmen waren gewaltig, die Hamburg zwischen 1882 bis zum Zollanschluss 1888 zu leisten hatte. Im großzügig ausgelegten Freihafengebiet gab es nach dem Zollanschluss, vor allem südlich der Elbe, zunächst noch größere ungenutzte Areale.[14] Das neu abgegrenzte Freihafengebiet umfasste 300 ha Wasser- und 700 ha Landfläche.

Anders als in England, wo die Firmen die Zollabfertigung durchführten und die Hafenarbeiter kontrollierten, war dies in Hamburg eine staatliche Aufgabe. Planung, Umsiedlung und Bau der Speicherstadt bilden eine großartige logistische Leistung, die kleinräumliche Versinnbildlichung des Welthandels, nicht nur eines der größten Speicherstadtquartiere der Welt, sondern neben großartigen ingenieurbautechnischen Leistungen auch ein Quartier von beeindruckender einheitlicher Gestaltqualität und Ensemblewirkung unter dem obersten Planer und Gestalter Franz Ferdinand Andreas Meyer.[15]

Abb. 4: Gesamtansicht der Speicherstadt mit Zollkanal

Die Speichernutzungen wurden damit stadträumlich separiert, wie später auch andere Nutzungen. „In Wirklichkeit nimmt ihre Zahl (der Speicher) sehr rasch ab, weil seit dem Zollanschluß Hamburgs der größte Teil unserer Einfuhr im Freihafen gelagert wird und für Speicher innerhalb der Zollstadt nur verhältnismäßig geringer Bedarf verblieben ist. Sie werden also abgerissen, um anders gearteten Gebäuden Platz zu machen, besonders Kontorhäusern (…)".[16]

Neben dem Güterumschlag bildeten die Werften den bedeutendsten Wirtschaftsfaktor im Hafengebiet. Sie waren seit Beginn des 19. Jahrhunderts auf dem südlichen Elbufer auf Steinwerder angesiedelt. Bis 1870 gab es fünfzehn Werften auf Steinwerder und am

Reiherstieg. 1877 kam die Werft Blohm & Voss hinzu, die bald Weltgeltung besitzen sollte und 1907 mit der Filiale der Stettiner Vulkan-Werft eine weitere Großwerft. 1912 lief hier unter großer Anteilnahme der Bevölkerung das größte Schiff der Welt die IMPERATOR vom Stapel. Deutschland als „latecomer" unter den Großmächten suchte nach 1900 die Ansprüche auf Kolonien und Weltmachtgeltung mittels einer Flottenbaupolitik zu untermauern. „Mein Feld ist die Welt" erklärte der einflussreiche Reeder und Generaldirektor der Hapag Lloyd Albert Ballin, der vom Nobody zum „Souverän der Seefahrt" aufstieg und auch „des Kaisers Reeder" tituliert wurde.[17]

Abb. 5: 1911 fertig gestellter erster Elbtunnel

Lebens- und Arbeitswelten im und am Hafen

Auch in Hamburg mussten die Hafenarbeiter – wie in allen Seehafenstädten – um die schwankende Zahl der Arbeitsplätze kämpfen.[18] Große Streiks hatten die Aufmerksamkeit auf die Lage der Hafenarbeiter gelenkt und Streiks in London 1889 und in Hamburg 1896/97 hatten Verbesserungen im Bereich der Arbeitsvermittlung und -Organisation erbracht, allerdings wenig am Strukturproblem des unterschiedlichen Anfalls der Arbeit ändern können. Es stand ein ständiges Überangebot an nicht spezialisierten Arbeitskräften zur Verfügung, je nach Bedarf wurden Arbeitskräfte eingestellt und entlassen. Die Arbeitssuche („Umschau") erfolgte auf den Straßen am Hafen oder in Gaststätten. Die Wirte hatten entsprechend ein Interesse an hohen Zechen und einer verzögerten Vermittlung – bei der die Zechschulden den Arbeitssuchenden direkt vom Lohn abgezogen wurden. Auch die Lohnauszahlung fand häufig in Wirtschaften statt. Die langen Wartezeiten setzten die Arbeiter „sittlichen Gefahren" aus und verführten zu „Müßiggang und Trunk".[19] Gleichwohl waren Kneipe und Wirtshaus für Hafenarbeiter auch wichtige soziale Institutionen, wo Informationen und Erfahrungen ausgetauscht wurden.

Erst 1906 wurden Löhne und Arbeitszeiten tarifvertraglich geregelt. 1902 hatte der Verein für Socialpolitik eine umfangreiche Enquete gestartet, um die Lage der in der Seeschifffahrt beschäftigten Arbeiter wie die wirtschaftliche und technische Entwicklung der Seeschifffahrt zu untersuchen. Die Arbeit im Hafen und beim Güterumschlag war vielseitig, nicht ungefährlich und körperlich anstrengend. Folgende Berufsgruppen wurden unterschieden: Schauerleute, Ewerführer, Speicherarbeiter, Kaiarbeiter, Getreidearbeiter, Kohlenarbeiter, Schiffsmaler, Schiffsreiniger, Kesselreiniger und Maschinisten.[20]

Unzureichende Verkehrsverbindungen zum und im Hafen verlängerten Anfahrtswege. Bis ins 20. Jahrhundert hinein gab es „Ruderboot-Fahrgemeinschaften" um zu den Schiffen zu gelangen, die zu be- und entladen waren. Die Mahlzeiten konnten in Speisehallen („Kaffeeklappen") eingenommen werden, wo kein Alkohol ausgeschenkt wurde. Die Arbeit erfolgte in Gruppen („Gängen") von 8 bis 10 Arbeitern. Die Fertigstellung des Elbtunnels 1911, gebaut nach Vorbildern in Glasgow und London – dessen 100-jähriges Jubiläum 2011 gefeiert wurde – bildete einen weiteren Höhepunkt ingenieurbautechnischer Leistungen.[21] Die Regelung der zunehmenden Verkehrsströme zwischen beiden Seiten der Elbe, wie von den Wohngebieten der Hafenarbeiter zu den Werften und Schiffen wurde damit – ohne störende kreuzende Hafenfähren und witterungsunabhängig – deutlich verbessert.

Ab Mitte des 19. Jahrhunderts war auch die Auswanderung nach Amerika zu einem wichtigen Geschäftszweig geworden. Zwischen 1871 und 1914 war Hamburg wichtigster Transithafen für über zwei Millionen osteuropäischer Auswanderer. 1901 wurde südlich der Elbe auf der Veddel von der Schifffahrtsgesellschaft HAPAG eine „Auswandererstadt" mit Pavillons errichtet, die zeitweise 5 000 Menschen beherbergte, die auf eine Passage warteten. Heute ist das Areal als Auswanderungsmuseum nachgebaut worden und als Museum zu bestaunen.

Integraler Bestandteil des Hafenkomplexes waren auch „besondere" hafennahe Viertel („sailor towns"). Höchst international orientiert bildeten sie ein Konglomerat aus einer Fülle von Funktionen und Dienstleistungen, das Geschäfte für Bekleidung, Genussmittel und Souvenirs, Seemannskirchen, Unterkünfte, Wirtshäuser, Tätowierstuben, Wirtshäuser, Tanzpaläste und Bordelle umfasste. Jüdische, chinesische, schwarze und dunkelhäutige Menschen anderer Kulturen waren mit ihren Lebens-, Ess-, und Arbeits- und Wohnweisen in Seehäfen längst präsent, während sie im Binnenland noch als „exotisch" bestaunt wurden. Hafenviertel galten „als gefährlich" und hatten häufig den Ruf unsicher und „unmoralisch" zu sein, zugleich bildeten sie erste „Trittsteine" für die Neuankömmlinge, die Chancen für Prozesse von informeller Aneignung und die Herausbildung ethnischer Ökonomien eröffneten.

Als „Folge und Ergänzung" zur Arbeitswelt entstand die Gegenwelt nördlich am Hafen, der „Red light district" mit Vergnügungsbetrieben, Tanzhallen, Wirtshäusern, Matrosenkneipen, Bordellen und Theatern. Die Reeperbahn trug zum Ruf St. Paulis als „Armenhaus" und „Schandfleck" zugleich bei. Das Laster und Vergnügen, das Exotische und Fremde, lockte Hamburger aus der Stadt sowie Seeleute und Hafenarbeiter nach St. Pauli. Die Reeperbahn bildete das bekannteste Vergnügungsviertel der Welt.[22] In spanischsprachigen Ländern wird für diese Hafenviertel und Schlumpfwinkel der Andersartigkeit der Name „Barrio Chino" benutzt, der schon begrifflich Bezüge zur Internationalität – in diesem Fall nach China („Chinatown") – herstellt.[23] Um 1900 fuhren bereits ca. 5 000 fremde Seeleute auf deutschen Schiffen, vor allem als Heizer und Trimmer, da – so die biologistisch-rassistische Begründung – die „Kulis" besonders anspruchslos und „hitzebeständig" seien.[24] Auch ein „Chinesenviertel" entstand in der Nähe des Hafens.

Besonderheiten der Hafenarbeiterwohnungsfrage in Hamburg

Auch die Wohnungsfrage erhielt in Hamburg – wie in anderen Seehäfen – ihre besondere Ausprägung durch die lokale Ökonomie, vor allem durch den Hafen. Da Wohnungen im Hafen und Freihafen nicht zugelassen waren, mussten die im Hafen beschäftigten Arbeiter am Hafenrand „zusammenrücken" oder sich in weiter vom Hafen entfernten Gebieten eine neue Bleibe suchen.[25] Durch Wartezeiten im Hafen sowie die Abhängigkeit von Kneipenwirten für die Arbeitsvermittlung erhöhten sich die Kosten für Essen und Trinken.[26]

1892 brach in Hamburg eine Choleraepidemie aus, bei der über 8 000 Menschen starben. Die Cholera lenkte vor allem den Blick auf die Lebensverhältnisse der (Hafen-)Arbeiterschaft. Die Cholera bewirkte und beschleunigte so soziale Reformen, die nicht nur im hygienischen, wohnungspolitischen und städtebaulichen Bereich lagen. Die Unzulänglichkeiten der Strukturen der Hamburgischen Verwaltung waren durch die Epidemie offengelegt worden, hatten Veränderungen ermöglicht und den politischen Wandel forciert. Aber weniger die empirischen Untersuchungen, sondern vielmehr der große Hafenarbeiterstreik in Hamburg 1896 bewirkte eine erneute Diskussion der Wohnungsfrage und folgende staatliche Initiativen.[27] Unzufriedenheit über stagnierende Löhne bei steigender Arbeitsintensität und höheren Lebenshaltungskosten sowie Unterdrückung der Bildung von Gewerkschaften durch Einschränkung der Koalitionsfreiheit waren die Gründe für den Arbeitskampf, dessen Ausbruch zunächst von Unternehmerseite „bösen" englischen Agitatoren angelastet wurde.[28]

Ferdinand Toennies – einer der renommiertesten deutschen Soziologen – schrieb über den „Strike" und den Zusammenhang zwischen Hafenarbeit und Wohnungsnot: „Die Wohnungsnot der arbeitenden Klasse, charakteristisch für die kapitalistische Produktionsweise schlechthin, erfährt in Hafenstädten leicht eine besondere Verschärfung. Die Bedeutung der Gelegenheit, aber auch die Kürze der Pausen zwischen überlangen Arbeitszeiten, so oft drängende Arbeit vorhanden, machen ein nahes Wohnen, in höherem Grade als sonst, zur Bedingung der Arbeit selbst, auch abgesehen von der Konkurrenz Arbeitsuchender. Um Arbeitsmarkt und Arbeitsstätte drängen sich daher die Scharen der Hafenarbeiter und derer, die es werden wollen, dicht zusammen. Die Folgen in Gestalt von Notpreisen kleiner Wohnungen, Ueberbevölkerung des verfügbaren Raumes, Einschränkungen im sittlich notwendigsten Komfort, machen sich in jeder Hafenstadt bemerkbar."[29]

Robert Koch hatte erklärt, er vergesse, dass er sich in Europa befinde, wenn er die Hamburger Gängeviertelwohnungen sehen würde. Die Arbeit der „Sanierungskommission" beförderte schließlich die Einleitung von Sanierungen in drei Bereichen. Ab 1900 begann vor diesem Hintergrund in Hamburg die einzige bedeutende Flächensanierung in Deutschland vor dem Ersten Weltkrieg.

Aber in der Regel waren die nach der Sanierung errichteten neuen, gut ausgestatteten Kleinwohnungen für die unregelmäßig beschäftigten Hafenarbeiter zu teuer. Viele Bewohner hatten viele Jahre am Hafen gelebt und suchten nun vergeblich an der gewohnten hafennahen Wohnumgebung festzuhalten. Die Verdrängung der „kleinen Leute" und „Problemgruppen" aus dem Hafenviertel war ein durchaus erwünschter Nebeneffekt der Sanierung. Für die betroffenen Hafenarbeiter war diese „Modernisierung" ihrer Wohn- und Lebensverhältnisse entweder mit höheren Mietbelastungen verbunden, oder sie bewirkte einen zwangsweisen Umzug in die mietpreisgünstigeren, aber vom Hafen abgelegeneren Wohnquartiere. Eine Verdrängungswelle – heute würde man sie als Gentrification bezeichnen – aus den mietpreisgünstigen Wohnungen am Hafen folgte umgehend.

Pfadabhängigkeiten des offenen Tidehafens

1913 überholte Hamburg mit der Umschlagsmenge Rotterdam und Antwerpen und stieg nach London und New York zum drittgrößten Hafen der Welt auf. Im gleichen Jahr wurde Hamburg Millionenstadt, innerhalb von nur 20 Jahren hatte sich die Einwohnerzahl verdoppelt. Die folgenden Erweiterungen des Hamburger Hafens umfassten bald auch das Südufer der Elbe. Hamburgs Nachbarstädte Altona und Harburg betrieben eigenständige Hafen- und Stadtentwicklungspolitiken. Der Generalplan von 1908 richtete den Blick allerdings auch auf preußische Gebietsteile. Auf Kuhwerder, Steinwärder, später auf Neuhof und Waltershof entstanden dann nach dem Hamburgisch-Preußischen Köhlbrandvertrag neue Liegeplätze und Umschlagsmöglichkeiten auch für die Flussschifffahrt.

Hamburg schlug Mitte des 19. Jahrhunderts nach kontroversen Debatten eine andere Pfadentwicklung als englische Häfen – für den offenen Tidehafen – ein, die sich als zukunftsfähig erweisen sollte.[30] In Hamburg wurde der Hafen nicht zum Spielball privater Interessen, wie in anderen Seehafenstädten. „Was dem Hafen nützt, nützt auch Hamburg" galt als Leitlinie für die Hafenerweiterungen. Der Hafenbetrieb verblieb in der Hand der Stadt. Land und Infrastrukturen wurden von der Stadt verpachtet und nur ausnahmsweise verkauft. Neue, moderne Hafenanlagen konnten ohne Rücksicht auf den Schiffsverkehr hemmende Schleusen erstellt werden.

Im Handbuch des Seehafenbaus war 1911 über Hamburg vermerkt: „Beispiel eines erstklassigen Binnensee-Handelshafens im Ebbe- und Flutgebiet mit offenen Hafenbecken, zum größten Teil künstlich gegraben mit besonders umfangreicher Berücksichtigung der Bedürfnisse des Umschlags von Seeschiff zu Flussschiff und einiger großer Schiffahrtsgesellschaften".[31] Auch international galten die Hamburger Hafenanlagen als innovativ und vorbildlich. So wurde in einem Buch für ein nordamerikanisches Publikum betont: „this book was written with the conviction that the much-needed modernization of our ocean and Great Lakes terminals must be along the lines followed in Hamburg (…)".[32]

Netzwerke und Internationalisierung

Nicht nur Güter wurden bewegt, gehandelt und ausgetauscht, auch Ideen und Konzepte wurden transferiert. Detaillierte Kenntnisse über Hafenplanungen und -betrieb im internationalen Vergleich wurden in den entsprechenden Fachzeitschriften, über Tagungen, Ausstellungen und Fachexkursionen ausgetauscht. Seit Mitte des 19. Jahrhunderts gab es Expertennetzwerke, in denen international Erfahrungen diskutiert und jeweils lokale Lösungen optimiert wurden.

Einen systematischen Überblick über bedeutende Seehäfen weltweit gab A. Dorn in seinem zweibändigen Werk. Ging es in seinem Werk eher um eine Beschreibung der Häfen, suchen andere Autoren gezielt Umschlag und Hafenbetrieb zu verbessern und hier von „best practices" zu lernen. Der Hamburger Hafen gilt bezüglich der Betriebsabläufe und Organisation international durchweg als vorbildlich. So schrieb der spätere hamburgische Wasserbaudirektor Bubendey 1885: "So sehenswürdig die großen Lagerräume der London Docks in kaufmännischer Beziehung sind, so wenig vermag die Art des Betriebes den Ingenieur, welcher die neueren Einrichtungen anderer Häfen kennt, zu befriedigen".[33]

Unterschiedliche Arbeits- und Lebenswelten, Lebensstile und Kulturen bestehen in allen Seehäfen nebeneinander. Das enge Beieinander von Fremdem und Exotischem am Hafen zog viele Menschen an. Hafen und Uferzonen waren nicht von der Stadt getrennt, sondern öffentliche Räume und Schauplatz des Austausches. In Hafenstädten war man früher und offener gewohnt mit Fremdheit und Andersartigkeit umzugehen, während Phänomene des „Fremden" für Menschen im Binnenland ungewohnt, „anormal", exotisch und teilweise bedrohlich erschienen. Das wiederum implizierte für die „Fremden" zunächst Probleme der Assimilation, der Diskriminierung und Kriminalisierung.

Die Hafengebiete bildeten somit Besonderheiten im Stadtgefüge: Zwischenräume und Austausch- und Übergangszonen zur bürgerlichen Normalität, Diasporen, Andersartigkeiten mit besonderen (Sub-)Kulturen und sozialen Netzwerken. „Mit der Globalisierung wird die Welt zusehends „kleiner", und Entferntes wird stärker miteinander verknüpft. Zugleich wird sie „größer", weil wir noch niemals weitere Horizonte überschauen konnten".[34] Eine Internationalität auf „kleinstem Raum" nahmen die Hafenviertel vorweg, zugleich beförderten die hier dominanten Milieus von Kaufleuten, Industriellen und Reedern immer internationale und schließlich globale Vernetzungen und Austauschbeziehungen. Die „Globalisierung der Meere" ist wechselseitig mit den infrastrukturellen Voraussetzungen in Häfen verbunden. Seehäfen bilden wiederum zentrale Knotenpunkte im vielgliedrigen System zunehmend internationaler und globaler Arbeitsteilung.

Die historischen baulich-räumlichen Infrastrukturen, Kais, Hafenbecken und Speichergebäude wurden in den letzten Jahrzehnten überformt und nicht selten zur Unkenntlichkeit entstellt. Das authentische Hafenambiente weicht einer nostalgischen Inszenierung. Bilder und Szenen von Hamburg sind ohne Hafen kaum vorstellbar. Es gibt ein ganzes Genre von Belletristik über Hamburg als „Tor zur Welt", über hafenstädtisches Milieu, die „Welthafenstadt" und das besondere Ambiente, das die „Warenmarke Hamburg" und das Image ausmacht. Siegfried Lenz hat es im „Der Mann im Strom" unnachahmlich literarisch gezeichnet: „(Ihm ...) sollte der Hafen gezeigt werden, er war der Stolz der großen Stadt, ihr Ruhm, ihre Schatzkammer von altersher; mit dem Hafen war verbunden, was Tradition hatte, was hier galt und bedeutend war, und der Hafen war sehenswert, ohne Zweifel (...) Alles war sorgsam berechnet in dieser Stadt – es hatte nie an fleißigen Rechnern gefehlt, an blonder Zuverlässigkeit".[35]

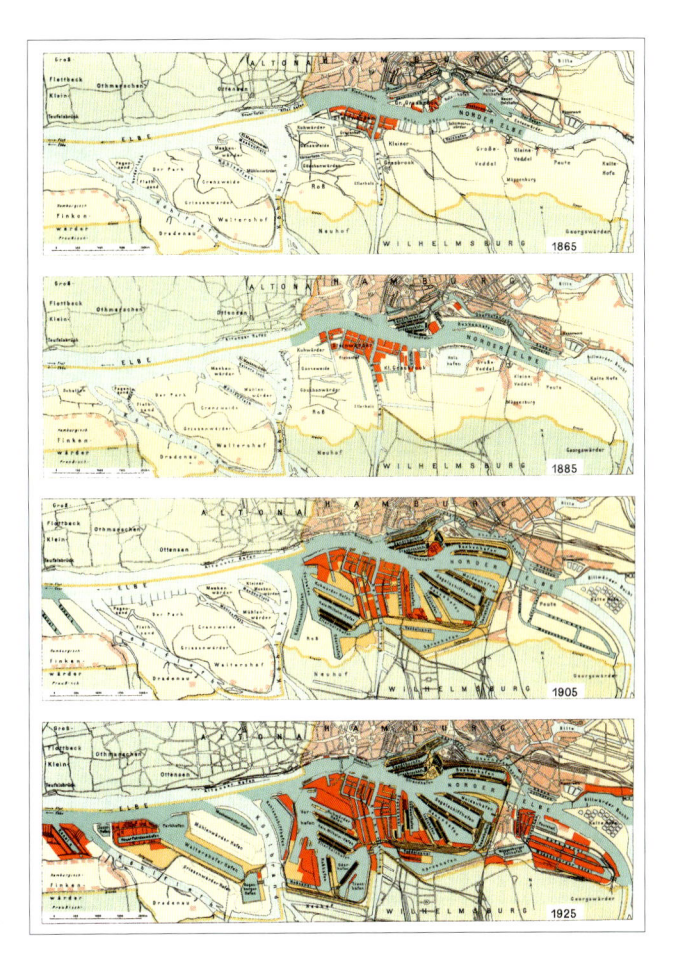

Abb. 6: Phasen des Hafenausbaus in Hamburg 1865–1925

Abstract

Hamburg – Amphibious city in an (inter-)national context

Each seaport has its own characteristics and there are no two cities with a seaport in the world that are the same. Rather, each has its very specific features that give it its own individual look and history. It is the different geographical contexts, the technical potential, historical developments, hinterland infrastructure and the constellation of players involved that together shape and determine the specific stages of development and restructuring of a seaport. Typically, seaport cities are amphibious and display a close dove-tailing of water and land based features.

Preserving buildings and infrastructures, some of which are listed, means opening up a unique potential to link and merge past, present and future thus creating a new unity with regard to architecture and construction features. Hamburg is a case in point. However, this endeavour means that some rather difficult choices have to be made if one wishes to, on the one hand side, be mindful of maritime heritage and its authenticity and, on the other, if current demands made by urban development and the real estate industry are to be taken into consideration.

This presentation takes Hamburg's city and port history as a starting point: How can the special development paths of Hamburg, its buildings and spatial particularities as well as the listed parts of the city be placed into an international context? What similarities and differences are there when comparing Hamburg to other seaport cities?

Literaturverzeichnis

ALTSTAEDT, K. Heinrich, Schauerlüd, Schutenschupser und Kaitorten. Arbeiter im Hamburger Hafen, Erfurt 2011.

AMENDA, Lars, Fremd-Wahr-Nehmung und Eigen-Sinn. Das „Chinesenviertel" und chinesische Migration in Hamburg, 1910–1960, in: Angelika EDER (Hrsg.), „Wir sind auch noch da!". Über das Leben von und mit Migranten in europäischen Großstädten, Hamburg 2003, S. 73–94.

BADURA, Sven, Der alte Elbtunnel Hamburg, Berlin 2011.

BESELIN, Oskar, Franz Andreas Meyer, Ein Baumeister der Großstadt Hamburg, Hamburg 1974.

BORSCHEID, Peter, Das Tempo-Virus. Eine Kulturgeschichte der Beschleunigung, Frankfurt am Main 2004.

BRAUN, Harry, Dorothée ENGEL, Vom Brook zur Speicherstadt, Erfurt 2010.

BUBENDEY, Johann Friedrich, Die Häfen von London, in: Deutsche Bauzeitung No. 95, 1885, S. 570.

CLAPP, Edwin J., The Port of Hamburg, New Haven, London, Oxford 1911.

CHRISTIANSEN, Flemming, Chinatown Europe. Identity of the European Chinese towards the beginning of the twenty-first century, London 2003.

DORN, Alexander, Die Seehäfen des Weltverkehrs, Bd. 1, Wien 1891.

EBERSTADT, Hermann, Hamburgs Anschluß an das deutsche Zollgebiet, Hamburg 1981.

EMMERICH, Walter, Der Freihafen, Hamburg 1960.

EVANS, Richard, Tod in Hamburg. Stadt, Gesellschaft und Politik in den Cholera-Jahren 1830–1910, Reinbek 1990.

FISCHER, H. E., Sittengeschichte des Hafens, in: L. SCHIDROWITZ (Hrsg.), Sittengeschichte des Hafens und der Reise, Wien 1927.

FITGER, E., Die wirtschaftliche und technische Entwicklung der Seeschiffahrt, Leipzig 1902.

FLÜGEL, Heinrich, Die deutschen Welthäfen Hamburg und Bremen, Jena 1914.

HEIMERDINGER, Timo, Der Seemann. Ein Berufsstand und seine kulturelle Inszenierung (1844–2003), Köln, Weimar, Wien 2005.

GRÜTTNER, Michael, Arbeitswelt an der Wasserkante. Sozialgeschichte der Hamburger Hafenarbeiter 1886–1914, Göttingen 1984.

KLUDAS, Arnold, Dieter MAASS, Susanne SABISCH, Hafen Hamburg. Die Geschichte des Hamburger Freihafens von den Anfängen bis zur Gegenwart, Hamburg 1988.

LAFRENZ, Jürgen, Die Speicherstadt in Hamburg, in: Die alte Stadt 4/1994, S. 318–338.

LEE, Robert, The socio-economic and demographic characteristics of port cities: a typology for comparative analysis, in: Urban History 25/2, 1998, S. 147–182.

LENZ, Siegfried, Der Mann im Strom, Hamburg 2002.

MAAK, Karin, Die Speicherstadt im Hamburger Hafen, Hamburg 1985.

MAASS, Dieter, Der Ausbau des Hamburger Hafens 1840–1910, Hamburg 1990.

MEYER, F. Andreas, Hamburg und die Zollanschlußbauten, in: Stahl und Eisen, Oktober 1888, S. 650–661.

OSTERHAMMEL, Jürgen, Niels P. PETERSSON, Geschichte der Globalisierung, Dimensionen, Prozesse, Epochen, München 2003.

PUDNEY, John, London's Docks, London 1975.

PUFFERT, Douglas, Pfadabhängigkeit in der Wirtschaftsgeschichte, in: C. HERMANN-PILLATH, M. LEHMANN-WAFFENSCHMIDT, (Hg.), Handbuch zur evolutorischen Ökonomik, Wien 2000.

RABE, Johs. E., Von alten hamburgischen Speichern und ihren Leuten, Hamburg 1913.

RATH, Jürgen, Arbeit im Hamburger Hafen. Eine historische Untersuchung, Hamburg 1998.

REINCKE, Heinrich, Hamburg. Ein Abriß der Stadtgeschichte von den Anfängen bis zur Gegenwart, Bremen 1926.

RUDOLPH, Wolfgang, Die Hafenstadt. Eine maritime Kulturgeschichte, Erfurt 1979.

SCHUBERT, Dirk, Seehafenstädte als Vorreiter der Globalisierung – Pfadabhängigkeiten der Hafen- und Stadtentwicklung in Hamburg und London, in: Ralf ROTH, (Hrsg.), Städte im europäischen Raum. Verkehr, Kommunikation und Urbanität im 19. und 20. Jahrhundert, S. 107–138, Stuttgart 2009.

SCHULZE, F. W., Seehafenbau. Bd. 1, Allgemeine Anordnung der Seehäfen, Berlin 1911.

STUBBE-DA LUZ, Helmut, Stadt und Hafen Hamburg in ausländischer Reiseliteratur vom 17. bis zum 19. Jahrhundert, in: Jürgen ELLERMEYER, Rainer POSTEL (Hrsg.), Stadt und Hafen. Hamburger Beiträge zur von Handel und Schiffahrt, Hamburg 1986.

TEUTEBERG, Hans J., Die Entstehung des modernen Hamburger Hafens 1866–1896, in: Tradition 17/1972, S. 257–291.

TOENNIES, Ferdinand, Die Enquete über die Zustände der Arbeit im Hamburger Hafen, in: Archiv für soziale Gesetzgebung und Statistik Bd. 12/1898, S. 303–348.

WIBORG, Susanne, Albert Ballin – der „Souverän der Seefahrt", Hamburg 2001.

Abbildungsnachweis

Abb. 1: Hamburg in frühen Photographien 1848–1888, Sammlung Bokelberg, Eingeleitet und kommentiert von Will Keller, im Verlag der Sammlung Bokelberg, Hamburg ohne Jahr

Abb. 2 bis Abb. 4: Bernhard Meyer-Marwitz, Hamburgs Weg zum Welthafen, Hamburg 1960, Verlag Okis Dr. Karl Josef Sattelmair

Abb. 5: Sven Bardua, Der alte Elbtunnel Hamburg, Berlin 2011, Historische Wahrzeichen der Ingenieurbaukunst in Deutschland Bd. 8

Abb. 6: L. Wendemuth, W. Böttcher, Der Hafen von Hamburg, Hamburg 1928 (Meissner & Christiansen)

* Die Abbildungsrechte sind vom Autor geklärt worden und liegen in dessen Verantwortung.

---

[1] Technische Standards, organisatorische Bedingungen und räumliche Allokationen sind pfadabhängig, wenn sie dauernde Auswirkungen auf spätere Entscheidungen haben. Pfadabhängigkeit ist damit ein Ansatz zur Erklärung nicht nur vergangener, sondern auch gegenwärtiger Ereignisse. Vgl. PUFFERT, Pfadabhängigkeit, Wien 2000.

[2] OSTERHAMMEL/PETERSSON, Geschichte, S. 14.

[3] Für die Seeleute bildete der Landgang und der Besuch der Vergnügungsviertel der Hafenstädte eine Ausnahmesituation gegenüber dem Alltag auf dem Schiff und auf See, die eine verzerrende Darstellung beförderte und einen „dankbaren Soff für pittoreske Ausmalungen und romantisierende Überformungen" bot. Vgl. HEIMERDINGER, Der Seemann, 2005, S. 77.

[4] BORSCHEID, Das Tempo-Virus, S. 110: „Auch auf den Meeren setzt sich das ‚dromologische' Gesetz durch: Jede höhere Geschwindigkeit grenzt zunächst niedrige Geschwindigkeiten aus, um sie schließlich zu verdrängen."

[5] Alle Daten FLÜGEL, Die deutschen Welthäfen, S. 293.

[6] TEUTEBERG, Die Entstehung, 1972, S. 271.

[7] So der aus Glasgow kommende Besucher John Strang. Zit. nach: STUBBE-DA LUZ, Stadt und Hafen, 1986, S. 200.

[8] REINCKE, Hamburg, 1926, S. 258.

[9] Vgl. PUDNEY, 1975.

[10] KLUDAS, MAASS, SABISCH, Hafen Hamburg, 1988, S. 22, HANSEN, Im Auf und Ab der Gezeiten, 1989 und WENDEMUTH, BÖTTCHER, Der Hafen von Hamburg, 1928.

[11] FITGER, Seeschiffahrt, S. 51.

[12] Vgl. LAFRENZ, Die Speicherstadt, S. 318–338 und MAAK, Die Speicherstadt im Hamburger Hafen, 1985 und EMMERICH, Der Freihafen, 1960.

[13] EBERSTADT, Hamburgs Anschluß an das deutsche Zollgebiet, 1981, S. 33.

[14] RATH, Arbeit im Hamburger Hafen, 1988.

[15] Vgl. BESELIN, Franz Andreas Meyer.

[16] RABE, Speicher, S. 5. Die Speicherstadt wurde nach 2002 wieder aus dem Freihafengebiet herausgenommen und gehört seither zum Zollinland.

[17] Vgl. WIBORG, Albert Ballin, 2001.

[18] Zu einem komparativen Vergleich von Hafenstädten und Besonderheiten der Bevölkerungsstruktur vgl. LEE, The socio-economic and demographic characteristics of port cities, S. 150 ff.

[19] RATH, Arbeit, S. 185.

[20] ALTSTAEDT, Schauerlüd, S. 7 ff.

[21] BARDURA, Elbtunnel, S. 27.

[22] FISCHER, Sittengeschichte des Hafens, 1927, S. 28.

[23] Derartige Chinatowns gab/gibt es in vielen Seehafenstädten Rotterdam (Katendrecht), Amsterdam, New York, Singapur, Bangkok, Havanna, Panama City und unter dem Namen „Barrio Chino" in Havanna und Barcelona (El Raval). Vgl. CHRISTIANSEN, Chinatown Europe, 2003.

[24] AMENDA, Fremd-Wahrnehmung, S. 75. In den 1920er Jahren wurde die Niederlassung von chinesischen Seeleuten als „wachsende Plage" wahrgenommen und im Rahmen der NS-Rassenpolitik war dann von „Verbrecherviertel", „Spielhöllen" und „Opiumhöhlen" die Rede. Vgl. AMENDA, Fremd-Wahrnehmung, S. 80 ff.

[25] TOENNIES, Die Enquete über die Zustände der Arbeit im Hamburger Hafen, 1896, S. 335.

[26] TOENNIES, a. a. O., S. 313 beschrieb diese „Umschau" wie folgt:, Dass „ein zuweilen 2 Tage langes Warten („Ausguck") auf avisierte Schiffe der Arbeit selber vorausgehen, Tage, die also eigentlich zum „Dienste" gehören, aber nicht bezahlt werden."

[27] EVANS, Tod in Hamburg, 1990, S. 643.

[28] GRÜTTNER, Arbeitswelt.

[29] TOENNIES, Hafenarbeiter und Seeleute in Hamburg, S. 179.

[30] SCHUBERT, Seehafenstädte, S. 108.

[31] SCHULZE, Seehafenbau, S. 86.

[32] CLAPP, The Port of Hamburg, S. vii.

[33] BUBENDEY, Die Häfen, S. 570.

[34] OSTERHAMMEL, PETERSSON, Geschichte, S. 8.

[35] LENZ, Der Mann, S. 18.

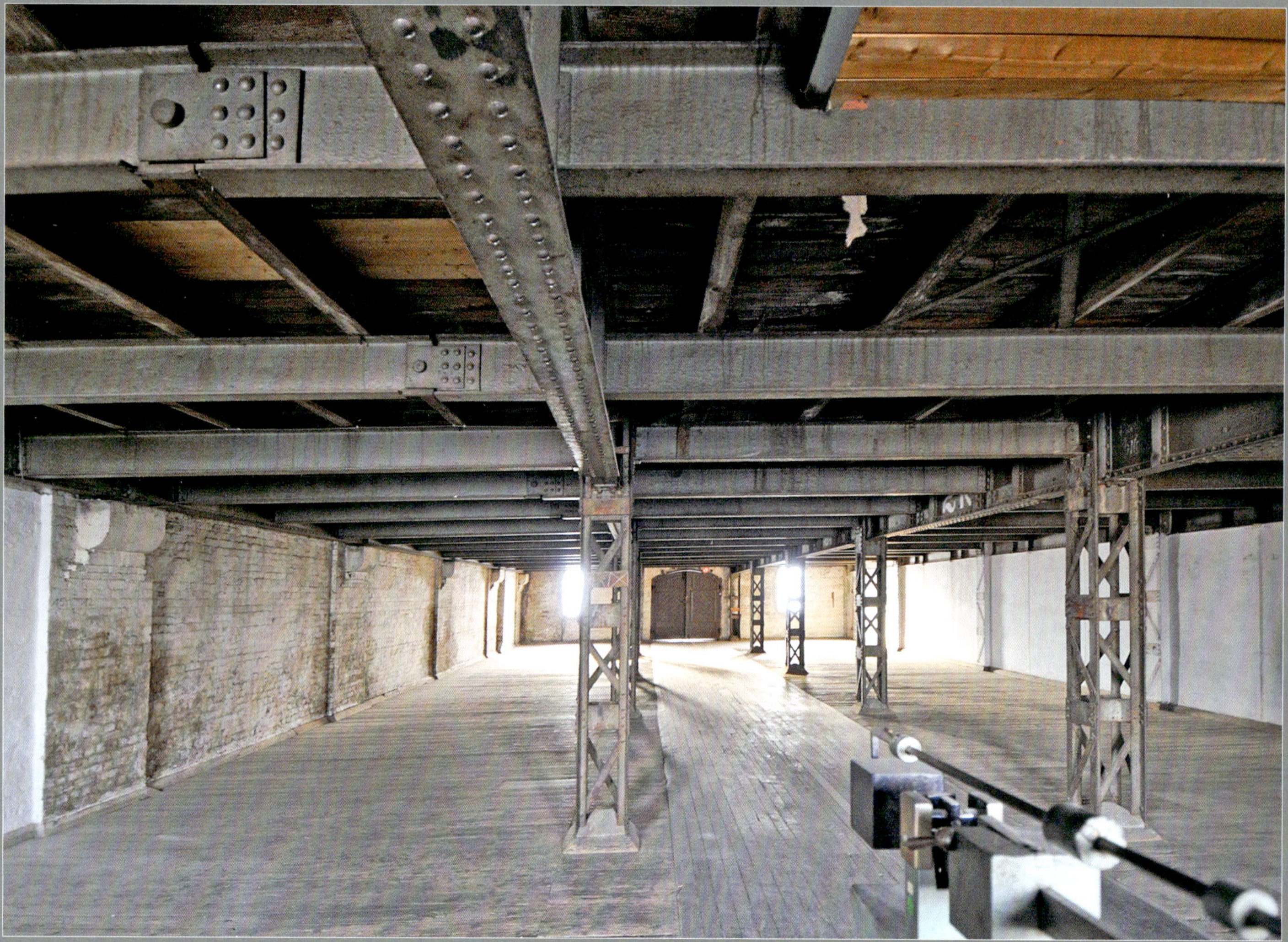

Speicherbauten/Warehouse Buildings:
**Deutsche Seehäfen und Speichergebäude
German Seaports and Warehouse Buildings**

Hamburg, Speicher

Ralf Lange

Die Hamburger Speicherstadt

Die Geschichte und Entwicklung der Speicherstadt

Die Speicherstadt wurde von 1885 bis 1927 in drei Bauabschnitten errichtet.[1] Sie bestand ursprünglich aus 17 Gebäudekomplexen mit Büro- und Lagerflächen, von denen heute noch 15 erhalten sind. Diese Komplexe werden traditionell Blöcke genannt und fortlaufend mit Buchstaben gekennzeichnet. Um Irritationen des Lesers vorzubeugen, sei darauf hingewiesen, dass die Buchstaben F und I nicht vergeben wurden und dass mit den Buchstaben A, B, C, J, K, M, N, Q und R nicht vollständige Blockeinheiten, sondern nur Blockabschnitte bezeichnet wurden.[2] Außerdem gehören zur Speicherstadt zahlreiche Brücken, die Zollgebäude am Alten Wandrahm und die Verwaltungs- und Betriebsgebäude der ehemaligen HFLG Hamburger Freihafen-Lagerhaus-Gesellschaft – der heutigen HHLA Hamburger Hafen und Logistik AG.

Der Bau der Speicherstadt war eine Folge des Zollanschlussvertrages, der 1881 zwischen der Stadt Hamburg und dem Deutschen Reich geschlossen wurde.[3] Hamburg und die preußischen Nachbarstädte Altona und Wandsbek sollten in das deutsche Zollgebiet eingegliedert werden, wofür eine Frist bis Oktober 1888 gesetzt wurde.[4] Da die Hamburger Wirtschaft nicht auf das bisherige Privileg verzichten wollte, Importgüter zollfrei umschlagen, lagern, veredeln und verarbeiten zu können, wurden große Teile der aktuellen und zukünftigen Hafenflächen als Freihafen ausgegrenzt: „Innerhalb dieses lediglich von außen zollamtlich zu bewachenden Bezirks ist die Bewegung der Schiffe und Waaren von jeder Zollcontrole befreit [...]."[5] Zölle und andere Einfuhrabgaben mussten erst entrichtet werden, wenn die Waren dieses

Abb. 1: Der Sandtorhafen mit Block O und dem ersten Verwaltungsgebäude der HFLG (rechts), die beide von Hanssen & Meerwein und Stammann & Zinnow stammten (1885–87, Aufnahme um 1890)

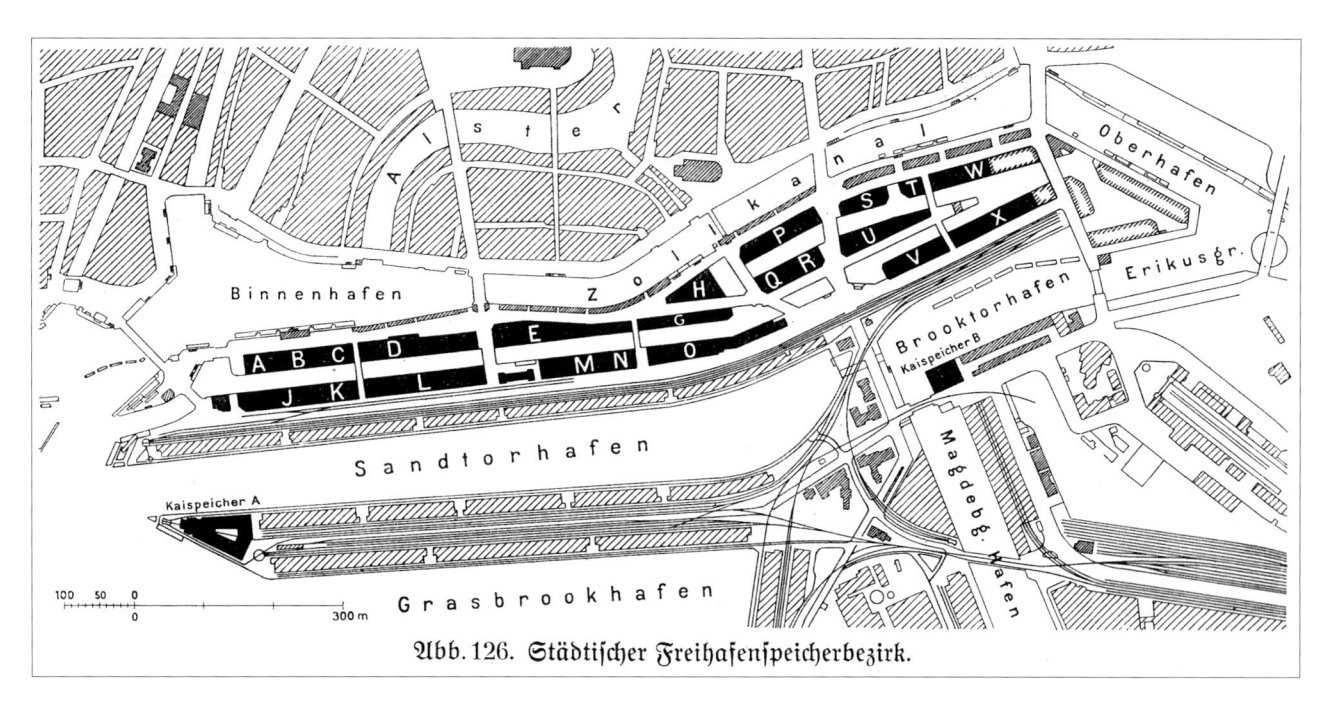

Abb. 2: Lageplan der Speicherstadt mit den Blockbezeichnungen (1914)

Gebiet verließen; bei Transitgütern für das Ausland entfielen diese von vornherein. Die Stadt legte außerdem Wert auf die Zollhoheit im Freihafen, befürchtete sie doch andernfalls eine „mit den Bedürfnissen des Großhandels nicht genügend vertraute Verwaltung".[6]

Der Bau der Speicherstadt war notwendig, weil sich die bisher genutzten Lagerflächen in der Innenstadt konzentrierten[7], wogegen es im zukünftigen Freihafengebiet kaum Lagerhäuser gab.[8] Es wurden zwar auch alternative Standorte für die Freihafenspeicher diskutiert[9]; der Senat hatte aber längst die Brookinseln ins Visier genommen, die verkehrsgünstig an der Nahtstelle zwischen den Häfen auf dem Großen Grasbrook und der südlichen Altstadt lagen, wo sich der Außenhandel konzentrierte.[10] Nachrangig war demgegenüber offenbar, dass diese Inselgruppe 16 000 Einwohnern zählte, die zunächst „disloeiert" werden mussten, bevor die Baumaßnahmen beginnen konnten.[11] Weiteren 2 500 Menschen drohte das gleiche Schicksal, weil außerdem die wasserseitige Bebauung vom Meßberg bis zu den Kajen dem Zollkanal und einer Uferstraße weichen sollte.[12]

Außer der Errichtung der Speicherstadt waren bis zum Zollanschluss noch zahlreiche weitere Baumaßnahmen zu bewältigen, von denen hier nur die wichtigsten genannt seien: – die Umfassung des Freihafengebiets mit Zollgrenzanlagen und Zollkontrollstationen; – der Bau des Segelschiffhafens auf dem Kleinen Grasbrook, um die Segelschiffe verlagern zu können, die bis dahin im Niederhafen vor der Neustadt ankerten; – der Bau des Zollkanals nördlich der späteren Speicherstadt, um Binnenschiffen eine Umfahrung des Freihafengebiets an seiner Nordseite zu ermöglichen, – der Bau der Norderelbbrücke, um den zukünftigen Freihafen vom Durchgangsverkehr zu entlasten.[13] Die Reichsregierung erklärte sich bereit, die Hälfte der Baukosten bis zu einer Summe von maximal 40 Millionen Mark zu übernehmen.[14] Das deckte jedoch nur einen weitaus geringeren Teil der tatsächlich entstehenden Kosten, die schon bald nach oben korrigiert werden mussten und schließlich mit 123 Millionen Mark veranschlagt wurden[15], wovon 54,5 Millionen Mark auf den Erwerb der Grundstücke für die Speicherstadt und den Zollkanal entfielen.[16]

Die Brookinseln vor dem Bau der Speicherstadt

Die Brookinseln waren noch im späten Mittelalter weitgehend ungenutztes Gelände, sieht man von den Schiffbauplätzen ab, die schon allein aus Brandschutzgründen vor den Toren der Stadt lagen.[17] Ab 1547 wurden sie in den Stadtwall einbezogen, der in Höhe des heutigen Sandtorkais und Brooktorkais aufgeschüttet wurde, wobei der Sandtorhafen den Verlauf des ehemaligen Wallgrabens markiert. Von 1615

Abb. 3: Die Straße Kehrwieder am Binnenhafen, die für den Bau der Speicherstadt abgebrochen wurde (1884)

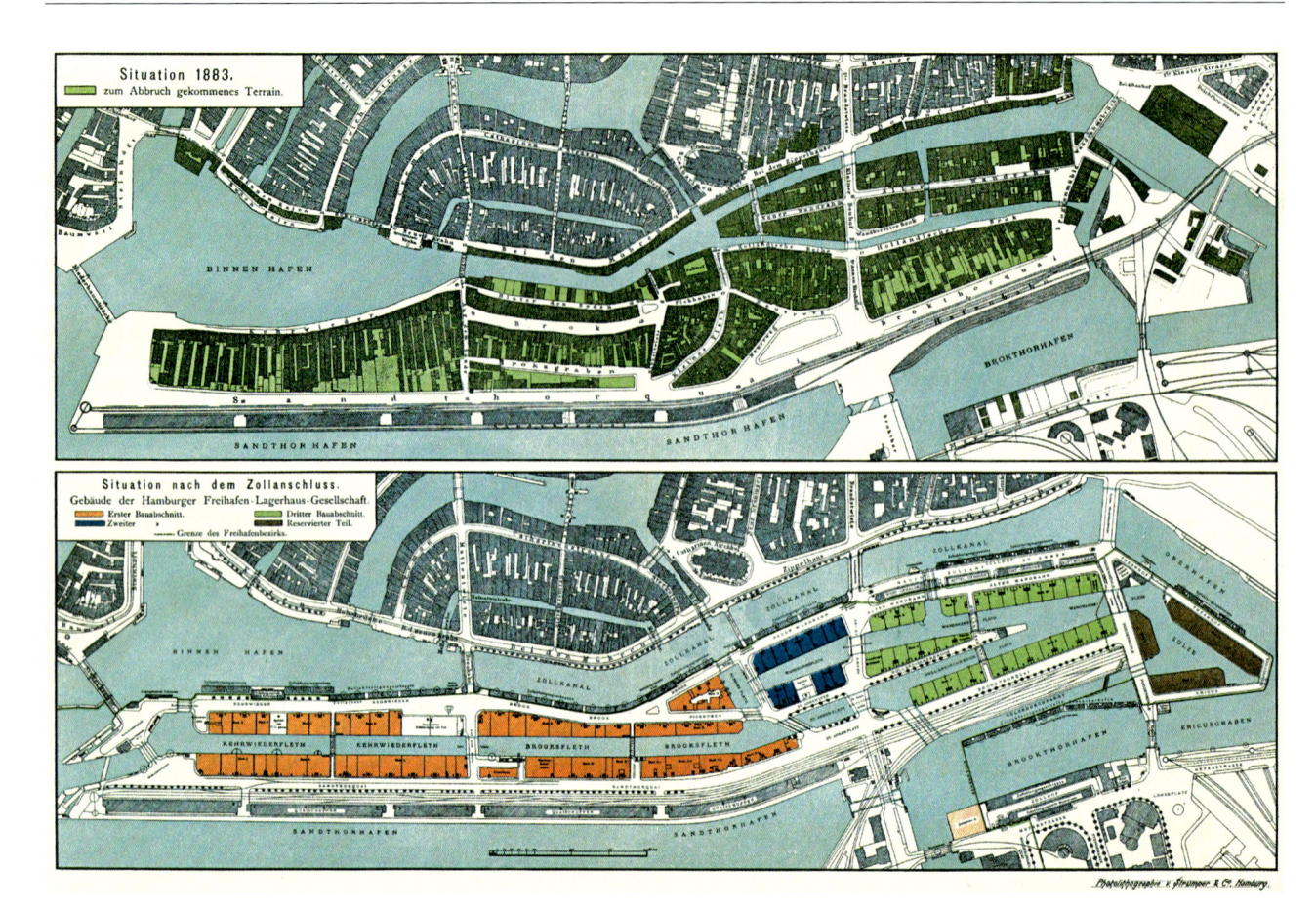

Abb. 4: Die Brookinseln vor dem Abbruch der Bebauung (1883, oben) und nach Fertigstellung der Speicherstadt. Die drei Bauabschnitte sind farbig markiert: Orange (1885–88), Blau (1891–96), Grün (1899–1927). Die braunen Blöcke auf der Ericusspitze wurden nicht realisiert

bis 1626 wurde die Stadtbefestigung erheblich erweitert, woran die Ericusspitze im Südosten der Speicherstadt erinnert, die ursprünglich eine der Bastionen war. Die systematische Besiedlung der Brookinseln setzte erst spät ein. Noch am Ende des 16. Jahrhunderts gab es hier große unbebaute Flächen, auf denen die „Gewandrahmen" standen: Trockengestelle für englische Wollstoffe, die in Hamburg gewalkt und gefärbt wurden. Hiervon leiten sich die Straßennamen Alter und Neuer Wandrahm ab.[18]

Sieht man von einigen gründerzeitlichen Bauten ab, herrschte um 1880 auf den Brookinseln eine geschlossene Bebauung aus dem 17. und 18. Jahrhundert vor.[19] Am Kehrwieder, am Brook und am Pickhuben standen Fachwerkhäuser, in denen neben dem Kleinbürgertum der Handwerker, Einzelhändler und Gastwirte vor allem Arbeiter wohnten. Die Innenhöfe dieser Häuser waren ebenfalls dicht bebaut und wurden mit internen Gassen erschlossen – den sogenannten Gängen –, die nur über Tore in den Vorderhäusern zugänglich waren. Am Neuen Wandrahm, an der Holländischen Reihe, am Holländischen Brook und am Alten Wandrahm standen dagegen repräsentative Bürgerhäuser im Barockstil, an die in der Regel rückwärtig Speicher anschlossen. Seit der Mitte des 19. Jahrhunderts wanderte das Bürgertum allerdings aus der südlichen Altstadt ab, und zog bevorzugt in die neuen Villenviertel an der Außenalster. Die historischen Bürgerhäuser wurden in Mietwohnungen aufgeteilt oder in Kontorhäuser umgewandelt.[20]

Die Vorbereitung der Baugelände

Der Abriss der Bebauung der Brookinseln begann am 1. November 1883 am Kehrwieder.[21] Bis Ende 1887 war das gesamte Gelände bis zur heutigen Straße Bei St. Annen freigeräumt, wodurch zugleich das Terrain für den zweiten Bauabschnitt (ab 1891) vorbereitet wurde. Da großer Zeitdruck herrschte, wurde mit dem Bau der Infrastrukturen begonnen, sobald ein größerer Abschnitt verfügbar war: „Den leitenden Gedanken bildete bei der Aufstellung des Arbeitsplanes das Bestreben, möglichst schnell Terrain für die Herrichtung von Freihafen-Speichern […] zu schaffen."[22] Auch der 25 Meter breite Hauptkanal der Speicherstadt, nach den angrenzenden Straßen abschnittsweise in Kehrwiederfleet, Brooksfleet und St. Annenfleet benannt, wurde sukzessive realisiert. Er erstreckte sich zunächst von der Kehrwiederspitze bis zur St. Annenbrücke, hinter der nach Süden abknickte, um in den Brooktorhafen zu münden, und wurde erst bei der Realisierung des dritten Bauabschnitts als Holländischbrookfleet nach Osten verlängert.

Weitere Zerstörungen brachte der Bau des Zollkanals nördlich der Speicherstadt mit sich, für den das Dovenfleet und das westlich anschließende Mührenfleet zu einem 45 Meter breiten Kanal vereinigt wurden, der im Westen in den Binnenhafen mündete.[23] Bereits 1883 wurde die Bebauung an der Nordseite des Dovenfleets abgebrochen; Ende des Jahres 1887 fielen am Katharinenkirchhof die letzten

Häuser.[24] Da sich hierdurch die willkommene Gelegenheit bot, eine neue Uferstraße vom Meßberg bis zu den Kajen anzulegen, wurde auch die wasserseitige Bebauung am Binnenhafen niedergelegt.

Die oben skizzierten Maßnahmen wiederholten sich im Prinzip, als östlich der Straße Bei St. Annen der dritte Bauabschnitt entstand; im Winter 1897/98 wurden hier die ersten Häuser abgerissen.[25] Die Speicherstadt sah ihrer Vollendung entgehen, als 1906 die „Aptierung" des restlichen Geländes für die östliche Hälfte von Block W und Block X in Angriff genommen wurde.[26] Tatsächlich verzögerte sich die Fertigstellung von Block W dann aber noch bis Mitte der 1920er Jahre (vgl. unten).

Die HLG und die Quartiersleute

1885 wurde die HFLG Hamburger Freihafen-Lagerhaus-Gesellschaft als Aktiengesellschaft gegründet, um den Bau der Speicherstadt privat zu finanzieren.[27] Das Gelände blieb dagegen städtisches Eigentum und wurde an die HFLG unter der Bedingung verpachtet, dass die Stadt am Gewinn beteiligt wurde und die Option erhielt, sukzessive sämtliche Aktien zu erwerben. Es gelang der Stadt zwar erst 1928, Alleineigentümer der HFLG zu werden. De facto agierte die Gesellschaft aber von vornherein wie ein stadteigenes Unternehmen, zumal dem Senat alle Baupläne und Kostenvoranschläge zur Genehmigung vorgelegt werden mussten und dieser auch über die Höhe der Mieten für die Lagerflächen und Kontore zu entscheiden hatte. 1935 wurde die HFLG mit der Staatlichen Kaiverwaltung vereinigt und 1939 in HHLA Hamburger Hafen- und Lagerhaus-Aktiengesellschaft umbenannt. Seit 2005 nennt sich der Konzern HHLA Hamburger Hafen und Logistik AG.

Die HFLG nutzte jedoch nur wenige Speicher in eigener Regie. Der größte Teil wurde an die Quartiersleute vermietet, wie sich die Lagerhalter im Hamburger Hafen bis heute nennen.[28] Die Quartiersleute lagerten, bemusterten und veredelten Importgüter „auf fremde Rechnung" und zählten somit zu den „Zwischenunternehmern", wie sie damals für den Hamburger Hafen typisch waren.[29] Ihre Kunden rekrutierten sich zumeist aus dem Außenhandel. Aber auch der produzierende Sektor vertraute ihnen seine Rohstoffe an.

Außerdem gab es drei Speicher in Privatbesitz: Am Kehrwieder ließen sich die Weinhandelsfirmen Jebens und Lorenz-Meyer eigene Lagerhäuser errichten (Block B) und am St. Annenufer investierten Hanssen & Studt in einen Kaffeespeicher (Block R3).[30] Die beiden Staatsspeicher am Kehrwieder und am Sandtorkai, bei denen die Lagerflächen mit einem Postamt und einer Zollabfertigung bzw. der Maschinenzentralstation der Speicherstadt kombiniert wurden, blieben dagegen im Besitz der Stadt.[31]

Die Architekten der Speicherstadt

Abgesehen von den Staatsbauten und Privatspeichern lag die Verantwortung für die Planung und Errichtung der Speicherstadt bei der HFLG – wenn auch „unter Aufsicht und Mitwirkung des Ingenieurwesens der Bau-Deputation."[32]

Die HFLG erhielt eine eigene Bauabteilung, die unter ihrem Chefingenieur Heinrich Hagn bis zur Fertigstellung des ersten Bauabschnitts Ende 1888 15 Ingenieure, 24 Architekten und 23 Bauaufseher beschäftigte.[33] Mit Georg Thielen, Hanssen & Meerwein und Gustav Schrader wurden aber auch freie Architekten hinzugezogen, die in erster Linie für die Gestaltung der Fassaden zuständig waren.[34] Von Thielen stammten die Blöcke A, C, D, E, G, H, J, K, L, M und P, von Hanssen & Meerwein die Blöcke N, O, Q, R, U und V sowie die beiden Verwaltungsgebäude der HFLG und von Gustav Schrader die Blöcke S, T und W. Dabei mussten sich Hanssen & Meerwein die Aufträge für die Blöcke N und O sowie für das erste Verwaltungsgebäude der HFLG mit Stammann & Zinnow teilen und beim Bau des zweiten Gebäudes der HFLG mit Johannes Grotjan kooperieren.[35]

Für die Staatsbauten wie die erwähnten Staatsspeicher, die technischen Gebäude (vgl. unten), die Brücken oder die Gebäude für die Zollabfertigung zeichnete dagegen Franz Andreas Meyer verantwortlich, der Oberingenieur der Baudeputation (vergleichbar mit der späteren Baubehörde). Außerdem wurden Meyer alle Pläne der HFLG zur Begutachtung vorgelegt, was ihm kontinuierlichen Einfluss auf die Entwicklung der Speicherstadt sicherte.[36] Als Meyer 1901 starb, wurde sein Stellvertreter Eduard Vermehren zum Oberingenieur ernannt.[37] Vermehrens Nachfolger Friedrich Sperber (ab 1907) konnte dagegen kaum noch Akzente setzen, da die Speicherstadt nun fast vollständig realisiert war. Dies trifft, mutatis mutandis, auch auf Raywood zu, den späteren Chefingenieur der HFLG, der nur noch Block X (1908–12) und die östliche Hälfte von Block W (1925–27) realisieren konnte.[38] Vermutlich war Raywood auch am vierten Bauabschnitt der Speicherstadt beteiligt, der seit 1905 auf der Ericusspitze geplant war[39], aufgrund des Kriegsausbruchs 1914 und der Wirtschaftskrisen der Weimarer Republik aber Makulatur blieb.

Meyer, Vermehren und Thielen hatten die Polytechnische Schule in Hannover absolviert[40], die damals durch die Lehrtätigkeit von Conrad Wilhelm Hase geprägt wurde. Hases Leitbild war die norddeutsche Backsteingotik, wobei es ihm jedoch nicht nur um die Übernahme bestimmter historischer Formen bzw. deren Adaption an die modernen Bauaufgaben ging, sondern vor allem auch um das materialgerechte Gestalten mit Sichtmauerwerk, für das das mittelalterliche Bauen viele Anregungen bot.[41] Man findet deshalb in der Speicherstadt relativ selten explizit gotische Motive wie Kreuzrippengewölbe oder Spitzbogen. Entscheidender war, dass die Fassaden ausschließlich aus Backsteinen gefügt wurden. Dieses gleichsam modulare Gestaltungsprinzip, bei dem alle gliedernden und dekorativen Details konsequent aus dem genormten Format der Ziegel abgeleitet sind, macht die spezifische Qualität der „Hannoverschen Schule" aus: „[Hase] erhob das Einhalten dieser Maße zum Grundsatz; die Schichtenfugen gaben ihm beim Entwurf das Netz für alle Höhenabmessungen; ihnen hat sich jede Schmuckform, jede Gliederung unterzuordnen [...]".[42]

Mit dem Wiederaufbau der Speicherstadt, die im Zweiten Weltkrieg schwere Schäden erlitten hatte, wurde Werner Kallmorgen beauftragt.[43] Das war ein Glücksfall, lag der Komplex doch außerhalb des Blickfelds der damaligen Denkmalpflege.[44] Kallmorgen war dagegen um eine objek-

Abb. 5: Speicherstadt – erster Bauabschnitt: Block G (Mitte) und Block H (rechts) von Georg Thielen (1886/87 bzw. 1887/88, Aufnahme 1932). Block G wurde 1943 zur Hälfte zerstört. Heute steht hier die Kaffeebörse (vgl. Abb. 13)

tivere Beurteilung der historistischen Bauten der Kaiserzeit bemüht, sprach von „der lustigen liebevollen Architektur der 80er Jahre" und konstatierte anerkennend, diese Speicher seien „wirkliche Architektur".[45] Dabei schreckte er auch vor der originalgetreuen Rekonstruktion der Gebäude nicht zurück, wogegen er bei den Neubauten bestrebt war, diese zwar modern zu gestalten, aber mit Konzessionen an den „Genius loci", was er vor allem durch rote Backsteinfassaden und bestimmte Gliederungen leistete. Auch die Bauabteilung der HHLA, die einige Blöcke in eigener Regie wiederherstellte, hielt sich an sein Konzept.

Die technische Ausrüstung der Speicherstadt

Der vertikale Transport der Waren auf die einzelnen Lagergeschosse erfolgte mit Hilfe von außen liegenden Winden, so dass jeder Speicher an der Wasser- und an der Landseite über große Schiebe- oder Klapptüren verfügt, die übereinander angeordnet sind – die so genannten Luken. Diese senkrechten Lukenachsen münden in Giebel mit Windenauslegern, die von kleinen Kupferhauben als Witterungsschutz überdeckt werden. Heute sind allerdings nur noch die landseitigen Winden in Betrieb, so dass an den Wasserseiten in der Regel

die Stahlseile mit den charakteristischen weißen Stahlkugeln fehlen, die dafür sorgen, dass die Seile auch ohne Last straff hängen. Ein weiteres typisches Detail der Speicherstadt sind die Bedienungsstangen für die Winden, die außen neben den Luken angebracht sind und bis zum Dachgeschoss reichen, wo eine Verbindung zum Windenantrieb besteht. Schiebt man die Stange nach oben, bewegt sich auch das Lastseil der Winde in diese Richtung – und vice versa.

Die Speicherwinden wurden mit Druckwasser angetrieben, in den Kellern gab es außerdem hydraulische Hubbühnen. Höchsten technischen Ansprüchen genügte auch die Beleuchtung der Speicher, die aus Sicherheitsgründen bereits 1888 voll elektrifiziert war.[46] Die Speicherstadt erhielt deshalb eine eigene Maschinenzentralstation, in der die elektrischen Generatoren und die Pumpen für die Windenhydraulik standen, die mit Dampf aus dem benachbarten Kesselhaus angetrieben wurden. Da im Laufe der Zeit immer mehr Firmen in elektrische Sortiermaschinen investierten, z. B. zum Sieben oder Schälen von Rohkaffee, wurde 1901 noch zusätzlich eine Unterstation in Block U in Betrieb genommen, in der ein mit Stadtgas betriebener elektrischer Generator stand.[47] 1953 wurden die Winden auf Elektromotoren umgerüstet und die ursprüngliche technische Ausrüstung der Speicherstadt wohl bald darauf verschrottet.[48]

Allgemeine Kennzeichen der Speicherarchitektur

Die Speicherfassaden kennzeichnen sich nahezu durchgängig durch ein einheitliches Schema, wobei die land- und wasserseitigen Fassaden im Prinzip gleich gestaltet sind. Über ein oder zwei Sockelgeschossen mit großen Fenstern, die sich für die Kontore anboten, aber auch zum Lagern genutzt wurden, erheben sich drei bzw. vier weitere „Normalgeschosse", die ausschließlich als Lagerflächen dienten und deshalb kleinere Fenster haben. Die vertikalen Lukenachsen, die sich in der Regel vom Erdgeschoss bis zu den Windengiebeln erstrecken, verklammern die heterogenen Fassadenzonen. Die Schmalseiten der Blöcke werden durch Giebel und Türme akzentuiert, sofern diese eine exponierte Lage haben. Während der erste Bauabschnitt durchgängig steile Dächer aufweist, wurden die späteren Blöcke mit flach geneigten Dächern errichtet, wodurch die Zahl der Normalgeschosse von fünf auf sieben erhöht werden konnte.

Nahezu sämtliche Bauten sind mit rotem Backstein verblendet. Für die Kellergeschosse, die quasi die Stoßkanten der Gebäude bilden, wurde der hart gebrannte und somit besonders widerstandsfähige dunkelrote Klinker gewählt. Während diese Zonen schmucklos sind, weisen die darüber liegenden Fassadenabschnitte eine kraftvolle Gliederung aus Vorlagen, Wasserschlägen, Gesimsen, Friesen und Konsolen im Sinne der „Hannoverschen Schule" auf (vgl. oben). Bänder und Ornamente aus andersfarbigen Ziegeln oder vereinzelt auch grünen Glasplättchen (Block E und Block L) setzen Akzente im Sichtmauerwerk. Seltener wurden Glasurziegel verwandt. Dabei spiegelt die Gestaltung die Hierarchie der Bauaufgaben wieder. Während sich die Speicher in der damals üblichen Terminologie als „Backsteinrohbauten" charakterisieren lassen[49], d.h. ihre Fassaden sind nahezu ausschließlich aus Ziegeln gestaltet, werden die Verwaltungsgebäude der HFLG durch Gliederungen aus Werkstein nobilitiert.

Die Grundrisse und die Konstruktion der Speicher

Die meisten Gebäude in der Speicherstadt wurden in Skelettbauweise errichtet, um möglichst flexibel nutzbare, ungeteilte Lagerflächen zu erhalten. Aus dem gleichen Grund wurden die Treppenhäuser mit den Schächten für die

Abb. 6: Das Kesselhaus von Franz Andreas Meyer (1886/87). Das Gebäude büßte nach dem Zweiten Weltkrieg seine Schornsteine ein, die bei der Restaurierung durch gmp Architekten als Stahlgitterkonstruktionen nachempfunden wurden (1999–2001)

Abb. 7: Block D von Georg Thielen (1887/88). Deutlich ist die horizontale Zweiteilung in Büro- und Lagergeschosse zu erkennen

Abb. 8: Schnitt durch Block D von Georg Thielen (1887/88). Neben den hydraulischen Winden verfügten die Speicher im ersten Bauabschnitt noch zusätzlich über Haspelwinden für den manuellen Betrieb

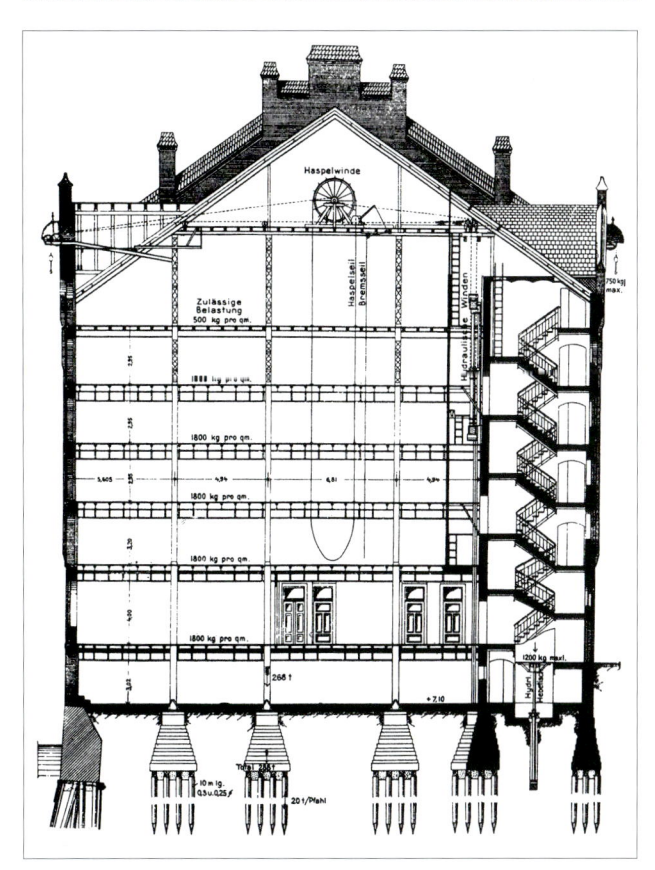

Abb. 9: Block E von Georg Thielen im Bau (um 1888).
Die Stahlelemente wurden vorgefertigt an die Baustelle
geliefert

Windenhydraulik und den Toiletten, die an den Zwischenpodesten der Treppen angeordnet sind, zu kompakten Kernzonen zusammengefasst. Nottreppenhäuser gab es anfänglich nicht.[50]

Mit den Blöcken Q und R (1894–96) wurden auf Anregung von Adolph Libert Westphalen, dem Branddirektor der Hamburger Feuerwehr, der übrigens selbst Architekt war, die „Westphalentürme" eingeführt: runde Türme, die zur Hälfte in die Geschossflächen integriert sind und Wendeltreppen als Notausgänge umschließen, wobei eiserne Balkone als externe Zugänge dienen.[51] Vor allem der dritte Bauabschnitt wird durch diese malerischen Türme geprägt, die sich ausschließlich an den Wasserseiten der Blöcke befinden.

Die gesamte Speicherstadt steht auf Holzpfahlgründungen aus zwölf Meter langen Stämmen, die mit Dampframmen in den Boden getrieben wurden.[52] Diese erlitten im Zweiten Weltkrieg nur relativ geringe Schäden und konnten deshalb beim Wiederaufbau mitsamt den Kaimauern weiter verwendet werden.[53] Unterschiede bestehen dagegen hinsichtlich der Konstruktion der Blöcke, die zunächst in Stahlskelettbauweise mit genieteten Gitterstützen, Deckenträgern und Unterzügen errichtet wurden.[54] Welche Risiken die unverkleideten Stahlkonstruktionen bargen, zeigte sich 1891 beim Brand des Staatsspeichers am Sandtorkai, als die Stahlstützen einknickten.[55] Bei den Speichern Q, R, S, T und U sowie dem Privatspeicher von Hanssen & Studt wurde deshalb nahezu durchgängig Holz für den Innenausbau gewählt, das im Brandfall bessere Eigenschaften aufweist als unverkleideter Stahl. Bei den Blöcken V und W kamen feuersicher ummantelte Gusseisenstützen zum Einsatz, bei Block X erneut Stahlstützen, die jedoch mit Beton ausgegossen und mit Blech verkleidet wurden. Abgesehen von der östlichen Hälfte von Block W (1925–27) spielte Stahlbeton vor dem Zweiten Weltkrieg keine Rolle.

Die Verwaltungsgebäude der HFLG

Das erste Verwaltungsgebäude der HFLG, ein Entwurf von Hanssen & Meerwein und Stammann & Zinnow (1886/87, vgl. Abb. 1), wurde wie ein Kopfbau an Block O gefügt, so dass es sich nach drei Seiten hin architektonisch entfalten konnte.[56] Auffällig im Vergleich mit den übrigen Bauten in der Speicherstadt sind die Sandsteingliederungen, die das Gebäude in dem Ensemble hervorheben und seinen besonderen Rang unterstreichen. Die Dachhäuschen und zwei kegelförmige Helme, die einen Turm bzw. einen Runderker bekrönen, verleihen dem relativ kleinen Bau einen malerischen Umriss und somit eine starke Präsenz. Ungewöhnlich für den Norden sind die neogotischen Motive, die auf süddeutsche Vorbilder verweisen, wie die Kreuzblume auf dem Dreiecksgiebel oder der polygonale Erker, der an ein Nürnberger „Chörlein" erinnert. Die Skulptur in der Nische am Fleet stellt die Hl. Anna mit ihrer Tochter Maria dar als Reminiszenz an die St.-Annen-Kapelle, die bis zum Abbruch 1869 auf dem Gelände der späteren Speicherstadt stand.[57] Der Bildhauer ist nicht bekannt.

Von Hanssen & Meerwein – in Kooperation mit Johannes Grotjan – stammte auch das zweite Verwaltungsgebäude der HFLG, das am westlichen Ende von Block U entstand (1902–04).[58] Das Gebäude sollte sich zwar „in würdiger Weise den bereits im nördlichen Freihafengebiet entstandenen Gebäuden anpassen."[59] Dies gewährleistet aber nur die

Abb. 10: Das zweite Verwaltungsgebäude der HFLG von
Hanssen & Meerwein und Johannes Grotjan (1902–04)

Abb. 11: Die Ruine von Block R (1944)

Abb. 12: Das Freihafenamt in Block R von Werner Kallmorgen (1952/53)

Kombination von rotem Verblendmauerwerk mit Sandsteingliederungen, die in der Wettbewerbsausschreibung übrigens auch gefordert war, wogegen der für die Speicherstadt ungewöhnliche Renaissance-Charakter das Gebäude zu einem Fremdkörper in seinem Umfeld macht. Das Treppenhaus und die Eingangshalle wurden mit Granitsäulen, Kreuzrippengewölben, Jugendstilfliesen und schmiedeeisernen Geländern repräsentativ ausgestattet. Heute ist das Gebäude mit dem angrenzenden Block U, der von gmp Architekten in ein Bürohaus umgewandelt wurde (2000–02), zur Unternehmenszentrale der HHLA vereinigt.[60]

Die Kriegszerstörungen und der Wiederaufbau

Im Zweiten Weltkrieg wurde die Speicherstadt wiederholt das Ziel von Bombenangriffen. Die schwersten Schäden waren bei der britisch-amerikanischen Luftoffensive vom 25. Juli bis 3. August 1943 – der „Operation Gomorrha" – sowie bei den Angriffen am 13. Dezember 1943 und am 18. Juni 1944 zu verzeichnen.[61] Die Zerstörungen konzentrierten sich im ersten und zweiten Bauabschnitt, was wohl auch an den Stahlskeletten der Gebäude lag, die den Bränden nicht standgehalten hatten. Die Blöcke A, B, C, J, K und M sowie die östliche Hälfte von Block G waren als Totalschäden zu verbuchen. Auch die Blöcke O und R waren zum größten Teil zerstört. In den Blöcken D, E, L und P klafften große Lücken. Im westlichen Teil von Block H waren die oberen Geschosse eingestürzt. Der dritte Bauabschnitt wies dagegen einen weitaus geringeren Zerstörungsgrad auf. Lediglich zwei Abschnitte in Block U, einer in Block W und der kleine Block T zählten hier zu den Verlusten.

Für den Wiederaufbau der Speicher zeichnete, wie oben dargestellt, neben der Bauabteilung der HHLA vor allem Werner Kallmorgen verantwortlich, der den Anspruch, hatte, von der historischen Architektur so viel wie möglich wiederherzustellen.[62] Die teilzerstörten Blöcke D, E, H, L, P und U wurden rekonstruiert; lediglich die Dachgeschosse wurden vereinfacht, insbesondere die Windengiebel. Von Block M und dem ehemaligen Speicher von Hanssen & Studt (Block R 3) ließen sich zumindest die Straßenfassaden erhalten, wogegen die Fassaden an der Wasserseite neu gestaltet wurden, wenn auch mit Windenhäuschen und Luken wie bei den historischen Speichern. Der Innenausbau erfolgte in Stahlbetonskelettbauweise, sofern die Konstruktionen irreversibel geschädigt waren. Auf diese Weise entstand eine Collage aus unterschiedlichen Bauschichten, die das wechselvolle Schicksal der Gebäude dokumentiert

Völlig neu konzipiert wurden dagegen Block T sowie die völlig zerstörten Abschnitte der Blöcke G, O und R, zumal hier Büros statt der ursprünglichen Lagerflächen entstehen sollten. Während das Bürohaus in Block O eine Skelettfassade aus dunkelgrau gefärbtem Stahlbeton erhielt, die in Brüstungshöhe mit roten Ziegeln ausgefacht wurde, entwickelte Kallmorgen für die neuen Bürohäuser in den Blöcken G, T und R Rasterfassaden aus Backstein (vgl. Abb. 12 und 14). Auffällig ist der betont handwerkliche Charakter der Ausführung: Die Stürze der Rasteröffnungen sind mit Rollschichten auf Stich gemauert, was der Architektur eine traditionalistische Note verleiht. Die Präzision, mit der alle Fassadendetails aus den genormten Ziegelmaßen entwickelt sind, erinnert an die „Hannoversche Schule". Die gekuppelten Fenster der Blöcke R und T sowie der wiederhergestellten Ostfassade von Block P wirken wie Paraphrasen auf die historische Speicherarchitektur. Vergleichbare Fenster finden sich auch an den Speichern aus der Zeit vor dem Ersten Weltkrieg.

Das ehemalige Zentrum des Kaffeehandels

Eine Sonderrolle spielten die Blöcke N und O von Hanssen & Meerwein und Stammann & Zinnow (1886/87, vgl. Abb.

1), die auf Betreiben der Kaffeehändler errichtet wurden.⁶³ Beide Blöcke waren ursprünglich identisch gestaltet, was sich jedoch kaum noch vermittelt, weil Block O im Zweiten Weltkrieg bis auf einen kleinen Rest zerstört und durch Neubauten ersetzt wurde. Block N blieb dagegen unversehrt. Auffällig ist die schmucklose Backsteinarchitektur, die zu den Straßen hin lediglich durch hell gestrichene Putzflächen, u. a. neogotische Blendbogen, akzentuiert wird, wogegen die wasserseitigen Fassaden völlig schlicht sind. Das Erdgeschoss und die ersten beiden Obergeschosse enthielten Kontore, was sich an den größeren Fenstern ablesen lässt, während in den darüber liegenden Geschossen mit den Luken der Kaffee lagerte. Außerdem war der Saal der Kaffeebörse in Block O untergebracht.

Beim Wiederaufbau von Block O durch Werner Kallmorgen (1955–59, vgl. Abb. 13) wurden die Lager- und Büroflächen auf eigenständige Baukörper aufgeteilt und der Börsensaal in einen Neubau ausgegliedert, der anstelle der zerstörten Osthälfte von Block G entstand.⁶⁴ Die neue Kaffeebörse, ein Entwurf von Kallmorgen und Schramm & Elingius (1955/56), wurde mit verglasten Fußgängerbrücken über das Brooksfleet und die Straße Pickhuben hinweg an die Kontore in den Blöcken O und H angebunden. Hinsichtlich des flachen Tonnendachs und der mit Werkstein verkleideten Stahlbetonskelettfassaden zitiert das Gebäude den südlichen Annex des Rathauses in Aarhus von Arne Jacobsen und Erik Møller (1938–42), das als ein Leitbau der deutschen Nachkriegsarchitektur gelten kann.⁶⁵ Die Ausstattung des Börsensaals ist erhalten, wenn auch derzeit ausgelagert. Eine untergehängte Schalldecke aus Holzstäben zeichnet den Schwung der Dachschale nach. Ein farbiges Glasbild der Firma Kuball, das Kaffeepflücker bei der Arbeit zeigt, dominiert die östliche Stirnwand.

Die aktuelle Entwicklung der Speicherstadt

In den 1980er Jahren zeichnete sich deutlich ab, dass die Speicherstadt gegenüber anderen Lagereinrichtungen im Hamburger Hafen nicht mehr konkurrenzfähig war. Während immer mehr Quartiersleute in moderne Flachlager abwanderten oder ihre Betriebe aufgaben, weitete sich zugleich der internationale Orientteppichhandel aus, der bis dahin nur eine marginale Rolle gespielt hatte, so dass schließlich 60 Prozent der vermietbaren Flächen, d. h. ohne die Dachböden und Keller gerechnet, für die Lagerung von Teppichen genutzt wurden.⁶⁶ Seit 2000 ist auch diese Branche stark rückläufig, zumal die Speicherstadt seit 2003 nicht mehr zum Freihafen gehört. Seitdem werden immer mehr Lagerböden in Büroflächen umgewandelt und sporadisch auch Gastronomie und Einzelhandel angesiedelt. Kultur- und Freizeitangebote sorgen für touristische Anziehungspunkte. Wohnungen bleiben dagegen die Ausnahme, weil die Speicherstadt sturmflutgefährdet ist und die meisten Gebäude bei einer Überflutung nicht von Rettungsfahrzeugen erreicht werden können.

Die Umwandlung der Speicherblöcke erfolgt in Abstimmung mit der Denkmalpflege unter größtmöglichem Erhalt der historischen Bausubstanz. Das äußere Erscheinungsbild der Gebäude bleibt unangetastet, und auch im Innern prägen die originalen Skelettkonstruktionen aus Holz, Stahl oder Gusseisenstützen weiterhin den Raumeindruck.⁶⁷ Bei den erforderlichen Einbauten wird Wert darauf gelegt, dass sich diese hinsichtlich der Materialien und Strukturen von dem ursprünglichen Bau abheben, so dass diese nachträglichen Veränderungen „lesbar" bleiben. Tiefere Eingriffe in die Gebäudesubstanz sind vor allem dann erforderlich, wenn die Sanitäranlagen und Erschließungen verbessert werden müssen, z. B. durch den Einbau von Fahrstuhlschächten. Nach

Abb. 13: Das ehemalige Zentrum des Kaffeehandels in der Speicherstadt: das Bürohaus in Block O (links) von Werner Kallmorgen (1954/55) und die Kaffeebörse von Kallmorgen und Schramm & Elingius (1955/56). Im Hintergrund befindet sich der Kaffeespeicher in Block O im Bau (Aufnahme um 1956)

Abb. 14: Der dritte Bauabschnitt der Speicherstadt mit den Blöcken S, U und W, die ab 2000 in Bürohäuser umgewandelt wurden, sowie Block X (links) wurden. Das kubische Gebäude (Hintergrund rechts) ist Block T von Kallmorgen & Partner (1967)

diesen Kriterien wurden bereits die Blöcke D, P, Q, R, S, U und W (westliche Hälfte) revitalisiert.

Eine vorläufige Bewertung

Aufgrund ihrer Größe, ihrer baulichen Geschlossenheit und ihres guten Erhaltungszustands stellt die Speicherstadt ein auch international einzigartiges maritimes Baudenkmal dar. Lediglich in Liverpool und Triest sind mit den Docks bzw. dem Porto Vecchio vergleichbare Ensembles erhalten.[68] Allerdings waren die Lagerhäuser am Mersey und an der Adria integrale Bestandteile der Seeschiffshäfen. In Hamburg wurden Speicher am seeschiffstiefen Wasser dagegen als nicht notwendig erachtet, weil die Ladung eines Schiffes selten für ein einziges Lagerhaus bestimmt war und somit ohnehin auf mehrere Orte verteilt werden musste.[69] Deshalb erhielt der Freihafen mit der Speicherstadt und den heute bis auf Lagerhaus G nicht mehr erhaltenen Speicherblöcken am Dessauer und Melniker Ufer zwei zentrale Lagerhausviertel, die neben den Landwegen vor allem mit Binnenschiffen erreichbar waren.[70] Die seeschiffstiefen Kais waren dagegen ausschließlich für Schuppen reserviert, in denen die Güter kurzfristig zwischengelagert wurden, bis sie an die Empfänger im Hinterland gingen oder verschifft wurden.[71]

Ein weiteres Alleinstellungsmerkmal der Speicherstadt ist ihre repräsentative Architektur.[72] Während die Lagerhauskomplexe in Liverpool und Triest betont gleichförmig wirken und die Gliederung der Fassaden primär funktionalen Aspekten folgt – wenn auch in Triest nobilitert durch Anleihen an das Palastschema -, waren die Architekten in Hamburg bestrebt, ein möglichst abwechslungsreich gestaltetes Ensemble zu entwerfen, dem Türme, hohe Dächer und Giebel überdies eine starke Fernwirkung verleihen. Diese Gestaltung war nicht nur der exponierten Lage der Speicherstadt auf einer Inselgruppe am Rand der City geschuldet. Sie machte das Viertel auch gleichsam zum architektonischen Aushängeschild des Welthafens Hamburg, der damals die führende Rolle nach London und New York behauptete – im Wettlauf mit Rotterdam[73] – und zudem einer der bedeutendsten Außenhandelsplätze war.

In kunsthistorischer Hinsicht lässt sich der Rang der Speicherstadt am besten greifen, wenn man sie als ein herausragendes Beispiel der „protomodernen" Architektur wertet, die gerade im Industrie- und Gewerbebau des 19. Jahrhunderts Lösungen hervorgebracht hat, die aus einer späteren, zugegebenermaßen verkürzenden Sicht, wie Pioniertaten der architektonischen Moderne wirken.[74] Charakteristische Merkmale dieser „Protomoderne" der Speicherstadt sind die Skelettbauweise aus vorgefertigten Stahlelementen, die hierdurch bedingte Entlastung der Außenwände von ihrer statischen Funktion – die somit nur noch als Klimahüllen fungieren – und die modularen Strukturen der Fassaden, deren Maße im Sinne der „Hannoverschen Schule" konsequent aus dem genormten Ziegelformat abgeleitet sind. Nicht zu vergessen die standardisierten Grundrisse, für die Franz Andreas Meyer das verbindliche Muster entwickelt hatte.[75] Dieser prinzipiell moderne Charakter der Speicherstadt wurde Ende der 1940er Jahre von Werner Kallmorgen erkannt und von ihm für den Wiederaufbau des schwer zerstörten Viertels fruchtbar gemacht.

Abstract

Hamburg Warehouse District (The Speicherstadt)

Trade and shipping have always had a strong influence on Hamburg's development. This process gained particular momentum in the course of the 19th century when the Port of Hamburg came to be rated among the most important ones in the world, ranking third only to London and New York. With its 15 blocks of warehouses the *Speicherstadt* is clear evidence of this. The blocks have been preserved to this day and form the largest integrated complex of warehouse buildings the world over. The *Speicherstadt* also includes administrative buildings belonging to the port owner and operator HHLA (formerly HFLG) and buildings that were formerly used by customs and for technical purposes.

The *Speicherstadt* was an up-front investment anticipating the integration of Hamburg into the German Customs Union (Deutsches Zollgebiet) which was completed on October 15, 1888. Before, in many parts of Hamburg imported goods could be introduced, stored and processed duty-free. After 1888, this privilege obtained only within the port area which was the reason why many warehouse operators had to move there. The *Brookinseln* (islands) to the South of the Old Town were chosen as the area where the new Free Port warehouses would be built. In 1881, there were some 16 000 people who inhabited those islands. All the buildings on the islands were torn down and the islands were integrated into the port area.

The demolition process began in 1883. Construction of the first group of warehouses – blocks A to O – was started in 1885 and completed in time for the integration into the German Customs Union in 1888. The second group – blocks P, Q and R – were built between 1891 and 1896. Due to WW I and the subsequent economic crises, the completion of the third group of warehouses – blocks S to X – was delayed till 1927. However, by 1912, with the exception of the Eastern half of block W (1925–1927), large part of this section of the *Speicherstadt* was almost complete. Blocks Y and Z were no longer needed after WW I and plans to build them were abandoned.

The *Speicherstadt* is among the main oeuvres of the *Hannoversche Schule* – this was the name of the neo-Gothic architecture taught by the *Technische Hochschule Hannover* at the time. Two of the most senior architects involved in building the *Speicherstadt* had studied in Hannover: Franz Andreas Meyer, Senior Engineer of the City of Hamburg, and Georg Thielen who was responsible for nearly the entire first group of warehouses plus block P. The *Hannoversche Schule* was not so much concerned about style, but focused mainly on what it considered to be appropriate ways of using brick as a design feature. In this regard, much inspiration was to be had in the north from medieval architecture.

Most buildings within the *Speicherstadt* were built with skeleton frames in order to produce large office spaces that could be compartmentalised as needed and thus offered maximum flexibility of use. To begin with the steel frames consisted of riveted pillars, supporting beams and girders which were prefabricated and delivered from the Ruhr District. For reasons of fire protection, as of 1891 wooden constructions were preferred. From 1904 onwards warehouses were built with fire-proofed jacketed pillars. Hoists for the lifting of goods to the warehouses were hydraulically powered, i.e. by water. Illumination was fully electrified as early as 1888.

In 1945, fifty per cent of the *Speicherstadt* was in ruins. Werner Kallmorgen was put in charge of reconstructing the *Speicherstadt*. He saw to it that the neo-Gothic facades some of which had collapsed were restored true to their original versions. An exception were the roofs: They were simplified and some of the ornamental turrets and gables were left out. However, when it came to replacing those warehouses which had been completely destroyed, Kallmorgen opted for an uncompromisingly modern design. Yet his brick facades and certain other design elements and structures of his office and warehouse buildings easily fit in with the historical ensemble.

Literaturverzeichnis

ALTSTAEDT, K. Heinrich, Quartiersmann in der Hamburger Speicherstadt, Hamburg 2003.

ARCHITEKTEN- UND INGENIEUR-VEREIN in Hbg., Versammlung am 4. Novb. 1885. Herr Hagn macht Mittheilungen über: die in der Ausführung begriffenen Speicherbauten der Hamburger Freihafen-Lagerhaus-Gesellschaft, in: Deutsche Bauzeitung, 1885, Nr. 95, S. 575–576, 1885.

BECKERSHAUS, Horst, Die Hamburger Straßennamen. Woher sie kommen und was sie bedeuten, 4. Aufl., Hamburg 2000.

BESELIN, Oskar, Franz Andreas Meyer. Ein Baumeister der Großstadt Hamburg, Hamburg 1974.

BOLLE, Arved, Der Generalplan für den Ausbau des Hamburger Hafens im Wandel der Zeiten, in: Jahrbuch der Hafenbautechnischen Gesellschaft, 1950/51, Bd. 21/22, Berlin – Göttingen – Heidelberg 1953, S. 34–50.

BRACKER, Jörgen, Das Kirchspiel St. Katharinen, in: Das Kirchspiel St. Katharinen. Der Hafen, die Speicherstadt und die Kirche, Unter dem gekrönten Turm, Hamburgs Geschichte, Menschen damals und heute, Unternehmen, Hrsg. von Axel Denecke, Peter Stolt und der Hamburger Hafen- und Lagerhaus-AG, Hamburg 2000.

BURMESTER, Andreas (Hrsg.), Die grossen Speicherbauten Hamburg's und Altona's. Eine Sammlung von Ansichten, Grundrissen und Schnitten, Hamburg 1890.

CORNEHL, Ulrich, „Raummassagen". Der Architekt Werner Kallmorgen 1902–1979 (Schriftenreihe des Hamburgischen Architekturarchivs), Hamburg 2003.

Thielen, Georg, in: DENKSCHRIFT zum 50jährigen Stiftungsfest des Architekten- und Ingenieur-Vereins zu Hamburg am 18. April 1909, Hamburg 1909, S. 93–94.

EILERT, P., Die Entwicklung der bau- und maschinentechnischen Anlagen der Hamburger Freihafen-Lagerhaus-Gesellschaft, in: Zeitschrift des Vereines Deutscher Ingenieure, 1910, Nr. 50, S. 2081–2089, S. 2135–2143 u. S. 2176–2183.

ENGELS, H., Eduard Vermehren †, in: Zentralblatt der Bauverwaltung, 1918, Nr. 11/12, S. 56.

GURLITT, Cornelius, Die deutsche Kunst des Neunzehnten Jahrhunderts. Ihre Ziele und Thaten (Das Neunzehnte Jahrhundert in Deutschlands Entwicklung. Bd. 2), Berlin 1899.

HAGN, Zum Speicherbrand in Hamburg, in: Deutsche Bauzeitung, 1891, Nr. 52, S. 313–314.

HAMBURG UND SEINE BAUTEN, unter Berücksichtigung der Nachbarstädte Altona und Wandsbeck. Zur IX. Wanderversammlung des Verbandes deutscher Architekten- und Ingenieur-Vereine in Hamburg vom 24. bis 28. August 1890, Hrsg. vom Architekten- und Ingenieur-Verein zu Hamburg, Hamburg 1890.

HAMBURG UND SEINE BAUTEN unter Berücksichtigung der Nachbarstädte Altona und Wandsbek 1914, Hrsg. vom Architekten und Ingenieur-Verein Hamburg, 2 Bde., Hamburg 1914.

HANSEN, Theodor, Hamburg und die zollpolitische Entwicklung Hamburgs im 19. Jahrhundert, Hamburg 1913.

HENCKE, Joachim, Der Wiederaufbau der Speicherstadt im Hamburger Hafen, in: Handbuch für Hafenbau und Umschlagstechnik, Bd. IX, Hamburg 1963, S. 146–154.

HERTZ, Paul, Unser Elternhaus (Hamburgische Hausbibliothek), Hamburg 1902.

HINZ, Frank M., Planung und Finanzierung der Speicherstadt in Hamburg. Gemischtwirtschaftliche Unternehmensgründungen im 19. Jahrhundert unter besonderer Berücksichtigung der Hamburger Freihafen-Lagerhaus-Gesellschaft (Veröffentlichungen des Hamburger Arbeitskreises für Regionalgeschichte, Bd. 7), Münster – Hamburg – London 2000.

HIPP, Hermann, Amtliche Erinnerung. Denkmalpflege und Stadtplanung in Hamburg vor und nach dem Zweiten Weltkrieg, in: Peter Reichel (Hrsg.): Das Gedächtnis der Stadt. Hamburg im Umgang mit seiner nationalsozialistischen Vergangenheit (Schriftenreihe der Hamburgischen Kulturstiftung, Bd. 6), Hamburg 1997, S. 61–80.

INDUSTRIEBAU, Ausstellung veranstaltet von der Universität Stuttgart, Institut für Entwerfen und Konstruktion Professor Kurt Ackermann, 2. Aufl., Stuttgart 1984.

KLEMANN, Hein A. M., Wirtschaftliche Verflechtungen im Schatten zweier Kriege 1914 bis 1940, in: Hein A. M. Klemann und Friso Wielenga (Hrsg.), Deutschland und die Niederlande. Wirtschaftsbeziehungen im 19. und 20. Jahrhundert (Niederlande-Studien, Bd. 46), Münster 2009, S. 19–39.

KLOSTERMEIER, Collin und WIECKHORST, Thomas, Fabriken und Speicher neu genutzt. 13 industrielle Gebäude mit neuer Funktion (Edition Bauhandwerk, Bd. 2), Gütersloh 2008.

KOKKELINK, Günther und LEMKE-KOKKELINK, Monika, Baukunst in Norddeutschland. Architektur und Kunsthandwerk der Hannoverschen Schule 1850–1900, Hannover 1998.

LANGE, Ralf, Hamburgs Familiensilber wird poliert: Die aktuelle Entwicklung in der Speicherstadt, in: Architektur in Hamburg. Jahrbuch der Hamburgischen Architektenkammer, Hrsg. von der Hamburgischen Architektenkammer, Hamburg 2002, S. 130–135.

LANGE, Ralf, HafenCity und Speicherstadt. Das maritime Quartier in Hamburg, 3. erweiterte u. aktualisierte Aufl., Hamburg 2010.

MAAK, Karin, Die Speicherstadt im Hamburger Freihafen. Eine Stadt an Stelle der Stadt (Arbeitshefte zur Denkmalpflege in Hamburg, Nr. 7), Hamburg 1985.

MAASS, Dieter, Der Ausbau des Hamburger Hafens 1840 bis 1910. Entscheidung und Verwirklichung, Hamburg 1990.

MEYER-BRUNSWICK, Uwe, Palaisähnliche Hamburger Bürgerhäuser des 17. Jahrhunderts und ihre Geschichte, Hamburg 1990.

MITTHEILUNG DES SENATS AN DIE BÜRGERSCHAFT, betreffend die mit der Reichsregierung geführten Verhandlungen über den Anschluß Hamburgs an das deutsche Zollgebiet. NO. 46. Hamburg, den 27. Mai 1881, in: Verhandlungen zwischen Senat und Bürgerschaft im Jahre 1881, Hamburg 1882, S. 201–202.

MITTHEILUNG DES SENATS AN DIE BÜRGERSCHAFT. NO. 47. Hamburg, den 3. Juni 1881. Antrag, betreffend Genehmigung der mit der Reichsregierung über die Modalitäten des Anschlusses Hamburgs an das Deutsche Zollgebiet getroffenen Vereinbarung vom 25. Mai d. J., in: Verhandlungen zwischen Senat und Bürgerschaft im Jahre 1881, Hamburg 1882, S. 207–248.

MITTHEILUNG DES SENATS AN DIE BÜRGERSCHAFT. NO. 73. Hamburg, den 3. Juli 1882. Antrag, betreffend den Anschluß Hamburgs an das Deutsche Zollgebiet, insbesondere den Generalplan und Generalkostenanschlag, in: Verhandlungen zwischen Senat und Bürgerschaft im Jahre 1882, Hamburg 1883, S. 289–300.

MITTHEILUNG DES SENATS AN DIE BÜRGERSCHAFT. NO. 200. Hamburg, den 24. Nov. 1897. Bericht der Senats- und Bürgerschafts-Commission zur Ausführung des Zollanschlusses, betreffend die Aptirung der Wandrahminsel für Freihafenspeicher, in: Verhandlungen zwischen Senat und Bürgerschaft 1897, Bd. 2, Hamburg 1898, Bd. 2, S. 727–741.

MITTEILUNG DES SENATS AN DIE BÜRGERSCHAFT. NO. 255. Hamburg, den 29. November 1905. Bericht der Senats- und Bürgerschaftskommission zur Ausführung des Anschlusses Hamburgs an das deutsche Zollgebiet, betreffend die Aptirung des östlichen Teiles der Kehrwieder-Wandrahminsel für Freihafenspeicher, in: Verhandlungen zwischen Senat und Bürgerschaft 1905, Bd. 2, Hamburg 1906, S. 815–822.

RATH, Jürgen, Arbeit im Hamburger Hafen. Eine historische Untersuchung von Jürgen Rath (Hamburger Studien zur Geschichte der Arbeit, Bd. 1), Hamburg 1988.

THAU, Carsten und VINDUM, Kjeld: Arne Jacobsen, Copenhagen 2001.

WASMUTHS LEXIKON der Baukunst, 4 Bde., Berlin 1932.
WENDEMUTH, Ludwig und BÖTTCHER, Walter, Der Hamburger Hafen, 2. Aufl., Hamburg 1931.
Ueber die ZOLLANSCHLUSS-BAUTEN Hamburgs. Nach einem Vortrage des Ober-Ingen. F. A. Meyer, in: Deutsche Bauzeitung, 1884, Nr. 17, S. 97–99.

Abbildungsverzeichnis

Abb. 1, 3, 9, 11, 13: Speicherstadtmuseum
Abb. 2: Hamburg und seine Bauten 1914
Abb. 4: Die Hamburger Freihafen-Lagerhaus-Gesellschaft 1885–1910. Denkschrift zum 25-jährigen Jubiläum, Hamburg 1910.
Abb. 5: HHLA, Gustav Werbeck
Abb. 6: Klaus Frahm
Abb. 7, 12, 14: Elbe & Flut, Thomas Hampel
Abb. 8: Hamburg und seine Bauten 1890
Abb. 10: Heinz-Joachim Hettchen

* Die Abbildungsrechte sind vom Autor geklärt worden und liegen in dessen Verantwortung

[1] Einige zentrale Aspekte der Baugeschichte der Speicherstadt, insbesondere die Rolle von Oberingenieur Franz Andreas Meyer und die Standortdiskussion, sind Gegenstand von: MAAK, Speicherstadt, 1985. Maak wird jedoch nicht dem Anspruch einer umfassenden Darstellung der Speicherstadt gerecht, zumal sie nur einzelne Blöcke des ersten Bauabschnitts ausführlicher behandelt. Siehe deshalb im Folgenden vor allem: HAMBURG UND SEINE BAUTEN, 1890, S. 398 ff.; EILERT, Entwicklung, 1910; HAMBURG UND SEINE BAUTEN, 1914, Bd. 2, S. 76 ff.; LANGE, Speicherstadt, 2010, S. 57 ff.

[2] Vgl. den Plan mit den Blockbezeichnungen in: HAMBURG UND SEINE BAUTEN, 1914, Bd. 2, S. 77.

[3] Siehe auch im Folgenden: HANSEN, Entwicklung, 1913, S. 151 ff.

[4] Der Zollanschluss wurde auf einen noch zu bestimmenden Tag nach dem 1. Oktober 1888 terminiert. Der Bundesrat sollte den exakten Termin in Abstimmung mit dem Hamburger Senat festlegen. Siehe MITTHEILUNG, NO. 47, 1882, Anlage 1, S. 240.

[5] MITTHEILUNG, NO. 46, 1882, S. 202.

[6] MITTHEILUNG, NO. 47, 1882, S. 209.

[7] Vgl. BURMESTER, Speicherbauten, 1890.

[8] „Wir beschränken uns darauf zu constatiren, dass in dem projectirten Freigebiet, abgesehen von der verhältnismässig nur geringen Zahl und Größe der in den Quartieren Kehrwieder und Brook belegenen Privatspeicher, bis jetzt ausser den Lagerschuppen auf Steinwärder für Guano, Salpeter und dergl. nur der Speicher am Kaiserquai für Waarenlagerung und der Silospeicher am Brooktorhafen für Kornlagerung existirt […]." Bemerkungen und Erläuterungen zu einem Plan und Kostenanschlag betreffend den Anschluß Hamburgs an das Reichszollgebiet, unterzeichnet von Franz Andreas Meyer und Christian Nehls, Hamburg, 12. Mai 1881. Zitiert nach MAAK, Speicherstadt, 1985, S. 20.

[9] Zur kontroversen Diskussion um den Standort der Freihafenlagerhäuser siehe: MAAK, Speicherstadt, 1985, S. 15 ff. und S. 41 ff.

[10] So stand bereits zu Beginn der Planungen fest, dass die Brookinseln zumindest teilweise in den Freihafen einbezogen werden: „Der Freihafenbezirk umfaßt die Norderelbe bei Hamburg, den Hafen und die Quaianlagen, einen von Hamburg noch näher zu bestimmenden Theil der zwischen den Quaianlagen [auf dem Großen Grasbrook, R. L.] und dem vom Binnenhafen nach dem Oberhafen sich erstreckenden Flethzug [dem späteren Zollkanal, R. L.] belegenen Straßen und Häusercomplexe, sowie die der Stadt gegenüber belegenen Elbinseln." MITTHEILUNG, NO. 46, 1882, S. 201.

[11] MITTHEILUNG, NO. 73, Anlage A, 1883, S. 15.

[12] MITTHEILUNG, NO. 73, Anlage A, 1883, S. 15.

[13] Hierzu ausführlicher: MAASS, Ausbau, 1990, S. 90 ff. Allerdings beschränkt sich Dieter Maass auf den eigentlichen Hafenausbau und geht nicht auf die Norderelbbrücke ein, die unter der Leitung von Franz Andreas Meyer errichtet wurde. Siehe ZOLLANSCHLUSS-BAUTEN, 1884, S. 97.

[14] MITTHEILUNG, NO. 47, 1882, S. 231.

[15] Die Kosten waren davon abhängig, in welchem Umfang die Brookinseln für die geplanten Freihafenspeicher abgebrochen wurden. Als im Mai 1881 die ersten konkreten Planungen vorlagen, wurden die Kosten auf 93 bis 104 Millionen Mark geschätzt. Siehe MAAK, 1885, S. 24 ff. 1882 beliefen sich die Schätzungen bereits auf 100,3 bis 123 Millionen Mark. Siehe MITTHEILUNG, NO. 73, 1883, S. 289.

[16] 54,5 Millionen Mark waren die kalkulierten Kosten für die gesamten Brookinseln sowie für die Grundstücke, die für den Ausbau des Zollkanals benötigt wurden, also diejenigen Flächen, die später auch tatsächlich in Anspruch genommen wurden. Siehe MITTHEILUNG, NO. 73, Anlage A, 1883, S. 15.

[17] Zur Geschichte der Brookinseln siehe auch im Folgenden: BRACKER, Kirchspiel, 2000, S. 16 ff.

[18] BECKERSHAUS, Straßennamen, 2000, S. 16 f. und S. 259 f.

[19] Der Zustand der Brookinseln kurz vor dem Abriss ist besonders gut belegt, weil Georg Koppmann von der Baudeputation mit einer fotografischen Dokumentation beauftragt wurde. Weitere Aufnahmen liegen von Friedrich Strumper vor. Siehe MAAK, 1985, S. 30 ff.

[20] Exemplarisch belegen lässt sich diese Entwicklung anhand des besonders repräsentativen Bürgerhauses Neuer Wandrahm 6 (um 1680), das um 1870 von Hanssen & Meerwein für Kontorzwecke umgebaut und von mehreren Firmen, darunter auch das Architekturbüro selbst, genutzt wurde. Siehe MEYER-BRUNSWICK, Bürgerhäuser, 1990, S. 199 f. Zum sozialen Wandel der Brookinseln siehe auch die Erinnerungen von Paul Hertz, dessen Familie

am Holländischen Brook wohnte: HERTZ, Elternhaus, 1902.
21 Siehe auch im Folgenden: MAAK, Speicherstadt, 1985, S. 82
22 ZOLLANSCHLUSS-BAUTEN, 1884, S. 97.
23 MAASS, Ausbau, 1990, S. 95 ff.
24 MAAK, Speicherstadt, S. 82. Die sukzessive Realisierung des Zollkanals resultierte aus dem Umstand, dass der Verkehr auf dem Mührenfleet und dem Dovenfleet möglichst wenig beeinträchtigt werden sollte. Siehe ZOLLANSCHLUSS-BAUTEN, 1884, S. 99.
25 Diese Erweiterung wurde vom Senat und von der Bürgerschaft am 19. bzw. 24. Juni 1897 beschlossen. Siehe MITTHEILUNG, NR. 200, 1898, S. S. 727. Am 1. November 1897 wurden die Häuser am Alten Wandrahm und am Wandbereiterbrook gekündigt. Mit dem Abriss sollte unverzüglich begonnen werden. Die Häuser am Holländischen Brook und am Brooktorkai folgten erst ein Jahr später. Siehe ebd., S. 727.
26 Siehe MITTEILUNG, NR. 255, 1906, S. S. 815.
27 Siehe hierzu auch im Folgenden: HINZ, Planung, 2000, S. 193 ff. u. S. 290 f.
28 Diese dominante Rolle der Quartiersleute in der Speicherstadt war allerdings anfänglich nicht intendiert und musste von ihnen erst erstritten werden. Siehe HINZ, Planung, 2000, S. 137 ff.
29 Siehe RATH, Arbeit, 1988, S. 288 ff. Zum Beruf und zur Tradition der Quartiersleute siehe auch allgemein: ALTSTAEDT; Quartiersmann, 2003.
30 Zu den Speichern von Jebens und Lorenz Meyer, die übrigens von Gustav Schrader bzw. Puttfarcken & Janda stammten, siehe: HAMBURG UND SEINE BAUTEN, 1890, S. 404 und S. 414 f; HINZ, Planung, 2000, S. 213 ff. Zum Engagement der Firma Hanssen & Studt in der Speicherstadt siehe: HINZ, Planung, 2000, S. 233 ff.
31 Siehe im Einzelnen: HAMBURG UND SEINE BAUTEN, 1890, S. 416 f.; HINZ, Planung, 2000, S. 234 f. u. 245 f. Der Speicher am Sandtorkai wurde 1891 durch einen Brand zerstört und die Maschinenzentralstation danach ohne Lagergeschosse wiederhergestellt.
32 HAMBURG UND SEINE BAUTEN, 1890, S. 401 ff.
33 EILERT, Entwicklung, 1910, S. 2083 f.
34 Siehe auch im Folgenden: LANGE, Speicherstadt, 2010, S. 82 f. u. 96 ff.
35 Um Entwürfe für den späteren Block O und das Verwaltungsgebäude der HFLG wurden die Architekten Hanssen & Meerwein, Stammann & Zinnow und Carl Elvers gebeten. Franz Andreas Meyer favorisierte den Entwurf von Hanssen & Meerwein. Die HFLG wollte aber auch Stammann & Zinnow an der Realisierung beteiligen. Siehe ARCHITEKTEN- UND INGENIEUR-VEREIN, 1885, S. 575 f. Zum zweiten Verwaltungsgebäude der HFLG wie Anm. 56.
36 MAAK, Speicherstadt, S. 79 ff.
37 Zur Biographie von Franz Eduard Vermehren (1847–1918) siehe: ENGELS, Vermehren, 1918, S. 56; KOKKELINK und LEMKE-KOKKELINK, Baukunst, 1998, S. 572.
38 Nach dem bisherigen Forschungsstand ist über Raywood kaum mehr bekannt als seine Unterschriften auf den Plänen zu den erwähnten Speicherblöcken. Außerdem hat er für die HFLG Speicher am Melniker Ufer realisiert.
39 Der Planung des vierten Bauabschnitts wurde 1905 in Angriff genommen, wenn auch zunächst nur im Hinblick auf die Infrastrukturen, die 1910 fertiggestellt sein sollten. Siehe MITTEILUNG, NR. 255, 1906, S. S. 820. Pläne für die auf der Ericusspitze geplanten Blöcke Y und Z sind nach dem bisherigen Stand der Forschung nicht überliefert.
40 Zur Biographie von Franz Andreas Meyer (1837-1901) siehe: BESELIN, Meyer, 1974. Zur Biographie von Georg Thielen (1855–1901) siehe: DENKSCHRIFT, 1909, S. 93 f. Zur Biographie von Franz Eduard Vermehren wie Anm. 37.
41 Siehe KOKKELINK und LEMKE-KOKKELINK, Baukunst, 1998, insbes. S. 11 ff. u. S. 87 ff.
42 GURLITT, Kunst, 1899, S. 455.
43 Zu Biographie und Werk von Werner Kallmorgen (1902–1977) siehe: CORNEHL, Raummassagen, 2003.
44 So reagierte Günther Grundmann, von 1950 bis 1959 Landesdenkmalpfleger in Hamburg, mit Unverständnis, als er 1950 in einem Radiointerview auf die Speicherstadt angesprochen wurde, die er offenbar nicht als denkmalschutzwürdig erachtete. Siehe HIPP, Erinnerung, 1997, S. 74.
45 Hamburgisches Architekturarchiv, Bestand Werner Kallmorgen, S 021, Moderne Häfen. Bau und Erscheinungsbild, Vortrag im Kunstverein Göttingen am 19. 11. 1973, Typoskript, S. 7 f.
46 Zur technischen Ausrüstung der Speicherstadt siehe auch im Folgenden: HAMBURG UND SEINE BAUTEN, 1890, S. 417 ff. u. S. 422 f.; EILERT, Entwicklung, 1910, S. 2139 ff.
47 EILERT, Entwicklung, 1910, S. 2143.
48 Zur technischen Ausrüstung der Speicherstadt siehe: EILERT, Entwicklung, 1910, S. 2139 ff. u. S. 2176 ff. Zur Umrüstung der Winden auf Elektromotoren siehe: HENCKE, Speicherstadt, 1963, S. 152.
49 „Ziegelrohbau, Backsteinrohbau bezeichnen den Reinbau in Ziegeln, ohne oder mit nur ganz untergeordneter Verwendung anderer Baustoffe zur Herstellung des Mauerwerks, das also im wesentlichen einheitlich gebildet ist, aus Ziegeln im Verbande besteht und diesen Verband in der Ansicht zeigt." WASMUTHS LEXIKON, Bd. IV, 1932, S. 744
50 Die Blöcke P, Q und R waren die ersten Speicherblöcke, die sowohl an der Land- als auch an der Wasserseite über feuerfeste Treppenhäuser verfügten. Siehe EILERT, Entwicklung, 1910, S. 2136.
51 Vgl. HAMBURG UND SEINE BAUTEN, 1914, Bd. 2, S. 80. Zur Biographie von Adolph Libert Westphalen, der seit 1893 Hamburger Branddirektor war, siehe: http://feuerwehrhistoriker.de/historie.html. Aufgerufen am 02. Februar 2012. In diesem Artikel werden auch die „Westphalentürme" erwähnt.
52 EILERT, Entwicklung, 1910, S. 2087.
53 HENCKE, Speicherstadt, 1963, S. 148.
54 Siehe auch im Folgenden: EILERT, Entwicklung, 1910, S. 2088 f.
55 Hierzu ausführlicher: HAGN, Speicherbrand, 1891.

⁵⁶ Zur Planungsgeschichte des HFLG-Gebäudes, das zusammen mit Block O, entstand, siehe: MAAK, Speicherstadt, 1985, S. 87 ff.

⁵⁷ BRACKER, Kirchspiel, 2000, S. 18 f.

⁵⁸ Im Wettbewerb wurden zwei gleiche erste Preise an Hanssen & Meerwein und Johannes Grotjan verliehen, die sich daraufhin das Projekt teilten. Siehe: WETTBEWERB, 1902, S. 200. Zu dem Gebäude siehe auch: HAMBURG UND SEINE BAUTEN, 1914, Bd. 1, S. 474.

⁵⁹ Siehe auch im Folgenden: WETTBEWERB, 1902, S. 16.

⁶⁰ LANGE, Familiensilber, 2002, S. 135. KLOSTERMEIER und WIECKHORST, Fabriken und Speicher, 2008, S. 102 ff.

⁶¹ Siehe auch im Folgenden: HENCKE, Speicherstadt, 1963, S. 148.

⁶² CORNEHL, Raummassagen, 2003, S. 71 ff. Vgl. auch LANGE, Speicherstadt, 2010, S. 96 ff.

⁶³ Die Planungsgeschichte der Blöcke O und N und die Umstände, die zu ihrer Errichtung geführt haben, werden ausführlich dargestellt in: MAACK, Speicherstadt, 1985, S. 87 ff.; HINZ, Planung, 2000, S. 226 ff.

⁶⁴ CORNEHL, Raummassagen, Hamburg 2003, S. 318 f. u. S. 326 f.

⁶⁵ Vgl. THAU und VINDUM, Jacobsen, 2001, S. 98 ff. u. S. 272 ff.

⁶⁶ LANGE, Familiensilber, 2002, S. 130 f.

⁶⁷ Vgl. auch im Folgenden: LANGE, Familiensilber, 2002; KLOSTERMEIER und WIECKHORST, Fabriken und Speicher, 2008, S. 99 ff.

⁶⁸ Vgl. die betreffenden Artikel in diesem Band.

⁶⁹ Diese Ansicht vertrat z. B. die einflussreiche Deputation für Handel und Schifffahrt. Siehe MITTHEILUNG, NO. 73, 1882, Anlage B, S. 4.

⁷⁰ Zu den Speichern A bis E am Melnicker Ufer und den Speicher F bis H am Dessauer Ufer, die zeitgleich mit der Speicherstadt entstanden (1888–1910) und von der HFLG in eigener Regie bewirtschaftet wurden, siehe: EILERT, Entwicklung, 1901, S. 2085 f. und S. 2135.

⁷¹ „Der Kaischuppen soll nicht zur längeren Lagerung der Güter dienen, sondern nur zur kurzfristigen Aufnahme von Löschgut bis zur Auslieferung an die Empfänger, von Ladegut bis zur Verschiffung. Er braucht also nicht größer zu sein, als die Aufnahme und die übersichtliche Ausbreitung einer vollen Schiffsladung auf eine Schiffslänge fordert. Dazu genügt erfahrungsgemäß bei den größten Schiffen eine Schuppenbreite von etwa 50 Metern." WENDEMUTH und BÖTTCHER, Hafen, 1931, S. 60 ff.

⁷² Dieses Urteil reflektiert allerdings heutige Maßstäbe. Die damaligen Kritiker urteilten noch völlig anders: „Bezüglich der äußeren Erscheinung der Speicher waltete das Bestreben vor, die großen Gebäudekomplexe vor nüchterner Kahlheit zu bewahren, wenn auch im Ganzen nur auf eine günstige Massenwirkung hingearbeitet werden konnte, und von der Anwendung weitergehenden Schmuckes, als der Bestimmung der Gebäude nicht entsprechend, abgesehen werden mußte." HAMBURG UND SEINE BAUTEN, 1890, S. 407. Zur zeitgenössischen Rezeption der Speicherstadt siehe auch: MAAK, Speicherstadt, 1985, S. 117 ff.

⁷³ 1913 wurden in den Groß-Hamburger Häfen, d.h. einschließlich Altona und Harburg, 27,7 Mio. Tonnen umgeschlagen. Siehe BOLLE, Generalplan, 1953, S. 40. In Rotterdam waren es 23 Mio. Tonnen. Siehe KLEMANN, Verflechtungen 2009, S. 23.

⁷⁴ Siehe hierzu als beispielhaft: INDUSTRIEBAU, 1984, S. 11 ff.

⁷⁵ „Die Grundbedingungen für die Einrichtung der Speicher wurden bereits vor Konstituierung der Freihafen-Lagerhaus-Gesellschaft an der Hand eines vom Ingenieurwesen der Bau-Deputation ausgearbeiteten Entwurfes zu einem Speicherkomplex festgestellt [...]. Im Wesentlichen handelte es sich dabei um die Geschoßhöhen, die relative Höhenlage des Raumes [gemeint ist das Erdgeschoss, R. L.] zur Straße und die Maximalbelastungen der einzelnen Böden, um die Art und Vertheilung der Brandmauern und der feuersicher anzulegenden Treppenhäuser." HAMBURG UND SEINE BAUTEN, 1890, S. 405 f.

Georg Skalecki

Speicherbauten in Bremen

Bei dem Titel des Beitrages „Speicherbauten in Bremen" denkt man vielleicht zunächst an die großen Hafenspeicher, wie man sie zum Beispiel in der sogenannten Bremer Überseestadt vorfindet, also sehr große Lagergebäude für industriell betriebene Häfen des 19. und 20. Jahrhunderts. Auch vom Hamburger Thema und der Dimension der Speicherstadt ausgehend, scheint auf der Tagung der großvolumige Speicher zunächst eher zentraler Betrachtungsgegenstand.

Einleitend will ich aber auch kurz auf die wenigen Reste älterer und kleinerer Pack- und Lagerhäuser eingehen. Da Bremen, wenn auch verstreut, hoch bedeutende Zeugnisse älterer Hafenspeicher des 15. bis 19. Jahrhunderts besitzt, wird zur Einführung ins Thema ein knapper Einblick in die Entwicklung der Typologie ermöglicht. Die Begrifflichkeit darf uns dabei nicht irritieren, wir sprechen von Packhaus, Lagerhaus, Speicher, letztlich ist immer das gleiche gemeint. Speicher sind Funktionsbauten, deren wesentliche Merkmale seit dem Mittelalter die gleichen sind: geschossweise sollen Waren, welcher Art auch immer, gelagert werden. Dazu benötigt man ebene, belastbare Flächen, die gut zu erreichen sind. Speicher liegen deshalb in der Nähe der Verladeeinrichtungen, in unserem Falle nahe der Hafenbecken, haben große Ladeluken, über die in der Regel mit Winden oder Kränen die Waren direkt auf die verschiedenen Lagerebenen gehoben werden können. Die Bauten haben stabile Decken, früher in Holz, später in Beton. Trotz der gewünschten hohen Belastbarkeit versucht man relativ große Stützenweiten zu erreichen, da die Stützen das Hantieren behindern. Ob die Speicher von der Giebel- oder der Langseite beschickt werden, ist oftmals den topographischen Gegebenheiten geschuldet. Eine innere Vertikalerschließung ist eher unüblich. Im Prinzip ist der Typus so schon von Anbeginn festgelegt und wird über die Jahrhunderte nur durch technische Fortentwicklungen oder spezielle Einzelanforderungen leicht variiert. Varianten kommen auch durch Kombinationen mit anderen Nutzungen vor, wenn z. B. Wohnungen, Werkstätten oder Verkaufsmöglichkeiten hinzukommen. So kann das Lagerhaus zum Kontor werden.

Mit der nun folgenden Aufzählung werden Bremer Beispiele mit unterschiedlichen Nutzungen vorgeführt, und es wird am Rande zugleich auch auf die aktuelle denkmalpflegerische Problematik, meist der Nach- oder Umnutzung, eingegangen. En passant wird auch etwas in die Hafengeschichte Bremens eingeführt und ein knapper Überblick über die unterschiedlichen Standorte gegeben.

Die mittelalterliche älteste Anlegestelle in Bremen war der Ufermarkt, wo ein kleiner Nebenarm der Weser, die Balge, ein geschütztes Entladen von Lastkähnen ermöglichte. Am südlichen Ende des heutigen Marktplatzes, zwischen Schüt-

Abb. 1: Bremen, Schnoor: Speicher, Anfang 15. Jh.

ting und Böttcherstraße, befand sich diese Anlegestelle. Das bedeutendste Fundstück dazu ist der heute im Deutschen Schiffahrtsmuseum in Bremerhaven gezeigte Lastkahn „Karl", nach Karl dem Großen, dem Gründer Bremens, benannt, der mit seiner dendrochronologischen Datierung von 808 ein sehr frühes Zeugnis von Hafenumschlag in Bremen ist.

Nur wenig später, im hohen Mittelalter, entwickelte sich der heute sogenannte Schnoor zu einem kleinen Handelsquartier. Lastkähne konnten auf der Balge bis in dieses Quartier hineinfahren und wurden dort direkt in sogenannte

80 *Speicherbauten in Bremen*

Abb. 2: Bremen, Schnoor: Jacobus-Packhaus, um 1800

Abb. 4: Bremen, Vegesack, Thiele-Speicher um 1800

Abb. 3: Bremen, Vegesack, Speicher 17. Jh.

Abb. 5: Bremen, Vegesack, Thiele-Speicher um 1800, innen

Packhäuser entladen, wovon sich ein älteres Zeugnis in rudimentären Resten erhalten hat. Der Wasserlauf ermöglichte das Entladen der Waren in das rückwärtige Lagerhaus. Das Gebäude „Hinter der Balge" stammt im Kern aus dem frühen 15. Jahrhundert und besaß einen giebelständigen Packhausteil, wo über Seilwinden die Waren auf die verschiedenen Lagerböden gehoben wurden. Das Gebäude reicht nach vorne bis zur Straße, wo dann schließlich die

Waren nach Lagerung oder Bearbeitung auf Karren verladen und abtransportiert werden konnten. Hier waren also Lager, Arbeitsstelle, Wohnhaus alles unter einem Dach verbunden, die Ausrichtung mit dem rückwärtigen Giebel zum Wasserlauf und dem vorderen Eingang zur Straße eine typische Erscheinung. Zunächst diente das Vorderhaus auch als Lager, später kam ein rückwärtiger Anbau hinzu. Reste der inneren Gebäudestrukturen sowie eine Winde zeugen von der ursprünglichen Funktion. Nach Verfüllung der Balge 1837 ist der rückwärtige Teil dieses Gebäudes verändert worden. Die benachbarten Häuser an der Balge dürften zum Teil ähnlich organisiert gewesen sein, jedoch hat sich davon kaum noch etwas erhalten.

Dafür gibt es im Schnoor-Viertel in Bremen noch ein großes Packhaus, das kurz nach 1800 erbaut wurde und nur wenig entfernt von der Weser liegt. Die Anbindung an den Fluss wurde durch spätere Straßenneubaumaßnahmen stark gestört und ist heute abgetrennt. Der verputzte Bau wurde über die Giebelseiten beschickt und besitzt bis heute die hohen und stark belastbaren originalen hölzernen Lagerböden. Mit der Höhe und der großen Tiefenerstreckung ist dies ein stattlicher Vertreter dieses Bautyps, auch angesichts der Erbauungszeit im frühen 19. Jahrhundert.

Nach Anwachsen der Schiffsgrößen durch Entwicklung der mittelalterlichen Koggen, die bis zu 200 Tonnen Last transportieren konnten und hochseetauglich waren, wurde ab dem 13. Jahrhundert in Bremen ein neuer Hafen angelegt, der sogenannte Schlachtehafen, direkt an der Weser. Auch hierzu gab es inzwischen mehrere spektakuläre Schiffsfunde, so die sogenannte Hansekogge von 1380, heute ebenfalls im Deutschen Schiffahrtsmuseum in Bremerhaven. Historische Ansichten, wie die von Hogenberg aus dem Jahr 1598, zeigen eine lange Kajenmauer, also die Anlegestelle des Flusshafens und den regen Schiffsverkehr auf der Weser. Unmittelbar hinter der Kaje standen giebelständige Häuser, in die die Waren sofort umgeschlagen wurden. Dort entstand ein spezieller Typus mit Lagerhaus und Kontorhausfunktionen. Allerdings haben sich an der Schlachte keine älteren Bauten erhalten, sondern es finden sich dort nur noch reine Kontore des frühen 20. Jahrhunderts, die jedoch zumindest optisch mit ihrer Giebelständigkeit zur Weser noch an die älteren Situationen erinnern.

Den nächsten Entwicklungsschritt erlebte Bremen mit dem Bau eines ersten künstlichen Hafenbeckens im Stadtteil Vegesack, flussabwärts gelegen. Hier entstand im 16. Jahrhundert der wohl europaweit älteste künstliche Hafen, der in der Regel wegen der größeren Meeresnähe eisfrei blieb, und so auch als Winterhafen genutzt werden konnte. Im Umfeld des Vegesacker Hafens haben sich einige Speichergebäude in mehr oder weniger authentischem Zustand erhalten. Sie zeigen die typischen Merkmale: Mehrgeschossigkeit, große Gebäudetiefe, hohe Giebel, über die in der Regel die Speicher beschickt wurden, gelegentlich gab es auch Ladeluken und Winden an den Langseiten der Gebäude.

In der alten Hafenstraße in Vegesack, in unmittelbarer Nähe des Hafenbeckens, haben sich drei bemerkenswerte Beispiele erhalten, so das älteste Packhaus, das im Kern aus dem 17. Jahrhundert stammt und Mitte des 18. Jahrhunderts etwas umgebaut wurde, das Portal stammt von 1740. Der langgestreckte dreigeschossige Bau mit hohem Satteldach wurde an der Langseite beschickt, Luken und eine Winde ermöglichten die Einlagerung der Waren. Im Inneren sind trotz mehrfacher Umbauten noch Reste des konstruktiven Holzwerks, der Packböden und des Dachstuhls vorhanden.

Der nächste Vegesacker Speicher stammt aus der Zeit um 1800. Er besitzt große Ladeluken und eine giebelständige Beschickung, wodurch die drei Vollgeschosse und die zwei Dachgeschosse erreicht werden konnten. Das hervorragend

Abb. 6: Bremen, Vegesack, Speicher, Anfang 19. Jh., Fassade 1860

erhaltene Innere zeigt authentisch einen über 200 Jahre alten Speicher. Er gehörte einem privaten Handelshaus und bezeugt mit seiner Größe die Blüte des Vegesacker Hafens.

Ein weiteres Beispiel stammt wohl vom Anfang des 19. Jahrhunderts, die dekorative neogotische Fassade wurde allerdings erst um 1860 dem bestehenden Bau vorgelegt. Auch hier erfolgte das Einlagern der Waren über Seilwinden über die Giebelseite, wobei über drei Luken die Obergeschosse bedient wurden. Der Bau wurde schon Mitte des 19. Jahrhunderts umgenutzt. Heute ist keine originale Innensubstanz mehr erhalten.

Unweit entfernt, mit unmittelbarer Wasserlage an der Einmündung der Aue in die Weser, liegt ein weiterer Speicher in Vegesack, der nicht nur ideal diesen Bautypus zeigt, sondern mit gut erhaltener Originalsubstanz und geschickter Neunutzung aufwartet. Der sogenannte Lange-Speicher entstand kurz nach 1805 als Lager einer Schiffsbauwerft. Der viergeschossige Bau liegt parallel zum Wasser und hat somit eine Erschließung an der Langseite. Symmetrisch gegliedert mit Ladeluken und Seilwinde wurden die Waren über die Mitte des Speichers eingelagert. Nach Niedergang der Werft 1870 wurde der Bau mehrfach von unterschiedlichen

Abb. 7: Bremen, Vegesack, Lange-Speicher, 1805

Abb. 8: Bremen, Vegesack, Lange-Speicher, 1805, Innenkonstruktion mit Winde

Nutzern, aber immer als Lager verwendet. Dabei blieb die innere Holzkonstruktion unangetastet. Nach mehrjährigem Leerstand wurde 2007 nach einem Architekturwettbewerb eine zukunftsträchtige Umnutzung realisiert. Da die einzelnen Etagen des Speichers von außen beschickt wurden, gab es nie eine richtige innere Vertikalerschließung. Wunsch der Denkmalpflege war es, besonders die Holzkonstruktion der Böden unverändert zu erhalten, trotz der Probleme von Brandschutz und Erschließung. Geschickt schlug das siegreiche Architekturbüro eine externe Treppen- und Aufgangsanlage an der Stelle vor, wo auch die Waren früher auf- und abgehievt wurden. Heute arbeiten in dem Gebäude Yachtdesigner und Bootsausstatter im originalen Ambiente der unverändert erhaltenen und unverkleideten Lagerböden.

Mit dem heute allerdings stark veränderten Hafenbecken existiert in Bremen-Vegesack somit eine durchaus bemerkenswerte Gruppe von alten Hafenspeichern des 17. bis 19. Jahrhunderts. Die Beispiele haben heute unterschiedliche Nutzungen und unterschiedliche Erhaltungszustände, sie legen aber unverändert anschaulich Zeugnis der älteren Hafenarchitektur ab. Der Typus war im Grunde seit dem Mittelalter angelegt, nur die Größe variierte. Dies lag daran, dass die Speicher unabhängig in privater Regie von einzelnen Kaufleuten betrieben wurden. Mit Einführung der staatlich organisierten Hafenwirtschaft änderte sich die Situation.

1888 beschloss man in Bremen die Weserregulierung, Begradigung und Vertiefung des Flusses sowie die Anlage eines neuen großen Hafenbereichs. Dieser Hafen nördlich und unweit der Bremer Altstadt wurde als Freihafen konzipiert und erhielt drei große Hafenbecken, den Europahafen, den Überseehafen und den Industriehafen. Planer war Ludwig Franzius, der ein neues logistisches System entwickelte, mit dem eine erhebliche Beschleunigung des Warendurchlaufs ermöglicht wurde. Im großen Stil wurden Umschlagsanlagen entwickelt, mit langen Kajen und angrenzenden Schuppen sowie zahlreichen flexiblen Halbportalkränen. Damit wurde der industriell betriebene Großhafen eingeführt. Die Waren, die noch als Stückgut angeliefert wurden, konnten sehr schnell vollständig aus den Schiffen entladen werden und ohne Zeitverzögerungen durch langsame Verladung und Zuordnung auf Fahrzeuge, wurden sie in den großflächigen Schuppen rasch abgestellt. Dort konnte dann das Stückgut sortiert und für die Weiterverwendung vorbereitet werden. Hinter den Schuppen lagen ausgedehnte Gleisanlagen und hier war auch für eine optimale Straßenanbindung gesorgt, wo die Waren, die sofort weiter transportiert werden sollten, aus den Schuppen auf Zug oder LKW geladen werden konnten. Hinter den Gleisanlagen folgten dann wiederum die bis zu 400 Meter langen mehrgeschossigen Hafenspeicher, wo auf den einzelnen Ebenen und über mehrere Ladeluken das Gut eingelagert wurde. Nach einer gewissen Verweildauer konnten später die Waren umgekehrt wieder aus dem Speicher geholt werden, um dann auf Zügen oder Straßen gebracht zu werden oder auch wieder zurück in andere Schiffe zum Weitertransport. Schnelligkeit und Zeitersparnis war damals als entscheidender Faktor zur Kostenreduzierung ausgemacht. Wegen seiner Vorteile wurde das Bremer System nach 1888 in vielen Welthäfen nachgeahmt.

Der Bremer Überseehafen wurde 1888 bis 1917 vollständig ausgebaut, allerdings auf der Höhe seiner Leistungsfähigkeit ab 1944 in großen Teilen zerstört. Nach Kriegsende unterstützten die Amerikaner einen sehr schnellen Wiederaufbau, da sie über Bremen ihren Nachschub organisierten. So wurden ab 1946 neue Schuppen und neue Speicher erbaut, die aber nach dem gleichen System arbeiteten. Lediglich die Konstruktionen der Bauten wurden dem Stand der modernen Technik angepasst.

Es ist noch zu erwähnen, dass der gesamte Bereich des Überseehafens nach dem Siegeszug des Containers 1999 stillgelegt wurde, die Freihandelszone aufgehoben wurde und seit dem Jahr 2000 dieses Stadtentwicklungsgebiet von ca. 300 ha Fläche unter dem Namen „Überseestadt" zum neuen Quartier umfunktioniert wird. Büro und Gewerbe, aber auch Wohnen sollen hier wassernah und auf historischer Fläche zu einem neuen Stadtteil werden. Dazu entwickelte die Stadtplanung einen Masterplan, der zunächst weitestgehend ohne Berücksichtigung der historischen Bauten entstand. Das Areal war allerdings auch wegen der großen Verkehrsflächen und wegen der schon früheren Abbrüche sehr weitläufig und nur partiell mit historischem Bestand besetzt. Dennoch versuchte die Denkmalpflege, gemeinsam mit einem externen Gutachter denkmalwürdige Bauten für den Erhalt zu empfehlen.

Schauen wir uns die erhaltenen, denkmalgeschützten und auch bereits in Abstimmung mit der Denkmalpflege umgenutzten Bauten der Reihe nach an, zugleich auch in ihrem heutigen Zustand.

Wie erwähnt, gehören zum Bremer System die Schuppen zum kurzfristigen Abstellen der Waren, Sortieren und Weitertransport. Diese großflächigen Anlagen zur Kurzzeitlagerung liegen direkt an der Kaje und müssen zum ungehinderten Ablauf der logistischen Kette beidseitig große Öffnung haben.

Der Schuppen 2 ist der älteste erhaltene Schuppen, denn kein Vorkriegsschuppen hat den Krieg überdauert. Diese sehr simple Architektur hat natürlich in der Vermarktung einen schweren Stand. Dennoch ist es gelungen, auch hier repräsentativ diesen Bautyp zu bewahren. Der Schuppen 2 ist der Standardtyp und mit seinem Erbauungsjahr von 1951 ein früher Vertreter. Wegen des Baustoffmangels unmittelbar nach dem Krieg verbaute man hier in Zweitverwendung Stahlprofile von Vorkriegsschuppen. Große Schiebetüren zur Kaje und Kräne stellten eine schnelle Löschung der Waren sicher. In dem großflächigen Schuppen wurden die Waren sortiert und kurz zwischengelagert, um sie dann auf der anderen Seite abzutransportieren. Zweckmäßig waren deshalb große Stützenweiten und viel Licht über die Lichtkuppeln. Nach einer zurückhaltenden Sanierung wurde der Schuppen in vermietbare, unterschiedlich große Teile durch reversible Zwischenwände getrennt. Jedoch blieben die Segmente so groß, dass etwas von der ursprünglichen Weite eines Schuppens auch heute noch zu erahnen ist. Ein Mix an Gewerbe, wie zum Beispiel die Korpuswerkstatt der Silberwarenmanufaktur Koch & Bergfeld oder die Ideenschmiede von nextpractice, wo Psychologen die Anforderungen und Wünsche an Produkte der Zukunft erforschen, zeigt den Aufbruch in eine neue Zeit.

Ein weiteres Beispiel, zugleich eine Sonderform, stellt Schuppen 1 dar. 1959 entstand dieser Bau, der, das ist ungewöhnlich, als zweigeschossige Anlage konzipiert wurde. Dies war nötig, weil hier ein besonders hoher Warendurchsatz gewährleistet werden musste. So entstand ein übereinander gestapelter Doppelschuppen. Die Deckenkonstruktion musste natürlich für besonders hohe Lasten konzipiert werden. Dieser Schuppen hat eine Länge von 405 Metern und eine Nutzfläche von über 36.000 Quadratmetern. Ein Kopfbau für die Verwaltung macht ihn besonders prägnant, ebenso die abgeschrägte Ecke, die dem Gleisverlauf geschuldet ist. Im Erdgeschoss ist dem Schuppen eine Rampe vorgelagert, wo die Kräne das Gut abstellen konn-

Abb. 9: Bremen, Überseestadt, Speicher 11

ten, bevor es mit Staplern ins Innere gefahren wurde. Um für das Obergeschoss eine ebensolche Rampe zu erhalten, wurde dieses Geschoss etwas verschoben. So entstand dort eine eigene Ladebühne. Auf der Wasserseite besitzen beide Geschosse große Schiebetore, zur Langseite hat das Erdgeschoss Tore und Rampen und für das Obergeschoss wurden große Lastenaufzüge notwendig. An dieser Seite lagen wiederum Rampen für die Verladung auf Zug und Lkw.

Auch dieser Bau ist inzwischen umgenutzt. Mit einem Architekturwettbewerb wurden Lösungen für die Nutzungsideen zweier Investoren gesucht. In einer Hälfte des Schuppens wird unter dem Stichwort „Faszination Auto" alles um das klassische Automobil angeboten: Restaurierung, Wartung, Verkauf, jegliches Zubehör und Einlagerung sowie Automuseum. Im Obergeschoss kann der Oldtimer-Liebhaber ein Wohnloft erwerben, wo er mit dem Auto in die Wohnung fahren kann. Für die Denkmalpflege war es auch hier besonders wichtig, dass in Bereichen etwas von der Großzügigkeit und der Weite eines solchen Schuppens erhalten bleibt. Die Hauptachse wird deshalb als Boulevard

Abb. 10: Bremen, Überseestadt, Schuppen 1, innen

Abb. 11: Bremen, Überseestadt, Speicher I

die zentrale Erschließung übernehmen und die seitlichen Einbauten werden durch Glas und große Offenheit ein hohes Maß an Filigranität und Transparenz bewahren. Auch hier wurden die Umnutzungen auf größtmögliche Einfachheit hin entwickelt. Die herbe Schlichtheit der Industriearchitektur wird weitestgehend bewahrt. Dort wo es notwendig ist, werden moderne Gestaltungselemente hinzu entwickelt.

Die Schuppen waren wie ausgeführt keine Gebäude für langfristige Warenlagerung. Diese Funktion übernahmen die Speicher, die in der zweiten Reihe standen. Von den Bremer Speichern in der Überseestadt hat sich ein Vorkriegsbeispiel erhalten. Genauer gesagt sind es zwei, denn der heutige Speicher XI entstand aus der Verbindung durch einen Zwischenbau von ehemals zwei selbständigen Bauten, den Speicher XI und XIII. 1910–1912 wurden diese Gebäude errichtet und 1947 zusammengefasst (siehe Abb. 9). Damit entstand ein Bau von 400 Metern Länge und einer Lagerfläche von 37 000 Quadratmetern. Die Eisenbetonkonstruktion als Innenskelett und die massiven Backsteinaußenwände prägen das Erscheinungsbild. Ein flaches Pultdach und eine ursprünglich vollständig geschlossene Nordwand als Brandwand sind als weitere Merkmale zu benennen. Die Waren wurden in dem Speicher eingelagert und nach einer bestimmten Lagerzeit zum Weitertransport verladen. Dies erfolgte von einer Seite, deshalb zeigt die Südseite mehrere Erschließungsachsen von denen immer zwei Segmente beschickt wurden. Dort waren Treppenhäuser, Lastenaufzüge sowie eine Ladeplattform und Ladeluken angeordnet. Auf vier Ebenen wurden die Waren eingelagert.

Ab dem Jahr 2001 wurde dieser Bau langsam saniert und umgenutzt. Es wurden aber keine modernen Bürostandards angestrebt, sondern wie selbstverständlich wurden die historischen Gegebenheiten akzeptiert und daran Neugestaltungen angepasst. Die unterschiedlichen Nutzer fügen sich ein in den historischen Rahmen ohne diesen zu sprengen.

Hochschule, Büros, Gewerbe, Handel, Museum, Gastronomie, Flächen für Veranstaltungen finden hier eine Unterkunft und können das historische Ambiente für sich selbst gewinnbringend nutzen. Alle Details der Gestaltung wurden sensibel entwickelt. Die Hauptfassade wurde nur zurückhaltend aufbereitet. Dabei stand Reparatur stets vor Erneuerung. Die Laderampen und Andienungsbalkone wurden in die neue Erschließung integriert. Die ehemalige Segmentunterteilung in Einzelhäuser und Brandabschnitte konnte dabei auch erhalten werden. Die alten Industriefenster wurden ebenfalls nur aufbereitet, Fußböden zum großen Teil erhalten und historische Oberflächen belassen, notwendige Installationen wurden passend zum industriellen Bild schlicht auf Putz gelegt, um die Arbeitsatmosphäre eines Hafengebäudes weiterleben zu lassen. Für die innere Nutzung war eine bessere Belichtung unumgänglich. An der ehemals vollständig geschlossenen Nordwand wurden mit Diamantsägen Fensteröffnungen geschnitten, die in ihrem unverputzten Zustand belassen wurden, sodass sich dem Betrachter die Veränderungen und Vorgehensweise sofort erschließen. Die historische Identität des Speichers wird durch die Veränderung nirgends gestört. Bei der Umnutzung dieses Speichers wurde ein Umgangsmodell entwickelt, das vorbildlich auch für die darauffolgenden Projekte wurde. Die Investitionsbereitschaft von Privatunternehmen, die durch langfristige Mietverträge der öffentlichen Hand gefördert wurde, wäre ein eigenes Thema und kann hier nicht weiter vertieft werden.

Der nächste Speichertyp, den ich vorstellen möchte, ist der älteste Nachkriegsspeicher. 1947 wurde eine neue Konzeption für den Hafenausbau nach dem Krieg entwickelt, wobei, wie schon erwähnt, das Bremer System beibehalten wurde. 1948 entstand dann der Prototyp mit dem Bau von Speicher I als Stahlbetonskelettkonstruktion nach den Plänen des renommierten Büros Säume und Hafemann. An der Stelle eines Vorgängers entstand so ein Neubau, der mit einer klaren, allein der Funktionalität geschuldeten Gestalt viele Nachfolger fand. Das klare Rasterskelett wurde mit Backstein ausgefacht und sparsam befenstert. Der gleichförmige Rhythmus unterstreicht die Monumentalität. So wie der Bau seinerzeit abschnittsweise fertiggestellt und abschnittsweise in Betrieb genommen wurde, sollte er auch langsam in Teilabschnitten saniert und umgenutzt werden. Die extrem große Nachfrage nach solchen Bürolofts ließ jedoch eine rasche Komplettsanierung des Speichers zu. Das Vorgehen des neuen Betreibers war von Speicher XI geleitet. Die Fassadenstruktur mit den horizontalen Fensterbändern und darunter liegenden Wandausfachungen wurden als Modul genommen und dafür neue Fensterelemente entwickelt, die diesen Aufteilungen folgten. Jede dritte Achse des Bauwerks wurde unberührt gelassen, die dazwischen liegenden wurden geöffnet, um eine geeignete Belichtung für die neuen Arbeitsplätze zu schaffen. Die neuen Fensterelemente erhielten einen massiven Kämpfer in der Höhe, wo die alten Wandflächen endeten, so dass darüber wieder das historische Motiv des horizontalen Fensterbandes auftaucht. Bei herabgelassenen Jalousien, die sich in den Kämpferelementen befinden, ist die historische Anmutung und originale Rhythmisierung von geschlossenen und offenen Feldern wieder nachzuvollziehen. Bei der Ausgestaltung des Inneren übte man sich in größter Zurückhaltung und verschonte den Bau weitestgehend vor Veränderungen. Die Oberflächen der Wände wurden original und unbehandelt belassen, die historischen Holzböden nur aufbereitet, Stahlschiebetüren und Beschriftung blieben ebenso authentisch erhalten, wie die alten Aufzüge und Treppen. Teeküchen und Sanitäranlagen in den einzelnen Mieteinheiten sind in Boxen untergebracht, die wie abgestellte Holzkisten wirken.

Zum Schluss werfen wir noch einen Blick auf eine Gruppe kleinerer Speicher, die sog. Bachmannspeicher, eine Reihe von ehemaligen Baumwoll- und Tabakspeicher aus der Zeit ab 1903. Sie zeigen das Spektrum der Speicherarchitektur auf. Da wegen Kriegszerstörungen zwei Bauten in dieser Reihe durch Nachkriegsbauten ersetzt wurden, ergibt sich ein Ensemble, das geradezu wie ein Kaleidoskop die Geschichte historischer Hafenspeicher anschaulich macht. Die Architektursprache entspricht dem Stand der Zeit der Jahrhundertwende mit Backsteingliederungen oder in einem Fall als Putzbau. Auch hier sind einige Speicher bereits umgenutzt, wobei die notwendigen Eingriffe meist die Belichtung der großen Raumtiefen betreffen, so dass mit wenigen zusätzlichen Fenstern und Lichthöfen gearbeitet werden musste. Innenstrukturen und Außenerscheinungen waren jedoch kaum betroffen.

Dieser kleine Überblick macht deutlich, dass in Bremen noch eine Reihe bemerkenswerter unterschiedlicher Speicher vom 15. bis zum 20. Jahrhundert existieren, jedoch in der Regel als Einzelbauten, wenn man von dem kleinen Ensemble in Vegesack absieht. Das zum Teil hohe Alter hebt diese Bauten jedoch weit heraus. Daneben legen die Bauten in der Überseestadt Zeugnis vom industriell betriebenen Hafen ab und zeigen wegen ihrer geglückten Umnutzung auch Wege für den denkmalpflegerischen Umgang mit solch schwierigen, weil großflächigen Objekten auf.

Abb. 12: Bremen, Fabrikenhafen, Bachmannspeicher

Abstract

Warehouse buildings in Bremen

The city of Bremen can boast a number of important warehouses that date from the 15th to the 20th centuries. They are scattered over a fairly large area. The presentation gives an introduction to the warehouses that have been preserved to this day and a succinct overview of the different types and developments from loft (Packhaus) to storage facility to warehouse. There are some examples of buildings which were used for secondary purposes, too, and this presentation touches upon the problems of preservation that can arise in connection with a later or a changed use of these historical buildings. Another side aspect is the history of the Bremen Port as a whole. Also, a short overview of its different locations is given.

Port warehouses are functional buildings whose main features have not changed much since the Middle Ages: Their purpose is to provide for the storage of different goods on several storeys. This requires large, even surfaces that can cope with great loads and which are at the same time easily accessible. This is why warehouses tend to be located close to points of transhipment and in areas where the necessary equipment is available, in the case of Bremen this means near the docks. Warehouses can be accessed through big loading doors from which the goods can be lifted or lowered directly with the help of winches and pulleys. The wooden, later concrete floors and ceilings are very substantial. Because pillars would have hindered the handling of goods, the challenge lay in minimising their number while at the same time achieving high load capacities.

The list of examples comprises warehouses from the Schnoor district whose core was built in the 15th century, larger warehouses located in the oldest artificial dock of the 17th century in Vegesack, all the way to the very large warehouses in the so-called *Überseestadt* which stem from the early 20th century to the post-WWII-period.

Abbildungsverzeichnis

Alle Photos: Landesamt für Denkmalpflege Bremen

* Die Abbildungsrechte sind vom Autor geklärt worden und liegen in dessen Verantwortung

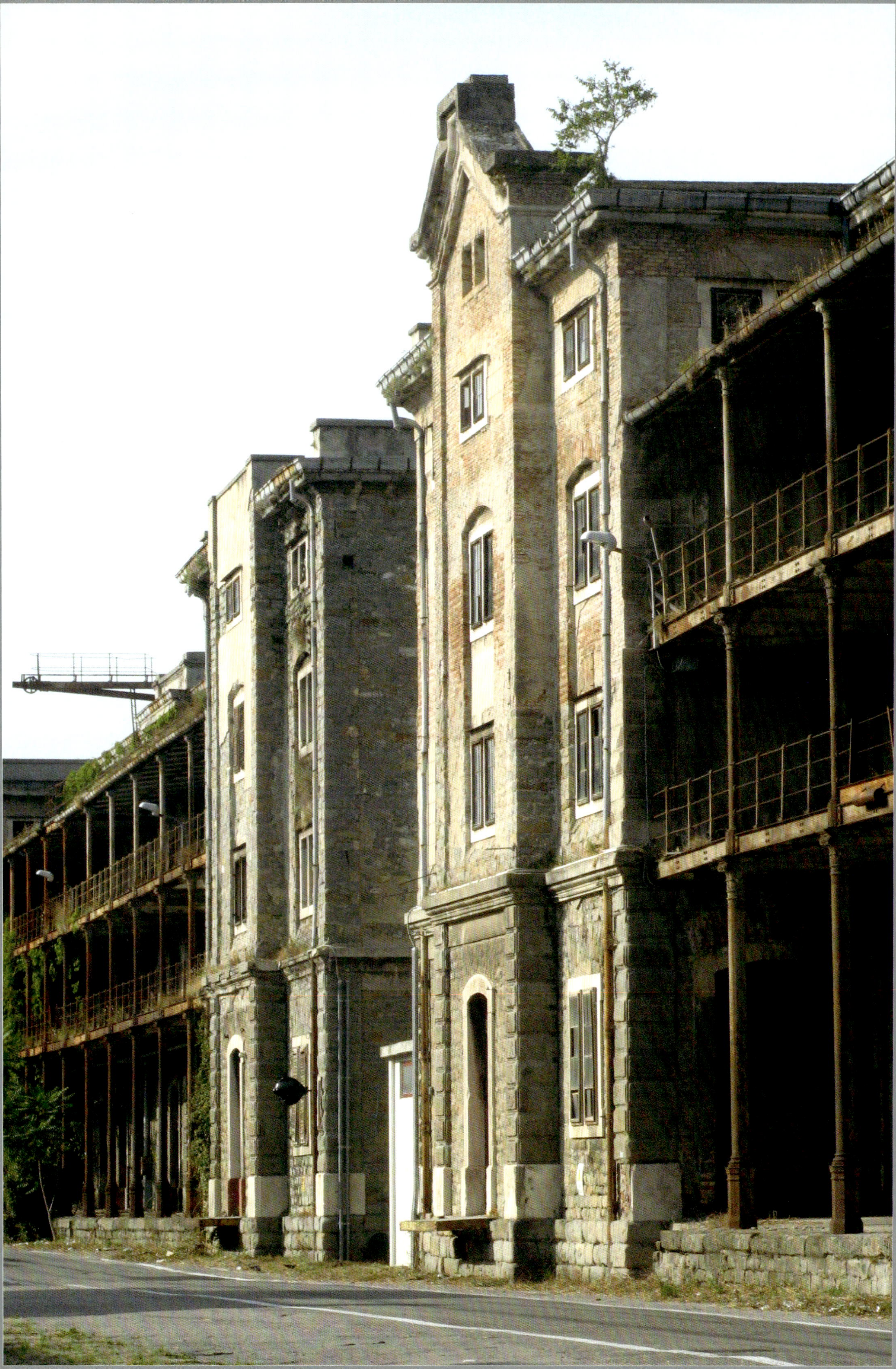

**Speichergebäude und -komplexe
in europäischen Seehäfen
Warehouse Buildings and Districts
in European Seaports**

Trieste, Old Port

Antonella Caroli Palladini

The Old Port of Trieste: Characteristics and Specificities of the Hydrodynamic Power Station and the Warehouse District

Introduction

In Trieste, the historical and architectural heritage of the Old Port has been at the heart of several political debates for about forty years and has been seen as an occasion for ephemeral projects, which have not resulted in either the rehabilitation or the redevelopment of the area yet. The time seems to be ripe for making a more efficient use of the site. Fortunately, the restoration of Warehouse 26, that is currently hosting the "Biennale diffusa" art exhibition, of the Hangar 1 on Pier IV, and the restoration of the hydrodynamic plant have been completed.

Actions by Italia Nostra, the Italian cultural association and non-profit organization for the protection of the national historical and architectural heritage, my studies conducted on the historical archives of the city and of the northern ports, in collaboration with the Speicherstadtmuseum, Hamburg's HafenCity and Professor Dirk Schubert, initiated and sped up the rehabilitation of the Old Port. Study and research activities have not only resulted in the implementation of protection measures but also lead the way to raise funds for the restoration and redevelopment of the site.

In October 2010, an international scientific committee gathered in Trieste, consisting of leading international experts on historic ports and waterfront districts. This tech-

Figure 1: Trieste, Old Port, Alexander von Schroeder, 1874 map of Trieste port

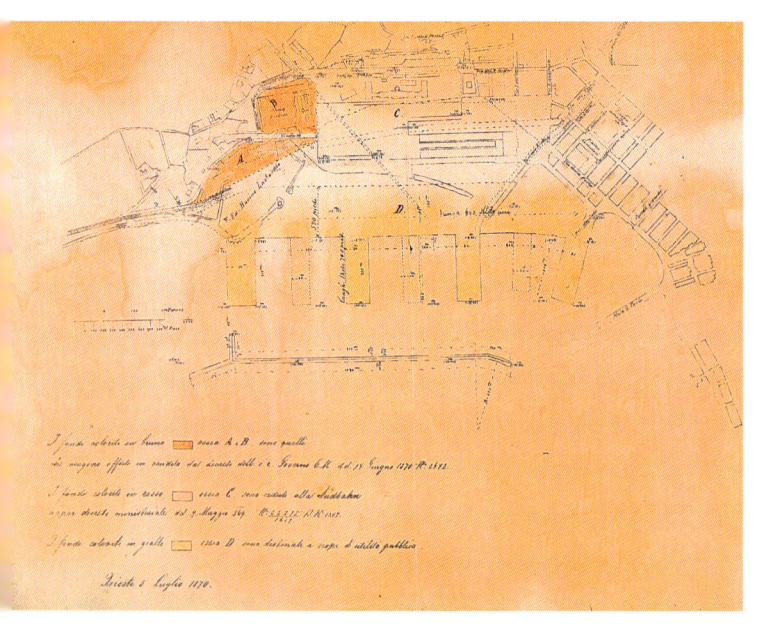

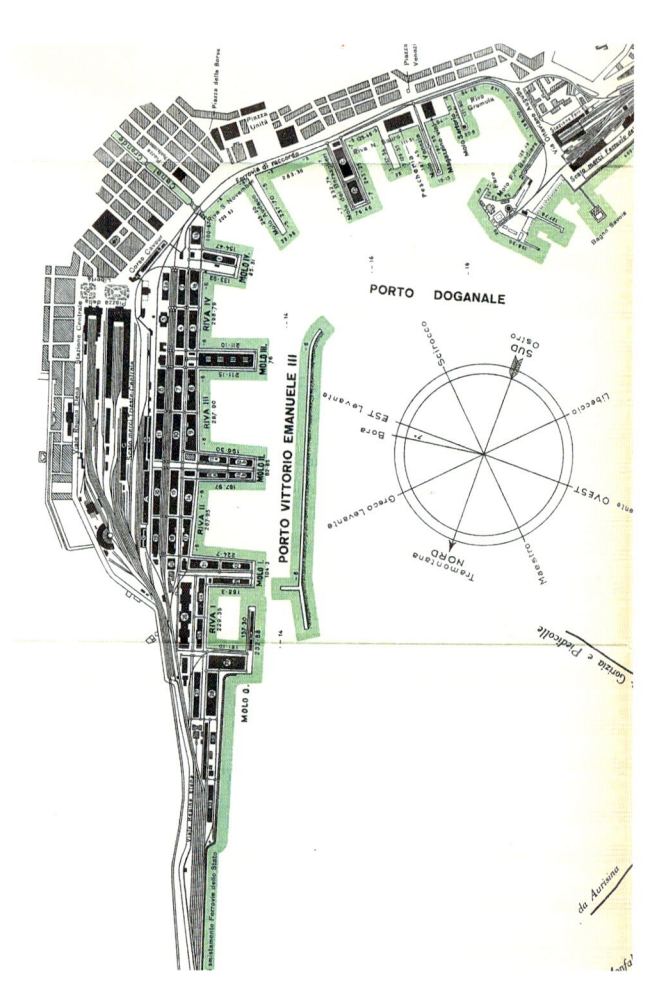

Figure 2: Trieste, Old Port, historic map of Port Trieste, archive of Port Trieste

nical-scientific body, that held a second meeting in Hamburg in June, will support the rehabilitation and redevelopment of the Old Port of Trieste, with the collaboration of Trieste's Port Authority, the Ministry for Cultural Heritage and Activities and "Portocittà", the 70-year concessionaire of the area.

The old Port of Trieste

The Old Port of Trieste represents an excellent witness of nineteenth century European industrial port architecture. It is a valuable example, unique of its kind, of a port facility built with the most advanced equipment, technology and materials of its time.

Figure 3: Trieste, Old Port, Warehouse no. 26, archive of Port Trieste

The Old Port, "Porto Vecchio" in Italian, is different from other ports of the Mediterranean area because it was built after the model of the Lagerhäuser, town districts designated as strategic areas for goods traffic in the Northern European ports, in particular the Hamburg Speicherstadt.

Built during the Habsburg period, between 1868 and 1887 after a thorough planning phase, the Old Port covers an area of about 600,000 square meters, spreading from the Ponte Rosso Channel to the suburban quarter of Barcola. It includes five piers (Pier 0, I, II, III, IV), approximately 3,100 metres of quays, twenty-three main buildings comprising hangars, warehouses and other facilities. The Old Port, protected by an offshore seawall, is directly connected to the old railway (1857).

The impact of the port construction caused some changes in the coastline after a large area was dredged and reclamation works took place.

The old port area and the nineteenth-century warehouses have lost their original function related to commercial traffic so they must open up to new opportunities. A re-visioning of the area must take place with the overall port strategy of Trieste. For a long time the cultural association "Italia Nostra", through the constant efforts of its volunteers, has been fighting for the preservation of this important historic port site. At last, as from August 2001, most of the buildings and the urban structure of the Old Port area fall under the protection of the national cultural heritage authorities.

"Italia Nostra" remains firmly committed to the restoration of the Old Port and to the preservation of its historic warehouses. "Italia Nostra" also chose the city of Hamburg as its reference partner for a correct redevelopment of the area and has established an international committee that can be involved in the selection of the restoration projects. In this regard it has already arranged a second international meeting "Trieste and Hamburg, port cities in comparison" which took place in June 2011 in Hamburg.

The Lagerhäuser of Trieste

The spirit that governed the project, probably thanks to the contributions of Hamburg citizen Alexander von Schöreder, in its guidelines was the idea that the port was to be seen as a city district and, therefore, as a set of Lagerhäuser.

Figure 4: Bremen, Speicher XI

Figure 5: Hamburg, Speicherstadt

Figure 6: Trieste, Old Port, warehouse no. 7

Figure 7: Trieste, Old Port, hydraulic power plant

The term Lagerhäuser has been used since the early plan stages and refers to the urban infrastructures dedicated to the loading, handling, storage and warehousing of goods in multi-storey lagers or hangars.

In the Northern European ports, the Speicher, Lagerhäuser, the Kältespeicher warehouses, except the six-storey Kaispeicher, were built far from the large basin and over the shallow canals. In particular, the six or eight storey Lagerhausgesellschaft warehouses were large and equipped with elevators. The Hamburg port facilities, and also the port of Bremen, while displaying monumental features, successfully matched the urban construction typologies and styles, so that the Staatsspeicher and the hangars merged with the urban fabric along the Elbe river channels.

The warehouses and the deposits were divided into four main categories: the hangars (100–400 metres long, with an height of 12 metres), the Staatsspeicher, the Kaispeicher (A and B) and the Lagerhausgesellschaft warehouses, which served mainly as depots for coffee, tobacco, wine and manufactured products.

The first project of Warehouse 26 of the port of Trieste recalled the stylistic features of the Speicherstadt warehouses.

The similarities of Warehouse 26 with Bremen's Speicher XI (now restored and dedicated to cultural activities and a museum) and Hamburg's Kesselhaus, a restored hydrodynamic plant and now used as an Info-centre.

In Trieste, each hangar was equipped on both sides with railway tracks which were used to load goods directly from wagons into the cargo ships. The hydraulic cranes, both portal or cranes of the "lame goat" type, were located on the edge of the quays and were steam-driven. Also on the land, a system of cranes and hoists facilitated the load-ing and unloading of heavy goods. Of all this electromechanical equipment, the hydraulic crane in front of Warehouse 6 of the old port and the floating pontoon "Ursus" are the only ones which are still in existence; the latter has been put under ministerial protection and will soon be restored.

The four main groups of port buildings

The warehouses and the hangars were placed on three roads, which were parallel to one another: a wider road in the middle and two narrower ones on both sides, one of which is adjacent to the railroad tracks.

1) one-storey buildings, above the ground level
2) two- or three-storey buildings with basement, attic, and balconies, located between the foreparts and supported by cast iron columns
3) four-storey buildings with basement, ground floor and four upper floors with balconies.
4) special buildings, such as the hydrodynamic plant and power conversion substations.

In addition, the "customs stands" are also worth noticing, which are symmetrical to the piers, together with isolated buildings, such as the "battery charger", the "lathe room", the inns and the additional buildings, leaning on the front lines, dedicated to various activities. The main road, which passes in front of the central administration building of the General Stores, is 1450 m long and over 30 m wide; the second road is 1000 m long and 30 m wide; and the third road, that is adjacent to the railway tracks, is 800 m long.

The port included a total number of 20 warehouses, 18 hangars and 17 other buildings. The warehouses were lent to traders, who had duty-free deposits and offices.

The hangars were built in nine months; the warehouses, according to their size, took 12 to 28 months for their construction. The delivery deadlines, that had been set on July 1st, 1891 (date of termination of the Free Port), was not met due to the difficulties of the foundational works.

The construction of these warehouses took on great importance not only for the adoption of new construction methods and the use of new materials, such as concrete, but also for the particular hydraulic and consolidation works carried out to overcome the difficulties posed by the underground conditions.

At that time, the foundations were thought to be the more inflexible and rigid, the safer, even when the soft ground received stress more easily. The trapezoidal configurations of some hangar plans near the shore are worth noticing, as they depend on the soil characteristics.

Stylistic remarks regarding the late 19th century power station architecture

A study of the industrial buildings of that period, especially the hydrodynamic and electrical power stations, built in Germany during the same period, such as Hamburg's Kesselhaus, reveals the diverse natura of those special buildings and facilities, which were intended to enhance the performance of factories and ports. An analysis of the buildings of that period shows that the stylistic and construction techniques were intended to camouflage bulky and modern pieces of machinery (visually somewhat aggressive) which would then result in one of the mainstream technological trends. At the time of construction (1890) of the hydrodynamic plant, only a few years after the 1881 Paris Universal Exhibition and the creation of the first electric engine designed by Galileo Ferraris in 1885, the ports of Hamburg, Buenos Aires, Calcutta and Genoa alone adopted this kind of equipment.

The work was unexpectedly important at the time of its construction, especially because it was connected to new production and industrial port activities. Indeed no detailed documentation about it is available in the port archive.

The hydrodynamic plant building

The hydrodynamic plant consists of three buildings, located and organized according to their functions: the first section of the building, that is on the left when looking coastward, is the former electrical conversion plant; the central building hosts the boiler room; while the building that is symmetrical to the gable, on the right side of the building, hosts the engine room and two water accumulator towers.

The distribution of geometric spaces, also on the plans, recalls the elements of Hamburg's Kesselhaus, that today serves as an information centre for the Speicherstadt.

Figure 8: Trieste, Old Port, hydraulic power plant, machinery room

Figure 9: Trieste, Old Port, hydraulic power plant, (1890) machine Breitfeld & Danek – Karolinental – Prag

Figure 10: Trieste, Old Port, hydraulic power plant, (1890) auxiliary machine Breitfeld & Danek – Karolinental – Prag

During the construction of the hydrodynamic plant (between 1887 and 1890) setting work activities according to the destination, the size and the hierarchy of operations

Figure 11: Trieste, Old Port, hydraulic power plant (1890), particular of auxiliary machine Breitfeld & Danek – Karolinental – Prag

Figure 12: Trieste, Old Port, the boiler room

Figure 13: Trieste, Old Port, power plant

was necessary, providing at the same time a proper distribution of internal spaces.

Therefore, it was necessary to build an engine room, a boiler room, a chimney, a coal store-room and a repair shop. The study and construction of the foundations was just as important, as it was necessary to provide for a firm, stress-resilient floor, which was able to support the weight of the four machines produced by "Aktien Maschinenbau-Gesellschaft vormals Breitfeld Danek & Co" Prague-Karolinenthal, the Cornwall-type boilers, the accumulators, the tanks, and the huge amount of water that was required to operate the cranes.

Three of the main devices and the auxiliary one were installed in 1891, while the fourth was initiated in 1904. The Cornwall-type boiler group, equipped with two chimneys, built by St. Jaschka & Sohn – Wien, provided a 7-bar steam power.

The plant was equipped with inlet channels, water release tubes, and water overflow devices.

The roof structure was also defined according to the requirements of the equipment that had to be installed inside the building. Therefore, the plant displays two gabled symmetrical bodies, of equal height, with parallel ridge lines, corresponding to the engine room and power substation, while the roof layout of the boiler rooms is orthogonal to the ridge line of the other ones. Also the south-east towers, leaning against the factory building through an intermediate structure, were sized bearing in mind that the hydraulic accumulators were to be installed there.

Over time, the hydrodynamic plant turned out, however, to lack the required space to match its expansion. Therefore, around 1913, a new power conversion substation was built.

The water used by the system, coming from the urban piping, was drawn in by the Port's return piping system, but also by two tanks, which supplied only enough water to cover the inevitable losses along the way.

The water pressure that was used to power the lifting equipment was distributed across the port through pipes of different diameters. The delivery and return pipes ran through underground shafts, which were wide enough to allow maintenance personnel to perform a complete and comprehensive inspection.

The high cost of this system and technical progress persuaded the port administration to replace, between 1936 and 1939, the steam engine with more suitable electric motors.

Only three of the four main engines were then electrified, as it was deemed appropriate to keep a steam reservoir in case of power failure. A perfectly preserved unit is still existing.

According to the manuals of that time, the driving power plants had to be near (preferably in adjacent rooms) a repair shop to perform minor repairs but also to rapidly manufacture spare parts.

Those buildings had to be equipped with a transport system between different rooms.

As far as users are concerned, until 1988 the station provided power to cranes, located outside the warehouses to lift goods to the upper floors, and elevators, located inside different port warehouses.

Restoration works to create the port museum centre are currently underway.

Improvement proposal as a cultural asset – establishment of a historical port site of national and international interest

During the past years, Italia Nostra has put forward a number of proposals, such as a request for protection measures to be applied to all the warehouses of the Old Port and also the recovery of the hydrodynamic plant of Trieste, inspired by Hamburg's Kesselhaus.

The hydrodynamic plant of the Old Port of Trieste is the only example in the world of a energy generator, fully preserved in its original building.

Figure 14: Trieste, Old Port, power plant

The Italia Nostra association, in 2004, in collaboration with public institutions, started an improvement project of this important cultural asset, currently under protection measures, which is intended to fully recover the building and to expand its uses including, in terms of tourist-cultural-port activities, the creation of a permanent exhibition, an archive of historical materials and the organization of guided tours. The establishment of a "historic port site of international interest" for the whole old port district could be put forward, starting its recovery and revitalization.

Abstract

Der Alte Hafen von Triest: Charakteristika und Besonderheiten des hydrodynamischen Kraftwerkes und des Lagerhausviertels

Der historische Hafen von Triest dokumentiert auf herausragende Weise die Industriehafenarchitektur des neunzehnten Jahrhunderts in Europa. Er ist ein wertvolles, ja einzigartiges Beispiel für einen Hafen, der mit den damals modernsten Geräten, der fortschrittlichsten Technik und den neuesten Materialien gebaut wurde.

Der Alte Hafen „Porto Vecchio" in Italien unterscheidet sich von anderen Mittelmeerhäfen, weil er nach dem Vorbild der nordeuropäischen Lagerhaus-Viertel entstand: Letztere waren praktisch ausschließlich dem Warenumschlag gewidmet. Insbesondere stand die Hamburger Speicherstadt Pate bei Entwurf und Bau des „Porto Vecchio".

Der Hafen entstand nach sorgfältiger Planung während der Habsburger Monarchie in den Jahren zwischen 1868 und 1887. Er umfasst eine Fläche von 600 000 qm und erstreckt sich vom Ponte Rosso Kanal bis zum Vorstadtviertel Barcola. Zum Hafen gehören insgesamt fünf Brücken (Pier 0, I, II, III, IV), Kais mit einer Länge von 3 100 Metern, 23 Gebäude, hierunter Hangars, Lagerhäuser sowie weitere Anlagen und Nebengebäude. Der Alte Hafen ist durch eine Außenmole gegen die offene See geschützt und direkt an die alte Eisenbahnlinie von 1857 angebunden.

Durch den Bau des Hafens veränderte sich der Küstenverlauf, da in großem Umfang ausgebaggert und Land hinzugewonnen wurde.

Figure 15: Trieste, Old Port, warehouse no. 26 after restoration (2011)

Figure 16: Trieste, Old Port, old warehouse no. 26 after restoration (2011)

Das ehemalige Hafengebiet und die Speicherstadt aus dem 19. Jahrhundert sind inzwischen vom Stadtzentrum umschlossen und haben ihre ursprüngliche Funktion für den gewerblichen Verkehr eingebüßt. Sie müssen sich deshalb für neue Nutzungen und Chancen öffnen, die im größeren

Figure 17: Trieste, Old Port, old warehouse no. 26 after restoration (2011)

Figure 18: Trieste, Old Port, hydraulic power plant, works for restoration (2011)

des Hafens von Triest bezeugen. Sogar die Auswahl der Baumaterialien, konstruktive Details sowie Zoll- und andere vertragliche Regelungen erlauben interessante Einblicke in die Hafenaktivitäten von Triest.

Der Kulturverband „Italia Nostra" und die in ihm organisierten ehrenamtlichen Mitglieder kämpfen seit langem unermüdlich für die Erhaltung dieses wichtigen historischen Hafens. Am 23. August 2001 gelang es endlich, die meisten der Gebäude sowie die städtebauliche Struktur des Alten Hafens unter den Schutz der nationalen Denkmalschutzbehörde zu stellen.

„Italia Nostra" engagiert sich weiterhin dezidiert für die Restaurierung des Alten Hafens und die Erhaltung der historischen Lagerhäuser. „Italia Nostra" hat sich bewusst mit Hamburg als Referenzpartnerstadt zusammengetan, um bei der Umwidmung des Hafengeländes den richtigen Weg einzuschlagen. Es wurde ein international besetzter Ausschuss eingerichtet, der bei der Wahl der Restaurierungs-Projekte einbezogen wird.

Bibliography

AMODEO, Fabio – CAROLI, Antonella "Trieste e il porto. Una storia per immagini", La biblioteca del Piccolo, volumi 1 e 2, editoriale FVG S. p. a., Trieste, 2007

CAROLI, Antonella "Punto Franco Vecchio-Tipologie, Sistemi costruttivi, Opere professionale e Normativa nel Porto di Trieste" – ed. La Mongolfiera, Trieste, 1996

CAROLI, Antonella "Trieste e Amburgo: mito e realtà delle città porto" – ed. Italo Svevo,Trieste, 2005 (Celebrazione del cinquantenario di Italia Nostra)

CAROLI, Antonella "Guida storica del Porto Vecchio di Trieste"- ed. Italo Svevo, Trieste, 2009

CAROLI, Antonella "La centrale idrodinamica del porto di Trieste" ed. Italo Svevo, Trieste, 2009

CAROLI, Antonella "Il progetto e la storia del Polo museale del porto di Trieste"– ed. Italo Svevo,Trieste, 2010

Meeting Trieste 1999 "Gli Hangars del Porto Vecchio di Trieste" ed. Battello Stampatore, Trieste, 2002

Sources of illustrations

Archives port of Trieste
Archives of Trieste city
Archives K. K. Staats Gewerbeschule -Trieste
Archives and institute „Alvar Aalto" – Torino
Archives of Guard coast Trieste

* The photo rights have been clarified by the author and she has the responsibility

Zusammenhang mit der traditionellen Bedeutung von Triest als Hafenstadt stehen. Sichtbare Zeugnisse des alten Hafengeländes existieren auch ohne gegenwärtige Nutzung fort: historische Lagerhäuser, Hangars, das Kesselhaus, Kaikräne, elektromechanisches Gerät und die alten Silospeicher mit ihrer charakteristischen Architektur.

Die Lagerhäuser, Hangars und bis zu vierstöckigen Gebäude bilden Parallelachsen, von denen die landseitig innerste in direkter Nachbarschaft zum Schienenstrang verläuft.

Bei allen diesen Gebäuden, Anlagen und Ausrüstungsgegenständen handelt es sich um unersetzbare Beispiele einer Industrie- und Technikarchitektur, die die große Tradition

John Hinchliffe

Liverpool Maritime Mercantile City World Heritage Site: Lessons for the conservation and management of port cities

ALL YOU NEED IS DOCKS – The long and winding road to the conservation of Liverpool's historic port city

Sea ports are an essential component in the broad cultural heritage of humanity. They are a pre-requisite of international civilisation, as they are the interface between land and sea, where goods and people are transferred and where global trading links are anchored.

By necessity, seaports must have docks where ships can moor and transfer their cargo. Some ports have natural sheltered deep water and can operate successfully using simple quays or piers but others, such as Liverpool, have a high tidal range and can only operate successfully by constructing enclosed wet docks to maintain a constant water level adjacent to the quays.

Brief History of Liverpool

Liverpool was founded by King John in 1207, as a port from which to sail to Ireland and Wales, but few noteworthy developments occurred there in the first 500 years! A map of 1577 shows that in the 16th century, the nearby Chester on the River Dee was busier than Liverpool on the River Mersey. Liverpool's growth as a port was hampered by the high tidal range of the river and the lack of protected moorings for ships.

However, in 1715 the Town Council opened the world's first commercial enclosed wet dock (which later became known as Old Dock), constructed within an infilled tidal pool, and Liverpool began its rise to become one of the greatest international port cities.

By the end of the 18th century, Liverpool had constructed a further five enclosed docks along the tidal margins. By the end of the 19th century, seven miles of enclosed docks had been completed in a continuous line along the east bank of the river. It was a remarkable achievement of civil engineering and municipal enterprise.

Figure 1: Liverpool 1682

The tangible evidence of Liverpool's global significance as an international seaport survives in many forms, especially in its surviving docks and warehouses. Liverpool has examples of many types of warehouses which demonstrate innovation and the evolution of warehouses as a building typology:

1. Warehouses in merchants' houses
2. Warehouses attached to merchants' houses
3. Warehouses detached from merchants' houses
4. Early fireproof warehouses
5. Bonded Warehouses
6. Monumental dockside warehouses
7. Inland warehouses combined with showrooms
8. Specialist warehouses

Liverpool's spirit of place is also a product of its intangible heritage: the memories and echoes of the lives of its dock

Figure 2: Old Dock

Figure 3: Waterloo Warehouse

Figure 4: Albert Dock circa 1980, prior to comprehensive restoration

Figure 5: Branding of WHS to enable business to show pride in the status

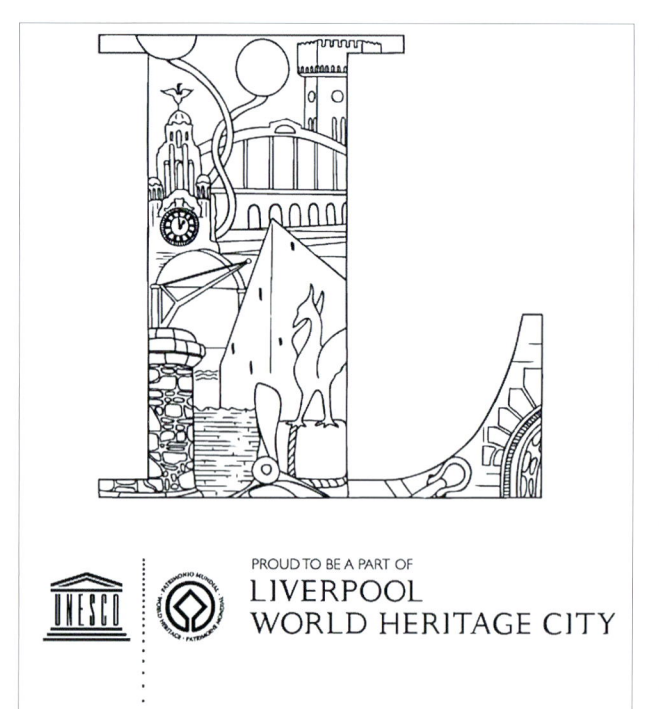

workers, merchants and sailors and the impacts on the millions of emigrants and enslaved Africans whose lives were transformed by their trans-Atlantic journeys on Liverpool-owned ships.

Liverpool's economic decline and population loss during the 20th century created a desperate need for urban regeneration and for the city to find a new identity and purpose. Liverpool's renaissance has been based on realising the communal, economic, townscape and historic value of its port heritage, as a unique and irreplaceable resource. The seed pearl of Liverpool's regeneration began the 1980's when the Albert Dock Warehouses were saved, conserved and converted into a mix of new uses, accessible to the public. The work of revitalising Liverpool's port heritage has continued since that time and, although much of the waterfront has been rejuvenated, it is still "work in progress". In the course of conserving, managing and regenerating the vast maritime heritage of Liverpool over the last thirty years, many lessons have been learnt, which could usefully be studied by other port cities. Many of these lessons will be obvious to port historians and conservationists but the benefit of stating the obvious is the avoidance of doubt!

The Lessons from Liverpool:

Lesson 1 – Be proud of your maritime heritage – encourage it to be valued

The citizens of Liverpool are traditionally proud of their maritime heritage but years of economic and social problems in the late 20th Century led to the fading of the communal memory of the city's past glories. Liverpool City Council and its partners, notably English Heritage, foresaw that if Liverpool could become a World Heritage Site (WHS), this international recognition would lead to a return of civic pride in the city and could be an inspiration for heritage-led regeneration. Verification of Liverpool's claim of the global significance of its docks was provided by Dr Ray Bondin (ICOMOS Assessor) who confirmed in 2003 that Liverpool has "The biggest and most complete system of historic docks in the world." Following much hard work by many people, the international significance of the port and city of Liverpool was recognized by UNESCO in 2004, when its historic waterfront, commercial centre and cultural quarter were inscribed onto the World Heritage list as "the supreme example of a commercial port of the 18th, 19th and early 20th centuries."

Building owners in Liverpool's WHS are now displaying pride in the WHS status, through a new branding initiative which encourages them to put up window stickers to proclaim "Proud to be part of Liverpool World Heritage City".

Lesson 2 – Celebrate and enjoy your maritime heritage – make the most of the "soft values"

Liverpool City Council capitalizes on Liverpool's maritime heritage by organizing regular events such as river festivals, Tall Ships Races and the *On The Waterfront* festivals, which use the historic port as a venue and a backdrop. Spectacular films of the events are sometimes made available

Figure 6: Sound and light projection at the On The Waterfront Festival 2011

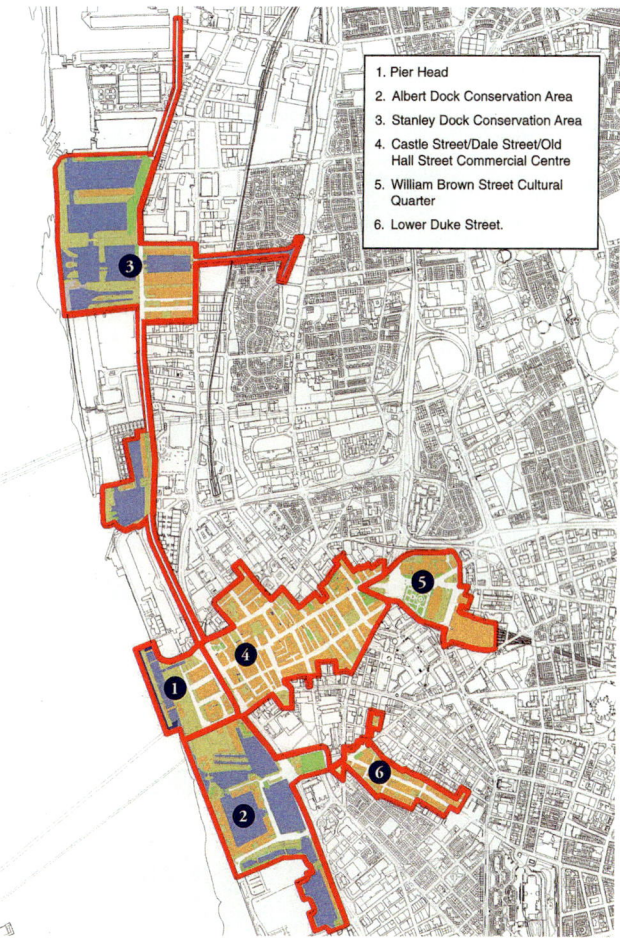

Figure 7: The six areas of distinctive townscape character of Liverpool's World Heritage Site

online so that even those who cannot attend can enjoy the events. (See the unmissable clips from 2011 at: http://vimeo.com/26827092 and http://vimeo.com/26884619.) Such events harness local pride but also contribute to the visitor economy, with hundreds of thousands of visitors.

This lesson is part of the wider concept promoted by Eric van Hooydonk in his *Soft Values of Seaports*. He rightly advocates that the public will show greater support and appreciation of operational seaports if full advantage is taken of the opportunities offered by those ports in connection with their heritage, nature, education, art and employment.

Lesson 3 – Understand the wider urban landscape of your port city – Undertake detailed studies of the urban fabric and landscape

As part of Liverpool's nomination process to become a WHS, the candidate site was assessed and subsequently divided into six areas of distinct townscape character, which had evolved as a result of different historic uses:

1. The Pier Head – the visual and spiritual focal point of the city
2. Albert Dock Conservation Area – an ensemble of docks and warehouses south of the Pier Head
3. Stanley Dock Conservation Area – an ensemble of docks and warehouses north of the Pier Head
4. Castle Street Commercial Centre – the palaces of commerce
5. The William Brown Street Cultural Quarter – Liverpool's historic expression of its interest cultural values
6. Lower Duke Street Merchants Quarter – early inland warehouses and merchants' houses

The identification of these six areas and their morphology assisted in the proper description, understanding and planning for those historic "quarters" of the city, which still have different characteristics of form and function.

Lesson 4 – Understand the port city's historic and intangible significance

UNESCO considers that Liverpool has *Outstanding Universal Value* because Liverpool:

1. Played a leading role in the development of dock construction, port management and international trading systems in the 18th and 19th centuries
2. The buildings and structures of the port and the city are an exceptional testimony to mercantile culture.

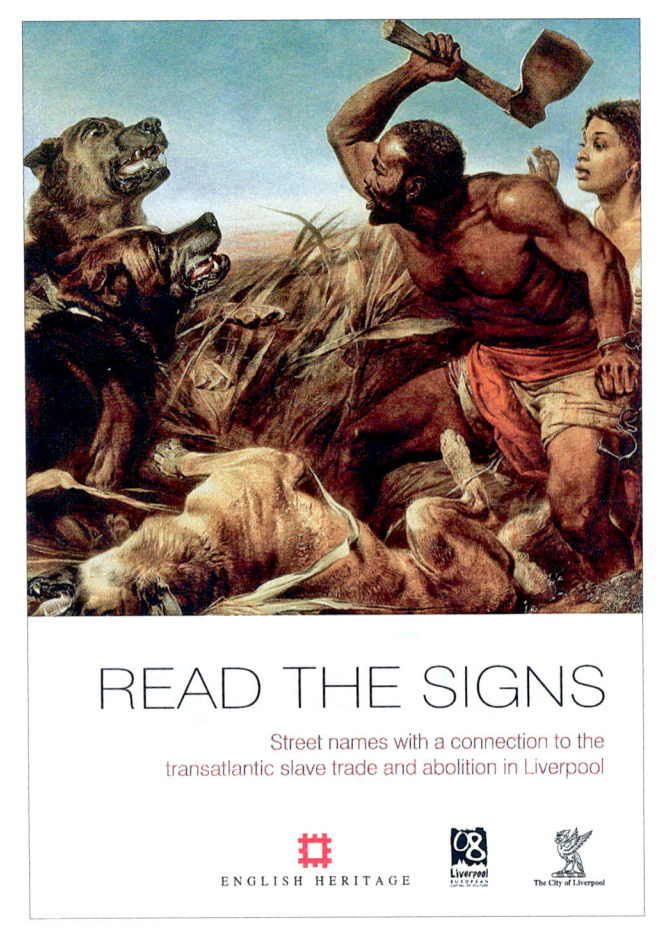

Figure 8: Identify intangible heritage of the port

3. Liverpool played a major role in influencing globally significant demographic changes in the 18th and 19th centuries, through: a) its involvement in the Trans-Atlantic Slave Trade and b) its involvement as the leading port of mass European emigration to the New World.

Visitors come to Liverpool to trace their *Genealogical Roots* and the *Geographical Routes* of their ancestors!

It is important to encourage understanding and interpretation of historic and intangible heritage, especially through events, displays, museums and publications as well as through urban planning and building conservation.

Lesson 5 – Ensure that better understanding of port heritage leads to informed conservation and better planning

English Heritage was the lead partner in the *Historic Environment of Liverpool Project* (HELP) from 2001 until 2010 which was established to encourage better understanding, management and celebration of the city's extraordinary cultural heritage.

HELP was an umbrella programme which:

1. Encouraged partnership working of major public sector organisations
2. Public engagement and
3. Brought together around 15 interlinked projects.

HELP was grouped into three key themes:

1. Investigation and Characterisation
2. Managing the Historic Environment
3. Access and Celebration of cultural heritage

A key output of the project was the publication of a series of popular books on Informed Conservation, which has enhanced knowledge and enabled more informed planning decisions.

The improved knowledge, management and celebration of the historic environment have enabled better planning decisions to be made.

Lesson 6 – Get statutory protection for historic port structures

A survey of all buildings in the WHS in 2005 demonstrated that many of the unlisted buildings were of significant architectural or historic interest but, because they were not listed, did not benefit from full legal protection. The HELP Programme resulted in a subsequent review of listed buildings within the WHS and the addition of many historic port buildings on to the statutory list, such as inland warehouses and the early fireproof warehouse at Vulcan Street/ Waterloo Road.

Lesson 7 – The public are attracted to mixed uses in historic buildings with a waterside setting

In the early 1980s, much of Liverpool's historic port was abandoned, dis-used and derelict. This was a symptom of industrial obsolescence and the future for the historic port looked bleak. The Merseyside Development Corporation (MDC) took a massive leap of faith to invest much public money into the restoration and creative re-use of several historic docks and warehouses on the premise that the public are attracted to mixed uses in historic buildings with a waterside setting. The MDC was proved right as the restoration of the Albert Dock in particular has been an outstanding success. Its restoration was undertaken in accordance with clear conservation principles. It annually attracts over 4 million visitors a year and is an international icon of heritage-led regeneration.

Lesson 8 – Public authorities should deliver regeneration of under-used port heritage by any means necessary

Public authorities should deliver regeneration of disused historic ports *by any means necessary,* using a wide range of planning and conservation tools:

1. Regeneration frameworks – such as Liverpool Vision's Strategic Regeneration Framework, which established the principle of reclaiming the waterfront
2. Planning policies – such as those in Liverpool's Unitary Development Plan which established regeneration and conservation policies
3. Management Plans – such as the Liverpool WHS Management which has the vision for the future that "The

organisations and people responsible for the management of the World Heritage Site are committed to ensuring that *Liverpool – Maritime Mercantile City* will be managed as an exemplary demonstration of sustainable development and heritage-led regeneration."

4. Detailed Planning guidance – such as the Liverpool WHS Supplementary Planning Document (2009) which addresses the key planning, regeneration and conservation issues which affect the WHS and clarifies the policies for the benefit of developers, building owners and decision-makers
5. Public Funding – a cocktail of funding from a variety of sources has transformed much of Liverpool's port heritage
6. Private Sector – the private sector of developers and landowners have primary responsibility for maintaining and enhancing their land and buildings and a constructive working relationship is required so that mutually shared objectives can be agreed and achieved

The establishment of a consensual management framework for port heritage is the most important requirement.

Lesson 9 – Carry out a comprehensive townscape analysis to identify key planning and conservation issues

The key planning and conservation issues will vary between port cities and so solutions or policies from elsewhere cannot necessarily be imported from elsewhere. It will always be necessary to undertake a comprehensive planning and townscape analysis to establish key issues and policies. As a pre-requisite of preparing the Liverpool WHS Supplementary Planning Document, an Evidential Report was produced, which formed a base-line of townscape information. The Evidential Report identified that the key planning and conservation issues for Liverpool included:

1. The need for design guidance
2. The need for policies for tall buildings
3. Building heights in the WHS
4. The protection of views
5. The future of the redundant historic water-spaces.
6. The replacement of existing buildings
7. The re-use of Historic Buildings
8. The Dock Wall
9. Archaeology
10. Conservation standards
11. The Liverpool Waters site

It is also essential that developers for developers undertake their own detailed view analysis and heritage impact analysis to assess the impact of proposed development on the historic port.

Lesson 10 – Identify buildings that make a negative contribution to the historic urban landscape and encourage their remodelling or removal/replacement

Not all buildings within Liverpool's historic port are heritage assets or contribute to the outstanding universal value

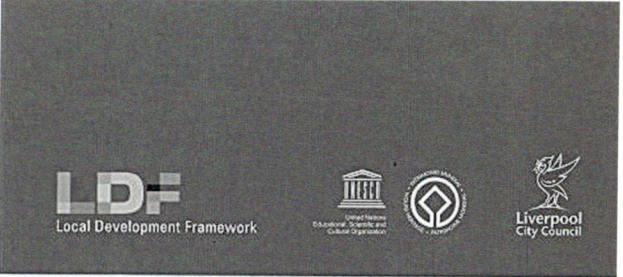

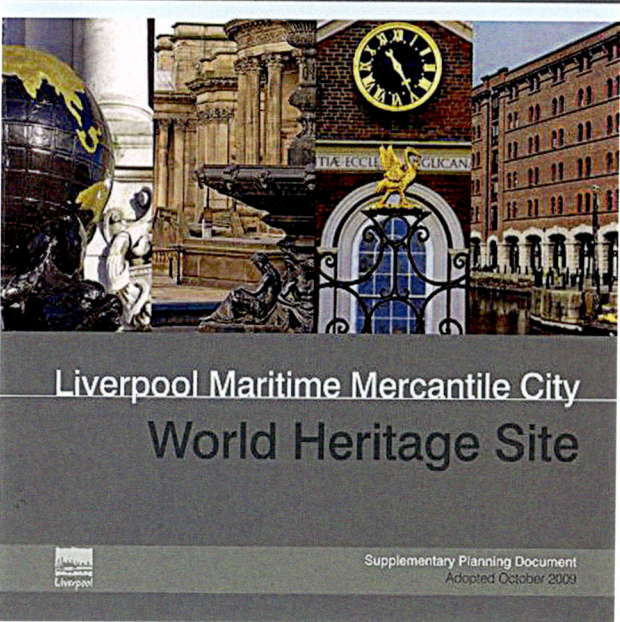

Figure 9: Produce detailed planning guidance for development, regeneration and conservation

of the WHS. Liverpool City Council commissioned a study to identify those building which make a neutral or negative contribution to the historic urban landscape. It then confirmed that it would not object in principle to their remodelling or demolition and replacement.

Conclusions

1. The conservation and management of Liverpool's port heritage are based upon the principle of the "virtuous circle of cultural heritage"
Improved Understanding of Cultural Heritage results in More Enjoyment of Cultural Heritage, which results in- Greater Valuing of Cultural Heritage, which results in- Better Caring for Cultural Heritage which results in and Improved Understanding of Cultural Heritage and so the circle goes on!
2. The public authorities in Liverpool are always keen to learn and share best practice in the conservation and management of its cultural heritage. From 2008 until 2011, Liverpool was a member of URBACT's HerO (Heritage as Opportunity) Project, which was a European networking project to develop sustainable strategies for living historic cities, including the port cities of Naples and Valletta. The outputs of the HerO Project should be of interest to everyone who is responsible for the conservation

and management of historic cities. Those outputs include a paper on *The Untapped Potential of Cultural Heritage* and a guidebook on how to prepare Integrated Cultural Heritage Management Plans.
3. All historic ports and all historic cities are unique, but many have common characteristics and face similar challenges. Liverpool does not claim to have all the answers nor to have achieved perfect solutions and it still has many challenges ahead. UNESCO welcomed Liverpool as case study in the conservation of port heritage *in progress* and so it is pleased to share its experiences and the lessons it has learnt to provide a communal reservoir of knowledge for other port cities to study and benefit from.

For further information, visit www.liverpoolworldheritage.com and www.urbact.eu/hero or contact jnshinchliffe@gmail.com

Abstract

Welterbestätte Liverpool Maritime Mercantile City: Lehren für die Erhaltung und Bewirtschaftung von Hafenstädten
ALL YOU NEED IS DOCKS – Der steinige Weg hin zur Bewahrung von Liverpools historischem Hafenviertel

Seehäfen stellen im umfassenden kulturellen Erbe der Menschheit eine essenzielle Komponente dar. Sie sind Voraussetzung für eine international ausgerichtete Zivilisation, denn sie bilden die Schnittstelle zwischen Land und Meer, über die Güter und Menschen überführt werden und an der weltweite Handelsbeziehungen ihre Verankerung haben.

Die internationale Bedeutung des Hafens und der Stadt Liverpool wurde von der UNESCO im Jahr 2004 anerkannt, als das historische Hafenviertel und Handelszentrum als „herausragendes Beispiel eines Handelshafens des 18., 19. und frühen 20. Jahrhunderts" in die Liste der Weltkulturerbestätten aufgenommen wurde.

Der Vortrag gibt einen kurzen Abriss der Geschichte Liverpools, von der Eröffnung des weltweit ersten Schwimmdocks 1715 bis hin zum Status der Stadt als eine der großen Hafenstädte der Welt am Ende des 19. Jahrhunderts. Der Niedergang im Verlauf des 20. Jahrhunderts machte eine tiefgreifende Erneuerung der Stadt erforderlich. Sie musste eine neue Identität und Bestimmung finden. Die Wiedergeburt Liverpools basierte auf der Realisierung des kommunalen, wirtschaftlichen, stadtlandschaftlichen und historischen Werts seines Hafens. Er stellt ein einzigartiges und nicht zu ersetzendes Kapital dar.

Die Erneuerung Liverpools begann in den 1980er Jahren, als die Lagerhäuser des Albert Docks gerettet, erhalten, einer Reihe neuer Verwendungen zugeführt und für die Öffentlichkeit zugänglich gemacht wurden. Die Wiederbelebung des Hafens wurde seitdem fortgeführt. Und obwohl ein großer Teil des Gebiets verjüngt wurde, ist vieles immer noch „im Bau". Im Verlauf der Erhaltung, Bewirtschaftung und Erneuerung des riesigen maritimen Erbes Liverpools wurden Erfahrungen gesammelt, die auch anderen Hafenstädten von Nutzen sein können:

Lektion 1 – Sei stolz auf Dein maritimes Erbe.
Lektion 2 – Genieße und feiere Dein maritimes Erbe.
Lektion 3 – Entwickle ein Verständnis für die urbane Landschaft Deiner Hafenstadt.
Lektion 4 – Erkenne die historische und unangreifbare Bedeutung der Hafenstadt.
Lektion 5 – Stelle sicher, dass ein besseres Verständnis des Erbes, das der Hafen darstellt, zu einer von Kenntnisreichtum geprägten Erhaltung und zu besserer Planung führt.
Lektion 6 – Sorge dafür, dass historische Hafenstrukturen gesetzlich geschützt werden.
Lektion 7 – Am Wasser gelegene historische Gebäude, die verschiedenartig genutzt werden, sind für die Menschen besonders attraktiv.
Lektion 8 – Die Behörden sollten alles daran setzen, eine Erneuerung durchzuführen.
Lektion 9 – Nimm eine umfassende Analyse des Stadtbilds vor, um wichtige Planungsfragen zu ermitteln.
Lektion 10 – Ermittle Gebäude, die sich auf die historische urbane Landschaft negativ auswirken und ermutige dazu, sie zu beseitigen/ersetzen.

Zwar sind alle historischen Häfen und Städte einzigartig, viele haben jedoch die gleichen Merkmale und stehen vor ähnlichen Herausforderungen. Liverpool gibt weder vor, auf alles eine Antwort noch perfekte Lösungen gefunden zu haben. Viele Herausforderungen liegen noch vor uns. Die UNESCO sieht Liverpool als Fallbeispiel für eine fortlaufende Bewahrung des Hafenerbes. Die in Liverpool gemachten Erfahrungen stellen ein Wissensreservoir dar, das andere Hafenstädte nutzen und von dem sie profitieren können.

Weitere Informationen erhalten Sie unter www.liverpoolworldheritage.com, oder setzen Sie sich mit John Hinchliffe unter jnshinchliffe@gmail.com in Verbindung.

Sources of Illustrations

Fig. 1; Fig. 2: National Museum Liverpool
Fig. 3: English Heritage
Fig. 4; Fig. 5; Fig. 6; Fig. 7; Fig. 8; Fig. 9: Liverpool City Council

* The photo rights have been clarified by the author and he has the responsibility

Axel Föhl

Der Hafen von Antwerpen

Hafenentwicklung

In der Staffel der Nordseehäfen zwischen Hamburg und Le Havre kommt Antwerpen schon früh hohe Bedeutung zu. Die 726 erstmals urkundlich erwähnte Stadt erlangte mit dem Aufschwung Brabants nach der Schlacht von Worringen 1288 wachsende wirtschaftliche Bedeutung und zog seit dem Beginn des 14. Jahrhunderts große Teile des Zwischenhandels mit Deutschland auf sich. Stadtrechte erhielt sie 1291, das Stapelrecht für englische Wolle 1295. Der Förderung durch die burgundischen Herzöge verdankte sie die Vorrangstellung gegenüber der bis dahin bedeutenderen, aber durch die Versandung des Zwin benachteiligten Handelsstadt Brügge. Die 1460 gegründete Handelsbörse war die erste in Europa. Um 1550 hatten mehr als tausend ausländische Handelshäuser einen Sitz in Antwerpen, darunter die Fugger und Welser, Antwerpen galt als reichste Handelsstadt der christlichen Welt. Dank ihrer geographischen Lage am Kreuzungspunkt der Handelswege Westeuropa-Ostseeländer und England-Mitteleuropa und nach der Entdeckung Amerikas wuchs die Stadt von 46 000 Einwohnern im Jahr 1496 auf 125 000 im Jahr 1568. Damit war allerdings zunächst der Zenit überschritten. Die Unterdrückung der Reformation durch die Spanier vertrieb zahlreiche Handelshäuser, 1585 wurde die Stadt spanisch. Die von den Niederländern errichtete Scheldeblockade traf die Stadt zugunsten von Amsterdam empfindlich, erst 1863 kaufte man den Niederländern den Scheldezoll ab. Die Napoleonzeit hatte einen vorübergehenden, gegen England gerichteten Entwicklungsschub gebracht, aber erst mit dem nach der Jahrhundertmitte abschnittsweise angelegten "Eisernen Rhein", einer Schienenverbindung in die deutschen Schwerindustriegebiete, begann der neuerliche Aufstieg Antwerpens, die Einwohnerzahl wuchs bis 1880 auf 178 000.[1] Um 1870 hatte der Seegüterverkehr bereits einen Umfang von 2 Millionen Tonnen, bis zum Ersten Weltkrieg stieg er auf 19 Millionen.

Sowohl die deutsche Besetzung von 1914–1918, als auch die von 1940–1944 dauernde zweite deutsche Okkupation ließen Antwerpen und seine Hafenanlagen weitestgehend intakt, ein Schicksal, das – was die Erhaltung historischer Substanz anbelangt – dieses Hafenareal deutlich von denen in Hamburg oder Rotterdam unterscheidet.

Die prosperierende Entwicklung nach 1945 brachte auch Antwerpen bedeutende Entfaltungsmöglichkeiten, seit 1950 wurde der Hafenausbau zunehmend von den Modalitäten des Containerumschlages geprägt, die Entwicklung ging scheldeabwärts weg von den historischen Arealen nördlich der Innenstadt in Richtung der holländischen Scheldemündung.

Nach Rotterdam steht Antwerpen heute europaweit an zweiter, weltweit an vierter Stelle beim Güterumschlag.

Hafenanlagen

Jahrhundertelang, von 1263 bis ins 16. Jahrhundert, wurde die flußseitige Ansicht der Stadt vom mittelalterlichen Kran auf dem sogenannten „werf" bestimmt (Abb. 1). Dies war eine ca. 0,2 ha umfassende Landzunge am rechten Scheldeufer, „werp" oder auch „kranenhoofd" genannt. Eine der Theorien über die Etymologie des Stadtnamens geht davon aus, daß Antwerpen seinen Namen von der Ortslagenbezeichnung „aan t' werp" – „am Werft" ableitet. Die erste signifikante Erweiterung der Hafenanlagen bestand dann zwischen 1543 und 1545 in der Erweiterung dreier Fleete aus der Mitte des 13. Jahrhunderts auf ca. 25 ha Fläche, dem „Koolvliet", dem „St. Jansvliet" und dem „St. Petersvliet"[2]. Die weiter oben erwähnten politischen Entwicklungen brachten mit der spanischen Herrschaft die Entwicklung dann für 250 Jahre zum Stillstand. Erst mit Napoleons Besuch im Juli 1803 veränderte sich die Lage. Antwerpen, von Napoleon zunächst als „afrikanisches Dorf" bezeichnet, wurde mit den Plänen zur Kontinentalsperre unversehens zur „Pistole, gerichtet auf Englands Herz". Noch im gleichen Monat erfolgte die kaiserliche Ordre zur Errichtung

Abb. 1: Antwerpens "waterfront" um 1518

Abb. 2: Bonaparteschleuse, Napoleon- und Willemdock, 1967

eines Schleusendocks sowie die Anlage eines anderthalb Kilometer langen Kais längs der Schelde, das bei Bedarf auch als Geschützbatterie zu verwenden sein sollte. Hier, an der Schwelle des Industriezeitalters, klang bereits ein Motiv an, das im Laufe des 19. Jahrhunderts wieder und wieder angeschlagen werden sollte: zur Anlage des napoleonischen Docks mußten auf dem höhergelegenen Grund der Antwerpener „Nieuwstad" 1300 Behausungen Platz machen, ein Vorgang, der sich bei der Anlage der 1868 eröffneten St. Pancras Eisenbahnstation in London wiederholen sollte, wo die 20000 Bewohner von Agar Town schlicht verdrängt wurden.[3] Eine nahezu gleiche Zahl von angestammten Bewohnern hatte auch der ab 1863 in Angriff genommenen Anlage der Hamburger Speicherstadt zu weichen.[4]

1811 wurde die Antwerpener „Bonapartesluis" mit der Passage eines in der gleichen Stadt auf Kiel gelegten Kriegsschiffes mit achtzig Kanonen in Betrieb genommen. Die 17,4 Meter lange Schleuse wurde 1974 verfüllt. Das anschließende erste Dock maß 145 auf 173 Meter bei einem Tiefgang von 6,18 Metern. Von 1808 bis 1810 entstand das zweite, 155 auf 378 Meter messende Dock. 1815 gelangten beide Docks samt Schleuse durch Schenkung Willems II. der Niederlande an die Stadt. Bis 1837 wurden die meistenteils mit Böschungen versehenen Becken durch Kaimauern ersetzt (Abb. 2). Zur Hundertjahrfeier 1903 taufte man die bislang „Klein Dok" und „Groot Dok" benannten Anlagen in „Bonapartedok" und „Willemdok" um.[5]

Auf den Aufschwung nach 1850 und die Ablösung des Scheldezolls und die Anlage des „Eisernen Rheins" reagierte die Stadt Antwerpen mit der Anlage eines zweiten Dockkomplexes als Kernstück des späteren „Kattendijkdoks". Er lag außerhalb der Festungszone im Norden und bestand zunächst aus einem 140 auf 500 Meter messenden Dock. Dieses 1856 bis 1860 angelegte Dock wurde bereits 1863 um insgesamt drei Trockendocks sowie das zunächst „Mexicodok", bald aber wegen seiner Bestimmung „Houtdok" – „Holzdock" genannte Hafenbecken vergrößert. Den Hintergrund hierfür bildete die rapide Zunahme des nun auch mit Dampfkraft betriebenen Schiffsverkehrs. 1864 erbrachten 2753 Seeschiffe einen Güterumschlag von fast 900000 Tonnen. Wichtig zu erwähnen in diesem Zusammenhang sind auch die 1843 in Angriff genommenen Güterbahnanlagen in Verbindung mit der dann 1847 in Betrieb genommenen Bahnverbindung mit Köln. In der ersten Hälfte des 20. Jahrhunderts sollten dann noch Kanalverbindungen ins Hinterland dazu kommen.

Neben den wasserbaulichen Arbeiten war man aber seit der Jahrhundertmitte auch zum Bau von Lagerhäusern geschritten.[6] Damit wurde eine Tradition wiederaufgenommen, deren erhaltene Sachzeugen bis in das 16. Jahrhundert zurückreichen. Unweit des seit 2006 im historischen St.-Felix-Lagerhaus untergebrachten Stadtarchivs wurde 1564 das „Hessenhuis" als Bestimmungsort aus Deutschland kommender Waren erbaut. Den Niedergang nach 1585 überdauerte es als Kaserne, bis es im 19. Jahrhundert wieder seiner ursprünglichen Bestimmung zur Warenlagerung zugeführt wurde, der es bis um 1950 diente. Seither finden hier alle Arten von Ausstellungen statt. Der unmittelbare Nachbar des „Hessenhuis" ist das 1910 als backsteinverkleideter Betonbau errichtete, eckturmbekrönte Lagerhaus der „Magasins et Entrepôts Réunis La Cloche". Somit ist im

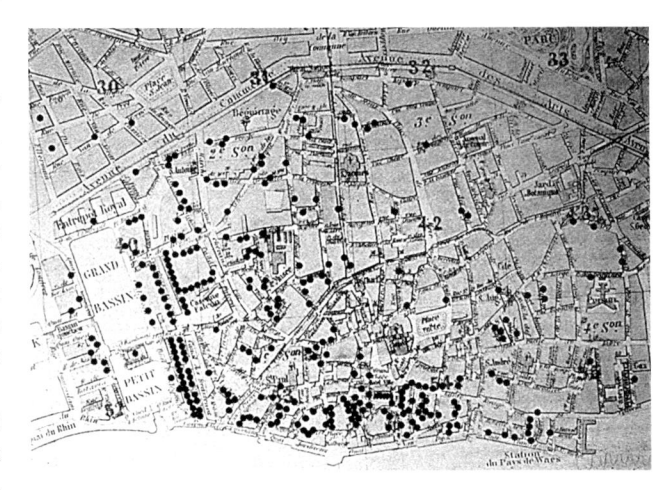

Abb. 3: Verteilung der Lagerhäuser um den Antwerpener Hafen, 1874

Abb. 4: Das 1882 angelegte, 1967 verfüllte „Zuiderdok", im Hintergrund die monumentale Hydraulik-Zentrale

Zuge einer einzigen Straße der charakteristische Typus des Lagerhauses in seiner Erscheinungsform über fast fünf Jahrhunderten hin vertreten. Eine 1874 entstandene Karte zeigt die dichte Verteilung der zahlreichen Lagerhäuser entlang von Schelde und Hafenbecken (Abb. 3). Erwähnenswert vor allem das „Entrepôt St. Felix" am Willemdok, ursprünglich errichtet 1858, nach Brand wieder aufgebaut 1863. Einen einschneidenden Verlust stellt der 1990 erfolgte Abbruch des „Entrepôt Royal", des königlichen Lagerhauses dar, das, 1830 erbaut, nach einem Brand im Jahr 1900 erneut entstanden war und einer Wohnbebauung des Architekten Hans Kollhoff weichen mußte. Das Dockareal nördlich der Stadt vergrößerte sich 1887 um das 6,9 ha umfassende Amerikadock und das über 10 ha messende Lefèbvredock. Ersteres diente vor allem der Petroleumeinfuhr, ein Gewerbe, das seit 1861 erstmals für Europa in Antwerpen betrieben wurde. Nach einigen Brand- und Explosionskatastrophen verlagerte man den Erdölumschlag an das südliche Ende des Scheldekais. Dieses war zwischen 1877 und 1888 als noch heute das Erscheinungsbild der Stadt maßgeblich bestimmende Element an der Schelde zwischen dem Kattendijkdok und der Südstation errichtet worden. 600 Gebäude und die weiter oben erwähnte Werft verschwanden dabei zugunsten eines hundert Meter breiten, mit offenen Eisenschuppen, Ladekränen, Eisenbahngleisen und einer Fahrstraße versehenen Uferstreifens. Vom Abbruch verschont blieb einzig das 1520 angelegte Burggebäude des „Steen", das, im 19. Jahrhundert kräftig romantisiert, seit 1864 als Museum und seit 1952 als Schiffahrtsmuseum diente. Die umfangreiche Sammlung maritimer Fahrzeuge ging 2011 an das neueröffnete „MAS", das „Museum aan de Stroom", die neuartige Konzeption eines Stadtmuseums über. Zur Aufnahme des durch die kilometerlange Kaianlage verdrängten Werftverkehrs entstand auch das „Zuiderdok", ein ab 1882 angelegtes System dreier Docks von zusammen 4,1 ha Oberfläche (Abb. 4). Bedauerlicherweise verfüllte man noch 1968 dieses Dock und schuf eine bis heute öde wirkende Freifläche.

Die weitere Entwicklung führt in das nördlich der Stadt gelegene Terrain bis zur Grenze mit den Niederlanden und soll hier nur mit einer Übersichtskarte aus dem Jahr 1984 vorgestellt werden, die klarmacht, daß das als historisch erhaltenswert geltende Areal, ähnlich wie in Hamburg, nur einen flächenmäßig winzigen Teil der Gesamtanlage des Antwerpener Hafens bildet (Abb. 5).[7] Auch nach 1984 ging die Entwicklung weiter, bemerkenswert ist dabei das Übergreifen auf das linke Scheldeufer sowie die nunmehrige Erstreckung des Hafensystems bis zur Grenze mit den Niederlanden, hier vor allem in Form von langgestreckten Kanaldocks, so die Docks B1, B2 und B3 mit ihrer nördlichen Verbindung zur Schelde. Diese erfolgte 1967 mit dem Bau der 500 Meter langen „Zandvlietsluis" und der 1989 eröffneten Berendrechtsluis", der mit 500 zu 68 Metern größten Schleuse weltweit.[8]

Aufgeführt werden als erhaltenswerte Hafenstrukturen müssen aber noch neben den Hafenbecken, Umschlagseinrichtungen und Lagerhäusern die bestehen gebliebenen Einrichtungen des Hydrauliknetzes, das einst umfangreiche Hafenbezirke mit Kraftwasser versorgte, ähnlich den Anlagen in Liverpool, London, Bremen oder Hamburg. Unter den ursprünglich acht Anlagen ist als prominentestes und

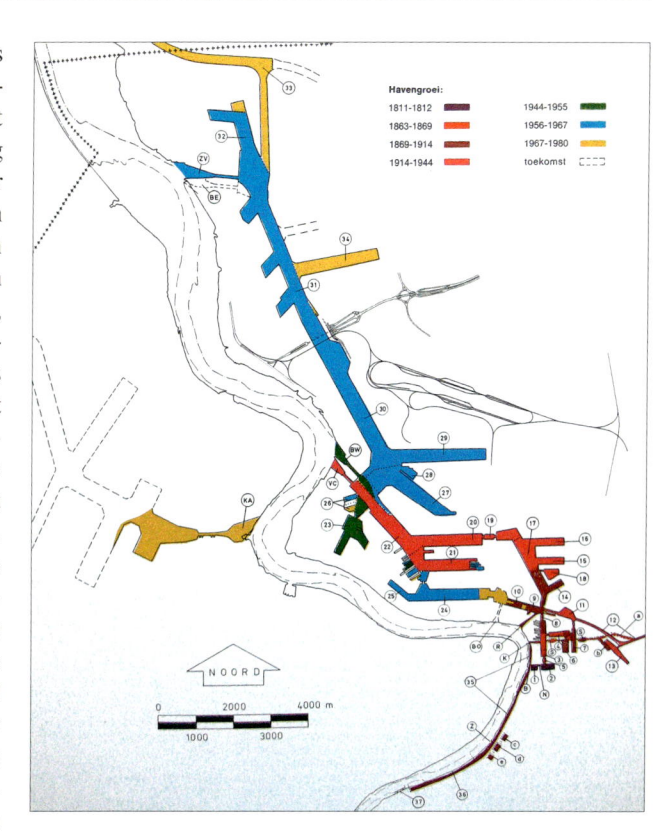

Abb. 5: Hafenentwicklung 1811–1980

Abb. 6: Zwischen Renaissance und Revolutionsarchitektur: das „Zuiderpershuis"

Abb. 7: Speisehaus für Arbeiter, 1907, heute Restaurant und Festsaal

architektonisch den europäischen Durchschnitt weit überragendes Beispiel das „Zuiderpershuis" zu nennen, die hydraulische Kraftzentrale am 1968/69 verfüllten Zuiderdok. Gleichzeitig mit dessen Anlage schufen der Ingenieur Paul de Witt und der Architekt Ernest Dieltiens in den Formen einer eklektizistischen Neorenaissance mit Anleihen bei der Revolutionsarchitektur die gewaltigen, die Akkumulatoren der Hydraulikanlage beherbergenden Doppeltürme mit ihrem löwenhauptbewachten Giebelportal (Abb. 6), das seit 1883 u. a. dem Betrieb von 156 Kranen, sechs Schleusen und drei Brücken diente. Bis 1977 versorgte die 1958 von Dampf- auf Elektroantrieb umgerüstete Druckzentrale noch die Nassaubrücke mit Antriebskraft. Zu diesem Zeitpunkt ging übrigens auch die letzte Londoner Hydraulikzentrale außer Betrieb, sie hatte so lange noch die Eisernen Vorhänge der Westend-Theater versorgt.[9]

1979 unter Schutz gestellt, dient der Bau des Zuiderpershuis seither vielfältigen kulturellen Zwecken, der Umbau erfolgte unter Wahrung des technischen Charakters der Anlage. Gegenstück zur Südzentrale ist das 1878 errichtet, ebenfalls erhaltene „Noorderpershuis" als reichverzierter Backsteinbau mit Sandsteinappliken und einem ebenfalls prominent in Erscheinung tretenden Akkumulatorenturm.

Ähnlich wie im Albertdock in Liverpool haben sich in Antwerpen auch die „Endstücke" des Hydrauliksystems teilweise erhalten, so im Lichthof des Lagerhauses St. Felix.

Erhaltungsbestrebungen

Um die Mitte der 1970er Jahre entwickelten sich unter englischem Einfluß auch in Antwerpen Bestrebungen zur Inventarisierung und Erhaltung von Zeugen der Hafengeschichte. Insbesondere der Direktor des Zentrums für Betriebsgeschichte an der katholischen Universität Antwerpen (Universitaire faculteiten Sint-Ignatius-UFSIA), Roland Baetens koordinierte einige an der Hafengeschichte interessierte und qualifizierte Protagonisten zu einem 1975 abgehaltenen Kolloquium, das mit Erhaltungsbestrebungen auf den rapidem Veränderungsdruck am Hafen reagierte.[10] Die Ergebnisse wurden breit publiziert. Mit der üblichen Verzögerung reagierte die Politik auf die wissenschaftlichen Impulse. Erst gegen Ende der 1970er Jahre evaluierte die Antwerpener Stadtplanung unter dem Arbeitsbegriff „Het Eilandje" nach dem Vorbild der von „free enterprise" getragenen Konzepte für die Verwertung der Londoner „Docklands" die Möglichkeiten einer Entwicklung des Kern-gebietes des historischen Hafens mit der 1974 geschlossenen Bonaparteschleuse. Gelegentlich der nationalen 150-Jahrfeiern richteten Stadtarchiv und Museumsdienst eine große historische Ausstellung aus, die die Hafenentwicklung ins Zentrum stellte und ihre Bedeutung für die Gesamtstadt eindringlich betonte.[11] Es sollte aber dann doch noch einmal gute zehn Jahre dauern, bis diese Impulse in entschiedeneres politisch-planerisches Handeln umgesetzt werden konnten.

Abb. 8: Die Front der Lagerhäuser entlang dem Willemdock, sämtlich neugenutzt

Unter dem Motto „Stad aan de Stroom" – Stadt am Fluß – wurde für das Eilandje ein Wettbewerb ausgeschrieben, den der katalanische Architekt und Städtebauer Manuel de Solà Morales gewann, der mit der Öffnung Barcelonas zum Meer seit Anfang der 1980er Jahre sein Verständnis für hafengeprägte Areale und ihre Integration in eine zukunftsoffene Stadtentwicklung unter Beweis gestellt hatte. 1994 wurde der Realisierung dieser Pläne aber erst einmal der finanzielle Riegel vorgeschoben. Wie häufig in Antwerpen, reagierte die Wirtschaft schneller als die Politik: Um „Willemdok" und „Napoleondok" wurden zahlreiche Lagerhäuser zu Büros und Veranstaltungsstätten umgewandelt, so wurde z. B. ein kirchenartiges ehemaliges Speisehaus für Dockarbeiter aus dem Jahr 1908 zu einem Restaurant mit angeschlossenem Festsaal (Abb. 7).

Zu einer Attraktion wurde auch ab 2001 die Konversion des ehemaligen Pumpenhauses am Nordende des Kattendijkdok zu einem Speiserestaurant, das den Dinierenden den Blick erlaubt auf die vollständig erhaltene Maschinenebene des 1918 errichteten Baues mit den drei 11 000 Kubikmeter Wasser pro Minute bewegenden Zentrifugalpumpen, die bis 1982 ihren Dienst taten.[12] Von hier aus bietet sich bis heute auch ein guter Beobachtungspunkt des Hafengeschehens ähnlich wie bei dem in Rotterdam aus dem ehemaligen Empfangsgebäude der Holland-Amerika-Linie seit 1993 entwickelten Hotel „New York".

Die 1872 gegründete „Red Star Line", in deren Auftrag das Pumpenhaus einst erbaut wurde, beförderte fast drei Millionen Auswanderer via Antwerpen in die neue Welt, eine Vergangenheit, die das am Rijnkaai projektierte Migrantenmuseum am ehemaligen Sitz der Schiffahrtsgesellschaft thematisieren soll – die Ballinstadt läßt grüßen.[13]

Eine als hochgradig gelungen zu bezeichnende Umnutzung erfuhr das 1858 von Architekt Felix Pauwels errichtete und nach Brand 1863 neuerbaute Lagerhaus „St. Felix", das für die Aufbewahrung von Kaffee, Wein und Tabak bestimmt war. Der siebengeschossige Backsteinbau besitzt auf Gußeisenstützen aufgelagerte Holzböden. 1912 übernimmt die Stadt bei bis 1950 gleichbleibender Bestimmung den Bau, was den noch bis in die 1980er Jahre deutlich wahrnehmbaren Geruch nach Tabak erklärt. Ab der Mitte der 1970er Jahre wird das Lagerhaus geräumt und steht – ab 1976 förmlich unter Denkmalschutz – leer. Nach Planungen seit 1998 fällt 2002 die Entscheidung, im Zuge der Aufwertung des „Eilandje"-Areals das Stadtarchiv im Entrepôt St. Felix einzurichten. Zusammen mit der Denkmalpflege finden die Architekten Paul Robbrecht und Hilde Daem Mittel und Wege, die mit hohen Gewichten belastbaren Ebenen unter Beibehaltung der zwischen 1863 und 1895 entstandenen Gesamtkonstruktion aus 815 hölzernen und 700 gußeisernen Stützen mit 18 Beton-Containern zu bestücken, die das Archivgut beherbergen. 2006 wird das Archiv eröffnet. Die zentrale überdachte Ladestraße wird für das Publikum geöffnet, im Erdgeschoß siedelt sich Gastronomie an.[14] Einen Hinweis auf die früher omnipräsente Antriebskraft der Hydraulik bieten hier historische Konsolkräne.

Abb. 9: Die eisernen Lagerschuppen entlang des 1877–1988 erbauten Scheldekais

Abb. 10: Königliches Lagerhaus von 1906, nach Abbruch 1989 im Jahr 2004 durch ein Apartmenthaus ersetzt

Abb. 11: Zentrale Hafen-Feuerwache, 1922, soll mit einem Zaha-Hadid-„Wolkenbügel" bekrönt werden

Bestimmt das Lagerhaus St. Felix zusammen mit weiteren, dem 19. und frühen 20. Jahrhundert entstammenden Lagerhäusern die flußabgewandte Längsseite des heute von Marinafunktionen bestimmten Willemdoks (Abb. 8), so widerfuhr seinem östlichen Ende ein weniger schonend mit der Vergangenheit verfahrendes Schicksal. Hier war 1830 ein mit dominantem Dreiecksgiebel versehenes Lagerhaus, das vom niederländischen König Willem I. eingeweihte „Koninklijke Entrepôt" errichtet worden, das nach Brand im Jahr 1902–1906 in historisierend-repräsentativen Formen, aber in einer frühen Eisenbetonbaubauweise und mit Eisenbahnanschlüssen verbunden, wiederaufgebaut wurde (Abb. 10).[15] Im Zuge des Konzepts von „Stad aan de Stroom" entstand ein vom amerikanischen Architekten Richard Meier verfaßter Masterplan zur Bebauung des „Eilandje". Trotz starken in- und ausländischen Protestes demolierte man 1989 das königliche Lagerhaus und ersetzte es 2004 durch einen von dem deutschen Architekten Hans Kollhoff entworfenen, in etwa der ehemaligen Kubatur folgenden Appartement-Neubau mit öd-monotonen Rasterfassaden.

Unter den dem Meierschen Masterplan folgenden vielen Hochhausbauten östlich der beiden historischen Docks ragt das im Mai 2011 eröffnete „MAS", das „Museum aan de Stroom" heraus. Dem Wettbewerbsgewinner von 1990, Manuel de Solà Morales folgend, entwickeln die beiden niederländischen Architekten Willem Jan Neutelings und Michiel Riedijk sein Konzept einer „kulturellen Achse" zwischen Stadtzentrum und altem Hafen weiter. Zwischen Napoleon- und Willemdock, anstelle des 1568 errichteten, 1893 abgebrochenen Hansehauses, steht nun ein mit rotem Sandstein verkleideter, kräftiger Turmbau, der trotz seiner turmartigen Vertikalwirkung der Monumentalität durch spiralförmig angeordnete Fensterbänder, die den Bau erheblich leichter erscheinen lassen, entkommt.

Die Wiederzugänglichmachung der sechs Kilometer langen Kaizone längs der Schelde mit ihren vielfach gereihten, offenen eisernen Lagerschuppen (Abb. 9) erfolgt, wie bereits mit dem Konzept „Stad aan de Stroom" 1990 angedacht, als Wiedergewinnung einer Verbindung zwischen Stadt und Schelde-Fluß nach dem Muster zahlreicher anderer europäischer Städte. Sie folgt den Festlegungen eines 2007 abgehaltenen Wettbewerbes, der gleichzeitig mit der Notwendigkeit in Verbindung steht, die Hochwasserschutzeinrichtungen zu verbessern. Weiter nördlich werden zwei relativ moderne Umschlageinrichtungen, der „Hangar 26" und der „Hangar 27", jeweils holzverkleidete Lagerhäuser auf schlanken Betonstützen seit dem Jahr 1993, dem Jahr, in dem Antwerpen Kulturhauptstadt Europas war, für vielfältige Zwecke zwischen Gastronomie, Ausstellung, Büros und Bildung genutzt.

Im Nordosten des Stadtzentrums entstand nach 1873 ein großer Rangierbahnhof, der im Zuge der Nordwanderung des Hafens ebenfalls nach Norden ausweichen mußte. Das brachgefallene Areal im Stadtteil Dam bildete lange eine Barriere für die Stadtentwicklung. Unter intensiver öffentlicher Beteiligung entstand hier bis 2009 nach Plänen der Wettbewerbssieger Bernardo Secchi und Paola Viganò ein 16 ha großer, dem Sport, der Freizeit und Veranstaltungen gewidmeter Park mit dem an den historischen Eisenbahnbetrieb gemahnenden Namen „Park Spoor Nord". Bemerkenswert ist hier die zitatweise Überlieferung einiger der alten Gleisverbindungen und der Einbezug historischer Bauten des ehemaligen Bahnbetriebes. Das Vorgehen erinnert an den Umgang mit dem Weinhändlerquartier Bercy in Paris vor dreißig Jahren, aber auch einen solchen mit Schwerindustriebrachen im Ruhrgebiet.

Ausblick

Der hier versuchte Überblick über das vielfältige Geschehen in der „Stadt am Strom", seit man sich Mitte der 1970er Jahre der Bedeutung des historischen Hafens bewußt geworden war, ist notwendig unvollständig. Zahlreiche Strukturen weiter im Norden des Stadtzentrums, z. B. im Bereich der „Montevideo"-Lagerhäuser werden unter Einbezug der Nutzung historischer Bauten weiterentwickelt. Auch die unvermeidliche Zaha Hadid steht mit einem Projekt des Aufsetzens eines ihrer schroff gezackten Gebilde auf ein gigantisches, 1922 errichtetes Feuerwehrgebäude[16] im nördlichen Hafenbereich am Kai Nr. 63 ante portas, das als künftiger Sitz der Hafenbehörde schier die Elbphilharmonie in den Schatten zu stellen droht. Das Projekt soll einen „landmark"-Charakter entwickeln, wobei man sich fragen kann, ob der neoklassische, vierflügelige Feuerwachen-Bau des Architekten E. van Averbeeke, der inspiriert war durch das 1893 abgebrannte, 1568 errichtete Gebäude der deutschen Hanse am Napoleondok, nicht bereits „landmark"-Charakter genug besitzt (Abb. 11).

Unter die Zukunftsprojekte zählt auch der Plan, das 1968 verfüllte „Zuiderdok" erneut zu öffnen. Dies würde der Ödnis des durch das Zuschütten entstandenen Stadtraums ein Ende bereiten und dem prächtigen Hydraulik-Palast des „Zuiderpershuis" wieder seinen angestammten Rahmen bieten, von der Attraktion einer Wasserfläche inmitten einer im Aufwind befindlichen Wohngegend einmal ganz abgesehen.

Unerwähnt bleiben müssen hier auch die zahlreichen und hochinteressanten Brückenbauten des Hafens, unter anderem signifikante Vertreter der sog. „Rollklappbrücken". Weiter gibt es auch historische, teils sogar noch in Betrieb befindliche Trockendocks und viele weitere mit dem Dockbetrieb zusammenhängende Hilfsbauten.

Antwerpens Umgang mit seinen historisch wertvollen Hafenteilen war nicht immer von planmäßigem Vorgehen geprägt. Das in beträchtlichem Umfang vorhandene Erbe wurde durch die Stadt erst in mehrfachen Anläufen gewürdigt und beplant, immer wieder waren es kommerzielle Aktivitäten, die einen Anfang setzten. Das Scheldeufer, das „Eilandje" genannte Quartier sowie die Zone nördlich und südlich hiervon entwickeln sich aber mittlerweile zu einem mehr oder weniger zusammenhängenden Gebiet, das von einer im europäischen Maßstab bedeutenden Vergangenheit des Hafens geprägt wird. Es wird versucht, eine maßvolle Balance zu halten zwischen Alt und Neu in einer Stadt, die nach langem Stillstand wirtschaftlich wieder prosperiert und damit auch beträchtlichen Druck auf das Baugeschehen ausübt.

Die historischen Hafenelemente verleihen Antwerpen ein deutlich wahrnehmbares und eigenständiges Gepräge. Durchaus selbstbewußt postuliert Antwerpen, allen voran der Marinejurist und Hochschullehrer Eric van Hooydonk, unter dem Begriff von der „Internationalen Hafenikone Antwerpen"[17] eine führende Stellung unter den historisch geprägten Hafenstädten der Welt. Sein 2007 erschienener Hafen-Überblick klassifiziert Antwerpen, Hamburg und Rotterdam wie folgt: Antwerpen – the Finest, Hamburg – the Proudest, Rotterdam – the Biggest. Ein stichhaltiges Argument für den hier vorgetragenen Stolz ist dabei neben dem durch den Zweiten Weltkrieg nur wenig zerstörten historischen Reichtum auch die unverminderte Fortdauer der aktuellen Bedeutung des Hafens.

Abstract

The Port of Antwerp

Since the Middle Ages Antwerp has been an important trading hub. Its importance grew in Napoleonic times: from 1863 till the end of the 19th century and, further downstream on the Schelde, from the 1950s.

Since the 1970s the historical port's significance for the city and its architectural heritage has been highlighted. Urban planning began to respond to this recognition in the „Het Eilandje" region, but only in a piecemeal fashion. Not before the 1990s did the comprehensive concept of „Stad aan de stroom" see the light of day which, together with a number of newly introduced competitions, served as a base for urban planning. In the vicinity of the two docks from Napoleonic times a zone for new uses was created which included historical elements such as the „Entrepôt St. Felix" which became the city archives. The northern part of the former shunting yard was converted into the „Park Spoor Noord" that has attracted a great deal of attention. The next step will be the reconversion of the „Zuiderdoks" which were filled in 1969. The Schelde Quays with their characteristic rows of cast iron sheds outside of the city centre will be the subject of additional competitions.

Bibliographie

ANTWERPEN. Tijdschrift van de stad Antwerpen XXI, April 1975, S. 2–68

CITY OF ANTWERP/STADSARCHIEF, Felixarchief, architecture and history, Antwerpen 2011

DE LLOYD, Dagblad voor Transporteconomie. Sondernummer zum Tag des offenen Hafens 24.–26. Juni 1983, S. 2

DEPAUW, Carl, De Antwerpse stapelhuizen tijdens de 19de eeuw: een architectuur-historisch onderzoek, in: Monumenten & Landschappen, 1986, S. 45

HIMLER, Albert, Verkeer. Goederenverkeer. De Haven, in: Stadt Antwerpen (Hrsg.), Antwerpen 1830–1980, Ausstellungskatalog Antwerpen 1980

HOOYDONK, Eric van, Antwerpen, internationaal havenikoon. Een visie op de identiteit van Antwerpen als havenstad, Löwen 2008

HOOYDONK, Eric van / Verhoeven, Patrick, The Ports Portable. A cultural travel guide to the port cities of Antwerp, Hamburg & Rotterdam, o. O. 2007

KENNES, H., u. a., Inventaris van het cultuurbezit in België, architectuur, Stad Antwerpen, fusiegemeenten, Bouwen door de eeuwen heen in Vlaanderen 3ND, Brüssel/Turnhout 1992

MAAK, Karin, Die Speicherstadt im Hamburger Freihafen. Eine Stadt an Stelle der Stadt, in: Jürgen Ellermeyer, Rainer Postel (Hrsg.), Stadt und Hafen. Hamburger Beiträge zur Geschichte von Handel und Schiffahrt (Arbeitshefte zur Denkmalpflege in Hamburg, Nr. 8) Hamburg 1985

PRIMS, F., Geschiedenis van Antwerpen, Antwerpen 1927–1949, 28 Bde., Registerband; Neuauflage Brüssel 1977

SIMMONS, Jack, St. Pancras Station, London 2003

STADT ANTWERPEN, Hafenroute, Antwerpen 1990, 7. Aufl.

TRINDER, Barrie, FÖHL, Axel, u. a., The Blackwell Encyclopedia of Industrial Archaeology, Oxford 1992, Stichwort Hydraulic Power, S. 341 f.

VIAENE, Patrick, Industriële Archeologie in België, Gent 1986

Abbildungsnachweis

Abb. 1: Nationaal Scheepvaartmuseum Antwerpen
Abb. 2: Technische Dienst Havenbedrijf, Antwerpen 1967
Abb. 3: Antwerpen. Tijdschrift der Stad Antwerpen XXI, 1975, S. 15
Abb. 4: Archief Zuiderpershuis
Abb. 5: De Lloyd, extra editie, 23. 6. 1983
Abb. 6 bis Abb. 11: Axel Föhl

* Die Abbildungsrechte sind vom Autor geklärt worden und liegen in dessen Verantwortung

[1] Floris PRIMS, Geschiedenis, 1977, Bd. 26, S. 567
[2] Albert HIMLER, in Stadt Antwerpen, 1980, S. 36
[3] Vgl. Jack SIMMONS, 2003, S. 26 ff.
[4] Vgl. Karin MAAK, 1986, S. 115 ff.
[5] HIMLER, a. a. O., S. 37
[6] DEPAUW, 1986, S. 45
[7] DE LLOYD, 1983, S. 14
[8] Vgl. dazu Hafenkarte von 1990
[9] Vgl. TRINDER, FÖHL, u. a., 1992, S. 341 f.
[10] Tijdschrift van de stad Antwerpen, 1975, S. 2–68
[11] Stad Antwerpen, 1980, S. 3–95
[12] KENNES, u. a. 1992, S. 124
[13] HOOYDONK, Ports Portable, 2007, S. 109 f.
[14] Stadsarchief, 2011, S. 5
[15] VIAENE, 1986, S. 99
[16] KENNES, a. a. O., S. 156
[17] HOOYDONK, 2008, S. 111

Paul Meurs

Rotterdam: from Port City to Harbor Landscape

The port of Rotterdam does not have and never had any warehouse-area comparable to the Speicherstadt in Hamburg. At first sight, the Speicherstadt looks like an architectonic work, based on the typology of dense and vertical warehouses, grouped together into one homogeneous urban complex. The water and public spaces seem to be carved out of these volumes, as streets in a historic city. Other port cities, like Liverpool, are more urban in their layout, having the docks and harbor basins as dominant public spaces within the urban tissue. Rotterdam partly has a similar urban layout, but from 1895 onwards developed into a different direction – creating a harbor landscape of such a scale and impact, that it gradually lost contact with the city. The 20th century port of Rotterdam developed as a maritime landscape, dedicated to transit cargo (without much need for storage on land). The warehouses that were developed stand as isolated objects in the wide and open landscape of the port.

There are some major developments that gave an impulse to the development of the port of Rotterdam in the late 19th and early 20th centuries. On the long run Rotterdam even became the biggest port in the world. The first development was the creation of a direct access to the sea, with the completion of the Nieuwe Waterweg in 1872. From that moment on ships could reach Rotterdam directly, without the need to pass locks or docks – as the tidal difference is only one meter. Second, the intensification of global commerce and the rapid industrialization in Europe meant a continuous growth in transportation and Rotterdam happened to be very well located. The city had and still has an enormous hinterland, including the German Ruhr-area. Rotterdam could develop into a gateway for raw materials (grain, coal, ore, wood and fuels), manufactured cargo and passengers. During the period 1880–1910 the port of Rotterdam was smaller than those of Hamburg and Antwerp. The city opted for a strategy to compete on speed, concentrating on the mechanization of handling goods and the rapid transit of cargo – which in many cases was directly loaded into smaller ships.

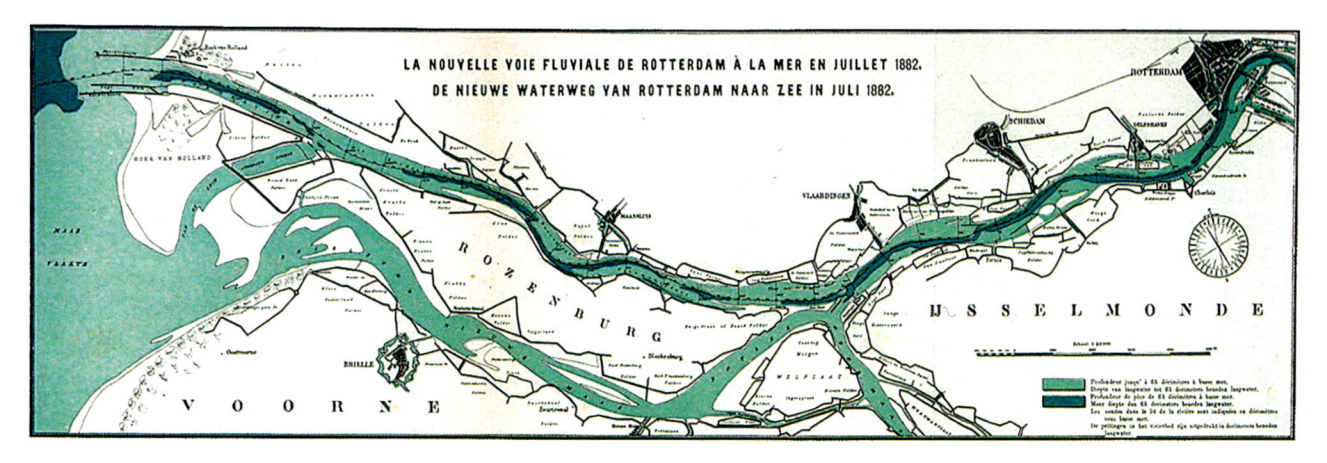

Figure 1: Nieuwe Waterweg, a direct connection from Rotterdam to the sea was completed in 1872

This was the third development: Rotterdam opted to become a transit harbor and this choice made the harbor competitive and successful. Innovations were achieved in mechanization, civil engineering, infrastructure – and incidentally in the construction of large scale warehouses (with big concrete spans).

Up to 1872, the harbors of Rotterdam were a part of the city and located on the northern bank of the river Maas. The so-called Watercity (the city built outside the protection of the dikes) showed a mixture of warehouses and quays with luxurious merchant's houses and the major public spaces of the city. The riverfront, stretching along the old city core and beyond, was the stage for harbor activities, as well as the place to be for the Rotterdammers. They could enjoy the beauty of the river in a series of linear parks and green public spaces. That is the reason why the riverfront is called Boompjes (Little Trees). After the inauguration of the Nieuwe Waterweg, the modernization of the harbor took mainly place at the south bank of the river Maas. There was plenty of space available here. In just a few years' time, the southern shores of the Maas faced a complete makeover. New harbors were dug out of the land – creating a functional landscape. The land between the water basins was covered with infrastructure of quays, rail, roads, storage areas and warehouses. The Koningshaven, Bin-

Figure 2: Haringvliet, one of the harbours in the watercity

Figure 3: Boompjes, riverfront as port area and urban public space

Figure 4: Boompjes, riverfront with the major green space downtown

nenhaven, Entrepothaven and Spoorhaven were realized from 1874 until 1879, creating a new island in the river Maas ('Noordereiland') and the area known as 'Kop van Zuid' ('Head of South'). The interventions were the fruit of public-private investments, initiated by the entrepreneur Lodewijk Pincoffs (1827–1911), founder of the Rotterdamsche Handelsvereening (Rotterdam Trade Association) in 1872. Part of these works was the construction of bridges by the city to connect the north bank with the Noordereiland and the south bank (1878). The trade association (RHV) opened office and storage buildings in 1879. The offices were in the 'Poortgebouw' ('gate-building'), designed by the architect J.S.C. van de Wall. For storage, the RHV opened entrepot 'De vijf werelden' ('The Five Worlds'), a large complex of warehouses for coffee, tea, sugar and spices, designed by T.J. Stieltjes. The harbor developments initiated by the trade association RHV differ from the older harbor installations at the north bank, creating a world on its own, opposed to the old city. But the investments never paid off. The enterprise collapsed in the same year, 1879, in financial scandals. Pincoff fled to America. The possessions in the harbor were passed over to the municipality in 1882.

The failure of the private trade association RHV made the city of Rotterdam reconsider its role in the development of the port and municipalize the harbor. G.J. de Jongh, director of public works from 1879 until 1910, took up the public task to extend the harbor. He is seen as the visionary and main architect of the modernization of Rotterdam around 1900. De Jongh was a leading figure in the city, leaving a strong mark on today's appearance of both the city and the port of Rotterdam. He was responsible for the construction of a number of harbors west of the inner city: Parkhaven (1893), Jobshaven (1908) and Schiehaven (1909). For De Jongh, the economy of the harbor was this important, that he did not hesitate to bring railroads into the richer residential areas. For him, Rotterdam was a city of work, where money had to be earned. Those who longed for historic cities should go to Delft or Gouda, those who wanted luxurious living areas should better move to The Hague – as he publicly stated. The main achievements of De Jongh were realised at the south bank, with the creation of harbor basins of unprecedented dimensions: Rijnhaven (1895, 28 ha), Maashaven (1905, 60 ha) and Waalhaven (1907–1930, 310 ha). Pictures of these ports in the pre-war period show that the innovation was in the harbor itself, where very large cranes and floating elevators could handle bulk cargo very quickly and reload it in river vessels.

The main warehouses constructed over the first decades of the 20th century are large in scale, but remained isolated landmarks in the landscape of the port. Some examples are the Blauwhoedenveem in the Jobshaven (architect J.J. Kanters, 1912) and the Grainsilo in the Maashaven (JP Stok, 1906; extension M. Brinkman, 1919). The Wilhelminapier, created by the construction of the Rijnhaven, is perhaps the most urban part in this area. No wonder, as it housed the major passenger terminals of the city, operated by the Holland America Line (HAL). The space along the pier is divided in lower warehouses along the Rijnhaven and the river Maas, separated by a row of higher warehouses in the centre. The head of the pier contains the former head office of the HAL, built from 1901 until 1919 (architect C.B. van der Tak). Other buildings at the Wilhelminapier are Pakhuis Meesteren (warehouse, 1940), Las Palmas (workshops HAL, 1950–1953) and the passenger terminal Rotterdam (1946–49).

The destruction of Rotterdam during the Second World War affected the inner city and many of the port installations. After the war, the port expanded westwards towards the sea and eventually into the sea with the construction of the Maasvlakte, more than 40 kilometres away from the city centre. The main large-scale warehouses of the pre-war period survived the war, but meanwhile have lost their original function. Most of them are now listed monuments and have been refurbished into apartments (Blauwhoedenveem, Poortgebouw), a shopping area (Entrepotgebouw), discothèques (Maassilo), a hotel (HAL head offices) or a cultural centre (Las Palmas). New urban development has come to the Kop van Zuid and some other harbor areas – bringing the city into the former areas of the port. If a comparison with the Speicherstadt would have to be made, only the area of the Kop van Zuid and the Wilhelminapier can be taken in consideration. But both in layout, age of warehouses, urban fabric, architecture and current heritage this region differs from the Hamburg case.

Abstract

Rotterdam:
Von der Hafenstadt zur Hafenlandschaft

Der Hafen von Rotterdam hat nie ein mit der Hamburger Speicherstadt vergleichbares Lagerhausviertel besessen. Bereits auf den ersten Blick bildet die Speicherstadt eine architektonische Einheit. Dafür sorgt die Typologie der verdichteten und vertikalen Lagergebäude, die sich zu einem homogenen städtischen Ensemble zusammenfügen. Wasserflächen und öffentliche Räume in der Speicherstadt wirken, als seien sie aus den Gebäudekomplexen herausgeschnitten – wie Straßen in einer historischen Stadt. Andere Hafenstädte wie Liverpool sind stärker urban angelegt, da Docks und Hafenbecken hier den öffentlichen städtischen Raum strukturell beherrschen. Rotterdam hat eine ähnliche städtische Struktur, jedoch ging die Entwicklung dort seit 1895 in eine andere Richtung: In Rotterdam wurde eine Hafenlandschaft von so großen und eindrucksvollen Ausmaßen geschaffen, dass der Kontakt mit der Stadt allmählich verloren ging. Der Rotterdamer Hafen hat sich dann im 20. Jahrhundert zu einer maritim geprägten Industrielandschaft weiter entwickelt, die hauptsächlich dem Umschlag von Transitwaren gewidmet ist (so dass wenig Bedarf an Lagerkapazitäten an Land bestand und besteht). Die vorhandenen Lagerhäuser stehen jeweils isoliert in der großen offenen Fläche des Hafengeländes.

Bibliography

DEKKING, H. (editor) The Port of Rotterdam, the continental centre of world-shipping and world-commerce, one of the most flourishing cities in the world; published on the occasion of the Olympiade, Rotterdam 1928

EDZES, Harry; Vrij Entrepot, 'n stukje geschiedenis van Rotterdam, Rotterdam 1979

KLERK, Len de; LAAR; Paul van der; and MOSCOVITER, Herman, Jongh, G. J. de; havenbouwer en stadsontwikkelaar in Rotterdam, Rotterdam 2008

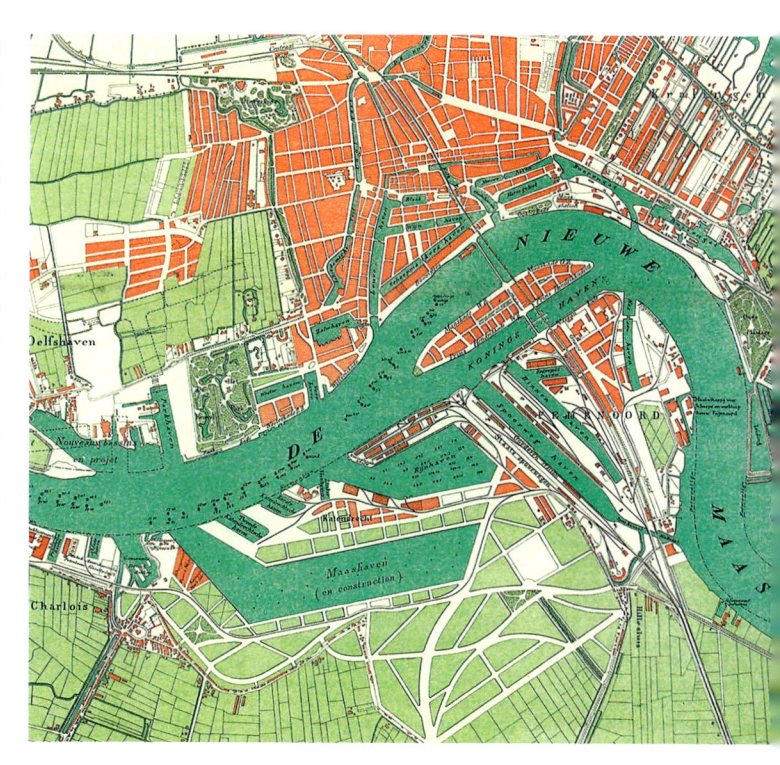

Figure 5: Rotterdam in 1898, showing the extensions of the port on the southern bank of the river

Figure 6: De Hef and the Koningsbrug, two bridges in the Koningshaven

Figure 7: Rijnhaven, 1910

Figure 8: Office building Holland Amerika Lijn, Wilhelminapier

Figure 9: Rijnhaven, grain silos Nederlandsche Veem, built in 1900

Figure 10: Warehouse Jobsveem, constructed in 1912

LAAR, Paul van der, Stad van formaat, vol.2, geschiedenis van Rotterdam in de negentiende en twintigste eeuw, Zwolle 2000

MEURS, Paul, De moderne historische stad, ontwerpen voor vernieuwing en behoud 1883–1940, Rotterdam 2000

MEYER, Han; De stad en de haven, stedebouw als culturele opgave in Londen, Barcelona, New York en Rotterdam: veranderende relaties tussen stedelijke openbare ruimte en grootschalige infrastructuur, Rotterdam 1996

L. C. J. van Ravesteyn, Rotterdam in de negentiende eeuw, de ontwikkeling der stad, Rotterdam 1924

M. M. A. Voogd and W. Ringlever, Album de Rotterdam, Rotterdam 1911

Sources of illustrations

Fig. 1: VOOGD, A. and RINGLEVER, W., Rotterdam 1911
Fig. 2 to Fig. 10: Collection SteenhuisMeurs

Axel Priebs

Der Südliche Freihafen in Kopenhagen

Einleitung

Wenn es um historische Lagerhausensembles geht, hat Kopenhagen viel zu bieten. Den Inneren Hafen prägt eine Reihe von Lagerhäusern aus dem 18. Jahrhundert, die überwiegend gut erhalten und sinnvoll genutzt sind. Auch der Bereich des heute nur noch zu einem kleinen Teil von der Marine genutzten innenstadtnahen Bereichs Holmen weist eine Reihe gut erhaltener maritimer Gebäude und Anlagen auf. Wahrscheinlich hat gerade diese Präsenz des maritimen Erbes mitten in der Stadt dazu geführt, dass der Bereich des Südlichen Freihafens, der erst seit dem ausgehenden 19. Jahrhundert entstanden ist, deutlich weniger öffentliche Aufmerksamkeit erfahren hat. Für die Bewertung der Hamburger Speicherstadt, die ebenfalls am Ende des 19. Jahrhunderts entstanden ist und durchaus Bedeutung für die Kopenhagener Debatte um die Hafenentwicklung hatte, ist aber gerade der Südliche Freihafen von großem Interesse. Die thematischen und zeitlichen Verbindungen waren der Grund dafür, dieses Beispiel für die Hamburger Konferenz „Stadtentwicklung zur Moderne – Zur Entstehung großstädtischer Hafen- und Kontorhausquartiere" aufzuarbeiten. Dabei soll zum einen die Entstehung des Südlichen Freihafens und deren Rahmenbedingungen nachgezeichnet werden und zum anderen der Frage nachgegangen werden, wie die Entwicklung dieses Hafenbereichs seit dem Niedergang des traditionellen Stückgut- und Massengutumschlages verlaufen ist.

Vorgeschichte des Freihafens[1]

Die historische Keimzelle des Kopenhagener Hafens liegt nahe dem Stadtzentrum in der Nähe des heutigen Schlosses Christiansborg. Eigentliche Hafenanlagen entstanden erst seit dem 16. Jahrhundert. Insbesondere in der langen Regierungszeit von König Christian IV. (1588–1648) wurden der erste geschützte Kriegshafen am Zeughaus, der durch Kanäle und Hafenbecken charakterisierte neue Stadtteil Christianshavn sowie die Marinestation Holmen gebaut. In der blühenden Handelsperiode in der zweiten Hälfte des 18. Jahrhunderts wurden beidseits des Inneren Hafens, d. h. sowohl an der Uferlinie der Frederiksstad als auch auf Christianshavn, monumentale Lagerhäuser errichtet. Mit der 1864 erfolgten Verlagerung der Maschinenfabrik B & W nach Christianshavn zog auch die Industrie in den Bereich des Inneren Hafens ein, wo sie über viele Jahrhunderte das Stadtbild bestimmte.

Sowohl die geringe Wassertiefe als auch die völlig unzureichende Zahl der Liegeplätze im Hafen erzeugten in der zweiten Hälfte des 19. Jahrhunderts dringenden Handlungsbedarf. Deswegen wurden zwischen Kaufmannschaft, Hafenverwaltung und Regierung intensiv die Ausbau- und Erweiterungsmöglichkeiten des Hafens erörtert. 1862 lag ein von Hafenbaumeister Lüders und Hafenkapitän Garde erarbeiteter erster Hafenplan vor. Dieser enthielt umfangreiche Maßnahmen zur Leistungssteigerung des Innenhafens, die in den Jahren 1865–80 realisiert wurden[2]. Allerdings stieß der alte Innenhafen damit endgültig an seine Kapazitätsgrenzen, womit nur noch eine Hafenerweiterung außerhalb des die Altstadt umgebenden Wallringes in Frage kam. Um dieses Projekt und im Zusammenhang damit die schon früher diskutierte Anlage eines Freihafens zu erörtern, wurde eine Kommission eingesetzt. Diese schlug 1881 den Bau eines Freihafens nördlich des Kastells, d. h. außerhalb des Wallringes, vor. Allerdings blieb diese Empfehlung ohne konkrete Folgen; vielmehr wurden auch weiterhin andere Lösungen diskutiert – so etwa ein Hafenausbau nördlich des Marinehafens Holmen unter teilweiser Überplanung der militärischen Anlagen[3].

Zu einer Entscheidung führte erst der Druck, der sich in den 1880er Jahren durch Entwicklungen außerhalb des Königreichs aufbaute[4]. Insbesondere ließen die Planung und die 1888 begonnene Realisierung des Nord-Ostsee-Kanals quer durch Schleswig-Holstein einen drastischen Bedeutungsverlust des Kopenhagener Hafens befürchten, weil die Route durch den Kanal deutlich kürzer und gefahrloser war als die Passage um das Skagerrak und durch den Öresund. Damit zeichnete sich ab, dass Kopenhagen ins Abseits der Handelsströme geraten würde. Gleichzeitig sorgten der verstärkte Ausbau des Hamburger Hafens und die dortigen Pläne für die Anlage eines Freihafens (im Zusammenhang mit dem ebenfalls im Jahr 1888 realisierten Anschluss Hamburgs an das Zollgebiet des Deutschen Reichs) für Unruhe in dänischen Wirtschaftskreisen, weil es im 19. Jahrhundert gerade erst gelungen war, den Einfluss Hamburgs auf die dänische Wirtschaft zurückzudrängen. Vor dem Hintergrund dieser aus dänischer Sicht bedrohlichen Entwicklungen kam es nach einer entsprechenden Denkschrift des Kopenhagener Hafenkapitäns im Jahr 1888 zu einem Parlamentsbeschluss, mit dem die erforderlichen Mittel für vorbereitende Untersuchungen zur Anlage eines Freihafens in Kopenhagen bereit gestellt wurden. Drei Jahre später beschloss das Parlament dann auch den eigentlichen Bau des Kopenhagener Freihafens.

Bau des Freihafens[5]

Nach nur gut dreijähriger Bauzeit konnte der Freihafen 1894 seiner Bestimmung übergeben werden. Er gilt als

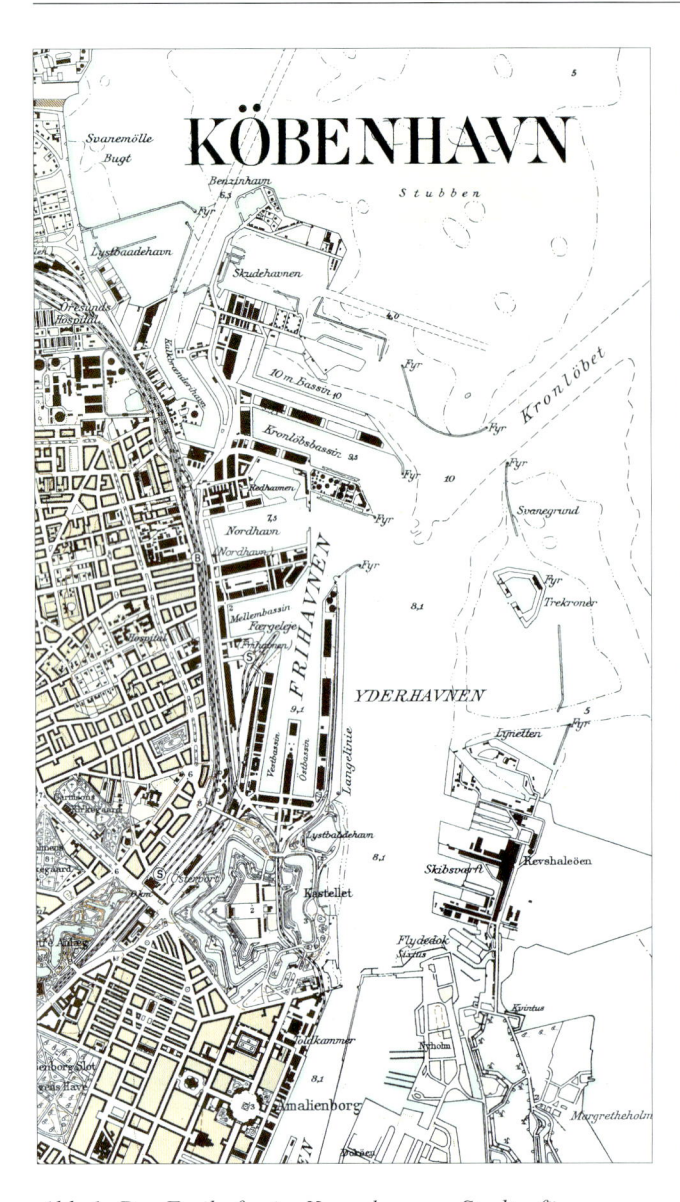

Abb. 1: Der Freihafen im Kopenhagener Stadtgefüge (1964), Ausschnitt aus der Topographischen Karte (Originalmaßstab 1 : 20 000 verkleinert)
(© Kort & Matrikel-styrelsen (621)

Abb. 2: Luftbild des Kopenhagener Freihafens Blickrichtung Westen, (Juni 1936), Foto: Det kgl. Bibliothek, Kopenhagen

„eine der bestgeglückten Anlagen in der Geschichte des Kopenhagener Hafens", der nach umfassender Abwägung verschiedener Gesichtspunkte und Wettbewerbsbeiträge als durchdachte Einheit geplant und angelegt wurde[6]. Angelegt wurde der Freihafen vor der alten Küstenlinie in Anschluss an den Stadtteil Østerbro entsprechend den damals aktuellen technischen Erkenntnissen in Form von Fingerpiers. Neben zwei großen, angenähert in Nord-Süd-Richtung verlaufenden Hafenbecken wurden zwei kürzere Becken in Ost-West-Richtung angelegt (Abb. 1 und 2). Der Freihafen ist damit ein klassisches Beispiel des stückgutorientierten Hafentyps im Industriezeitalter, in dem der Umschlagbetrieb einschließlich der Behandlung und Zwischenlagerung der Waren ein arbeitsintensiver Prozess war. Zur Unterscheidung von den nördlichen Hafenerweiterungen wird nachfolgend – entsprechend der offiziellen Diktion – der älteste Teil des Freihafens als „Südlicher Freihafen" bezeichnet.

Die Hochbauten des Freihafens lassen sich in Lagerhäuser, Büro- und Funktionsgebäude sowie Industriegebäude unterscheiden. Bedeutendster Architekt in der ersten Bauphase des Freihafens war Vilhelm Dahlerup, der durch den Hafenbaumeister H. C. V. Møller unterstützt wurde. Dahlerup entwarf die beiden südlichen Lagerhäuser auf der Ostmole, das Elektrizitätswerk am Dampfærgevej sowie das markante Silolagerhaus auf der Mittelmole (Abb. 3). Der Langelinieschuppen auf der Ostmole wurde von Dahlerup gemeinsam mit H. C. V. Møller entworfen. Dieser Schuppen diente zusammen mit dem Zollgitter der Abgrenzung des Freihafens nach Osten, außerdem wurde über das Dach des ca. 250 m langen Schuppens auch die insgesamt ca. 1 km lange Langelinie-Promenade angelegt. Diese war der Kopenhagener Bevölkerung im Zusammenhang mit den Diskussionen um den Bau des Freihafens als Ersatz für den verloren gegangenen Zugang zum Öresund an der Stelle des Freihafens versprochen worden. Östlich der Promenade wurden Anlegestellen am tieferen Fahrwasser vorgesehen, die heute von großen Kreuzfahrtschiffen genutzt werden. Für die meisten – eher etwas im Hintergrund gelegenen – Büro- und Funktionsgebäude des Freihafens, darunter das große Zollamt, zeichnete der Architekt Erik Schiødte verantwortlich. Die Gebäude der Gründungsphase wurden weitestgehend von der Freihafengesellschaft selbst in Auftrag gegeben, was – trotz unterschiedlicher Architekturstile von Dahlerup und Schiødte – zu einem sehr einheitlichen Erscheinungsbild des frühen Freihafens führte[7]. In der zweiten Bauphase des Freihafens trat besonders der Architekt Frederik L. Levy in Erscheinung, der um 1900 drei große Gebäude auf dem Westkai (Amerikakai) entwarf, nämlich das Manufakturhaus, ein wegen der Ausprägung seines Baukörpers als „Domkirche" bezeichnetes Lagerhaus (Pakhus A) sowie ein weiteres sehr ausdrucksstarkes Silolagerhaus (Silopakhus B), das wegen seiner zwei Türme seit geraumer Zeit ebenfalls als „Domkirche" bezeichnet wird (Abb. 4). Unter den seinerzeit entstandenen Gewerbebauten am westlichen Rand des Freihafengebiets ist das 1901 errichtete markante Fabrikgebäude der Fa. Nordisk Fjer besonders erwähnenswert.

Zur unverzichtbaren Infrastrukturausstattung des neuen Freihafens gehörte natürlich auch der Anschluss an das Eisenbahnnetz[8]. Besondere Bedeutung hatte die 1894 erfolgte Anlage des Fährbetts für die Eisenbahnfähre Kopenhagen – Malmö durch die Dänischen Staatsbahnen (DSB), die im folgenden Jahr ihren Betrieb aufnahm. Dabei entstand auch ein kleines, aber markantes Bahnhofsgebäude, das von Heinrich Wenck, dem Architekten des Kopenhagener Hauptbahnhofs, entworfen wurde (vgl. Abb. 13). 1895 wurde auch eine Gleisverbindung vom Freihafen zum Inneren Hafen (Søndre Toldbod) in Betrieb genommen. Parallel zu dieser Strecke verlief ein Gleis, das für den Rangierbetrieb auf den Freihafenkais erforderlich war. Nach einem aus heutiger Sicht höchst brutalen Eingriff in die östliche Wallanlage wurde das Kastell fortan durch eine eingezäunte Gleistrasse zerschnitten. Südlich der Freihafenbecken entstand eine kleine Gleisharfe, die auch den schiefwinkligen, den Gleisanlagen angepassten Grundriss eines 1916 durch Ove Huus entworfenen Lagerhauses erklärt (Abb. 5).

Trotz moderner Anlagen und internationaler Werbung verlief die Entwicklung des Umschlaggeschäfts zu Beginn zögerlich und verstärkte sich erst Anfang des 20. Jahrhunderts, woraufhin eine neuerliche Hafenerweiterung in nördlicher Richtung in Angriff genommen wurde. In den Jahren 1915–18 entstand das Kronløbsbassin, 1919–22 das Orientbassin. Waren schon in der ersten Bauphase des Freihafens, etwa auf der nördlichen Ostmole, auch deutlich einfachere, flache Lagerschuppen gebaut worden, wurden ähnliche Gebäude auch im Zuge der nördlichen Erweiterung des Freihafens errichtet.

Strukturwandel und politische Diskussion zur Revitalisierung [9]

Erste Anzeichen eines tief in das Stadtgefüge eingreifenden Strukturwandels waren im Kopenhagener Hafen bereits kurz nach dem 2. Weltkrieg erkennbar, als der schmale, kanalartige Nyhavn seine Umschlagfunktionen verlor. Hier wurde 1971 das erste Hotel in einem Lagerhaus eröffnet. Eine zunehmende Deindustrialisierung führte seit den 1960er Jahren dazu, dass im Inneren Hafen und später im Südhafen Brachflächen entstanden, die für neue Nutzungen zur Verfügung standen. Auch die 1967 erfolgte Verlagerung des Fleischexports nach Esbjerg sowie die Einstellung der DFDS-Fährlinien nach Ålborg und Århus im Jahr 1970 trugen dazu bei, dass der Innere Hafen wesentliche Funktionen verlor. Den wohl weitreichendsten Einschnitt für den Hafenumschlag in allen älteren Hafenbereichen aber brachte das Aufkommen des Containertransports seit Mitte der 1960er Jahre mit sich, da der konventionelle Stückgutumschlag seine vormalige Bedeutung verlor und die hierfür eingerichteten Umschlaganlagen, Lagerhäuser und Lagerschuppen nicht mehr den neuen logistischen Ansprüchen genügten.

In der Folge wurde in Kopenhagen immer intensiver über die Umstrukturierung und erneute Inwertsetzung der nur noch extensiv genutzten Flächen entlang des Inneren Hafens sowie des unweit gelegenen Südlichen Freihafens diskutiert. Während eine interessierte Öffentlichkeit mit Unterstützung kritischer Planer und Architekten ein Gesamtkonzept einforderte und der Stadt ein inkrementalistisches Vorgehen vorwarf, versuchte sich die politisch sehr selbständig agierende Hafenverwaltung der stadtplanerischen Einflussnahme zu

Abb. 3: Der Kopenhagener Freihafen mit dem Dahlerup-Silolagerhaus auf der Mittelmole um 1912 (rechts)

Abb. 4: Der Kopenhagener Freihafen mit den Gebäuden von Levy auf dem Amerikakai um 1921 (links)

Abb. 5: Das ehemalige Lagerhaus von Ove Huus (rechts) und Funktionsgebäude im südlichsten Bereich des Freihafens (1991)

Abb. 6: Die 4 Lagerhäuser auf der Ostmole (1991)

Abb. 7: Verfallene Dahlerup-Lagerhäuser auf der Ostmole (1990)

entziehen. Die Diskussion eskalierte in den 1980er Jahren, als die Hafenverwaltung der finanziell ausgebluteten Stadt einige Kaigrundstücke zu hohen Marktpreisen anbot und in anderen strategischen Bereichen langfristige Pachtverträge mit wenig stadtverträglichen Nutzern abschloss. Über mehr als ein Jahrzehnt blockierten sich Hafen und Stadtplanung vor den Augen einer kritischen Öffentlichkeit gegenseitig, wobei sich in dieser Zeit punktuell in einigen Teilbereichen des Hafens aber schon neue Nutzungen etablierten. Ein wichtiger Durchbruch bezüglich der Umstrukturierung der Hafenfläche ergab sich erst aus den Empfehlungen einer 1988 eingesetzten Hafenkommission[10]. Danach sollten die eigentlichen Hafenaktivitäten im Nord- und Osthafen konzentriert werden, während in den übrigen älteren Hafenbereichen auch Wohnnutzungen möglich wurden, was zuvor sowohl von wesentlichen Akteuren der Stadt als auch vom Hafen abgelehnt worden war.

Das Unbehagen über das Agieren der Hafenverwaltung führte Anfang der 90er zu einer Gesetzesinitiative, mit der brachgefallene Hafenflächen in eine privatrechtliche Entwicklungsgesellschaft überführt werden sollten. Da dieser Weg politisch nicht durchsetzbar war, wurde 1993 eine andere Richtung eingeschlagen. Verabschiedet wurde nun ein Gesetz, mit dem die Hafenverwaltung zusätzlich zum Hafenbetrieb auch für die Entwicklung der aufgegebenen Hafengebiete verantwortlich wurde. Damit erhielt sie einen breiten finanziellen Handlungsspielraum, musste sich aber fortan innerhalb des von der Stadtplanung vorgegebenen Rahmens bewegen. Dass diese Weichenstellung richtig und erfolgreich war, zeigte sich darin, dass sowohl Stadt als auch Hafenverwaltung in der Folge ein hohes Tempo bei der Umstrukturierung der aufgegebenen Hafenflächen vorlegten. Nachdem die Stadt in ihrem Stadtentwicklungsplan 1993 die „Stadt am Wasser" zu einem der vier vorrangigen Planungsthemen erklärt hatte, legte die Hafenverwaltung 1994 ihre Überlegungen für die im Gesetz geforderte Umnutzungsstrategie vor und zeigte damit, dass sie ihre neue Rolle schnell gefunden hatte. Seitdem hat sie zwar auch aufgegebene Grundstücke an andere Nutzer verkauft, in zentralen Flächen aber selbst den Part als Projektentwickler im Sinne der Stadtentwicklung übernommen und erhebliche Investitionen auf nicht mehr hafenwirtschaftlich genutzten Flächen getätigt. Dieses starke Engagement ist natürlich auch darauf zurück zu führen, dass die Hafenverwaltung mit den erzielten Renditen dringend benötigte Mittel für die Investitionen im eigentlichen Hafenbereich erwirtschaften konnte.

Die Umgestaltung des Südlichen Freihafens

Der Bereich des Südlichen Freihafens ist ein sehr markantes Beispiel dafür, dass die aufgegebenen Kopenhagener Hafengebiete nach Jahren einer zermürbenden Diskussion und des weitgehenden Stillstandes tatsächlich innerhalb relativ kurzer Zeit in eine dauerhafte urbane Nutzung überführt wurden. Wie bereits erwähnt, hatte der Niedergang des Stückgutverkehrs auch in Kopenhagen in den 1960er Jahren eingesetzt. Schon damals musste die älteste Bausubstanz des Freihafens zwei schwere Einbußen hinnehmen: Nachdem 1965 das als „Domkirche" bezeichnete Lagerhaus von Levy abgerissen worden war, wurde drei Jahre später das Silolagerhaus von Vilhelm Dahlerup auf der Mittelmole durch Brand zerstört und anschließend ebenfalls abgerissen. Die vier Lagerhäuser auf der Ostmole wurden zunehmend extensiv und seit 1975 gar nicht mehr genutzt. Sie bildeten zwar ein interessantes, geschlossenes Ensemble (Abb. 6), der jeweilige architektonische Wert der einzelnen Gebäude wurde aber unterschiedlich bewertet. Dies zeigte sich auch darin, dass der Magistrat der Stadt Kopenhagen im Jahr 1977 für zwei dieser Lagerhäuser eine Abrissgenehmigung erteilte. Anlass war die Absicht der Hafenverwaltung, das östliche Hafenbecken zu verfüllen und auf der dadurch gewonnenen Fläche den Umschlag japanischer Importfahrzeuge zu konzentrieren. Dieses Vorhaben scheiterte jedoch an den Vorschriften des neuen Planungsgesetzes, das für dieses Vorhaben einen Lokalplan (entspricht einem Bebauungsplan nach deutschem Recht) voraussetzte. Die Hafenverwaltung brachte ihre Verärgerung über diese Entwicklung dadurch zum Ausdruck, dass sie auf der Ostmole den Verfall für sich arbeiten ließ[11], wovon die verwaisten und zum Teil verfallenden Anlagen die ganzen 1980er Jahre hindurch ein trauriges Zeugnis ablegten (Abb. 7).

Da sich die hafenwirtschaftlichen Aktivitäten bereits in den Nordhafen verlagert hatten, konnte der größte Teil des Südlichen Freihafens im Frühjahr 1985 förmlich aus dem Freihafengebiet ausgegliedert werden, wobei die Flächen jedoch im Besitz der Hafenverwaltung blieben. In diesem Jahr entbrannte eine heftige Diskussion um die zukünftige Funktion dieses stadtnahen, über den Bahnhof Østerport gut erschlossenen Gebietes. Nunmehr wurden in der Presse Pläne des Architekten Jørn Utzon für ein Hotel- und Kongresszentrum mit 70 000 qm Bruttogeschossfläche an Stelle der vier Lagerhäuser auf der Langeliniemole vorgestellt. Diese Pläne stießen bei der Bevölkerung insbesondere im angrenzenden Stadtteil Østerbro auf erheblichen Widerstand. Einige Vereine und Initiativen sahen in dem Verlust der hafenwirtschaftlichen Funktionen nämlich die Chance, den dicht bebauten Stadtteil wieder zum Wasser zu öffnen und attraktive Naherholungsbereiche zu schaffen. Die Initiative „Langelinie den Kopenhagenern", eine Dachorganisation von 33 Initiativen und Vereinigungen, konzentrierte sich in der Diskussion u. a. auf die Zukunft der leer stehenden Lagerhäuser. Bei Teilen der Kommunalpolitik und der Verwaltungsspitze stieß sie mit diesem Anliegen auf offene Ohren. Die gleiche Magistratsabteilung, die acht Jahre zuvor dem Abriss von zwei Lagerhäusern zugestimmt hatte, legte 1986 – unter neuer politischer Leitung – einen Vorschlag für die Erhaltung der vier Lagerhäuser vor, in dem der beabsichtigten wirtschaftlichen bzw. touristischen Nutzung eine Inwertsetzung für die Kopenhagener Bevölkerung gegenübergestellt wurde. In engem Kontakt mit den Initiativen wurden Überlegungen entwickelt, die vier Lagerhäuser jeweils als Kreativ-/Musikzentrum, als Ökohaus, als internationales Zentrum sowie als Kinderhaus zu nutzen. Für den Fall des Abrisses von zwei Lagerhäusern wurden auch Pläne für den Bau eines Museums für moderne Kunst sowie eines als „Orangerie" bezeichneten Restaurants entwickelt[12].

In der Diskussion um die vier Lagerhäuser setzte sich schließlich der für die Stadtplanung zuständige Oberbürgermeister als Promotor des Utzon-Projektes gegenüber seiner Magistratskollegin durch, die für den Erhalt und die genannte Nachnutzung der Lagerhäuser plädierte. Damit war die Bahn frei für das Utzon-Projekt, das dem 1987 eingeleiteten Lokalplanverfahren für den größten Teil des Südlichen Freihafens zugrunde lag. Zwar hatte Utzon sein Projekt inzwischen so weit umgearbeitet, dass Dahlerups Lagerhaus ganz und die übrigen Lagerhäuser teilweise in die Planungen integriert wurden, doch musste das gesamte Vorhaben nunmehr wegen eines Dissenses zwischen der Stadt und dem Umweltministerium als Genehmigungsbehörde des Stadtentwicklungsplans erst einmal auf Eis gelegt werden – die Lagerhäuser auf der Ostmole blieben weiter ungenutzt stehen, die Kais wurden gelegentlich als Liegeplatz für Schiffe, jedoch ohne eigentliches Umschlaggeschäft, genutzt.

Erst 1989 kam es zu einer Einigung zwischen Stadt und Umweltministerium im Genehmigungsverfahren für den Stadtentwicklungsplan. In der Anlage zum Genehmigungserlass wurden wesentliche Eckpunkte für die Umnutzung

Abb. 8: Neubauten auf der Mittelmole (1998)

des Südlichen Freihafens skizziert, wie sie später dann auch im Bebauungsplan konkretisiert wurden[13]:

– Freihaltung des Südlichen Freihafens von Hafenfunktionen südlich des Atlaskais im Hinblick auf die angestrebte Lokalisierung anderer urbaner Nutzungen
– Änderung der Nutzung auf der Westseite des Südlichen Freihafens von „Hafennutzung" in „Wohnen/Dienstleistungen"
– Verhältnis von Wohnungen und Dienstleistungen im gesamten Bereich im Verhältnis von 40 zu 60, um eine Durchmischung zu erreichen
– Erhaltung des großen Dahlerup-Lagerhauses auf der Ostmole und dessen Einbeziehung in die Umstrukturierung
– Eröffnung der Möglichkeit zur Anlage einer durchgehenden Straßenverbindung am Westrand des Südlichen Freihafens

Nach der Genehmigung des Stadtentwicklungsplans war das Utzon-Projekt für die Langelinie – u. a. wegen eines Wechsels bei den Kapitaleignern des Langeliniekonsortiums – nicht mehr aktuell. Im November 1990 wurde ein neuer Lokalplanentwurf vorgelegt, der die genannten Eckpunkte sowie die Pläne des ØK-Konzerns aufgriff, auf der Mittelmole eine neue Konzernzentrale zu bauen; dieser Plan wurde im Dezember 1991 in der Stadtvertretung beschlossen[14]. Obwohl von Experten im Jahr 1993 noch einmal die Unterschutzstellung aller vier Lagerhäuser auf der Ostmole empfohlen worden war, entschied die Stadt im selben Jahr endgültig, nur Dahlerups Lagerhaus sowie die Langeliniepromenade unter Denkmalschutz zu stellen. Die übrigen drei Lagerhäuser wurden im Herbst 1993 abgerissen[15]. Zu erwähnen ist, dass die Hafenverwaltung in dem vom Bebauungsplan nicht erfassten westlichen Freihafenbereich sowie für den Südbereich im Jahr 1991 einen eigenen Plan für die Umstrukturierung (vorrangig für Büros und hafenorientierte Dienstleistungen) vorlegte.

Abb. 9: Neue Wohngebäude am Indiakai (2011)

Abb. 10: Blick auf den Südlichen Freihafen mit der ehemaligen Nordisk Fjer-Fabrik (links) und dem DFDS-Bürogebäude vorne rechts (2007)

Büronutzungen, dazu aber auch Wohnungen (Abb. 8). An der Südseite der beiden ehemaligen Hafenbecken, wo ebenfalls die Lagerschuppen abgerissen worden waren, konnten Anfang 1994 die ersten Wohngebäude auf dem Indiakai fertiggestellt werden (Abb. 9).

Nachdem 1994 am Westrand des Freihafengeländes eine neue 4-spurige Entlastungs- und Erschließungsstraße entlang des früheren Freihafenzauns (deswegen die Bezeichnung „Gittervej") ihrer Bestimmung übergeben worden war, konnte die Umstrukturierung des westlichen Hafengeländes zielstrebig vorangetrieben werden. Für neue Flächenpotenziale sorgte insbesondere die Entfernung der umfangreichen Gleisanlagen, nachdem der Danlink-Fährverkehr nach Schweden wegen der Eröffnung der Öresundbrücke eingestellt worden war. Hier entstanden mehrere Neubauten, aber auch einige früher hafenwirtschaftlich bzw. industriell genutzte Gebäude wurden für eine dauerhafte und hochwertige Nutzung umgebaut (Abb. 10). Besonders bemerkenswert sind die Umnutzung des von Levy gebauten Silolagerhauses und des großen Fabrikgebäudes von „Nordisk Fjer" für Bürozwecke.

Auf der Ostmole, wo nur das große Dahlerup-Lagerhaus erhalten geblieben war, wurden Wohngebäude errichtet. Zu erwähnen ist, dass nach der Einstellung des Bahnverkehrs im Freihafen auch die Restaurierung der zerstörten Wallanlagen des Kastells möglich wurde. Der erste Abschnitt der Restaurierung erfolgte 1988, der zweite 1998. Heute zeugen nur noch die Freiräume zwischen den Gebäuden im südlichsten Teil des Freihafengeländes sowie eine Brücke über die ehemaligen Gleisanlagen südlich des Kastells von dem starken Eingriff in die historische Bausubstanz, der angesichts der Umstände beim Bau des Freihafens Ende des 19. Jahrhunderts vertretbar erschien.

Gebäudesubstanz

Nach der weitestgehend abgeschlossenen Umstrukturierung des Südlichen Freihafens stellt sich die Frage, wie mit der Besonderheit dieses Ortes und der historischen Bausubstanz umgegangen worden ist. Ein Blick auf das Gelände, wie es sich heute darstellt, zeigt zuerst einmal die gründliche Umstrukturierung. Unzweifelhaft ist der Bereich des Südlichen Freihafens ein lebendiges Quartier mit zahlreichen Büroarbeitsplätzen und Wohnnutzung geworden. Bei den Gebäuden dominieren auf den ersten Blick die Neubauten der beiden letzten Jahrzehnte, die unterschiedlich sensibel in die Umgebung eingefügt wurden.

Nachdem Ende 1991 durch den Lokalplan 197 die planungsrechtlichen Voraussetzungen für die Umstrukturierung und Revitalisierung des Südlichen Freihafens geschaffen worden waren, wurden nach jahrelangen Diskussionen um das richtige Konzept schnell tatsächliche Veränderungen erkennbar. Als erstes wurde im Mai 1992 mit der Verbreiterung der Mittelmole begonnen, auf der zuvor die noch bestehenden Lagerschuppen abgerissen worden waren. Hier entstanden mit dem großen Gebäudekomplex der ØK

Während bei den massiven Gebäuden auf der Mittelmole und im südlichen Hafenrandbereich überwiegend gelbe Bau- und Verblendmaterialien verwendet wurden, orientieren sich die Neubauten auf der Ostmole sowohl in den Proportionen als auch mit der Wahl von roten Ziegeln als Verblendmaterial an dem erhaltenen Dahlerup-Lagerhaus. Dieses wurde einer außerordentlich sorgfältigen und aufwändigen Restaurierung unterzogen, dient einer Behörde als Bürohaus und stellt ein Schmuckstück der Ostmole dar[16] (Abb. 11). Auch die Räumlichkeiten unter der Langelinie-Promenade wurden renoviert und in Wert gesetzt. Als Infrastruktur der sich stürmisch entwickelnden Kreuzschifffahrt, aber auch als Attraktion für Spaziergänger und Touristen wurden hier Läden und Restaurants eingerichtet.

Eine besonders interessante Umnutzung erfuhr das erwähnte, von F. L. Levy entworfene Silolagerhaus auf dem Amerikakai. Da die vertikalen Strukturen des Kornsilos nicht mit anderen Nutzungen kompatibel waren, wurde das Gebäude in seinem Mittelteil „entkernt". Während hier 1995 „nach innen" ein heutigen funktionalen Gesichtspunkten entsprechendes Bürogebäude für einen kommunalen Spitzenverband entstand, konnte „nach außen" das markante Profil des Gebäudes bewahrt werden. Wie erwähnt, wird das Gebäude mit seine beiden markanten Türmen heute häufig als Domkirche des Freihafens bezeichnet, obwohl dieser Beiname ursprünglich für das erwähnte und schon früh abgerissenes Nachbargebäude des selben Architekten geprägt worden war. Etwas beeinträchtigt wird der positive Ansatz beim Silolagerhaus durch die sehr heterogene Bebauung in der Nachbarschaft des Amerikakais, die insgesamt einen sehr unruhigen Eindruck dieses Bereichs zumindest von der Kaiseite vermittelt (Abb. 12). Etwas verloren wirkt nach seiner Translozierung auch das weiter nördlich gelegene kleine Freihafen-Bahnhofsgebäude zwischen den großen Neubauten (Abb. 13).

Aus heutiger Sicht ist es zu bedauern, dass schon in den 1960er Jahren zwei besonders markante Lagegebäude verloren gingen. Auch über die Erhaltungswürdigkeit des Ensembles der vier Lagerhäuser auf der Ostmole würde heute möglicherweise anders geurteilt als in den 1990er Jahren. Trotz des Verschwindens dieser historischen Bausubstanz und der umfassenden Nutzungsänderungen weist das Freihafengelände allerdings noch eine größere Zahl von Gebäuden aus der Gründungszeit auf. Neben einigen umgenutzten Lager- und Fabrikgebäuden sind insbesondere die Funktions- und Bürogebäude im südlichsten Teil des Geländes erwähnenswert (Abb. 5 und 14). Zu nennen sind das alte Zollamt, das ehemalige Post- und Telegrafenamt, das frühere Freihafen-Elektrizitätswerk sowie das Capella-Gebäude, eines der nicht sehr zahlreichen vom Jugendstil geprägten Gebäude in Kopenhagen. Das DFDS-Bürohaus am Amerikakai (Abb. 10) ist ebenso wie das schiefwinklige und für Bürozwecke umgenutzte Lagerhaus von Ove Huus (Abb. 5), dessen östliche Fassade ca. 5 Meter länger ist als die die Westfassade, ein Schmuckstück des Geländes.

Zu fragen ist auch, ob der maritime Charakter des Geländes nach den Umgestaltungen erhalten geblieben ist. Natürlich lässt sich schon durch die nur wenig verkleinerte Wasserfläche der ehemaligen Hafenbecken der ursprüngliche Nutzungszweck des Geländes nicht verleugnen. Die neuen Gebäude selbst nehmen diese historischen Nutzungen aber nur wenig auf. Für den Charakter des Geländes muss es sicher als Glücksfall gesehen werden, dass auch nach Aufgabe der Eisenbahnfähre die Funktion des Südlichen Freihafens als Fährhafen erhalten wurde. Seit der Verlagerung der Fähren nach Oslo aus dem Inneren Hafen legen hier regelmäßig große Kraftfahrzeug-Fährschiffe an, was den maritimen Charakter des Quartiers ebenso stärkt wie die Segelboote, die vor allem im Sommerhalbjahr die großen Wasserflächen beleben (Abb. 15). Auch die großen Kreuzfahrtschiffe, die auf der Ostseite am Langeliniekai anlegen, sind aus vielen Teilen des Südlichen Freihafens gut sichtbar.

Abb. 11: Restauriertes Dahlerup-Lagerhaus mit benachbarten Neubauten auf der Ostmole (2010)

Abb. 12: Neu- und Altbauten auf dem Amerikakai; in der Bildmitte das umgebaute ehemalige Silo Lagerhaus von Levy (auch „Domkirche des Freihafens" genannt) (2007)

Abb. 13: Etwas verloren wirkt das translozierte Freihafen-Bahnhofsgebäude vor der Kulisse der Neubauten (2007)

Bilanz

Obwohl noch eine Reihe von Gebäuden der Ursprungsphase erhalten ist, hat der Südliche Freihafen in den beiden letzten

Abb. 14: Blick von Süden auf den Freihafen mit dem vierspurigen Gittervej. Gebäude von links: altes Zollamt, Domkirche, Manufakturhaus, ehem. Elektrizitätswerk, Capella-Haus (2007)

Abb. 15: Blick auf Amerikai und Oslo-Fähre (2011)

Jahrzehnten seinen Charakter gründlich verändert. Bereits in den 1960er Jahren wurde das Ensemble der Gründungszeit durch den Abriss von zwei besonders markanten Gebäuden empfindlich beeinträchtigt. Da die entscheidenden stadtentwicklungspolitischen Diskussionen in einer besonders konjunkturschwachen Zeit geführt wurden, hatte die Stadt nicht die erforderlichen Mittel, um mit öffentlichen Investitionen und Nutzungen wirksam Einfluss auf die künftige Richtung der Entwicklung Einfluss zu nehmen. Obwohl die Umgestaltung des Hafens durchaus ein breit diskutiertes öffentliches Thema war, stand beim Südlichen Freihafen der Erhalt der Hafenanlagen und -gebäude aus der Gründungszeit nicht im Mittelpunkt der Diskussion. Dies dürfte daran liegen, dass der historische Hafen Kopenhagens im Zentrum der Stadt liegt und dort eine größere Zahl sehenswerter ehemaliger Lagerhäuser aus dem 18. Jahrhundert erhalten ist, die im öffentlichen Bewusstsein offenbar einen deutlich höheren Stellenwert hatten als die Gebäude des Südlichen Freihafens aus dem späten 19. und frühen 20. Jahrhundert.

Mit dem erneuten Wachstumsschub der Stadt ab 1992/93 erfuhr der Südliche Freihafen eine rasante Entwicklung, wodurch er zum Pionier der Hafenrevitalisierung in Kopenhagen avancierte. In der Folge kam es zu einer tiefgreifenden Umgestaltung, in der einige der noch verbliebenen Lagerhäuser und -schuppen aus den frühen Jahrzehnten verschwanden und durch Neubauten mit massiver Nutzungsdichte ersetzt wurden. Obwohl die Architektur der Wohn- und Bürogebäude an der Südseite und auf der Mittelmole mit ihren Proportionen und dem für diesen Bereich untypischen gelben Ziegelstein nicht unumstritten ist und die zusätzliche Barrierewirkung des vierspurig ausgebauten Gittervej kritisiert wird, ist hervorzuheben, dass nach langen Jahren der Diskussion und der Kritik an den Umstrukturierungsplänen ein neuer Stadtteil mit guter Funktionsmischung entstanden ist, der durchaus zeigt, dass eine Revitalisierung aufgegebener, stadtnaher Hafengebiete sinnvoll und möglich ist. Kehrseite der Entwicklung ist, dass die alte Bausubstanz nur noch in wenigen Teilbereichen den Charakter des Südlichen Freihafens bestimmt.

Abstract

The Southern Free Port of Copenhagen

The Copenhagen Free Port is characterised by finger-shaped piers. It was built in the years 1891 till 1894, the decision in its favour being sped on by the building of the Kiel Canal and the Free Port of Hamburg which, it was feared, would weaken Copenhagen's role as a trading hub. The first buildings to be erected in the new Free Port (two warehouses, the large shed on Langelinje on the East Pier, the imposing grain silo on the Middle Pier plus a power plant) were commissioned by the Free Port Association and designed by the renowned architect Vilhelm Dahlerup. The other warehouses, administrative buildings and production facilities were erected by other developers. Around the turn of the century the architect Frederik L. Levy designed three very conspicuous buildings for the Western part of the port, i.e. the so-called Manufakturhus, a warehouse that came to be known as the "Free Port Dome" plus a silo-warehouse-building.

The advent of container transport in the Sixties saw the Southern part of the Free Port and most of its buildings lose their function. In 1965 the „Free Port Dome" was demolished, the grain silo plus warehouse on the Middle Pier followed in 1968 after a devastating fire. In 1977, the City authorised the demolition of two of the four remaining warehouses on the Eastern Pier which were no longer in use. The Port Authority wanted to fill the Eastern Dock thus reclaiming the land and allowing for the building of a large-scale transhipment facility for imported cars. However, planning permission was never granted and the Port Authority left the area to decay. Jørn Utzon's plans for a hotel and conference center on the Langelinie-Mole were not put into practice either.

The restructuring of the Southern Free Port did not start before 1991 when the first office blocks and residential buildings were erected. In 1993 the recommendation that all four warehouses should be be protected was reiterated, but as a result of the significant pressure put on the authorities by potential investors it was decided only to list the biggest warehouse, i.e. Dahlerup Warehouse plus Langelinie Promenade. The other three warehouses were torn down. The Dahlerup Warehouse was thoroughly renovated. In 1995, when developments in the Western part of the port were beginning to take shape, the central part of the grain silo which was to house up-to-date offices was completely gutted. The characteristic shell of the building, however, was preserved.

While some of the buildings from the original building phase have survived, the Southern Free Port has changed fundamentally in character over the last two decades.

Literaturverzeichnis

BISGAARD, Holger, Københavns genrejsning, o.O. 2010.
JENSEN, Sigurd, SMIDT, Claus M.: Rammerne sprænges. Københavns historie, bd. 4 1830–1900, København 1982.
LORENZ, G.: Københavns Havn og dens udvikling. København 1929.
MADSEN, Hans Helge: Østerbro før og nu – og aldrig. København 1993.
MØLLER, H.C.V.: Kjøbenhavns Havns Udvikling i Fortid og Nutid samt Forslag til Havnens fremtidige Udvidelse. Kjøbenhavn 1917.
PLANSTYRELSEN (Hrsg.): Bygninger og anlæg i Københavns Havn. Registrant nr. 2. København 1988.
POULSEN, John: Byens Baner. Jernbanen i København i 150 år. København 1997.
PRIEBS, Axel: Strukturwandel und Revitalisierung innenstadtnaher Hafenflächen – das Fallbeispiel Kopenhagen. In: Erdkunde (46) 1992, S. 91–103.
PRIEBS, Axel: Die Entwicklung des Innenhafens von Kopenhagen im Kontext der historischen Stadtgeographie. Entstehung, Differenzierung und Transformation einer maritimen Stadtlandschaft. In: Siedlungsforschung Bd. 15, 1997, S. 131–152.
SMIDT, M. Claus: Christianshavn. København før og nu – og aldrig, bd. 7, København 1989.
THOSTRUP, Sven: Holmen og Orlogsværftet. København før og nu – og aldrig, bd. 8, København 1989.
VOSS, Henry: Dahlerups Pakhus i Frihavnen – et fortidsminde med fremtid. Søborg 1999.

Abbildungsnachweis

Abb. 1: Geodætisk Institut 1964
Abb. 2: Foto: Det kgl. Bibliothek, Kopenhagen
Abb. 3: Ansichtskarte um 1912
Abb. 4: Ansichtskarte um 1921
Abb. 5 bis Abb. 15: Fotos: Prof. Dr. Axel Priebs

* Die Abbildungsrechte sind vom Autor geklärt worden und liegen in dessen Verantwortung.

---

[1] Vgl. ausführlicher PRIEBS, Die Entwicklung, 1997
[2] LORENZ, Københavns Havn, 1929, S. 14
[3] THOSTRUP, Holmen, 1989, S. 143
[4] JENSEN/SMIDT, Rammerne, 1982, S. 245
[5] Vgl. ausführlich zur Baugeschichte des Freihafens: Planstyrelsen, Bygninger, 1988, und MADSEN, Østerbro, 1993
[6] Planstyrelsen, Bygninger, 1988, S. 30
[7] Planstyrelsen, Bygninger,1988, S. 37
[8] vgl. zu den folgenden Ausführungen POULSEN, Byens baner, 1997
[9] Vgl. hierzu PRIEBS, Strukturwandel, 1992
[10] BISGAARD, Københavns genrejsning, 2010, S. 95
[11] MADSEN, Østerbro, 1993, S. 265
[12] MADSEN, Østerbro, 1993, S. 265
[13] Schreiben des Umweltministeriums vom 9.10.1989, Anlage zur Genehmigung des Kopenhagener Stadtentwicklungsplans, veröffentlicht in der Drucksache 644/89 des Kopenhagener Magistrats vom 23.10.1989
[14] Københavns Kommune, Lokalplan Nr. 197
[15] MADSEN, Østerbro, 1993, S. 266
[16] VOSS, Dahlerups Pakhus, 1999

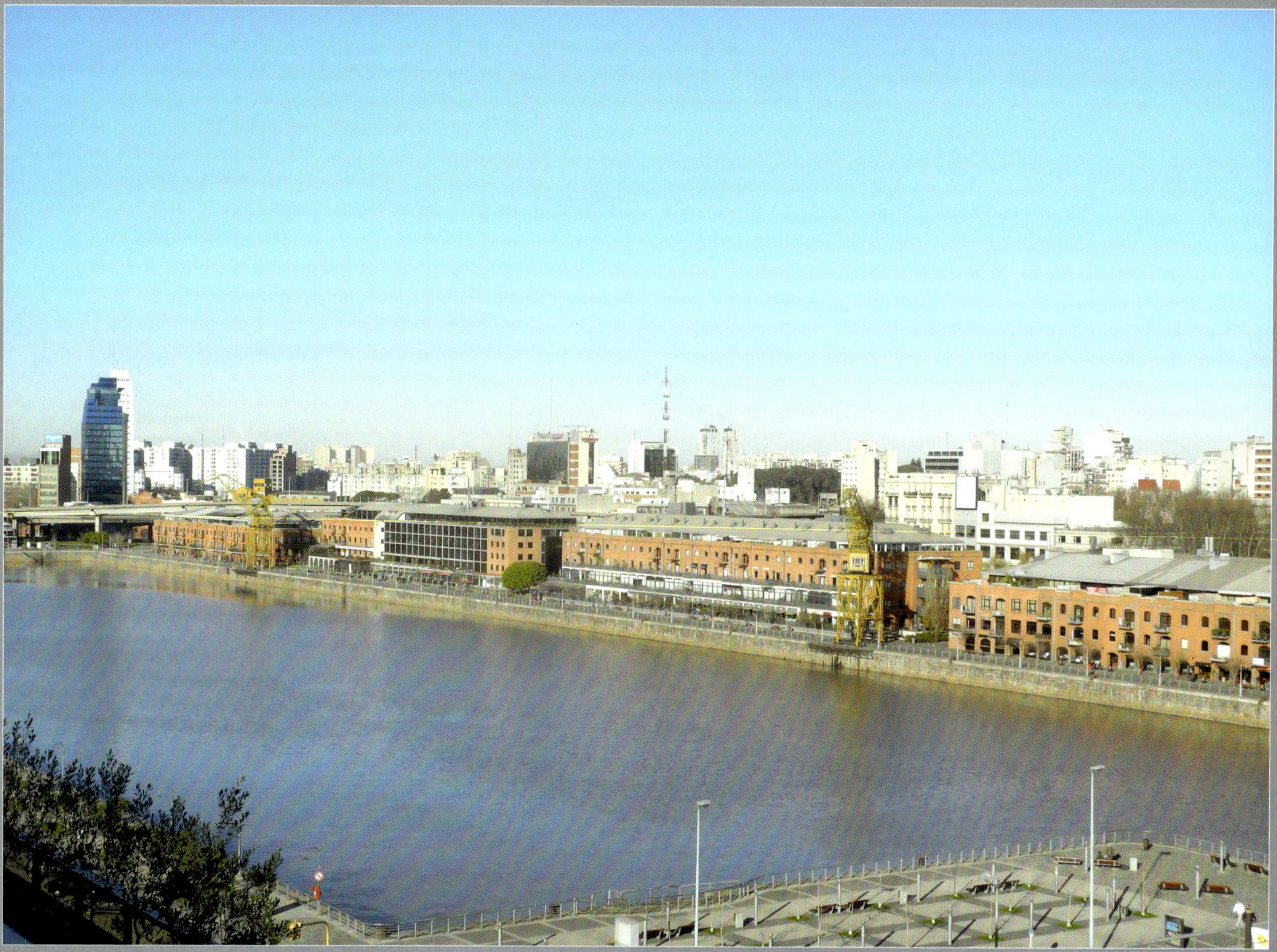

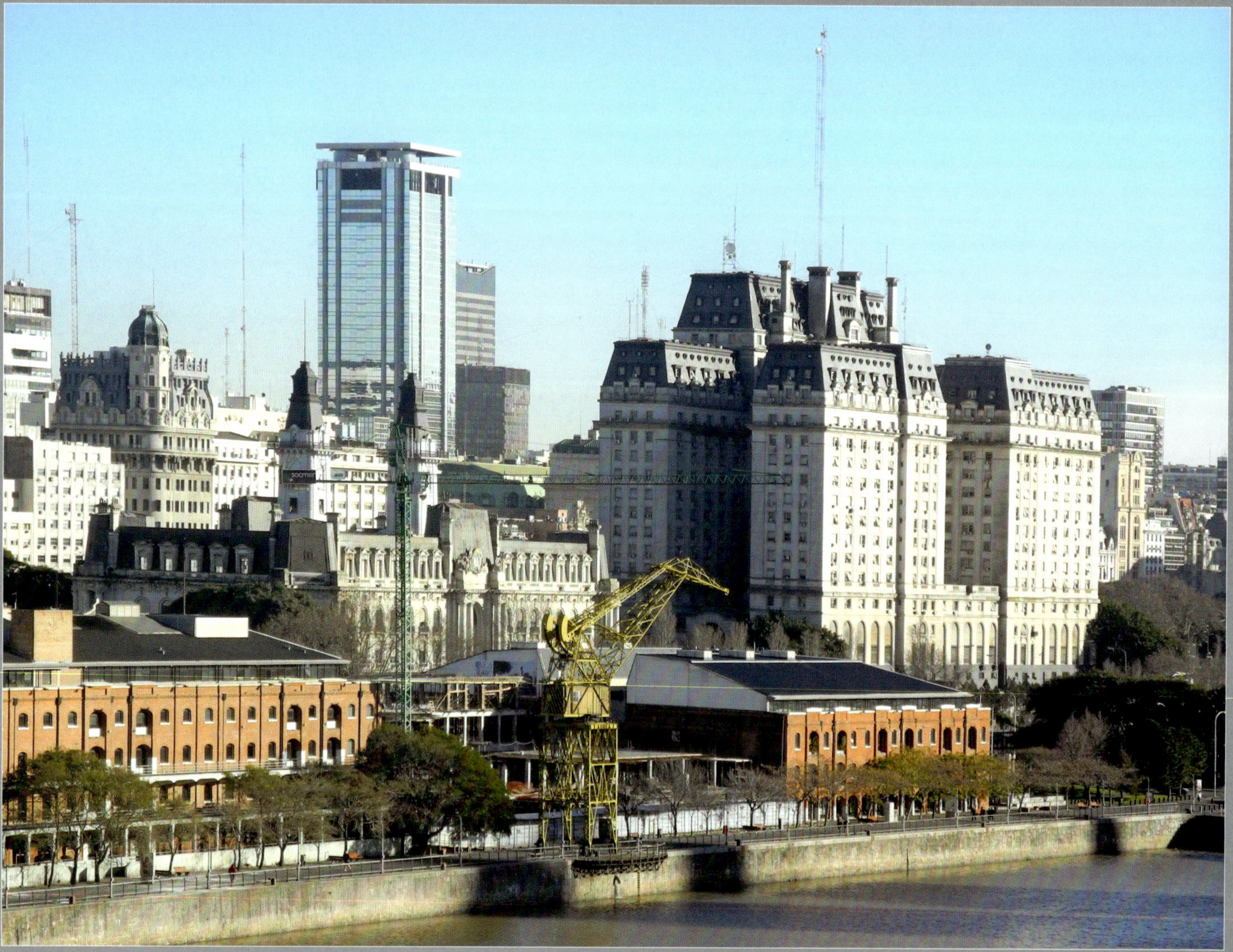

Speicher- und Lagerkomplexe außerhalb Europas
Warehouse and Storage Districts Beyond Europe

Buenos Aires

Sara E. Wermiel

Shaped by Function: Boston's Historic Warehouses

This paper discusses the history of warehouses built before 1920 in Boston, Massachusetts, U.S.A., with a focus on those in the Fort Point Channel Landmark District (FPCLD). The FPCLD is a roughly 55-acre (22.3 hectares) area in the South Boston neighborhood of the city, and it contains 85 had the leading port. Boston's port remained one of the busiest through the nineteenth century, and in the latter nineteenth century, port facilities – including piers, warehouses, and railroad service – expanded in the South Boston area. In the twentieth century, other North American ports grew

Figure 1: Warehouses in Fort Point Channel District, photo 1925

historic warehouses and lofts, which were built between 1880 and 1930. This is the largest collection of warehouses in a definable area in the city, and it probably is also one of the most intact warehouse districts in the United States. Before discussing the history of the FPCLD, the paper presents an overview of the development of Boston's old harbor and the distinctive warehouse blocks that were once a prominent feature of it. Until the mid-eighteenth century, Boston was the most populous North American town and

to outrank Boston. Today, most of the wharves and facilities of the old harbor have disappeared. In South Boston, the warehouses and lofts of the FPCLD survive. Although they now serve purposes other than storage and manufacturing, these warehouses and lofts continue to physically represent a time when maritime commerce and industry dominated the city's economy. These building feature a special form of heavy-timber interior framing, adapted from a regional construction tradition.

Boston's Historic Port and Its Warehouses

Boston is a commercial city, established where it was because of the harbor. In 1630, Europeans settled permanently at the small peninsula that became Boston. The harbor was the town's hub: streets with names like Fish Street, Ship Street, Sea Street, and Mackrill (mackerel) Lane (after a fish that was abundant in colonial times) radiated from the harbor and followed its edge. Over time, filling in around the periphery of the peninsula – a process of making land – obliterated the outlines of Boston's original topography, including that of the old harbor. As the new land was developed for contemporary, and not necessarily maritime, purposes, the physical connections between the harbor and the city broke down. Today, although some of the old streets remain, the destinations are gone, so the logic of their locations has been obscured. As author and historian William H. Bunting noted, "Few Bostonians today view the harbor as an integral geographical part of the city, or much less – as in the past – view the city as a component of the harbor."[1] Many of the structures and facilities built for the traffic of the old port have been demolished. Those that remain, no longer serving their original purposes, are like fish that missed the outgoing tide, left stranded on a beach.

Among the old structures stranded in the modern city is a type that was once a vital component of the port: the warehouse. Warehouses were built in the earliest days of European settlement and eventually lined Boston's streets and wharves. Today, after demolition and new construction, few streets in the old port area contain enough historic fabric to suggest that past time.

One relatively large and intact district of former warehouses and loft buildings still stands, and it is the focus of this paper.[2] The district, commonly called the Fort Point Channel District, is located on the eastern shore of a body of water, the Fort Point Channel, in the South Boston neighborhood of the city. (Fig. 1) Boston's port expanded into South Boston in the latter part of the nineteenth century. The land on which the historic warehouses stand was made by a private company, the Boston Wharf Company.[3] Boston Wharf Company not only made the land there, but subdivided it into lots, planned and built the streets, and erected most of the buildings on it.

Because of its large extent, and the good state of preservation of the original buildings, the Fort Point Channel District admirably represents the look and feel of Boston's waterfront of the late nineteenth and early twentieth centuries. For this reason, it has been listed on the National Register of Historic Places (2004), and it is the first non-residential area in Boston to be designated a local landmark district.[4] Like the warehouses that once filled Boston's old harbor area, the buildings of the Fort Point Channel District have lost their original reasons for being. But the buildings are being adapted and reused for new purposes: residential, office, retail, and cultural. The warehouses and lofts of the District contain features that were common to warehouses as a building type, but also some that were special to Boston warehouses in the period in which they were built: specifically, their heavy timber interior framing was an adaptation of a regional construction tradition called "slow-burning construction."

This paper discusses the old harbor and its warehouses, and then treats the development of the Fort Point Channel District, its warehouses and lofts, and their special characteristics.

The Colonial Port

The Port of Boston is an ocean port, located at the head of Massachusetts Bay, on the Atlantic Ocean. The place that became the city of Boston, originally a small peninsula, was settled by English colonists in 1630. (Fig. 2) The peninsula featured an excellent harbor, described as "safe and capacious …, sheltered from the ocean by clusters of well wooded islands."[5] Also, the Bay had deep (for that period) natural channels, and the harbor islands created many sheltered anchorages. While settlements sprouted up around Massachusetts Bay, Boston became the trading center. It was in Boston where the provincial governor lived and the local government was established.

Maritime activities dominated life in the colonial settlement. Fishing was an important industry, as fish were one of the few resources colonists had to trade. Settlers immediately began to build facilities where boats could be loaded and unloaded. These were concentrated on the eastern side of the peninsula, facing the ocean, in a semi-circular inlet. This inlet became the main harbor, and it was known by several names but principally as Town Cove.

The local topography and tides, and the small draft of even ocean-going vessels in the seventeenth and eighteenth centuries, allowed the construction of wharves, or piers, that projected far into the water. The special topographic feature that made this construction relatively easy and inexpensive was the gradually sloping ground surrounding the shoreline. (Fig. 2) Wharves were built on simple foundations called cribs or cribwork, which were made of logs. Logs formed the outside frame and were also laid at intervals inside the frame and connected by transverse timbers, all notched

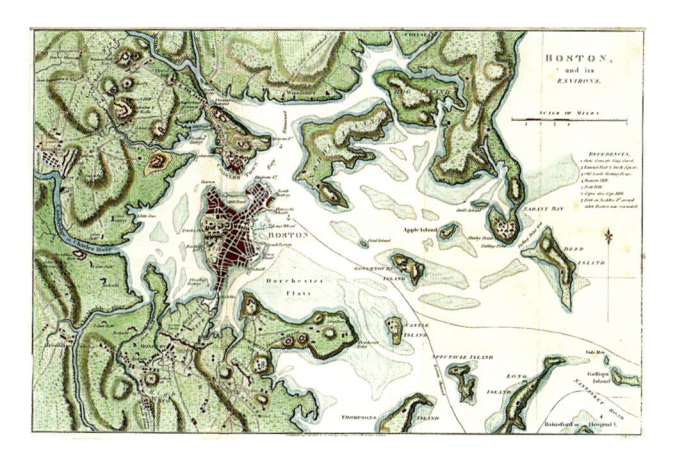

Figure 2: Boston is the peninsula, mostly brown-colored. The light green around the landmasses signifies shallow areas, including "flats" that might be dry at low tide

Figure 3: Warehouses on the north side of Long Wharf (center) in Boston Harbor and along other wharves

Figure 4: Remains of former warehouses, Central Wharf (now on Milk Street), built 1815–1817

Colonial-era and Early Nineteenth-century Warehouses

Warehouses are ancient structures – perhaps the oldest kind of purpose-built building for business and industry. A unique feature of warehouses was that they were open on the interior, often with floors supported by posts rather than bearing partition walls. Other features that were common to warehouses built before the twentieth century were large doors to bring goods through; doors stacked one above the other (in multi-story buildings); heavy construction, because of the great weight of goods kept inside; and equipment for hoisting and lowering goods.

Bostonians built warehouses on or near the wharves at an early date. By 1638, a group of investors had built a wharf, crane, and warehouse at the Town Dock.[10] By the 1680s, warehouses lined the wharf that for a time stretched across the Town Cove, and later, Long Wharf filled with warehouses. (Fig. 3)

What were the early warehouses like? Today, there are no warehouses (indeed, very few structures at all) in Boston that were built before 1800. Written materials and contemporary drawings provide few details of their structural characteristics. Probably, as shown in drawings, they were like boxes with pitched roofs. And most were built of wood, with wood plank walls enclosing wooden frames. Boston's timber warehouses were demolished and replaced, but they also disappeared in great fires. After conflagrations, laws often were passed to outlaw combustible building materials; nevertheless, Boston continued to be predominantly a wooden town until the opening of the nineteenth century. Some owners tried to make their warehouse more fire-resistive. One warehouse known to have brick walls was the Triangular Warehouse, built in the Town Dock area after the great fire of 1679 destroyed that neighborhood. A writer who knew the warehouse firsthand noted that, "It was constructed with great strength, the bricks were of a larger size than those now used…" Another warehouse built after the 1679 fire, known as the Old Feather Store, had wood exterior walls covered with "rough-cast:" mortar mixed with bits of glass from broken old bottles. Both buildings were demolished in the nineteenth century.[11]

Boston's maritime enterprise included the carrying-trade (vessels hired to transport goods), fishing, and also a particular kind of trading: speculative trading voyages in which merchants owned the ships and the cargo. Merchants in this last category sent goods out from America – dried fish, timber, agricultural products, rum, and imported goods – to places that wanted them – the West Indies, Europe, Africa, and so on – to exchange for goods that were wanted at home. Such trading was undertaken through the eighteenth century, but declined in the second half as Great Britain repressed it through force and regulation. Following political independence in 1783, Boston merchants became more ambitious, making trading voyages to more remote locations. One storied route involved sending goods around Cape Horn to the northwest coast of North America to exchange for animal furs, which were traded for tea, silk, chinaware, and so on in China; these Chinese goods were brought back to the East Coast of North America for sale. The China trade, and the

together and fastened. Some of the cells of the framework had floors. The cribs could be built on land and floated to their destination, at which point rocks were dumped into the cells with the floors, and this sank the crib and held it in place.[6] Then a deck would be built on top.

In a few instances, the colonists built what may have been closed docks, such as were later built in Liverpool and London. The famous closed docks of Liverpool, beginning with the 1715 Old Dock, were walled basins with gates, through which boats could enter only with the tides. Bostonians built several basins in the 1600s, including Town Dock at the head of Town Cove, but it is not known if these basins had gates or were open at their ends.[7] The main facility for docking boats and ships were finger wharves or piers. Boston, like Hamburg, could have an open harbor with wharves that could be approached at all times even by large ships.[8] At the end of the seventeenth century, Boston had 63 wharves, with another 14 wharves located across the harbor in Charlestown (now part of Boston).[9] Early in the following century, what came to be called Long Wharf was built (1710–1715), which, when completed, extended about 1,600 feet (487.7 m). It ended in a platform with a crane for handling cargo.

general revival of trade with distant places, called forth an active shipbuilding and outfitting industry in Boston and its region. Many merchants accumulated great fortunes from this business.

These prosperous businessmen needed places to store their goods, and invest their money, and in the early nineteenth century, a higher class of warehouse began to be built in Boston. Brick and stone exterior walls became the norm. A number of former warehouses from this period survive, for example, eight buildings that stood on Central Wharf. (Fig. 4)

Beginnings of Land-making and the Rise of the Warehouse Block

A notable change in harbor development also occurred in the early nineteenth century: major land-making projects commenced. As previously noted, the shoreline around Boston sloped gradually, and in many places, the ground was exposed at low tide. This tidal land was called "flats." To encourage wharf and pier construction, and therefore maritime commerce, colonial lawmakers granted owners of waterfront property the right to build on the flats adjoining their land. And as a result, many wharves were built around Town Cove and beyond. Then in the early nineteenth century, landowners began to fill the flats to make new land to build on. The way they did this, typically, was by erecting a barrier, or seawall, of stone or timber around the perimeter of the area to be filled. Stone and gravel (or anything else) was dumped between dry land and the wall, to raise the new ground above high tide. While rubbish and other poor materials often were used for fill, Boston was fortunate to have another topographical feature that facilitated land-making: many high, rocky hills located near the shore. These hills were cut down, and the soil, gravel, and rocks carted to the waterfront. (Fig. 5)

Some of the early land-making projects were undertaken by government – Boston or the Commonwealth of Massachusetts – but most were carried out by groups of private investors. Investors came together to undertake speculative land-making projects just as they did for speculative trading voyages. Already in the early eighteenth century, investors had joined together to construct Long Wharf; in the early nineteenth century, development companies formed for more ambitious construction projects. These investor-owned real estate companies became a Boston specialty. The companies made land, laid out streets, subdivided land into lots, and sold the lots or erected and sold buildings.

The first example of private land-making on Boston's waterfront was India Wharf. Built between 1803 and 1807 on the southern side of Town Cove, the project consisted of a deep-water wharf and blocks of brick warehouses. The wharf was a great success, and its investors undertook similar projects, for example, at Broad and India streets.[12]

At this time, a distinctive kind of warehouse emerged: the monumental warehouse block. These buildings contained many stores, but were built by real estate development companies rather than by individual owners, and were designed to appear to be single, large buildings. A precursor to this

Figure 5: Cutting down Boston's Beacon Hill ca 1811 to fill the Mill Pond

Figure 6: India Wharf warehouses, built 1805–ca 1807: although consisting of many separate stores, the stores were grouped and treated as one building

idea was the group of warehouses built on Long Wharf, some of which had been completed by 1711. (Fig. 3) The investors who built the wharf sold lots on its north side and, to assure uniformity in the warehouses developed there, imposed conditions on the buyers. The lots measured 40 x 20 feet [12.2 x 6.1 m] on the west end and 24.5 x 20 feet [7.5 x 6.1 m] on the harbor end, and the buildings erected on them had to be 21.5 feet (6.6 m) high with a roof pitch of five feet (1.5 m). This approach – selling land with conditions as to the buildings that could be erected – became a usual one, and it resulted in uniform-looking blocks.

But when a development company itself built the warehouses and sold the individual stores, it controlled the overall design, and from the company-built projects, the monumental warehouse block emerged. Charles Bulfinch, Boston's leading architect in the early nineteenth century, may have originated the idea of the warehouse block. He designed what was probably the first example at India Wharf (1805–1807). The block had 32 separate stores, but with a pedimented dormer in its center, it looked like a monumental Georgian-style building, composed of a central pavilion and wings. (Fig. 6) Another early example, also designed by Bulfinch, was Central Wharf (1815–1817), which originally had 54 stores. (Fig. 4) Frank H. Forbes, a contemporary who had worked at merchant firms on the waterfront,

Figure 7: Granite walls, and monolithic piers and lintels, of the Custom House Block on Long Wharf, completed 1848

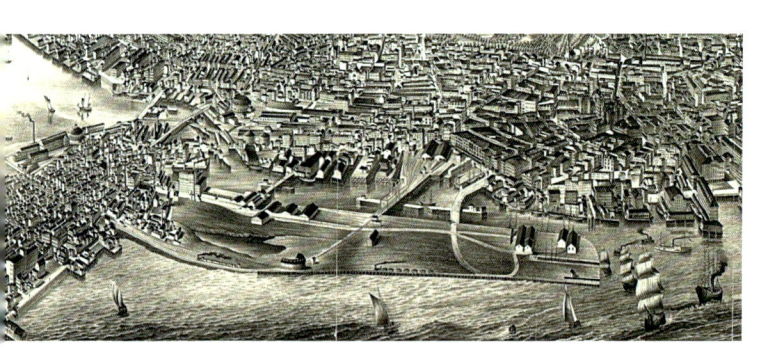

Figure 8: View of Boston Wharf Co. and Commonwealth of Massachusetts's made-land, looking west, ca 1880. The curved piece of land is Fan Pier

described Central Wharf as "the most conspicuous and the most attractive of the old Boston wharves" and "the largest continuous block of warehouses in the country." Other examples of these blocks were built through the first half of the nineteenth century. With improved techniques for quarrying and cutting granite (a hard but abundant stone in New England), it became a popular material for the walls of these buildings. The stones were cut in enormous pieces, which added to the imposing presence of the warehouse blocks. In his reminiscences, Forbes recalled how the "spacious docks and wharves," as well as the "fine warehouses that flanked them," created "a magnificent water front," "the pride of the city."[13] These warehouse blocks, expressions of Boston's successful maritime enterprise in the first half of the nineteenth century, characterized the architecture of the central harbor.

Construction of warehouse blocks came to an end in the 1850s. Over time, as the waterfront was filled in and new streets were constructed, this distinctive architecture lost its visual coherence. India Wharf and Central Wharf, severed when construction of Atlantic Avenue began in 1868, have (except for a fragment) since disappeared.[14]

Some of the monumental blocks remain, and one example is the Custom House Block on Long Wharf. (Fig. 7) Completed in 1848, it reflects the more elaborate design and materials of the mid-nineteenth century. It is 224 feet long (68.3 m), 80 feet (24.4 m) wide on its eastern end and 60 feet (18.3 m) wide on its western end, and has a five-story center section and four-story wings. The south (principal) façade was built with massive granite blocks, the rear with brick. It contained 14 stores originally. Inside, wood joists are supported on brick walls that divide the space into separate stores. The building has been remodeled and lost its cupola. It took its current form in the 1970s, when it was renovated for shops and apartments.[15]

Development of the Fort Point Channel Area

In the second half of the nineteenth century, land-making proceeded steadily along Boston's shoreline and included some massive projects, like the filling of Back Bay and South Bay; but the section of the city that increased the most by land-making is South Boston. In South Boston, over 1,000 acres (4 square kilometers) of land, intended for port and water-oriented uses, were added. This neighborhood, annexed by Boston in 1804, is separated from Boston proper by the Fort Point Channel. Wharves dotted the west (Boston) side of the Channel, and after bridges were built to join the two land masses, manufacturing firms started up on the east (South Boston) side. Land-making in the area proceeded from south to north and west to east, starting at the Fort Point Channel and continuing across the South Boston Flats. Railroads served the area, and additional road and railroad bridges were built across the Channel as new land materialized. The bridges made the new land accessible and encouraged development, but they also interfered with ship traffic in the Channel and diminished the value of the Channel's wharves for port purposes.

Boston Wharf Company Develops the Fort Point Channel District

One of the companies that made land in South Boston was the Boston Wharf Company (BWCo).[16] A private real estate company incorporated in 1836, BWCo purchased land and adjoining flats east and north of the Free Bridge that connected Boston to South Boston, with the intention of building wharves for docking and warehousing. By 1837, it completed two large wharves that extended roughly north from First Street into the Channel.[17] BWCo built its wharves by constructing a stone seawall, then filling in behind it. The flats adjoining its property, by colonial law, belonged to the company, and over time, BWCo increased its land by building seawalls farther north and filling in. Around 1855, the Midland Railroad laid tracks along the western edge BWCo's site.

Boston Wharf Co. was not the only party interested in filling the South Boston Flats. In the late 1860s, the Commonwealth of Massachusetts adopted a plan to fill the Flats, including an area north of BWCo's property. The rationale for this ambitious project was to improve the harbor, especially to deepen the main ship channel, which many believed was becoming shallower due to land-making. The process of filling the South Boston Flats by the Commonwealth and other land owners went on for years. In 1873, the Commonwealth began construction of the curved end of the seawall, a site called Fan Pier, as well as a dock along the main ship channel.[18] Filling of this area and BWCo's site were completed by 1882. (Fig. 8.) Flats to the east were sold to the Boston and Albany Railroad, which filled its site and developed a railroad terminal for transferring goods from ship to train.

Before the 1880s, BWCo's business was operating wharves and storage, and it developed a specialty in handling sugar and molasses. BWCo built large, wooden sheds along their docks to handle these imports. Not coincidentally, there were two large sugar refineries located nearby.

In the 1880s, as BWCo completed its land-making, it started to change the nature of its business, from a builder of wharves and sheds along the Channel, to a developer of industrial and warehouse buildings served by rail and trucks. The opening of Congress Street Bridge in 1875, located at the northern end of BWCo's new land, made BWCo's site practically an extension of Boston's downtown. In 1882, the first warehouse in the District with brick walls went up, near the foot of Congress Street Bridge, on land BWCo sold to the developer. Called Dorr's Stores, this four-story building was used for storing wool, cotton, and general merchandise. By 1890, several brick warehouses and lofts had been built along or near Congress Street, by private owners on lots BWCo sold to them, or by BWCo for specific tenants. An example of the latter was a building for Atlas Stores (1890). (Fig. 11)

Manufacturers also came to the area, and they tended to build their own lofts. During the 1890s, the southern end of the District became a manufacturing zone. A notable project there was undertaken in the mid-1890s by Samuel Wormwood and associates on a roughly three-acre (1.2 hectare) site purchased from the BWCo. The project consisted of five principal buildings, all six-story brick lofts. Known as the Factory Buildings Trust, the complex offered factory space for rent and provided tenants with electric light and power from its own power plant.

By this time, as it announced with an electric sign on the roof of its office building, BWCo was an "industrial real estate" company. It planned and built streets. It built structures to suit specific tenants, which it leased or sold to them. These were designed in the company's architectural department. BWCo also sold land, which the new owners developed. The District was attractively located for commercial and industrial firms. As well as being near the piers, it was served by rail, and rail spurs ran right up to the sides of many buildings.

The pace of loft construction got a boost around 1900 when the Summer Street Bridge opened and Summer Street was extended from downtown Boston across BWCo's land. Unlike Congress Street, Summer Street was built at a raised grade through BWCo's site and crossed the railroad tracks east of the site on a viaduct, thereby avoiding interference

Figure 9: Summer Street in the FPCD, with Melcher Street curving from its raised grade down to A Street. Boston Wharf Co.'s offices were located in the red brick building (center), which features the company's electric advertising sign on the roof

Figure 10: Summer Street in the FPCD, looking west

from the trains. This made Summer Street an important thoroughfare. And the raised grade created its most striking urban design feature: a road curving from the elevated Summer Street down to grade at A Street. Named Melcher Street for BWCo's Superintendent, Lewis Melcher, this curving road was laid out in 1897. (Fig. 9)

BWCo developed Summer Street as a monumental city street. (Fig. 10.) The lofts in the District up to this time had been six stories or less, but Summer Street had nine-story lofts. These were intended for wool merchants. Boston was a hub of the wool trade, and wool merchants liked to be together. Jeremiah Williams & Co., a large wool trading firm, built the first nine-story loft building on Summer Street in 1898. (Fig. 14) BWCo then developed the rest of the block with lofts for the wool dealers. In the early twentieth century, wool merchants relocated practically en masse to the FPCD, and Summer Street became famous internationally as a center of the wool trade. The tall Summer Street buildings were fireproof and had a high level of architectural finish.

Figure 11: Patterned brick at the corner does little to relieve the plainness of the Atlas Stores, FPCD, the first part of which was built in 1890 by BWCo

Figure 12: "Ordinary" floors of closely-spaced joists and bridging

Figure 13: "Warehouse" framing, consisting of large girders and beams, and tongue-and-groove boards making the floor deck; Stillings Building, FPCD, built 1901

The south side of Summer Street developed later, between 1903 and 1910, but with buildings of proportions and finish like those on the north side. BWCo took offices in the prominent 1905 building at the corner of Summer and Melcher streets. (Fig. 9)

By the 1950s, development of the District for warehousing and manufacturing had come to an end. A reinforced concrete building at 51 Sleeper Street, built in 1929, turned out to be the last of the lofts. The Great Depression, World War II, and the changing regional and national economies, stalled and then ended loft development.

Then the traditional tenants began to leave the buildings. New England's wool textile industry declined, and along with it, Boston's wool market. Manufacturers and wholesalers preferred suburban locations with better highway access. Vacancies became widespread. In the 1970s, artists discovered the area, and by 1980, so many artists had moved into the District that an Open Studios event could be held. In the first decade of the twenty-first century, BWCo began to sell off its property. Today, the FPCD has been transformed into a neighborhood of office, residential, retail, cultural, and artist live/work spaces.

Physical Features of the Fort Point Channel District Warehouses

As a result of the limited range of purposes for the buildings (warehousing and manufacturing), and the fact that most were built during a relatively short time period (the late 1880s to 1920), developed by one company (BWCo), and designed by its employees, there is great uniformity in the buildings of the District. In this respect, its development was like that of Speicherstadt, which similarly was developed by one owner, with buildings for a single purposes (warehousing), and in exactly the same time period. The FPCD buildings have features that are characteristic of warehouses and lofts generally: tiers of doors for loading goods; pulleys and lifts for raising and lowering goods; doors at the ground floor elevated to the level of railroad car and truck beds; and little or superficial architectural embellishment. (Fig. 11.) And, like most warehouses, they had open interiors, usually framed (except for firewalls) and little interior finish. The interior construction of the buildings was either fireproof (i. e., all structural parts – frame, floor, roof, partitions, stairways – were made of noncombustible materials) or timber. Most were timber-framed, which was also typical of warehouses of their time.

Of those with timber frames, most were built with "warehouse" framing. Eighty percent of the extant historic warehouses and lofts in the District (68 of 85 buildings) have these floors. Only two have "ordinary" floors, meaning floors made of closely-spaced joists. (Fig. 12) The warehouse-framed floors consist of girders, typically 14 inches deep, and beams, typically 12 or 14 inches deep, which are spaced roughly three to four feet (0.9 to 1.2 m) apart. The frame is decked with thick plank. There would be no ceiling under the beams – the frame was left exposed. (Fig. 13) In the earliest examples of this type of framing, the beams rest on top of the girders. Later, metal hangers were used to hold the beams. In most buildings, the posts are timber, square in section with chamfered corners. Very few buildings have cast iron columns even though by the 1880s, cast iron columns were commonplace and widely used in urban lofts elsewhere.

Warehouse framing may have originated in Boston, although this is uncertain. Probably it evolved from a somewhat similar framing system, also a regional specialty, known as "mill construction" or "slow-burning construction." That system was used universally in the construction of textile mills in New England. In mill construction, the floors typically consisted of girders only, spaced eight to ten feet (2.4 to 3 m) apart, covered with a deck of 3- or 4-inch plank, then topped with a finish floor. There would be no ceiling under the girders. The system was created as an affordable alternative to fireproof construction: a way to make textile mills safer without using expensive, noncombustible construction materials. Heavy timber was found to burn slowly, and when protected with automatic sprinklers and other extinguishing apparatus, made a comparatively safe structure. The wide spacing of the floor girders created unobstructed panels in which sprinkler heads could spray water effectively. Automatic sprinklers had become widespread in textile factories in the 1890s. No slow-burning frame was found in Fort Point Channel District.

Warehouse framing appears to be a variation of slow-burning construction, adapted for urban lofts. Although they did not have sprinklers originally, and the iron hangers made the floors more vulnerable to failure in a fire, nevertheless the heavy timber floors of the FPCD lofts would have burned more slowly than ordinary floors. And using girders and beams made stronger floors with fewer posts than girder-only floors. The first architect for BWCo, Morton Safford, used warehouse floors in the earliest extant building he designed in the District: the J. S. Williams Stores of 1888. No building he designed had ordinary framing.

Fireproof construction, more expensive than timber framing, was used only in the tall buildings, as required by law. Fifteen of the extant historic lofts, all of them eight stories or higher, are fireproof. Most have steel frames and concrete floors; two have reinforced concrete frames. The block of wool warehouses on the north side of Summer Street, between the Channel and A Street, are fireproof. The architecturally distinguished Jeremiah Williams & Co. Building (1898) is representative of the fireproof buildings. (Fig. 14.) It has a steel frame, Columbian concrete fireproof floors, and a stair made of Guastavino (timbrel vaulted) tiles.

The buildings of the District for the most part fill their lots. BWCo's control over the land allowed it to maximize land coverage and therefore the available floor area of the properties they developed. The result of the density, rectilinearity, and uniform mass was a visual coherence that is especially notable in the streetscapes of Summer and Melcher streets. (Figs. 9, 10, and 14)

Coherence was also achieved by the generally reserved architectural ornamentation and limited number of styles represented, and thus the recurring decorative effects, like projecting cornices and stilted arches over window openings. The most prevalent architectural styles are Classical Revival and Stylized Classical, which were in vogue during

Figure 14: Jeremiah Williams & Co. Building, a fireproof wool warehouse, FPCD, built 1898; it has two more stories on its rear side

Figure 15: A tier of loading doors that has been changed to windows after renovation; Dwinell-Wright Co. Building, FPCD, built 1904

the period of greatest expansion – from the 1890s through the 1920s. Ornamentation was generally confined to façades along principal streets. The buildings BWCo developed were designed by their staff architects, first Morton D. Safford (1842–1921), then Howard B. Prescott (1874–1956), who worked for the company from 1893–1917 and 1917–1939, respectively.

Loading docks and hoistways are common features of the buildings. Loading docks are situated above the ground, at the level of a cart, truck, or railway car. These are even found on the principal façades of buildings, when this was the best access. A common feature of the lofts is the tiers of doors, one over the other, with a pulley (locally known as "whips") at the top. (Fig. 15)

Conclusion

The warehouses and lofts of the Fort Point Channel Landmark District were shaped by their function, having features that are characteristic of warehouses generally, and also a local variation of heavy timber floor framing, which probably was introduced to make the buildings safer in a fire. The District is remarkable for its visually coherent streetscapes, created by buildings of similar materials, massing, styles, and purposes. What makes the District especially noteworthy is the large number of these buildings in a well-defined area. Not only individual buildings, but entire streetscapes survive largely intact, preserving the visual identity of the area as a loft neighborhood. FPCLD is significant as an unusually coherent and well-preserved collection of late-nineteenth and early twentieth-century warehouses and lofts. It represents Boston's former status as a major maritime trading center and is a rare example in the United States of a relatively intact warehouse district from this period. However, compared to Speicherstadt, it is much smaller and was never considered a model of port organization as the Port of Hamburg was at the turn of the twentieth century.

Abstract

Geprägt von Funktion: Bostons historische Lagerhäuser

Der vorliegende Artikel befasst sich mit der Geschichte der vor 1920 in Boston, Massachusetts, errichteten Speicher, und zwar im besonderen mit denjenigen des Fort Point Channel Landmark District (FPCLD). Hierbei handelt es sich um eine 22,3 Hektar große Fläche im südlichen Teil von Boston City mit 87 historischen Gebäuden, die in der Zeit von 1880 und 1930 entstanden und hauptsächlich Speicher und Schuppen (lofts) umfasst. Dies ist die größte zusammenhängende Ansammlung von Speichern und Schuppen in Boston und wahrscheinlich eine der intaktesten Speicherstädte in den USA. Bevor der Artikel sich dem FPCLD widmet, wird ein Überblick gegeben über die Entwicklung des alten Hafens von Boston und die einzigartigen Speicher und Schuppen, die einst zu seinen charakteristischsten Merkmalen gehörten. Bis in die Mitte des achtzehnten Jahrhunderts hinein war Boston die bevölkerungsreichste Stadt Nordamerikas und der Hafen der Stadt war führend. Auch im neunzehnten Jahrhundert gehörte der Bostoner Hafen zu den umschlagreichsten, wurde dann aber im zwanzigsten durch andere nordamerikanische Häfen in seiner Bedeutung überholt. Die meisten Kais und Hafenanlagen, die einst die Skyline des Bostoner Hafens bildeten, sind inzwischen verschwunden. Im südlichen Teil der Stadt hat mit dem FPCLD jedoch ein gewachsenes Stück Hafeninfrastruktur überlebt, das noch heute physisch von einer Zeit zeugt, in der Seehandel und Industrie das Wirtschaftsleben Bostons bestimmten. Die Speicher und Schuppen mit ihrem ganz eigenen Gepräge sind Belege für den Baustil Bostons im späten neunzehnten Jahrhundert.

Bibliography

"Boston's Old Wharves," Boston Daily Globe (March 14, 1894): 6.

BUNTING, William H., Portrait of a Port: Boston, 1852–1914 (Cambridge, Mass.: Belknap Press of Harvard University Press, 1971).

CLAPP, Edwin J., The Port of Hamburg (New Haven: Yale University Press, 1911).

FORBES, Frank H., "The Old Boston Water Front, 1840–1850,"in William Rossiter, ed., Days and Ways in Old Boston (Boston: R..H. Stearns & Co., 1915).

GOODRICH, S. G., A Pictorial History of America; Embracing Both the Northern and Southern Portions of the New World (Hartford: E. Strong, 1844).

GREENE, Carleton, Wharves and Piers; Their Design, Construction, and Equipment (New York: McGraw-Hill Book Co., 1917).

HILL, Hamilton A., The Trade and Commerce of Boston, 1630 to 1890 (Boston: Damrell & Upham, 1895).

KRIEGER, Alex and David Cobb, Mapping Boston (Cambridge, Mass.: MIT Press, 1999).

MATHERLEY, Polly and Marie Frank, "Long Wharf and Custom House Block (NHL)," 1989, National Register of Historic Places, National Park Service, Washington, D.C.

SEASHOLES, Nancy S., Gaining Ground: a History of Landmaking in Boston (Cambridge, Mass.: MIT Press, 2003).

SHURTLEFF, Nathaniel B., A Topographical and Historical Description of Boston (Boston, 1871).

SNOW, Caleb H., A History of Boston, 2nd edition (Boston: Abel Bowen, 1828).

WERMIEL, Sara E. and Susan M. Ceccacci, "Fort Point Channel Landmark District Study Report, Final Draft," August 2003, prepared for the Boston Landmarks Commission, Boston, Massachusetts.

WHITEHILL, Walter M., Boston; a Topographical History, 2nd edition (Cambridge, Mass.: Belknap Press of Harvard University Press, 1968).

Sources of illustrations

Fig. 1.: Fairchild Aerial Surveys, Inc., "Boston. South Boston," 1925. Boston Public Library, Boston, Massachusetts.

Fig. 2.: "Boston and its environs," from Thomas Page's Revolutionary War-era surveys, R. Phillips publisher, 1806. Boston Public Library, Boston, Massachusetts.

Fig. 3.: "A View of Part of the Town of Boston…" reproduction of a 1768 engraving by Paul Revere. Boston Public Library, Boston, Massachusetts.

Fig. 4.; Fig. 7.; Fig. 9. to Fig. 15.: S. Wermiel, 2011.

Fig. 5.: "Beacon Hill, from Mt. Vernon Street…," J. H. Bufford's Lithography, from John R. Smith drawing of 1811-1812; Smith, Knight & Tappan publisher, 1858. Boston Public Library, Boston, Massachusetts.

Fig. 6.: HABS/HAER, "Copied by Survey Photographer…, HABS MASS,13-BOST,6-3," before 1868. Library of Congress, Washington, D. C.

Fig. 8.: "View of Boston, Massachusetts 1880," drawn & published by H. H. Rowley & Co., lithographed by Beck & Pauli. Library of Congress, Washington, D. C.

* The photo rights have been clarified by the author and she has the responsibility

---

[1] BUNTING, Portrait of a Port: Boston, p. xvii.

[2] The term "loft" means an open floor, with few if any partitions; and a stack of such open floors constitutes a loft building or simply loft. In this paper, the term loft is used to mean the whole building. Because the space in lofts is unspecialized, these buildings could be used for diverse purposes, but generally (originally) they were used for warehousing and manufacturing. Purpose-built storage warehouses might be more specialized than lofts, and had features such as interior fire partitions, small windows, and low floor-to-ceiling heights, which lofts would not have.

[3] "Made land" is a term of art that refers to land created by filling in ground originally covered with water, like marshes and tidal flats.

[4] The Fort Point Channel Landmark District was designated by the Boston Landmarks Commission on December 9, 2008 and confirmed by the mayor and approved by City Council on January 28, 2009. In 2003, it contained 95 building, of which 85 (those built between 1880 and 1930) are historic. Since 2003, some new buildings have been constructed in the District.

[5] GOODRICH, A Pictorial History of America, 1844, p. 379.

[6] GREENE, Wharves and Piers, 1917, pp. 52–55.

[7] SEASHOLES, Gaining Ground, 2003, pp. 22–24.

[8] CLAPP, The Port of Hamburg, 1911, pp. 10–11.

[9] HILL, The Trade and Commerce of Boston, 1895, p. 39.

[10] SEASHOLES, Gaining Ground, 2003, p. 22.

[11] SNOW, A History of Boston, 1828, pp. 107–108, 167; SHURTLEFF, A Topographical and Historical Description of Boston, 1871, pp. 639–645.

[12] SEASHOLES, Gaining Ground, 2003, pp. 41–49.

[13] FORBES, "The Old Boston Water Front," 1915, pp. 51, 45–46; "Boston's Old Wharves," 1894, p. 6.

[14] WHITEHILL, Boston; a Topographical History, 1968, p. 88.

[15] MATHERLY and Frank, "Long Wharf and Custom House Block (NHL)," 1989, pp. 7–2 – 7–3.

[16] This section draws on WERMIEL and Ceccacci, "Fort Point Channel Landmark District Study Report," 2003.

[17] KRIEGER and Cobb, Mapping Boston, 1999, plate 22, p. 113.

[18] SEASHOLES, Gaining Ground, 2003, pp. 300–306.

Alfredo Conti

Puerto Madero, Buenos Aires, Evolution of a Warehouse Area

Introduction

Puerto Madero is the port area of the city of Buenos Aires inaugurated at the end of the 19th century. A few decades after inauguration, it became evident that the port had become obsolete, especially on account of the changes of ships dimensions and maritime transportation technology. Since a new port had been constructed next to Puerto

Figure 1: Buenos Aires in 1750

Madero, the latter was gradually abandoned until it became a degraded area next to Buenos Aires' downtown. Projects of redevelopment of the area were implemented from the mid 1980s onwards, including a master plan approved in 1991. The area was completely redeveloped and became a new and fashionable neighbourhood of the city. The aim of this text is to introduce the origin and development of Puerto Madero as a port and warehouse district up to its present situation.

Buenos Aires, a port city

Buenos Aires, the capital city of Argentina, is located by the Plata River, which is in this area some 45 km wide. A first Spanish settlement had been established in 1536 and abandoned some years later. The formal foundation of the town, according to Spanish laws, took place in 1580. The site selected for the location of the town was a plateau some 15 m higher than the river bank, which is characterised by its shallowness. The embouchure of a tributary river constituted the harbour which made possible the protection of ships. The urban layout of the village responded to the prescription of the Spanish laws: a grid of parallel streets forming square blocks and a plaza, located next to the river bank, which concentrated the main institutional buildings: the cathedral, the *cabildo* (town hall) and the residence of the Spanish authorities (Fig. 1).

The town had a slow development over its first 200 years. Located between the river and the vast plains scarcely colonised by the Spaniards, the town had mainly a strategic importance, to control the entrance to the Parana and Uruguay rivers and the attempts of Portugal to occupy Spanish territories next to Plata River. The economic policies of Spain concentrated the economic activities in a few ports of the Americas, especially located in the Caribbean area. Buenos Aires harbour had scarce activity, especially limited to regional commerce. The situation changed at the end of 18th century; in 1776 Buenos Aires was declared capital city of the Rio de la Plata Vice-Royalty and in 1778 the King of Spain habilitated the port for direct commerce with the metropolis.

Argentina declared the independence from Spain in 1816. From this time onwards, a process of colonisation of the planes started and the young country became progressively a producer of agricultural goods. By the mid 19th century a pier was constructed to serve as a new port next to the city downtown. Nevertheless, the shallow coast of the river prevented ships to approach the pier and passengers and goods were taken from ships by boats. A new customs building was then constructed at the entrance of the town for the pier, according to the Italian influences in architecture prevailing at that period.

By 1880, Argentina started a process of modernisation designed and implemented by the national bourgeoisie and based on the production and exportation of agricultural goods. This process was characterised by the total occupation of the national territory, an economic increase, the arrival of millions of immigrants and the openness to European influences in architecture and styles of life. Buenos Aires became the official capital city in 1880 and started a process of expansion and modernisation that converted it, in the span of a few decades, into one of the most cosmopolitan cities in the world. This cosmopolitanism is clearly expressed in the architectural renovation experienced not only by Buenos Aires but also by other Argentine cities; the prevailing eclecticism of the period was used by Italian, French, English or German architects settled in the country or by local architects trained in prestigious European schools. The railway network, introduced in Argentina at the end of the 1850s, was extended along the country to link the productive areas with the ports. A fan system was in place by 1890 where the port city of Buenos Aires was the main converging point.

It became evident that the old harbour was not appropriate for a country and a city which were at a rapid process of growth; the construction of a new modern port became necessary. Several projects for a new port had been proposed since the end of the 1850s; in 1882 Eduardo Madero presented a project that consisted in a series of docks on a piece of land gained to the river; the project included two entrance canals, north and south, a defensive external seawall, one basin and four docks linked by short canals and floodgates (Fig. 2). The final project was elaborated by the English agency Hawkshaw, Son and Hayter.

The western bank of the docks was dedicated to an alignment of warehouses while the eastern bank was reserved to the location of flour mills, warehouses and silos. The construction of the new port started in 1887 and the works were finished gradually between 1890 and 1897. The inauguration of Puerto Madero implied not only a new port but the extension of the city to the river through a new port and warehouses district (Fig. 3). Office buildings related to the port and the new customs building were located on urban blocks next to Puerto Madero.

The warehouses on the west bank

On the western bank of the docks warehouses were built according to the project of the agency Hawkshaw, Son and Hayter from England. Four warehouses were located in relation with each of the docks, thus forming an alignment that characterises the image of Puerto Madero up to date. The buildings were constructed by the German enterprise Weyss und Freitag between 1900 and 1905. All of them have a rectangular plan with a structure combining steel and concrete and brick facades (Fig. 4, 5, 6). Along the docks, cranes provided by the firm Armstrong & Mitchell were located to connect warehouses and ships. The buildings on the eastern bank of the docks were constructed throughout the same period included warehouses belonging to flour mills companies and silos, some of them constructed in corrugated iron. Next to the north entrance of the port, an immigrants' hotel was erected to serve as temporary accommodation for people who massively arrived in Argentina at that time.

Ten years after the inauguration, it was evident that Puerto Madero was becoming obsolete, especially because of its docks system and the changes of ship dimensions, for which the docks appeared insufficient. A new port was constructed next to Puerto Madero using a different layout; instead of docks parallel to the river bank, a finger pier system was employed, which resulted more suitably to the conditions of the site. The new port is up to date the active port of the city and the main port of the country; Puerto Madero, instead, was gradually abandoned as an active port district.

Between 1925 and the 1980s, several projects to revitalise the area were elaborated, but none of them implemented. It is worth mentioning that when Le Corbusier visited Buenos Aires in 1929 he imagined an extension of the city towards the river, an idea that he retook in his plan for Buenos Aires

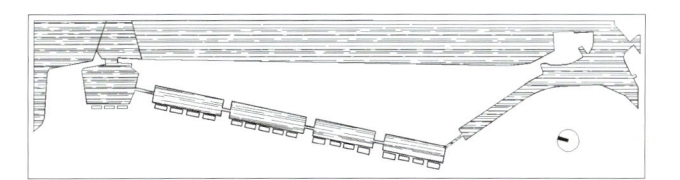

Figure 2: The port proposed by Eduardo Madero

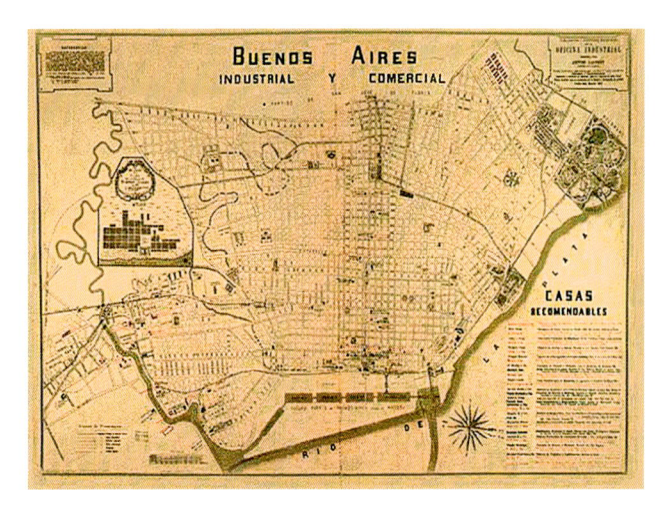

Figure 3: The city of Buenos Aires in 1890 with Puerto Madero

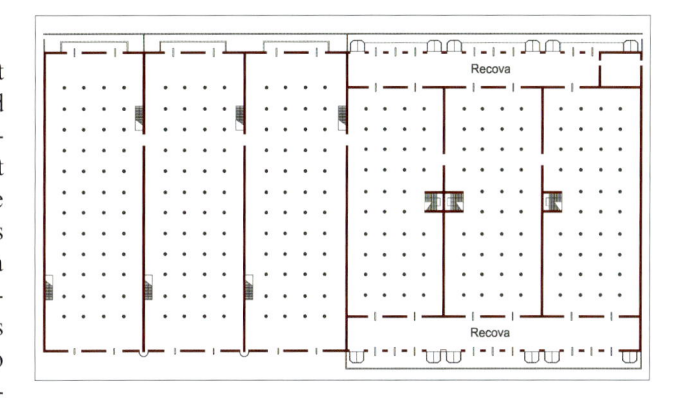

Figure 4: Original plan of warehouses

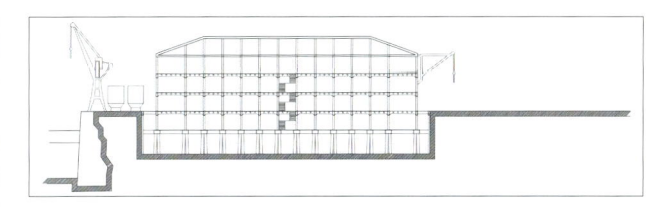

Figure 5: Section of a warehouse

in 1937. Le Corbusier proposed to preserve the system of docks and convert the area in a green park by demolishing the existing buildings.

The reconversion of the area

After several decades of abandonment and degradation and several projects for revitalization, the actions for the revi-

Figure 6: Façade of a warehouse

Figure 7: Warehouses on the western bank

Figure 8: Pedestrian promenade along the dock

talization of the area started in 1989, with the creation of a corporation integrated by the national and local governments. The area was then transferred to the corporation and the City of Buenos Aires was committed to elaborate the norms for urban development. Some plots were transferred to private investors.

The local government began, with the assistance of the City of Barcelona, studies for the revitalisation plan and convened in 1991 a national competition of ideas, from which resulted the master plan for the new neighbourhood. The realization of this plan constitutes the largest project of its kind ever held in Buenos Aires; numerous streets and avenues were opened and parks and plazas created. The area became a major centre of trade expansion with the additions of offices, flats and cultural facilities, also creating a new tourist attraction. During the recession faced by Argentina between 1998 and 2002 many major plans and projects were suspended, but a new impetus started after the recovery experienced by the country's economy since 2003.

The old warehouses of the western bank were preserved (Fig. 7). In 1991, the local government of the city of Buenos Aires approved specific protection guidelines to ensure proper interventions on the sixteen remaining buildings. A special decree protects since then all the buildings and their environment including all elements that bear testimony to the old port.

The interventions on buildings were based on strict conditions of respect to their facades and original materials to maintain the historic character of the area. Original materials were used for new pedestrian pavements and the existing cranes and minor components of the old port were restored (Fig. 8). It was established that rehabilitation works should ensure consolidation and maintenance of facades, galleries and arcades, respecting their materials and design; the existing doors and windows were respected in shape and dimensions (Fig. 9). It was accepted that new windows could be opened on the walls at the extremes of the warehouses provided that their design is contextual with the original appearance (Fig. 10). Former warehouses house today flats, offices, and restaurants and cafés on the ground floors, something that made of Puerto Madero one of the main and most renowned gastronomic districts of the city. Two buildings were bought and restored by the Argentine Catholic University to house headquarters and colleges.

On the eastern bank, most historic buildings had been demolished over the period of abandonment of the port activities. This area was considered as an opportunity for new developments: streets and avenues were opened and parks and squares created. The few remaining historic buildings were preserved; the most important is a former warehouse reconverted into a luxury hotel designed by Philip Starck. A first stage of construction of new buildings was based on the repetition of proportions and volumes of the facing old warehouses of the western bank (Fig. 11). At the beginning of the 21st century high rise buildings started to be erected, a process that has continued up to date. New facilities within the area include three five-star hotels, one university, one fine arts museum, designed by Rafael Viñoly, shops, restaurants and cafés. A pedestrian bridge linking the two banks of the docks, designed by Santiago Calatrava and dedicated to the International Day for Women, was inaugurated in 2005 (Fig. 12). Puerto Madero is today the most expensive neighbourhood of the city of Buenos Aires; for the coming years, several hotels, shops and a cinema complex are planned.

The construction of high rise buildings has completely changed the scale and the atmosphere of the district (Fig. 13).

Figure 9: Detail of restored façade

Figure 10: Treatment of an extreme of warehouse

The conclusion on the revitalisation of Puerto Madero district is that it could be considered at the same time a successful and unsuccessful intervention. From an economic point of view, the intervention has been successful: what used to be a degraded area became the most fashionable and expensive district of the city, open to residents and visitors who enjoy the promenade along the docks, parks and gastronomic and cultural facilities. It is also important as the redefinition of a new relationship between the city and the river, something lost when Puerto Madero was constructed.

From a heritage point of view, Puerto Madero is an example of a partial vision that contemplated preservation of architectural components and part of the remaining infrastructure, like the cranes, that bear testimony to the old port. Nevertheless, the redevelopment of the eastern bank makes the old warehouses, although properly preserved, appear like anecdotes in a completely new district (Fig. 14). Even if many buildings were lost prior to the master plan the integrity and authenticity of the area have completely changed. Although Puerto Madero is considered an example or urban

Figure 11: Contrast between first and second stages of construction of new buildings on the eastern bank

Figure 12: Bridge by Santiago Calatrava

Figure 13: New high rise buildings

Figure 14: General view of the current state of the area

restructuring at international level, pressures coming from real estate buildings were and are in this case more powerful than the heritage vision; and this could constitute a warning for similar cases: the big challenge is how to balance preservation with development and, in this framework, it is evident that Puerto Madero is not a proper example.

Abstract

Puerto Madero, Buenos Aires: Entwicklung eines Lagerhaus-Areals

Puerto Madero ist das Hafenviertel der Stadt Buenos Aires. Es ist nach Eduardo Madero benannt, nach dessen Plänen der Hafen am Ende des 19. Jahrhunderts gebaut wurde. Buenos Aires sollte damals neue Hafeneinrichtungen erhalten, um der wirtschaftlichen Entwicklung und Modernisierung Rechnung zu tragen, die sich in Argentinien in den letzten Dekaden des Jahrhunderts vollzog. Aufgrund der flachen Ufer des La Plata konnte für den Bau des Hafens Land gewonnen und die Stadt über ihre natürlichen Grenzen hinaus erweitert werden. Der neue Hafen umfasste eine Reihe zusammenhängender Docks, Fluttore und Schwenkbrücken, an denen sich Lagerhäuser, Getreidemühlen und Silos befanden, alle gebaut von englischen und deutschen Unternehmen. Als er fertig war, galt der Hafen als eine der beeindruckendsten Ingenieursleistungen der damaligen Zeit. Einige Jahrzehnte später jedoch war Puerto Madero schon wieder veraltet, weil mittlerweile noch größere Schiffe gebaut wurden und sich die maritime Transporttechnologie verändert hatte. Als Konsequenz wurde neben Puerto Madero ein neuer Hafen gebaut. Das alte Hafengebiet wurde nach und nach aufgegeben und verfiel allmählich. Ab Mitte der 1980er Jahre wurden Projekte und Maßnahmen umgesetzt, um das Gebiet zu sanieren, darunter auch ein 1991 genehmigter Bebauungsplan. Ehemalige Lagerhäuser wurden in Büros, Lofts und gewerblich genutzte Anlagen umgewandelt. Der alte Hafen erblühte zu einem neuen, lebendigen Stadtviertel. Nach der schweren Wirtschaftskrise, die Argentinien zu Beginn des 21. Jahrhunderts traf, bot sich in Puerto Madero erneut die Möglichkeit, Entwicklungsprojekte umzusetzen. Im Laufe dieser zweiten Interventionsphase wurden einige gegenüber den Lagergebäuden am Ufer gelegene Baudenkmäler unglücklicherweise abgerissen, um Platz für Hotels, gewerbliche und kulturelle Einrichtungen, Wohngebäude und Parks zu schaffen. Das neue, trendige Stadtviertel wurde zum Ziel der Immobilienprojektentwicklung. Dementsprechend wurden in den letzten Jahren mehrere Hochhäuser errichtet. Heute ist Puerto Madero das teuerste Stadtviertel von Buenos Aires und ein Muss für Touristen. Obwohl die Anordnung der Docks praktisch unverändert geblieben ist, sind im Zuge des Wiederbelebungsprozesses viele interessante Gebäude verloren gegangen. Nur die Reihe der Lagerhäuser auf der Westseite der Docks zeugt von der Industriearchitektur am Ende des 19. Jahrhunderts und erinnert zusammen mit einigen Kränen und kleineren Objekten an die ursprüngliche Funktion des Gebiets.

Bibliography

GAZANEO; J. y M. Scarone (1966): *La arquitectura de la Revolución Industrial.* Buenos Aires, IAAIE.

LA TRANSFORMACIÓN de la ciudad. Puerto Madero. Arquis, Arquitectura y Urbanismo, enero 1994. Buenos Aires, Universidad de Palermo.

LIERNUR J. F. y F. Aliata (Compiladores) (2004): *Diccionario de Arquitectura en Argentina. Estilos, obras, biografías, instituciones, ciudades.* Buenos Aires: Clarín. Volúmenes 1–6.

MADERO G., 1955: *Historia del puerto de Buenos Aires.* Buenos Aires, edición del autor.

MOLINARI R. L., 1980: *Buenos Aires, 4 siglos.* Buenos Aires, Tea.

WEBSITE http://www.puertomadero.com/ (Visited August and September 2011)

Sources of Illustations

Fig. 1: http://www.la-floresta.com.ar/cronologia.htm
Fig. 2: Mercedes Ferrara
Fig. 3: http://www.skyscraperlife.com/argentina/11050-mapas-y-proyectos-antiguos-de-buenos-aires.html
Fig. 4: Gisel Andrade
Fig. 5: Natalia Isasmendi
Fig. 6 to Fig. 14: Alfredo Conti

* The photo rights have been clarified by the author and he has the responsibility

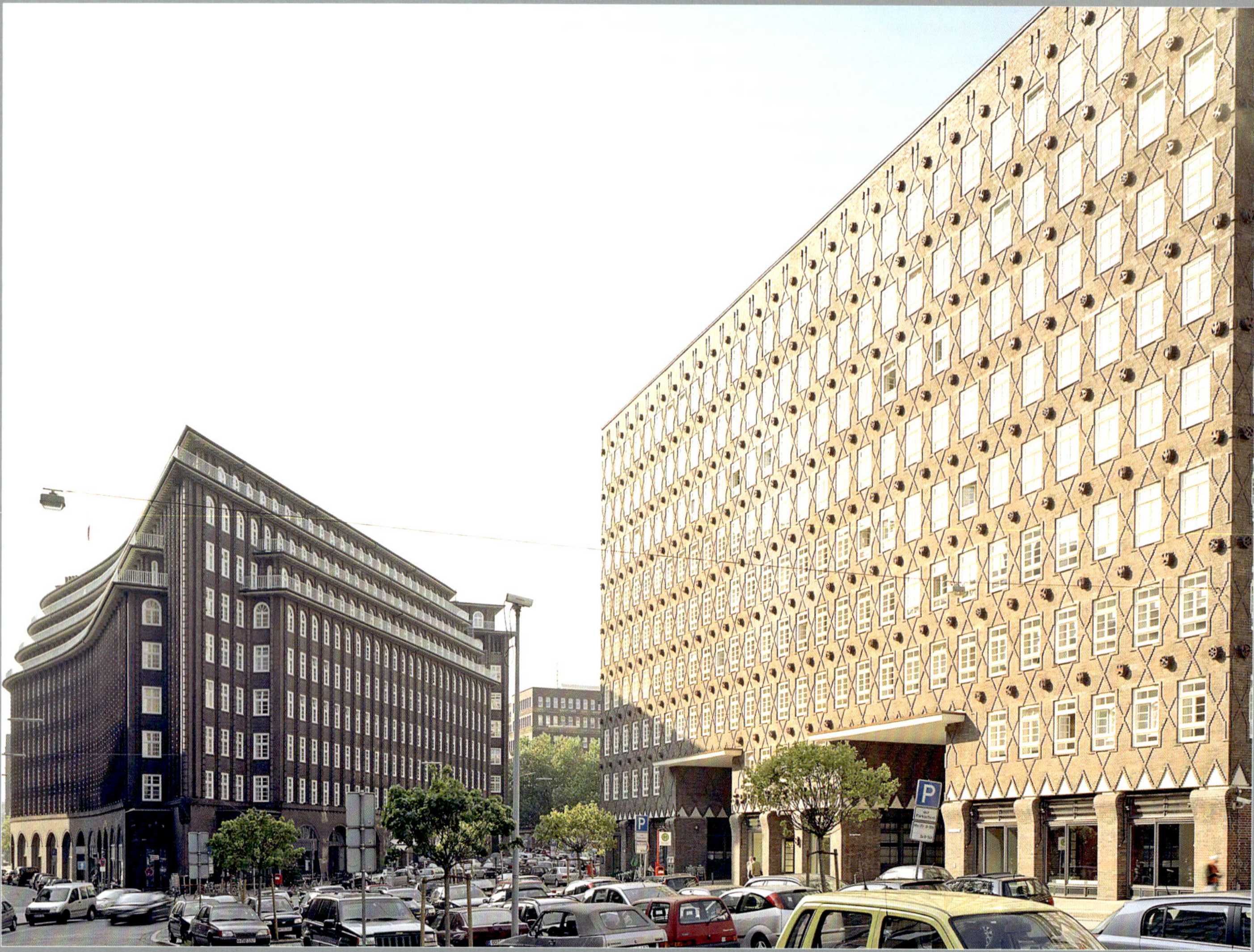

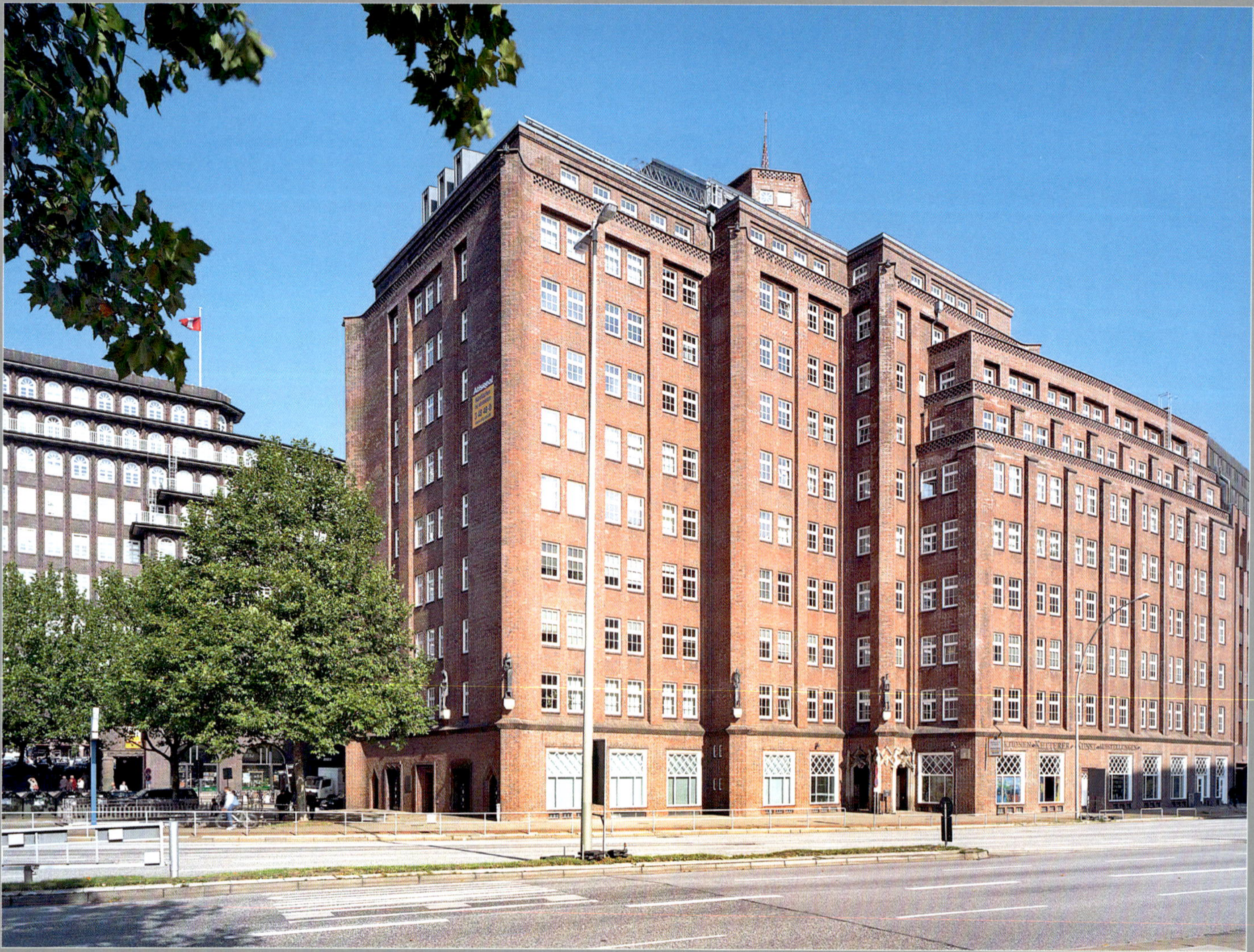

Bürohausbauten/Office Buildings:
**Das Hamburger Kontorhaus im
(inter-)nationalen Vergleich
The Hamburg Office Building in
(Inter-)national Comparison**

Hamburg

Carol Herselle Krinsky

The Office Building Architecture of the Early 20th Century in New York

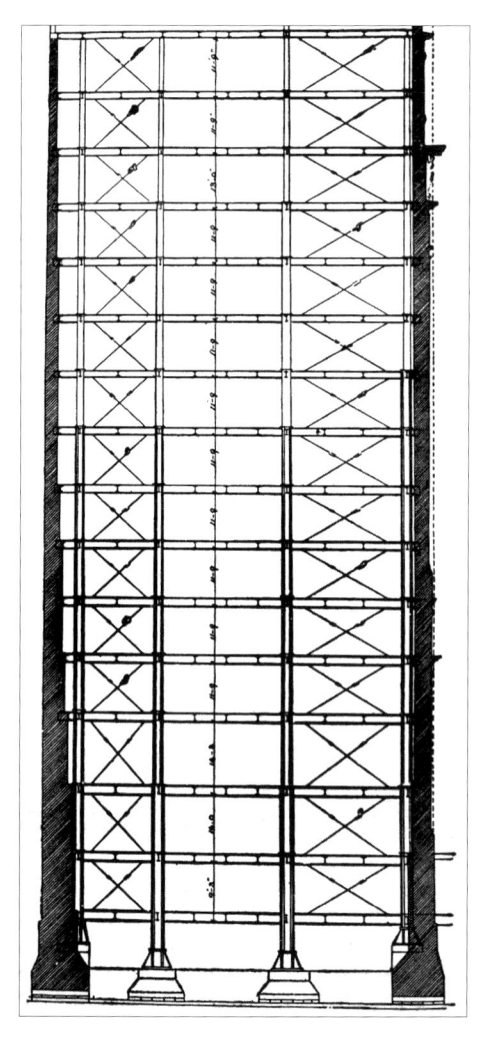

Figure 1: Structural diagram from Landau & Condit, Rise of the New York Skyscraper, p. 165

This brief account must start with the fact that the technology for skyscrapers originated at the same time in New York as in Chicago. This was brought to modern attention by my retired colleague, Sarah Bradford Landau who enlarged and corrected the work of her predecessor, Carl Condit, in the book, *The Rise of the New York Skyscraper*, which they published together in 1996. To qualify as a skyscraper, the building had to have a (Fig. 1) *skeleton frame* that carried both the floors and the outer surface. It had to be *taller than wide*. *Wind-bracing* had to be provided, often done through the floors. To get people upstairs, the building needed an *elevator with safety brakes*. *Water pumps* were required to get water to the roof for use in washrooms and water foun-

tains or to power hydraulic elevators. Materials had to be as *fireproof* as possible, and fireproofing material was developed to surround the steel columns because fire-fighting equipment could not reach the top of these buildings. The first elevator office building (Fig. 2) was the Equitable Life Insurance Building in New York, of 1868–70 by Gilman & Kendall with George B. Post, though it had a masonry frame. Post also designed New York's first building to use large-scale skeleton construction, the Produce Exchange of 1883, although it was not used for the entire building (Fig. 3). William LeBaron Jenney's Home Insurance Building in Chicago finished two years later was both entirely skeleton-framed, and vertical. Two years after that, in 1887, Bradford Lee Gilbert designed the Tower Building in New York, an early example of effective wind-bracing in which the weight of walls and floors was transmitted to the foundation by metal posts and beams (Fig. 4).

By 1900, tall buildings proliferated in the business district of the city, widely known as Wall Street, in southern Manhattan. That had become the business district because it was close to the docks, warehouses, shipping companies, and freight companies. Related facilities were on its outer borders, and a freight railroad reached to the western edge of the area.

The years before the First World War saw an enormous increase in the number and height and width of these office buildings. Citizens complained about crowded streets and

Figure 2: Equitable Building, New York City, by Gilman & Kendall with George B. Post, 1870

Figure 3: Home Insurance Building, Chicago, William LeBaron Jenney, 1885

Figure 4: Tower Building, New York City, Bradford Lee Gilbert, 1887

sidewalks because twice as many people worked in ten storey buildings as in five storey buildings. Doctors worried about the lack of sunlight and ventilating breezes, or about mental problems that they thought could be traced to overcrowding. The danger of fires beyond the reach of fire engine hoses troubled many people. Aesthetes lamented the end of classical proportions that were no longer possible because of the stretched vertical shape of the new buildings, and they were also concerned about the appearance of a crowded city.

The most famous aesthetic response was by Louis Sullivan of Chicago during the 1890s, who worked with the German-born engineer, Dankmar Adler. Their tall office buildings in St. Louis in the Midwest (Fig. 5), and Buffalo in western New York State at the end of the Great Lakes emphasized height, bringing forward the vertical lines of the supporting steel and adding intermediate verticals to make the buildings into what Sullivan saw as "proud and soaring thing[s]." He may have derived inspiration from the Tower building's vertical elements. Other architects preferred to pile small elements on top of each other, or to imitate Romanesque architecture – often German Romanesque – in which tall arches embraced several floors. Often, skyscraper designs reflected training in classical and Renaissance architecture, in which there was an element of a base, a shaft, and a capital even if the building details were in one of the medieval styles – Romanesque or Gothic. One of a few exceptions (Fig. 6) is the Woolworth Building, the tallest building in the world between 1913, when it was finished, and 1931 when the Empire State Building was finished. Covered in terra cotta plaques that can be washed clean, the Woolworth Building is Gothic in style, emphasizing vertical lines, small-scale decoration, and pointed spires. It soon acquired

Figure 5: Wainwright Building, St. Louis MO, by Adler & Sullivan, 1891

ened architects, government leaders, property owners, and civic observers understood that in time, the early skyscrapers could ruin each other financially. The first skyscraper on a block would benefit from air, sunlight, and prestige, but a second one built next to it would cut off 25% of the light, air, and visibility. Three more skyscrapers built around it would reduce the value of the first building, especially as the newer ones were, well, newer and perhaps had better water pumps, faster elevators, and more modern design. If that happened, city property tax revenues would fall because each building would be worth less, and therefore would pay less tax. Architects were interested in beauty, civic observers were interested in logic and urban amenity, the government was interested in a predictable and reliable tax base, and building owners wanted to maintain their buildings' value. They gathered from 1913 to 1916 to find ways to regulate the growth of skyscrapers. One problem was that no legislature would restrict what private property owners could do with their land because they were afraid that building owners would insure their defeat in the next election. So the civic leaders instituted changes through a resolution, a legal statement, by the City Council which had the force of law, even if it was not actually a law. The rules governed what one could build in a given district, and how much of it could be built: low houses here, high-rise office buildings there. The areas for high buildings were set around Wall Street and in the center of Manhattan, between Third and Eighth Avenues, from 34th Street (where the Empire State Building is) to 59th Street, just south of Central Park.

Figure 6: Woolworth Building, New York City, by Cass Gilbert, 1913

Figure 7: Metropolitan Life Insurance Building, New York City by Pierre Lebrun, 1907–09

the nickname "Cathedral of Commerce." True, its tower was so narrow that only small companies could rent offices there, but in those days, many companies were still small. Besides, the tower was built for prestige, not only for income. The demolished Singer Tower of 1906–8 by Ernest Flagg was similarly a box with a tower. Other early 20th century buildings were simply tall square towers (Fig. 7) such as those for the Metropolitan Life Insurance Company (1907–09 by Pierre Lebrun) and Bankers Trust Company on Wall Street by Trowbridge & Livingston, 1910–12. But most early high-rises such as the Equitable insurance company's second building finished in 1915 by Graham, Burnham & Co. were bulky, so as to squeeze the most profit from the building site.

In 1916 came a change in architectural form. Aesthetics and public well-being were not the only reasons. Enlight-

Figure 8: Hugh Ferriss, zoning possibilities, drawing

Instead of having a building rise straight up, covering the entire site, now buildings had to follow rules that allowed straight-up buildings to be only fairly low. If a building occupied the whole site, it could only rise straight up for a few floors, depending upon the width of the street. The wider the street, the higher the building could rise straight up (Fig. 8). After that limit, the building would have to set back under a sloping line drawn from the center of the street to the first height limit. Then all other floors would have to fit under that slope until the building set back to only 25 percent of the site. From that point, a tower could rise to any height, as this image shows. This explains the design of the Chrysler (Fig. 9) and Empire State Buildings. They are on sites large enough to make towers worth building, because the 25 % towers are wide enough to contain fairly large offices. In any case, their sponsors were interested in prestige, not only in rentable square meters.

Therefore, buildings did look different after 1916, or rather, after 1922 when large-scale building began again after the War. But the change did not affect building owners' profits as much as you might think. That's because before air-conditioning, a big square building included a lot of space that could not be rented. The reason is that people did not want to work more than nine meters from a window. If a building was fifty meters wide and about 30 meters deep, with only one indentation for light, that meant a lot of space that could not be used. And if it could not be used, it could not be rented profitably. The lower floors used some of the space in the middle for elevators which need no air or light. But higher up, fewer elevators are needed so it was all right to set the building back to reflect the loss of elevators.

As for architectural style, architects realized that they could no longer build Renaissance or Romanesque buildings under the new rules. The emphasis on vertical elements to suggest height received new attention (Fig. 10). A model for the new buildings came from Eliel Saarinen's second prize entry of 1922 for the Chicago Tribune newspaper building

Figure 9: Chrysler Building, New York City, William van Alen, 1931

Figure 10: 2ⁿᵈ Prize Entry for the Chicago Tribune Building competition, Eliel Saarinen, 1922

Figure 11: Lever House, New York City, Gordon Bunshaft for Skidmore Owings & Merrill, 1949–52

Figure 12: Seagram Building, L. Mies van der Rohe with Philip Johnson

competition. His design showed vertical lines that in some cases terminated in sculptural figures. This surely inspired designers in New York after 1922 such as the Graybar Building adjacent to Grand Central Terminal. Other designers left out the figures, since few people believed in the allegories that various naked and clothed figures were supposed to represent. They used plant forms or exotic decorations taken from Asia or from the Paris Exposition International des Arts Industriels et Decoratifs to embellish the vertical lines that emphasized the steel frames underneath. Most office buildings focused decoration at the entrance where it would be seen by passers-by, and on the tops, as at the Chrysler or the McGraw-Hill Publishing Company on West 42ⁿᵈ Street, built in 1930–31 by Raymond Hood. Tops would be distinctive and visible from a distance. The designs could be more or less classical, simply geometric, as on the Empire State Building, Assyrian because of the ziggurat building shape, as on the Fred F. French Building on 5ᵗʰ Avenue, designed by

Sloan & Robertson and Douglas Ives, finished in 1927. They could be faintly plantlike as at the top of Rockefeller Center, although the doorways there have elaborate classically-based figure compositions, because the conservative owner agreed that art enhanced the value of an office building. Spiky decorations could suggest industry, as on the General Electric, formerly Radio Corporation Building by Cross & Cross, finished in 1931 on Lexington Avenue, which has a top that suggests electrical currents zigzagging through the air. None of this was profound or entirely serious; the designs were meant to capture public attention and to make the building attractive to tenants. Part of the reason for the abundant art and the huge Christmas tree at Rockefeller Center was to make it a great monument for future rental, because when it was built in the 1930s, few businesses needed new office space and fewer wanted to move. Incidentally, the plan of Rockefeller Center with some high and some low buildings, is almost entirely related to zoning rules, as I have explained elsewhere.

The rules remained in place until 1961. By that time, business companies had grown and wanted all employees on one floor. Most setback buildings could not accommodate them in their narrow towers. Tenants wanted air-conditioning but very few of the setback buildings were air-conditioned. People admired Lever House by Skidmore Owings & Merrill (Fig. 11) and the Seagram Building by Ludwig Mies van der Rohe with Philip Johnson. They have open plazas, and citizens wanted more plazas. So the city changed its zoning rules, and that is why the famous setback skyscrapers are confined to the years 1916–1961.

Abstract

Bürohausarchitektur des frühen 20. Jahrhunderts in New York City

New York und Chicago entwickelten die technischen Elemente des Wolkenkratzers zur gleichen Zeit, vornehmlich in den 1880ern. Hierzu gehörten Stahlgerüste (später mit feuerfestem Material verkleidet), Vorhangfassaden, Windsicherungen, Fahrstühle mit Sicherheitsbremsen und Wasserbehälter auf den Dächern. Die Architekten verfeinerten die technischen Elemente und erprobten viele künstlerische Lösungen für diese neue architektonische Form. Im Jahre 1916 führte New York Baugesetze ein, die vorschrieben, dass Gebäude um ein im Verhältnis zur Straßenbreite bestimmtes Maß zurück versetzt werden mussten. Dieses führte zur Entstehung von besonderen Hochhausgebieten wie auch zu den pyramidenartig zurückgesetzten Wolkenkratzern, wie z. B. das Chrysler Building und das Empire State Building.

Die Regeln förderten nicht-historische, exotische oder geometrisch-modernistische Dekorstile, meistens gepaart mit der kommerziellen Absicht, Aufmerksamkeit zu erregen. Diese Regeln galten bis 1961, als neue technische und kommerzielle Anforderungen weitere Änderungen in der Gestaltung von Bürohäusern erforderlich machten.

Bibliography

Encyclopedia of New York City, ed. Kenneth T. JACKSON, 2nd ed., New Haven, Yale University Press, 2010

BURROWS; Edwin G. and Mike WALLACE, Gotham: I: A History of New York City to 1898, New York, Oxford University Press, 2000

Rise of an American Architecture, ed. Edgar KAUFMANN Jr. and Henry-Russell Hitchcock, New York, Praeger/Metropolitan Museum of Art, 1976

LANDAU, Sarah Bradford and CONDIT, Carl, Jr. Rise

PHELPS STOKES; Isaac Newton, Iconography of Manhattan island, 1408–1909, New York, Robert H. Dodd, 1915–1928 (6 volumes)

BLETTER; Rosemarie Haag and ROBINSON; Cervin, Skyscraper Style: Art Deco New York, New York, Oxford University Press, 1975

ADAMS; Nicholas; Skidmore Owings & Merrill: The Experiment since 1936, Milan, Electa, 2006

Sources of illustrations

Figures 1, 3, 4, 8, 10: Department of Art History, New York University image bank

Figures 2, 6, 7: Library of Congress Prints & Photographs Collection

Figures 5, 9, 11: Carol Herselle Krinsky

* The photo rights have been clarified by the author and she has the responsibility

Kristen Schaffer

The Early Chicago Tall Office Building: Artistically and Functionally Considered

Figure 1: Exterior, Homes Insurance Building, Chicago (1883–85) William LeBaron Jenney, with added upper floors (demolished)

In architectural and urban histories, two points stand out about Chicago: the city's rapid growth and the development of the tall office building there. Founded as a settlement only in 1803, by the end of the 19th century Chicago's population exceeded one and a half million and the city had claimed its position as the second city of the United States and rival to New York.[1] This rivalry appears in histories of architecture, especially with regard to the development of the tall office building, or early skyscraper, as both cities claimed its origin. What matters here, however, is not the question of origin but Chicago's identity and architectural sensibility. New York was closer to Europe both geographically and culturally, and the influence of European architectural preferences was greater there. Chicago expressed itself through its architecture as being more pragmatic and less historical than that of New York, a bit tougher, and, especially in these early years, more in tune with the economic demands of modernity.

In this context it is necessary to observe the difference between modernity and modernism. Modernity refers to the industrial revolution, the changes in the means of production, and the harnessing of new forms of energy, as well as the dislocations and economic restructuring that caused great social changes. The effects of the industrial revolution were exaggerated in the United States by the its rapid development, its great numbers of immigrants, and its seemingly unlimited resources. This contributed to rapidly growing Chicago and to the development of the tall office building, especially the speculative building which was expected to produce revenue. Modernism, on the other hand (as in "international style modernism"), was an aesthetic sensibility of philosophical, intellectual, and artistic origins.

The tall office building did not originate as a work of art, but as a response to economic pressure and rising land values caused by expanding business and population. In the years of rebuilding after the great fire of 1871, the Loop (or business district) became more purely commercial, but its area was limited by Lake Michigan on the east, branches of the Chicago River on the north and west, and a bulwark of railroad yards on the south. Because so much of business required face-to-face contact, the only way to accommodate growth was to go up. Building up was made possible by the more economical production of steel, advancements in structural wind bracing and foundations, and the development of fireproofing, as well as by technological advancements in plumbing, heating, ventilating, and perhaps most important of all, in the safety, reliability, and speed of the elevator.

These forces also created the demand for larger, more complex speculative office buildings: revenue-producing machines that architects designed, and contractors built to meet client specifications, often represented by a building and rental agent. Yet architecture is an art, and the plans, sections, and elevations required the work of an architect to make the buildings not only functional and sound, but culturally legible and acceptable. More than that, in the context of the office building, it had to be desirable. This is not just a reiteration of the Vitruvian triad of 'commodity, firmness, and delight.'[2] Delight, or desirability, was now part of the design's function to attract tenants and produce revenue.

The history of the tall office building in Chicago can be encapsulated in a comparison of two of its most prominent firms: Adler & Sullivan and Burnham & Root. Dankmar Adler hired Louis H. Sullivan in 1879, and they formed the firm of Adler and Sullivan in 1881.[3] Daniel H. Burnham and John W. Root formed their firm in 1873.[4] With a few modest diversions, these Chicago local firms will be the focus of this discussion.

The firms competed for the same projects, but the principals had different strengths. Sullivan disparaged Burnham for thinking of architecture as a business. From the outset Burnham strove for larger projects: "my idea is to work up a big business, to handle big things, deal with big businessmen, and to build up a big organization, for you can't handle big things unless you have an organization." The business corporation was the model for the large architectural offices. Not intending any flattery, Sullivan observed that "the only architect in Chicago to catch the significance of this movement was Daniel Burnham, for in its tendency toward bigness, organization, delegation and intense commercialism, he sensed the reciprocal workings of his own mind."[5] On the other hand, Sullivan admired Root's "great versatility and restrained originality" in design.

Adler's position was somewhat similar to Burnham's. He understood that the "architect is not only an artist ... but also an engineer, a man of science, a man of affairs." He continued his definition – and this was after his split from Sullivan – by saying that the architect was not just a "clear thinker and brilliant writer."[6] This was a barb at Sullivan, implying that he was an artist but not an architect. Given the size and level of complexity of the new tall office buildings, it became clear that it was more than a single architect could handle. A contemporary architect observed that "individual have been supplanted. It now takes several men to make a good architect."[7] Architectural offices became larger and now often included structural engineers and technicians.

Early in their young careers, both Burnham and Sullivan had worked for William LeBaron Jenney, a Chicago architect trained as an engineer. Jenney designed the Home Insurance Building (1883–85), one of the earliest uses of steel, at least for part of its frame structure (Fig. 1). Although the technological problems of structure were solved rather quickly, the architect had a more difficult time with the facade. The structural metal frame was separate from the enclosing walls. This disengagement of enclosing envelope from structural support was liberating, but not easy. In the long tradition of masonry load bearing walls, structure and enclosure were one and the same; and with thousands of years of experience, there were hundreds of good examples of architectural composition and proportion. The tall building, with its new "curtain wall," was a new artistic problem. Coupled with the need for light and the extreme proportions of the new building type, architects struggled to find appropriate articulation and expression. Chicago's German speakers translated and published portions of the work of Gottfried Semper, whose writings provided theoretical direction, but the architectural problem of the facade was difficult to solve. Jenney's solution, in its layer cake-like stacking, was on the whole unsatisfactory.

Figure 2: Exterior, Marshall Fields Wholesale Store (1885–87), Chicago, H. H. Richardson (demolished)

Figure 3: Exterior, Auditorium Building (1886–89), Chicago, Adler & Sullivan

A building in Chicago had an exemplary facade, by the master of the masonry load-bearing wall, the Boston-based architect H. H. Richardson. His Marshall Fields Wholesale Store (1885–87) (Fig. 2) provided architects with a useful facade strategy. The grouping of the windows of multiple stories under a single arch provided offered a way to rethink facade composition. This creates the illusion of shorter and more traditional scale of facade. This insight[8] was evident on a Chicago street. Facade composition, as a cultural language, may begin in the context of structure and materials, but as an aesthetic form it accrues meaning unto itself, and in providing precedents for architects, develops a legacy of its own. The meaningfulness of Richardson's facade was based on his preference for masonry architecture, but its appeal was broader and, as a model, was disengaged from structure by those who found it inspirational.

Richardson's facade organization appears rather quickly in works by Adler & Sullivan and Burnham & Root.[9] The most

Figure 4: Exterior, Guaranty Building (1894–96), Buffalo, N.Y., Adler & Sullivan

Figure 5: Exterior, The Rookery (1885–1888), Chicago, Burnham & Root

notable example is Adler & Sullivan's Auditorium Building (1886–89) in Chicago (Fig. 3).[10]

The Auditorium Building was commissioned by a consortium of businessmen to provide Chicago with a suitable cultural venue. This mixed use complex contained an important hotel and rental office space, whose revenues would support the Auditorium theater itself. The building's facade wraps its three street faces and unifies the different functions. Richardson's Marshall Field Wholesale Store provided Adler & Sullivan with a way of organizing this expansive facade into a compositional whole, but there were limits as to how far it could be expanded.

In the firm, it was Sullivan who was responsible for the design of facades, and he made a major breakthrough in facade design, first in the Wainwright Building (1890–92) in St. Louis and then in the Guaranty Building (1894–96) in Buffalo (Fig. 4).[11] The Wainwright was praised for its simple composition and plain treatment, for "its superior coherence and unity."[12] Frank Lloyd Wright would say it was "Sullivan's greatest moment – his greatest effort. The 'skyscraper' was a new thing under the sun, an entity with ... beauty all its own".[13] The Guaranty (later Prudential) Building developed this new idiom to greater perfection. One critic was enthralled: "I know of no steel-framed building in which the metallic construction is more palpably felt through the envelope of baked clay."[14]

In these facades, Sullivan departed from the Richardsonian model, and created a strategy that he explained was based on function. In his article "The Tall Office Building Artistically Considered,"[15] he stated "form ever follows function." He divided the facade into three zones: the first two floors that relate to the street; the top floor; and the repetitive floors of offices that is the tall middle zone. It is in this middle zone that Sullivan offered a new strategy by grouping these floors all together, no matter how many, and by emphasizing the height of the building with uninterrupted piers that extended through the full height of the building's midsection.

What is curious about Sullivan's article is that he only minimally discusses function. He explains it in terms of the three zones, but he assumes that the plans have all been worked out already. This is curious in that the careful working out of a design to produce a maximum amount rental space was done in the arrangement of the building's plans. Sullivan addresses the modernism of the building in the artistic composition of the facade, but does not directly engage the modernity of this building type in its need to be an efficiently organized revenue-producer.

The architect who does take up this issue is Root of Burnham & Root, in his article "A Great Architectural Problem."[16] He discusses the layouts of a series of offices around a light court based on the limits and orientation of the site, at the same time "enumerat[ing] some of the structural and commercial conditions which lie at the beginning of a typical architectural problem of the present." His article reveals the stringent limitations under which the architects worked in order to create a maximum of high-quality rentable space. Compared to facade composition, the development of the floor plan to provide adequate light and air has enjoyed somewhat less discussion in architectural histories.[17]

The Rookery (1885–1888) by Burnham & Root is a Chicago building that was noted by contemporaries for the development of its plan. Its exterior wall is still a combination of some load-bearing elements and a curtain wall on frame, and, earlier than the Auditorium, the facade is not so well composed (Fig. 5). However, the building was praised in its own time by architectural critic Montgomery Schuyler for the "Roman-largeness of its plan and the thoroughness with which it was carried out."[18] The first two floors take up the entire site, while the offices on the floors above are arrayed around a large open court (Figs. 6, 7). At the center on the ground floor is a two-story atrium covered with iron and glass and surrounded by an interior balcony giving access to the first (American second) floor (Fig. 8).

The Rookery's plan proved enduring. The hollow square plan was subsequently widely used, by Burnham and Root as well as by others. So powerful was its effect in the Rookery, that Schuyler incorrectly attributed the invention of this plan type to Burnham and Root: If it is not so uniquely impressive now, it is because such a project, when it has once been successfully executed, becomes common property, and may be reproduced and varied until, much more than in purely artistic successes, the spectator is apt to forget the original inventor, and the fact that the arrangement he takes for granted was not always a commonplace but originally an individual invention.[19] However incorrect the attribution of origin, the plan had great impact.

A comparison of the plan of the Rookery with that of the Guaranty-Prudential Building (Figs. 9, 10) in this regard may seem unfair as the Guaranty is so much smaller, but it is instructional nevertheless. In the upper floors, both plans respond to the same stringent requirements for light and air, requiring a court and limiting the depth of the offices from the exterior to the corridor wall.[20] But the differences in the ground floors is striking. The Rookery plan is organized around the atrium which provides a strong sense of place, a destination that is clear. Despite the relatively large amount of space (given its small size) devoted to public access, there is no sense of destination in the Guaranty.[21] One is confronted almost immediately with the bank of elevators, and the rest of the ground floor public sequence has the spatial dimension of a corridor. The interior is disappointing; the surfaces are well-ornamented but the space is not well-defined.

This difference is even more apparent in section. Schuyler's phrase "Roman largeness" characterizes the generosity of the sectional development of the Rookery as well (Fig. 11). The building possesses a well-developed spatial sequence of varying height and width, of compression and then release, into the spatial and visual expansion of the two-story atrium.

In the section of the Guaranty, the sensibility of the corridor prevails (Fig. 12). Although it is a generous single story, it is still just a single story. Despite Sullivan's theory about how the first two stories both relate to the street, there is no connection of the first (American second) floor to that of the street level, no two-story space; no spatial connection. The floors remain separate. The only place the floor plate is cut is at the stairs where, by necessity, they must pass through from one floor to the next. Despite Sullivan's statement that the first two stories have a relation to the street, that have little relation to one another, and there is no real architectural difference between this first floor (American second floor) and the repetitive floors above.

The connect of the first two floors at the Rookery is well-developed and takes place mostly in the atrium, but also in the entry vestibule. In the atrium, the stair to the first (American second) floor is placed on axis with the entrance, providing direct access to the balcony that wraps the space. Desirable by virtue of its location in this major public space, this

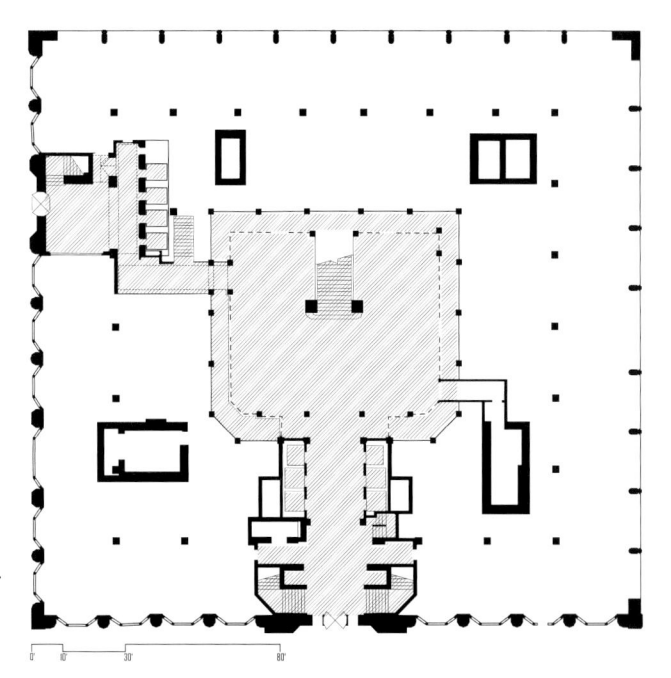

Figure 6: Ground floor plan, The Rookery (1885–1888), Chicago, Burnham & Root

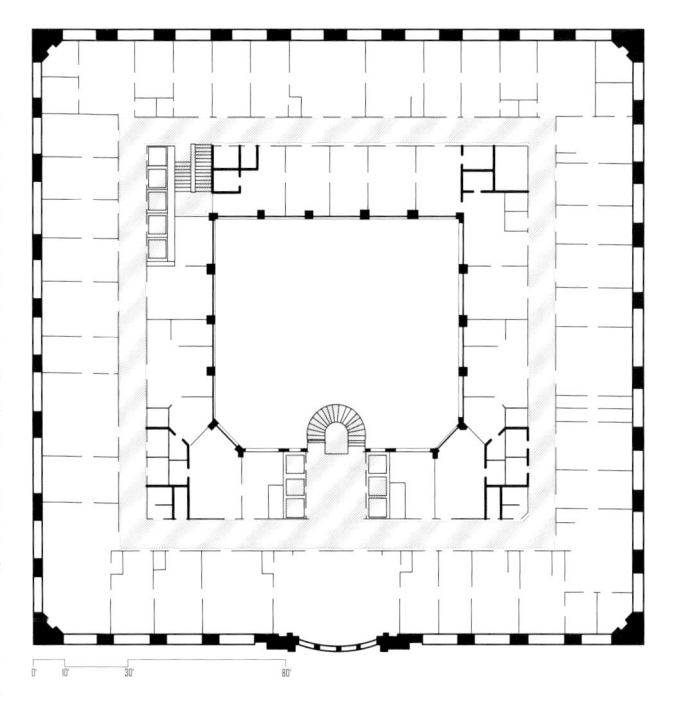

Figure 7: Typical floor plan, The Rookery (1885–1888), Chicago, Burnham & Root

Figure 8: Interior, The Rookery (1885–1888), Chicago, Burnham & Root

upper level of the atrium acts as a second ground floor by virtue of its clear visual connection and clear sequence. The dissolution of the floor plate here, and the sectional development, create a first (American second) floor that relates well to the street.[22]

This sectional development and open center plan was used by Burnham & Root in the Masonic Temple Building completed after Root's death (1890–1892), and in D. H. Burnham & Co.'s Railway Exchange, later Santa Fe, Building (1903–04), both in Chicago. In the later Continental & Commercial National Bank, now 208 S. La Salle St., Chicago (1911–1914), Burnham makes the connection between the ground floor with a public passage and the grand two-story sky-lit banking hall above.[23] The continuity in the work of the firm is as striking as the lack of sectional development in the work of Adler & Sullivan. It is curious that the Rookery, a speculative office building, has a more elaborately developed section than the presumably more ceremonial Auditorium Building with its theater and hotel lobbies. Adler & Sullivan's Stock Exchange Building with its important trading room also lacked spatial connections between the levels of the building. One could well ask why Adler & Sullivan did not avail themselves of this architectural opportunity; but perhaps the more interesting question is how Burnham & Root were able to devote so much space (both in area and height) to non-rental public space in buildings designed to produce revenue.

The answer lies in the person of Owen Aldis and what Burnham in particular learned from him. Aldis was a property manager and building agent, notably for Peter and Shepherd Brooks, the investors who commissioned from Burnham and Root the Grannis Building (1880–81), the Montauk Block (1881–82), the Monadnock Building (1884–92), and the Rookery. By 1902, Aldis & Company produced and managed "more than one-fifth of Chicago's office space."[24]

Burnham & Root's first major commission for an office building was the Grannis Block and in that context they learned a great deal about the requirements of a speculative office building and benefitted greatly from Aldis' knowledge. The architects organized this seven-story building around a light court and also attempted to create two first floors so that prime rental rates could be charged for both the low storefronts and the tall banking floor above them. Another look at the Rookery plan and section reveals how the architects were able to refine that strategy. In the Rookery, the ground floor was again devoted to retail. These tenants could be charged the highest rate as they had direct access to the exterior and pedestrian traffic, and some to the atrium as well. The floor above was designed as an American version of the *piano nobile*, the most important level of an urban building, and with the goal of almost duplicating the revenue the ground floor produced. Here the floor-to-ceiling height is greater than that of the ground floor and the rental spaces were larger. Banks were the major tenants of these spaces. This strategy also contributed to the life of the street as retail tends to enliven the sidewalk while banks, which do not engage the passer-by with window displays, were one floor up but still contributed to foot traffic.

The Rookery's well-developed spatial sequence of varying height and width is a marker of the building's and, by association, the tenants' status. Tenants were attracted by the way the atrium would act as their lobby and prolong the architectural promenade to their doors. The atrium created a desirable public space and provided a building lobby at a scale appropriate to the new tall office building and one that resonates at the urban level as well. It advertised the desirability of the building. The clients and architects strove not for the most economical solution in the meanest terms, but for something grander and more monumental that would yield higher revenues. The Rookery contained a considerable amount of "wasted" (that is to say, non-rentable) public space. Yet this unoccupied space had another function. Representative of decorum and status, space became an indicator of a building's place within the hierarchy of the city's structures.[25]

This understanding of the larger picture comes from Aldis. The Rookery exemplifies one of his rules for Profitable Building Management: "Second class space costs as much to build as first class space. Therefore build no second class space."[26] Aldis was, of course, knowledgeable about the cost effectiveness of a plan, square footage returns, and the price of maintenance and upkeep. He knew, however, that such a focus on economics would not be enough to attract the best tenants. While most commercial buildings had minimal lobbies so that more space was devoted to the highest income-producing rentals like restaurants and shops, Aldis believed in making the public spaces high-quality, especially the lobby.[27] Aldis developed the fundamental criteria of office building design from the point of view of profitable economic return by emphasizing "good light and air, attractive lobbies and corridors, easy circulation, and good building service and maintenance." He preferred a large number of small tenants as they could be charged a higher rate per square foot.

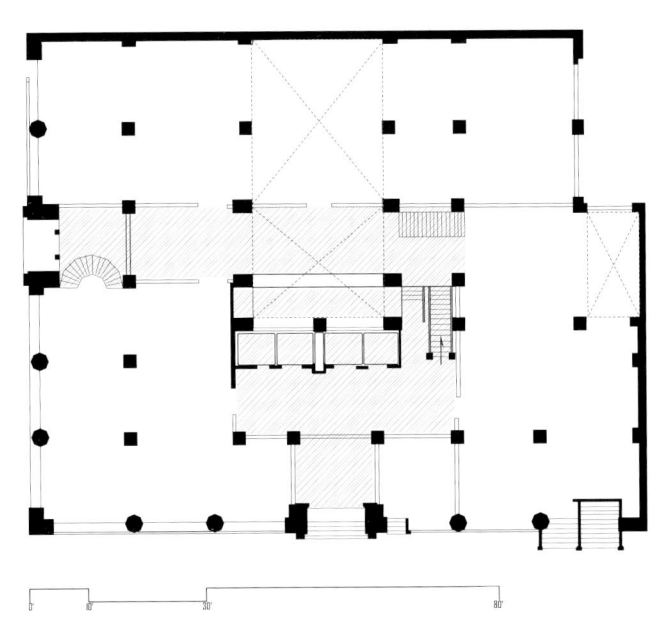

Figure 9: Ground floor plan, Guaranty Building (1894–96), Buffalo, N.Y., Adler & Sullivan

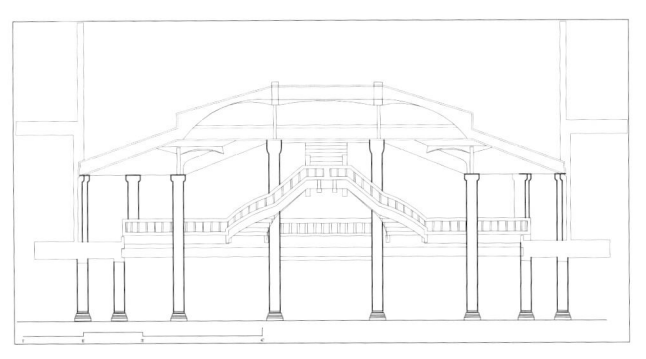

Figure 11: Section through ground floor, The Rookery (1885–1888), Chicago, Burnham & Root

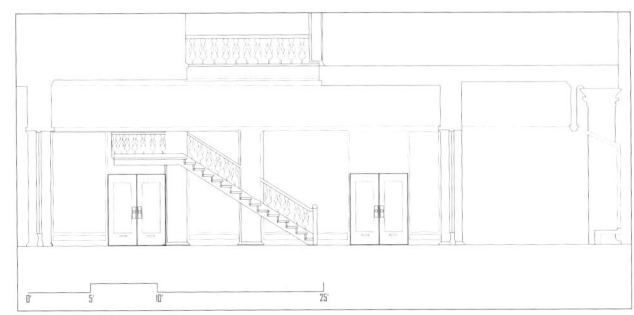

Figure 12: Section through ground floor, Guaranty Building (1894–96), Buffalo, N.Y., Adler & Sullivan

The rules of Profitable Building Management were written for the Marquette Building (1893–1895, addition 1906), Chicago, designed by Holabird & Roche (Fig. 13).[28] Here, although not as elaborate as the public space of the Rookery atrium, the plan reveals a vestibule, stairs to the first (American second) floor, and a spacious elevator lobby. What the plan does not reveal is that the elevator lobby is of double height, linking the two floors and relating the upper level to the lower. In its own time the building was noted as having fulfilled both the demands of artistry and commerce.[29]

Aldis advocated high-quality interiors, and tenants began to clamor for them. Perhaps in reaction to the bald speculative quality of earlier, ornamentation as well as good quality materials and finishes were demanded for buildings of the first class rental category. There was a recognized commercial value to beauty; the economic problem needed an artistic solution.[30]

The tall speculative office building was part of the major changes that occurred in architecture by the end of the

Figure 10: Typical floor plan, Guaranty Building (1894–96), Buffalo, N.Y., Adler & Sullivan

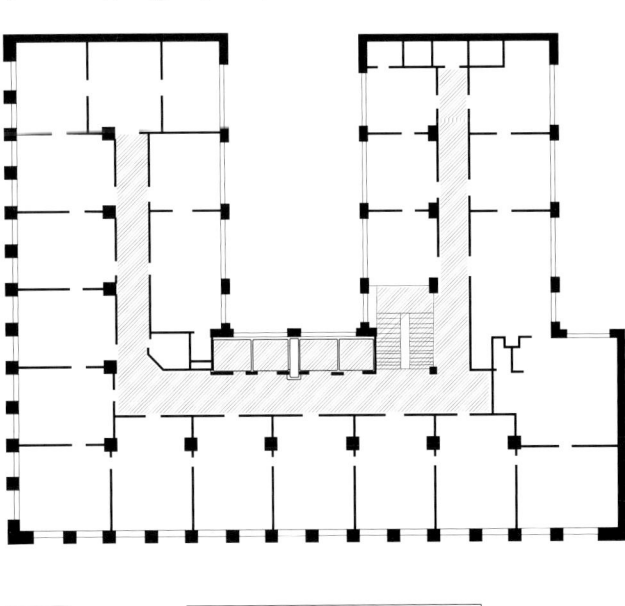

Figure 13: Ground floor plan, Marquette Building (1893–1895, addition 1906), Chicago, Holabird & Roche

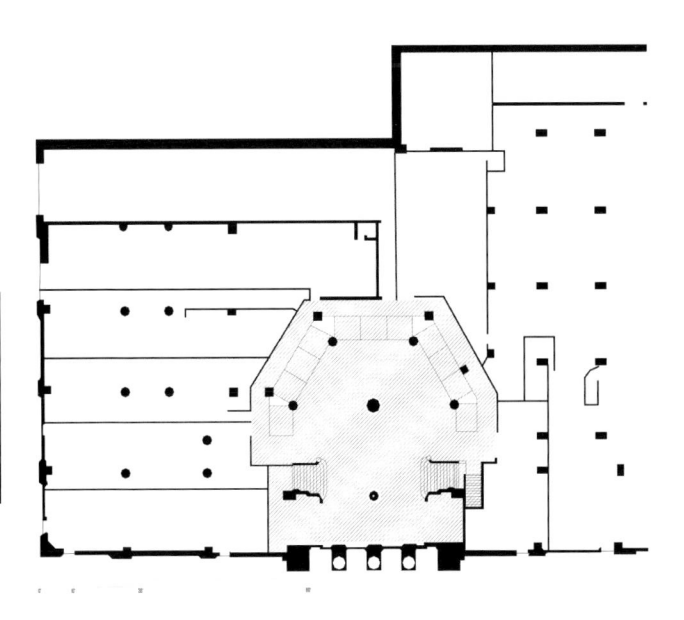

19th century. An architectural writer remarked at the time that: Current American architecture is not a matter of art, but of business. A building must pay or there will be no investor ready with the money to meet its cost. This is at once the curse and the glory of American architecture.[31] Another writer remarked how "in this strictly utilitarian building the requirements are imposed with a stringency elsewhere unknown in the same degree," and yet, it was, he thought, "very greatly to the advantage of the architecture." In particular, he recognized the "very great share" Chicago businessman (even more than New York) had in the "evolution of commercial architecture" through the insistence on accepting functional and economic requirements.[32] All recognized the changing demands on the profession by the effects on modernity, at the same time there were calls for a contemporary American architecture mostly in terms of a new style. In succeeding years, in art and architectural histories, the meeting of the new demands of modernity was too often separated from the appearance of modernity, or modernism.

That separation has tended to extract architecture from its context. This artificial separation contradicts the fact that our buildings are deeply a part of our entire cultural, social, political, and economic contexts. They are not solely artistic artifacts. And as large and largely permanent construction, architecture has shaped our cities. And, perhaps most importantly, such buildings are a repository of architectural and urban knowledge, waiting to be rediscovered and to correct our path when we go astray in the design of our human environment.

Abstract

Das große Bürogebäude im frühen Chicago aus künstlerischer und funktionaler Sicht

Das große Bürogebäude als Spekulationsobjekt verwies schon per definitionem auf die Aspekte Höhe und Rentabilität in ihrer extremen Form. Es stellte die Architekten in puncto Bauentwurf und -ausführung vor neue Herausforderungen und architektonische Prinzipien und Dimensionen, die sich über Jahrhunderte für fünf- oder sechsgeschossige Strukturen entwickelt hatten, wurden durch die hohe Fassade eines solchen Gebäudes gesprengt. Die fein abstimmbare Quadratmetermiete, die dann mit Geschossflächen und Etagen multipliziert wurde, verlangte erstmals eine Flächenplanung, über die genau Rechenschaft abzulegen war.

Diese zwei wichtigen Aspekte – Fassade und Grundriss – in der Entwicklung der großen Bürogebäude im Chicago des späten 19. und sehr frühen 20. Jahrhunderts sind Thema dieses Vortrags. Im Mittelpunkt der Diskussion steht dabei hauptsächlich die Arbeit der Firmen Adler & Sullivan sowie Burnham & Root (später D. H. Burnham & Co.).

Bibliography

BERGER, Miles L., *They Built Chicago: Entrepreneurs Who Shaped A Great City's Architecture* (Chicago: Bonus Books, 1992).

BLUESTONE, Daniel, *Constructing Chicago* (New Haven: Yale University Press, 1991).

BRUEGMANN, Robert, *The Architects of the City: Holabird & Roche of Chicago, 1880–1918* (Chicago: The University of Chicago Press, 1997).

CHAPPELL, Sally A. Kitt, *Architecture and Planning of Graham, Anderson, Probst and White, 1912–1936: Transforming Tradition* (Chicago: The University of Chicago Press, 1992).

FREI, Hans, *Louis Henry Sullivan* (Zurich: Artemis Verlags-AG, 1992).

GILBERT, James, Perfect Cities (Chicago: The University of Chicago Press, 1991).

HOFFMANN, Donald, *The Architecture of John Wellborn Root* (Baltimore: The Johns Hopkins University Press, 1973).

HOFFMANN, Donald, ed., *The Meanings of Architecture: Buildings and Writings by John Wellborn Root* (New York: Horizon Press, 1967).

MAYER, Harold M. and WADE, Richard C., Chicago: Growth of a Metropolis (Chicago: University of Chicago Press, 1969).

REBORI, A.N., „The Work of Burnham & Root, D. H. Burnham, D. H. Burnham & Co., and Graham, Burnham & Co.", *Architectural Record* XXXVIII (July 1915) 33–168.

ROOT, John W., „A Great Architectural Problem," *The Inland Architect and News Record* XV: 5 (June 1890) 67–71, reprinted in Donald Hoffmann, ed., *The Meanings of Architecture: Buildings and Writings by John Wellborn Root* (New York: Horizon Press, 1967).

SALTON, Deborah, "Burnham and Root and the Rookery," in John S. GARNER, ed., *The Midwest in American Architecture* (Chicago: University of Illinois Press, 1991) 76–97.

SCHAFFER, Kristen, *Daniel H. Burnham: Visionary Architect and Planner*. Photographs by Paul Rocheleau, introduction by Scott Tilden. New York: Rizzoli International Publications, Inc., 2003.

SCHULTZ Earle and SIMMONS, Walter, Offices in the Sky (New York: The New Bobbs-Merrill Co., 1959).

SCHUYLER, Montgomery, *American Architecture and Other Writings*, William H. Jordy and Ralph Coe, eds., (Cambridge, Massachusetts: The Belknap Press of Harvard University Press, 1961).

SCHUYLER, Montgomery, "Great American Architects Series: Part I – Architecture in Chicago" *Architectural Record* (December 1895).

SCHUYLER, Montgomery, "Great American Architects Series: Part II. – D. H. Burnham & Co.," *Architectural Record* (December 1895).

SULLIVAN, Louis H., *The Autobiography of an Idea* (New York: Dover Publications, Inc., 1956 [1924]).

SULLIVAN, Louis H, "The Tall Office Building Artistically Considered" in *Louis Sullivan: The Public Papers*, Robert Twombly, ed. (Chicago: The University of Chicago Press, 1988) pp. 103–113.

TWOMBLY, Robert, *Louis Sullivan: His Life and Work* (New York: Viking Penguin, Inc., 1986).

TWOMBLY, Robert, ed. *Louis Sullivan: The Public Papers*. (Chicago: The University of Chicago Press, 1988)

WIGHT, Peter B., "Daniel Hudson Burnham: An Appreciation." *Architectural Record* XXXII (August 1912) 178–183.

WILLIS, Carol, *Form Follows Finance: Skyscrapers and Skylines in New York and Chicago* (New York: Princeton Architectural Press, 1995).

WOODS, Mary N., *From Craft to Profession: The Practice of Architecture in Nineteenth-Century America* (Berkeley: University of California Press, 1999).

Sources of illustrations

All drawings were commissioned by and are reproduced courtesy of the author. They were produced by Matteo Rapallini. All photographs used with the permission of the Art Institute of Chicago, Ryerson & Burnham Archives.

* The photo rights have been clarified by the author and she has the responsibility

---

[1] Chicago was incorporated in 1833. By 1850, the city had less than 30,000 inhabitants, but between 1850 and 1870, the population grew tenfold, to about 300,000 inhabitants. It grew to 1,000,000 inhabitants by 1890, and by 1900 the population had reached 1,700,000. Some of this growth, especially in the period from 1880 to 1890, was due to the annexation of adjacent townships. During that period, the increase of population within the old city limits was 57%, but in the increase from annexation was 650%. MAYER and WADE, Chicago, 30, 35 & 176; GILBERT, Perfect Cities, 27.

[2] I am referring to the first century BCE Roman architect Vitruvius whose definition of architecture, as utilitas, firmitas, and venustas, was translated into English in the early 17th century by Sir Henry Wotton, as commodity, firmness and delight.

[3] SULLIVAN, Autobiography, 255–257. The partnership lasted until 1895. Adler died in 1900. Sullivan faced increasing difficulties after the split but practiced until 1922. He died in 1924.

[4] WIGHT, „Burnham: An Appreciation," 178. Their partnership and friendship ended with Root's death in 1891. Burnham continued practicing as D. H. Burnham & Co. until his death in 1912.

[5] SULLIVAN, *Autobiography*, 285–286, 314. WOODS, *From Craft to Profession*, 118–120. Casting this same trait in a different light, a former employee recalled that "Burnham was one of the first architects to build up a highly efficient and well-equipped office organization to satisfy the needs of a rapidly increasing business." Burnham helped engineered the transition to the modern large architectural practice. REBORI, "Work of Burnham & Root," 34.

[6] Quoted in TWOMBLY, Sullivan: Life & Work, 331, from a paper Adler delivered before the American Institute of Architects in October 1896.

[7] This was the East Coast architect Robert S. Peabody. See WOODS, 138; also 161.

[8] I am not claiming that it is the first or the only such insight; only that it was powerful.

[9] Other examples are the McCormick Offices and Warehouse (1886) by Burnham & Root, and the Walker Warehouse (1888–89) by Adler & Sullivan, both in Chicago.

[10] According to Adler, the facade design was suggested by the client, the Chicago Grand Auditorium Association. FREI, Sullivan, 68, citing Adler's remarks in Architectural Record, 1892.

[11] Although neither of these building are in Chicago, they were produced by Chicago architects and are considered among the best examples of what is known as the Chicago school.

[12] SCHUYLER, „Architecture Chicago: Adler & Sullivan" in JORDY & COE, American Architecture, 390.

[13] Quoted in TWOMBLY, Sullivan: Life & Work, 285.

[14] SCHUYLER, „Architecture in Chicago: Adler & Sullivan" in JORDY & COE, American Architecture, 393. The whole quotation: "The Guaranty building at Buffalo is in its scheme a variant upon that of the Wainwright, the main difference being the substitution of terra cotta for the masonry of the basement and for the brickwork of the superstructure. The more facile material is recognized throughout in the treatment by reticulations of surface ornament differing in density and character of design, according to the function of the surface treated and to the function of what is behind it. I know of no steel-framed building in which the metallic construction is more palpably felt through the envelope of baked clay."

[15] SULLIVAN, „The Tall Office Building Artistically Considered" was first published in Lippincott's Magazine (March 1896) and then in *Inland Architect & News Record* (May 1896). It is reprinted in TWOMBLY, ed., *Sullivan: Public Papers*, 103–13, among other places. The quoted phrase appears on pp. 111 & 112.

[16] ROOT, „A Great Architectural Problem," was published in The Inland Architect and News Record, XV:5 (June 1890) 67–71; and reprinted in HOFFMANN, ed., Meanings of Architecture, 130–42. The quotation is on 133.

[17] WILLIS, in Form Follows Finance, has given this issue greater publicity, but it has always been the concern of historian Robert BRUEGMANN, see especially his Architects of the City.

[18] SCHUYLER, „Great American Architects – D. H. Burnham & Co.," 50.

[19] SCHUYLER, „Great American Architects – D. H. Burnham & Co.," 53.

[20] A major planning problem for the tall office building was the penetration of sunlight into interior work spaces. This limited office depth and arrangement. Given standard floor-to-ceiling heights of ten to twelve feet, the maximum depth from exterior window to corridor wall ranged between twenty and twenty-eight feet. Despite being a new technological wonder made possible by gas and later electrical lights, and by mechanical heating and sometimes

cooling systems, the tall office building still relied heavily on natural light and air. Cooling was not air conditioning, which was a later invention. WILLIS, *Form Follows Finance*, 24–27; BLUESTONE, *Constructing Chicago*, 132.

[21] ADLER & SULLIVAN'S plan for the earlier Wainwright Building was very similar to that of the Guaranty.

[22] Unfortunately Frank Lloyd Wright's renovation of the interior (1905–07) destroyed some aspects of the original unifying lightness and airiness that Root achieved with the use of open ironwork. Root's floor design has been reproduced in the latest restoration. See SALTON, „Burnham and Root and the Rookery," in GARNER, ed., *Midwest in American Architecture*, 76–97.

[23] That Burnham continues with this strategy after Root's death has allowed me to argue for Burnham's role in the design of the firm's buildings. See SCHAFFER, Daniel H. Burnham.

[24] BERGER, They Built Chicago, 39.

[25] BRUEGMANN, *Architects of the City*, 70 & 114–15; BLUESTONE, *Constructing Chicago*, 140. See also CHAPPELL, *Graham, Anderson, Probst and White*, 2, for another discussion of building hierarchy.

[26] Aldis' rules for Profitable Building Management: "First: The office that gives up the most for light and air is the best investment. Second: Second-class space costs as much to build and operate as first-class space. Therefore, build no second-class space. Third: The parts every person entering sees must make a lasting impression. Entrance, first floor lobby, elevator cabs, elevator service, public corridors, toilet rooms must be very good. Fourth: Generally, office space should be about 24 feet deep from good light. Fifth: Operating expenses must be constantly borne in mind. Use proper materials and details to simplify the work. Sixth: Carefully consider and provide for changes in location of corridor doors, partitions, light, plumbing and telephones. Seventh: Arrange typical layout for intensive use. A large number of small tenants is more desirable than large space for large tenants because: a) A higher rate per square foot can be added for small tenants. b) They do not move in a body and leave the building with a large vacant space when hard times hit. c) They do not swamp your elevators by coming and going by the clock. Eighth: Upkeep of an office is most important. Janitor service must be of high quality, elevator operators of good personality. Management progressive." SCHULTZ and SIMMONS, Offices in the Sky, 33–34.

[27] BERGER, They Built Chicago, 39–48

[28] Martin ROCHE worked for Jenney at the same time as Sullivan.

[29] BRUEGMANN, Architects of the City, 124.

[30] Quoted in WILLIS, *Form Follows Finance*, 29–30. See also BLUESTONE, *Constructing Chicago*, 128–132.

[31] Barr Ferre in an address to the AIA convention in 1893, quoted in WILLIS, Form Follows Finance, 15.

[32] SCHUYLER, „Great American Architects – Architecture in Chicago," 8.

Christopher Woodward

The Office Building Architecture of the Early 20th Century in London
The London office building 1900–30 and a case study of
an urban ensemble: Kingsway

Introduction

This paper has two parts; each illustrates the sharp *differences* between individual buildings and urban development in London and Hamburg during the period 1900 to 1930.

The first part is an introduction to three broad themes that inform the construction of the London office building in the period, followed by a chronological survey of about twenty significant office buildings of the period. The majority were built for particular commercial clients – banks, insurance and trading companies – otherwise speculatively. Buildings for the state are referred to in passing. The survey is illustrated by recent photographs, supplemented where possible by plans and other material from contemporary journals and magazines.

The second part is, as a contrast with the commercial district associated with the Chilehaus and Sprinkenhof etc, a case study of an early twentieth-century urban ensemble constituted almost entirely of office buildings: Kingsway, one of the series of 'improvements' – new streets – begun at the beginning of the nineteenth century. These were intended to relieve traffic congestion, improve the commercial building stock and to remove areas of slums, dispersing their inhabitants or rehousing the 'deserving poor' in new philanthropically-inspired developments.

Fig. 1: Capitol, Rome, Michelangelo Buonarroti and Giacomo della Porta, 1539–92

Fig. 2: Palazzo Massimo alle Colonne, Rome, Baldassare Peruzzi, 1532–36

1 Three themes and a survey

1.1 Plans and forms of organisation, types

While the twenty selected buildings are extraordinarily diverse, some common themes can be discerned. These include the development of types and methods of organising spaces for the activities of large, complex commercial, hierarchical entities. Techniques for these had first emerged in England in the early- and mid-19th century in the plans of, for example, museums, law courts, town halls, ministries and hospitals, particularly in the work of John Soane (1753–1837), in his Bank of England and Law Courts, and later of Alfred Waterhouse (1830–1905). These new plans were without exception developed within the framework of the street, always extending to the boundaries of their sites, the 'building lines'. Their ranges were about 9m thick and daylit either from the perimeter or from the 'light wells' that penetrated the block.

Fig. 3: Palazzo Chigi-Odescalchi, Rome, Carlo Maderna, G. L. Bernini and others, 1622–29, 1644–66

Fig. 4: Rashtrapati Bhavan (former Viceroy's House), New Delhi, India, Edwin Lutyens, 1912–31

1.2 Building technology

The Ritz Hotel of 1906, designed by Mewès and Davis, was the first London's building in which a steel frame clad in redundant conventional masonry was used. A year later year same architects' offices for the *Morning Post* newspaper were completed (Fig. 6), also built with a steel frame. While since the Industrial Revolution England had much experience of industrial and warehouse buildings constructed with cast-iron frames, the use of the fireproofed steel frame almost certainly followed the example of the rebuilding of Chicago after the fire of 1871. The layouts of these frames tended use the square bays of the warehouse, and until buildings such as Broadway House (Fig. 15) and were rarely based on particular planning ideas about use or sub-division. This form of construction became *de rigueur* in commercial buildings until 1945 when shortages of steel provoked the substitution of the reinforced concrete frame.

While the white stone from Portland in Dorset had first been introduced in London's monumental architecture by Inigo Jones in Whitehall Banqueting House of 1623–27, until the end of the nineteenth century its use remained limited mainly to the cladding of churches and large houses. By the beginning of the twentieth century it had become widely used as a general covering for the street fronts of commercial buildings, as most of the examples here show, while humbler materials such as light-reflecting white glazed brick were used for lining their light wells. Windows to the street were usually made of drawn bronze or hardwood while the first steel frames first appeared in light wells.

1.3 Style: imperial dreams

By 1900 the gothic revival had finally expired, first challenged in the 1860s in official circles by a form of Italianate classicism, and in domestic architecture by the various practitioners of the Arts and Crafts, including Waterhouse's near contemporary Richard Norman Shaw (1831–1912).

Edward VII, successor to Queen Victoria, was crowned in 1901 and the period of his reign until his death in 1910, now known as the 'Edwardian', was characterised by both what in retrospect was seen as the apogee of British imperialism, and those political and cultural forces which were eventually to lead to its demise. In matters of both urban form and architecture, the search for an appropriate "imperial" style in town planning inevitably suggested the use of axes and vistas. The buildings that formed these were to be dressed in an amalgam of various but exclusively classical forms originating in Italy and France and transmuted through the École des Beaux Arts (Figs. 1, 2 and 3).

It was, though, from 1911 when New Delhi, the new capital of India was founded, that these megalomaniac dreams were most fully realised, chiefly and most astutely by Edwin Lutyens (1869–1944) – the dream described by Nikolaus Pevsner as the '*folie de grandeur imperiale*' (Fig. 4).

1.4 Survey

The following examples have been chosen largely for their architectural significance: they show the variety of approaches to the design of office buildings in London in the period 1900 to about 1930.

Sources of plans and other information available in the literature are indicated.

Abbreviations
AR: *Architectural Review* magazine
Butler: A S G BUTLER, The Architecture of Sir Edwin Lutyens, volume 3: Town and public buildings, London 1950

Fig. 5
Offices, shops and flats 1903
R Norman Shaw with Ernest Newton
St. James's Street SW1
Corner site, in Shaw's late Baroque style, five storeys around a single light well, loadbearing masonry (?), Portland stone cladding.
Plans and elevations in: vol. 21 AR 1907, pp. 46–9

Fig. 6
Newspaper offices 1906–7
Mewès and Davis
Aldwych WC2
Triangular corner site, seven storeys (top mansard later addition); early use of steel frame.

Fig. 7
Kodak House 1911
Sir John Burnet Tait
65 Kingsway WC2
End of block, six storeys (top floor later addition). Steel frame, 'warehouse' construction. Portland stone clad piers with bronze-clad spandrels and window frames between.

Fig. 9 / Fig. 10
Britannic House 1924–27, 1987–89
Edwin Lutyens; Peter lnskip and Peter Jenkins
Moorgate and Fisbury Circus EC2
Originally built as headquarters of an oil company. End of block. Three differentiated façades, the most elaborate that to Finsbury circus. Originally two light-wells, separated by major rooms, one now covered by atrium roof. Steel frame, Portland stone cladding. Plans in: AR vol. 57 1925, p. 192 ff.

Fig. 11 / Fig. 12
Adelaide House 1924–25
John Burnet, Tait and Partners
King William Street EC4
End of block. Eleven storeys, corers and ends of façades emphasized, closely-spaced piers between, 'Egyptian cornice', 'warehouse' type steel frame, Portland stone cladding.
Plans in: AR vol. 57 1925, p. 68–73

Fig. 13
ex **Midland Bank Head Office** 1924–39
Lutyens; executive architects Gotch and Saunders
Poultry and Princes Street EC3
Site spans between two streets each having different, sophisticated astylar elevations, the more intricate to Poultry. Two main light wells. Suite for board and chairman's office on top floor, board room crowned with flat dome. Steel frame, Portland stone cladding. Empty in 2011, with plans for conversion into a hotel.
Plans, elevations and details in: Hussey, vol. 3, plates XXIX–XXX etc

Fig. 14
Bush House 1925–35
Helmle and Corbett
American architects for an American client. Large development on Aldwych island site. Steel frame, Portland stone cladding. Central north-south range with U-shaped offices to west and east. Main entrance on axis of Kingsway marked with magnificent screened exedra.
Plans and contemporary photos in: AR vol 55 1924, p. 132 ff.

Fig. 15
Broadway House 1927–9
Charles Holden
55 Broadway SW1
Built as new headquarters of London transport. Modern plan: irregular cruciform wings radiating from core, all standing on single-story podium above Underground station. Wings organised as rooms on either side of a corridor. No light-wells: all rooms have un-restricted views. Steel frame, Portland stone cladding.
Plans in: AR vol. 66 1929, pp. 225–6

Fig. 16
Unilever House 1930–31
J Lomax Simpson with John Burnet, Tait and Lorne
New Bridge Street and Embankment EC4
Island site, curved façade facing bridge with magnificent 3-storey high giant colonnade. Originally planned round two light wells, one of these now an atrium. Steel frame, Portland stone cladding.

2 A case study, a new office district: Kingsway and Aldwych, started 1898

In London, and until the formation of the Board of Metropolitan Works in 1855, there was no central agency to promote public works of infrastructure (including improving the poor drainage responsible for the two cholera outbreaks of 1854), or to address the unsatisfactory housing conditions of the poor. Having addressed the first with the major works to the new Thames Embankment, the Board continued with the establishment of several new streets designed to demolish areas of poverty and establish new traffic routes.

The elected London County Council (LCC) replaced the Board in 1889, the same year that the campaigner Charles Booth published his polemical 'Descriptive Map of London Poverty'. With wider powers than the Board, the LCC undertook schemes of social housing (previously provided by charitable trusts), and in 1898 published its plan identify-

Fig. 8: ex County Hall 1911–22 and 1931–33,
Ralph Knott, Westminster Bridge SE1
Built as headquarters of London County Council, now hotel. Island site with frontage to Thames; six storeys plus two in huge roof, planned round multiple light-wells. Steel frame, Portland stone cladding

ing the area roughly midway between the West End and the City as an opportunity to provide a useful north-south traffic link and to eradicate slums to the east of Covent Garden. The council bought up sufficient land to provide for a new road, 'Kingsway' 100 feet (30 metres) wide, and lined with irregular plots on which developers were invited to build offices. Kingsway was to be a modern road, of ample width for pedestrians and traffic below which ran two new sewers and a tram tunnel; two ample vaults were provided for piped services. Large basements below the pavements extended from the building plots.

While the road was aligned on the Baroque church of St Mary to the south, a connection to Waterloo Bridge was provided by a new quarter-crescent to the west, reflected to the east. The resulting crescent was called 'Aldwych'.

Site clearance began immediately the plan was published, and the new road opened in 1905. The scheme provoked much discussion and criticism in the professional press, most of it detailed. (For example, the mandatory splayed block corners intended to help traffic movement were censured for breaking the street-line.) An unofficial competition for the design of the Aldwych block produced mediocre results: most entries proposed uniform buildings with regular cornice-lines and dressed and with feeble classical motifs, all vaguely French.

Development began rapidly at the south end with buildings on the two crescents. In the period up to 1914 it continued northwards on Kingsway, after which supplies of material became increasingly restricted. Suggestions for uniform development of form, for example a continuous cornice line 80 feet (24 metres) above the ground were not realised, but building lines *were* strictly observed, and every building is clad in the traditional material of London for non-domestic properties: Portland stone, introduced to London by Inigo Jones for the facings of his Banqueting House, 1619 and used ever since for institutional and many commercial buildings.

The architectural quality of many of the mainly seven- to nine-storey office buildings with shops on the ground floor is tentative and undistinguished, the work of Trehearne and Preston. A few buildings, however, show some ambition. Lutyens' Dorlond House of 1906, for the head office of a gardening magazine, completed two years after the larger *Country Life* offices of two years earlier (Fig. 8). Its facade is layered: fortified Sanmicheli on the ground; eighteenth-century palace above, topped by an Arts and Crafts classical synthesis (Fig. 17). Contemporaries criticised the design for failing to provide large enough windows at street level, and this was indeed a perennial concern since the classical language yielded few suggestions.

The single building which has entered respectable histories, and of which Nikolaus Pevsner approved is the 'proto-modern' Kodak House of 1910, designed by the Scot John Burnet. Its bland warehouse structure is clad to the street with an assured composition of base, middle and top which at pavement level on either side of the central entrance suavely incorporates very wide windows for the display of camera equipment. This is separated by an intermediate floor from the four storeys of office accommodation where near-featureless pilasters separate full-height bronze panels and widow frames. The whole is capped with an Egyptoid cornice.

In the 1920s the southern termination of Kingsway was provided by an American developer, Irving T. Bush, proprietor of a large distribution (logistics) company for whose proposed 'trade center' his American architects brought to London their grand American classical style with their magnificent exedra (but without the planned ambitious tower) (Fig. 7).

The best example of the type that underlies most of the commercial buildings of the period 1900–1910 is perhaps that of Australia House on the triangular site on the east side of Aldwych, started in 1913 and completed in 1918 (Fig. 18). Its plan can be regarded as a solid carved out by three light wells, or as a perimeter block with an additional central range. The crucial point to note is that the light wells are strictly utilitarian, their workaday architecture a sharp contrast with the stone 'imperial' pomp presented to the street. Moreover, they do not extend to the ground but stop at first floor level to allow light to penetrate into the continuous, publicly-accessible ground floor. At Australia House, this ground floor is of some magnificence, and a vaulted and marble-lined, Doric-ordered route extends right through the building from east to west.

This pattern of internal light-wells, adapted to suit particular site conditions, provided the pattern for the offices of most of the period from 1900 to 1930. While by no means confined to London, it is sufficient to distinguish the type from, say, that of the Hanseatic open courts, 'die hanseatischen Höfe', of Hamburg's Chilehaus, and accentuate the particularity of the latter's type.

Fig. 17: Dorlond House, Kingsway, London WC2, Edwin Lutyens, 1906

Fig. 18: Australia House, Aldwych, London WC2, A M and A G R Mackenzie, 1913–18

Abstract

Bürohausarchitektur des frühen 20. Jahrhunderts in London

Diese chronologische Untersuchung von bemerkenswerten Bürogebäuden in London, die zwischen 1900 und 1930 entstanden, betrachtet sowohl Gebäudeart, -form und -funktionen als auch deren architektonischen Stil. Haben diese Gebäude einen Beitrag zum Ensemble oder gar zur Stadtlandschaft geleistet? Es wird eine Studie zum letzten ehrgeizigen „imperialen" städteplanerischen Ensemble Londons vorgestellt, nämlich dem städtischen Sanierungskonzept für die neuen Straßen „Aldwych and Kingsway", wozu Gebäude und Infrastrukturmaßnahmen gehören. Die Arbeiten begannen im Jahre 1906, jedoch entstanden große Teile erst später und die Nachkriegsbauten – fast ausschließlich Geschäftshäuser – sind zeitgenössisch. Sie heben sich sehr deutlich vom Hamburger Kontorhausviertel ab und sind einzigartig.

Bibliography

Simon BRADLEY and Nikolaus PEVSNER, The Buildings of England: London, 6 vols, London 1997

A S G BUTLER, The Architecture of Sir Edwin Lutyens, 3 vols, vol 3 Town and public buildings, London 1950

Elain HARWOOD and Andrew SAINT, Exploring England's Heritage, London 1991

Edward JONES and Christopher WOODWARD, A Guide to the Architecture of London, 4th edition, London 2009

Alistair SERVICE, Edwardian Architecture, London 1977

Alistair SERVICE, The Architects of London, London 1979

Picture credits

All photos © Christopher Woodward; Figs. 5–18 from Edward JONES and Christopher WOODWARD, A Guide to the Architecture of London, 4th edition, London 2009.

* The photo rights have been clarified by the author and he has the responsibility

Herman van Bergeijk

Dutch Office Building 1900–1940.
A Question of Style or Mentality?[1]

In 1915 a newspaper in Rotterdam opened an article on office building with the following sentence: 'Awareness of power expresses itself in a lust for building and as the trade companies in Rotterdam are growing in size and influence, they will establish in our city office palaces that already on the street side show what they have to mean'.[2] The article is a token to the importance given to office building in the city on the Maas. Remarkably enough it was preceded by an article on the architecture of the public authorities suggesting a relationship between the two.

Yet to state that the question of the office building has been a recurrent theme within Dutch architectural debates would be an exaggeration. On the contrary, it seems that the topic has hardly been worth discussing. Architectural magazines and books regularly present office buildings but it is not a topic that ranks high on the professional agenda. And in history? For different reasons in the typically one-sided histories of modern architecture office building plays a marginal role. In general, office buildings follow the stylistic developments and only a few examples, isolated phenomena, can be considered 'ahead of their time'. As far as the Netherlands are concerned, the focus points in history are those which were affected by innovative legislation, and in particular the famous 'Woningwet' (Housing Law).

Office building is dependent on a client who is willing to put an extra effort in the question of representation and who wants to combine aesthetic qualities with usefulness. This can either be the government or a company that needs administrative facilities. Office building belongs in the capitalistic world or as the architect Jan Wils noted in 1920, there is a close link between the modern businessman and the modern artist. The artist sublimes the intentions of the merchant and Wils listed buildings that could be considered a 'plus for commercial enterprises'.[3] The facades of office buildings are often a token of richness and a representation of a certain ideology. Due to its particular nature, in some cases, office building will even become an object of speculation for private entrepreneurs. Such is surely the case of the so called 'White House' in Rotterdam (Fig. 1), designed by Willem Molenbroek and constructed around 1900. This building was beyond any doubt an important beacon in the city. It was the first high-rise building in the Netherlands and was considered to be inspired by American skyscraper examples. Clearly the developers saw the potential of high-rise for office building, but the Netherlands were not the United States and the project was not a great success. It was difficult

Figure 1: W. Molenbroek, 'White House', Rotterdam, 1897–1900

Figure 2: J. S. C. van de Wal, gate building/later main office building of the Holland-Amerika Lijn (Poortgebouw), Rotterdam, 1878

Figure 3: J.A. Brinkman and L.C. van der Vlugt, Office building of the Van Nelle factory, Rotterdam, 1926–1929

Figure 4: A.J. Kropholler, Main office building of the bank Mees & Co, Rotterdam, 1929–1933

to find renters. The prominent position was deliberately chosen. It increased its potential to be used for advertisements. The white building with its massive roof that functioned as a panorama platform – a belvedere – was visible from great distances along the main river. With an elevator one could rush to the top and admire the spectacular view. It was a billboard in more than one way. Yet, the architectural world hardly took notice of the building. The White House did not in any way represent the character of this port-city, but neither did the gate building (Poortgebouw) (Fig. 2) that was finished in 1878, which for many years would be the main office building of the Holland-Amerika Lijn.

Although for many years the White House remained an important icon in the city of Rotterdam, it would be substituted at the end of the nineteen twenties by the famous Van Nelle factory of J.A. Brinkman and L.C. van der Vlugt (Fig. 3) that represented a more modern and contemporary approach to the problem. The factory had a separate administration block that showed the same transparency. From heaviness the accent had moved towards lightness, the same lightness that was considered to be fundamental for products of a modern industrialized society. The contrast between the White House and the Van Nelle factory cannot be bigger but nevertheless both were seen, in their time, as examples of modern architecture. Between these two extremes there was a broad spectrum of other possibilities. It seems that Rotterdam was the city of extremes. This can also be exemplified by two office buildings of the bank Mees & Co. On the one hand one has the modern bank building of Brinkman and Van der Vlugt (Fig. 4) and on the other the brick main office of the same bank at the Blaak designed by A.J. Kropholler. Both buildings were built in approximately the same years. This dualism between heaviness and lightness characterizes the two sides of a city that after World War II has done much to portray itself as a modern town. Architects like W. Kromhout and H.F. Mertens belong to the group in the centre between these extremes. Their work shows in the masonry the influence of the more expressionistic architecture of the Amsterdam School. Kromhout was the architect of the amazing Noordzee building (1916) and of the office of the navigation association (Fig. 5) built in

1920, and Mertens was the house architect of the Rotterdam Bank Association and the architect of the remarkable Unilever building. These buildings certainly bring a touch of Amsterdam to its rival city in the south-west. The interesting buildings of Kromhout bear more connotations to ships than the Scheepvaarthuis. The critic and architect Willem Retera was ecstatic in his opinion. According to him 'these buildings are no more blocks where people talk and do their business [...] but buildings that open up in atmosphere and space, and that have taken in the stimulating times and radiate it again'.[4]

Responsible for this gaze towards the capital was the construction of the Scheepvaarthuis, the collective housing of several shipping companies, from 1912 onwards (Fig. 6). The commission had been given to the well established firm of J. N. and A. D. N. van Gendt. Van Gendt had and would build many big buildings. They were specialized in structural engineering. In order to achieve an aesthecally gratifying image it was decided that J. M. van der Mey would design the facades. Van der Mey, a talented draughtsman, had hardly built but he had been the aesthetic advisor of the city and was probably also related to one of the directors of the shipping companies. The building was the overture to an architectural fashion that was especially heralded in the beautiful magazine *Wendingen*. Michel de Klerk, Piet Kramer and many other artists worked under the supervision of Van der Mey in the design of many architectural details. The building was overloaded by all kinds of ornament and expensive materials. The history of Dutch shipping was illustrated in many sculptural elements although in its overall setting the building did not embody any reference to a naval metaphor, there were many aspects that connected to the companies that were housed in the building. Some details like the ropelike edge of the roof and the undulating movement of the same can be seen as derived from a marine inspiration and there were many allegorical scenes. The main entrance was marked by a truncated tower in which one could find a luxurious staircase to all the different floors. Although some people have tried to read the building as an analogy to a ship, this likeness is less apparent than in the famous building of Höger. With a little fantasy one could see in the Chilehaus the bow of a ship with which Henry B. Sloman transported his goods from South America. But whereas the Chilehaus forms an ensemble with its environment the Scheepvaarthuis in Amsterdam remains an isolated object. The manner in which ornament and decorations were applied in the building in Amsterdam is totally different from the way Höger and the brothers Gerson had used it in their buildings. They work more with patterns and texture. A building that does have a Hamburg flavor is the head office of Siemens on the Huygenspark (Fig. 7) in The Hague, built in 1922. It is still unknown who the architect was. Schumacher was well appreciated in The Hague where an exhibition of his work was organized in the same year 1922. Yet it is well known that Hans Hertlein was the architect of many Siemens buildings in Germany.

The impact of the Scheepvaarthuis on the cityscape was also less evident than that of the White House. Besides their location along the waterfront the buildings had little in common and similarities are hard to find. Although both made

Figure 5: W. Kromhout, Office of a navigation association, Rotterdam, 1920

use of the advanced technologies of their time these were draped in different kind of dresses. The White House wanted to be international, whereas the Scheepvaarthuis tried to establish and connect itself to a Dutch tradition without falling into a specific historicism. It is an example of 'Backsteinarchitektur' in the same way as the famous Stock Exchange of H. P. Berlage (Fig. 8) had been but it left the sober and rationalized style of Berlage far behind, at least as far as the facades and ornament went because the concrete skeleton of the construction belonged to another tradition. In fact it was a total neglect of the principles of Berlage, a fact that was acknowledged by Van der Mey when he admitted that 'the

Figure 6: J. N. and A. D. N. van Gendt / J. M. van der Mey, Scheepvaarthuis (collective housing of several shipping companies), Amsterdam, 1912–1916

Figure 7: Hans Hertlein, head office of Siemens, The Hague, 1922

façade had nothing else to carry than its own weight and that it was supported by the core construction'.[5] Like in many other buildings of architects that are considered to be a part of the Amsterdam School there is no relationship between the outside and the inside. This was however an attitude that not many Dutch architects would approve of, even if some German critic saw it as 'natural means of expression of a healthy brick art'.[6] The main office of the Dutch railroad in Utrecht, designed by the civil engineer George W. van Heukelom in 1921, is a witness that brick could also be applied in a more rigorous way without becoming immediately orna-

Figure 8: H.P. Berlage, Stock Exchange, Amsterdam 1896–1903

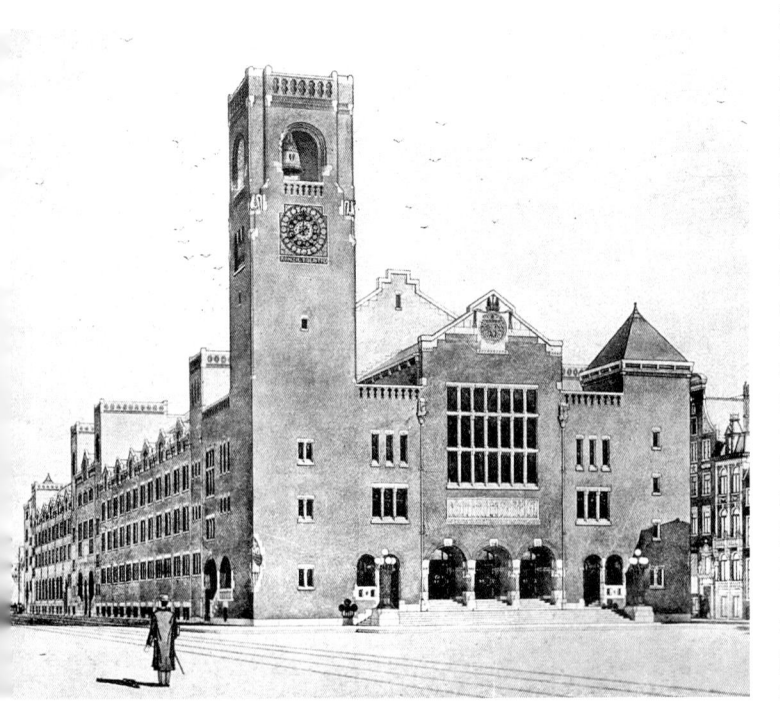

mental. In its vertical articulation it is similar to the Stumm-Konzern building of Paul Bonatz in Düsseldorf. It stands in great contrast to, for example, the post office building of the government architect J. Crouwel (1924) in the same city of Utrecht.

The reception of the Scheepvaarthuis differed greatly. Whereas the architect J. Luthmann saw it as the expression of 'a tense and very personal spirit', in 1941 it was seen as a reaction to the work of Berlage. All truth in architecture had been thrown overboard, according to H. M. Kraayvanger. And K. P. C. de Bazel once stated that is was pure 'virtuosity, without deeper grounds, ingenious, but without conviction'[7]

The engineering office of the brothers Van Gendt would also be responsible for the structure of the construction of the Dutch Trading Company (de Nederlandsche Handel Maatschappij), in the center of Amsterdam in the years 1919 to 1926 (Fig. 9). This enormous and impressive building was to be one of the last works of K. P. C. de Bazel, an architect who was a member of the Theosophical Society. The zoning of the upper floors gave the building a more Borobudur, temple like appearance, but inside the light courts showed the influence of Frank Lloyd Wright's Larkin building in Buffalo, which in many aspects also resembled a temple. Compared with the head office of the oil company Esso in The Hague, built in the same years by the Rotterdam office of De Roos and Overeynder (Fig. 10), we notice that the building of De Bazel is more compact and less expressive in volume. Yet what the buildings have in common is that again the structure is made of concrete and the façade is just a visual component. The Esso building functions, thanks to the deep red color of the used bricks and the massive tower, as a beacon to all those who come to the city, but in relation to its environment it has a certain ambivalence that was noticed and well worded by the reviewer in *Bouwkundig Weekblad*.[8]

Another office building with a structural skeleton designed by the office Van Gendt was the building of 'De Nederlanden van 1845' in The Hague. Here the relationship between outside and inside was much stricter which should not surprise us when we know that H.P. Berlage was the architect (Fig. 11). Berlage created the corporate identity of several insurance companies from 1895 onwards and was responsible for the office building of the Wm. H. Müller & Co. in London in 1914 that had an almost classical appearance. Imaging becomes important. Whereas brick had been the main component in these buildings, in 1925 he chose to express also the concrete structure in the façade. Two years after his trip to the Dutch Indies Berlage made an extraordinary achievement and proved to still be an inspiring figure in Dutch architecture. Thanks to the structure the building was flexible in its use and in 1954 a second floor was added by the Hilversum architect W.M. Dudok. It is an extension that is not obtrusive at all. When the project of Berlage was published in the newspapers it was seen as an experiment in which 'the always living wood' had been substituted by 'the dead concrete'.[9] The sober building had nevertheless not lost its aesthetic effect and that had also been the main purpose of the architect who was continuously looking for new beauty.

In this overview of Dutch office buildings we started in Rotterdam that profiled itself as port city, then went to the more culturally oriented Amsterdam and now will end in The Hague. It is in this last city that certainly the most remarkable office buildings have been realized thanks to the presence of the government and many international banking and oil companies. Generally speaking, these clients tended to be more inclined towards a more conservative and solid appearance. Tradition was a key word. In that light should also be mentioned the big building that J. J. P. Oud designed for the B. I. M. (Bataafse Import Maatschappij) in 1938 (Fig. 12) in the periphery of The Hague and that marked a turning point in his career. The board of directors wanted a building that was 'simple, sober and in line with the new management culture that the company represented'. It should be different from the large office of the B. P. M. that the brothers Van Nieukerken had designed in 1915 (Fig. 13) and that was in a sort of Dutch neo-Renaissance style. A competition was held and the project of Oud was awarded the first prize. The scheme that the architect had applied permitted a building in phases. Besides, Oud did not want the building to look like housing and in spite of his attempts to rationalize his decisions the building was heavily criticized by his former friends. In their eyes the building had become a question of style and not the proper result of an attitude that wanted to be seen as modern. Especially the application of ornament was considered to be a betrayal of the principles of modernism. A radical architect had become in their eyes a reactionary, illustrating the problems of 'affiliation' in a more and more politically complicated society just before the national-socialistic Barbarism. Also Van Nieukerken expressed in his unpublished memoirs a negative judgment on the building: 'For the exterior I have no admiration and the inside is sober objectivity. [...] When I see the cold objectivity I am reminded of the ink coolie in a paper warehouse, a slave of the office in modern life that has made economy and speed to the highest ideals'.[10] Oud seemed unable to please anybody.

His building is maybe the last building in which representation was embodied within ornament. After the Second World War the ordering of volumes will be the main issue for architects to deal with. Their solution will be, according to their own opinions, purely architectural in nature and easy to read for the common passer by. The tendency towards abstraction was victorious.

In order to take decisions regarding what we should do with these kinds of buildings after that they have lost their original function it is absolutely necessary to learn to read, decipher and understand what they have been telling us all along and what they are telling us in this moment. To do that we need certain skills and should not act too hastily based on only a superficial opinion, as in the case of the Scheepvaarthuis – the building has been recently transformed into a hotel. Where once decisions where taken, people now sleep and dream away. The rich decoration helps them on their way into the somatic realm of oblivion.

What we can learn from this short overview – and I deliberately use the thin worn word of Venturi 'learning' – is that some buildings have captured the spirit of the place and some have been capable of installing a new one, but that is

Figure 9: K. P. C. de Bazel, Nederlandsche Handel Maatschappij (Dutch Trading Company), Amsterdam, 1919–1926

Figure 10: De Roos and Overeynder, head office of the oil company Esso, The Hague, 1919–1925

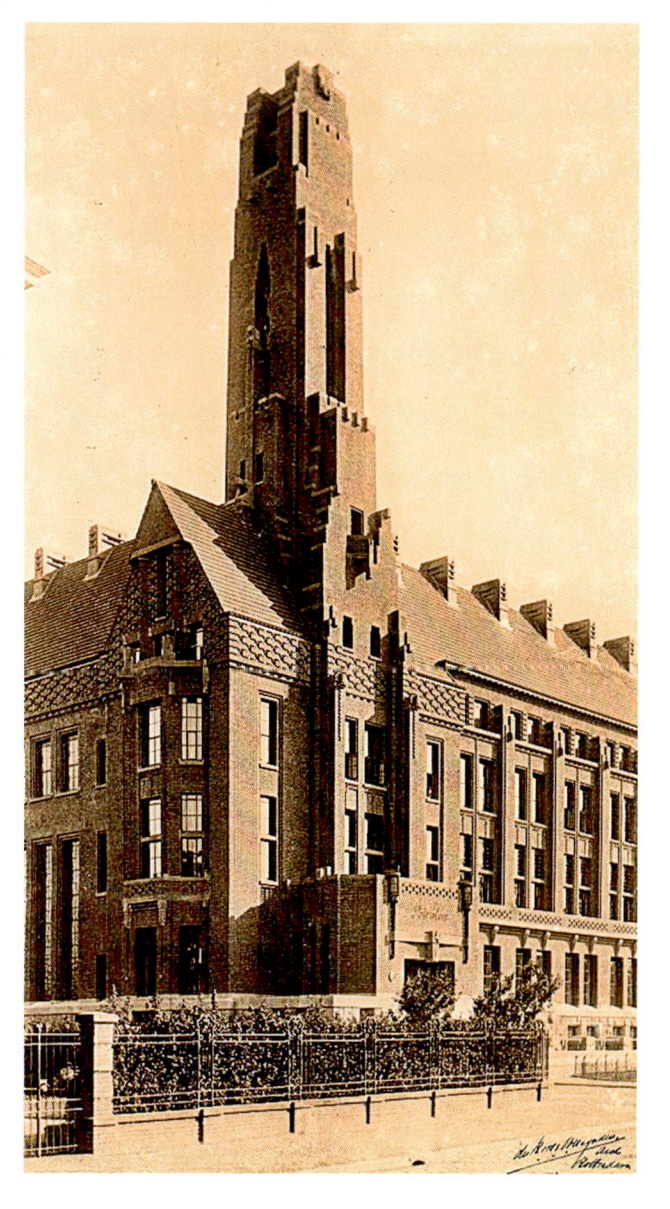

Figure 11: H.P. Berlage, office building of 'De Nederlanden van 1845', The Hague, 1920/1924–1927

of great importance to take into account the specific context through a more than random observation. Whereas in The Hague and Rotterdam there is a strong tendency to put isolated objects in an urban context that has a totally different character, in Amsterdam this is less the case.

Abstract

Niederländische Bürogebäude 1900–1940. Eine Frage des Stils?

Der vorliegende Beitrag über niederländische Bürogebäude aus der ersten Hälfte des zwanzigsten Jahrhunderts versucht, einen kurzen Überblick über diesen Teil der Großstadtarchitektur in den Niederlanden zu geben und die gestaltenden Kräfte dahinter zu erforschen. Im Zuge der Entwicklung eines neuen Management-Kapitalismus entstanden große, oft international tätige Unternehmen wie Banken, Versicherungen und Mineralölgesellschaften, die große Büroflächen benötigten. Diese dienten nicht nur repräsentativen Zwecken, sondern wurden in dem Bestreben errichtet, das charakteristische Gepräge der städtebaulichen Umgebung zu berücksichtigen und ihm etwas Neues hinzuzufügen. Das führte zu einer Heterogenität, die einerseits Abbild der stilistischen Vielfalt der Zeit sowie der Debatte darüber ist und andererseits die veränderte Haltung zur Rolle der städtischen Architektur widerspiegelt. In Amsterdam neigte man dem Expressionismus zu, in Rotterdam lässt sich ein eher funktionaler Stil erkennen. In Den Haag wiederum wird die Suche nach einer historisch orientierten Monumenta-

Figure 12: J.J.P. Oud, head office of the B.I.M. (Bataafse Import Maatschappij), The Hague, 1938

lität deutlich. Es waren meist die Bauunternehmer, die für Entwurf, statische Berechnungen und Erstellung der Stahlrahmenkonstruktion verantwortlich zeichneten, aber den Architekten kam die Aufgabe zu, sich um die Ästhetik zu kümmern. Auf diese Weise ergab sich ein subtiler Dialog zwischen der eher neutralen Konstruktion und dem repräsentativen Charakter der Fassaden, bei dem Architekten, Auftraggeber, Baumeister und städtische Behörden zu Wort kamen und wo Technik und Ästhetik zusammentrafen.

Literature

BANK, J./BUUREN, M. van, *1900: The Age of Bourgeois Culture*, Assen 2004.
d. CL., 'Kantoorgebouw Petrolea', in: *Bouwkundig Weekblad*, 1925, nr. 13, pp. 197–206
EEDEN, F. van, *Dagboek*, part III, 1911–1918, Culemborg 1971
JOBST, G., *Kleinwohnungsbau in Holland*, Berlin 1922
Kantoren, banken, administratiegebouwen, Rotterdam 1933
'Kantoorbouw', in: *Rotterdamsch Nieuwsblad*, 1915, 16 June.
KRAAYVANGER, H.M., 'De Nederlandsche bouwkunst na Berlage', in: *Nederland bouwt in baksteen 1800–1940*, Rotterdam 1941
LUTHMANN, J., 'Overzicht van de ontwikkeling der bouwkunst in Nederland', in: *Moderne Bouwkunst in Nederland*, part 1, Rotterdam 1932
'Nieuw gebouw De Nederlanden van 1845', in: *Het Vaderland*, 1924, April 19th, p. 1.

Figure 13: M.A. and J. van Nieukerken, office building of the B.P.M. (Bataafse Petroleum Maatschappij), 1915–1917

RETERA, W., *W. Kromhout Czn.*, Amsterdam 1925.
WILS, Jan, 'Handel, verkeerswezen en bouwkunst', in: *Het Vaderland*, October 7th 1920, avondblad B, p. 2.

Sources of illustrations

All reproductions stem from the collection of the IHAAU/TU Delft or from the private collection of the author.

* The photo rights have been clarified by the author and he has the responsibility

---

[1] This paper is a shortened version of a longer article that will be published elsewhere. A short overview is given in: *Kantoren*, in de serie 'Moderne Bouwkunst) in the series 'Moderne Bouwkunst.
[2] 'Kantoorbouw'.
[3] See: WILS, 'Handel'.
[4] RETERA, *Kromhout Czn.*, p. 54.
[5] See: BANK/BUUREN, *1900*, p. 190.
[6] See: JOBST, *Kleinwohnungsbau*, p. 23.
[7] See: LUTHMANN, KRAAYVANGER, p. XII and, for the remarks of De Bazel: EEDEN, p. 1503
[8] See: d. CL., 'Kantoorgebouw', pp. 197–206.
[9] 'Nieuw gebouw'.
[10] See the typoscript 'Van leven, bouwen, strijden en ontvangen in een architectenfamilie', in: NAi, Archive Van Nieukerken, nr. 584, p. 759.

Vladimir Slapeta

Prag, die Entstehung der neuen Metropole

„Die heutige Phase der Architektur charakterisiert der leise, aber erbitterte Kampf zwischen der aristokratischen und der demokratischen Auffassung" schrieb im Jahre 1924 der Architekt Josef Chochol, eine der führenden Persönlichkeiten des vorkriegszeitlichen Prager Kubismus, in seinem Text „Zur Demokratisierung der Architektur"[1], und führte weiter aus: „Die aristokratische Auffassung ist ein Überrest aus der Zeit des historischen Individualismus und ihr Merkmal ist Ausschließlichkeit, ein selbstständiges Trennen von den Anderen, „niedriger" Stehenden. Diese Eigenschaft ist undemokratisch, dem Fühlen und auch dem Denken unserer Zeit fremd, sogar gegenläufig, kurz unmodern. Einfach Anachronismus. Moderne und demokratische Auffassung der Architektur und ihrer Ausdrucksmittel kennzeichnen extreme Sachlichkeit und starker Wille zur Kollektivität. Der Grundzug ist, völlig dem vom praktischen Leben gegebenen Zweck zu genügen, nicht die sogenannten Gewöhnlichkeiten des Alltaglebens zu vermeiden, und sich mit der Lage zufrieden zu geben, die uns allen gleich gemeinsam ist."

In der Polarität zwischen diesen zwei Auffassungen – dem auslaufenden aristokratischen Konzept und dem entstehenden demokratischen Konzept, bewegt sich das Planen und

Abb. 1: Josef Zitek, Josef Schulz – Rudolfinum 1881–1883

Bauen in Prag seit der Wende vom 19. zum 20. Jahrhundert. Die übereilte Entwicklung der Stadt und ihre Transformation in die moderne Metropole hing, noch in der zweiten Hälfte des neunzehnten Jahrhunderts, mit der wachsenden wirtschaftlichen und politischen Bedeutung Prags als Zentrum der tschechischen Länder in der Zeit der industriellen Revolution zusammen. Das zeigte sich durch ihren inneren Umbau nach dem Abbau der theresianischen Fortifikation, durch den Bau des internationalen Eisenbahnknotens, durch die Beseitigung des jüdischen Ghettos, schließlich auch durch die Regulation der Moldau sowie die Einführung des öffentlichen Verkehrswesens und des elektrischen Netzwerkes.

Diese großen Veränderungen der städtischen Infrastruktur, begleitet vom sozialen Wandel und dem Anwachsen des Marktes, führten auch zur Maßstabsänderung der Verwaltungs-, Handels-, Verkehrs-, aber auch der Kulturgebäude. Die neuen Gebäude begannen vor allem die regulierten Ufer der Moldau zu säumen – auf der linken Seite entstand die Straka-Akademie (heute der Sitz der Regierung), auf dem rechten Ufer dann die Gebäude des tschechischen Nationaltheaters und des Konzertsaales Rudolfinum (Abb. 1), beide nach dem Entwurf von Josef Zítek, Professor der deutschen Technischen Hochschule in Prag und in Deutschland bekannt auch als Architekt des Landesmuseums in Weimar. Zíteks Gebäude führten in Prag die Ideen Gottfried Sempers ein. Andere Möglichkeiten zum Bauen bot der Abbau der theresianischen Fortifikationen, an deren Stelle zum Beispiel das Gebäude des Hauptbahnhofs entstand und schließlich auch das Nationalmuseum nach dem Entwurf von Josef Schulz. Mit seiner großzügigen Auffassung und dem großstädtischen Maßstab ist ihm der allmähliche Umbau des Pferdemarktes, jetzt schon Wenzelsplatz, zum Hauptboulevard der neustädtischen Handelscity zu verdanken.

Die drei- bis viergeschossigen Bürgerhäuser aus der Zeit des Barocks und Klassizismus wurden allmählich in großzügiger Weise durch eine etwa sechsstöckige Bebauung ersetzt. Josef Schulz hat auch gegenüber dem Rudolfinum an der Grenze der Jüdischen Altstadt das Kunstgewerbemuseum gebaut. Die Beseitigung des jüdischen Ghettos hat – nach dem Vorbild des Pariser Umbaus durch Baron Hausmann – zum Durchbruch der Pariser Straße als neuer Achse der Altstadt zur Moldau geführt. Auch hat die Stadt hat begonnen, sich in den Industrievierteln Karlín und Smíchov zu entwickeln. Bis zum Anfang des Ersten Weltkrieges wurden neue Stadtpaläste zu neuen Dominanten und Orientierungspunkten sowohl in der Struktur der historischen Stadt als auch in den neu entstehenden Stadtbezirken. Beispiele sind der Palast des Wiener Bankvereins (Abb. 2) in der Straße Na Příkopě „Am Graben" des Architekten Josef Zasche aus den Jahren 1906–08 oder der Palast des Versicherungsvereins der Zuckerindustrie auf Senovážné náměstí aus den Jahren 1911–12, der in der Zusammenarbeit des Münchner Architekten Theodor Fischer mit Zasche entstand, oder auf dem Ufer der mit einem kubistischen Portal versehene Palast der

Allgemeinen Pensionsanstalt aus den Jahren 1912–14, welcher Josef Zasche zusammen mit Jan Kotěra entwarf. Die Neubauten dieser Zeit entstanden auch direkt am wichtigsten Handelsboulevard der tschechischen Metropole, dem Wenzelsplatz. Ladenpassagen verbanden diese Paläste mit dem Straßennetz der Neuen Stadt und bereicherten damit bedeutend das städtische Parterre. Diese Tradition hat man auch in der Zwischenkriegszeit fortgeführt.

Den Koruna-Palast (Krone-Palast, Abb. 3) mit einer eleganten Passage zur Straße Na Příkopě hat nach dem Wettbewerb mit Jan Kotěra Antonin Pfeifer gebaut. Der Großvater des ehemaligen Präsidenten Václav Havel hat die populäre Lucerna-Passage gebaut, die durch den Block die Štěpánská- mit der Vodičkova-Straße verbindet. Vielleicht die interessanteste Intervention aus der Zeit kurz vor dem Ersten Weltkrieg stellt in der engen Nachbarschaft das Haus der Mährischen Versicherungsanstalt an der Ecke Wenzelsplatz und Štěpánská-Straße dar. Sein die Ecke beherrschender, plastisch runder und monumental entwickelter Tambur, der möglicherweise von Plečniks Zacherl-Haus in Wien beeinflusst wurde, gab der Umgebung einen bisher unüblichen großzügigen Großstadtcharakter. Möglicherweise ist bis heute der Architekt unbekannt.

Die Gründung der Tschechoslowakei hatte Prag als Metropole des neuen und ökonomisch prosperierenden Staates einen Impuls zum systematischen Aufbau der neuen Verwaltungspaläste für dessen politische und ökonomische Führung gegeben. Für den Bau der neuen Ministerien wurden vor allem die Grundstücke entlang des neu regulierten rechten Ufers der Moldau ausersehen – im Vordergrund die Palacký-Brücke, auf dem altstädtischen Vordergrund die Franz Josef I.-Brücke und weitere im Petersviertel, für welche die neuen Regulationen ausgearbeitet wurden. Diese Aufgaben wurden den etablierten Architekten der Mittelgeneration anvertraut, die Josef Chochol zweifellos in die mit der aristokratischen, traditionellen architektonischen Sprache verbundenen Auffassung einordnen würde, wenngleich sie teilweise auf der Wiener Akademie bei Otto Wagner erzogen wurden. Wagners Schüler Bohumil Hübschmann hat am Ende der zwanziger Jahre die klassizierende Komposition des Sozialministeriums und des Landesamtes um das Emmauskloster gebaut, obwohl für dieses Gebiet schon eine Studie im kubistischen Stil aus den Jahren 1917–19 von Vlastislav Hofman existierte. Josef Fanta, der Schöpfer des Prager Wilson-Hauptbahnhofs, wurde mit dem Bau des Handelsministeriums an der Einmündung der Revoluční-Straße zur Moldau beauftragt; er hat das Gebäude sehr konservativ im Geiste des klassizistischen Neobarocks aufgefasst. In der Fortsetzung dieses Ufers im Petersviertel haben in der ersten Hälfte der zwanziger Jahre die drei Wagner-Schüler Bohumil Hübschmann, Antonín Engel und František Roith den Entwurf der Regulation dieses exponierten Geländes für den Bau dreier Ministeriengebäude ausgearbeitet: für das Landwirtschaftsministerium (František Roith), das Verkehrsministerium (Abb. 6), das später mit seinen gigantischen Ausmaßen dem Zentralkomitee der Kommunistischen Partei gedient hatte (Antonín Engel) und schließlich das Ministerium für Öffentliche Arbeiten, das jedoch nicht gebaut wurde und um welches gerade der Konflikt zwischen der demokratischen und aristokratischen Auffassung der Architektur ausgetragen

Abb. 2: Josef Zasche – Wiener Bankverein, 1906

Abb. 3: Antonín Pfeiffer – Koruna Palace 1911–12

wurde: gegen das konservative Konzept von Hübschmann stand der modern gestimmte Entwurf von Kamil Roškot.

Ein weiteres Entwicklungsgebiet, in dem man mit dem Bau der Monumentalgebäude rechnete, war das Prager „Westend" – Dejvice, das Antonín Engel zwar in konservativem Geiste, aber großzügig mit einem zentral gelegenen Platz entworfen hat, den das Generalstabsgebäude dominiert, und aus welchem sich der neue Campus der tschechischen Technischen Universität entwickelte.

Mit der Stadtentwickelung durch Neubau rechnete man auch auf dem linken Ufer der Moldau in Holešovice: die drei architektonischen Wettbewerbe in Jahren 1924–1926 sind wieder ein Beweis des Konfliktes zwischen den beiden von Josef Chochol erwähnten architektonischen Auffassungen. Der erste war der Wettbewerb für das Gebäude der Arbeiter-

Abb. 4: Jan Kotěra – Mozarteum, 1911–13

Abb. 5: Pavel Janák, Josef Zasche – Réunione adriatica di Sicurta ADRIA Palace, 1922–24

Abb. 6: Antonin Engel – Verkehrsministerium, 1925–31

unfallversicherungsanstalt (Abb. 7). Den ersten Preis bekam Oldřich Liska aus Königgrätz (der in Dresden studiert hatte) für den gegen das Ufer symmetrisch geordneten und mit der Terrassenordnung der beiden Giebelmauern abschließenden Entwurf, während die anderen preisgekrönten Entwürfe der Kotěras-Schüler Jaromír Krejcar und Kamil Roškot eine gewisse moderate Variante der Moderne präsentierten.

Eine Sensation dieses Wettbewerbes war aber der Entwurf von dem Gočár-Schüler F. M. Černý, der ein mutiges Konzept in dem Geiste des Theo van Doesburg entworfen hatte, dessen Werk Karel Teige gerade in das tschechische Milieu einführte. Aber trotz der Ergebnisse des Wettbewerbes wurde in die zweite Runde neben Liska und Gočár überraschend auch Jaroslav Rössler eingeladen. Auch wenn Gočár in der zweiten Runde einen ungewöhnlich graziösen, in seiner Geometrie und Rationalität fast „Ungers'schen" Entwurf abgab, bekam letztendlich den Auftrag der konservative Architekt Jaroslav Roessler und erweiterte so die Reihe der traditionell aufgefassten Verwaltungspaläste des neuen Prag.

Hatte hier die moderne Auffassung nicht den Widerhall gefunden, so hatte sie sich in den beiden anderen Wett-bewerben in Holešovice letztlich doch durchgesetzt. Im zweistufigen Wettbewerb für den Palast der Prager Mustermessen hatte in der zweiten Runde der Entwurf von Oldřich Tyl und Josef Fuchs gegen die konservativere Arbeit von Alois Dryák gewonnen. Er wurde in den folgenden vier Jahren ausgeführt. Nach der Rekonstruktion dient der Palast heute als Moderne Galerie (Abb. 8). Die interessanteste seiner Räumlichkeiten ist die von dem Erd- bis zum achten Geschoss durchgehende sogenannte kleine Zentralhalle.

Als Le Corbusier im Jahre 1928 zum dritten Mal nach Prag kam, war er vom Maßstab dieses Palastes beeindruckt – bisher konnte er davon nur träumen. Trotzdem äußerte er sich kritisch: Es sei ein sehr interessantes Gebäude, aber es sei noch nicht die Architektur... und kritisierte vor allem die Treppen anstelle der von ihm propagierten Rampen und auch die quadratischen Fenster in dem nördlichen Teil des Gebäudes anstelle der von ihm bevorzugten Bandfenster.

Die moderne Auffassung von einem Bürogebäude hat sich auch in dem engeren Wettbewerb für den Palast der Prager Elektrischen Betriebe durchgesetzt, wo Gočárs Schüler Adolf Benš mit Josef Kříž gewonnen hat (Abb. 10). Sie entwarfen auf dem Vorgebiet der kubistischen Hlávka-Brücke eine symmetrische Komposition mit großzügiger Gliederung. Vor den T-förmigen Hauptblock sind zwei niedrigere Flügel mit Atrien gesetzt und so entsteht eine plastische Komposition, die in der sanften Senke gut zum neogotischen Kirchengebäude von St. Antonius und zur Stadtbebauung passt. Die Seitenfront bildet den Hintergrund der Brücke und die Hinterfront reflektiert sensibel die Achse der Kirche. Der Eingang ist dann aus der Hauptstraße heraus komponiert, aus dem ein wenig abgeschrittenen cour d'honneur. Der ursprüngliche Entwurf setzte auch ein symmetrisch situiertes Gebäude gegenüber der Eingangsachse voraus. Es ging um einen mit höchstem technologischem Standard durchgeführten Bau – es war das erste klimatisierte Gebäude in Prag. Seine Architektur ist von dem lapidaren Takt der standardisierten Fensteröffnungen in dem bekannten Stahlbetonskelett gegeben, von dem eleganten Aufschwung der niedrigeren Flügel und der keramischen Bekleidung. Kurz nach der Eröffnung im Sommer 1935 fand hier ein großer Empfang aus Anlass des Kongresses der Internationalen Föderation für Wohnungspflege und Städtebau IFHTP statt.

Während im Palast der Prager Elektrischen Betriebe noch die Konzeption der zwar sehr modernen und teilweise offenen aber trotzdem blockförmigen Struktur verfolgt wurde, wurde im Palast der Allgemeinen Pensionsanstalt zum ersten Mal das Konzept des offenen kreuzförmigen Grundrisses im Grünen durchgesetzt, wie es Le Corbusier und die CIAM-Gruppe postulierten. In einem eingeladenen Wettbewerb unter neun Architekten zur Jahreswende 1928–29 wurde der gemeinsame Entwurf von Josef Havlíček und Karel Honzík gewählt, zu dem ein eleganter Entwurf von Havlíčeks Lehrer und Grandseigneur der tschechoslowakischen Architekturszene Josef Gočár in Konkurrenz stand.

Der Direktor des Institutes soll damals erklärt haben, dass der gewinnende Entwurf unheimlich hässlich, aber dass er der billigste sei, und deswegen hat man entschieden ihn zu bauen. Havlíček und Honzík haben mit ihrem Entwurf zu einer Änderung der ursprünglich blockformigen Regulation gezwungen. Der Palast ist in der Form des offenen Kreuzes gebaut, dessen höherer Flügel bis zu 12 Stockwerke erreicht. Das Kreuz wird noch von niedrigen Wohn- und Ladenflügeln umrahmt. Dieses Gebäude wurde zu einem Manifest der tschechoslowakischen CIAM-Gruppe, zum Symbol der Betätigung der urbanistischen Doktrin Le Corbusiers und zur meistpublizierten Architektur der Tschechoslowakei der Zwischenkriegszeit. Sogar auch die deutsche Zeitschrift „Moderne Bauformen" hat ihm die ganze Doppelnummer zu Beginn des Jahres 1935 gewidmet, vielleicht zum ersten Mal auch mit Farbfotografien.

Wenn im März 1935 Oldřich Starý, der Chefredakteur der avantgardistischen Revue Stavba, die Ergebnisse des Prager Verwaltungsgebäudebaus in der neuen Republik bilanzierte, konnte er die Vorhersage von Josef Chochol nur bestätigen und die Kritik zufügen: „Der Staat hat der Stadt Prag nicht die Gebäude solcher Qualität gegeben, zu der er dem Prager Aufbau verpflichtet war. Nehmen wir die Ministerien (es gab keinen einzigen öffentlichen Wettbewerb!). Das Finanzministerium ist so gänzlich in der Tiefe des Gartens bei den Englischen Jungfrauen ersoffen, dass es, trotz der riesigen Kosten, für den Stadtaufbau überhaupt nichts bedeutet (Architekt F. Roith). Das Landwirtschaftsministerium von demselben Autor ist so schematisch ausdrucksvoll, dass es aus der gegebenen hervorragenden Lage ebenso nichts schafft.

Das Verkehrsministerium hat einen konservativen architektonischen Ausbau. Von dem Handelsministerium schämt man sich zu reden ... usw."[2] Nur die rücksichtsvolle Erweiterung des Černín Palastes für das Außenministerium von Pavel Janák hat Starý gelobt.

Im Vergleich zum Staat haben die Handelsgesellschaften die moderne Architektur, jene demokratische Auffassung Josef Chochols bevorzugt. Und so entstand im Zentrum Prags eine Menge von modernen Palästen, die mit Witz und Verständnis in die historische Struktur der Stadt eingebaut wurde, oft mit großzügig konzipierten Ladenpassagen im Parterre. Ich meine hier z. B. den Palast Černárůže Na Příkopech (Am Graben) von Oldřich Tyl mit der Sequenz der drei groß angelegten Räume mit Galerien, bedeckt mit einem Gewölbe aus Glasziegeln, oder das Haus des tschechoslowakischen Werkbundes auf der National- Straße (Národní třída) mit einem ausziehbaren Passagendach von

Abb. 7: Jaroslav Roessler – Arbeiterunfallversicherungsanstalt, 1925–29

Abb. 8: Oldřich Tyl, Josef Fuchs – Messepalast / heute Moderne Galerie, 1924–28

Abb. 9: František Roith – Die Gewerbebank / heute Nationalbank, 1929–38

Oldřich Starý oder den Palast Moldavia Genereli in der Straße Na Příkopech / arch. Kozák-A. Černý / mit der Broadway-Passage zur Celetná-Straße (Abb. 12).

Abb. 10: Adolf Benš, Josef Kříž – Elektrizitaetsbetriebe der Stadt Prag, 1926–35

Abb. 12: Bohumír Kozák, Antonín Černý – Passagge Broadway 1934–35

Abb. 11: Oldřich Tyl – Passagge Die schwarze Rose 1929–30

Abb. 13: Jaroslav Fragner – Merkur Palast 1935

Ein anderes herausragendes Beispiel ist der MERKUR-Palast von Jaroslav Fragner, der die westliche Hälfte des Hintergrundes der damals noch englischen Kettenbrücke (später Štefánik-Brücke) bildet (Abb.13).

Die Identifikation der jungen tschechoslowakischen Bourgeoisie und der jungen Intelligenz mit der modernen Architektur der Neues Bauen und CIAM-Bewegungen, ist ein spezifisches Phänomen der zwischenkriegszeitlichen Tschechoslowakei.

Es bleibt hier aber das Paradox, dass die programmatischen Gebäude, wie zum Beispiel der Palast des Allgemeinen Pensionsinstitutes von Havlíček und Honzík, die mit ihrer Publizität auch international mehr bekannt waren, vielleicht – im historischen Blick zurück – schneller alt geworden sind als diejenigen, die so unauffällig in den historischen Kontext Prags hineinkomponiert und mit völliger Selbstverständlichkeit in das Mosaik seiner Gebäude eingefügt sind. Hierin besteht der Zauber der Prager Moderne. Der Idee des Le Corbusier'schen Städtebaus mit kreuzformigen Grundrissen im Grünen wurde bis zur Zeit des Stalinismus weiterhin fast verbissen gefolgt. Sogar im letzten großen städtebaulichen Wettbewerb für die Regulation des Gebietes von Žižkov hinter dem Allgemeinen Pensionsinstitut für die Zwecke der Finanz- und Justizbehörden, zum Jahreswechsel 1939–1940 unter Kontrolle der deutschen Okkupationsbehörden, war in fast allen Entwürfen die Idee der freien Bebauung vertreten. Josef Havlíček hat dann unmittelbar nach dem Krieg in der ersten Nummer der Zeitschrift Architekt SIA im Jahr 1946 demonstrativ seine Studie für den Umbau Prags im Geiste von Le Corbusiers Plan Voisin mit neuen vertikalen Akzenten pyramidenförmiger Wolkenkratzer veröffentlicht. Zur Ausführung kam es aber wegen der nachkriegszeitlichen politischen Entwicklung nicht, und nach der kurzen Peripetie der Versuche um die stalinistische Tortenarchitektur blieb zumindest das zentrale Prag vor radikalen Eingriffen bewahrt, so seinem zauberhaften „Genius Loci" treu bleibend.

* Die Abbildungsrechte sind vom Autor geklärt worden und liegen in dessen Verantwortung

[1] Architekt SIA, r. 23/1924/, s. 1–5
[2] Oldřich STARY: Plán a kvalita ve výstavbě Prahy. Stavba, Praha r. 12/1935/, č. 8, s. 113–122

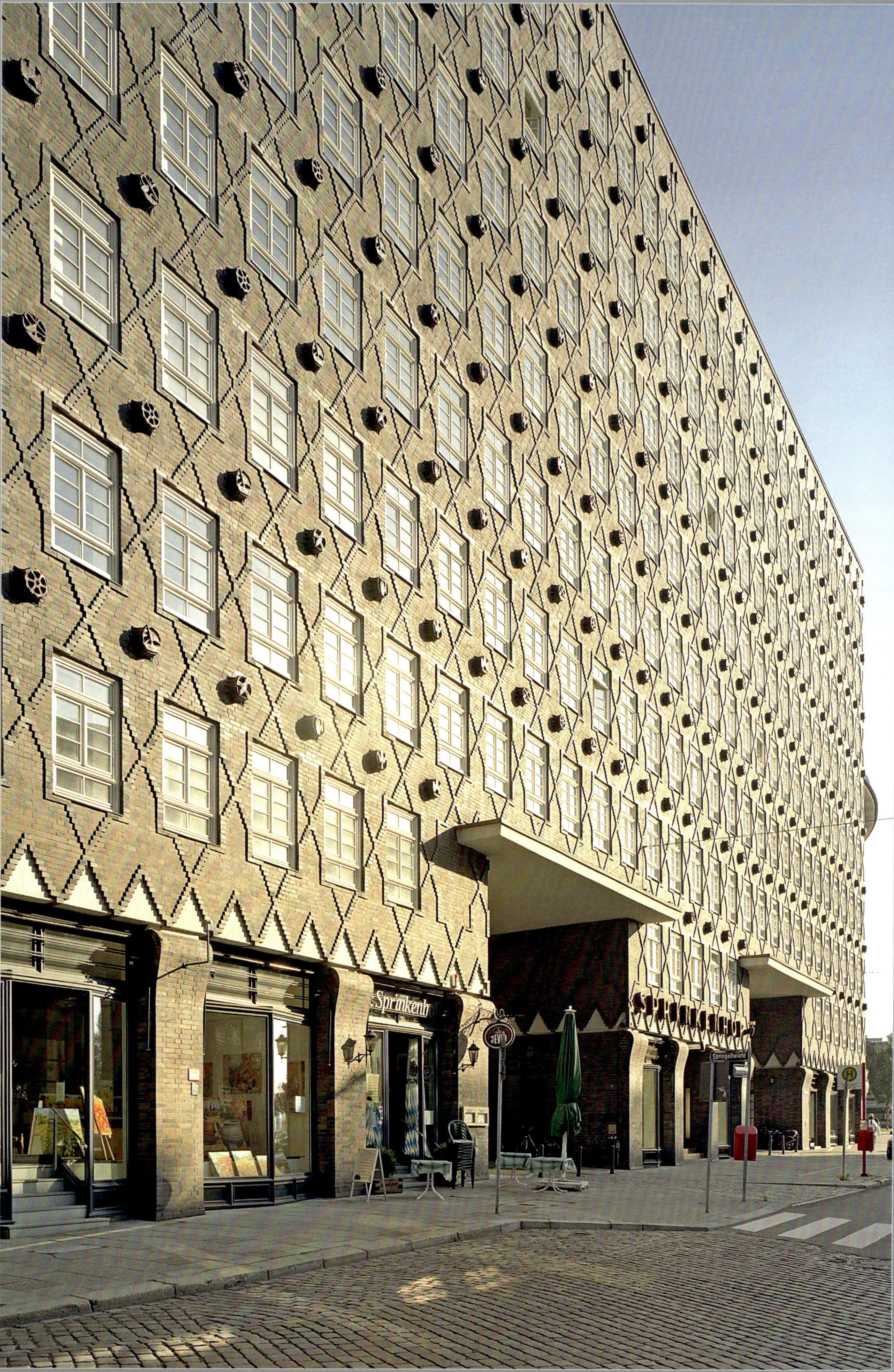

Deutsche Bürohausarchitektur
German Office Building Architecture

Hamburg

Wolfgang Pehnt

Sehnsucht nach dem Anderen –
Bürohäuser in den Jahren des Expressionismus

Bürohäuser, sollte man denken, bieten wenig Anlass, die Ausdruckskräfte zu mobilisieren. Leitz-Ordner und Kundenkarteien – bringt das die Phantasie auf Höchstleistungen? Die Zwecke lagen fest und waren alles andere als inspirierend. In der zeitgenössischen Literatur waren sie diskutiert und man konnte damals annehmen: ausdiskutiert worden, obwohl reine Bürohäuser noch als Seltenheit galten. Dass *sie* – und nicht die großen Bauten der Gemeinschaft wie Kirchen, Rathäuser, Gildehäuser – künftig die Cities bestimmen würden, war aber bereits deutlich. Der so genannte tertiäre Sektor, der die Dienstleistungen der verwalteten Welt übernahm, war schon damals im Vormarsch begriffen. In Deutschland kamen im Jahr 1907 bereits zwei Millionen Angestellte und Beamte auf dreizehn Millionen Arbeiter.[1] Heute erfasst der tertiäre Sektor mit Handel, Bank- und Kreditwesen, Verkehr, Tourismus und Kommunikation in den Industriegesellschaften an die 70 Prozent der Beschäftigten.

Alfred Wiener, ein gut informierter Autor, wies 1912 in seiner Monographie über Geschäftshäuser darauf, gerade bei dieser Bauaufgabe gelte es, „einer großen Menge sich vielfach widersprechender technischer Anforderungen zu genügen und dabei doch übersichtliche, also tunlichst einfache Gebilde zu schaffen". „Die Eigenart und Neuheit des Zweckes", die baupolizeilichen Vorschriften, die Notwendigkeit, Wege innerhalb der Bauten störungsfrei zu regeln und für die Sicherheit der im Bau verkehrenden Personen zu sorgen, das alles lasse Fragen des Stils in den Hintergrund treten.[2] Flexibilität war erste Bedingung. Denn Geschäftsentwicklung und künftiger Raumbedarf waren nicht von vornherein abzuschätzen, nicht wenn der Bauherr das ganze Gebäude benötigte und erst recht nicht, wenn ein solches Haus verschiedene Mieter aufnahm. Raumeinteilungen durften daher im Grundriss nicht ein für allemal festgelegt sein. Trennwände mussten versetzt werden können. Tragende Pfeiler waren auf das statisch unerlässliche Minimum zu beschränken. An den Fassaden durften die flexiblen Zwischenwände nicht auf große Glasscheiben treffen, sondern bedingten schmalere Fenster, deren Zwischenpfeiler die Anschlüsse der Trennwände aufnehmen konnten.

Ein Bau wie das Mannesmann-Verwaltungsgebäude in Düsseldorf, Baujahre 1911/12, zeigt, wie sehr solche funktionalen Bedingungen die Erscheinung eines Gebäudes prägten (Abb. 1). Sein Architekt Peter Behrens gewann aus der gebotenen Reihung schmaler Achsen seine Form. Die so entstandene „kubische Geschlossenheit und Großkörperlichkeit", wie Behrens-Biograf Fritz Hoeber formulierte,[3] ergab sich aus der Berücksichtigung und Inszenierung der neuen Bedingungen. Sie ließ sich jedoch auch als eine Darstellung der Potenz des Auftraggebers lesen, vergleichbar den Palazzi der mächtigen Florentiner Bankiers im Quattrocento. „Die monumentale Kunst findet naturgemäß ihren Ausdruck an der Stelle, die einem Volke am höchsten steht, die es am tiefsten ergreift, von der aus es bewegt wird. Es kann der Ort sein, von dem Macht ausgeht oder dem auch inbrünstige Verehrung zugetragen wird", schrieb Behrens in diesen Jahren.[4] Unter solchen Aspekten gewann nun auch das profane Bauwerk des Verwaltungsgebäudes seine Ausdrucksqualitäten – freilich noch nicht die, die später der Architekturexpressionismus entwickelte.

Ein Bürohaus, das genau gleichzeitig mit der Mannesmann-Administration entstand, Hans Poelzigs Geschäftshaus in Breslau, galt den Zeitgenossen und auch den späteren Historikern als Vorläufer sachlicher Verwaltungsbauten, ähnlich wie das Mannesmann-Haus, als „Meilenstein auf dem Weg ... zur Moderne".[5] So kann man es in der Tat sehen: ein Bau, der elegant um eine Straßenecke kurvt, Brüstungsbänder entwickelt und damit die Horizontale betont – ein Vorgänger jener rasanter Geschäftshaus-Architektur, wie sie in den 1920er Jahren vor allem Erich Mendelsohn gepflegt hat.

Aber wie das Düsseldorfer Mannesmann-Gebäude kann man den Breslauer Poelzig-Bau auch ganz anders lesen: als eine kraftvolle Verdeutlichung, ja Übertreibung hier mehr der konstruktiven als der funktionalen Gegebenheiten. Poelzig sucht sich die Momente aus, die zur Expression taugen. Er türmt Stockwerk um Stockwerk Betonrahmen aufeinander, und zwar so, dass sie in den vier unteren Etagen an den Straßenseiten jeweils übereinander auskragen, wie ein mittelalterlicher Fachwerkbau. Die Stützenbreite nimmt nach oben hin ab (Abb. 2). Jede Brüstung wird von reliefierten Konsolen gestützt, einer Art verrutschter Triglyphen. Es wirkt, als stemme ein Schwergewichtler gut abgestützt, aber ächzend die Last in die Höhe.

Behrens zeigte übrigens, wie innerhalb weniger Jahre aus Gebilden der eisernen Notwendigkeit wie seinem Mannesmann-Haus in Düsseldorf oder seiner Continental-Verwaltung in Hannover ein zutiefst expressives – und man darf ungeniert sagen – expressionistisches Gebilde werden konnte. Auftraggeber war auch diesmal ein Konzern, der auf dem Wege zu weltwirtschaftlicher Geltung war, die Farbwerke Hoechst (Abb. 3, 4). Behrens, eben noch Baumeister im Dienst machtbewusster Industrieimperien, hatte unter dem Eindruck der Kriegskatastrophe eine der vielen Volten seiner Karriere vollzogen. Jetzt sagte der Architekt der kaiserzeitlichen Großindustrie – Mannesmann, AEG, Continental – vorübergehend dem „ästhetischen Imperialismus" ab und bekannte epochenkonform seine „tiefe Sehnsucht nach dem Anderen, das nicht auf dieser platten Erde ist".[6]

„Das Andere" zeigt sich in der äußeren Gestalt im Farbspiel der Materialien; in der Verwendung der Parabel bei den Fenstern des obersten Stockwerks, den Schall-Löchern des Turmes und der die Straße überspringenden Brücke; überhaupt in der romantisierenden Gruppierung der Bauvolumen, in dieser Anmutung von Sakralität und Burgenromantik. Über Jahrzehnte hinweg haben die Farbwerke Hoechst mit einem Markenzeichen Werbung gemacht, das diesen Turm und dieses Stadttor stilisierte. Dass Bauten der Imagepflege dienen und für Werbung eingesetzt werden konnten, war auch in jenen Jahren schon bekannt.

Volle Register zog Behrens in der Innenhalle. Der Funktion nach ist sie der Verteilerraum für die verschiedenen Geschosse dieses Gebäudes, das nicht einmal den Hauptsitz der Verwaltung bildet – der befindet sich jenseits der Straße, gegenüber. Hier waren vielmehr Techniker und Bürokaufleute untergebracht, allerdings auch ein Konferenzsaal des Unternehmens. In der Treppenhalle perlt das Licht von drei sternförmigen Glaskuppeln die chromatisch eingefärbten Steinbüschel der Bündelpfeiler herab. „Taten und Leiden des Lichts" hat Goethe, im nahen Frankfurt geboren, die Farben genannt. „Jeder reine Farbenklang ist ein Ton aus dem Universum, etwas Letztes, Entscheidendes", schrieb der Kritiker Adolf Behne 1919.[7] Aber darüber darf man nicht vergessen, dass der Bau, der „Bote letzter kosmischer Dinge" auch von der Produktpalette der Farbwerke Hoechst zu künden hatte.

Wie kamen der Architekt und sein allmächtiger Bauherr, der Hoechster Generaldirektor Geheimrat Dr. Adolf Haeuser, darauf, aus diesem Gebäude der Technischen Verwaltung ein bis ins Detail durchgeformtes Gesamtkunstwerk zu machen, ein geheimnisvoll durchleuchtetes Raumgebilde, eine Kathedrale der Farben und des Lichtes? Der hohen Halle war ein niedrigerer, dreischiffiger Saal angeschlossen, der dem Gedächtnis der im Ersten Weltkrieg gefallenen Werksangehörigen gewidmet war. Die numinose Stimmung breitete sich von diesem Totengedenkort, diesem geheiligten Kern des ganzen Bauwerks, auf die Räume des beruflichen Alltags aus. Auch profane Architektur stand in diesen ersten Jahren nach 1918 *sub specie aeternitatis*.[8]

So setzte Max Taut – aber nicht nur er – das zeittypische Motiv des Kristalls für das Berliner Gewerkschaftshaus des ADGB ein (1921–23). Kristall galt als die verdichtete Form des Glases. Das eine teilte mit dem anderen den erhabenen Nimbus. Wo immer die bauenden Zeitgenossen mit Glas umgingen, assoziierten sie einen weiten Horizont von Bedeutungen, der über die Gralsmystik und Edelsteinsymbolik von Romantik und Mittelalter bis zur Metaphorik des Hohen Liedes Salomonis und der Offenbarung des Johannes zurückführte: eine „Stadt von lauterem Golde, gleich dem reinen Glase", ein „Strom lebendigen Wassers, klar wie Kristall". Der Große Sitzungssaal in Tauts ADGB-Haus ist durch winklig gebrochene und von Dreiecksgiebeln bekrönte Hochfenster hervorgehoben, als tagte dort König Artus Gralsrunde. Dass der Auftrag von einer Vertretung der Arbeiterschaft kam, hatte für Taut und seine Freunde Bedeutung, schien damit doch der ersehnte Kontakt zum Volke angebahnt. Als die Neue Sachlichkeit die Optik der Fachgenossen zu bestimmen begann, sah man den Bau eher als ein Beispiel früher Gerüst- und Rasterkonstruktion.

Abb. 1: Peter Behrens, Mannesmann Verwaltungsgebäude, Düsseldorf, 1911/12

Abb. 2: Hans Poelzig, Geschäftshaus in der Junckernstraße, Breslau, 1911–13

Und Hamburg? Hamburg nahm im Geschäftshausbau schon vor dem Ersten Weltkrieg eine Vorreiter-Rolle ein, resümierte Wiener in seinem einschlägigen Fachbuch. Er verweist auf den Dovenhof schon aus dem Jahre 1885. Auch heute befänden sich in Hamburg „die besten und zahlreichsten Bürohäuser". „Heute", das war 1912, also sogar bevor die Totalsanierung im Meßbergviertel eingesetzt hatte. In den Stadtmythologien galt Berlin immer als die Stadt, die sich ständig neu erfindet, stets im Werden befindlich ist. Aber die größte zusammenhängende Abbruch- und Neubaumaßnahme in Kaiserreich und Weimarer Republik bot nicht Berlin, sondern Hamburg, wo „Alt-Amsterdam" erst dem Zollhafen und dann den Kontorhäusern am Meßberg weichen musste.

Wenn sich das Bürohaus – oder richtiger: wenn einige Bürohäuser einen Assoziationshorizont anpeilten, der einen eindrucksvollen Auftritt ermöglichte und sie in die Bauaufgaben eines höheren Anspruchsniveaus wie Kirche, Volkshaus, Theater einreihte, so gab es einen Bautypus, der diese Entwicklung von vornherein stützen konnte: das Hochhaus. Die „tiefe Sehnsucht nach dem Anderen, das nicht auf dieser platten Erde ist" ließ sich ganz wörtlich mit dem Bürohaus als Hochhaus befriedigen, und der Wunsch, aus knapper werdenden Grundstücken in Citylage höheren Profit zu ziehen, natürlich auch.

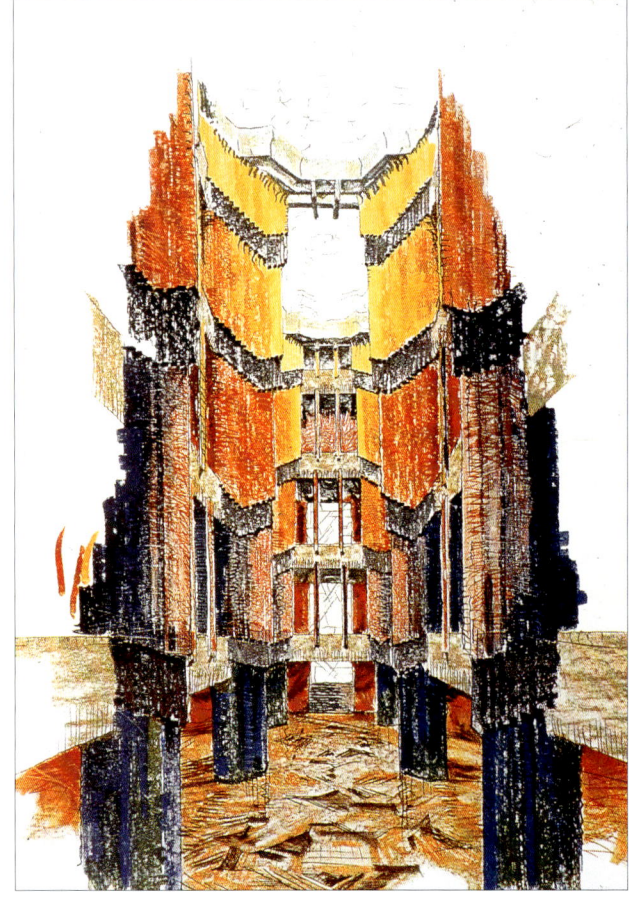

Es gab und gibt viele Gründe, hohe Häuser und Türme zu bauen, praktische und ideelle. Einige haben sich im Laufe der Geschichte erledigt, andere gelten noch heute. Verteidigungsgründe wie bei den Geschlechtertürmen wird heute kaum jemand geltend machen. Der Überblick, die weite Sicht, die aus der Höhe zu gewinnen war, stellte einen weiteren Grund dar. Aus der Höhe konnte man erkennen, was auf einen zukam: Freund oder Feind, Feuer, Unwetter, und entsprechende Informationen erteilen: akustische oder optische Signale, Glockengeläut, Hornblasen oder Leuchtfeuer. Auch dieses Motiv ist nicht mehr aktuell. Ein weiteres Argument für das Hochhaus hat mit Nähe, Dichte, Erreichbarkeit zu tun, zu Anfang des 20. Jahrhunderts allemal. Wo die Stadt sich baulich konzentriert, können ihre Massenverkehrsmittel besser genutzt und ausgebaut werden. Denn wenn alles gleichmäßig in die Fläche gestreut wäre, gäbe es mehr und länger ausgeübten individuellen Verkehr und damit Energieverbrauch, um von einem Punkt zum anderen zu gelangen. Darin liegt auch ein ökologischer Vorteil des Hochhauses, vielleicht der einzige, der wirklich zählt, trotz aller energetischer Aufrüstung auch der Hochhäuser.

Aber was wären alle diese Motive ohne das Haupt- und Staatsmotiv: das symbolische Potential des hohen Gebäudes? Das 1. Buch Mose, Kapitel 11 war immer dabei: „Wir bauen uns eine Stadt mit einem Turm, der bis an den Himmel reicht!" Wer hoch baute, war den Göttern näher, verbündete sich mit den Mächten der Höhe, mit Sonne und Licht: Pyramide und Zikkurat. Er erwies dem Höchsten die Ehre: der Kirchturm vom frühmittelalterlichen Campanile bis zum modernen Kirchenbau. Er erging sich in Imponiergebärden, Drohgesten und Machtansprüchen: der Turmbau von Babylon, die Geschlechtertürme, die Rathaustürme, die seit dem 14. Jahrhundert mit Glocken und Uhrwerk, den Instrumenten der Zeitbeherrschung, verbunden waren. Von anderer subkutaner Symbolik zu schweigen, die sich aus körperlichen Analogien herleitet (Abb. 5).

An allen diesen Welten partizipieren die deutschen Beispiele, wenn auch in Anspruch und Auftritt herabgedimmt. Gegenüber den USA war Europa sowieso im Verzug. Zwar gab es einzelne Gebäude, die es auf zehn, zwölf Stockwerke brachten, etwa das Witte Huis in Rotterdam von 1898 mit 48 m, das mehrere Jahre lang Europas höchstes Bürohochhaus war. Aber soviel hatte das Equitable Life Building in Manhattan schon dreißig Jahre zuvor geschafft! Die eigentlichen Hochhäuser in Europa waren die Kathedralen, die im 19. Jahrhundert fertig gestellt wurden: der Ulmer Münsterturm mit 162 m, die Kölner Domtürme mit 157 m. Ein Kunststück für sich war der Gerüstbau um die Türme, Holzgerüste, auf die auch die Dombaumeister besonders stolz waren. Zeitweise hatte die Kölner Baustelle 700 Beschäftigte. Diesmal kamen die Fachleute aus Amerika, und nicht umgekehrt, um den Baustellenbetrieb zu studieren.

Doch die normale Reise-Richtung der Hochhaus-Experten war Europa – USA. Allein vor dem Ersten Weltkrieg hatten

Abb. 3 und 4: Peter Behrens. Verwaltungsgebäude Farbwerke Hoechst. Ffm-Höchst, 1920–24

Peter Behrens, Werner Hegemann, Bruno Möhring, Bruno Schmitz, Josef Stübben – der Planer der Kölner Neustadt – und andere Amerika besucht; nach 1918 waren es bis in unsere Tage Hunderte von Fachkollegen. „Es waren steinerne Leuchttürme, die uns die neue Welt drüben entzündet hat", schrieb der Schriftsteller Herbert Eulenberg, als es 1924 die Einweihung des Wilhelm-Marx-Hochhauses in Düsseldorf zu feiern galt. Von den Amerikanern konnte man die Praxis des Hochhausbaus lernen, die Fundamentierung, die Konstruktion, die Grundrissausbildung, die Baustellenorganisation und die Haustechnik. Aber den Deutschen sei aufgetragen, so weiter Eulenberg, die Synthese zu finden zwischen der „Turmaufgabe des deutschen gotischen Geistes" und den „erdschweren horizontalen Tatsachen", „um aus dem Gedankenfluge und seiner materiellen Bindung das Meisterwerk der Zukunft hervorgehen zu lassen."[9]

Hochhäuser waren vor dem Ersten Weltkrieg in Preußen noch nicht realisierbar, konstruktiv sicherlich, aber genehmigungsfähig waren sie noch nicht. Die baurechtlichen Voraussetzungen wurden erst in den frühen 1920er Jahren geschaffen. Das Preußische Ministerium für Volkswohlfahrt verfügte mit einem Erlass 1921, dass „vielgeschossige Häuser (Hochhäuser)" auf dem Wege des Dispenses zugelassen werden dürften. Die einzelne Entscheidung behielt sich das Ministerium vor.

Nicht jedes acht- oder neungeschossige Haus wird man als Hochhaus empfinden. Es kommt auch auf sein Verhältnis zur Nachbarschaft an, auf seine Alleinstellung, auf sein Verhältnis von Breite zu Höhe und nicht nur auf die absolute Höhe, ob wir ein Hochhaus als Hochhaus oder als Turmhaus oder gar als Wolkenkratzer einschätzen. Ich würde gern den Test machen, ob Passanten eigentlich das Chilehaus als Hochhaus oder nur als hohes Haus empfinden. Der bürokratischen Definition – „Aufenthaltsraum mehr als 22 m über der Geländeoberfläche" – entspricht es mit seinen zehn Geschossen und ca. 33 Metern Bauhöhe natürlich voll und ganz.

Der sozusagen vorbestimmte Ort für Hochhäuser war in Deutschland respektive in Preußen natürlich die Reichshauptstadt. In Berlin ließ die Preußische Akademie des Bauwesens 1920 von Bruno Möhring ein Gutachten anfertigen, in dem eine Kette von zwanzig Hochhäusern entlang der Spree vorgeschlagen wurde. Auf Möhrings Vorarbeiten fußte ein Jahr später der berühmte Wettbewerb für ein dreieckiges Grundstück an der Friedrichstraße, zu dem Mies van der Rohe, Hans Poelzig, die Brüder Luckhardt, Hugo Häring oder Hans Scharoun sensationelle Entwürfe einreichten. Dieser Wettbewerb führte zu nichts weiter als einem Bretterzaun um die Baustelle.

Auch in der übrigen Stadt scheiterten jahrelang fast alle Projekte. Die ersten, auch vom Auftritt her imponierenden Hochhäuser entstanden an der Peripherie, wie der Borsig-Turm in Berlin-Tegel von Eugen Schmohl (Abb. 6) und danach sein Ullstein-Hochhaus in Tempelhof – also dort, wo von der ausreichend verfügbaren Fläche her eigentlich keine Notwendigkeit bestand, hoch zu bauen. Der Borsigturm, elf Stockwerke und 65 Meter hoch, trägt eine gezackte Krone, die einen Saal aufnimmt. Dass man dem Typus Turmhaus noch mit Vorsicht begegnete, zeigen in der Gestaltung die Unterteilung durch mehrere horizontale Gesimse und in der

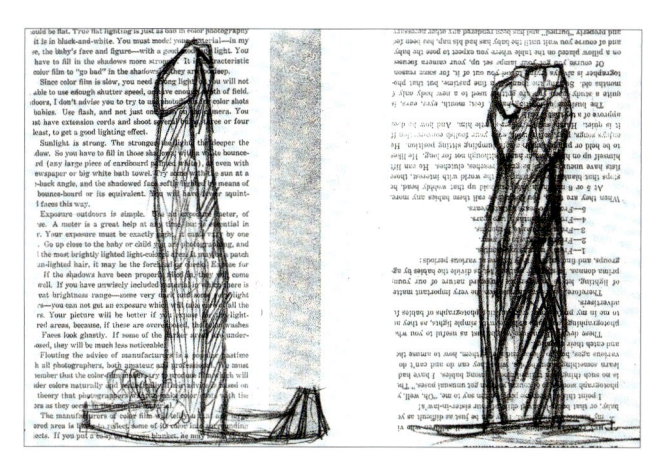

Abb. 5: Hans Hollein, Projekt für einen Wolkenkratzer in Chicago, Zeichnung, 1958

Abb. 6: Eugen Schmohl, Borsigturm, Berlin-Tegel, 1922–24

Konstruktion die Mischung aus selbsttragender Klinkerfassade und innerem Stahlskelett.

Merkwürdig ist, dass *der* Landesteil, in dem die meisten frühen Hochhäuser tatsächlich gebaut wurden, der Westen war und nicht die Reichshauptstadt. In Düsseldorf[10] entstand 1922–24 das Wilhelm-Marx-Haus, benannt nach einem Düsseldorfer Oberbürgermeister, der im Jahr der Fertigstellung gestorben war (Abb. 7). Der Architekt gehörte zur rheini-

Abb. 7: Wilhelm Kreis, Wilhelm-Marx-Haus, Düsseldorf, 1922–24

schen Prominenz, Wilhelm Kreis, später der Architekt des Düsseldorfer Ehrenhofes und vieler anderer Bauten. Der Turm hat zwölf Stockwerke und kommt auf 56 Meter, also auf mehr als das doppelte Maß, ab dem ein Haus als Hochhaus gilt. Die tragende Konstruktion bildet ein Stahlbetonskelett, verkleidet ist es mit Ziegelstein. Gesimsbänder aus Kunststein betonen allerdings auch hier eher die Schichtung der Stockwerke als den Drang zur Höhe. Zeittypisches Maßwerk bildet die Krone, dahinter verbirgt sich ein spitzer Turmhelm, das Wasserreservoir. Der Düsseldorfer Volksmund nannte es das „Tiroler Hütchen".

Köln ließ diese Konkurrenz nicht ruhen. Der Streit um die Führungsrolle der Städte im Westen war in vollem Gange. Oberbürgermeister Konrad Adenauer setzte sich vehement für Hochhäuser ein. Er ließ den Städtebauer Fritz Schumacher, den er für drei Jahre aus Hamburg auslieh (1920–23), schwergewichtige Hochbauten am Aachener Weiher wie am Brückenkopf Heumarkt entwerfen (Abb. 8).[11] Schumachers mächtige Versionen für den Heumarkt sahen erst ein Doppelhochhaus vor, dann eine einzige Hochhausscheibe. Jedes Mal wurde die Straße, die auf die Rheinbrücke führt, niedrig überbrückt. Die Baumasse wirkte wie ein überdimensioniertes Stadttor, ein Brückenverschluss eher als ein Brückenkopf.

Auf den Protest der Fachkollegen hin verzichtete Schumacher auf den Auftrag; ich denke, man hätte ihm diese Brückenfestungen auch in Hamburg nicht abgenommen. Da man die Sache als nationale Frage betrachtete, wurde ein deutschlandweiter Ideenwettbewerb ausgeschrieben. Nicht weniger als 412 Architekten beteiligten sich am Kölner „Hochhaus-Karneval", darunter prominente Baumeister wie Poelzig, Kreis oder Scharoun. Ein Auftrag entwickelte sich nicht daraus, unter anderem, weil die Ausschreibung ein zu großes Raumvolumen vorgegeben hatte. Zwangsläufig hätte es – wie bei Schumacher – zu Hochhäusern führen müssen und schreckte mögliche Bauherren ab.

Doch mit dem Hansa-Hochhaus am Ring erhielt die Stadt Köln ohne größere Diskussionen ein massives Bauwerk (Abb. 9). Der Turm schließt einen Breitbau ab: klinkerverkleidet, leicht gotisierend mit Strebepfeilern an den Turmkanten und Lochfenstern, die in den jeweils oben abschließenden Reihen als Dreiecksfensterchen ausgebildet sind. Dreieckig sind auch die Stürze über den Fenstern im Ladengeschoss. Das Traggerüst ist aus Stahlbeton. Die Entscheidung über das Baumaterial hing von den jeweiligen Materialpreisen ab; in den späteren zwanziger Jahren war es dann wieder wirtschaftlicher, in Stahl zu bauen. In seinem Programm folgte das Hansa-Hochhaus amerikanischen Vorbildern. Es mischte die Nutzungen, Büros, Kino, Café, Bank, Läden – heute übrigens auch Hotel. Mit 17 Geschossen und 65 Metern war das Hansa-Hochhaus für kurze Zeit das höchste Bürohaus in Europa. Der Sieg über Düsseldorf war damit für dieses Dezennium gesichert. Sein Architekt, Jacob Koerfer, arbeitete zugleich als Immobilienbesitzer und Bauunternehmer. Planung und Finanzierung kamen aus einer Hand. Seit dem erfolgreichen Hansa-Hochhaus galt Koerfer in Westdeutschland als Spezialist fürs hohe Bauen und baute auch in Aachen, Essen, Dortmund.

Was unterschied solche Bauten von den beneideten amerikanischen Vorbildern, abgesehen davon, dass sie nie die Höhe der amerikanischen Spitzenbauten erreichten? Das New Yorker Woolworth Building reckte schon seit anderthalb Jahrzehnten seine 241 Meter in die Höhe. Aber der nord-amerikanische *skyscraper* stellte sich in europäischer Lesart als schnöde Ausgeburt kommerzieller Interessen dar, bewundert zwar, doch ungeformt. Es waren, so Siegfried Kracauer, „Ungetüme, die ihr Dasein dem ungezügelten Machtwillen raubtierhaften Unternehmertums verdanken".[12] Aufgabe der Europäer und speziell der Deutschen war es, die gigantischen quantitativen Leistungen Amerikas zu einem Werk künstlerischen und disziplinierten Ausdruckswillens zu veredeln. Zeitgenössisches Zitat: „Wieder einmal erscheint es Deutschland vorbehalten zu sein, ein neues Problem mit deutscher Gründlichkeit und Gestaltungskraft zu lösen."[13]

Das *deutsche* Hochhaus sollte bildmäßige Wirkungen entfalten. Es sollte in bedeutenden städtebaulichen Lagen als monumentales Wahrzeichen wirken und den Städten zu einer Ablesbarkeit verhelfen, die sie seit ihrer explosionsartigen Ausbreitung im 19. Jahrhundert verloren hatten. Dass private Grundeigentümer durch bisher ungekannte Bebauungsdichten unmoralische Spekulationsgewinne einstreichen könnten, wollten sozial denkende Planer wie Max Berg vermeiden, indem sie sich als Bauherren der Turmhäuser öffentliche Bauherren vorstellten. Dazu kam es aber fast nie. Man tröstete sich mit der Hoffnung, die unverdiente Wertschöpfung, die durch die hohe Überbauung der Grund-

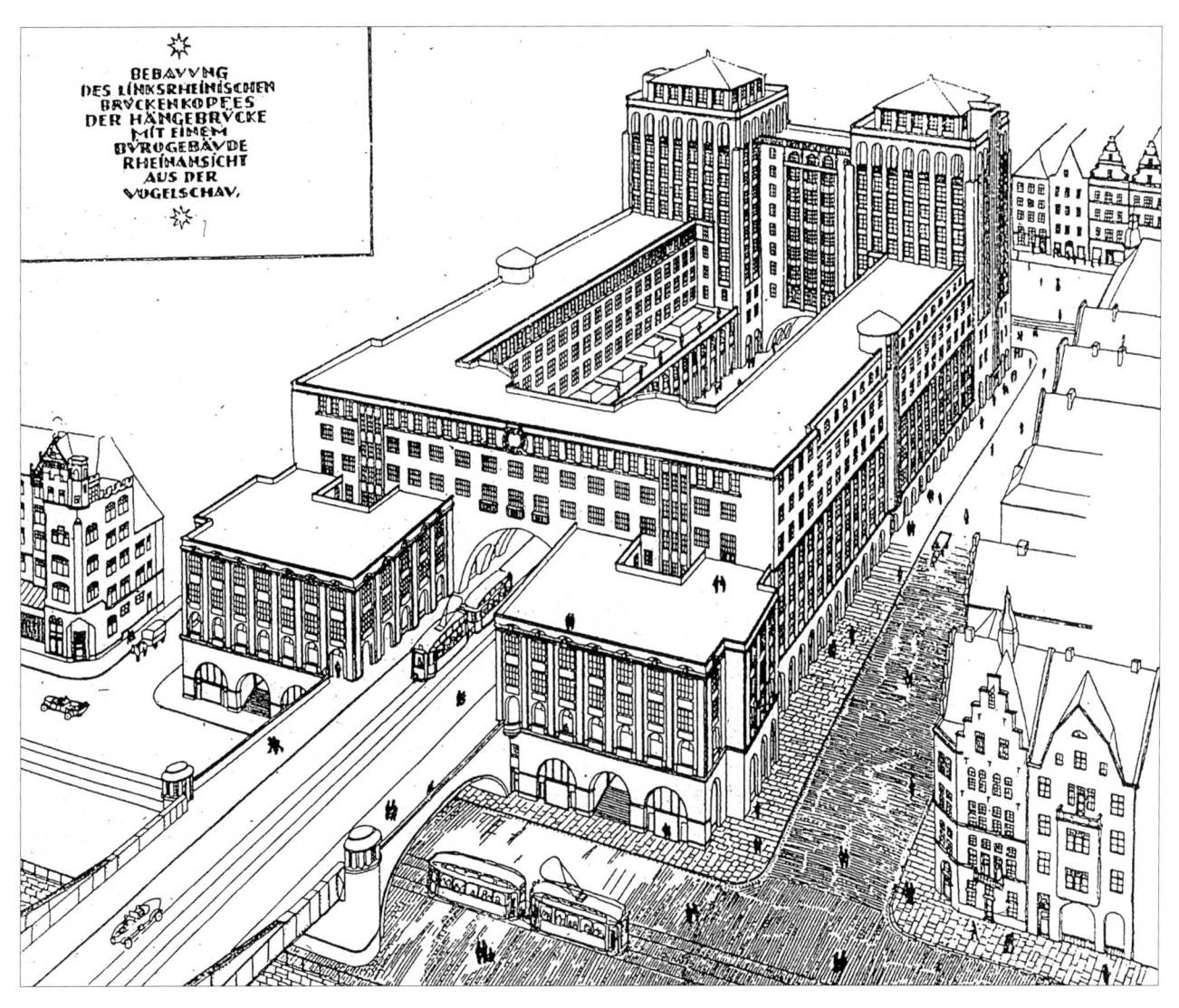

Abb. 8: Fritz Schumacher, Projekt Brückenkopf Heumarkt, Köln, 1921

stücke entstand, zugunsten der Allgemeinheit abschöpfen zu können. „Hier liegt die Steuer, die die Stirn des Kämmerers wieder glättet."[14] Auch schrieb man den neuen Bürohochhäusern soziale Wirkungen zu. Villen und Miethäuser, die bisher von Verwaltungen belegt waren, würden nun freigemacht und die Wohnungen dem knappen Wohnungsmarkt zurückgegeben werden.

Fast alle gebauten Hochhäuser dieser Jahre nahmen eine Haltung ein, die uns heute als konservativ erscheint. Zur Avantgarde, die sich ja bei den einschlägigen Wettbewerben der frühen zwanziger Jahre schon zu Wort meldete, lässt sich keines von ihnen zählen. Von ihrer Skelettkonstruktion geben sie nichts nach außen preis. Heimischer Backstein oder Klinker wurden bevorzugt. Die Bauten sollten sich als Werke der Baukunst präsentieren. Und sie sollten deutschen Selbstbehauptungswillen dokumentieren. Bei der Einweihung des Wilhelm-Marx-Hauses hieß es: „Unglücklicher Krieg und drückender Friede brachen aus stolzem Bau manchen Stein. Aber ungebeugter deutscher Bürgersinn, der unzerbrechlicher Wille und zäher Fleiss ist, lässt nicht von seinem Werke."[15]

Die Bauleistung in den westdeutschen Großstädten ist umso imposanter, als „der Schrei nach dem Hochhaus" (eine Artikelüberschrift von 1921[16]) in politisch verzweiflungsvoller Lage erscholl. Nach dem Ersten Weltkrieg waren das linksrheinische Rheinland und drei Brückenköpfe im Rechtsrheinischen von der Entente besetzt. 1921 und 1923 verschärfte die zusätzliche Besetzung erst des Raumes Düsseldorf-Duisburg und dann des Ruhrgebiets durch französische und belgische Truppen die Lage. Vollständig zogen die Besatzungstruppen erst 1930 ab. Bis dahin wurde der Westen durch Streiks, durch Produktionszusammenbrüche, durch den „Ruhrkampf" erschüttert.

Dagegen stand ein erstaunlicher Optimismus. Fritz Schumacher rechnete für Köln mit zwei Millionen Einwohnern. In Düsseldorf, das Verwaltungen der großen Ruhrkonzerne in die angenehmere Lage am Rhein ziehen konnte und sich zum „Schreibtisch" des Industriereviers entwickelt hatte, schätzte man die künftige Bevölkerungszahl auf eine Million. Beide Male blieb es bei der Hälfte. Architektur, vor allem die neuen „Riesenhäuser", sollten die Überlebenskraft der Region dokumentieren. Charakteristisch sind die Namen, die man ihnen gab: das Deutschlandhaus in Essen, das Haus Grenzwacht in Aachen. Turmhäuser hielten die Wacht am Rhein, *deutsch immerdar. Lieb Vaterland, magst ruhig sein.* Auch für die Bauten des Hamburger Kontorhaus-

Abb 9: Jacob Koerfer, Hansa-Hochhaus, Köln, 1924/25

viertels – der Poet Rudolf G. Binding nannte Fritz Högers Chilehaus ein „Denkmal eingeborener Kraft einer Stadt, eines Volkes"[17] – galt der patriotische Auftrag: Sie korrespondierten mit dem Wiederaufbau der deutschen Flotte nach dem Ersten Weltkrieg und hielten die Wacht an der Elbe.

Abstract

Longing for the Other – Office buildings in the years of expressionism

Do cardboard files and file cards made by Leitz inspire architects' creative forces? You may think that office buildings are not the ideal playing field for our powers of expression, but it was becoming increasingly clear at the turn from the nineteenth to the twentieth century that office rather than communal buildings such as churches, town halls and guildhalls were to dominate our cityscapes in the future. As early as 1907, roughly one in seven gainfully employed persons in Germany was a salaried employee (two million employees compared with thirteen million workers). Commercial buildings for the service industry were typically erected for a multitude of individual tenants. It was often impossible to predict how these different businesses would fare and whether they would expand and need more office space at a later stage which is why flexibility was of the essence. This was best achieved with dividable skeleton constructions. But people still wanted "imposing monuments in conspicuous places". Through their *mise en scène* of existing constructive and functional elements, architects such as Peter Behrens and Hans Poelzig created buildings which can be considered milestones on the path towards architectural modernity.

Shortly before, and certainly after WW I, a new architectural format arrived on the German scene which allowed for impressive *entries*: The high-rise building. The expectation and "deep-rooted taste for something different that is not of this flat Earth" could now be met in the shape of office buildings. The early Twenties saw the introduction of new building laws which permitted the building of high-rise buildings. The US introduced such legislation much earlier and as a result became the Mecca of high-rise office buildings to be visited by numerous German architects. But Europeans and Germans particularly, increasingly seemed to feel their role was in uplifting the truly gigantic American achievements by turning modern office architecture into works of creative cityscaping and art. A contemporary patriot enthusiastically commented thus on the first high-rise buildings in Berlin, Hamburg and the Ruhr district: "Again, Germany seems privileged in being the country to solve this new problem with characteristic thoroughness and creativity."

Literaturverzeichnis

BEHNE, Adolf, Die Wiederkehr der Kunst, Leipzig 1919.
BEHRENS, Peter, Was ist monumentale Kunst?, in: Kunstgewerbeblatt, Neue Folge 20, Heft 3, 1908–09, S. 46 ff.
BEHRENS, Peter, Das Ethos und die Umlagerung der künstlerischen Probleme, in: Graf Hermann KEYSERLING (Hg.), Der Leuchter. Jahrbuch der Schule der Weisheit, Darmstadt 1920 (1921), S. 315 ff.
BINDING, Rudolf G., Das Chile-Haus in Hamburg (1924), in: Carl J. H. WESTPHAL (Hg.), Fritz Höger. Der niederdeutsche Backstein-Baumeister, Wolfshagen-Scharbeutz, 1938, S. 13.
Berlins dritte Dimension, Berlin o. J. (1912).
CHAMRAD, Evelyn, WINDORF, Wiebke, Der „Schrei nach dem Turmhaus": gebaute und geplante Hochhäuser der 20er Jahre in Düsseldorf, in: Jürgen WIENER (Hg.), Die Gesolei und die Düsseldorfer Architektur der 20er Jahre, Köln 2001, S. 84 ff.
EULENBERG, Herbert, Der Gedanke des Hochhauses, in: Das Wilhelm-Marx-Haus, Düsseldorf o. J.
FRANK, Hartmut, Vom sozialen Gesamtkunstwerk zur Stadtlandschaft. Fritz Schumachers Generalplan für Köln, in: Hartmut FRANK (Hg.), Fritz Schumacher. Reformkultur und Moderne, Stuttgart 1994, S. 133 ff.
HOEBER, Fritz, Peter Behrens, München 1913.
HOHL, Reinhard, Bürogebäude – international, Stuttgart 1968.
KRACAUER, Siegfried, Über Turmhäuser, in: Frankfurter Zeitung, 2. 3. 1921.
NEUMANN, Dietrich, Deutsche Hochhäuser der zwanziger Jahre, Diss. TU München, 1989.
PEHNT, Wolfgang, Taten und Leiden des Lichts, in: Bernhard BUDERATH (Hg.), Peter Behrens. Umbautes Licht, Das Verwaltungsgebäude der Hoechst AG. München, Kat. Verwaltungsgebäude Hoechst, 1990. S. 169 ff.
POELLNITZ, Hans von, Der Schrei nach dem Hochhaus, in: Bauwelt, Jg. 12. 1921, S. 47.
RAPPOLD, Otto, Der Bau der Wolkenkratzer. Kurze Darstellung auf Grund einer Studienreise für Ingenieure und Architekten, München, Berlin 1913.
RODENSTEIN, Marianne (Hg.), Hochhäuser in Deutschland. Zukunft oder Ruin der Städte?, Stuttgart 2000

SCHMAL, Peter Cachola, Wolfgang VOIGT, Immer eine große Linie, in: Wolfgang PEHNT, Matthias SCHIRREN (Hg.), Hans Poelzig. Architekt Lehrer Künstler, München 2007, S. 112 ff.

STOMMER, Rainer, Dieter MAYER-GÜRR, Hochhaus. Der Beginn in Deutschland, Marburg 1990.

WIENER, Alfred, Das Warenhaus. Kauf-, Geschäfts-, Büro-Haus, Berlin 1912.

Die Wolkenkratzer kommen! Deutsche Hochhäuser der zwanziger Jahre. Debatten, Projekte, Bauten, Braunschweig Wiesbaden 1995.

WOLF, Paul, Hochhäuser, in: Bauamt und Gemeindebau, 1922. S. 43.

ZIMMERMANN, Florian (Hg.), Der Schrei nach dem Turmhaus. Der Ideenwettbewerb Hochhaus am Bahnhof Friedrichstraße Berlin 1921/22, Kat. Bauhaus-Archiv, Berlin 1988.

Abbildungsnachweis

Abb. 1; Abb. 2; Abb. 3; Abb. 6; Abb. 7; Abb. 9: Prof. Dr. Wolfgang Pehnt

Abb. 4: Paul Joseph Cremers. Peter Behrens. Sein Werk von 1909 bis zur Gegenwart. Essen, 1928, Tafel nach S. 8

Abb. 5: Hans Hollein, Wien

Abb. 8: Fritz Schumacher. Köln. Entwicklungsfragen einer Großstadt. München, 1923, S. 258

* Die Abbildungsrechte sind vom Autor geklärt worden und liegen in dessen Verantwortung

---

[1] HOHL, Bürogebäude – international, 1968, S. 7.
[2] WIENER, Das Warenhaus, 1912. S. V.
[3] HOEBER, Peter Behrens, 1913, S. 172 f.
[4] BEHRENS, Was ist monumentale Kunst?, 1908–09, S. 46.
[5] SCHMAL, VOIGT, Immer eine große Linie, in: PEHNT, SCHIRREN, Hans Poelzig, 2007, S. 114.
[6] BEHRENS, Das Ethos, in: KEYSERLING (Hg.), Der Leuchter, 1920 (1921), S. 322.
[7] BEHNE, Die Wiederkehr der Kunst, 1919, S. 102.
[8] Ausführlich siehe PEHNT, Taten und Leiden des Lichts, in: BUDERATH, 1990, S. 169 ff.
[9] EULENBERG, Der Gedanke des Hochhauses, in: Das Wilhelm-Marx-Haus. Düsseldorf, o. J.
[10] CHAMRAD, WINDORF, Der „Schrei nach dem Turmhaus", in: WIENER (Hg.), Die Gesolei, 2001, S. 84 ff.
[11] FRANK, Fritz Schumachers Generalplan für Köln, in: FRANK (Hg.), Fritz Schumacher, 1994.
[12] KRACAUER, Über Turmhäuser, 1921.
[13] WOLF, Hochhäuser, zit. in: ZIMMERMANN (Hg.), 1988, S. 197.
[14] Berlins dritte Dimension, (1912), S. 7.
[15] zit. in: STOMMER, MAYER-GÜRR, Hochhaus, 1990, S. 106.
[16] POELLNITZ, Der Schrei nach dem Hochhaus, 1921, S. 47.
[17] BINDING, Das Chile-Haus in Hamburg, 1924, S. 13.

Wolfgang Voigt

Deutsche Bürohausarchitektur 1924–1940

Entstehung und Wandlungen eines neuen Bautyps: Bürohäuser zwischen 1924 und 1940

„Hunderttausende von Angestellten bevölkern tagtäglich die Straßen (...), und doch ist ihr Leben unbekannter als das der primitiven Volksstämme, deren Sitten die Angestellten

Abb. 1: Hermann Seeger, Bürohäuser der privaten Wirtschaft

in den Filmen bewundern."[1] Seit der Jahrhundertwende um 1900 vermehrten sich in den Großstädten die Beschäftigen mit *„white collar jobs"* in Handel, Industrie, Verwaltung und Verkehr. Siegfried Kracauer nahm sie 1930 zum Gegenstand seines berühmten Essays *Die Angestellten. Aus dem neuesten Deutschland*, dem das am Anfang stehende Zitat entnommen ist. Viele der Frauen und Männer, deren massenhaftes Auftreten dem ethnologischen Blick von Kracauer aufgefallen war, verbrachten den Tag in Büros und Schreib-

sälen in einer schnell wachsenden neuen Gattung von Bauten, die ihre Ausprägung erst in den Jahren vor und nach dem Ersten Weltkrieg bekommen hatte. In Karl Schefflers Richtung weisendem Buch *Architektur der Großstadt*[2] aus dem Jahre 1913 hießen diese noch *Geschäftshäuser* oder *Kontorhäuser*, bevor nach dem Ersten Weltkrieg die noch heute übliche Bezeichnung *Bürohäuser* in Gebrauch kam.

Um 1930 war infolge der beschleunigten Citybildung in einigen großen Städten die Ausbreitung der Bürohäuser nicht mehr zu übersehen. Die Herausgeber des *Handbuches der Architektur* nahmen daraufhin zwei neue Bände ins Programm, den ersten für die *Bürohäuser der privaten Wirtschaft*[3] (Abb. 1) und einen weiteren für *Öffentliche Verwaltungsgebäude*. Im 1933 erschienenen ersten Band zog der Autor Hermann Seeger im Abschnitt „Bürohaus und Baukunst" Bilanz über die herausragenden Bauten seit dem Ersten Weltkrieg und nannte an allererster Stelle das Hamburger Kontorhausviertel, wo nur mit Klinker-Bürohäusern in „nordischer Schwere" eines der eindrucksvollsten Städtebilder Deutschlands geschaffen worden sei.[4] Unter 49 Beispielen, mit denen die neue Gattung der Bürohäusern vorgestellt wurde, gab deren regionale Häufung einen Hinweis auf Orte mit expliziter Citybildung: 14 befanden sich in Berlin, sieben in Hamburg – davon allein vier im Kontorhausviertel; dann fünf in Städten des Ruhrgebiets und je drei in Köln und in Frankfurt am Main.

Karl Scheffler hatte 1913 gefordert, beim Geschäftshaus seien Konstruktion und Materialcharakter „rückhaltlos zu bekennen".[5] Stattdessen werde jedoch „heute (...) in ganz wenigen Punkten erst mit kompromissloser Sachlichkeit gestaltet (...); fast überall weicht man vor der konsequenten Unbedingtheit noch zurück."[6] Zwar konnte er sich bereits „Kontorhausfassaden [vorstellen], in denen jede Fenstergruppe gleichen Wert hat, in der es weder dekorative Aufbauten noch überflüssigen Schmuck" geben würde. Allerdings setzte er voraus, die durch Funktion und Konstruktion gesetzten Vorgaben seien, „gewissermaßen innerhalb der Grenzen einer monumentalen Prosa, kunstmäßig zu gliedern."[7] Nach dieser Devise, die dem Konsens des Deutschen Werkbundes entsprach, waren vor 1914 die vielen ersten Kaufhäuser in den Großstädten gestaltet worden und auch die Kernbauten des expressionistisch gestimmten Hamburger Kontorhausviertels wird man unter diese Überschrift stellen können.

Eine Voraussetzung des Bürohauses war der schon vor 1914 begonnene Wechsel vom Massivbau zu Skelettkonstruktionen aus armiertem Beton, an dessen Stelle ab Mitte der 1920er Jahre auch reine Stahlkonstruktionen auftraten. Hier kam es zwischen der Zementindustrie und der Stahl-branche zu einem permanenten Wettbewerb um die Gunst der Architekten, der unentschieden geblieben ist. Insbesondere die Betriebe der Stahlindustrie suchten verständlicherweise Kompensationen für die gewaltigen Kapazitäten, die sie vor und während des Ersten Weltkrieges aufgebaut hatten. Die Skelettkonstruktionen, wie sie in der Hamburger Speicherstadt und in den Kaufhäusern vor 1914 vorgebildet waren, erlaubten nun auch in den Bürohäusern flexible Grundrisse mit leichten Trennwänden, die sich jederzeit entfernen oder verschieben ließen.

Die zunehmende Rationalisierung der Büroarbeit, die im Einsatz von Schreib- und Rechenmaschinen oder in der 1922 vorgenommenen Normung der Papierformate nach DIN ihren Ausdruck fand, begünstigte eine tayloristische Sicht auf die Bauaufgabe. Der massenhaft addierte Normalarbeitsplatz – ein Schlüsselbegriff des Bürohauses – sei nun „die Zelle, aus dem der gesamte „Organismus des Bürohauses" entwickelt werde (Seeger).[8] Und es kommt noch eine anderes neues Leitbild ins Spiel, der von Adolf Behne formulierte Funktionalismus in der Architektur mit dem absoluten Vorrang der Zwecke.[9] Das alles dominierte den einzelnen Bau nun stärker als Karl Schefflers monumentale Prosa, die nur im Konzert mit anderen Monumenten der Großstadt einen Sinn ergab. Der perfekte Grundriss des Gebäudes gewann, während der Grundriss des Stadtraumes, der im Kontorhausviertel in Hamburg für ein so virtuoses Zusammenspiel der Bauten sorgte, an Bedeutung verlor. Wohin das langfristig führte, konnte man ab 1930 im Konzept der Bandstadt[10] sehen, die nicht mehr Räume komponierte, sondern Funktionen sauber getrennt nebeneinander gestellt sehen wollte.

Schefflers „konsequente Unbedingtheit" zeigte sich bald im Regiment der normierten, aus den Abmessungen des einzelnen Schreibplatzes gewonnenen Raumachsen, die immer häufiger das Achsmaß der Fassaden bestimmten. Als Vorläufer ist hier Peter Behrens zu nennen, der in der Düsseldorfer Mannesmann-Zentrale (1911/12) in den Obergeschossen der noch massiv aus Naturstein konstruierten Fassade lange Reihen besonders schmaler Pfeilerfenster anordnete, hinter denen flexible Unterteilungen vom großen Schreibsaal bis zur engsten Raumzelle möglich wurden.[11] Wo in den 1920er Jahren noch experimentiert wurde, argumentierte Ernst Neufert in seiner ab 1936 immer wieder aufgelegten *Bauentwurfslehre* mit erprobten Standardmaßen, die aus dem minimierten Raumbedarf des einzelnen Angestellten und seines Arbeitstisches entwickelt waren.[12] Die kürzeste Raumachse mit 1,30 Metern erlaubte nicht nur die engste Reihung der Tische, sondern auch die elastischste Teilung von Räumen.

Ab der zweiten Hälfte der 1920er Jahre wurden enge Fensterstellungen, die auf solchen Maßen beruhen, immer häufiger angewendet. Wo das Chilehaus noch drei Fenster auf sechs Metern Breite hatte, gab es in Erich zu Putlitz' Mohlenhof in Hamburg (1928) bereits vier Fenster auf nur noch fünf Metern (Abb. 2). Im gleichen Maße, wie die Sachlichkeitsmaxime des Neuen Bauens eine Tendenz zu glatten Lochfassaden bewirkte, blieben als einzige Gliederung die manchmal endlosen Reihen vertikaler Fenster übrig. Dass dies bei großen Bauten in der Horizontale zu ermüdenden Wirkungen für das Auge führen konnte, hatte 1913 Friedrich Ostendorf vorausgesehen, als er in seinen *Sechs Bücher vom Bauen* dem Mannesmann-Bau von Behrens „öde Lang-

Abb. 2: Friedrich Ostendorf, Zeichnung der Mannesmann-Hauptverwaltung Düsseldorf (1911) in seinem Werk Sechs Bücher vom Bauen, Bd. 2, 1914

Abb. 3: Schoch & Putlitz, Kontorhaus Mohlenhof, Hamburg, 1928

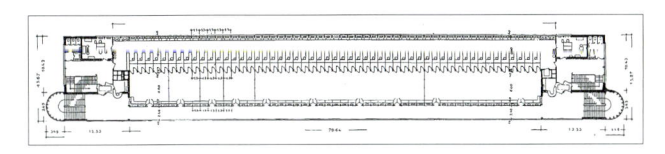

Abb. 4: Rudolf Schroeder und Willy Hahn: Arbeitsamt Kiel, 1928–30, Grundriss 1. OG

weiligkeit" unterstellte[13] (Abb. 3). Ostendorfs Bücher waren voller solcher Attacken auf seine Kollegen – u. a. auf Hermann Muthesius und Theodor Fischer – ohne dass deren Namen genannt wurden. Ihre Bauten waren jeweils mit einer seiner charakteristischen Strichzeichnungen nachgezeichnet und anonymisiert, aber die Zeitgenossen erkannten sehr schnell, wer gemeint war.

Ein besonders konsequentes Beispiel serieller Architektur aus der Addition von Arbeitsplätzen, wie sie nun an der

Abb. 5: Ludwig Mies van der Rohe, Entwurf für ein Bürohaus, 1922

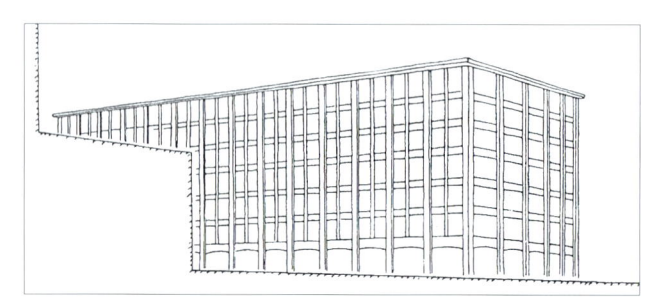

Abb. 6: Wilhelm Stortz, Konstruktion und Gestaltung großer Geschoßbauten in Eisenbeton, Stuttgart 1930. Alternative zur Konstruktion des Bürohausprojekts von Mies

Abb. 7: Emil Fahrenkamp, Shellhaus, Berlin 1930–32

Tagesordnung war, war das wie eine Bandstadt perfekt organisierte Arbeitsamt in Kiel von Rudolf Schröder und Willy Hahn (1928–30) (Abb. 4). Hier waren 48 Arbeitsplätze der Beamten ebenso vielen „Sprechkojen" für Arbeitsuchende zugeordnet, die durch eine Drehtür aus den Warteräumen betreten werden konnten. Veränderte sich der Bedarf bestimmter Branchen und Berufe, wurden durch das Verschieben von Querwänden immer wieder anders dimensionierte Warteräume geschaffen, zu denen man über eine außen liegende Galerie gelangte.[14]

In Mies van der Rohes Entwurf eines Bürohochhauses aus dem Jahre 1922 sollte es, anstelle der addierten Fenster, um das Gebäude gelegte Fensterbänder mit nur noch dünnen Metallsprossen geben (Abb. 5). In die Kernzone gestellte Stützenreihen, die weit auskragende Betondecken tragen würden, sorgten für einen rundum freien Grundriss und

erlaubten, „die horizontale Schichtung (…) aufs energischste" zu betonen und „zur beherrschenden Gestaltungsgrundlage" zu machen. Form und Konstruktion seien unmittelbar eins geworden, so das Lob Ludwig Hilberseimers in seiner *Großstadtarchitektur* (1927).[15]

Das Projekt fand nicht ungeteilte Zustimmung. Wilhelm Stortz, ein an der Technischen Hochschule Stuttgart lehrender Bauingenieur, der der von Paul Bonatz und Paul Schmitthenner dominierten konservativen „Stuttgarter Schule" verbunden war, nannte den Entwurf von Mies 1930 eine „Übertreibung einer an sich richtigen Konstruktionsidee", die der Form zuliebe einen unwirtschaftlichen Mehraufwand gegenüber konventionellen Betonstützen in der Fassade erfordere. Und er publizierte einen Mies korrigierenden Entwurf, der die aufwendigen, auf Biegung beanspruchten Elemente stark reduzierte (Abb. 6). Von der im Sinne der Avantgarde modernen Erscheinung des Projekts, die ihm und ihrem Architekten einen Platz in der Architekturgeschichte der Moderne sicherte, blieb dabei allerdings nichts übrig.[16]

Der Entwurf von Mies blieb damals ungebaut, aber die hier angeregte horizontale Bänderung lieferte der Architekturmoderne eine immer neu interpretierte, in aller Welt anzutreffende Form. Eine virtuose Variation, die von Mies' Purismus allerdings weit entfernt war, entstand 1930–32 am Shell-Haus von Emil Fahrenkamp in Berlin (Abb. 7). Die mit Travertin verkleidete Fassade einer elfgeschossigen Hochhausscheibe ließ er in eine Zeile mit abgetreppten Obergeschossen und regelmäßigen Rücksprüngen übergehen. Das Ergebnis war eine wellenförmige Front mit weichen Übergängen und besonderer Eleganz.[17]

Mehr als das von manchen als opulent angesehene Shell-Haus war Erich Mendelsohns Bürohaus am Potsdamer Platz (1929–31) der Neuen Sachlichkeit verpflichtet.[18] Die unregelmäßige Krümmung in der Fassade dieses „Columbushauses" war durch die Fluchtlinie vorgegeben (Abb. 8). Le Corbusiers Forderung, die Architekten sollten sich am Vorbild der Werke der Technik und des Verkehrs ein Beispiel nehmen, schien hier in Erfüllung gegangen zu sein. Denn der Blick in einen noch nicht bezogenen Großraum mit dem Fensterband im Hintergrund ähnelt auf frappierende Weise jener Aufnahme des offenen Dampferdecks aus *Vers une architecture* (1923), mit dem Le Corbusier seine Mahnung an die „Augen, die nicht sehen", illustriert hatte[19] (Abb. 9, 10).

Für die Entwicklung der Gattung ebenso wichtig wie das Projekt von Mies wurde Hans Poelzigs IG-Farben-Zentrale in Frankfurt am Main (1928-30), die für damalige Verhältnisse eine Ansammlung von Superlativen repräsentierte, in denen die Konzentrationsprozesse in der Industrie ihren baulichen Ausdruck fanden[20] (Abb. 11). Als Bauherr fungierte der in der Chemie angesiedelte größte Konzern Europas, der innerhalb der gemessen an Technik und Wissenschaft fortschrittlichsten Branche der Epoche entstanden war.

Hier entstand das größte Verwaltungsgebäude des Kontinents als symmetrische Großform in einem Parkgelände, errichtet als reine Stahlkonstruktion, die in der Rekordzeit von vier Monaten aufgestellt werden konnte. Der siebengeschossige, mit dünnen Travertinplatten verkleidete Baukörper bestand aus einem schmalen, 254 Meter langen Riegel mit gleichmäßiger Krümmung, in den sechs geringfügig höhere Querbauten in einheitlichem Rhythmus eingeschoben waren. Die kammartige Figur des Baukörpers, folgte dem Beispiel des Verwaltungsgebäudes von General Motors, das nach einem Entwurf von Albert Kahn 1920 in Detroit gebaut worden war. Die Kurve im Grundriss sollte ein Maximum Maximum an Sonnenlicht einfangen, um auch den Großraumbüros in den Querflügeln mit ihrer erheblichen Raumtiefe natürliches Licht zu geben. Die Erschließung erfolgte über sechs dezentrale Treppenhäuser mit Paternoster-Aufzügen; dagegen blieb der Zugang über das durch einen Portikus markierte Mittelportal mit einer Vorfahrt für Automobile den Direktoren und ihren Gästen vorbehalten.

Einem amerikanischen Vorbild verdankte auch der Hauptsitz des Elektrokonzerns Philips im niederländischen Eindhoven (1926–28) sein ungewöhnliches Innenleben. Von Frank Lloyd Wrights Larkin Building in Buffalo (1903/04) ließ sich dessen Architekt Dirk Roosenburg zur Anlage eines fünf Geschosse hohen, mit Glas überdachten Atriums anregen. Die Schreibtische der Angestellten standen auf dem Boden der Halle und in den Geschossen darüber, die als offene Galerien an die Halle grenzten. Es sollte ein halbes Jahrhundert dauern, bis der Gedanke der Atriumhalle und des konsequenten Großraumbüros in Europa wieder aufgenommen wurde.[21]

Moderne Bürohäuser entstanden nicht nur für die öffentliche Verwaltung und für Auftraggeber aus der Wirtschaft, sondern auch für die in der Weimarer Republik erstmals zugelassenen Vertretungen der Arbeiter und Angestellten. Allein die nach Millionen zählende Mitgliederverwaltung legte den Aufbau zentraler Verwaltungen nahe. In Frankfurt am Main errichtete der Allgemeinde Deutsche Gewerkschaftsbund (ADGB) in den Jahren 1929–31 ein achtgeschossigen Hochhaus mit unverkleidetem Betonskelett, in dem die Branchengewerkschaften eigene Büros unterhielten, die mit neuester Technik ausgestattet wurden[22] (Abb. 12). Während Poelzigs Bau den Chefs des größten Trusts einen präsidialen Auftritt erlaubte, sorgte hier der Architekt Max Taut für einen betont sachlichen Ausdruck für diejenigen Verbände, die den Firmenleitungen in den Auseinandersetzungen um Lohn und Arbeitszeit gegenüberstanden. Wie bei Erich Mendelsohns Hauptsitz des Metallarbeiterverbandes (Berlin, 1928–30)[23] ging es darum, der Kapitalseite mit einer selbstbewussten Architektur auf Augenhöhe gegenüberzutreten.

Eine Bemerkung zu Hochhäusern: Die meisten der hier behandelten Bürobauten galten als Hochhäuser, die aus Gründen des Brandschutzes nur mit Ausnahmegenehmigung errichtet werden durften, sobald sie Aufenthaltsräume oberhalb einer Höhe von 22 Metern Höhe über dem Straßenniveau besaßen. Die Hochhauseuphorie der Jahre nach dem Ersten Weltkrieg war ebenso wie im übrigen Europa weder ein flächendeckendes Phänomen, noch führte es zu einer großen Zahl von wirklich hohen Bauten mit deutlich mehr als zehn Geschossen.

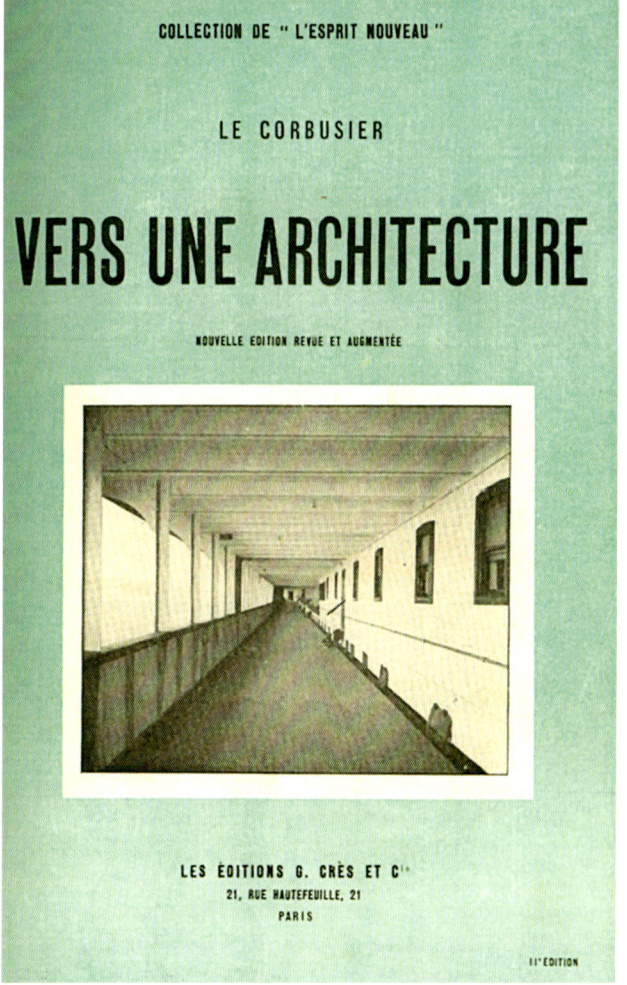

Abb. 8: Erich Mendelsohn, Columbushaus, Berlin 1929–31
Abb. 9: Le Corbusier, Vers une Architecture, 1923,
Umschlag mit Schiffsdeck

Abb. 10: Erich Mendelsohn, Columbushaus, „Geschoßsaal"

Abb. 11: Hans Poelzig: IG Farben-Verwaltungsgebäude, Frankfurt am Main, 1928–30

Abb. 12: Max Taut, ADGB-Haus Frankfurt am Main, 1928–30

Die ganzheitliche Betrachtung des Städtebaus – einer vor 1914 maßgeblich in Deutschland entwickelten, und in den kommunalen Bauverwaltungen bereits gut verankerten akademischen Disziplin – sorgte dafür, dass auch die Nachteile einer schrankenlosen Hochhausentwicklung im Blick blieben. Wer auch immer in den 1920er Jahren aus Deutschland in die USA reiste – ob Ernst May oder Martin Wagner, berichtete von der beeindruckend modernen Bautechnik der *Riesenbauten Amerikas* (so ein Buchtitel von 1930) [24], aber auch vom Verkehrschaos in Manhattan, von einer hypertrophen Hausse der Bodenwerte, die man nicht importieren wollte und von der zwangsläufigen Verschattung der niedrigen Nachbarn, was in der Hochblüte der Licht-Luft-Sonne-Begeisterung ein unverzeihlicher Mangel war.

Die ersten europäischen Bürohäuser, die es in der Höhe und äußeren Erscheinung mit den amerikanischen Vorbildern aufnehmen wollten, entstanden daher nicht in Berlin, sondern in Madrid (Hochhaus an der Gran Via von Ignacio de Cardénas Pastor, 1929) und in Antwerpen (Jan van Hoenacker, Kredietbank, 1929–32, Höhe: 87 Meter). Von den Hochhäusern in deutschen Großstädten wurde in der Regel verlangt, dass sie mit den existierenden Türmen der historischen Kernstadt dialogfähig waren und diese nicht übertrumpften. Nicht selten bedienten die Hochhausprojekte Vorstellungen einer neuen Stadtkrone, eines Ringes neuer Stadttore (wie in Stuttgart, Breslau und München) einer modernen Stadtmauer (Messehausprojekt und in Hamburg) oder eines Brückenkopfes am großen Fluss (Köln).[25] Erst Ende der 1930er Jahre änderte die Überbietungsmanier der Nationalsozialisten diese Haltung, als in Hamburg mit dem Gau-Hochhaus der NSDAP ein veritabler Wolkenkratzer von 250 Metern Höhe geplant war (Konstanty Gutschow, 1937 ff.), der alle Bürotürme des Kontinents übertreffen und die Stadt auf den Rang der US-Metropolen heben wollte.[26]

Wo Nordamerika in die Höhe baute, hatte Hans Poelzigs gekurvtes Gebäude vorgeführt, wie ein sehr großes Volumen bei mittlerer Höhe in die Breite entwickelt werden konnte. Die IG-Farben-Zentrale wirkte als starkes Vorbild für die Gliederung großer und noch größerer Verwaltungskomplexe, die durch kammartige Strukturen gegliedert wurden. Unter dem Einfluss des Frankfurter Beispiels wurde 1931 ein Ideenwettbewerb für ein riesiges Justizzentrum in Berlin-Moabit veranstaltet, das zahlreiche Gerichte der Stadt in einem Gebäude vereinigen sollte.[27] Die meisten Teilnehmer lösten die Aufgabe durch parallel gestellte Hochhausscheiben, die durch einen querlaufenden Trakt zu einem einfachen oder doppelten Kamm von bis zu 500 Metern Länge verbunden wurden (Abb. 13). Der Wettbewerb war für die konkret gestellte Aufgabe folgenlos, denn der Gedanke des Justizzentrums wurde nicht weiter verfolgt. Für die Gliederung großer Verwaltungskomplexe zeigte er jedoch Möglichkeiten auf, die später aufgegriffen wurden.

Der Bau weiterer privater Bürohäuser wurde während der Weltwirtschaftskrise durch die Reichsregierung für die Dauer einiger Jahre untersagt.[28] Zu groß war der krisenbedingte Leerstand im frisch gebauten Bestand, der erst abgebaut werden sollte. Wenn in den folgenden Jahren trotzdem gebaut wurde, war in der Regel der nationalsozialistische Staat der Bauherr. Als das Dritte Reich daran ging, im Rahmen der Kriegsvorbereitung dem Militär eine neue Infrastruktur zu geben, verursachte dies eine Welle von Verwaltungsneubauten erheblicher Größe, die sich zur Gliederung der Baumassen oft am IG-Farben-Gebäude und am Moabiter

Wettbewerb orientierten. Die Kammstruktur wurde oft durch eine Folge von geschlossenen oder nach einer Seite offenen Höfen ergänzt, wie bei Ernst Sagebiels Reichsluftfahrtministerium in Berlin (1934/35).[29] Das von Wilhelm Kreis entworfene Luftgaukommando IV in Dresden (1935–38) wurde um eine Aufmarschachse gruppiert, die von identischen Kammbauten flankiert war. Das ebenfalls von Kreis geplante Oberkommando des Heeres (1938ff.), das als eines der größten Einzelbauten innerhalb der Speerschen Neugestaltung Berlins vorgesehen war, folgte einem ähnlichen Schema, wobei geschlossene Höfe an die Stelle der Zeilen des Kammes traten[30] (Abb. 14).

Stilistisch waren die öffentlichen Verwaltungsbauten ebenso wie die zentralen Bauten der NS-Partei seit Mitte der 1930er Jahre auf einen repräsentativen Neoklassizismus festgelegt, der den Bauten einen deutlichen Ausdruck von Macht und hierarchischer Ordnung geben sollte. Dabei waren die Anforderungen an Herrschaftssymbolik je nach Status der Institution verschieden. Das Verwaltungsgebäude der NSDAP in München (Paul Ludwig Troost, 1934–35)[31] erhielt einen deutlich mächtigeren Auftritt als eine nachgeordnete Verwaltung in der Provinz (z. B. die Reichsbahndirektion Dresden, ca. 1935), bei der ein leicht monumentalisiertes Portal genügte, um ein funktional konzipiertes Bürohaus mit Fensterbändern als Bauleistung des Dritten Reiches zu kennzeichnen.[32] Achsensymmetrische Gruppierungen der Baumassen und andere Elemente monumental bestimmten Bauens waren indessen keine neuen Phänomene, denn sie waren auch während der Weimarer Republik stets präsent geblieben (z. B. Oberpostdirektion Erfurt, ca. 1930; Rathaus Wilhelmshaven 1928–29, Entwurf Fritz Höger).[33]

Außerhalb des staatlichen Sektors entstanden in Deutschland ebenso wie in anderen Ländern Europas weiterhin Bürohäuser in einem unmonumentalen, sachlichen Gewand, in denen das raumökonomische Denken der 1920er Jahre auch dort die Architektur bestimmte, wo die puristische Ästhetik der neuen Sachlichkeit nicht mehr gefragt war[34] (Abb. 15). Dagegen war der funktionalistisch bestimmte Diskurs in den Architekturmedien nicht mehr präsent. Der 1933 angekündigte, aber erst zehn Jahre später während des Zweiten Weltkrieges erschienene, wiederum von Hermann Seeger verfasste zweite Band über *Öffentliche Verwaltungsgebäude* in der Serie des *Handbuches der Architektur* ist charakteristisch für diesen Themenwechsel.[35] Er bietet, beginnend mit der Neuen Reichskanzlei Albert Speers, eine hierarchisch gegliederte Übersicht über die seit 1933 entstandenen Beispiele von Staats- und Parteibauten, denen einige noch zu Zeiten der Republik gebaute Kreis- und Kommunalverwaltungen, Polizeipräsidien und Finanzämter beigemischt waren.

Die zuvor zentrale Frage nach den Anforderungen an den Arbeitsplatz, nach Raumachsen und anderen für den Entwurf bestimmenden Faktoren war indessen nicht verschwunden. Die Logik der Standards hatte sich durchgesetzt und regierte oft auch hinter monumentalisierten Fassaden. Dafür sorgte ab 1936 das wirkungsreichste Handbuch der Architekturgeschichte, die bald auch in andere Sprachen übersetzte *Bauentwurfslehre* Ernst Neuferts, die sich bald als eine von den meisten praktisch tätigen Architekten befragte

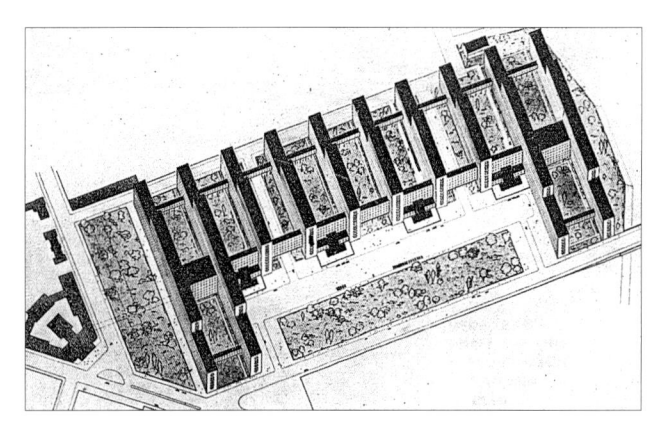

Abb 13: W. W. Zschimmer, Berlin: Beitrag zum Wettbewerb Justizzentrum Moabit, 1. Preis, 1930

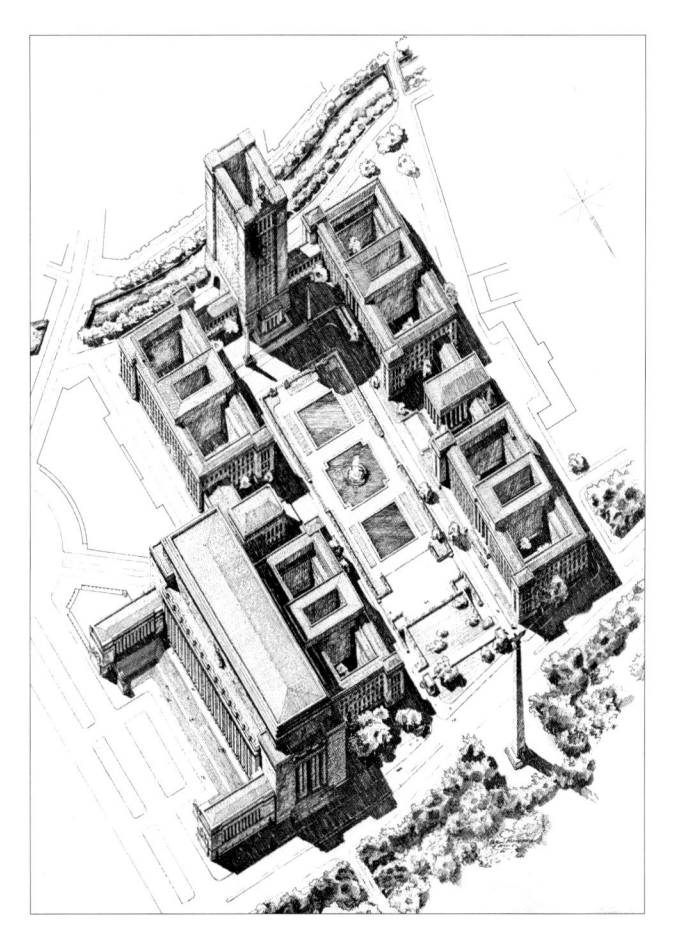

Abb. 14: Wilhelm Kreis, Oberkommando des Heeres, Berlin 1938

Autorität etablierte. Wie ein Bürohaus zu planen war, welche Grundrisse empfehlenswert waren, welche Alternativen für die Erschließung bestanden, welche Konstellationen spezialisierter Möbel sinnvoll und ökonomisch waren, alles das präsentierte die *Bauentwurfslehre* im Abschnitt „Bürohäuser" in 118 Miniaturdarstellungen, die für dieses Buch so typisch sind[36] (Abb. 16). Bezeichnenderweise geschah dies nicht an aktuellen Beispielen, sondern ausschließlich an solchen aus der Zeit der untergegangenen Republik, in denen das Bürohaus seine architektonische Form gefunden hatte.

Abb. 15: Bernhard Pfau, Pressehaus Düsseldorf, ca. 1936

Abstract

German office building architecture 1924–1940

Siegfried Kracauer wrote an essay in 1930 entitled *The Salaried Masses*. It was about the men and women who spent their working days in the large office halls of a new type of building which was conceived and started sprouting up before and during WW I. In *The Architecture of Metropolises*, written in 1913, Karl Scheffler still called these buildings *Geschäftshäuser* or *Kontorhäuser* (business or office houses). Only later, namely after WW I, did the composite noun *Bürohäuser* come into use – it is still the usual German term today. As a result of the rapid formation of modern city centres in some large towns, at the end of the 1920s this type of building had become very conspicuous. Scheffler demanded that these office blocks "unreservedly own up to what they are" both in terms of their construction and the materials they used. The *Speicherstadt* (warehouse district) in Hamburg and the department stores built before 1914 pioneered the skeleton frame construction using reinforced concrete. Partition walls were lightweight and could easily be removed or shifted, thus allowing for flexible ground planes. The standardised work place – a key feature and a term often used in the context of these new office buildings – was replicated in large numbers and became the stem cell from which the office block evolved as an organism. Also, a new model started to emerge, namely Adolf Behne's functionalism which meant that architecture fully embraced the supremacy of purpose in all construction. After 1933, there was no such thing any longer as a functionalism-centred debate in the specialist architecture media, but functionalism did continue to exert its influence at the practical construction level. Standards and their logical rationale – expressed in their most extreme form by Ernst Neufert in his *Bauentwurfslehre* (Teaching Construction Design) – had won the day and ruled also behind those facades that now took on a certain monumentalism.

Literaturverzeichnis

(ARBEITSAMT) „Das Arbeitsamt in Kiel. Architekten: Willy Hahn† und Rudolf Schröder, Kiel", in: Wasmuths Monatshefte für Baukunst 15 (1931), S. 25–30.

ARNDT, Karl „Problematischer Ruhm – die Großaufträge in Berlin 1937–1943", in: Winfried Nerdinger, Ekkehard Mai (Hg.): Wilhelm Kreis. Architekt zwischen Kaiserreich und Demokratie 1873–1955, München/Berlin 1994.

Abb. 16: Platzbedarf in Bürohäusern, in: Ernst Neufert, Bauentwurfslehre (1936)

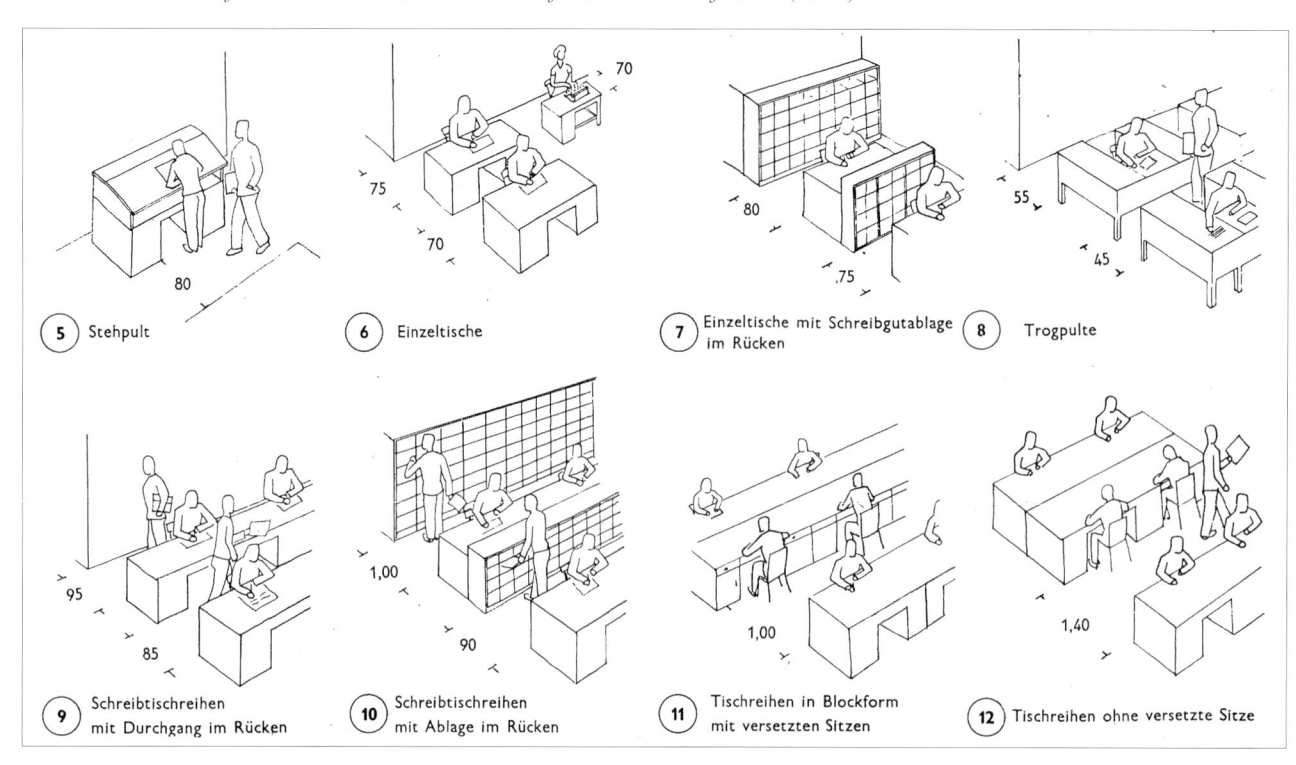

BEHNE, Adolf, Der moderne Zweckbau, Berlin 1926.

BEHNE, Adolf „Max Taut's Gewerkschaftshaus in Frankfurt am Main", in: Wasmuths Monatshefte für Baukunst 15 (1931), S. 481–96.

(COLUMBUSHAUS) „Das Columbushaus in Berlin in 29 Bildern von Erich Mendelsohn", in: Wasmuths Monatshefte für Baukunst und Städtebau 17 (1933), S. 81–88.

DITTRICH, Elke, Ernst Sagebiel, Berlin 2005.

FRANK, Hartmut „‚Das Tor zur Welt'. Die Planungen für eine Hängebrücke über die Elbe und für ein Hamburger ‚Gauforum' 1933–1945", in: Ulrich HÖHNS (Hg.), Das ungebaute Hamburg. Visionen einer anderen Stadt in architektonischen Entwürfen der letzten hundertfünfzig Jahre. Hamburg 1991, S. 78–99.

HILBERSEIMER, Ludwig, Großstadtarchitektur, Stuttgart 1927.

HOEBER, Fritz (Hrsg.), Peter Behrens (Moderne Architekten Bd. 1), München 1913.

HÖHNS, Ulrich, Rudolf Schroeder. Neues Bauen für Kiel 1930–1960, Hamburg 1998.

HÖHNS, Ulrich, „Klinkerland. Fritz Höger in der norddeutschen Provinz", in: Claudia TURTENWALD (Hrsg.): Fritz Höger (1877–1949). Moderne Monumente, Hamburg 2003, S. 65–82.

VAN HOOGSTRATEN, Dorine: Dirk Roosenburg 1887–1962, Rotterdam 2005.

JACOB, Brigitte, Emil Fahrenkamp. Bauten und Projekte für Berlin, Berlin 2007.

(JUSTIZGEBÄUDE) „Zentrales Justizgebäude in Berlin-Moabit", in: Wettbewerbe für Baukunst und Schwesterkünste. Beilage zu: Deutsche Bauzeitung 64 (1930), Nr. 50, S. 50–64.

JAMES, Kathleen, Erich Mendelsohn and the Architecture of German Modernism, Cambridge MA 1997.

KRACAUER, Siegfried, Die Angestellten. Aus dem neuesten Deutschland. Frankfurt 1971 (Erstveröffentlichung 1929).

LE CORBUSIER, Vers une architecture. Paris 1923.

N. MILJUTIN, Nikolaj, Sozgorod. Basel 1992 (Erstveröffentlichung 1930/1932).

NEUFERT, Ernst, Bauentwurfslehre, Berlin 1936.

(OBERPOSTDIREKTION) „Oberpostdirektionsgebäude in Erfurt", in: Deutsche Bauzeitung 64 (1930), S. 669–675.

OSTENDORF, Friedrich, Die äussere Erscheinung der einräumigen Bauten. Allgemeines und einräumige Bauten (Sechs Bücher vom Bauen, Bd. 2), Berlin 1914.

PAULSEN, Friedrich, „Das Luftfahrtministerium als Werk der Baukunst", in: Bauwelt 28 (1937), H. 8, S. 11–17.

(RATHAUS) „Das Rathaus zu Rüstringen. Architekt Fritz Höger, Hamburg", in: Deutsche Bauzeitung 64 (1930).

SCHEFFLER, Karl, Die Architektur der Großstadt. Berlin 1913.

SCHMAL, Peter Cachola, VOIGT, Wolfgang „Immer eine große Linie. Das Verwaltungsgebäude der I. G. Farbenindustrie in Frankfurt am Main und andere Verwaltungsbauten", in: Wolfgang PEHNT, Matthias SCHIRREN (Hrsg.): Hans Poelzig 1869 bis 1936. Architekt Lehrer Künstler, München 2007, S. 112–125.

SEEGER, Hermann, Bürohäuser der privaten Wirtschaft, (Handbuch der Architektur, IV. Teil, 7. Halbband, Heft 1a), Leipzig 1933.

SEEGER, Hermann, Öffentliche Verwaltungsgebäude (Handbuch der Architektur, IV. Teil, 7. Halbband, Heft 1b), Leipzig 1943

SPEER, Albert (Hrsg.): Neue deutsche Baukunst, Berlin 1941

STEPHAN, Regina „‚Wir glauben an Berlin!'. Das Metallarbeiterhaus, das Columbushaus und andere Geschäftshäuser in Berlin", in: Regina STEPHAN (Hrsg.) Erich Mendelsohn Architekt 1887–1953. Gebaute Welten, Ostfildern-Ruit 1998, S. 144–166.

STOMMER, Rainer, Hochhaus. Der Beginn in Deutschland, Marburg 1990.

STORTZ, Wilhelm, Konstruktion und Gestaltung großer Geschoßbauten in Eisenbeton, Stuttgart 1930.

TURTENWALD, Claudia (Hrsg.), Fritz Höger (1877–1949). Moderne Monumente, Hamburg 2003.

WASHBURN, Frank, Riesenbauten Nordamerikas (Schaubücher Bd. 59), Zürich/Leipzig 1930.

Abbildungsnachweis

Abb. 1: Hermann Seeger: *Bürohäuser der privaten Wirtschaft, (Handbuch der Architektur, IV. Teil, 7. Halbband, Heft 1a),* Leipzig 1933. Umschlag

Abb. 2: Friedrich Ostendorf, *Sechs Bücher vom Bauen,* Bd. 2, 1914.

Abb. 3: Wolfgang Voigt

Abb. 4: Wasmuths Monatshefte für Baukunst 15 (1931)

Abb. 5: Ludwig Hilberseimer, *Großstadt Architektur.* Stuttgart o. J. (1927)

Abb. 6: Wilhelm Stortz, *Konstruktion und Gestaltung großer Geschoßbauten in Eisenbeton,* Stuttgart 1930

Abb. 7: http://de.wikipedia.org/wiki/Shell-Haus

Abb. 8: *Wasmuths Monatshefte für Baukunst und Städtebau* 17 (1933)

Abb. 9: Le Corbusier, *Vers une Architecture,* 1923

Abb. 10: *Wasmuths Monatshefte für Baukunst und Städtebau* 17 (1933)

Abb. 11: Entwurfsskizze im Deutschen Architekturmuseum, Frankfurt am Main

Abb. 12: Wolfgang Voigt

Abb. 13: Deutsche Bauzeitung, 64 (1930), Beilage Wettbewerbe, Nr. 8, S. 57.

Abb. 14: Albert Speer: *Neue Deutsche Baukunst,* Prag 1943.

Abb. 15: Bauwelt, 1937

Abb. 16: Ernst Neufert: *Bauentwurfslehre,* 1936

* Die Abbildungsrechte sind vom Autor geklärt worden und liegen in dessen Verantwortung

---

[1] KRACAUER, Die Angestellten, 1929, S. 11.
[2] SCHEFFLER, Die Architektur der Großstadt, 1913.
[3] SEEGER, Bürohäuser der privaten Wirtschaft, 1933.
[4] SEEGER, Bürohäuser der privaten Wirtschaft,, 1933, S. 43.

[5] SCHEFFLER, Die Architektur der Großstadt, 1913, S. 46.
[6] SCHEFFLER, Die Architektur der Großstadt, 1913, S. 40.
[7] SCHEFFLER, Die Architektur der Großstadt, 1913, S. 46.
[8] SEEGER, Bürohäuser, 1933, S. 14.
[9] BEHNE, Der moderne Zweckbau, 1926.
[10] MILJUTIN, Sozgorod, 1930/1932.
[11] HOEBER, Peter Behrens, S. 172–174, 177–182.
[12] NEUFERT, Bauentwurfslehre, 1936.
[13] OSTENDORF, Sechs Bücher vom Bauen, 1914, S. 247, 250.
[14] ARBEITSAMT, 1931, S. 25–30. HÖHNS, Rudolf Schroeder. Neues Bauen für Kiel 1930–1960. 1998.
[15] HILBERSEIMER, Großstadtarchitektur, 1927, S. 60–62.
[16] STORTZ, Konstruktion und Gestaltung großer Geschoßbauten in Eisenbeton, 1930, S. 18, 25–26.
[17] JACOB, Emil Fahrenkamp. Bauten und Projekte für Berlin, 2007, S. 211–265.
[18] COLUMBUSHAUS, 1933, S. 81–88. JAMES, Erich Mendelsohn and the Architecture of German Modernism, 1997, S. 225–230. STEPHAN, „‚Wir glauben an Berlin!'. Das Metallarbeiterhaus, das Columbushaus und andere Geschäftshäuser in Berlin", 1998, S. 144–166.
[19] LE CORBUSIER, Vers une architecture, 1923.
[20] SCHMAL, VOIGT, „Immer eine große Linie. Das Verwaltungsgebäude der I. G. Farbenindustrie in Frankfurt am Main und andere Verwaltungsbauten", 2007, S. 112–125.
[21] VAN HOOGSTRAATEN: Dirk Roosenburg 1887–1962, 2005.
[22] BEHNE „Max Taut's Gewerkschaftshaus in Frankfurt am Main", 1931, 481–96.
[23] STEPHAN, „‚Wir glauben an Berlin!'. Das Metallarbeiterhaus, das Columbushaus und andere Geschäftshäuser in Berlin", 1998, ibid.
[24] WASHBURN, Riesenbauten Nordamerikas (Schaubücher Bd. 59), Zürich/Leipzig 1930.
[25] STOMMER, Hochhaus. Der Beginn in Deutschland, 1990.
[26] FRANK, „‚Das Tor zur Welt'. Die Planungen für eine Hängebrücke über die Elbe und für ein Hamburger ‚Gauforum' 1933–1945", 1991, S. 78–99.
[27] JUSTIZGEBÄUDE, 1930, S. 50–64.
[28] SEEGER, Bürohäuser der privaten Wirtschaft, 1933, S. 11.
[29] PAULSEN, „Das Luftfahrtministerium als Werk der Baukunst", 1937, S. 11–17. DITTRICH, Ernst Sagebiel, 2005.
[30] SPEER, Neue deutsche Baukunst, Berlin 1941, S. 54. ARNDT, „Problematischer Ruhm – die Großaufträge in Berlin 1937–1943", 1994.
[31] SPEER, Neue deutsche Baukunst, Berlin 1941, S. 20.
[32] SEEGER, Öffentliche Verwaltungsgebäude, Leipzig 1943, S. 109–111.
[33] OBERPOSTDIREKTION, 1930, S. 669–675. RATHAUS, 1930, S. 297–303. HÖHNS, „Klinkerland. Fritz Höger in der norddeutschen Provinz", 2003, S. 65-82.
[34] Vgl. z. B. das Pressehaus von Bernhard Pfau in Düsseldorf, in Bauwelt 31 (1940), H. 22, S. 1–4.
[35] SEEGER, Öffentliche Verwaltungsgebäude, Leipzig 1943.
[36] Vgl. „Bürobauten" bei NEUFERT, Bauentwurfslehre, 1936, S. 170–177.

Robert Habel

Berliner City-Architektur (1871–1933)

Nach der Reichsgründung 1871 entwickelte sich Berlin bis zum Ende der 1920er Jahre von einer beschaulichen Residenzstadt mit ungefähr 826 000 Einwohnern zur brausenden und brodelten Metropole mit ca. 4,3 Millionen Einwohnern. Hinter dieser steigenden Bevölkerungszahl verbarg sich ein rasanter wirtschaftlicher Aufschwung, von dem neben der Schwer- und Feinindustrie vor allem das gesamte Verkaufs- und Handelswesen profitierte. Ein sichtbares Zeugnis fand dieser Aufstieg in der vollständigen Umgestaltung der Innenstadt. Nahezu sämtliche Geschäftshäuser entlang der lukrativen Einkaufsmeilen wurden bis 1914 durch Neubauten ersetzt, wobei der neue Bautypus „Warenhaus" bis weit in die 1920er Jahre hinein eine stilprägende Wirkung auf die Berliner City-Architektur haben sollte. Gebäude, die ausschließlich einer büromäßigen Nutzung unterworfen waren, entstanden vorwiegend ab 1919. Zu den wenigen Bürogebäuden der Vorkriegszeit gehörten die Landesversicherungsanstalt Alfred Messels (1853–1909) von 1903, vis-à-vis vom Märkischen Museum,[1] und das Nordsternhaus in Schöneberg von Paul Mebes (1872–1938) aus den Jahren 1912–14.[2]

Die heute zum Berliner Mythos stilisierten „goldenen 20er Jahre" hatten auf das Erscheinungsbild des Innenstadtbereichs weit weniger Einfluss, als man dies vermuten könnte. Dafür sprechen allein schon die Zahlen der neu entstandenen Geschäfts- und Handelshäuser: Waren es vor dem Krieg etwa 16 Warenhausneubauten, 27 Kauf- und 24 Geschäftshäuser, kamen ab 1919 lediglich 5 Waren-, 7 Kauf- und 11 Geschäftshäuser zur Ausführung.[3]

Ein wesentlicher Grund für die große Wirkung des Warenhauses auf die gesamte Berliner Geschäftshausarchitektur lag zweifellos in den mangelnden Voraussetzungen einer für den Handel nutzbaren Architektur.

1871 traten bei den Geschäftshäusern der Berliner Innenstadt anstelle des bescheidenen Spätklassizismus Schinkelscher Prägung aufwändige und reich stuckierte Neorenaissance- oder Neobarockfassaden, bei denen für eine zweckmäßige Innennutzung lediglich die unteren Stockwerke mit Hilfe großer Schaufensterscheiben aufgerissen wurden.

Ein Geschäftshaus an der Leipziger Straße 106 von dem damals viel beschäftigten und renommierten Architekturbüro Heinrich Kayser (1842–1917) & Karl von Großheim (1841–1911) aus dem Jahr 1877 zeigt diesen Widerspruch zwischen der Wohn- Ladennutzung besonders prägnant (Abb. 1):[4] Während die unteren drei Etagen sich mit großen Schaufensterscheiben zur Straße öffneten, waren die darüber liegenden Geschosse mit der üblichen reichen Stuckatur eines städtischen Wohnhauses der frühen Gründerjahre überzogen worden. Für diese bauästhetisch höchst zwei-

Abb. 1: Berlin, Geschäftshaus, Leipziger Straße 106, Fassade, zerstört (Aufnahme 1888)

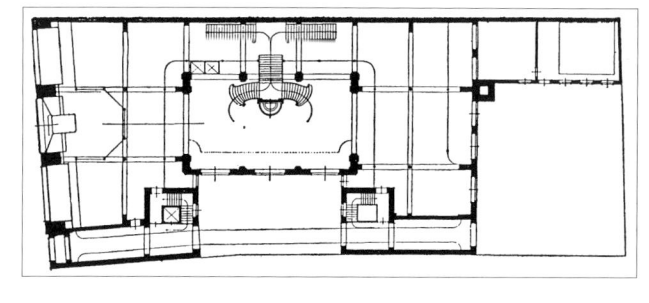

Abb. 2: Berlin, Warenhaus Wertheim, Oranienstraße 53–54, Grundriss, zerstört

felhafte Lösung übernahm der Schriftsteller und Architekt Hans Schliepmann (1855–1929) in seiner Publikation von 1913 über die Entwicklung des Geschäftshauses vom Ber-

Abb. 3: Berlin, Warenhaus Wertheim, Oranienstraße 53–54, Fassade, zerstört (Aufnahme vor 1900)

Abb. 4: Berlin, Warenhaus Wertheim, Leipziger Straße 132–133, Fassade mit Baustelle des Preußischen Herrenhauses [heute Bundesrat] im Vordergrund, zerstört (Aufnahme 1898)

liner Volksmund die treffende Bezeichnung vom „Haus auf Stelzen".[5]

Den Anfang der großen architektonischen Veränderung beim Berliner Geschäfts- und Handelshaus machte der Neubau für die Familie Wertheim an der Kreuzberger Oranienstraße. Als besonders glückliche Fügung sollte sich dabei die fruchtbare Zusammenarbeit zwischen der Wertheim-Familie und dem Architekten Alfred Messel erweisen,[6] der sich bereits zuvor durch zweckmäßige Innenraumaufteilungen und Fassadengestaltungen bei neuen Geschäftshäusern einen Namen gemacht hatte.[7] Im Unterschied zu den anderen Verkaufshäusern, die ebenfalls nach modernen, kapitalistischen Modalitäten organisiert waren, und die den Festpreis, die Preisauszeichnung und das Umtauschrecht als neue Verkaufsform eingeführt hatten, wurden die Geschäfte Georg Wertheims (1857–1939) – Spiritus Rector der Firma gleichen Namens – mit dem Namenszusatz „Warenhaus" versehen.[8]

Bei seinem Wertheimneubau übernahm Messel erstmals in Deutschland den in Paris bereits in den 1860er Jahren entwickelten Bautypus des Warenhauses. Das französische Warenhaus bestand aus einer eisernen Stützenkonstruktion, die weite, unverstellte Verkaufsräume bis ins obersten Stockwerk erlaubte. Für ausreichende Licht- und Luftzufuhr dienten geschossübergreifende Lichthöfe, an deren Seiten sich zugleich die repräsentativen Treppenaufgänge befanden. Auf dieses System griff Messel bei seinem ersten Warenhaus für die Firma Wertheim an der Oranienstraße 53–54 zurück. Größere Veränderungen zum französischen Vorbild ergaben sich in der Grundrissgestaltung, da das Grundstück aufgrund der preußischen Feuerschutzverordnungen nur zu zwei Dritteln bebaut werden durfte (Abb. 2).[9] Bei der Fassadengestaltung hielt sich Messel eng an das französische Vorbild – in diesem Fall dem Warenhaus *Au Printemps* von Paul Sédille (1836–1900) von 1881/82 – und gliederte seine Front in Form horizontaler Geschossbänder im Stil des Pariser Neubarock (Abb. 3). Neben den drei rundbogigen Sockelarkaden und den geschossübergreifenden Kolossalpilastern übernahm Messel auch die für den französischen Neubarock so typischen Ochsenaugenfenster in der Dachzone.

Nach der erfolgreichen Zusammenarbeit an der Oranienstraße beauftragte Georg Wertheim Messel im Jahr 1896 mit dem Bau eines neuen Verkaufshauses an der Leipziger Straße 132/133, der damaligen Haupteinkaufsmeile der aufstrebenden Spree-Metropole.

Bei der Grundrissdisposition griff Messel erneut auf das System von offenem Lichthof in Verbindung mit umlaufenden Verkaufsgeschossen zurück. Im Unterschied zu seinem ersten Wertheimhaus in Kreuzberg erschien der Anordnung der Räumlichkeiten hier wesentlich geordneter und einheitlicher. Beispielsweise lagen Haupteingang, Lichthof und der Treppenaufgang in die oberen Etagen auf einer zentralen Mittelachse, die im Bereich des schmaleren Lichthofs von je zwei rechteckigen Innenhöfen flankiert wurden. Über diese Höfe erfolgte der gesamte Warentransport.

Bei der Architektur der Straßenfront wählte Messel eine bis dahin in der deutschen Architektur ansatzweise nur bei Hinterhöfen anzutreffende Außengliederung (Abb. 4). Anstelle eines bis dahin üblichen, horizontalen Erscheinungsbildes gliederte er die Front seines Geschäfts- und Warenhauses mittels schmaler, gotisierender und durchlaufender Pfeiler, die im Wechsel mit vertikalen, breiten und gläsernen Schaufensterbändern standen. Mit diesem vertikalen Gliederungssystem gelang es Messel auf geschickte Weise, auch die eigentliche Bestimmung des Hauses – dem werbewirksamen Handel mit Waren – eine zweckmäßige Außenhülle zu geben. Die monumentalen, vertikalen Schaufensterbänder dienten aber nicht allein der Warenpräsentation, sondern erfüllten darüber hinaus die dringend notwendige Aufgabe, die Innenräume mit genügend Licht und Luft zu versorgen.

Die größte Wirkung zeigte das Wertheimhaus jedoch bei Dunkelheit: Über ein hausinternes Turbinensystem leuchtete das elektrisch erleuchtete Warenhausinnere auf die dunkle, damals lediglich von schwachen Gaslampen beleuchtete Leipziger Straße.

Sowohl von der Bevölkerung als auch von der zeitgenössischen Architekturkritik als Ausdruck einer modernen und zeitgemäßen Handelsarchitektur verstanden, beeinflusste diese Fassade mit ihrer offenen, vertikalen Gliederung ab 1897 maßgeblich das Erscheinungsbild fast sämtlicher neu entstehenden Geschäftshäuser im Berliner Innenstadtbereich und weit darüber hinaus. Henry van de Velde widmete in seinem Aufsatz über die „verstandesmäßigen und folgerechten Konstruktionsprizipien" Messels Wertheimbau eine höchst stimmungshafte Schilderung: „Im *Warenhaus Wertheim* scheint das Problem durch ein System gelöst zu sein, das epochemachend sein wird, und das ein vernünftig denkender Schöpfer finden musste. Man errichtete eine Reihe von hohen geraden Pfeilern, vom Boden ausgehend und bis zum Dache reichend, das sich frei auf sie lehnt und ein wenig überhängt. [...] Die Fassade des *Warenhauses Wertheim* ist die treffendste Kundgebung dessen, was der moderne Stil den logischen Folgen eines vernünftigen Urteilens entlehnt. Ihr einfacher rechtschaffener Karakter, der vielmehr zu einem einfachen äusseren Ansehen neigt, tritt klar hervor, und ich glaube nicht, dass ein modernes architektonisches Werk, welches aus ähnlichem Material wie das hier verwandte hergestellt ist, ein stärkeres Gefühl des Grossartigen und des fein Ersonnenen verursacht. [...] Ich kenne nur wenig Ergreifenderes, als den Anblick der hohen Pfeiler der Leipziger Strasse, welche ohne Anstrengung emporsteigen, um eine Last zu tragen, die ihnen so leicht und schön wie möglich ausgesonnen zu sein scheint."[10]

Zentraler Ort im Inneren war der prächtige, 400 Quadratmeter umfassende Lichthof, in dem sich – wie Gustav Stresemann berichtete[11] – sowohl die feine Damen aus den vornehmen westlichen Bezirken als auch die Arbeiterfrauen aus dem Wedding zum Kauf zusammenfanden. Als Point de Vue diente eine 6 Meter hohe, eherne Monumentalplastik der „Arbeit", die auf die Entwürfe Ludwig Manzels (1858–1936) zurückging und zu einem differenzierten plastischen Ausstattungsprogramm im Inneren und Äußeren des Wertheimhauses gehörte.

Eines der ersten Gebäude, das den großen Einfluss der Wertheimfassade auf die Berliner Geschäftshausarchitektur zeigt, ist die gut erhaltene Polnische Apotheke an der Friedrichstraße des Architekten Alfred Breslauer (1866–1954) von 1898 (Abb. 5). Breslauer, der 1896–1897 im Architekturbüro Messels mitgearbeitet hatte, war maßgeblich an der Organisation der Wertheimbaustelle beteiligt gewesen.[12] Die starke Vertikalbetonung der unteren drei Geschosse mit Hilfe durchlaufender Pfeiler in Verbindung mit den zurückliegenden, raumausfüllenden Fensterachsen zeigt den Messelschen Einfluss. Auf diese Übernahme hat bereits Henry van de Velde (1863–1957) in seinem in der „Innendekoration" von 1902 erschienenen und bereits angeführten Artikel über den Wertheimbau hingewiesen.[13]

Als der schärfste Konkurrent von Wertheim – der Warenhauskonzern Hermann Tietz – seine Firmenzentrale von München nach Berlin verlegte, wurde 1899/1900

Abb. 5: Berlin, Polnische Apotheke, Friedrichstraße 153a, Fassade, erhalten (Aufnahme um 1900)

Abb. 6: Berlin, Warenhaus Hermann Tietz, Leipziger Straße 46–49, Fassade, zerstört (Aufnahme um 1900)

Abb. 7: Berlin, Warenhaus Wertheim, Voßstraße 33, Fassade, zerstört (Aufnahme vor 1905)

Abb. 8: Berlin, Warenhaus Wertheim, Ansicht vom Leipziger Platz mit Eckpavillon, Gesamtansicht, zerstört (Aufnahme vor 1912)

beim Neubau am anderen Ende der Leipziger Straße die Grundrissdisposition des Messelbaues übernommen. Bei der Fassade setzte Tietz jedoch andere Akzente: Mit der Fassadengestaltung wurde nicht etwa das Architekturbüro Louis Lachmann (1860–1910) & Zauber beauftragt, das für die Gesamtkonzeption des Hauses verantwortlich blieb, sondern man bedachte Bernhard Sehring (1855–1941) mit dieser Aufgabe.[14] Um jede Nähe zu der Wertheimfassade an der Leipziger Straße zu vermeiden, löste Sehring das Fassadeproblem, indem er zwei riesige 26 Meter breite und 17 Meter hohe Glaswände zwischen einen steinernen Rahmen spannte, der in der Mitte zu einem neubarocken, reich skulpturierten, risalitartigen Eingang auswuchs, auf dessen Spitze für die Dimensionen des Hauses eine etwas zu groß geratene Weltkugel prangte (Abb. 6). Dieser erste kontinentaleuropäische Curtain-Wall erhielt bei der Architekturkritik wenig Beifall. Selbst der sich zur künstlerischen Avantgarde zählende Henry van de Velde fand den Tietzschen Neubau nur hassenswert: „Vergleiche würden sich aufdrängen, wenn uns Jemand in derselben Strasse weiter bis vor ein Gebäude führen würde, das eine ähnliche Bestimmung hat: das Warenhaus Tietz. Aber wenn wir alles zu sagen und zu bezeichnen hätten, was wir hassen, alles was es Schreckliches in der Welt gäbe, würde ich nie zu Ende kommen."[15] Für die große Ablehnung und den mangelnden Zuspruch dieses Gebäudes spricht zudem allerdings auch die nahezu fehlende Nachfolge in der Berliner Architektur.

Dazu war die Dominanz der Wertheimfassade einfach zu gewaltig, zumal Messel bei den Erweiterungen an der Leipziger Straße, bzw. Voßstraße von 1899/1900 und beim Eckpavillon am Leipziger Platz von 1904 weitere nachahmenswerte Alternativen zur vertikalen Gliederung des Urbaus von 1896 aufgezeigt hatte.

Während Messel bei der ersten Erweiterung von 1899 längs der Leipziger Straße das Prinzip der Pfeiler-Glasfassade weiter durchdeklinierte, galten an der rückwärtigen Voßstraße andere Gestaltungskriterien. An dieser noblen Adresse, die mehrere Gesandtschaften beherbergte, musste sich das Warenhaus als eine gutbürgerliche Residenz tarnen. Messel gelang dies, indem er die Pfeiler wieder einer Horizontalgliederung unterwarf, über einem breiten Gesims kleine Zwerchgiebel setzte und die Fensterachsen durch eine dreiteilige, gotisierende steinerne Gliederung akzentuierte (Abb. 7).[16]

Den nächsten Schritt von Messels Fassadenentwicklung markierte der 1904 ausgeführte Eckpavillon am Leipziger Platz (Abb. 8). Aufgrund des städtebaulich herausragenden Ortes am Eingang in die Leipziger Straße kam er zu der Lösung, ein mittelalterlich anmutendes, dunkles und massiges Gebäude zu entwerfen, das sowohl mit der Pfeiler-Glasfassade längs der Leipziger Straße im Einklang stand als auch diesen städtebaulich herausragenden Ort betonte. Über den reich skulptierten Eingangsarkaden öffnete Messel seinen Teppichsaal mit Hilfe eines eng stehenden Systems vertikaler Mauerstäbe. Nach oben hin schloss der Pavillon durch ein abrupt aufsitzendes, mächtiges und dunkles Mansarddach ab, was seine torhafte Wirkung deutlich unterstrich. Mit dieser Ecklösung schuf sich die Institution des Warenhauses einen wahrhaft kathedralartigen Eingang, der in seiner Monumentalität weitaus mehr aussagte, als der nahezu gleichzeitig vollendete Berliner Dom, was von einigen Architekturkennern durchaus spöttisch kommentiert wurde: „Die schärfste Kritik an der ‚neuen Dom- und Hofkirche' ist der Eckbau des Warenhauses Wertheim. Dort keine Spur jenes Andacht und Ehrfurcht erweckenden Eindrucks, den ein Gotteshaus erstreben soll, hier ein mit den Mitteln gothischer Kirchenarchitektur und erlesenstem modernen Feinempfinden errichtetes Gebäude, vor dem uns ein ähnlicher schöner Schauer packt, wie vor dem Straßburger Münster, dem Kölner Dom."[17]

Selbstverständlich führten auch die modifizierten Wertheimfassaden von 1899 und 1904 wieder zu einer reichen Nachfolge. Als Beispiel mag dafür das von Hermann Muthesius (1861–1927) 1912 umgebaute Damenkonfektionsgeschäft Kersten & Tuteur genannt werden (Abb. 9). Das vertikale Gliederungssystem der Messelschen Wertheimfassaden bildete für Muthesius das unmittelbare Vorbild. Julius Posener, der große Kenner der Berliner Architektur des 19. und 20. Jahrhunderts, würdigte dieses Haus als ein besonderes Beispiel für die zahlreichen, in seinen Worten „gemesselten" Fassaden der Berliner Geschäftshäuser der ersten Hälfte des 20. Jahrhunderts.[18]

Als 1907 am damals zu Charlottenburg gehörenden Wittenbergplatz das *Kaufhaus des Westens*, kurz *KaDeWe* genannt, eröffnet wurde, setzte damit nicht nur eine Entwicklung der vormals gutbürgerlichen Wohnstraßen Tauentzien und Kurfürstendamm zum zweiten Geschäftszentrum Berlins ein, was im Begriff der „West-City" bis in unsere Zeit nachvollziehbar ist, sondern bei seiner Fassadengestaltung versuchte der angehende Architekt Emil Schaudt (1871–1957) eine neue Variante im Geschäftshausbau aufzuzeigen. Anstelle einer auf vertikale Linien fußenden Erscheinung band Schaudt seinen Neubau in die horizontale Struktur der umliegenden Wohnbebauung ein. Ihm war es ein großes Bedürfnis, dass sein Gebäude, das 1907 noch als einsames Verkaufshaus in einer ausgesprochenen Wohngegend stand, architektonisch nicht zu sehr aus dem Verband der umliegenden, horizontal gegliederten Bebauung herausfallen sollte.[19] Gewisse Reminiszenzen an die Vertikalität der Geschäftshäuser der Innenstadt lassen sich aber auch bei dem Grundbau des häufig vergrößerten und umgebauten KaDeWe erkennen: So setzte Schaudt bei den das Hauptportal flankierenden, turmartigen Erkern die Vertikale als bestimmende Linie ein (Abb. 10). Ebenso versah er den hervortretenden Mittelbau seiner Seitenfassade zum Wittenbergplatz zitathaft mit vertikalen Mauerstegen. Dennoch stellte das von Adolf Jandorf (1870–1932) gegründete KaDeWe mit seiner Abfolge horizontal übereinander geschichteter Geschosse eine erste Alternative zum Vertikalismus Wertheimscher Prägung dar.

In den ersten Jahren nach dem Kriegsende 1918 kam die Bautätigkeit im Berliner Innenstadtbereich fast vollkommen zum Erliegen. Die Arbeit der Architekten beschränkte sich zwangsläufig auf den Entwurf. Dabei entstanden mitunter expressionistische Architekturphantasien, bei denen das rein Funktionelle zugunsten eines klaren, abstrakten und künstlerischen Formwillens interpretiert wurde, was sich in der Anwendung runder, konkaver und gezackter, kristalliner Formen manifestierte.

Abb. 9: Berlin, Kaufhaus Kersten & Tuteur, Leipziger Straße 36, Fassade, verändert erhalten (Aufnahme 1912)

Abb. 10: Berlin, KaDeWe, Tauentzienstraße 21–24, Fassade, stark verändert erhalten (Aufnahme 1908)

Bei einem Wettbewerb für einen vielgeschossigen Büroturm von über 80 Meter Höhe am Bahnhof Friedrichstraße beteiligte sich Ludwig Mies van der Rohe (1886–1969) im Jahr 1921 mit einem spektakulären Entwurf, dessen Ausführung allein schon an den damals fehlenden technischen Möglichkeiten gescheitert wäre, und auch in der Folge nicht ausgeführt wurde. Vielmehr erhoffte sich Mies durch seine künstlerisch sehr versierten Zeichnungen einem breiteren Publikum bekannt zu werden.

Gegenüber den dunklen Fassaden der umliegenden Altbauten projektierte Mies einen filigran aufstrebenden Turm, der im gleißenden Licht wie eine Vision erstrahlt wäre. Seine kristalline Struktur bestimmte nicht allein die äußere Hülle, sondern fand auch im Grundriss seine sinnvolle Ergänzung. Bei der Fassadengestaltung nahm Mies die Idee von der gläsernen Vorhangfassade des Tietzhauses wieder auf, jetzt

Abb. 11: Berlin, Mossehaus, Schützenstraße 18–25, Ansicht der Gebäudeecke, verändert erhalten (Aufnahme vor 1929)

aber um ein vielfaches gesteigert, da nirgends eine steinerne Einrahmung die kristalline Wirkung seines Hochhauses eingeschränkt hätte.[20]

In den Jahren 1921–1923 wurde Erich Mendelsohn (1887–1953) zusammen mit Richard Neutra (1892–1970) und dem Bildhauer Paul Rudolf Henning (1886–1986) mit dem Wiederaufbau der beim Spartakus-Aufstand durch Einschüsse stark in Mitleidenschaft gezogenen Gebäudeecke des Verlagshauses Mosse an der Schützenstraße beauftragt. In Verbindung mit dieser Baumaßnahme sah man ebenfalls eine Erhöhung des 1901–03 von Wilhelm Cremer (1845–1919) & Richard Wolffenstein (1846–1919) errichteten Gebäudes vor. Zur vertikal gegliederten Front des Altbaues, die ganz in der Tradition des Wertheimhauses an der Voßstraße stand, gestaltete Mendelsohn die Ecke bzw. die neu aufgeführten Dachgeschosse durch horizontal gegliederte und stark zurückliegende Fensterbänder (Abb. 11). Die Wirkung der neuen Fassadenteile gewann durch die Abschrägungen der oberen Gebäudekanten eine besondere Qualität und Dynamik, die sich in dem hervortretenden Eingangsdach und den kleinen Fensterbändern zum Altbau fortsetzte. Es ist auch nicht weiter verwunderlich, dass man mit dieser Erweiterung ein gewaltiges Schiff oder auch einen wahren Ozeandampfer assoziierte, der zufällig auf einer Berliner Straße gelandet sei.[21] Vor allem Mendelsohns dynamisch-expressive, horizontal gegliederte Fassade mit ihrem besonderen Effekt einer dramatisch gesteigerten Perspektive brach mit der bis dahin vorherr-

Abb. 12: Berlin, Ullsteinhaus, Mariendorfer Damm 1–3, Gesamtansicht, erhalten (Aufnahme Wolfgang Reuss 1986)

schenden Dominanz der vertikalen Linie bei der Berliner Geschäftshausarchitektur. Sie wurde von den zeitgenössischen Architekten als neue Möglichkeit der Fassadengestaltung betrachtet.

Neben der jetzt aktuellen Dominanz der horizontalen Linie gab es selbstverständlich eine Reihe von Büro- und Geschäftshäusern, die an die Traditionen der Vorkriegsarchitektur festhielten und diese im Stil einer gemäßigten *Neuen Sachlichkeit* interpretierten. Ab 1925 wurde nach Plänen des Messelschülers Eugen Schmohl (1880–1926) für den Ullstein-Konzern ein Druckhaus in Tempelhof errichtet.[22] Es verfügte neben einem prunkvollen Eingangspavillon als gewisse Referenz an das Ornament lediglich über schmale vertikale Mauerstäbe, welche in angedeuteter Form die Pfeilerfassade der Vorkriegsjahre zitierten (Abb. 12). Insgesamt war der Baukomplex aus rotem Backstein mit seinem alles überragenden Turm dennoch als horizontaler Stockwerksbau ausgeführt worden, was durch die abschließenden Rundbögen der Fenster- bzw. Pfeilerachsen unterstrichen wurde.

Als nach Plänen des Architekten Philipp Schaefer (1885–1952) der Karstadt-Konzern zwischen 1927 und 1929 ein Warenhaus am Hermannplatz errichten ließ, sah man in der Fassade des Eisenbetonbaus vor allem amerikanische Einflüsse, etwa dem Tribune-Tower in Chicago, verwirklicht (Abb. 13).[23] Handelte es sich bei Schaefers Fassade nicht vielmehr um eine Kombination Amerikanischer und Berliner Einflüsse? Schon beim Baumaterial ist eine Übereinstimmung mit Messels Wertheimpavillon zu erkennen. Bei beiden Fassaden wurde der in seiner Oberflächenstruktur porös und fleckig wirkende fränkische Muschelkalk verwendet – einer Gesteinsart, die durch Messels Eckpavillon ihren Siegeszug in Berlin angetreten hatte.[24] Eine weitere Gemeinsamkeit lässt sich in der von einfachen, senkrechten Mauerstegen getrennten, dreiteiligen Fensterzone erkennen, wenn diese auch bei Messel gedoppelt wurde. Beim Grundriss übernahm Schaefer schließlich die seit Wertheim in Berlin verwirklichte Anlage von Lichthöfen und Verkaufsgalerien. Amerikanische Einflüsse verrieten hingegen die beiden abgetreppten Türme, die für die Fernwirkung des Hauses von großer Bedeutung waren.

Dem Columbushaus Erich Mendelsohns am Potsdamer Platz war eine mehrjährige Planung vorausgegangen, bei der im Zusammenhang mit einem neuen Verkehrskonzept die alte mitunter chaotische Bebauung an den Platzwänden durch einheitliche Häuserbänder in Verbindung mit einem Punkthochhaus ersetzt werden sollte. Die Wirtschaftskrise 1929 verhinderte jedoch deren Ausführung. Lediglich mit dem Grundstück an der Nordwestecke hatte sich der Architekt Erich Mendelsohn bereits ab Mitte 1928 näher beschäftigt und plante dort zunächst einen zwölfgeschossigen Warenhausbau für den französischen Konzern *Galeries Lafayette*. Nachdem Lafayette sich wohl aufgrund der Intervention Georg Wertheims und der Krisensituation im Herbst 1929 endgültig von diesem Projekt verabschiedete, wurde die weitere Planung des Hauses 1930 von der Bellevue-Immobilien AG als Eigentümerin übernommen, 1931 begann man schließlich mit den Bauarbeiten des noch einmal von Mendelsohn überarbeiteten Hauses, das neben Laden- und Restaurationsräumen in den unteren beiden

Abb. 13: Berlin, Warenhaus Karstadt, Hermannplatz 10, Gesamtansicht, zerstört (Aufnahme um 1930 von Franz Stoedtner)

Abb. 14: Berlin, Columbushaus, Potsdamer Platz 1, Blick in die Ebertstraße, zerstört (Aufnahme 1933)

Geschossen in den oberen Etagen lediglich Büroraum enthalten sollte.[25]

Mendelsohn antwortete dem Symbol des Berliner Kaufwesens mit seiner ganz eigenen architektonischen Sprache, die aus einer horizontalen Schichtung von Fensterbändern und schmalen Putzstreifen bestand. Im Unterschied zum bereits vorgestellten Mossehaus gelang ihm dies beim

Columbushaus durch eine intelligente Verbindung eines kubischen und dynamischen Gliederungssystems. Während er die Platzecke lediglich durch die Gebäudekante betonte, fand der leicht gerundete Straßenverlauf der Friedrich-Ebert-Straße in der Fassade seine Entsprechung (Abb. 14). Dieses Gliederungsprinzip setzte Mendelsohn in den Abtreppungen des sehr viel höheren Columbushauses zur angrenzenden Altbausubstanz konsequent fort. Eine besondere Raffinesse lag im oberen Abschluss seines Gebäudes, der aus einer Terrasse bestand, die lediglich von einem schmalen Dach abgeschlossen wurde.

Entsprechend der Dachzone unterschieden sich die unteren beiden Geschosse von der übrigen Gliederung des Hauses. Anstelle der kleinteiligen Befensterung der Bürogeschosse verwendete Mendelsohn hier große Schaufensterscheiben. Diese waren fest in das Fassadensystem eingebunden, so dass von einer Renaissance des berüchtigten „Hauses auf Stelzen" bedenkenlos Abstand genommen werden konnte.

Zweifellos haben bei der Planung und Ausführung des Columbushauses für Mendelsohn städtebauliche Aspekte eine entscheidende Rolle gespielt, galt es doch der nordöstlichen Ecke des Leipziger Platzes mit dem Wertheimpavillon auf der nordwestlichen Seite des sich anschließenden Potsdamer Platzes ein adäquates Gebäude entgegenzusetzen. Mit seinen horizontalen Fensterbändern bildete das Columbushaus gleichsam einen Kontrapunkt zum platzbeherrschenden Warenhaus, was anhand der erhöhten Traufkante beider Gebäude deutlich wurde. Wie sehr ihre Dominanz die Platzanlage beherrscht hatte, wurde spätestens nach Abräumung der übrigen Bebauung 1954 offensichtlich. Bis zu seinem Abriss 1956 bildete die Ruine des Wertheimhauses den Eingang in die Leipziger Straße während das 1953 ausgebrannte und 1959 endgültig beseitigte Columbushaus den Übergang in die westliche Magistrale – die Potsdamer Straße – deren Ausgang markierte. Die bedeutendsten Bauten der Berliner Geschäftshausarchitektur lagen sich hier wie eine künstlerische Polarität gegenüber: Einerseits Messels vertikaler Pfeilerbau, andererseits Mendelsohn horizontal gegliedertes Büro- und Geschäftshaus. Beide Häuser wären für die nachfolgenden Generationen durchaus zu retten gewesen, wenn die Grenze zwischen Ost und West nicht gerade durch dieses Terrain verlaufen wäre.

Abstract

Berlin city architecture (1871–1933)

Berlin experienced an economic boom in the years after the establishment of the German Empire in 1871, but initially this had no major impact on the architecture of office buildings for commerce and trade. Blocks of rented apartments were still very much built in the style of the horizontally structured multi-storey buildings of previous periods. However, some ornamental elements were added to the facades and ground floors were opened up visually by using large shop windows. Popularly, these houses were dubbed "buildings on stilts" by Berliners. In 1893, Messel was the first architect in Germany to use the horizontal principle copied from French department stores when he built the *Wertheimbau* in *Oranienstrasse*. He then went on to build the second *Wertheimhaus* and from then on facades with pillars and large vertical rows of shop windows became the accepted model for German commercial and department store buildings. Despite the unanimous acclaim that Messel received from the media and the general public he changed tack when building the extensions that followed. He moved away from facades with pillars and glass. Contrary to everyone's expectations the corner building on *Leipziger Platz*, built in 1904, became the *Cathedral of Trade*: It was a massive, dark and externally hostile construction with a gigantic mansard roof.

Bernhard Sehring chose a different route when he designed the *Tietzhaus*. He had adopted the curtain wall from America, but the full glass facade remained unique. In 1906, Emil Schaudt, when designing *Kaufhaus des Westens* (KaDeWe), again reverted to a sequence of horizontally layered storeys. Emphasizing the horizontal dimension was to become one of the leading motifs of metropolitan architecture of the nineteen twenties. While Erich Mendelsohn was able to put into practice his idea of alternating lines of windows and balustrades when he built *Mosse-Haus*, Mies van der Rohe's fantasies of full glass facades remained largely fantasies when he built the high-rise building on *Friedrichstrasse*. But it was Messel's *Wertheimbau* that most architects in the twenties modelled their office buildings and department stores on. Philipp Schaefer modified the vertical pillar front the American way in the *Karstadthaus* on *Hermannplatz* which was built in 1927. The extension of *Wertheimhaus* on *Leipziger Platz* in 1926, too, followed Messel's precepts. The sheer number of office buildings and department stores built in Berlin in the late *Gründerzeit* is further evidence of their predominance: Before WWI there were some 16 department stores, 27 retail stores and 24 office buildings. After 1919 the number of new buildings of this type reached only 5, 7 and 11 respectively.

Literaturverzeichnis

BERLIN UND SEINE BAUTEN, Teil IX Industriebauten Bürohäuser, Architekten und Ingenieur-Verein zu Berlin (Hrsg.), Berlin – München – Düsseldorf 1971.

BERLIN UND SEINE BAUTEN, Teil VIII Bauten für Handel in Gewerbe, Bd. A Handel, Architekten und Ingenieur-Verein zu Berlin (Hrsg.), Berlin – München – Düsseldorf 1978.

BERLINER ARCHITEKTURWELT 3, 1901, S. 364.

DENKMALTOPOGRAPHIE BUNDESREPUBLIK DEUTSCHLAND, Denkmale in Berlin, Ortsteil Mitte, Landesdenkmalamt Berlin (Hrsg.), Petersberg 2003.

HABEL, Robert, Alfred Messels Wertheimbauten in Berlin – Der Beginn der Modernen Architektur in Deutschland. Mit einem Verzeichnis von Messels Werken, in: Die Bau- und Kunstdenkmäler von Berlin, Beiheft 32, Berlin 2009.

HOFMANN, Albert, Berliner Neubauten, in: Deutsche Bauzeitung 32, 1898, S. 217–219, 229–232.

KADEWE – Kaufhaus des Westens 1907–1932, Berlin 1932.

Max LUDWIG, Dom und Wertheim, in: Die Welt am Montag vom 6.3.1905, Nr. 10.

MENDELSOHN, Erich, Dynamik und Funktion, Realisierte Visionen eines kosmopolitischen Architekten, mit Beiträgen von Charlotte Benton, Ita Heinze-Greenberg, Kathleen James, Hans R. Morgenthaler und Regina Stephan, Ostfildern 2003.

MESSEL, Alfred, Werke, Berlin 1912.

MESSEL, Alfred 1853–1909 – Visionär der Großstadt (Ausstellungskatalog), Elke Blauert, Robert Habel und Hans-Dieter Nägelke in Zusammenarbeit mit Christiane Schmidt (Hrsg.), München 2009.

MESSEL, Alfred, Ein Führer zu seinen Bauten, Artur Gärtner, Robert Habel und Hans-Dieter Nägelke (Hrsg.), Kiel 2010.

MIES VAN DER ROHE, Ludwig, Die Berliner Jahre 1907–1938 (Ausstellungskatalog), Terence Riley und Barry Bergdoll (Hrsg.), München – Berlin – London – New York 2001.

Berliner Spaziergänge, in: NATIONAL-ZEITUNG vom 5.11.1907, Nr. 520.

NALBACH und NALBACH, Das Ullsteinhaus, Vom Druckhaus zum Modecenter, Helmut Engel (Hrsg.), Berlin 1998.

POSENER, Julius, Berlin auf dem Wege zu einer neuen Architektur, München 1978.

RAPSILBER, Maximilian, Alfred Messel, Berlin 1905.

SCHLIEPMANN, Hans, Geschäfts- und Warenhäuser, Berlin/Leipzig 1913.

STAHL, Fritz, Alfred Messel, Berlin 1911.

STRESEMANN, Gustav, Die Warenhäuser, in: Zeitschrift für die gesamte Staatswirtschaft 56, 1900, S. 696–733.

VAN DE VELDE, Henry, Die verstandesmäßigen und folgerechten Konstruktions-Prinzipien, in: Innendekoration 13, 1902, S. 101–109.

WIENER, Alfred, Alfred: Das französische Warenhaus im Gegensatz zum deutschen, in: Berliner Architekturwelt 15, 1913, S. 431–437.

Abbildungsnachweis

Abb. 1: Landesdenkmalamt Berlin, Fotoarchiv.
Abb. 2: Landesdenkmalamt Berlin, Fotoarchiv, Neg. Nr. LKB 3070/1962.
Abb. 3: Fritz Stahl, Alfred Messel, 1911, S. XIV.
Abb. 4: Landesdenkmalamt Berlin, Fotoarchiv, Neg. Nr. LKB 7192 D.
Abb. 5: Landesdenkmalamt Berlin, Fotoarchiv, Neg. Nr. 01/3417 [Magistrat].
Abb. 6: Landesdenkmalamt Berlin, Fotoarchiv.
Abb. 7: Maximilian Rapsilber, Alfred Messel, 1905, S. 78.
Abb. 8: Alfred Messel, Werke, 1912, Tf. XIa.
Abb. 9: Landesdenkmalamt Berlin, Fotoarchiv, Neg. Nr. II A 2227 [Magistrat].
Abb. 10: Berliner Architekturwelt 10, 1908, S. 85.
Abb. 11: Landesdenkmalamt Berlin, Fotoarchiv, Neg. Nr. 21343 R 02.
Abb. 12: Landesdenkmalamt Berlin, Fotoarchiv, Neg. Nr. 1105586.
Abb. 13: Landesdenkmalamt Berlin, Fotoarchiv, Neg. Nr. LKB 117244.
Abb. 14: Landesdenkmalamt Berlin, Fotoarchiv, Neg. Nr. 1112 B.

* Die Abbildungsrechte sind vom Autor geklärt worden und liegen in dessen Verantwortung

---

[1] MESSEL, Ein Führer zu seinen Bauten, 2010, S. 58–61.
[2] BERLIN UND SEINE BAUTEN, 1971, S. 132–133.
[3] siehe dazu: BERLIN UND SEINE BAUTEN, 1978. S. 71–82, 129–139.
[4] Für die Bereitstellung der überwiegenden Zahl der Abbildungen sei an dieser Stelle Frau Britta Kaden-Pohl und Herrn Wolfgang Bittner vom Fotoarchiv des Landesdenkmalamts Berlin herzlich gedankt.
[5] SCHLIEPMANN, 1913, S. 32.
[6] MESSEL 1854–1909 – Visionär der Großstadt, 2009
[7] Zu erwähnen wären hier besonders die sog. Werderhäuser. Siehe: HABEL, 2009, S. 43–47.
[8] HABEL, 2009, S. 101.
[9] WIENER, 1913, S. 431.
[10] VAN DE VELDE, 1902, S. 102–104.
[11] STRESEMANN, 1900, S. 714.
[12] HOFMANN, 1898, S. 231.
[13] VAN DE VELDE, 1902, S. 103–104.
[14] BERLIN UND SEINE BAUTEN, 1978, darin Peter Stürzebecher: Warenhäuser S. 16, sowie Klaus Konrad Weber und Peter Güttler: Die Architektur der Warenhäuser, S. 39.
[15] VAN DE VELDE, 1902, S. 104.
[16] BERLINER ARCHITEKTURWELT, 1901, S. 364.
[17] LUDWIG, 1905, o. S.
[18] POSENER, 1979, S. 477.
[19] KaDeWe, 1932, S. 19.
[20] MIES VAN DER ROHE, 2001, darin Vittorio Magnago Lampugnani: Die Moderne und die Großstadt, S. 42–43, sowie Dietrich Neumann. Hochhaus an der Friedrichstraße, Wabe, Projekt, Berlin-Mitte, 1921, S. 180.
[21] MENDELSOHN, 2003, darin Regina Stephan: „Denken an den Tag, wo Geschichte große Kurven schlägt und Hunderttausende unbefriedigt läßt" Frühe expressionistische Bauten in Luckenwalde, Berlin und Gleiwitz, S. 55–60.
[22] NALBACH UND NALBACH, 1998, darin Helmut Engel: Der Architekt des Ullsteinhauses, Eugen Schmohl, S. 13–27.
[23] BERLIN UND SEINE BAUTEN, 1978, darin Klaus Konrad Weber und Peter Güttler: Die Architektur der Warenhäuser, S. 60.
[24] NATIONAL-ZEITUNG, 1907.
[25] MENDELSOHN, 2003, darin Regina Stephan: „Wir glauben an Berlin" Das Metallarbeiterhaus, das Columbushaus und andere Geschäftshäuser in Berlin, S. 155–164.

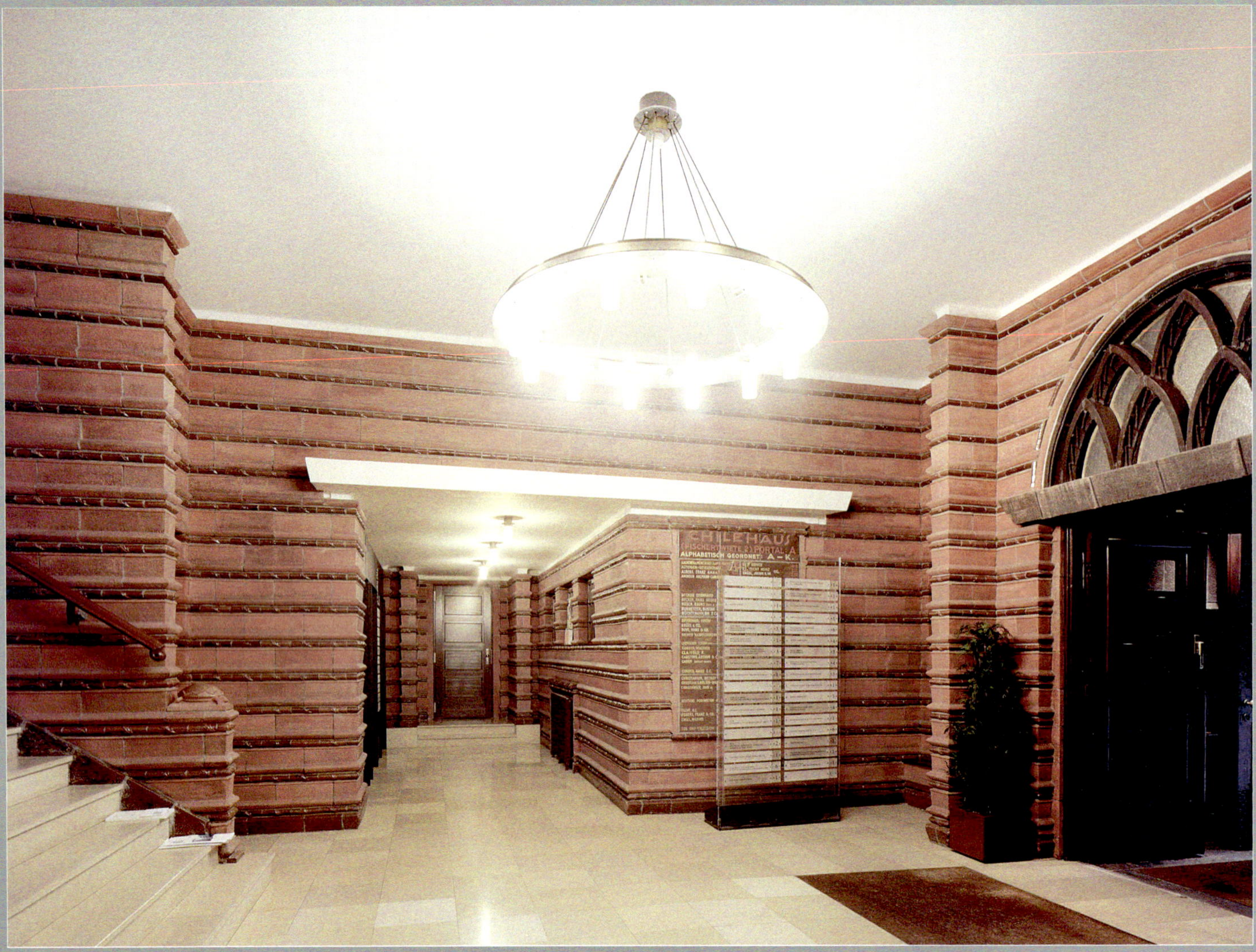

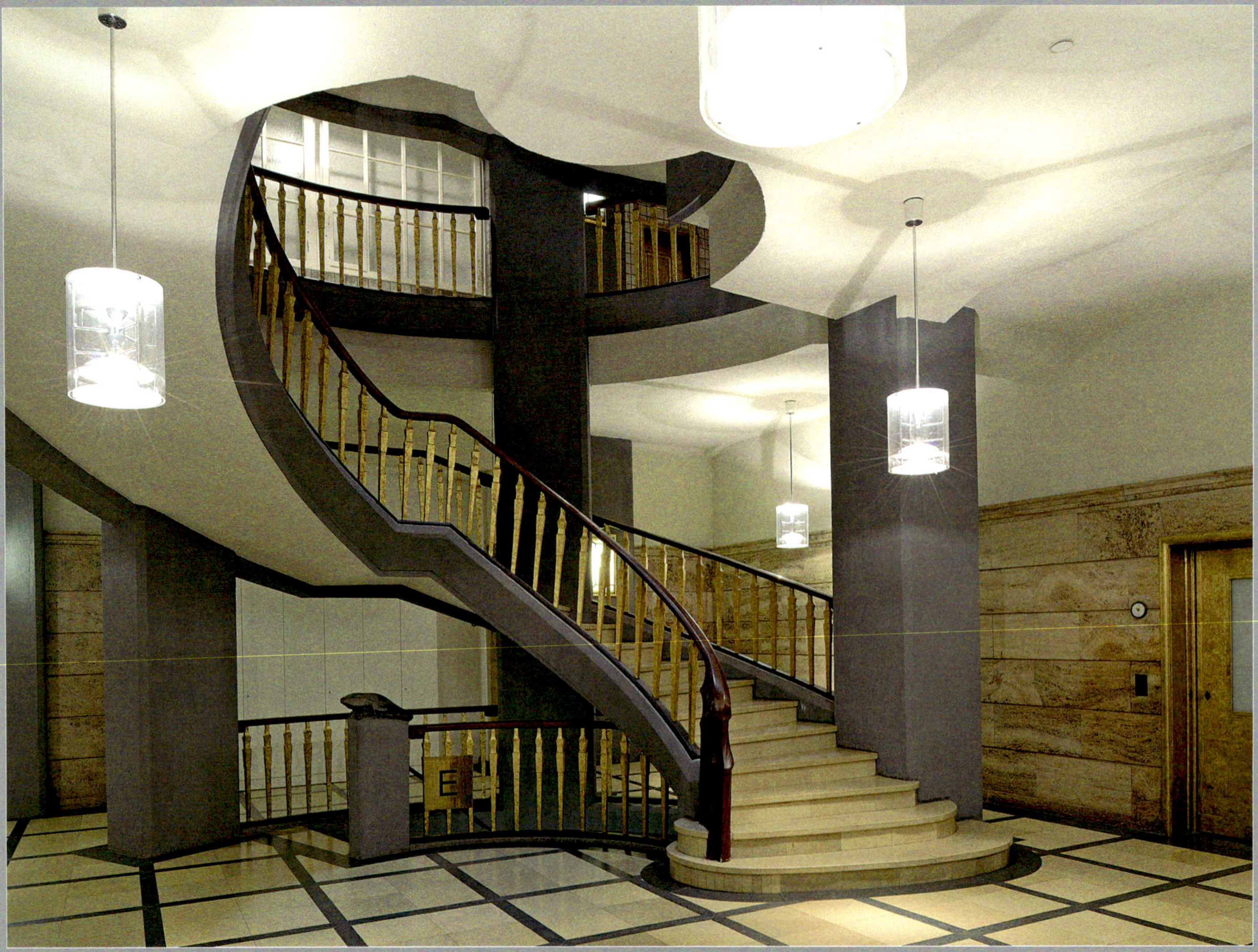

**Das Hamburger Kontorhaus
The Hamburg Office Buildings**

Hamburg

Jan Lubitz

Von der Kaufmannsstadt zur Handelsmetropole – Entwicklung des Hamburger Kontorhauses von 1886–1914

Als „Kontorhaus" wird in Hamburg ein Büro- und Geschäftshaus bezeichnet, das verschiedenen Firmen als Verwaltungsgebäude dient und üblicherweise auch über Ladenflächen im Sockelbereich verfügt. Der Bautypus „Bürohaus" ist dabei noch relativ jung. Während privatwirtschaftliche Verwaltungstätigkeiten über Jahrhunderte üblicherweise in den bürgerlichen Wohnhäusern oder Stadtpalästen angesiedelt waren, entwickelte sich erst im Zuge der Industriellen Revolution eine eigenständige Bauform für diese Aufgabe. Die Idee dafür „stammt aus England, wo sie nach den amerikanischen Großstädten verpflanzt wurde, um dann nach Deutschland zu kommen. In Deutschland sind es zuerst die Hansastädte Hamburg, Bremen und Lübeck, die den Gedanken aufnahmen."[1] Als erstes reines Bürohaus gilt das County Fire Office-Gebäude, das 1819 im Stadtzentrum von London nach einem Entwurf des Architekten Robert Abraham errichtet wurde.[2]

Der Ausdruck „Kontorhaus" leitet sich vom lateinischen „computare" ab, was mit „berechnen" übersetzt werden kann. Dieser Wortstamm ist auch in zahlreichen anderen Wörtern wie dem „Computer", dem „Konto" oder dem englischen „to count" zu entdecken. Obwohl Büro- und Geschäftshäuser auch in anderen Städten stehen, ist der Begriff „Kontorhaus" nur in Hamburg gebräuchlich. Bereits diese Tatsache deutet darauf hin, dass auch der Typus des Kontorhauses eine spezifisch Hamburgische Eigenart darstellt (Abb. 1).

Schon zur Hansezeit sprach man von „Kontoren". Gemeint waren damit die Handelsniederlassungen der hanseatischen Händler in fremden Städten. Die Hamburger Kaufleute nannten auch ihre Geschäftsräume in den für die Stadt charakteristischen Giebelhäusern „Kontore". Seit der Hansezeit und noch bis in das späte 19. Jahrhundert hinein beherrschte jener Bautyp das Hamburger Stadtbild. Das für

Abb. 1: Isometrie der Innenstadt von Hamburg, um 1860

diese Kaufmannshäuser typische enge räumliche Miteinander von Wohnen, Kontor und Lager geriet in den 1880er Jahren durch die Anlage der Speicherstadt in Auflösung. Mit der Speicherstadt entstand ein ausschließlich der Warenlagerung dienendes Areal, das eine funktionale Neuordnung des Stadtkerns auslöste.

Zuvor hatte schon 1861 die Aufhebung der Torsperren den Startschuss für einen tiefgreifenden Strukturwandel gesetzt, der eine neue räumliche Gliederung des Stadtgebiets bewirkte. Mit dem Ende der Torsperren strebten die wohlhabenden Hamburger Kaufleute zunehmend in die noch ländlich geprägten Vororte wie Rotherbaum, Hamm oder auf die Uhlenhorst, in denen sie sich neue Wohnhäuser und Landsitze erbauen ließen. Gleichzeitig boomte im 1871 gegründeten Kaiserreich die Wirtschaft, und Hamburg entwickelte sich zum größten deutschen Handelshafen. Dadurch entwickelte sich auch ein stetig wachsender Bedarf an neuen Büroflächen. „Viele Kaufleute bekamen ein großes Interesse, in nächster Fühlung mit den neuen großen Lagerhäusern des Freihafengebietes zu bleiben."[3] Die ersten neuzeitlichen Kontorhäuser wurden darum in den an die Speicherstadt angrenzenden Stadtbereichen errichtet.

Der Hamburger Kaufmann Heinrich Ohlendorff reagierte als erster auf die neuen Anforderungen, die sich aus dem in der Innenstadt anbahnenden Strukturwandel ergaben. Er beauftragte 1885 den renommierten Architekten Martin Haller mit dem Entwurf des Dovenhofs. Dieses erste Kontorhaus wurde an der Brandstwiete errichtet, einer im Zusammenhang mit dem Bau des Sandtorhafens 1868–69 neu ausgebauten Straße, die schon alleine dadurch in einem unmittelbaren Zusammenhang mit der Speicherstadt und den angrenzenden Hafenanlagen steht (Abb. 2).

Haller schuf mit dem Dovenhof einen Musterbau für alle nachfolgenden Hamburger Kontorhäuser. Die wesentlichen Innovationen des Gebäudes lagen in der inneren Gliederung, während die Fassaden mit ihrer Neorenaissance-Gestaltung noch relativ konventionell gehalten waren und sich nur wenig von den zeitgenössischen Bauten unterschieden. Allerdings verfügte der Bau mit seiner blockausfüllenden Bauweise schon über eine Dimension, die in der eng bebauten Altstadt aus dem Rahmen fiel. Das Grundstück wurde fast vollständig überbaut. Zwei kleine Innenhöfe sorgten dabei für die Belichtung der nach innen orientierten Büroräume. Die Grundrissstruktur mit den durch Zwischenwände individuell möblierbaren Büroflächen folgt rationalen Kriterien. Treppenhäuser und Nebenräume, vor allem die Toilettenanlagen, wurden räumlich gebündelt und in die sonst schlecht nutzbaren Ecken des Grundrisses gelegt. Da das Kontorhaus rein gewerblichen Zwecken dienen sollte, wurde auf repräsentative Gesten weitgehend verzichtet. Lediglich die Erschließungsflächen, also die mit Galerien versehenen Flure sowie die zentrale Eingangshalle mit dem angrenzenden Treppenhaus, wurden durch eine anspruchsvolle Innenausstattung räumlich aufgewertet. Als öffentlich zugängliche Bereiche dienten sie nämlich auch dem Kundenverkehr und stellten eine Art architektonische Visitenkarte des Hauses dar.

Hinzu kam eine für die Zeit hochmoderne Infrastruktur. Als erstes Gebäude in Deutschland wurden im Dovenhof Paternoster[4] eingebaut, mit denen nun auch die obe-

Abb. 2: Dovenhof, 1885–86, Architekt Martin Haller

Abb. 3: Wohn- und Geschäftshaus Brandstwiete, 1886–87, Architekt Albert Heidtmann

ren Geschosse bequem erschlossen werden konnten. Die Gebäudehöhe wurde dadurch erstmals durch städtebauliche Kriterien limitiert, nicht mehr durch praktische Fragen der Erreichbarkeit. Damit war in Hamburg der Startschuss für wachsende Gebäudehöhen gefallen. Technische Annehmlichkeiten wie eine Zentralheizung oder eine Rohrpostanlage trugen ebenfalls zur Modernität des Dovenhofs mit bei.

Der Dovenhof definierte mit seiner innovativen Konzeption die Bauaufgabe des großstädtischen Verwaltungsgebäudes neu. Weder in seiner Art noch in seiner Formgebung war das Gebäude an vorhandene Hamburger Vorbilder gebunden, „irgend ein in der Aufgabe liegender ästhetischer oder technischer Zusammenhang mit früherer hamburgischer Bauweise läßt sich nicht erbringen, denn das Kontorhaus bedeutet einen radikalen Bruch mit der Vergangenheit."[5] Die für die Bauzeit enorme Modernität offenbarte sich besonders durch direkte Vergleiche. So entstand 1886–87 gegenüber des Dovenhofs ein Wohn- und Geschäftshaus nach Entwurf des Architekten Albert Heidtmann. Neben

Abb. 4: Burstahhof, 1887–88, Architekten Bahre & Querfeld

Abb. 5: Johannishof, 1895–96, Architekt George Radel

Läden im Erdgeschoss waren dort in den oberen Etagen Kontore untergebracht, aber auch Wohnungen. Damit entsprach dieses Gebäude noch dem im späten 19. Jahrhundert vorherrschenden Typus eines gemischten Geschäftshauses, auf das die Innovationen des Dovenhofs zunächst keinen unmittelbaren Einfluss hatten. Auch die üppig ausstaffierte Neorenaissance-Fassade erfüllte vorrangig konventionelle Repräsentationsbedürfnisse, wenngleich sich im Fensterraster der Straßenfronten bereits die innere Gebäudelogik abzuzeichnen beginnt (Abb. 3).

Im Gegensatz zu diesen beiden großformatigen Baukomplexen an der neu ausgebauten Brandstwiete mussten die meisten in den 1880er und 1890er Jahren entstandenen Kontorhäuser in den bestehenden städtischen Kontext eingefügt werden. Die Neubautätigkeit beschränkte sich dabei auf die Bereiche unmittelbar nördlich der Speicherstadt sowie das Gebiet rund um die Börse. Auf einer typischen Altstadtparzelle zwischen dem Großen Burstah und dem rückwärtigen Alsterfleet wurde 1887–88 der Burstahhof errichtet. Bei diesem Kontorhaus haben die Architekten Bahre & Querfeld es bereits gewagt, die Fassaden vollständig in ein Skelettraster aufzulösen, um durch große Fensteröffnungen die tiefen Grundrisse ausreichend zu belichten. Erstmals wird beim Burstahhof zwischen breiten Primärstützen und schmalen Sekundärstützen unterschieden, die als Anschluss der individuell zu setzenden Innenwände dienen. Klassische Elemente wie Pilaster, Bossierungen oder Konsolgesimse deuten aber noch auf Bestrebungen hin, dieses ungewohnte Erscheinungsbild durch die Ausgestaltung mit historisierenden Details dem zeittypischen Geschmack anzupassen (Abb. 4).

Beeinflusst wurde diese Fassadenlösung wohl auch durch zeitgenössische Vorbilder der „Chicago School" und das dort geprägte Motto „form follows function"[6]. Vor allem das 1879 entstandene „First Leiter Building" scheint mit seiner Rasterfassade für die Gestaltung des Burstahhofs Pate gestanden zu haben. So entwickelt sich in Hamburg noch vor der Jahrhundertwende eine originäre Formensprache für die Kontorhäuser, „die einzig und allein aus den Zwecken dieser Gebäudeart und dem Bestreben, diesen Zwecken bis aufs äußerste zu dienen, hervorgegangen ist, ohne irgendwelche geschichtliche oder sentimentale Seitenblicke. Der Zweck hat also hier die Form gestaltet."[7]

Zu den funktionalen und baukünstlerischen Impulsen in der Entwicklung des Kontorhauses kam ab 1892 eine weitere wesentliche Komponente hinzu. In diesem Jahr grassierte eine Cholera-Epidemie, die den Anstoß zur Neugliederung der Hamburger Innenstadt gab. Der schon im Laufe des 19. Jahrhundert eingesetzte Entmischungsprozess des Stadtzentrums erfuhr dadurch eine erhebliche Beschleunigung. Infolge dieser Katastrophe wurden 1897 drei Sanierungsgebiete ausgewiesen, die den städtebaulichen Wandel von einer Kaufmannsstadt zu einer modernen Handelsmetropole weiter verstärkten. Mit dem Abriss der alten Gängeviertel entstanden Flächen, die nach einer neuen Nutzung verlangten, die ihrer zentralen Lage im Hamburger Stadtkern angemessen waren. Baumaßnahmen wie der 1897 vollendete Neubau des Rathauses oder der 1906 eröffnete Hauptbahnhof verstärkten die wachsende wirtschaftliche Bedeutung des Stadtzentrums.

Daraufhin gerieten auch Bereiche der Innenstadt in den Blickwinkel, die zuvor noch als abseitige Lagen galten. „Vom Jahre 1894 ab sieht man […] einzelne weitere Kontorhäuser entstehen […]. Aber erst etwa von 1900 an kann man von einer Hochkonjunktur des Kontorhauses sprechen".[8] Rund um das neue Rathaus wurden ab Mitte der 1890er Jahre verstärkt Neubauten wie der Johannishof errichtet, der 1895–96 nach einem Entwurf von George Radel entsteht. Mit seiner klaren dreizonigen Gliederung rezipierte der Bau noch gängige Gestaltungsmuster des Historismus, die aber auch in der zeitgenössischen amerikanischen Architektur der „Chicago School" Anwendung fanden. Allerdings ist bei diesem Kontorhaus die klassische Außenwand schon vollständig in ein stringentes Fensterraster aufgelöst, das gleichermaßen von einer horizontalen und einer vertikalen Lineatur überzogen ist. Gleichwohl ist die Natursteinfassade noch mit traditionellen Gliederungselementen ausgeschmückt (Abb. 5).

Auch das Kontorhaus Feigl, das 1899 nach Entwürfen von Walter Martens errichtet wurde, steht in einer dieser Nebenstraßen südlich des Rathauses. Dieses drei Jahre jüngere Kontorhaus verfügt bereits über eine eindeutig vertikal strukturierte Fassade. Die großformatigen Fensteröffnungen sind in senkrechten Bahnen zusammengefasst, auch wenn die vielgliedrige Ausgestaltung des Gebäudesockels diese Struktur etwas überspielt. Ein Attikageschoss bildet den oberen Abschluss der klaren dreizonigen Fassadengliederung. Als Fassadenmaterial kommen hier glasierte Ziegelsteine zur Anwendung, die das simple Fassadenraster mit einer eigenständigen ornamentalen Wirkung überziehen. Damit erweitert sich der Materialkanon, und ein neuer architektonischer Impuls findet Eingang in den Hamburger Kontorhausbau (Abb. 6).

Der funktionale, stadträumliche und architektonische Wandel der Innenstadt erfährt um die Jahrhundertwende eine massive Beschleunigung. An der Kaiser-Wilhelm-Straße, einer 1893 fertiggestellten Straßenverbindung zur expandierenden Vorstadt St. Pauli, wird 1901 der Holstenhof des Architekten Albert Lindhorst eingeweiht, der an dieser neuen Durchbruchstraße auch einen neuen Größenmaßstab erreicht. Während die Sockelzone bereits weitgehend für Schaufensterflächen verglast ist und nur durch einige gusseiserne Stützen sowie die Hauseingänge unterteilt wird, zeigen die Obergeschosse wieder das für Kontorhäuser in den späten 1890er Jahren üblich gewordene großformatige Fensterraster mit einer vertikalen Gliederung. Anstelle historisierenden Zierrats tauchen bei diesem Gebäude bereits figürliche und geometrische Ornamente auf, die maßgeblich vom zeitgenössischen Jugendstil beeinflusst sind (Abb. 7).

Die Suche nach neuen Architekturformen entwickelt sich in Hamburg parallel zum Entwicklungsprozess des Kontorhauses mit seiner rationalen Gebäudestruktur und den städtebaulichen Umbrüchen. Dabei löst der zeitgenössische Verlust weiter Teile des angestammten Hamburger Stadtbildes infolge der Sanierungsmaßnahmen eine Beschäftigung mit Alt-Hamburger Bautraditionen aus.[9] Als frühestes Resultat dieser aufkeimenden Hamburg-Romantik erhält das 1902–03 von Rambatz & Jollasse ausgeführte Kontorhaus Alsterhaus auf seiner Rückseite an der Ferdinandstraße eine Backsteinfassade, die mit Motiven der lokalen Baugeschichte ausgeschmückt wird. Der Entwurf dafür stammt vom Hamburger Bauinspektor Albert Erbe. Dadurch erhält die streng rationale Fassadenstruktur, die neben der typischen vertikalen Gliederung und horizontaler Zonierung auch wieder eine Differenzierung im Primär- und Sekundärstützen aufweist, erstmals eine spezifisch Hamburgische Note (Abb. 8).

Gleichzeitig führt der Architekt Hermann Wurzbach den „grès flammés"-Stein in Hamburg ein, einen gescheckten, bunten Glasurstein, der durch seine Unregelmäßigkeiten ein flirrendes Farbenspiel erzeugt. Verwendung findet dieses

Abb. 6: Kontorhaus Feigl, 1899, Architekt Walter Martens

Abb. 7: Holstenhof, 1900–01, Architekt Albert Lindhorst

Baumaterial unter anderem am Austral-Haus an der Poststraße von 1903–04, dem Gertig-Haus am Großen Burstah von 1905 und dem Kontorhaus Newman an der Schauenburgerstraße von 1906, die alle von dem Büro Frejtag & Wurzbach realisiert werden. Die Fassadenoberfläche wird bei diesen Bauten bereits als reine Verkleidung behandelt, die der tragenden Skelettstruktur vorgeblendet wird. Das konstruktive Skelett, das die Etagenflächen von tragenden Wänden freihält und somit flexibel einzurichten lässt, zeichnet sich in der Straßenfront durch die markanten Vertikalen der Pfeiler ab. Stützen, Fensterbrüstungen und Fenster sind in der Tiefe gestaffelt angeordnet, wodurch die Fassade eine plastische Gliederung erfährt. Auf historisierende Dekoration wird bereits vollständig verzichtet, das Erscheinungsbild wird nunmehr alleine durch die tektonische Struktur und das ornamentierend wirkende Fassadenmaterial geprägt (Abb. 9).

Um 1900 hat sich im Hamburger Kontorhausbau eine nüchterne Formensprache als architektonischer Standard etabliert. Die strenge, vertikal beherrschte Baustruktur mit ihren großformatigen Fensteröffnungen weist aber weiterhin eine klassische Gliederung in die drei Zonen Sockel, Hauptgeschosse und Gesims auf. Auch zeitgenössische Vorbilder der Büro- und Hochhaus-Architektur der USA, verbunden mit Architekten wie Louis Sullivan und Henry Hobson Richardson, aber auch Einflüsse der von Alfred Messel geprägten Architektur Berliner Warenhäuser werden von den Hamburger Architekten rezipiert. Neue Impulse werden dem Kontorhausbau nach 1900 hauptsächlich von der dynamischen städtebaulichen Entwicklung Hamburgs verliehen. Forciert durch die Stadtsanierungsmaßnahmen, durchlaufen weitere Gebiete in der Innenstadt einen Tertiärisierungsprozess. Auch das nach dem Brand von 1842 überwiegend mit bürgerlichen Wohnhäusern bebaute Gebiet östlich der Binnenalster wird durch Kontorhäuser wie dem Kirdorf-Haus, das 1901–05 nach Entwürfen der Architekten Lundt & Kallmorgen entsteht, allmählich in ein Büroquartier umgewandelt (Abb. 10).

Im Zusammenhang mit den neuen städtebaulichen Perspektiven werden für den Bau neuer Kontorhäuser auch zunehmend mehrere Parzellen zusammengefasst, um größere und besser nutzbare Baugrundstücke zu schaffen. Wurden die frühen Kontorhäuser noch in einen bestehenden stadträumlichen Kontext eingefügt, so werden nach 1900 zunehmend neue städtebauliche Situationen geschaffen. Das 1907–08 von Henry Grell am Neuen Wall errichtete Hübner-Haus steht an drei Seiten frei und grenzt lediglich mit seiner Rückwand an die vorhandenen Blockstrukturen. Aufgrund dieser Umstände erfährt die Baumasse eine bewusste plastische Durchformung. Während der Mittelteil sechsgeschossig ausgeführt ist, sind die um eine Etage niedrigeren Gebäudeecken gerundet. Das Fassadenbild wird von der inzwischen typisch gewordenen Vertikalität der Pfeiler dominiert. Dabei schafft das Wechselspiel von Haupt- und Nebenstützen ein eigenständiges gestalterisches Thema, das mit der baukörperlichen Gliederung korrespondiert (Abb. 11).

In den Jahren kurz nach 1900 ist der konstruktive und gestalterische Charakter des Kontorhauses bereits ausgereift. Sein charakteristisches Erkennungsmerkmal ist „eine ausgesprochen senkrechte Linienführung […], die sich aus dem Bedürfnis der größten inneren Teilungsmöglichkeit durch Querwände herausgestaltet hat".[10] Die Dimensionen sind jedoch noch im Wachstum begriffen. Während innerhalb des Stadtkerns der Maßstab der Bauten noch durch das vor-

Abb. 8: Alsterhaus, Rückfront, 1902–03, Architekt Albert Erbe

Abb. 9: Australhaus, 1903–04, Architekten Frejtag & Wurzbach

handene, engmaschige Straßennetz limitiert wird, zeigt das 1908–09 unmittelbar vor dem Wallring errichtete Bieber-Haus der Architekten Rambatz & Jollasse neue Perspektiven auf. Das Kontorhaus steht vollständig frei. Die um zwei Innenhöfe herum angeordnete Baumasse weist eine simpel gehaltene, aber effektive Rhythmisierung auf. Der strenge Rasterbau gehorcht dabei eher den Gesetzen des Industriebaus als den Anforderungen kaiserzeitlicher Baukunst und zeigt eine für die Bauzeit frappierende Modernität. Darum reift bereits in der Zeit vor dem Ersten Weltkrieg in Hamburg die Erkenntnis vom Kontorhaus als einem „Kind der Neuzeit, […] ein Bauwerk voller Regelmäßigkeit, Zweckmäßigkeit, Selbstverständlichkeit analog den Geschäftsbüchern des Kaufmanns"[11] (Abb. 12).

Als ab 1908 im ehemaligen Gängeviertel der Altstadt die Mönckebergstraße als Teil der Stadtsanierungsmaßnahmen nach der Cholera-Epidemie angelegt wird, entstehen auch im Stadtzentrum großzügige neue Bauflächen. Entlang der Straße werden bis zum Ausbruch des Ersten Weltkriegs zahlreiche großmaßstäbliche Kontorhäuser errichtet. Das gängige Muster wird dabei auch um neue architektonische Motive erweitert, die sich verstärkt auf lokale Bautraditionen berufen. Junge Architekten wie Henry Grell, Alfred Jacob und Otto Ameis oder Fritz Höger, der 1910 seine Ansichten über die zeitgemäße Gestaltung von Kontorhäusern in einem Buch veröffentlicht,[12] beginnen Alt-Hamburgische Bürgerhausmotive wie Volutengiebel, Sprossenfenster oder Backsteindetails zu adaptieren. Vor allem Fritz Höger kombiniert dabei die konstruktive Logik der für Hamburg so typischen historischen Fachwerkkonstruktion mit den Gesetzmäßigkeiten des modernen Skelettbaus (Abb. 13).

Dieser wachsende Einfluss der Heimatschutzbewegung fällt in eine Zeit umfassender Reformbemühungen, die 1907 in der Gründung des Deutschen Werkbundes kulminieren. Dadurch erfährt auch der Kontorhausbau eine wesentliche Erweiterung seiner architektonischen Ausdrucksmöglichkeiten. Die seit 1886 herausgebildeten Prinzipien des Kontorhauses – also die Skelettstruktur mit freiem Grundriss und nüchterner Rasterfassade – werden in diesen Jahren durch romantische, regional tradierte Elemente ergänzt. Einen entscheidenden Impuls erhält das Hamburger Bauschaffen durch den Backsteinbau, der nun als zentrales Element hanseatischer Baukultur identifiziert wird. „Der Backstein, der heute wieder in Gunst steht, wurde bis vor wenigen Jahren, trotz immer wiederholter Bemühungen vieler Architekten, von den Auftraggebern fast einmütig abgelehnt, bis schließlich einem Teil der Bauherren die Erkenntnis von dem Wert dieses Baustoffes in technischer wie in künstlerischer Hinsicht aufgegangen ist".[13]

Damit ist auch eine Abkehr vom als beliebig und internationalistisch empfundenen Historismus der Kaiserzeit verbunden. Ebenso beginnen sich die Ideale des Deutschen Werkbundes, der wiederentdeckte handwerkliche Qualitäten mit den Bedingungen moderner Produktionsweisen vereinen will, auf den Backsteinbau auszuwirken. Maßgeblich geprägt wird diese Entwicklung in Hamburg vom 1909 neu angetretenen Baudirektor Fritz Schumacher, einem der Mitbegründer des Werkbundes. Er schreibt über diesen Prozess: „Während die Mönckebergstraße entstand, begann in Hamburg mehr und mehr der Sinn für eine gesunde einsichtsvolle Neubelebung des Backsteinbaues einzusetzen. Man erkannte in ihm die Möglichkeiten, die gerade für unsere Küsten-

Abb. 10: Kirdorfhaus, 1901–05, Architekten Lundt & Kallmorgen

Abb. 11: Hübnerhaus, 1907–08, Architekt Henry Grell

Abb. 12: Bieberhaus, 1908–09, Architekten Rambatz & Jollasse

Abb. 13: Kontorhaus Glass, 1911, Architekt Fritz Höger

Abb. 14: Levantehaus, 1912–13, Architekten Franz Bach, Carl Gustav Bensel

striche von grundlegender Bedeutung werden können, und so war es ein Gebot der Stunde, diese Regungen nach Kräften zu fördern [...]. So liegt in der Buntscheckigkeit des Materials, die uns in der Mönckebergstraße entgegentritt, der Widerschein eines historischen Entwicklungsprozesses."[14]

Bis zum Ausbruch des Ersten Weltkriegs 1914 gehen diese verschiedenen Entwicklungsstränge im Hamburger Kontorhausbau eine einzigartige Synthese ein. Gerade die Mönckebergstraße bildet mit Bauten wie dem Levante-Haus der Architekten Franz Bach und Carl Gustav Bensel oder Fritz Högers Klöpper-Haus, beide 1912–13 errichtet, einen entscheidenden Katalysator in diesem Entwicklungsprozess. „Eingespannt wie eine Starkstromleitung zwischen zwei Polen des öffentlichen Lebens, dem Rathaus und dem Hauptbahnhof, ist sie gefüllt von Energien und Kunstwillen. Straßengrundriß und formale Gestaltung sind einheitlich im künstlerischen Entwurf und bilden einen einzigen Akkord"[15] (Abb. 14).

Noch vor Beginn des Ersten Weltkriegs gelangt in Hamburg mit dem Kontorhausbau eine neuartige Architektur zum Durchbruch, die auf rationalen Grundlagen basiert und eine eigenständige Formensprache entwickelt, die in dieser Art singulär ist. Die funktionalen Bedingungen der inneren Gebäudestruktur, die großformatige Baumasse, die plastische Behandlung der Baukörper, die nüchterne, vertikal geprägte Fassadenausbildung, das damit einhergehende bewusste Weglassen historistischer Details sowie die Neuentdeckung der Backsteinbauweise stellen um 1914 die wesentlichen Charakteristika des Hamburger Kontorhausbaus dar. Diese Entwicklungen erfolgen vor dem Hintergrund eines tiefgreifenden strukturellen Wandels, der Hamburg während der Kaiserzeit von einer noch mittelalterlich geprägten Kaufmannsstadt zu einer modernen Handelsmetropole werden lässt (Abb. 15).

Neben der dynamischen wirtschaftlichen Entwicklung der Stadt, deren Einwohnerzahl bereits 1910 die Millionengrenze übersteigt, tragen dazu verschiedene, miteinander in Wechselbeziehungen stehende Tendenzen bei. So wird die schon gegen Mitte des 19. Jahrhunderts begonnene funktionale Entflechtung des Stadtkerns durch eine zeitgleiche Modernisierung der öffentlichen Infrastruktur begünstigt. Elektrifizierung, Gas- und Wasserversorgung und der Bau eines leistungsfähigen Nahverkehrssytems mit dem 1912 eingeweihten Hochbahn-Ring schaffen nicht nur Grundlagen für eine Verdrängung des Wohnens an die Stadtränder, sondern ermöglichen auch im Umkehrschluss die Ausbildung einer vorrangig dem Geschäftsleben dienenden City. Der mit diesem Wandel einhergehende Verlust des mittelalterlichen Stadtbildes bildet wiederum die geistige Basis für eine Wiederentdeckung regionaler Traditionen, die in ein Streben nach der Entwicklung einer unverwechselbaren Hamburgischen Baukultur münden.

Dadurch wird in Hamburg in den Jahren nach der Jahrhundertwende die Abkehr vom kaiserzeitlichen Historismus mit weit größerer Konsequenz vollzogen als in den meisten anderen Regionen des Deutschen Reichs. Der vorrangig funktional begründete Citybildungsprozess verbindet sich hier mit der Entwicklung einer neuartigen Großstadt-Architektur, die den gewandelten Bedingungen der Zeit Ausdruck verleiht. Damit nimmt Hamburg nicht nur deutschlandweit, sondern auch im europäischen Kontext einer Vorreiterrolle ein. Die städtebaulichen, baukünstlerischen, soziologischen und infrastrukturellen Entwicklungsstränge der Zeit werden in der Stadt gebündelt und führen zu einem Durchbruch moderner Architektur, die nach dem Ersten Weltkrieg, unter den neuen politischen Vorzeichen der Weimarer Republik, mit dem Kontorhausviertel eine logische Fortsetzung findet.

Abstract

From Merchant City to Trade Centre – evolution of the Hamburg office building 1886–1914

During the latter part of the nineteenth century Hamburg underwent fundamental changes in terms of its urban development structure. While residents tended to move to the suburbs after rigid rules about living within the city gates had been abandoned, the city centre saw the development of a modern business district. The inauguration of the Port Warehouse District (Speicherstadt) in 1888 led to the development of many a new office and commercial building – in Hamburg parlance these are called *Kontorhäuser*.

The *Kontorhäuser* of this period typically provided office space that could be freely compartmentalised so that tenants could tailor them to their individual needs. *Kontorhäuser* have inner courtyards so that the rear part of the building, too, is lit by natural light, and their functional and streamlined development potential lends them a very rational structure. The requirements made on this type of office building led to dividable skeleton constructions made from steel or reinforced concrete. They were employed in the first *Kontorhäuser* as early as 1885.

This modern structural design and the very functional subdivision had consequences for the outer appearance of Hamburg *Kontorhäuser*: The facades with their vertical pillars were a reflection of the engineering methods and structural design on the inside. The first *Kontorhäuser* had to be integrated into an existing urban landscape, but the modernisation and rehabilitation efforts which started after the cholera epidemic, i.e. after 1892, were of a different order of magnitude and in the years leading up to WWI *Kontorhäuser* of rather bigger dimensions were built. They gave the city the novel character of a metropolis. The insertion, in 1909, of a whole new street, *Mönckebergstraße*, was a case in point.

From the architectural perspective, the building of *Kontorhäuser* in Hamburg started an entirely new development process which led to the end of historicism. The facades with their pillars were a consequence of rational planning and the structures were designed accordingly. Only few elements were copied from other historical periods. After the turn of the century, however, the homeland protection movement (Heimatschutzbewegung) came up due to the cognition of the increasing loss of local heritage. Therefore motifs typical of Hamburg were used in the *Kontorhäuser*.

Given these special circumstances, the *Kontorhäuser* developed into a unique architectural style which was unparalleled elsewhere in Germany. They significantly contributed to the shaping of Hamburg as a modern city, in terms of both urban planning and architectural design.

Literaturverzeichnis

Architekten- und Ingenieur-Verein zu Hamburg (Hrsg.), Das Hamburger Kontorhaus, Hamburg 1909.

BAHN, Hans, Von Hamburger Großbauten und ihren Schöpfern, in: Der Kreis, 1925, Heft 6–7, S. 10–29.

BRÖCKER, Paul, Fritz HÖGER, Die Architektur des Hamburgischen Geschäftshauses, Hamburg 1910.

ERBE, Albert, Christoph RANCK, Das Hamburger Bürgerhaus, Hamburg 1911.

HIPP, Hermann, Hans MEYER-VEDEN, Hamburger Kontorhäuser, Berlin 1988.

HIPP, Hermann, Freie und Hansestadt Hamburg. Kunst-Reiseführer, Köln 1989.

Abb. 15: Östliche Altstadt mit der Mönckebergstraße

KICK, Paul, Alphons SCHNEEGANS, Geschäfts- u. Warenhäuser, Messpaläste, Banken, (Handbuch der Architektur, Vierter Teil, 2. Halbband, 2. Heft), Leipzig 1923.

LANGE, Ralf, Vom Kontor zum Großraumbüro. Geschäftsviertel und Bürohäuser in Hamburg 1945–1970, Königstein (Taunus) 1999.

LÖWENGARD, Alfred, Geschäfts-, Kontor- und Warenhäuser, in: Architekten- und Ingenieur-Verein zu Hamburg (Hrsg.), Hamburg und seine Bauten unter Berücksichtigung der Nachbarstädte Altona und Wandsbek 1914. Erster Band, Hamburg 1914.

LUBITZ, Jan, Die Mönckebergstraße. Hamburgs Weg zur Großstadt, Hamburg 2009.

MELHOP, Wilhelm, Alt-Hamburgische Bauweise, Hamburg 1908.

NICOLAISEN, Dörte, Studien zur Architektur in Hamburg 1910 – 1930, Nijmegen 1985.

PALLMANN, Kurt, Hamburger Geschäftshaus-Neubauten, in: Deutsche Bauhütte, 1914, Heft 35–36, S. 427–341

PEVSNER, Nikolaus, Funktion und Form. Die Geschichte der Bauwerke des Westens, Hamburg 1998.

SCHUMACHER, Fritz, Das Entstehen einer Großstadt-Straße (Der Mönckebergstraßen-Durchbruch), Braunschweig – Hamburg 1922.

Abbildungsnachweis

Abb. 1, 2: Staatsarchiv Hamburg
Abb. 3–15: Jan Lubitz

* Die Abbildungsrechte sind vom Autor geklärt worden und liegen in dessen Verantwortung

---

[1] KICK, SCHNEEGANS, Geschäfts- u. Warenhäuser, Messpaläste, Banken, 1923, S. 196.

[2] Siehe auch hierzu PEVSNER, Funktion und Form, 1998, S. 213 f.

[3] KICK, SCHNEEGANS, Geschäfts- u. Warenhäuser, Messpaläste, Banken, 1923, S. 197.

[4] Der Paternoster wurde in England entwickelt und erstmals 1876 im General Post Office in London eingebaut. Der Begriff leitet sich vom Bewegungsmuster eines katholischen Rosenkranzes ab, bei dem zehn kleine Kugeln für die Ave Marias eine große Kugel für das Vaterunser („Paternoster") folgt.

[5] Architekten- und Ingenieur-Verein zu Hamburg (Hrsg.), Das Hamburger Kontorhaus, 1909, S. 2.

[6] Der Ausdruck wurde vom Chicagoer Architekten Louis Henri Sullivan 1896 in seinem Artikel „The tall office building artistically considered" geprägt, erschienen in der Zeitschrift „Lippincott's Magazine".

[7] LÖWENGARD, Geschäfts-, Kontor- und Warenhäuser, in: Architekten- und Ingenieur-Verein zu Hamburg (Hrsg.), Hamburg und seine Bauten unter Berücksichtigung der Nachbarstädte Altona und Wandsbek 1914. Erster Band, 1914, S. 432.

[8] Architekten- und Ingenieur-Verein zu Hamburg (Hrsg.), Das Hamburger Kontorhaus, 1909, S. 4 f.

[9] Siehe auch hierzu MELHOP, Alt-Hamburgische Bauweise, 1908; ERBE, RANCK, Das Hamburger Bürgerhaus, 1911.

[10] LÖWENGARD, Geschäfts-, Kontor- und Warenhäuser, in: Architekten- und Ingenieur-Verein zu Hamburg (Hrsg.), Hamburg und seine Bauten unter Berücksichtigung der Nachbarstädte Altona und Wandsbek 1914. Erster Band, 1914, S. 432.

[11] PALLMANN, Hamburger Geschäftshaus-Neubauten, in: Deutsche Bauhütte, 1914, Heft 35–36, S. 431.

[12] Siehe auch hierzu BRÖCKER, HÖGER, Die Architektur des Hamburgischen Geschäftshauses, 1910.

[13] LÖWENGARD, Geschäfts-, Kontor- und Warenhäuser, in: Architekten- und Ingenieur-Verein zu Hamburg (Hrsg.), Hamburg und seine Bauten unter Berücksichtigung der Nachbarstädte Altona und Wandsbek 1914. Erster Band, 1914, S. 432.

[14] SCHUMACHER, Das Entstehen einer Großstadt-Straße (Der Mönckebergstraßen-Durchbruch), 1922, S. 18 f.

[15] BAHN, Von Hamburger Großbauten und ihren Schöpfern, in: Der Kreis, 1925, Heft 6–7, S. 10.

Ralf Lange

„Steigerung zum Monumentalen" – Das Kontorhausviertel mit Chilehaus, Meßberghof, Sprinkenhof und Mohlenhof

Die Hamburger Kontorhausarchitektur und die Sanierung der Innenstadt nach der Cholera-Epidemie 1892

Das Chilehaus, der Sprinkenhof, der Mohlenhof und der Meßberghof – das ursprüngliche Ballinhaus[1] – sind charakteristische Zeugnisse der Architektur der Weimarer Republik, die auch im internationalen Vergleich herausragen. Zugleich dokumentieren sie das hohe konzeptionelle Niveau, das die Hamburger Bürohausarchitektur bereits vor dem Zweiten Weltkrieg auszeichnete. Allerdings sprach man an der Elbe nicht von Büro-, sondern von Kontorhäusern[2], womit Mietbürohäuser gemeint waren, deren Nutzer sich vorrangig aus den hafenabhängigen Branchen rekrutierten, die damals die Hamburger Wirtschaft dominierten: „Zahllose Ausfuhr- und Einfuhrgeschäfte, Agenten und Makler, Vertreter in- und ausländischer Firmen, Reedereien und Spediteure, Versicherungsbureaus und ähnliche Geschäfte, nicht zuletzt Rechtsanwälte brauchen für ein oft sehr wenig zahlreiches Personal bequem erreichbare, für sich abgeschlossene Kontorräume, die trotz ihrer geringen Ausdehnung einen behaglichen Eindruck machen sollen"[3] (Abb. 1 u. 2).

Da der Raum- und Flächenbedarf dieser zumeist relativ kleinen Unternehmen während des Entwurfs der Gebäude in der Regel noch unbekannt war, im Unterschied etwa zu einer Großverwaltung mit einer bestimmten Zahl an Mitarbeitern und klar definierten Abteilungen, wurde beim Entwurf der Kontorhäuser Wert auf ein Höchstmaß an Flexibilität hinsichtlich der Aufteilbarkeit der Geschossflächen gelegt. Folglich wurden die Gebäude in Stahlbeton- oder Stahlskelettbauweise errichtet und die Treppen, Aufzüge und Toiletten zu kompakten Kernbereichen zusammengefasst, um tragende Innenwände und sonstige störende Fixpunkte möglichst zu vermeiden. Weitere Kennzeichen des Kontorhauses sind der hohe Standard der Haustechnik, die sich bereits um 1900 durch Paternoster (Umlaufaufzüge), Zentralheizungen, elektrische Beleuchtung und Telefonanschlüsse auszeichnete, die besonders repräsentativ gestalteten Eingangsbereiche und die Skelettfassaden (wobei Letztere allerdings nur bedingt auf das Kontorhausviertel zutreffen, siehe unten).

Diese originär hamburgische Baugattung des Kontorhauses, die sich mit den Gebäuden des Kontorhausviertels in besonders ausgereifter Form manifestiert, ist sowohl Symptom als auch Katalysator eines Transformationsprozess, der aus der Hamburger Innenstadt, die um 1880 noch in großen Teilen vorindustriellen Charakter hatte, sukzessive ein monofunktionales Dienstleistungsviertel gemacht hat.[4] Forciert wurde diese Entwicklung noch, als der Senat nach

Abb. 1: Chilehaus, Portal C mit einer Terrakotta-Plastik von Richard Kuöhl

Abb. 2: Das Kontorhaus als gemeinsames Dach über einer Vielzahl kleinerer Unternehmen: Liste der Mieter am Treppenaufgang des Portals C. Das Schild wurde um 1950 in Pinseltechnik erstellt und bei einer Restaurierung freigelegt

der Cholera-Epidemie 1892, die rund 8 600 Todesopfer gefordert hatte, die Sanierung großer Teile der Innenstadt beschloss und systematisch diejenigen Grundstücke aufkaufte, die abgebrochen und städtebaulich neu geordnet wer-

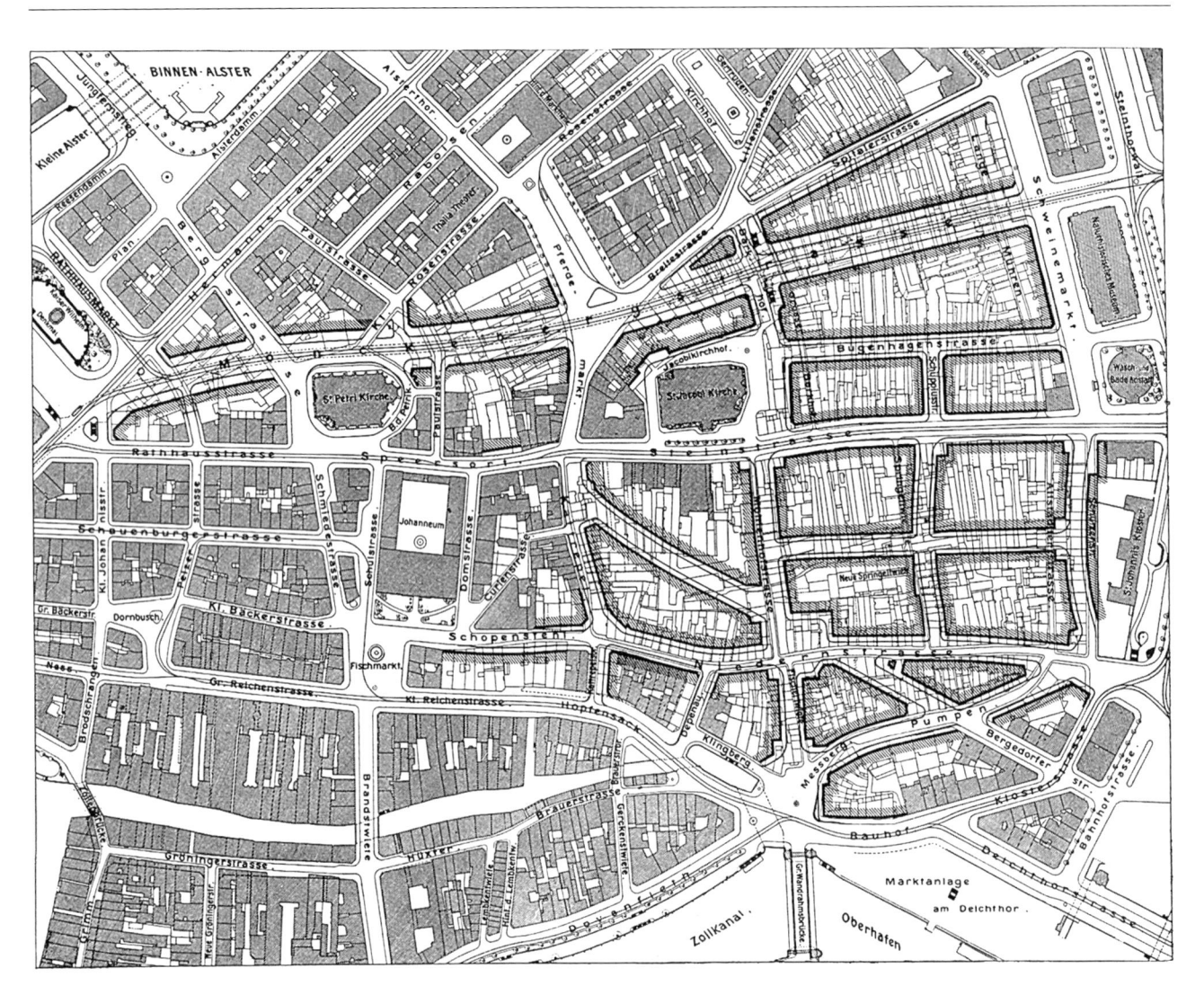

Abb. 3: Lageplan der Sanierungsgebiete in der Altstadt (um 1904). Im Südosten ist der geplante Straßenverlauf des Kontorhausviertels eingezeichnet, der später noch modifiziert wurde

den sollten.[5] Diese Maßnahmen betrafen auch die Anlage der Mönckebergstraße und ihrer Nebenstraßen (ab 1907),[6] die nahezu ausschließlich mit Kontorhäusern bebaut wurden, sowie das Kontorhausviertel, das sich von der Steinstraße bis zum Meßberg erstreckte und nach dem Ersten Weltkrieg realisiert wurde.[7]

Die Sanierung der südlichen Altstadt

Das Gebiet südlich der Steinstraße war ein so genanntes Gängeviertel, wie die Elendsquartiere der Innenstadt genannt wurden, deren Bebauung überwiegend aus Fachwerkhäusern des 16. bis 18. Jahrhunderts bestand.[8] Mit zunehmender Bevölkerung wurden in diesen Gebieten auch die Innenhöfe mit Gassen – den sogenannten Gängen – erschlossen und diese beidseitig mit zumeist mehrgeschossigen Wohnhäusern bebaut, so dass kaum noch größere Freiflächen übrig blieben. Als Zugänge dienten Tore oder schmale Durchlässe in den Vorderhäusern. Die Gängeviertel kennzeichneten sich durch besonders unhygienische Wohnverhältnisse und waren übervölkert, so dass die Cholera hier 1892 beste Voraussetzungen für ihre epidemische Ausbrei-

tung fand. Allerdings dauerte es noch zwei Jahrzehnte, bis die Sanierung in Angriff genommen wurde. 1913 wurden die ersten Häuser an der Niedernstraße abgerissen; 1917 sollte das gesamte Gebiet abgeräumt sein.[9] Die Abbruchmaßnahmen zogen sich jedoch, bedingt durch den Ersten Weltkrieg und die anschließend herrschende Wohnungsnot, bis Anfang der 1930er Jahre hin.

Nach dem Abriss der ursprünglichen Bebauung wurde das Straßennetz erneuert, wofür die bestehenden Straßen, etwa die Niedernstraße, die Mohlenhofstraße oder die Fischertwiete, in der Regel lediglich stark verbreitert und begradigt wurden (Abb. 3).[10] Völlig neu angelegt wurden die Altstädter Straße, der Burchardplatz und die Burchardstraße, die das gesamte Gebiet diagonal durchschnitt, um im Südosten in die heute nicht mehr vorhandene Bergedorfer Straße zu münden. Das Ergebnis dieses rigorosen Eingriffs in die überlieferten Stadtstrukturen waren schiefwinklige Grundstücke, die die Kreativität der Architekten herausforderten, was sich besonders deutlich am Chilehaus zeigte. 1912 erlangte dieser Plan, den das Ingenieurwesen der Baudeputation bereits 1904 vorgelegt hatte, Gesetzeskraft.[11] Fritz Schumacher, der 1909 zum Leiter des Hamburger Hochbauamtes und 1923 zum Oberbaudirektor ernannt wurde, konnte nur noch einige kleinere Korrekturen durchsetzen; u. a. wurde der Burchardplatz auf seine Initiative hin stark vergrößert und auf eine Bebauung der Fläche östlich des Chilehauses verzichtet, so dass dort ein weiterer öffentlicher Platz entstand, der das spektakuläre Gebäude besser zur Geltung brachte.¹²

Der städtebauliche Ideenwettbewerb 1914

Die südliche Altstadt sollte nach der Sanierung ursprünglich wieder als Wohnviertel dienen, wie bereits die Sanierungsgebiete in der südlichen Neustadt. Der Bürgerschaftsausschuss, der für die Sanierung eingesetzt worden war, machte allerdings auch deutlich, dass der Bedarf an günstigen Kleinwohnungen nicht unbedingt an dieser Stelle befriedigt werden müsste, zumal sich alternative Standorte anboten wie die hafennahen Stadtteile Veddel und Kleiner Grasbrook, die ab 1915 auch tatsächlich mit neuen Wohnblöcken bebaut wurden.¹³ Auch ein Zitat von Arnold Diestel, dem damaligen Präses der Finanzdeputation und späteren Ersten Bürgermeister (1920–24), deutet an, dass zumindest einzelne Mitglieder des Senats völlig andere Vorstellungen von der Zukunft der südlichen Altstadt hegten: „Dieses Gelände sollte man einer großzügigen einheitlichen Bebauung, die Rücksicht insbesondere auch auf die Marktinteressen nimmt, vorbehalten und die Einheitlichkeit nicht durch Häuser mit kleinen Wohnungen unterbrechen."¹⁴

1914 schrieb der Staat, quasi als Beschäftigungsmaßnahme für die Architekten während der ersten Kriegsmonate, einen städtebaulichen Ideenwettbewerb für dieses Gebiet aus (Abb. 4), um „ein möglichst reichhaltiges Studienmaterial zur Beurteilung der Frage zu erlangen, für welche Bedürfnisse die zu verkaufenden Plätze zuzuschneiden sind."¹⁵ Dabei wurde nur ein geringer Anteil an Kontorhäusern gefordert, denn durch den Bau der Mönckebergstraße sei „der Bedarf an Geschäftshäusern vorerst nahezu gedeckt"¹⁶. Als Vorbild diente offenbar die Sanierung der südlichen Neustadt, was sich auch an den gediegenen Details der Entwürfe zeigt, die mit traditionalistischen Fassaden, Erkern, Sprossenfenstern und einer ausgeprägten Dachlandschaft an die kurz zuvor errichteten Wohnblöcke in dem Sanierungsgebiet an der Martin-Luther-Straße und an der Rehhoffstraße erinnerten.¹⁷ Besonders gewürdigt wurde der Entwurf von Distel & Grubitz, der mit den Blöcken beiderseits der Fischertwiete bereits die Konturen des späteren Chilehauses aufscheinen lässt.¹⁸

Die Realisierung des Kontorhausviertels

Nach dem Ersten Weltkrieg war die Ansicht von Senator Diestel Konsens. Das Gebiet südlich der Steinstraße wurde bis zur Weltwirtschaftskrise als monofunktionales Kontorhausviertel entwickelt. Wohnungen wurden, wenn überhaupt, nur temporär von den Investoren toleriert. Im Chilehaus gab es zeitweilig 30 Wohnungen; von der ursprünglichen Auflage, zwei Drittel des Gebäudes in Wohnungen aufzuteilen, konnte sich der Bauherr Henry Brarens Sloman im August 1923 durch die Zahlung einer Ablösesumme von 2 Milliar-

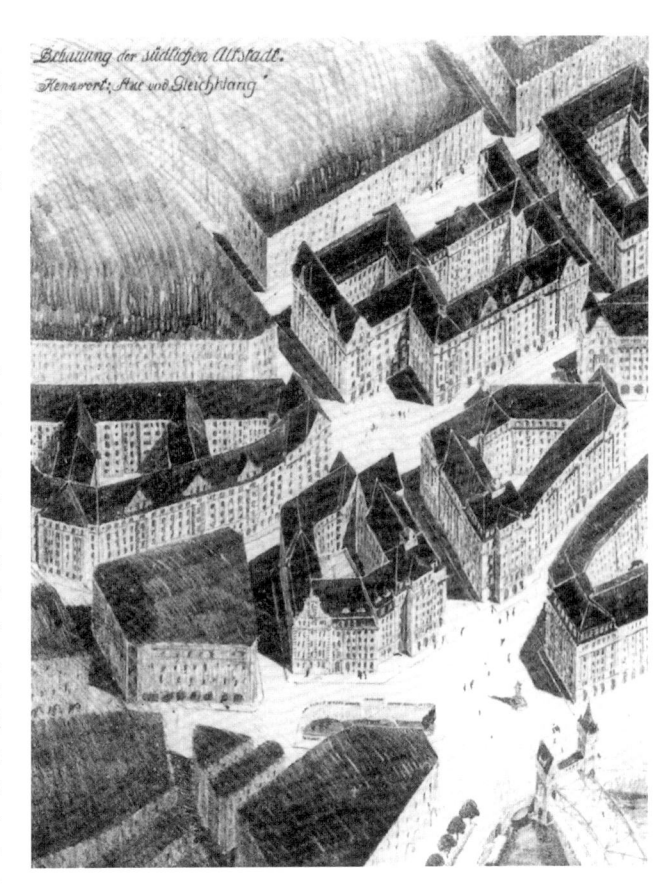

Abb. 4: Wettbewerb für die südliche Altstadt, Entwurf von Distel & Grubitz (1915)

den Mark an die Stadt, befreien.¹⁹ Anders sah es dagegen nach der Hyperinflation 1923 aus. Nun erzwang der herrschende Kapitalmangel eine größere Flexibilität der Investoren, was offenbar auch die Inanspruchnahme von Krediten für den Wohnungsbau nicht ausschloss.²⁰ Der Sprinkenhof wurde deshalb zunächst zu einem Großteil als Wohngebäude genutzt, wobei es sich in der Regel um Zwei-Zimmer-Wohnungen mit Küche und WC handelte.²¹ Um zu gewährleisten, dass diese Flächen später problemlos in Büroräume umgewandelt werden konnten, wurde in der Regel auf Bäder verzichtet.

Dass in diesen Krisenjahren überhaupt eine rege Baukonjunktur herrschte, verwundert nur auf den ersten Blick. Zum einen trat das Bürgertum die Flucht in die Sachwerte an. Zum anderen profitierte der Hamburger Hafen von der Exportorientierung der deutschen Wirtschaft, zumal der kontinuierliche Währungsverfall auch einen Wettbewerbsvorteil bei Ausfuhrgeschäften bedeutete.²² Bis Ende der Zwanzigerjahre erholte sich der Hafen von den Folgen des Ersten Weltkrieges und der Inflation, und 1929 gelang es sogar, den Hafenumschlag von 1913 zu übertreffen.²³ Allerdings warf bald darauf die Weltwirtschaftskrise den Außenhandel und die Schifffahrt erneut so stark zurück, dass dieser Spitzenwert bis zum Zweiten Weltkrieg nicht wieder erreicht wurde.²⁴ Hiervon wurde auch die Baukonjunktur betroffen. Bereits 1930 brach der Gewerbebau abrupt ein.²⁵ Und auch als sich die Wirtschaft Mitte der 1930er Jahre wieder zu erholen begann, wurden die letzten freien Flächen, die vor allem an der Steinstraße lagen, zunächst mit Wohnungen

Abb. 5: Luftbild des Kontorhausviertels mit Resten der ursprünglichen Bebauung (um 1929). Am unteren Bildrand sind der Montanhof, das Fernsprechamt Niedernstraße, der Mohlenhof, das Chilehaus und der Meßberghof zu sehen (von links nach rechts). Im Bildzentrum erhebt sich der kubische erste Bauabschnitt des Sprinkenhofs

gefüllt.[26] Ein Grundstück an der Burchardstraße blieb sogar bis Mitte der 1950er Jahre unbebaut.[27]

Der Baufortschritt im Kontorhausviertel spiegelt diese wechselvolle Entwicklung wider (Abb. 5).[28] In den Inflationsjahren wurden das Chilehaus von Fritz Höger (1922–24), der Meßberghof von Hans und Oskar Gerson (1922–24) sowie Haus Miramar von Max Bach (1922–24) errichtet. Aus den „Goldenen Zwanziger Jahren" stammen Haus Gülden Gerd von Zauleck & Hormann (1924/25), der Montanhof von Distel & Grubitz (1924/25), das Post- und Fernmeldeamt Niedernstraße von Postbaurat Martin Thieme (1924–26), der Mohlenhof von Klophaus, Schoch, zu Putlitz (1927/28) und die ersten beiden Bauabschnitte des Sprinkenhofs (1927/28 bzw. 1929/30), ein Gemeinschaftsprojekt von Höger und den Gebrüder Gerson. Während der Weltwirtschaftskrise konnten nur noch Haus Rodewald von Emil Neupert (1930/31) und Haus Hubertus von Bach & Wischer (1930/31) fertiggestellt werden. Dann stagnierte der Ausbau des Kontorhausviertels bis Ende der 1930er Jahre, sieht man von den erwähnten Wohnungen an der Steinstraße ab. Zum Teil bereits während der ersten Kriegsjahre entstanden noch das Bartholomay-Haus und das Pressehaus von Rudolf Klophaus (1937/38 bzw. 1938/39) sowie der dritte Bauabschnitt des Sprinkenhofs (1939–43), der von Höger allein stammte.

Allgemeine Kennzeichen des Kontorhausviertels

Bis auf wenige Ausnahmen ordneten sich alle bis 1931 errichteten Gebäude einem Leitbild unter, das Hans Bahn wie folgt umriss: „Das Dach wandelt sich zum flachen Kiesdach und wird den Lichtwinkeln entsprechend gestaffelt. [...] Statt liebenswürdiger Einzelmotive tritt die Steigerung zum Monumentalen durch gleichförmigen Rhythmus ein. Statt einzelner Häuser werden ganze Blöcke (Höfe) gestaltet."[29] Diese Entwicklung war nicht nur Zufall, denn im Sanierungsbiet der südlichen Altstadt konnte Fritz Schumacher sein Ideal einer einheitlichen Gestaltung mit Flachdächern und Klinkerfassaden ohne Abstriche umsetzen, für das er beim Bau der Mönckebergstraße noch vergeblich plädiert hatte.[30] So schrieb er über das zukünftige Kontorhausviertel: „Für die große Umgestaltungsarbeit, die hier demnächst vor sich gehen wird, liegen die Dinge hinsichtlich der Materialfrage anders als in der Mönckebergstraße. [...] Nichts steht im Wege, die mächtige Forderung einer einheitlichen Materialpolitik walten zu lassen [...]."[31] Kongeniale Mitstreiter fand Schumacher dabei in den Architekten Hans und Oskar Gerson und Fritz Höger, die bereits vor dem Ersten Weltkrieg dem Backstein in der Hamburger Architektur zu neuer Geltung verholfen hatten.[32]

Eine weitere Innovation der 1920er Jahre bedeuteten die Staffelgeschosse, die ein besonderes Anliegen der 1912 institutionalisierten Baupflegekommission waren (Abb. 6).[33] Die maximal zulässige Gebäudehöhe bis zur Traufkante betrug in der Hamburger Innenstadt 24 Meter. Abhängig von der Straßenbreite waren darüber hinaus aber noch Dachaufbauten erlaubt, sofern diese einen Neigungswinkel von mindestens 60 Grad zur Straße hin aufwiesen.[34] Die Konsequenz dieser Regelung waren „Nasendächer", die als gestalterisch unbefriedigend galten: „In Hamburg pflegte man bei allen Privatbauten ein nach der Straße zu nur verkrüppeltes mansardähnliches Scheindach und im übrigen eine flache Pappdeckung, mit der man alle Unregelmäßigkeiten einer wildgewordenen Grundrißbildung bequem überdecken konnte."[35] Als befriedigendere Alternative wurden Staffelgeschosse angesehen – vorausgesetzt, deren „Stufenprofil" blieb innerhalb des 60-Grad-Winkels, der ursprünglich für die Dachschrägen vorgeschrieben war.

Auffällig ist auch der Maßstab der Gebäude, der das Kontorhausviertel auch in städtebaulicher Hinsicht in der Innenstadt hervorhebt und zu einem signifikanten Ensemble zusammenschweißt. Boten die größten Kontorhäuser vor dem Ersten Weltkrieg, z. B. das Kaufmannshaus oder das Klöpperhaus, rund 20 000 bis 25 000 Quadratmeter Fläche[36], so sprengten das Chilehaus mit 36 000 Quadratmetern und der Sprinkenhof mit 52 000 Quadratmetern – nach Fertigstellung aller drei Bauabschnitte – alle bis dahin in Hamburg gültigen Rekorde.[37] Außerdem wurden jetzt großzügig Dispense von der Baugesetzgebung erteilt, so dass das Chilehaus zehn Geschosse erlangen konnte und somit eines der ersten Hochhäuser in Deutschland war.[38] Diese Hochhauseuphorie, die auch generell kennzeichnend für die deutsche Architektur der Zwanzigerjahre ist[39], ließ sich nach dem verlorenen Ersten Weltkrieg auch wirtschaftlich legitimieren: „Wir sind gezwungen, in den billigsten Raum, in die Höhe hineinzubauen, denn das Land, das Häuser tragen soll, können wir uns nicht mehr leisten."[40]

Das Chilehaus

Den unbestrittenen architektonischen Höhepunkt des Kontorhausviertels bildet das Chilehaus, das hinsichtlich der wie ein Bug auftragenden Spitze und der geschwungenen Südfassade an einen Schiffsrumpf erinnert (Abb. 7). Diese signifikante Gebäudeform war zwar das Ergebnis der irregulär geschnittenen Baufläche, die überdies durch die Fischertwiete geteilt wurde (ein Makel, den Höger zu beheben wusste, in dem er die Straße mit zwei großen Bogenöffnungen überbaute). Es ist aber zu kurz gegriffen, das Gebäude in erster Linie als Ergebnis dieser Zwänge zu interpretieren. Denn wie sich anhand der überlieferten Bauprüfakten belegen lässt, waren mehrere Dispense nötig, um auf den beiden Grundstücken, die ja, wie oben geschildert, ursprünglich für Wohngebäude vorgesehen waren, überhaupt ein Kontorhaus mit einem wirtschaftlichen Grundriss realisieren zu können.[41] Dabei hatte die Stadt anfänglich weder die dreieckige Spitze, noch die dynamische Fassadenkurve vorgesehen, so dass Henry Brarens Sloman zunächst mehrere kleinere Flächen zusätzlich erwerben musste, um Högers Entwurf

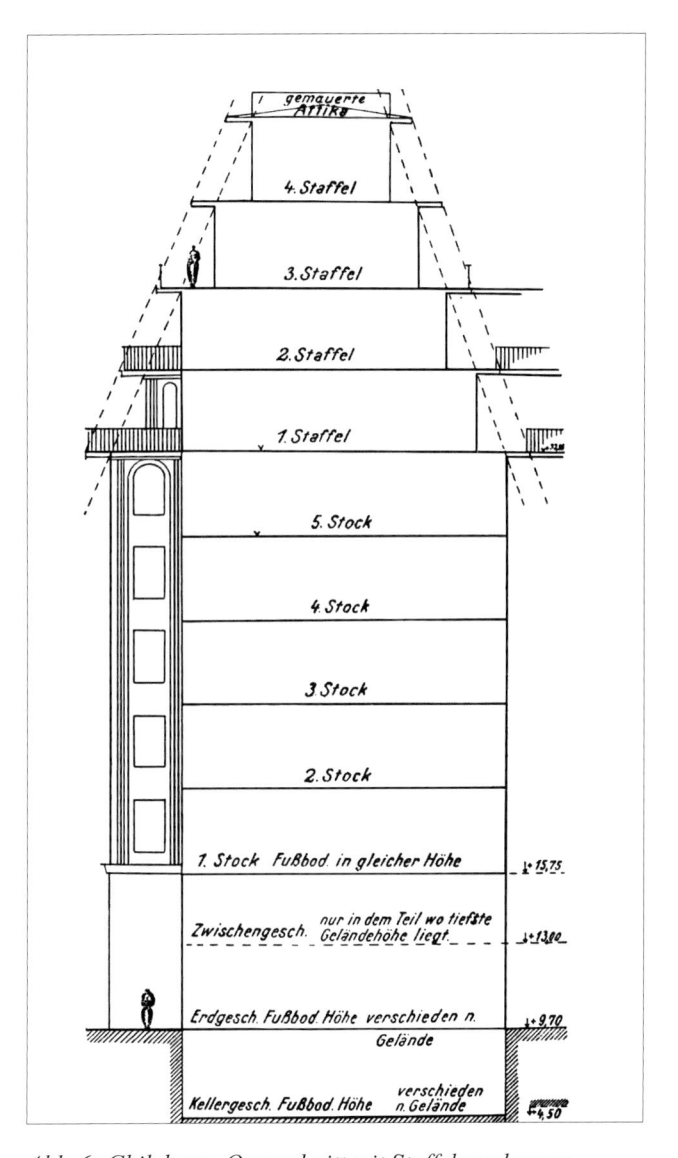

Abb. 6: Chilehaus, Querschnitt mit Staffelgeschossen

realisieren zu können. Selbst die heute so selbstverständlich anmutende Überbauung der Fischertwiete erforderte einen Dispens (Abb. 8).

Das Chilehaus ist ein Stahlbetonskelettbau, wobei die Fassaden jedoch zum größten Teil aus massivem Mauerwerk bestehen. Das Achsmaß der Konstruktion beträgt 6,18 m, was an den Fassaden aber nicht ablesbar ist, weil sämtliche Fassadenpfeiler die gleiche Breite von 0,72 m aufweisen.[42] Die Fassaden sind vollständig mit roten Klinkern verblendet, die in irisierenden bläulichen und bräunlichen Tönen changieren, wobei Ziegel minderer Wahl genommen wurden, deren rustikale, unregelmäßige Oberflächen damals besonders geschätzt wurden. An den Straßenseiten überspielen Vorlagen aus jeweils zwei parallelen Ziegeln pro Mauerschicht die relativ kompakten Pfeiler. Sie sind um 45 Grad gegenüber den Fassaden gedreht und wirken somit zu den Vorderseiten hin wie spitze Grate, wodurch die Außenhülle insbesondere an den Gebäudekanten einen feingliedrigen, geradezu vorhangartig anmutenden Charakter erhält. Da jede siebte Ziegellage rechtwinklig zu den Fassadenpfeilern gemauert wurde, um als Binder zu dienen, entstand ein ornamental wirkender Verband, der bei einer Schrägan-

Abb. 7: Chilehaus von Fritz Höger (1922–24)

Abb. 8: Chilehaus, Grundrisse des Erdgeschosses und eines Bürogeschosses

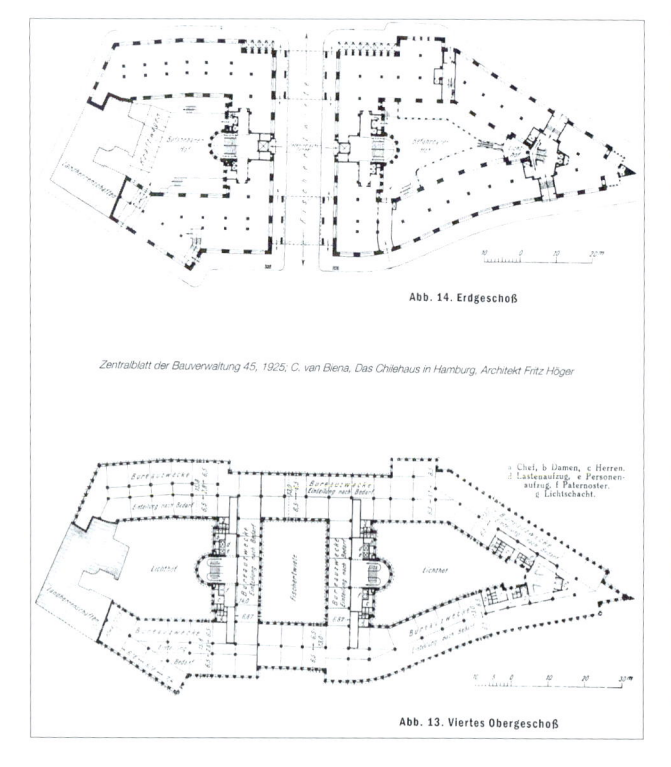

sicht zudem den verblüffenden Effekt hat, dass er diagonale Strukturen bildet, die sich über die gesamte Fassade ziehen.

Ein vergleichbares Vexierspiel bieten die Vorlagen, die je nach Blickwinkel des Betrachters entweder wie schlanke Fassadenpfeiler wirken oder sich so dicht zusammenschieben, dass die Fensterachsen nicht mehr zu sehen sind und der Eindruck einer homogenen Oberfläche aus Klinkern entsteht (Abb. 9). Oder wie es Höger selbst formuliert hat: „Im kleinachsigen Einzelrhythmus liegt auch der Hauptwesenszug der künstlerischen Qualität des Chilehauses. Nur durch den kleinachsigen Einzelrhythmus werden die durch viele Fenster gänzlich aufgelösten Fronten in der Verkürzung wieder zu ruhigen Flächen, und diese geschlossen, ergeben wieder den monumentalen Körper."[43] Diese Beschränkung auf ein einziges Gliederungsmotiv hebt das Chilehaus übrigens aus dem Werk von Höger hervor, der in den folgenden Jahren mit immer virtuoseren Ornamenten hervortrat.[44] Beim Chilehaus finden sich rein dekorativ aufgefasste Klinkerstrukturen dagegen nur an den unteren Fassadenzonen an der Fischertwiete, deren gestalterische Sonderbehandlung jedoch auch dadurch gerechtfertigt erscheint, dass hier die beiden Haupteingänge liegen.

Im Kontrast zu den Vorlagen hat Höger das Erdgeschoss durch ein flächiges Mauerwerk mit tief eingeschnittenen Segmentbogenöffnungen für die Schaufenster und Eingangsportale als Sockelgeschoss betont. Diese kompakte Zone legt sich gleichsam wie eine Banderole um die feingliedrigen Skelettfassaden und verklammert die unterschiedlichen Fassadenabschnitte. Die gleiche gestalterische Rolle spielen die Staffelgeschosse, die sich wie horizontale Bänder um den Komplex ziehen, wobei dieser Effekt noch durch die überkragenden Deckenplatten aus Stahlbeton verstärkt wird, die den Komplex mit ihrem scharfkantigen Profil konturieren. Maßstäblichkeit erhält diese signifikante Großform durch kleinteilige Details, wobei neben den Sprossenfenstern vor allem die Terrakotta-Plastiken von Richard Kuöhl hervorzuheben sind: die Figuren über den Portalen, die Terrakotta-Elemente der Arkaden am Burchardplatz und der beiden Pavillons, die die Gebäudespitze flankieren, sowie der Andenkondor – das Wappentier Chiles –, der wie eine Galionsfigur an dem „Bug" des Chilehauses angebracht ist und somit dessen Schiffssymbolik unterstreicht.[45]

Meßberghof, Sprinkenhof und Mohlenhof

Während die Fassaden des Chilehauses in relativ schmale Klinkerpfeiler mit spitzwinkligen Vorlagen aufgelöst sind, deren stakkato-artiger Rhythmus den dynamischen Charakter des Baukörpers unterstreicht, erhielten die benachbarten Gebäude aus gestalterischen Erwägungen flächige Fassaden. Den Auftakt machte der Meßberghof von Hans und Oskar Gerson (Abb. 10), dessen Kanten in Strebepfeiler auslaufen, die hinsichtlich ihrer gerundeten Anschlüsse wie in das Fassadenmauerwerk verschliffen wirken. Diese Pfeiler verleihen der Architektur einen nahezu sakral anmutenden, gotisierenden Zug, der ursprünglich noch durch die Pfeilerfiguren von Ludwig Kunstmann unterstrichen wurde.[46] Ansonsten blieb der Bau schmucklos, was sich zum einen durch eine gewollte Kontrastwirkung zum gleichzeitig errichteten Chilehaus erklären lässt, zum anderen aber auch dem künstlerischen Credo der Architekten entsprach, die bei ihren Entwürfen auch allgemein Wert auf eine flächige Wirkung des Mauerwerks legten: „Die Zusammensetzung der vielen nicht genau gleichen und verschieden getönten Steine mit dem Spiel der Fugen sichert der Fläche einen hohen ästhetischen Reiz. Wir [die Gebrüder Gerson, R. L.] empfinden diesen Reiz […] der Fläche so stark, daß wir im allgemeinen die Flächen nicht durch andere Mittel zu beleben versuchen und nach Möglichkeit vermeiden, die Körper [der Gebäude, R. L.] zu zergliedern."[47]

Der Sprinkenhof (Abb. 11, 12 u. 13), den die Gebrüder Gerson mit Fritz Höger entworfen haben, kennzeichnet sich dagegen im ersten Bauabschnitt durch eine ausgeprägte Lust am Ornament, wobei die Wahl auf diagonale, sich kreuzende Klinkerbänder fiel, die sowohl die Straßen- als auch die Hoffronten mit einem gleichmäßigen Muster überziehen. Runde Terrakottareliefs von Ludwig Kunstmann setzen Akzente. Ursprünglich hatten die Architekten Skelettfassaden entworfen, die aufgrund einer Intervention der Baupflegekommission jedoch flächig umgestaltet werden mussten, damit der Bau nicht zur Konkurrenz für das Chilehaus geriet.[48] Weitaus sachlicher präsentiert sich demgegenüber der zweite Bauabschnitt, der schmucklose Lochfassaden aufweist. Lediglich der Kopfbau am Burchardplatz wurde mit einem ornamentalen Verband aus Klinkern und goldfarbenen Ziegeln dekoriert, der sich auch an den Treppenhausfassaden des ersten Bauabschnitts findet. Beim dritten Bauabschnitt griff Höger Ende der 1930er Jahre mit diagonalen Fassadenmustern dagegen wieder auf das expressionistische Formenrepertoire zurück. Hier verdeutlicht sich ein anachronistischer Zug, der auch allgemein kennzeichnend für Högers Entwürfe in der NS-Zeit ist.[49]

Der Bannstrahl der Baupflegekommission traf auch den Entwurf für den Mohlenhof (Abb. 14), für den Klophaus, Schoch, zu Putlitz ursprünglich ebenfalls Pfeilerfassaden in expressionistischen Formen vorgesehen hatten, was in der unmittelbaren Nachbarschaft des Chilehauses aber als störend empfunden wurde.[50] Oder wie es in dem apodiktisch formulierten Schreiben der Baupolizei hieß, das sich nicht lange mit objektiv nachvollziehbaren Argumenten aufhielt: "Gegen die Errichtung des Geschäftshauses nach Maßgabe der eingereichten Vorlagen wird auf Grund § 2 Ziffer 1 des Baupflegegesetzes Einspruch erhoben mit der Wirkung, daß das Vorhaben in der beabsichtigten Art nicht ausgeführt werden darf. Begründung: Das Gebäude würde durch die Art der Gliederung, insbesondere durch die schräg gestellten Pfeiler und Fensterwände, das Platzbild verunstalten."[51] Der Mohlenhof erhielt stattdessen schmucklose Lochfassaden mit seriell gereihten, schmalen Fenstern, die erstmalig einen sachlichen Zug in die bis dahin ausgesprochen dekorationsfreudige Kontorhausarchitektur brachten.

Einen genaueren Blick lohnen schließlich auch die Eingangshallen und Treppenhäuser, die sich nun allerdings nicht mehr, wie noch in den Jahren vor dem Ersten Weltkrieg, durch Marmor, Mosaiken und Bronzeappliken auszeichnen, sondern durch Materialien mit einer rustikalen, bisweilen geradezu betont groben Qualität wie Keramikfliesen oder unglasierte Terrakotta-Elemente (wie im westlichen

Abb. 9: Chilehaus, Fassadendetails

Abb. 10: Meßberghof von Hans und Oskar Gerson (1922–24)

Eingang des Chilehauses). Nur in der Halle des Meßberghofs scheint mit der Wandverkleidung aus Travertin und den schlagvergoldeten Geländern und Türen noch einmal das Anspruchsniveau der Vorkriegsjahre auf, wenn auch konterkariert durch unverkleidete Stützen und Unterzüge aus scharriertem Sichtbeton.[52] Schule machte hier dagegen die gigantische Wendeltreppe, die sich über alle zehn Geschosse erstreckt. Vergleichbare Treppen finden sich auch im Sprinkenhof, wo sie ebenfalls sämtliche Geschosse wie überdimensionale Spiralen durchdringen. Oder wie es die Architekten selbst formulierten: „Das Haupttreppenhaus [...] als einziger großer Raum des Kontorhauses wird als verbindender Zentralraum durch die monumentale Durchsicht zur Geltung gebracht."[53]

Abb 11 Sprinkenhof von Fritz Höger und Hans und Oskar Gerson (1927–43)

Abb. 12: Sprinkenhof, Fassadendetails

Abb. 13: Sprinkenhof, Treppe im ersten Bauabschnitt

Die Rezeption und kunsthistorische Bedeutung der vier Kontorhäuser

Das Chilehaus und der Meßberghof waren Initialbauten der expressionistischen Architektur, wie diese Formensprache in nicht völlig schlüssiger Analogie zu den gleichnamigen Strömungen in der Literatur und in der bildenden Kunst heute bezeichnet wird.[54] Sie stehen am Anfang einer Kette vergleichbarer Bauten im gesamten Reichsgebiet. Etliche Details wurden sogar kopiert, was das Kölner Hansahochhaus belegt, bei dessen Entwurf sich Jacob Koerfer am Meßberghof orientiert hatte (1924/25).[55] Stärker noch als diese Stilvergleiche illustrieren jedoch die zahlreichen Veröffentlichungen in der zeitgenössischen Fachliteratur, welche herausragende Rolle das Kontorhausviertel in der damaligen deutschen Architektur spielte.[56] Dass diese Entwürfe auch außerhalb Deutschlands rezipiert wurden, belegt das Chilehaus, das in den 1950er Jahren gleich von vier internationalen Autoren, nämlich Arnold Whittick, Nikolaus Pevsner, Henry-Russel Hitchcock und Leonardo Benevolo, in den Kanon der beispielhaften Architekturen des 20. Jahrhunderts aufgenommen wurde.[57]

Der besondere Rang des Kontorhausviertels mit seinem zentralen Ensemble aus Chilehaus, Meßberghof, Sprinkenhof und Mohlenhof ist allerdings nicht nur in seiner architektonischen Qualität zu sehen, sondern auch in dem damals einzigartigen städtebaulichen Konzept, ein ganzes Stadtquartier ausschließlich für den Dienstleistungssektor zu reservieren. Vorläufer hatte das Kontorhausviertel in der Mönckebergstraße und in der Speicherstadt, die zwar in erster Linie als Lagerzentrum gedacht war, aber einen vergleichbar monofunktionalen Charakter hatte.[58] Diese Entwicklung war damals auch im internationalen Vergleich ohne Beispiel, sieht man von den hochgradig tertiärisierten Innenstädten einiger US-amerikanischer Metropolen wie New York oder Chicago ab. Diese Pionierstellung des Kontorhausviertels wird auch durch die temporäre Nutzung von Teilen des Chilehauses und des Sprinkenhofs für Wohnzwecke nicht geschmälert, da diese Bauten von vornherein als moderne Bürohäuser in Stahlbetonskelettbauweise mit zentralen Erschließungskernen konzipiert wurden und die Wohnungen somit lediglich einen provisorischen und reversiblen Charakter hatten.

Abstract

Chilehaus and office building district – office buildings after the First World War

The *Kontorhausviertel* is situated to the Southeast of the Old Town. After WW I it replaced the squalid und overpopulated *Gängeviertel*, a low quality housing area of narrow passages and with poor sanitation standards where the cholera epidemic of 1892 had claimed many more lives than elsewhere in the city. The *Gängeviertel* had been characterised by closed rows of half-timbered houses dating back to the 17th and 18th centuries, the only access to which was provided through narrow alleyways called *Gänge*. Back yards, too, were extremely densely built-up and you could only enter them through gates in the front houses.

Rehabilitation and modernisation of the southeasterly part of the Old Town was begun in 1913, but then stopped during WW I and the ensuing housing shortage to be finally completed during the 1930's. The narrow streets were significantly widened and plots amalgamated. *Burchardstrasse* was an entirely new street that cut diagonally through the area and prompted the exceptional ground plan of *Chilehaus*. As late as 1914 there were plans to erect residential buildings there, but after WW I a decision was taken to exclusively build office space. The only exception was *Steinstrasse* where residential houses were built during the world economic crisis.

The *Kontorhausviertel* includes 14 office buildings and two residential complexes nearly all of which were erected between 1922 and 1943. Four of them are conspicuous in terms of their architectural qualities. Together they form an ensemble within the *Kontorhausviertel*: *Chilehaus* by Fritz Höger (1922–24), *Meßberghof* by Hans und Oskar Gerson (1922–24), *Mohlenhof* by Klophaus, Schoch and zu Putlitz (1927/28) and *Sprinkenhof*. The first two sections of *Sprinkenhof* were built by Höger and the Gerson brothers (1927/28 and 1929/30 respectively), the third one was realised by Höger alone (1939–43).

These four office buildings, through their expressionist design, their unadorned brick facades and their rational ground planes which had become possible through modern reinforced concrete skeleton construction techniques were trendsetters for contemporary office architecture. At the same time, the erection of this monofunctional complex

Abb. 14: Mohlenhof von Klophaus, Schoch, zu Putlitz (1927/28, Aufnahme um 1929)

of office buildings was the culmination of a process in the course of which a city developed within the central part of Hamburg which was dominated for a large part by office buildings, shops and warehouses – a phenomenon that, at the time, only existed to the same extent in US metropolises and in London.

Literaturverzeichnis

BAHN, Hans. Groß-Kontorhäuser im Hamburger Sanierungsgebiet, in: Deutsche Bauhütte, 1929, H. 26, S. 410–411.

BAHN, Hans. Kontorhaus-Neubau „Der Mohlenhof" in Hamburg, in: Deutsche Bauzeitung, 1929, Nr. 78, S. 665–667.

BALLIN-HAUS – MESSBERGHOF. Denkmalpflege Hamburg, Hrsg. von der Kulturbehörde, Denkmalschutzamt, Hamburg 1997.

BENEVOLO, Leonardo. Geschichte der Architektur des 19. und 20. Jahrhunderts (dtv Wissenschaftliche Reihe), Bd. 1, München 1978.

BOLLE, Arved. Der Generalplan für den Ausbau des Hamburger Hafens im Wandel der Zeiten, in: Jahrbuch der Hafenbautechnischen Gesellschaft, 1950/51, Bd. 21/22, Berlin – Göttingen – Heidelberg 1953, S. 34–50.

BUCCIARELLI, Piergiacomo. Fritz Höger. Hanseatischer Baumeister 1877–1949, Berlin 1992.

BÜTTNER, Ursula. Die Finanzpolitik des Hamburger Senats in der Weltwirtschaftskrise 1929–1933, in: Zeitschrift des Vereins für Hamburgische Geschichte, Bd. 64, Hamburg 1978, S. 181–226.

BÜTTNER, Ursula. Der Stadtstaat als demokratische Republik, in: Werner Jochmann (Hrsg.), Hamburg. Geschichte der Stadt und ihrer Bewohner, Bd. 2, Vom Kaiserreich bis zur Gegenwart, Hamburg 1986, S. 131–264.

DISTEL, Hermann. Das hamburgische Kontorhaus, in: Deutsche Bauzeitung, 1926, H. 59, S. 485–488.

EVANS, Richard. Tod in Hamburg. Stadt, Gesellschaft und Politik in den Cholera-Jahren 1830–1910, Reinbek 1990.

FEDDERSEN, Martin. Das Chilehaus und das Ballinhaus. Zwei neue Hamburger Kontorhäuser, in: Moderne Bauformen, 1925, H. 1, S. 1–32.

FISCHER, Manfred F. Das Chilehaus in Hamburg. Architektur und Vision, Berlin 1999.

FRANK, Hartmut. Baukunst, Monumentalität und Heimatschutz. Die Architektur der Gebrüder Gerson und die Hamburger Schule, in: VOIGT, Gerson, 2000, S. 32–49.

GERSON, Hans und Oskar. Der „Sprinkenhof" in Hamburg, in: Wasmuths Monatshefte für Baukunst, 1929, H. 6, S. 225–229.

GERSON, Hans und Oskar. Ziegel und Architektenschaft, in: Tonindustrie-Zeitung, 1925, H. 49, S. 949–950.

GOETZ, Adolf. Das Ballinhaus, in: Bau-Rundschau, 1924, Hr. 8, S. 191–194.

HAMBURGER KONTORHAUS, Hrsg. vom Architekten- und Ingenieur-Verein zu Hamburg, Hamburg 1909.

HAMBURG UND SEINE BAUTEN unter Berücksichtigung der Nachbarstädte Altona und Wandsbek 1914, Hrsg. vom Architekten und Ingenieur-Verein Hamburg, 2 Bde., Hamburg 1914.

HAMBURG UND SEINE BAUTEN mit Altona, Wandsbek und Harburg-Wilhelmsburg 1918–1929, Hrsg. vom Architekten und Ingenieur-Verein in Hamburg, Hamburg 1929.

HAMBURG UND SEINE BAUTEN 1954–1968, Hrsg. vom Architekten und Ingenieur-Verein Hamburg e.V., Hamburg 1969.

HAMBURG UND SEINE BAUTEN 1969–1984, Hrsg. vom Architekten- und Ingenieurverein Hamburg e.V. und Hamburgische Gesellschaft zur Beförderung der Künste und Nützlichen Gewerbe Patriotische Gesellschaft von 1765, Hamburg 1984.

HARMS, Hans und SCHUBERT, Dirk. Wohnen in Hamburg – ein Stadtführer (Stadt – Planung – Geschichte, Bd. 11), Hamburg 1989.

HIPP, Hermann. Heimat in der City. Die Wandlung des Stadtbildes in der Hamburger Innenstadt um die Jahrhundertwende, in: Jürgen Ellermeyer und Rainer Postel, Stadt und Hafen. Hamburger Beiträge zur Geschichte von Hafen und Schiffahrt (Arbeitshefte zur Denkmalpflege in Hamburg, Nr. 8), Hamburg 1986, S. 127–141.

HIPP, Hermann. Wohnstadt Hamburg. Mietshäuser der zwanziger Jahre zwischen Inflation und Weltwirtschaftskrise (Hamburg-Inventar, Themen-Reihe Bd. 1), Hamburg 1982.

HITCHCOCK, Henry-Russell. Architecture: Nineteenth and Twentieth Centuries, Baltimore 1958.

HÖGER, Fritz. Einige sachliche Angaben zum Bau des Chilehauses in Hamburg, in: Zentralblatt der Bauverwaltung, 1925, Nr. 2, S. 13–16; Nr. 4, S. 34–37.

JAKSTEIN, Werner. Fritz Högers Arbeiten und ihre Wirkung auf die Entwicklung der Hamburger Architektur, in: Wasmuths Monatshefte für Baukunst, 1914/15, H. 3, S. 120–132.

KOCH, Hugo. Der Wiederaufbau der südlichen Altstadt in Hamburg, in: Bau-Rundschau, 1915, Nr. 13–15, S. 49–56, hier S. 49.

LANGE, Ralf. Das Hamburger Kontorhaus, Hamburg 2013 (in Vorbereitung).

LUBITZ, Jan. Die Mönckebergstraße. Hamburgs Weg zur Großstadt, Hamburg 2009.

MAYER, Martin. Das Hamburger Kontorhaus, in: Zentralblatt der Bauverwaltung, 1909, H. 89, S. 582–583.

MELHOP, Wilhelm. Alt-Hamburgische Bauweise. Kurze geschichtliche Entwicklung der Baustile in Hamburg dargestellt am Profanbau bis zum Wiedererstehen der Stadt nach dem großen Brande von 1842 nebst chronistisch-biographischen Notizen, Hamburg 1908.

MEYER-VEDEN, Hans und HIPP, Hermann. Hamburger Kontorhäuser. Fotos Hans Meyer-Veden, Text Hermann Hipp, Berlin 1988.

NEUMANN, Dietrich. Die Wolkenkratzer kommen! Deutsche Hochhäuser der zwanziger Jahre, Debatten – Projekte – Bauten, Braunschweig 1995.

NICOLAISEN, Dörte. Studien zur Architektur in Hamburg 1910–1930, Nijmegen 1985

PEHNT, Wolfgang. Die Architektur des Expressionismus, Ostfildern 1998.

PEVSNER, Nikolaus. Europäische Architektur von den Anfängen bis zur Gegenwart, München 1957.

RAUSCHNABEL, Kurt. Stadtgestalt durch Staatsgewalt? Das Hamburger Baupflegegesetz von 1912 (Arbeitshefte zur Denkmalpflege in Hamburg, Nr. 6), Hamburg 1984.

RUDHARD, Wolfgang. Das Bürgerhaus in Hamburg (Das deutsche Bürgerhaus, Bd. XXI), Tübingen 1975.

SCHRAMM, Jost. Schramm, v. Bassewitz, Hupertz. Häuser aus einem Hause, 100 Jahre eines Architektenbüros in Hamburg, Vorwort von Hermann Hipp, Bearbeitet von Christiane Leiska, Hamburg 1985.

SCHUBERT, Dirk. „Der Städtebaukunst dienen – und der Finanzdeputation eine Freude bereiten" oder: Die wechselvolle Geschichte der Sanierung der südlichen Altstadt, in: Ulrich Höhns (Hrsg.), Das ungebaute Hamburg. Visionen einer anderen Stadt in architektonischen Entwürfen der letzten hundertfünfzig Jahre, Hamburg 1991, S. 46–57.

SCHUMACHER, Fritz. Architektonisches von der Sanierung der Hamburger Altstadt, in: Deutsches Wohnungs-Archiv, 1926, H.5, S. 226–232.

STOMMER, Rainer und MAYER-GÜRR, Dieter. Hochhaus. Der Beginn in Deutschland, Marburg 1990.

TURTENWALD, Claudia (Hrsg.). Fritz Höger (1877–1949). Moderne Monumente (Schriftenreihe des Hamburgischen Architekturarchivs), Hamburg 2003.

VOIGT, Wolfgang (Hrsg.). Hans und Oskar Gerson. Hanseatische Moderne, Bauten in Hamburg und im kalifornischen Exil 1907 bis 1957, Mit Beiträgen von Hartmut Frank und Ulrich Höhns (Schriftenreihe des Hamburgischen Architekturarchivs), Hamburg 2000.

WHITTICK, Arnold. European Architecture in the Twentieth Century. Vol. 1, London 1950.

WINKELMANN, Friedrich. Wohnhaus und Bude in Alt-Hamburg. Die Entwicklung der Wohnverhältnisse von 1250 bis 1830. Berlin 1937.

WISCHERMANN, Clemens. Wohnen in Hamburg vor dem Ersten Weltkrieg (Studien zur Geschichte des Alltags, Bd. 2), Münster 1983.

Abbildungsnachweis

Abb. 1; Abb. 2; Abb. 10; Abb. 11: Heinz-Joachim Hettchen
Abb. 3: Hamburg und seine Bauten 1914
Abb. 4: Bau-Rundschau, 1915, Nr. 13–15
Abb. 5; Abb. 6; Abb. 7: Denkmalschutzamt Hamburg
Abb. 8: Zentralblatt der Bauverwaltung 1925, Nr. 45
Abb. 9: Wikimedia Commons, Wolfgang Meinhart
Abb. 12: Wikimedia Commons, SKopp
Abb. 13: Allianz Real Estate Germany GmbH
Abb. 14: Hamburgisches Architekturarchiv

* Die Abbildungsrechte sind vom Autor geklärt worden und liegen in dessen Verantwortung

[1] Das Ballinhaus musste 1938 auf Anweisung von Reichsstatthalter und Gauleiter Karl Kaufmann in Meßberghof umbenannt werden, weil Albert Ballin (1857–1918), der ehemalige Generaldirektor der HAPAG, Jude gewesen war. Siehe BALLIN-HAUS – MESSBERGHOF, 1997, S. 25 u. S. 65.

[2] Zur Definition, Architektur und Geschichte der Hamburger Kontorhäuser siehe auch im Folgenden: HAMBURGER KONTORHAUS, 1909; HAMBURG UND SEINE BAUTEN, 1914, Bd. 1, S. 432–486; MEYER-VEDEN und HIPP, Kontorhäuser, 1988; LANGE, Kontorhaus, 2013 (in Vorbereitung). Dieser Artikel fußt in Teilen auf dem letztgenannten Titel.

[3] MAYER, Kontorhaus, 1909, S. 583.

[4] HIPP, Heimat in der City, 1986. MEYER-VEDEN und HIPP, Kontorhäuser, 1988, S. 14 f. und S. 19 ff. Hierzu auch ausführlicher: LANGE, Kontorhaus, 2013.

[5] Hierzu ausführlicher: WISCHERMANN, Wohnen, 1983, S. 94 ff. Zur Cholera-Epidemie 1892 siehe auch: EVANS, Tod, 1990.

[6] Zur Geschichte der Mönckebergstraße siehe: SCHUMACHER, Großstadt-Straße, 1922; LUBITZ, Mönckebergstraße, 2009.

[7] Zur Sanierung der südlichen Altstadt siehe auch im Folgenden: HAMBURG UND SEINE BAUTEN, 1914, Bd. 2, S. 214 f.; HAMBURG UND SEINE BAUTEN, 1929, S. 594 ff. NICOLAISEN, Studien, 1985, S. 125 ff. SCHUBERT, Städtebaukunst, 1991.

[8] WINKELMANN, Wohnhaus, 1937, S. 25 f. Siehe auch: MELHOP, Bauweise, 1908, S. 304 ff; RUDHARD, Bürgerhaus, 1975, S. 111 ff.

[9] HAMBURG UND SEINE BAUTEN, 1914, S. 215.

[10] Vgl. die Pläne in: HAMBURG UND SEINE BAUTEN, 1914, Bd. 2, S. 201; HAMBURG UND SEINE BAUTEN, 1929, S. 18.

[11] NICOLAISEN, Studien, 1985, S. 126 u. S. 129.

[12] SCHUMACHER, Sanierung, 1926, S. 228 ff.

[13] Zu dieser Diskussion siehe: NICOLAISEN, Studien, 1985, S. 128 f. und Anm. 414. Gemeint sind die Wohnblöcke des Bauvereins zu Hamburg an der Harburger Chaussee, die von Ernst Vicenz stammen (1915–21), und die Großsiedlung Veddel (1927–31). Vgl. HARMS und SCHUBERT, Wohnen, 1989, S. 97 ff. u. S. 101 ff.

[14] Zitiert nach NICOLAISEN, Studien, 1985, S. 129

[15] KOCH, Wiederaufbau, 1915, S. 49. Zu dem Wettbewerb siehe auch: SCHUBERT, Städtebaukunst, 1991.

[16] KOCH, Wiederaufbau, 1915, S. 53.

[17] Vgl. HAMBURG UND SEINE BAUTEN, 1914, S. 580 u. S. 585 ff.

[18] KOCH, Wiederaufbau, 1915, S. 55.

[19] Bauprüfakten Klingberg 3, Fischertwiete 1 u. 2, Chilehaus, Bd. 3: Protokoll der Finanzdeputation, verhandelt den 4. August 1923.

[20] FRANK, Baukunst, 2000, S. 40.

[21] Im ersten Bauabschnitt des Sprinkenhofs diente lediglich der Trakt an der Burchardstraße, als Kontorhaus; der Rest war in Wohnungen aufgeteilt. Im zweiten Bauabschnitt wurde der Trakt an der Burchardstraße fast vollständig für Wohnzwecke ausgebaut. Vgl. auch im Folgenden die Grundrisse in: Bauprüfakten Burchardstraße 10–14, Sprinkenhof, Bd. 1 und 2; Bauprüfakten Burchardstraße 10–14, Sprinkenhof, Bd. 4.

[22] BÜTTNER, Stadtstaat, 1986, S. 205 u. S. 214.

[23] 1913 erreichte der Gesamtumschlag im Hamburger Hafen 27,7 Mio. Tonnen, 1929 28,6 Mio. Tonnen. Siehe BOLLE, Generalplan, 1953, S. 40.

[24] „Gegenüber dem Höchststand im Jahr 1929 schrumpfte der deutsche Außenhandel mengenmäßig bis 1931 um 28 % und bis 1932 sogar um 44 %, wegen der starken Preisverluste dem Wert nach sogar um 40 % bzw. 60 %." BÜTTNER, Finanzpolitik, 1978, S. 192. Dieser Einbruch spiegelt sich in den Umschlagszahlen des Hamburger Hafens wider. Der Gesamtumschlag im Hafen ging um rund ein Drittel von 28,6 Mio. Tonnen (1929) auf 19,6 Mio. Tonnen (1933) zurück und blieb trotz der Erholung seit 1934 im letzten Friedensjahr 1938 mit 25,7 Mio. Tonnen immer noch deutlich hinter dem Spitzenwert von 1929 zurück. Siehe BOLLE, Generalplan, 1953, S. 40.

[25] BÜTTNER, Finanzpolitik, 1978, S. 196, Anm. 48.

[26] Gemeint sind die Wohnbebauung an der Westseite der Mohlenhofstraße und der Altstädter Hof, die beide von Rudolf Klophaus stammen (1935/36 bzw. 1936/37). Vgl. HIPP, Wohnstadt, 1982, S. 125 f. und S. 150.

[27] Vgl. die offizielle Karte der Kriegsschäden in der Innenstadt, die diese Flächen als unbebaut ausweist, in:

SCHRAMM, Häuser, 1985, S. 84. An der Burchardstraße wurde nach dem Zweiten Weltkrieg das Valvo-Haus von Puls & Richter gebaut (1954/55).

[28] Auf einen Nachweis der einzelnen Gebäude wird im Folgenden verzichtet. Die Baudaten wurden anhand der betreffenden Bauprüfakten im Bezirksamt Mitte verifiziert.

[29] BAHN, Groß-Kontorhäuser, 1929, S. 410.

[30] SCHUMACHER, Großstadt-Straße, 1922, S. 13.

[31] SCHUMACHER, Großstadt-Straße, 1922, S. 20.

[32] Zum Werk von Fritz Höger siehe: BUCCIARELLI, Höger, 1992. TURTENWALD, Höger, 2003. Zu Hans und Oskar Gerson siehe: VOIGT, Gerson, 2000.

[33] RAUSCHNABEL, Stadtgestalt, 1984, S. 63 ff.

[34] Siehe auch im Folgenden: DISTEL, Kontorhaus, 1926, S. 488.

[35] JAKSTEIN, Arbeiten, 1914/15, S. 122.

[36] In der zeitgenössischen Literatur werden kaum Angaben über die Bruttogeschossflächen der Kontorhäuser gemacht. Diesbezügliche Werte liegen vor allem nach Umbauten vor, was nur bedingt Rückschlüsse auf den ursprünglichen Zustand erlaubt. So bot das Klöpperhaus nach der Entkernung und Umwandlung in ein Warenhaus 18 000 qm Verkaufsfläche, nicht gerechnet der Keller sowie das sechste Obergeschoss und das Dachgeschoss, die für die Verwaltung und die Sozialräume reserviert waren. Siehe HAMBURG UND SEINE BAUTEN, 1969, S. 509 f. Das Kaufmannshaus verfügte nach dem Umbau in ein Bürohaus mit Ladenpassage über eine Fläche von rund 23 600 qm in den Vollgeschossen. Siehe HAMBURG UND SEINE BAUTEN, 1984, S. 101.

[37] MÖLLER, Hamburg, 1999, S. 55.

[38] 1924, als das Chilehaus und der Meßberghof fertiggestellt wurden, konkurrierten gleich sechs Gebäude um den Rang, Deutschlands erstes Hochhaus zu sein: außer den beiden zuvor genannten noch das Borsig-Hochhaus in Berlin, das Wilhelm-Marx-Haus in Düsseldorf und das bereits 1923 fertiggestellte Industriehaus ebenda, das mit seinen sieben Vollgeschossen zumindest in baurechtlicher Hinsicht als Hochhaus gelten konnte. In Dresden wurde zudem der 1923/24 fertiggestellte Neubau der Ernemann-Werke als „Deutschlands erstes Turmhaus" gefeiert. Siehe NEUMANN, Wolkenkratzer, 1995, S. 31 ff.

[39] Hierzu allgemein mit zahlreichen Beispielen aus dem gesamten Reichsgebiet, u. a. auch aus dem Kontorhausviertel: STOMMER und MAYER-GÜRR, Hochhaus, 1990; NEUMANN, Wolkenkratzer, 1995. Zur Hochhausdebatte speziell in Hamburg siehe: NICOLAISEN, Studien, 1985, S. 135 f.

[40] GOETZ, Ballinhaus, 1924, S. 191.

[41] So sah der Bebauungsplan z.B. nur eine Gebäudetiefe von 12 Metern vor, wogegen das Chilehaus eine Tiefe von 13 bis 15,8 Meter aufweist. Siehe auch in Folgenden: Bauprüfakten Klingberg 3, Fischertwiete 1 u. 2, Chilehaus, Bde. 1–3.

[42] Siehe auch im Folgenden: Bauprüfakten Klingberg 3, Fischertwiete 1 u. 2, Chilehaus, Bd. 1.

[43] HÖGER, Angaben, 1925, S. 16.

[44] Wie Anm. 32.

[45] FISCHER, Chilehaus, 1999, S. 95 u. S. 107 ff.

[46] Der sakrale Charakter der Skulpturen fiel bereits der zeitgenössischen Kritik auf: „Mir scheint die Stilisierung dieser nur in wenigen Flächen zugeschnittenen Figuren zu weit zu gehen. [...] Vielleicht hätte der Künstler dann auch die Gefahr vermieden, an einem weltlichen Zweckbau Figuren von dem Ausdrucksgehalt kirchlicher Plastik anzubringen, wobei zugegeben werden soll, daß diese Gefahr durch den Platz, der für die Plastik bestimmt war, nämlich die an Strebepfeiler erinnernden Lisenen, sehr nahe lag." FEDDERSEN, Chilehaus und Ballinhaus, 1925, S. 2. Die Skulpturen wurden 1968 aufgrund starker Witterungsschäden entfernt und 1996/97 durch Neuschöpfungen von Lothar Fischer ersetzt. Zu den neuen wie den ursprünglichen Figuren siehe: BALLIN-HAUS – MESSBERGHOF, 1997, S. 24, S. 45 u. S. 54 ff.

[47] GERSON, Ziegel, 1925, S. 950.

[48] BAHN, Sprinkenhof, 1929, S. 485. Von dem ursprünglichen Entwurf mit Skelettfassaden sind aufgrund von Kriegsverlusten nur Fragmente überliefert, die in der Literatur bisher zwar jeweils anderen Gebäuden zugeordnet wurden, jedoch höchstwahrscheinlich eine frühe Entwurfsphase des Sprinkenhofs repräsentieren. Vgl. BUCCIARELLI, Höger, 1992, S. 184 (als Börse von Teheran); TURTENWALD, Höger, 2003, S. 158 (als undatiertes anonymes Geschäftshaus).

[49] Vgl. BUCCIARELLI, Höger, 1992, S. 166 ff.; TURTENWALD, Höger, 2003, S. 187 ff.

[50] BAHN, Mohlenhof, 1929, S. 666 f.; RAUSCHNABEL, Stadtgestalt, 1984, S. 63 ff.

[51] Schreiben der Baupolizeibehörde vom 17. September 1927, Einspruch Nr. 5787, in: Bauprüfakten Niedernstraße 8, Mohlenhof, Bd. 1.

[52] Siehe BALLIN-HAUS – MESSBERGHOF, 1997, S. 43 f.

[53] GERSON, Sprinkenhof, 1929, S. 229.

[54] Hierzu ausführlich: PEHNT, Expressionismus, 1998.

[55] Vgl. STOMMER und MAYER-GÜRR, Hochhaus, 1990, S. 43 ff.; NEUMANN, Wolkenkratzer, 1995, S. 178 (mit weiteren Literaturangaben).

[56] Über das Chilehaus erschienen bis zum Zweiten Weltkrieg mindestens 30 Beiträge in Fachzeitschriften und Fachbüchern, darunter auch einige internationale Veröffentlichungen. Der Meßberghof brachte es auf mindestens 20, der Mohlenhof auf mindestens acht und der Sprinkenhof auf mindestens 14 Fachveröffentlichungen, wobei der Fokus bei Letzterem auf dem ersten Bauabschnitt lag. Dieser Statistik liegen neben eigenen Recherchen vor allem die Angaben in der Sekundärliteratur zu Höger und den Gebrüder Gerson zugrunde (wie Anm. 32).

[57] WHITTICK, Architecture, 1950, S. 184; PEVSNER, Architektur, 1957, S. 677. HITCHCOCK, Architecture, 1958, S. 344; BENEVOLO, Geschichte, 1978, S. 178 f. (italienische Erstausgabe 1960).

[58] Vgl. den betreffenden Artikel des Verfassers in diesem Band.

Hartmut Frank

Die Hamburger Schule in der Architektur: Höger, Schumacher, Schneider und andere

Seit langem sind wir mit Begriffen wie dem der „Prairie-Schule" oder der „Amsterdamer Schule" vertraut, die übernommen aus der Kunstgeschichte und der Literatur ein gemeinsames Gestaltungsverständnis bezeichnen, das für eine Gruppe von Architekten zu einer Zeit und in einer gegebenen Region mehr oder weniger charakteristisch ist. Ohne weiteres verbinden wir Namen wie Frank Lloyd Wright oder Walter Burley Griffin mit der ersteren und Michel de Klerk oder Piet Kramer mit der anderen. Aber wir sind nicht gewohnt, auf gleiche Weise von einer Hamburger Schule zu sprechen, obwohl es dafür gute Gründe gäbe.

Seit dem Ende des 18. Jahrhundert wurden auf Initiative von Ernst Georg Sonnin und der Patriotischen Gesellschaft in Hamburg Bauzeichner ausgebildet, von denen einige später auch als Baumeister und Architekten arbeiteten. Aus dieser Ausbildungsstätte sind in der zweiten Hälfte des 19.Jahrhunderts sowohl eine Baugewerke-Schule wie eine Kunstgewerbeschule hervorgegangen, die beide lange Zeit gemeinsam mit dem Museum für Kunst und Gewerbe in einem Gebäude untergebracht waren. Aber bis in die 1970er Jahre gab es in Hamburg keinen Studiengang, in dem auf ähnliche Weise wie andernorts an den Technischen Hochschulen und Universitäten Architekten und Stadtplaner ausgebildet wurden. Zwar hatten an der Hamburger Kunstgewerbeschule namhafte Architekten wie Hugo Häring oder Karl Schneider gelehrt, aber nicht im Rahmen einer eigenen Ausbildung von Architekten, sondern in einer allgemeinen Lehre für Kunsthandwerker. Daneben bildete die Baugewerkeschule Handwerker zu Baumeistern und Bauleitern aus, die nur selten selbständige Architekten wurden. Die Mehrzahl der in Hamburg tätigen Architekten hatten ihre Ausbildung auswärts erfahren, etwa an den Technischen Hochschulen in Berlin, Dresden, Hannover oder Karlsruhe, wenn nicht sogar in Paris, London oder Kopenhagen, oder sie waren Autodidakten, die aus dem Handwerk kamen. Lange Zeit gab es in Hamburg keine Ausbildungsstätte, die in der Architektur schulbildend hätte wirken können. Ein universitärer Ausbildungsgang für Architekten wurde erst nach 1970 an der Hochschule für bildende Künste und für Stadtplaner ein weiteres Jahrzehnt später an der TU Hamburg-Harburg eingerichtet. Seit einigen Jahren befinden sich diese zusammengelegt mit Studiengängen der früheren Fachhochschule in der HafenCity Universität. Ob allerdings deren Absolventen eines fernen Tages als Schule gesehen und als solche die Gestalt der Stadt bestimmen werden, bleibt abzuwarten.

Trotz ihrer unterschiedlichen Ausbildungshintergründe haben viele der in Hamburg tätigen Architekten seit der Jahrhundertwende um 1900 viele Jahrzehnte lang, vor allem aber während der 20er Jahre, in ihrem generellen Architektur- und Gestaltungsverständnis erstaunliche Übereinstimmungen gezeigt. Im jeweilgen Werk der Brüder Fritz und Hermann Höger, in dem der gemeinsam arbeitenden Hans und Oskar Gerson, der Bürogemeinschaften Block & Hochfeld oder Klophaus, Schoch, zu Putlitz, aber auch in dem von Friedrich Ostermeyer oder Karl Schneider, um nur einige zu nennen, zeigen sich Gemeinsamkeiten, die sie deutlich von ihren Zeitgenossen in Berlin, München, Köln oder Frankfurt unterscheiden. Allen ihren Hamburger Bauten ist eine gewisse Schwere und Strenge gemeinsam. Sie gebrauchen ähnliche Materialien und tendieren dazu, deren Körperlichkeit zu vereinfachen und sie insgesamt schlicht erscheinen zu lassen. Auffällig ist die Verbindung dieser Eigenheiten mit einer fast vollständigen Abwesenheit von Gestaltungsmoden, die andernorts als avantgardistisch galten. Ohne Zweifel können die genannten Kennzeichen einer Hamburger Schule zu einem gewissen Grad dem generellen Einfluss und der Bauleitplanung von Fritz Schumacher und Gustav Oelssner, den Stadtbaudirektoren für Hamburg beziehungsweise für Altona, zugeschrieben werden. Aber das reicht bei weitem nicht, um die deutlichen Übereinstimmungen innerhalb der Hamburger Architektenschaft während nahezu eines halben Jahrhunderts zu erklären.

Hamburg war zu keiner Zeit ein Schaufenster des internationalen Stiles. Eine so gern zum Markenzeichen der Avantgarde des 20. Jahrhunderts erhobene weiße Moderne sucht man in der Stadt vergeblich und auch im stilistisch etwas weniger einheitlichen Altona kann man nur wenige Beispiele hierfür finden. Hamburg war zugleich die Hochburg einer nicht-avantgardistischen Moderne, die sich vergleichbar mit Bestrebungen in Skandinavien oder in den Niederlanden, aus regionalistischen Tendenzen heraus entwickelt hatte und deren Qualitäten zu lange Zeit und zu Unrecht von der zeitgenössischen Architektur-Geschichtsschreibung vernachlässigt worden sind. Die Debatte um eine charakteristische lokale Architektur reicht in die Zeit des Wiederaufbaus nach dem Großen Brand von 1842 zurück. Dieser hatte nicht nur mit einem neuen Wege- und Kanalisationsnetz, sondern auch mit einer neuen Bauordnung, das Gesicht der inneren Stadt radikal verändert. Ein Zurück zu dem zuvor üblichen, stets brandgefährdeten Holzfachwerk mit dekorativer Ziegelausfachung, das sich letztlich von der im Hamburger Umland üblichen ländlichen Bauweise herleiten ließ, war nicht denkbar. Der erste Hamburger Baudirektor Carl Ludwig Wimmel und der Vorsitzende der Wiederaufbaukommission Alexis de Chateauneuf, die beide Weinbrenners Karlsruher Schule entstammten, hatten deshalb einen keinesfalls regional verstandenen, der italienischen Renaissance entlehnten, sogenannten Rundbogenstil mit hellen Putz- und

Abb. 1: Theodor Bühlau, Patriotische Gesellschaft 1844–47, Aufstockung 1924 durch Erich zu Putlitz (Klophaus/Schoch/zu Putlitz)

Abb. 2: Franz Andreas Meyer, Portal der Brooktorbrücke über den Zollkanal der Speicherstadt, 1888

Ziegelbauten durchgesetzt, gegen den einige wenige, ‚neudeutsch' gedachte, neogotische Bauten, etwa das in dunklem Backstein von Theodor Bühlau am Ort des abgebrannten alten Rathauses errichtete Gebäude der Patriotischen Gesellschaft, sich kaum zur Geltung bringen konnte.[1]

Diese Tendenz änderte sich erst drei Jahrzehnte später. Sichtmauerwerk aus Backsteinen und neogotische Formen behaupteten sich zunehmend neben Putzbauten und detailreichem Natursteinmauerwerk, die sich trotz ihrer vorgeblich deutschen Neorenaissanceformen erkennbar an den Lehren der Pariser École des Beaux Arts orientiert hatten. Das in Hamburg traditionell stark beachtete englische Beispiel und der durch die industrialisierte Ziegelproduktion veränderte Markt der Baumaterialien unterstützten diese Veränderungen. Vor allem nahm der Einfluss von Architekten zu, die das Hannoversche Polytechnikum absolviert hatten und von den Ideen des dort lehrenden Neogotikers Conrad Wilhelm Hase geprägt waren. Einer der ihren, Franz Andreas Meyer, wurde Leiter des ‚Ingenieurwesens', jener Bauabteilung der Stadt, der sowohl die Anlage der technischen Infrastrukturen wie auch die Stadterweiterung unterstand und die das für die öffentlichen Bauten zuständige Hochbauamt unter dem an der Berliner Bauakademie ausgebildeten Carl Johann Christian Zimmermann mit seiner Vorliebe für die wilhelminische Neorenaissance an Bedeutung für die schnelle Modernisierung der Stadt übertraf. Das nach fünfzigjähriger Debatte und zahllosen Planungsvarianten schließlich 1900 fertiggestellte Hamburger Rathaus stellte das letzte und größte Monument jener unter der Ägide des Hochbauamtes entstanden Architekturen dar. Für diesen Entwurf zeichnete eine ganze Gruppe Hamburger Architekten verantwortlich, die sich unter dem in Paris ausgebildeten und mehrere Jahrzehnte lang bedeutendsten Hamburger Privatarchitekten Martin Haller zusammengefunden hatten.[2] Der für die Hamburger Reformdiskussion tonangebende Kunsthallendirektor Alfred Lichtwark hatte lange Zeit mit sehr mäßigem Erfolg versucht, dieses Projekt zum Ort und Ausgangspunkt einer Wiederbelebung Hamburger Kunst und Kultur zu nutzen. Ähnlich wie Justus Brinckmann, der Direktor des Museums für Kunst und Gewerbe, unternahm Lichtwark, von der Kritik am Rathausbau ausgehend, eine Vielzahl publizistischer und praktischer Aktivitäten, die neben der Förderung der Hamburger Kunst und des Kunstgewerbes auch auf ein neues Städtebau- und Architekturverständnis jenseits des vorherrschenden laissez-faire und Historismus gerichtet waren.[3]

Meyer hatte währenddessen den Bau der sogenannten Speicherstadt im neu eingerichteten Freihafen zu verantworten, der für die durch den Anschluss der Stadt an das Zollgebiet des 1871 neugegründeten Deutschen Reiches verlorenen Privilegien entschädigen sollte. Der Abbruch der bestehenden Bebauung auf den Elbinseln Kehrwieder und Wandrahm, einem vom Brand verschonten Teil der Altstadt, die Umsiedlung der dortigen Bewohner, die Anlage eines neuen Systems von Fleeten und die Errichtung eines eindrucksvollen, monofunktional allein zum Hafen gehörenden neuen Stadtteils zählen ohne Zweifel zu den bedeutendsten baukulturellen Ereignisse in der jüngeren Stadtgeschichte Hamburgs.[4] Die Speicherstadt veränderte nicht nur radikal die Topographie der Stadt und ihre Funktionszusammenhänge, sondern zugleich auch die Ästhetik ihrer Gesamterscheinung. Obwohl diese Speicher anfangs eher zur Arbeitswelt von Industrie und Hafen gezählt wurden als zur Baukunst, prägten sie die neue Wahrnehmung nachhaltig. Tatsächlich waren sie auch keine Ingenieurbauten wie die Krane, Kaimauern und Schuppen des übrigen Hafens, sondern durchaus bewusste Gestaltungsarbeiten von Archi-

Abb. 3: Titel zu Paul Bröcker/Ferdinand Sckopp, Über Hamburgs neue Architektur, 1908
Abb. 4: Titel zu Paul Bröcker/Fritz Höger: Die Architektur des Hamburgischen Geschäftshauses, 1910

tekten unter Meyers künstlerischer Oberleitung. Das rote Sichtmauerwerk ihrer Außenmauern und die grün oxydierten Kupferabdeckungen und Dächer schufen im Wechselspiel mit dem meist grauen Hamburger Himmel und dem dunklen Wasser der Fleete einen Gesamteindruck, dessen Wirkung auf die um die Jahrhundertewende einsetzende Suche nach einer spezifischen modernen Gestaltung der sich rasch ausdehnenden und verändernden Großstadt Hamburg nicht ausbleiben konnte.

Aus heutiger Sicht überrascht die geringe zeitgenössische Würdigung der Ästhetik der Speicherstadt durch die Protagonisten einer Hamburger Reformarchitektur. Diese bewegten sich in einer eigenartigen ideologischen Mischung von Ideen der aus England wirkenden Arts-and-Crafts- und der Gartenstadt-Bewegung mit der völkischen Romantik, wie sie unter anderem im Dürerbund und in der Heimatschutzbewegung blühte. Dazu kamen noch wie andernorts auch die Vorstellungen einer Sozial- und Kulturreform, die von den Wohnungs- und Bodenreformern, den Genossenschaften und den vielfältigen Lebensreformbewegungen propagiert wurden. In Hamburg wirkte nicht nur ein Heimatschutzverein, sondern gleich eine Vielzahl, die sich mit unterschiedlicher Schwerpunktsetzung auf die Stadt Hamburg, auf Altona, auf die Hamburger Geestlande und auf die Vier- und Marschlande bezogen. Im Gegensatz zu vielen Mitgliedern dieser Vereine waren einige der führenden Persönlichkeiten darin keine nostalgisch zurückblickenden Romantiker, sondern sich voll bewusst, dass eine bedeutende Großstadt wie Hamburg unausweichlich einer Modernisierung und einer angemessenen Neugestaltung bedurfte. Fortschrittsglauben liberaler und sozialistischer Provenienz mischten sich mit Lokalpatriotismus und niederdeutscher Traditionspflege. Trotz ihres nicht zu bezweifelnden fortschrittlichen Charakters aber konnte die Speicherstadt wohl wegen ihrer zugleich als historistisch verstandenen Gestaltung nicht als Vorbild für die ebenfalls durch die Absonderung der Hafenfunktionen von der historischen Stadt erforderlich gewordenen neuen Kontorhäuser dienen und schon gar nicht für den Massenwohnungsbau in den Stadterweiterungsgebieten im Norden und Osten der Stadt.

Besonders deutlich wird dies in den Veröffentlichungen der Architekten Fritz Höger, Ferdinand Sckopp und des Pädagogen und Journalisten Paul Bröcker zur Heimatpflege und zu den Problemen des modernen Kontorhausbaus in Hamburg. 1908 hatte Bröcker ein Bändchen: Über „Hamburgs neue Architektur" veröffentlicht und ihm als Titel

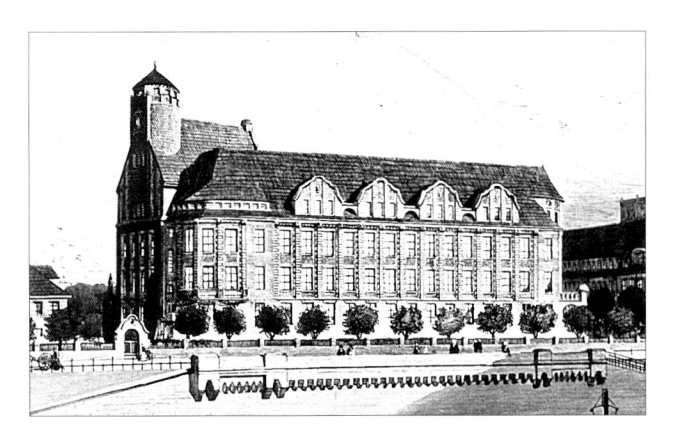

Abb. 5: Fritz Schumacher: Tropenkrankenhaus, Perspektive der 1. Fassung in Naturstein, 1909

eine Zeichnung von Ferdinand Sckopp vorangestellt.⁵ Diese zeigt überraschenderweise keine zeitgenössische Architektur, sondern ein fünfgeschossiges Hamburger Mietshaus aus der Mitte des 18. Jahrhunderts mit einem Doppelgiebel in unverputztem rotem Backstein und ohne Holzfachwerk. Es handelt sich um den sogenannten Paradieshof am Alten Steinweg, ein weder von seiner Nutzung noch von seiner Bauweise her besonders charakteristisches Alt-Hamburger Gebäude, das sich aber offensichtlich wegen seiner rationalen Fassadengliederung und der Materialwahl besonders gut als Vorbild in der damals aktuellen Debatte eignete. Bröckers „Heimatbuch" mit zahlreichen Federzeichnungen Sckopps von althamburger Bauten⁶ und „Fragen an die Heimat"⁷, eine bis in die Zwischenkriegszeit hinein erscheinende Schriftenreihe folgten 1910. Im gleichen Jahr erschien eine uns hier vorrangig interessierende Schrift mit dem barocken Titel: „Die Architektur des Hamburgischen Geschäftshauses. Ein zeitgemäßes Wort über die Ausbildung der Mönckebergstraße. Theoretische Betrachtungen von Paul Bröcker. Praktische Vorschläge von Fr. Höger Arch."⁸ Höger hatte diesem Band eine Reihe von Entwurfszeichnungen beigesteuert, die zeigen sollten, wie sich aus der spezifischen Hamburger Bautradition eine neue Geschäftshausarchitektur entwickeln ließe, die direkt beim Bau der großen neuen Durchbruchstraße von Rathausmarkt zum Hauptbahnhof mit ihrer neuen elektrischen Untergrundbahnlinie Anwendung finden könne. Keine aus der Neogotik entlehnten Schmuckformen wie in der Speicherstadt, sondern Adaptionen des bürgerlichen Spätbarock lieferten die stilistischen Vorgaben mit deren Hilfe die unumgänglichen Neubauten in der inneren Stadt mit den wenigen nach dem Brand verbliebenen Spuren historischer Bausubstanz harmonisch in Einklang gebracht werden sollten, um eine bessere Identifizierung der Hamburger mit ihrer sich schnell verändernden Lebensumwelt zu befördern. In den erläuternden Texten aber gehen die Autoren noch weiter zurück und bemühen sich um eine genealogische Ableitung dieser Neubauten von den niedersächsischen Bauernhäusern, die sie teilweise zu abenteuerlichen Theorien verleitet. Wichtig für die Architekturdiskussion aber war weniger die hier aufblühende Blut-und-Boden-Romantik, zu der Höger später noch zahlreiche Bonmots beisteuern wird, sondern die Überlegungen zu einer ortsbezogenen, historisch begründeten

Entwurfstypologie für die neue Bauaufgabe des modernen Geschäftshauses, die nicht nur neue Nutzungsformen, sondern auch zeitgemäße moderne Bautechnologien wie Stahl- und Betonfachwerk und zweischaliges Ziegelmauerwerk in ihre Überlegungen einbezog.

Mitten in diese laufenden Debatten hinein, die längst über die Hamburger Intellektuellenkreise hinaus auf die breite Öffentlichkeit wirkten, erfolgte 1909 die Berufung von Fritz Schumacher zum neuen Leiter des Hochbauamtes und Nachfolger Zimmermanns. Dieser hatte seine Aktivitäten aus gesundheitlichen Günden jahrelang seinem Stellvertreter Albert Erbe übertragen müssen, der sich, durchaus im Sinne der fachinternen Hamburger Debatten, bei den öffentlichen Bauten erfolgreich um eine Überwindung der Zimmermannschen Vorliebe für Formen der deutschen Renaissance bemüht hatte und diese durch eine leicht neobarock gefärbte Reformarchitektur ersetzt hatte. Bei seinem Amtsantritt betrat der gerade 40-jährige Schumacher ein Terrain, das sich nicht gerade als eine tabula rasa erwies, wo alle Welt nur auf seinen Auftritt gewartet hätte. Der aus Bremen stammende und als Sohn eines Diplomaten zeitweilig in New York aufgewachsene Professor der Technischen Hochschule Dresden war keineswegs die erste Wahl des Hamburger Senats für diese Stelle. Vor ihm hatte man ein gutes Dutzend anderer Kandidaten in Erwägung gezogen. Aber für Schumacher war es durchaus ein lange erträumtes Aufgabenfeld, das ihn in Hamburg erwartete und für das er eine erfolgreiche unbefristete Professur aufgab. Er hatte sich bereits in Dresden neben seiner Bautätigkeit aktiv um Fragen des modernen Städtebaus gekümmert, hatte zusammen mit Cornelius Gurlitt erste städtebauliche Seminare abgehalten und in Schriften und Vorträgen eine enge Verknüpfung von kommunaler Baupolitik mit den Bestrebungen der Kulturreform gefordert. Er hatte die Erste Deutsche Städteausstellung (1903) in Dresden initiiert und gehörte zu den maßgeblichen Organisatoren der bedeutenden Dritten Deutschen Kunstgewerbeausstellung (1906), aus der ein Jahr später der Deutsche Werkbund hervorging. An dessen Münchner Gründungsversammlung hatte er 1907 sein programmatisches Referat über die „Wiedereroberung harmonischer Kultur" gehalten.⁹

Bereits 1903 hatte er bei einer Tagung während der Städteausstellung eine neue gestaltungsorientierte Städtebaupolitik gefordert, die sich nicht länger vorrangig an pittoresken vorindustriellen Klein- und Mittelstädten orientieren, sondern statt dessen ihr Augenmerk gezielt auf die allgemein als hässlich geschmähten Industriestädte mit ihren Zusammenballungen zugewanderter „heimatloser" Proletarier richten sollte. In seinem Vortrag „Die architektonischen Aufgaben der Städte" hatte er gefordert, „Kunst und Leben wieder eng miteinander zu verbinden".¹⁰ Um dieses Ziel eines künstlerischen Städtebaus auf der Höhe der ökonomischen und technischen Möglichkeiten der Zeit zu erreichen, sei es unabdingbar, die entscheidenden Planungs- und Gestaltungsfragen in der Hand einer fähigen Künstlerpersönlichkeit zu vereinigen. Und fast prophetisch hatte er in diesem Zusammenhang Hamburg als den Ort erwähnt, an dem großartige Werke der Ingenieurkunst „einer kleinen, fremden, hilflosen Architektur" gegenüberstünden, ein Zustand den nur große Architekten wie Theodor Fischer oder Bruno

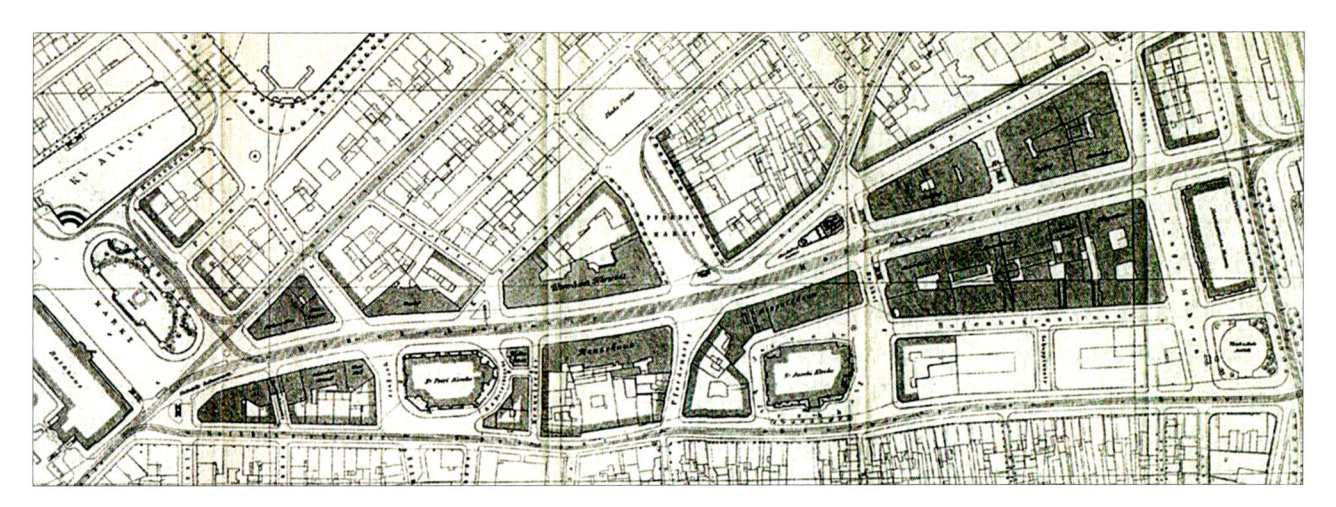

Abb. 6: Fritz Schumacher, Durchbruch der Mönckebergstraße, Gesamtplan (aus: Die Entstehung einer Großstadtstraße 1914)

Schmitz würden bewältigen können, nicht ahnend dass er selbst nur sechs Jahre später gerade diese Aufgabe übernehmen würde. Unerwartet schnell erarbeitete er sich gegen große Widerstände das erträumte Interventionsfeld, auf dem er die Ideale des Deutschen Werkbundes nicht wie bisher lediglich mit Entwürfen bürgerlicher Villen und ihrer Ausstattung zu kleinen Gesamtkunstwerken umsetzen konnte, sondern sich schrittweise an die Umgestaltung einer modernen Millionenstadt mit all ihren komplexen infrastrukturellen und sozialen Problemen machen konnte, nicht ohne sich zugleich selbst mit unermüdlicher paralleler schriftstellerischer und Vortragstätigkeit zu einem mythischen Helden zu stilisieren, der aus der modernen Hamburger Stadtgeschichte nicht mehr wegzudenken ist.

In kluger Voraussicht der ihn erwartenden Schwierigkeiten hatte er sich vor Amtsantritt einen neunmonatigen Urlaub ausbedungen, während dessen er in seinem Dresdener Büro nahezu ein Dutzend für Hamburg vorgesehener öffentlicher Bauten baureif bearbeitete, sodass er mit einem Feuerwerk von programmatisch verstandenen Projekten seinen Dienst antreten konnte. Weit entfernt von der später florierenden Idee, öffentliche Bauten als reine Zweckbauten anzusehen, hatte er ganz im Sinne seiner kulturreformerischen Überzeugungen diese als soziale Monumente konzipiert, mit denen der städtische Raum auf neue Weise inhaltlich definiert und den ihrer ländlichen Heimat entfremdeten Zuwanderermassen neue Identifikationsorte gegeben werden sollten. Formell waren diese Architekturen noch stark durch sein Dresdener Umfeld und die Nähe zu der dort von Wilhelm Kreis, Johann Jacob Erlwein oder Schilling & Graebner gepflegten Reformarchitektur mit neobarocken Anklängen geprägt. Ihre Formensprache widersprach so gesehen weder den kurz zuvor entstandenen Bauten des nahezu gleichaltrigen Albert Erbe noch den Vorschlägen des etwas jüngeren Fritz Höger, sie unterschied sich nur in der Wahl des in Dresden vorherrschenden Natursteins als generellem Baumaterial statt des in Hamburg von den Reformern vehement geforderten roten Backsteins. Es ist wohl bezeichnend für Schumachers Denk- und Arbeitsweise, wie schnell er sich in dieser Frage den lokalen Bedingungen angepasst hat, nicht etwa in Form eines an eine Niederlage grenzenden Kompromisses, sondern mit einer schnellen und gründlichen Übernahme des Backsteins in sein eigenes Entwurfsrepertoire. Er überarbeitete nicht nur unverzüglich die nach Hamburg mitgebrachten Entwürfe, sondern erforschte auch zugleich die Möglichkeiten einer modernen Backsteinarchitektur und machte, nicht unbedingt zur Freude anderer Hamburger „Backsteinfürsten", sich selbst zum wichtigsten Fürsprecher dieses Materials und das Backsteinrot zu einem entscheidenden Element einer Strategie, dem künftigen Hamburg einen einheitlichen Grundton zu geben. In seine Veröffentlichung „Das Wesen des neuzeitlichen Backsteinbaus" von 1920[11] fasste er diese Überlegungen zusammen, nicht ohne sich bei dieser Gelegenheit von den in Hamburg noch immer grassierenden heimatschützerischen Begründungen für die Verwendung dieses Materials entschieden zu distanzieren.

Schumacher stieß bei seinem Amtsantritt nicht allein auf den Widerstand der diversen Heimatschutz-Vereine, sondern sah sich zugleich in seinen Ambitionen, in Hamburg einen modernen Städtebau zu initiieren, durch Fritz Sperber behindert, der kurz vor ihm zum Leiter des Ingenieurbaus und Nachfolger von Franz Andreas Meyer ernannt worden war. Ihm unterstand mit dem Bau der technischen Infrastruktur der Stadt auch die Aufstellung neuer Bebauungspläne und die Anlage und der Unterhalt der städtischen Grünanlagen. Schumacher war explizit wegen des Städtebaus nach Hamburg gekommen, weshalb dieser Interessen-

Abb. 7: Fritz Höger: Rappolthaus an der Mönckebergstraße, 1910

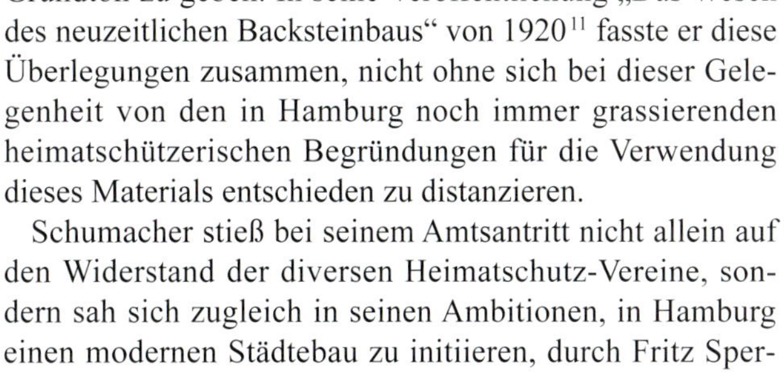

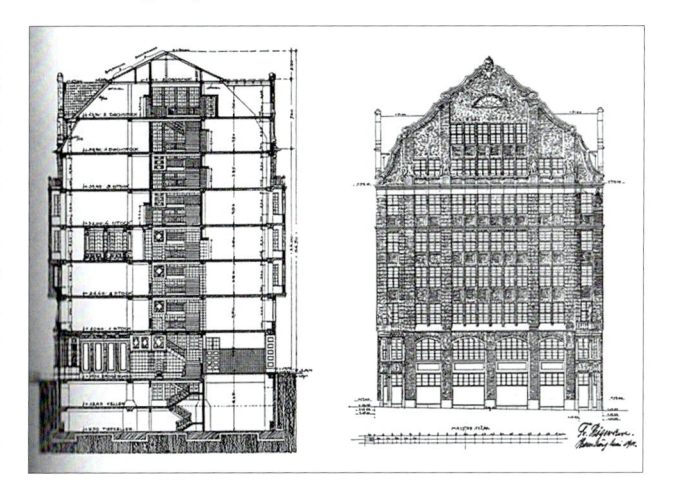

Abb. 8: Fritz Schumacher, Entwurf eines Verwaltungsgebäudes am Dammtorwall, 1912

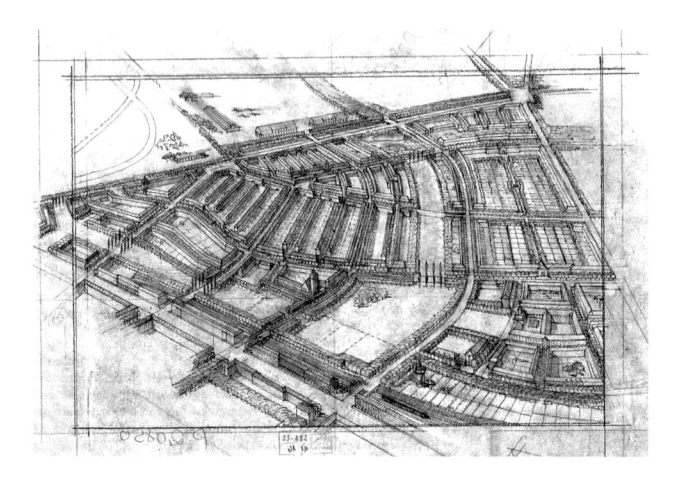

Abb. 9: Fritz Schumacher, Skizze zum B-Plan Hamburg Horn, ca. 1927

Abb. 10: Karl Schneider, Wohnungsbau am Habichtplatz, 1927/28, Luftphoto

konflikt für ihn eine größere Bedeutung bekommen musste als jener anfängliche mit dem Heimatschutz. Schumacher mischte sich jeweils mit dem Vorwand, die Interessen seines Hochbauamtes seien tangiert, in zahlreiche Projekte seines Kollegen ein und zog diese schrittweise an sich. Aus Dresden hatte er einen Kompromissvorschlag für die Gestaltung des seit zehn Jahren zwischen Anhängern des sogenannten englischen und des architektonischen Gartens umstrittenen Stadtparkprojektes mitgebracht, das er sehr zum Ärger Sperbers im Verlauf der Realisierung immer deutlicher als einen formalen Garten gestaltete, mit dem er die Raumkonzepte seiner späteren Siedlungsplanungen vorwegnahm und als ästhetisches Prinzip den Hamburgern vertraut machte. Dagegen konnte er sich beim Projekt einer Alsterstadt nicht gegen Sperber durchsetzen und musste seine Pläne resigniert aufgeben. Dessen Planungen für das Dulsberg-Gelände und für Barmbek-Nord jedoch konnte er radikal ändern und in den zwanziger Jahren auch tatsächlich realisieren.

Seine erste Bewährungsprobe hatte Schumacher beim Bau der Mönckebergstraße zu bestehen. Dieser Straßendurchbruch durch die Reste des Gängeviertels am Rande des Brandgebietes war längst beschlossen und bereits im Bau, als er sein Amt antrat. Er hatte keinen Einfluss auf die unglückliche Einführung der Trasse in den Rathausmarkt und auch nicht auf die spitzwinklige Einmündung der Spitaler Straße. Aber er konnte durchsetzen, dass die neuen Baulose entlang der Straße nicht in kleine Parzellen aufgeteilt wurden und dass für die Neubebauung eine strenge Gestaltsatzung Gebäudehöhen und Dachformen regulierte. Was er noch nicht durchsetzen konnte, war ein einheitliches Baumaterial. Er selbst fügte dem neuen Straßenbild der großen Kauf- und Kontorhäuser eine kleine Lesehalle mit dem Mönckeberg-Denkmal hinzu, gewissermaßen eine kulturpädagogische Ergänzung dieser von ihm als erster „Hamburger Großstadtstraße" bezeichneten modernen Konsumwelt. Schumacher durfte als städtischer Baubeamter keine privaten Planungsaufträge an dieser Straße übernehmen, dafür aber konnte Höger mit den Bauten des Rappolt- und des Klöpperhauses im Rahmen der städtebaulichen Vorgaben Schumachers zwei bemerkenswerte Beiträge zur Definition des modernen Hamburger Kontorhauses beisteuern. Der Planungsprozess der Mönckebergstraße war Schumacher so wichtig, dass er ihn nach Abschluss der Arbeiten in Brökkers kleiner Schriftenreihe „Fragen an die Heimat" veröffentlichte[12]. Hier konnte er ein erstes Mal in Hamburg seine Fähigkeit belegen, seine konkreten Planungserfahrungen zusammenzufassen und zu verallgemeinern. Er sprach nicht davon, aber hatte bei diesem Projekt zugleich gezeigt, dass er in der Lage war, die anfänglich gegnerischen Kräfte der Heimatschutz-Bewegung schrittweise in seine Planungskonzeptionen zu integrieren.

An der Mönckebergstraße, dann im Stadtpark und schließlich bei der Gestaltung der neuen „City" des Kontorhausviertels und beim Bau der Siedlungsgebiete seiner „Wohnstadt Hamburg" kann Schumacher seine Fähigkeiten als Koordinator der beteiligten freien Architekten immer perfekter unter Beweis stellen. Nach einer kurzzeitigen Beurlaubung nach Köln kehrte er 1923 nach Hamburg zurück und wurde zum Oberbaudirektor ernannt, wodurch er bis zu seiner Entlassung 1933 zehn Jahre lang endlich die planerische Machtfülle erhielt, die er sich von Anfang an für seine Tätigkeit in Hamburg gewünscht hatte. Mit den vor seinem Amtsantritt anfertigten Entwürfen für öffentliche Bauten hatte er bereits versucht, seine künstlerische Gestaltungslinie gewissermaßen an Pilotprojekten vorzustellen. Aber diese Projekte musste er insgesamt für die Realisierung umarbeiten und konnte sie nur nach und nach als exemplarisch in der Fachpresse veröffentlichen, wobei ihm allerdings seine Kontakte aus dem Deutschen Werkbund beste Dienste leisteten. Die freien Architekten und ihre Bauherren konnte er damit jedoch nur indirekt erreichen und zur Nachahmung veranlassen. Wollte er die gesamte Stadt seinem künstlerischen Gestaltungswollen unterwerfen, so musste er einerseits die private Entwurfstätigkeit der freien Architekten durch möglichst von allen Beteiligten anerkannte Regeln zu steuern suchen, oder besser, durch Überzeugungsarbeit ein Klima der Übereinstimmung erzeugen, das nicht als Zwang empfunden wurde, sondern als freie Zustimmung zu den von ihm verfochtenen Gestaltungsprinzipien.

Wir haben bereits angedeutet, wie Schumacher sich auch seinerseits bestimmten Prinzipien annäherte, über die bei seiner Ankunft unter den Hamburger Reformarchitekten ein weitgehender Konsens bestand. Er übernimmt deren generelle Präferenz für den roten Klinker, er passt seine großen öffentlichen Bauten, die traufseitig zur Straße hin angeordnet werden müssen, mit Reihen von Giebeln in hohen Dächern jenen Vorschlägen an, die Höger und andere zuvor gemacht haben, er führt die Prinzipien, die Erbe für die Schulneubauten eingeführt hat, noch bis zum Ersten Weltkrieg weiter und weicht von ihnen erst danach unter einem generell veränderten Gestaltungsklima ab, das heißt er gebärdet sich nicht als ein Gestaltungsdiktator, sondern arbeitet beharrlich in kleinen Schritten, mit beispielgebenden Projekten und mit neuen kooperativen Planungsverfahren an der Realisierung seiner Vorstellung einer modernen organischen Großstadt. Vor allem aber unterstützt er sie mit seinen Vorträgen und zahllosen Veröffentlichungen und entwirft im Laufe seiner Tätigkeit ein immer komplexeres Ideengebäude, das seine eigene Gestaltungsarbeit rechtfertigt und darüberhinaus seine gesamte Planungsarbeit argumentativ vorbereitet und die ihr zugrunde liegenden Vorstellungen öffentlich macht.[13]

Bei der sehr kontroversen Planungsarbeit für die einzelnen Bauabschnitte des Hamburger Stadtparks entwickelt Schumacher seine Methoden zur gemeinsamen Entwurfsarbeit mit allen Planungsbeteiligten. Diese halfen ihm, für seine Vorstellungen Zustimmung zu finden, sie gegebenenfalls zu modifizieren und auf diese Weise realisierbar zu machen. Die einzelnen Teilbereiche des Parks werden von ihm in Planskizzen entworfen, die dann in Plastilinmodelle übertragen werden, an denen Planer, Gärtner und politische Entscheidungsträger weiterarbeiten, bis ein Konsens gefunden ist. Dieses "modellmäßige Entwerfen" überträgt Schumacher später auf die Planungsprozesse für die „Wohnstadt", auf die Siedlungsprojekte für den Sozialen Wohnungsbau, die während der zweiten Hälfte der zwanziger Jahre in größerer Zahl in Hamburgs Norden und Osten errichtet werden. Hier arbeitet er mit den jeweiligen gemeinnützigen Bauträgern und den freien Architekten zusammen, denen anschließend die jeweiligen Baulose zur Realisierung übertragen werden. Nur in Ausnahmefällen, wie in der Jarrestadt, wurden diese Planungsprozesse durch offene Wettbewerbe eingeleitet. Der enge Dialog des Stadtplaners mit den Planungsbeteiligten, der in diesen Projekten nicht selbst als Architekt tätig werden darf, ist eine wichtige Erklärung für die relativ große gestalterische Homogenität der neuen Quartiere. Ihr liegt eine Übereinstimmung in Grundprinzipien zugrunde, ohne die die große Variationsbreite individueller Gestaltungen

Abb. 11: Fritz Schumacher, Volksschule Hamburg-Berne, 1930

Abb. 12: Kontorhausviertel um 1932, Luftphoto

durch die einzelnen beteiligten Architekten nicht möglich gewesen wäre. Die Lebendigkeit der nur auf einen flüchtigen ersten Blick hin homogen erscheinenden Quartiere ist weitgehend dieser kontrollierten Gestaltungsfreiheit geschuldet.

Schumacher hat für Hamburg nie einen Generalplan entwickeln können, der dem zu Anfang der 20er Jahre für Köln aufgestellten auch nur annähernd vergleichbar wäre.[14] Seine Planungstätigkeit war auf das Hamburger Staatsgebiet beschränkt, ein Fragment des gesamten Siedlungsraumes, das erst nach seinem Ausscheiden aus dem Amt mit dem

Groß-Hamburg-Gesetz von 1937 auf seine heutige Dimension ausgedehnt wurde. Aber er konnte dank der Kooperation eines entscheidenden Teils der Hamburger Architektenschaft dennoch ein Stadtbild schaffen, das selbst nach den Feuerstürmen des 2. Weltkrieges noch erkennbar ist. Nicht ein mit grenzenloser Macht ausgestatteter Oberbaudirektor stand hinter diesem Erfolg, sondern die Überzeugungskraft einer sehr diplomatischen Planerpersönlichkeit, die selbst immer wieder mit seiner eigenen Entwurfsarbeit für öffentliche Bauten bewiesen hatte, dass seine Gestaltungsauffassung nicht im Gegensatz zur Mehrzahl der freien Architekten der Stadt stand, sondern mit ihnen gemeinsame Ziele verfolgte, die wir heute durchaus als die einer „Hamburger Schule" bezeichnen können. Diese Schule hatte sich nach dem 1. Weltkrieg unter einem deutlich erkennbaren niederländischen und dänischen Einfluss immer stärker von ihrer anfänglichen Verankerung in einer engen und lokal verstandenen Heimatschutzbewegung emanzipiert und war gewissermaßen von einem analog argumentierenden Regionalismus zu einem abstrakteren, heute würde man sagen, kritischen Regionalismus geworden, den klare stereometrische Formen, eine einheitliche Verwendung des dunklen, roten Backsteins und eine ins Auge fallende Bodenhaftung und Schwere kennzeichnet.

Der dänische Architekt Steen Eiler Rasmussen wird in den 40er Jahren vom „Klump" sprechen, der als Gestaltungsprinzip hinter der spezifisch nordeuropäischen Variante der Moderne zu erkennen sei.[15] Ein Blick auf das Luftbild des Kontorhausviertel vom Ende der 20er Jahre macht deutlich, wie sehr die Bauten dieses bedeutendsten Ensembles der „Hamburger Schule", bestehend aus Chilehaus, Ballinhaus, Mohlenhof und Sprinkenhof, dem blockhaften Prinzip des Klump nahe kommen. Der Schumachersche Bebauungsplan ordnet lediglich die Baumassen zu einander, ihren unverwechselbaren Charakter aber erhalten sie durch die individuelle Gestaltung ihrer Architekturen, wobei Fritz Höger, die Gebrüder Gerson und die Bürogemeinschaft Klophaus, Schoch, zu Putlitz sich bei aller Gegensätzlichkeit ihrer Auffassungen doch einer gemeinsamen Generallinie unterwerfen, die diese Bauten bereits zum Zeitpunkt ihrer Fertigstellung zu einem Markenzeichen Hamburgs hat werden lassen.[16]

Abstract

The Hamburg School in Architecture: Höger, Schumacher, Schneider and the like

For a long time we have been familiar with terms like ‚Prairie School' or ‚Amsterdam School' borrowed from the historiography of Fine Art and from literature and transferred to the field of architecture, terms describing a common understanding of style more or less characteristic for a group of contemporaries in a given region. Easily we associate names like Frank Lloyd Wright or Walter Burley Griffin with the first and Michel de Klerk or Piet Kramer with the latter. But can we also speak about a Hamburg School in architecture?

Before the 1960s there was no institution in Hamburg educating architects and urban planners comparable to those of the Technical Universities in Berlin, Hanover, Stuttgart or elsewhere. Architects like Hugo Häring or Karl Schneider taught at the Kunstgewerbeschule (School of Applied Arts) but in a general design program and not in an architectural curriculum. The Baugewerkschule which existed parallel to the Kunstgewerbeschule trained Baumeister and Bauleiter, craftsmen who seldom became architects competing with those trained in the established Schools at the Technical Universities. For a long time there was nothing like an architectural school in the educational sense in Hamburg.

But notwithstanding their different educational background since about 1900 there are striking similarities in the general understanding of architecture and style in the work of many architects active in Hamburg. Architects like the individually working two Högers and the collaborating Gerson brothers, Block & Hochfeld, and Karl Schneider, to name just a few, despite their individualities have common characteristics in their architectural work, which distinguish it clearly from the work of their contemporaries in the other urban centres of Germany i. e. Berlin, Munich, Cologne or Frankfurt. Their common characteristics: a certain weight and seriousness, the use of similar materials and the tendency to simplify the volumetry combined with the absence of avant-garde attitudes, which to a certain degree can be attributed to the influence and regulations induced by personalities like Schumacher and Oelssner who as Stadtbaudirektoren (urban planning directors) of Hamburg and the neighbouring Altona defined the general planning and building policies through their master-plans and building control. But this doesn't explain all of these similarities. Already before their activities several organisations of the Heimatschutz-movement were active in the region and paved the way for the general use of the red brick in modern architecture which already since the mid-19th century had been a characteristic of the disciples of the neo-gothic Hase-School from Hanover working in Hamburg.

Hamburg was never a showcase of the architecture of the white avant-garde of the international style. By defining a Hamburg school it will be possible to describe a non-avant-garde modernism whose qualities has been been for too long overseen in contemporary architectural history.

---

[1] Vgl.: Eckhart HANNMANN, Carl Ludwig WIMMEL 1786 1845, Hamburgs erster Baudirektor, Prestel, München 1975; Hartmut FRANK, David KLEMM (Hrsg.), Alexis DE CHATEAUNEUF 1799–1853. Architekt in Hamburg, London und Oslo, Dölling und Galitz, Hamburg 2000; Ann-Kristin Maurer, Theodor Bühlau, Diss. Universität Hamburg 1987

[2] David KLEMM, Martin HALLER. Leben und Werk 1835–1925, Dölling und Galitz, Hamburg 1997

[3] Lichtwark veröffentlichte seit den 80er Jahren in Zeitschriften und Jahrbüchern eine größere Anzahl von Aufsätzen zu Themen der Architektur. Eine Auswahl findet sich in: Alfred LICHTWARK, Palastfenster und Flügeltür, 3. Auflage, Bruno Cassirer, Berlin 1905.

4 vgl. Karin MAAK, Die Speicherstadt im Hamburger Freihafen, Arbeitshefte zur Denkmalpflege in Hamburg, Nr. 7, Christians, Hamburg 1985
5 Paul BRÖCKER, Über Hamburgs neue Architektur. Zeitgemäße Betrachtungen eines Laien mit einem Geleitwort v. Landgerichtsdirektor Gustav Schiefler. Verlag Conrad H.A.Kloss, Hamburg 1908
6 Paul BRÖCKER, Mein Heimatbuch. Was die hamburgischen Bauten der Jugend und dem Volke von unserer Stammesart erzählen. Boysen & Maasch, Hamburg 1910
7 Paul BRÖCKER, Was uns das Gängeviertel erzählt, 1. Heft der Reihe Fragen an die Heimat. Herausgegeben vom Bund für Schulreform in Hamburg. Arbeitsgruppe für Heimatpflege, Selbstverlag 1910
8 Die Architektur des Hamburgischen Geschäftshauses. Ein zeitgemäßes Wort über die Ausbildung der Mönckebergstraße. Theoretische Betrachtungen von Paul Bröcker. Praktische Vorschläge von Fr. Höger Arch., Boysen & Maasch, Hamburg 1910
9 Fritz SCHUMACHER, Die Wiedereroberung harmonischer Kultur, in: Der Kunstwart, H. 21 (1907/08) 2. Viertel, S. 135–138
10 Fritz SCHUMACHER, Architektonische Aufgaben der Städte, in: Robert Wuttke (Hrsg.), Die deutschen Städte, Bd. 1, Leipzig 1904
11 Fritz SCHUMACHER, Das Wesen des neuzeitlichen Backsteinbaus, Callwey München 1920
12 Fritz SCHUMACHER, Das Entstehen einer Großstadt-Straße (Der Mönckebergstraßen-Durchbruch), in: Fragen an die Heimat, Herausgegeben vom Deutschen Bund für Erziehung und Unterricht, Ortgruppe Hamburg, 3. Heft, Georg Westermann, Braunschweig und Hamburg 1922
13 Zu Schumachers umfangreichem Schrifttum vgl. Werner Kayser, Fritz Schumacher. Architekt und Städtebauer. Eine Bibliographie. Arbeitshefte zur Denkmalpflege in Hamburg, Nr.5, Christians, Hamburg 1984
14 Fritz SCHUMACHER/Wilhelm ARNTZ, Köln. Entwicklungsfragen einer Großstadt, Callwey, München 1923
15 Vgl. hierzu das Kapitel III. Der Klump in: Steen Eiler RASMUSSEN, Nordische Baukunst. Beispiele und Gedanken zur Baukunst unserer Zeit in Dänemark und Schweden, Ernst Wasmuth, Berlin 1940

Redner/Speakers

Prof. Antonella Caroli Palladini
Italia Nostra and Ministry of Cultural Heritage
Via Murat 12, 34123 Trieste

Alfredi Luis Conti
ICOMOS Argentina
Jerez 514 – Ensenada Buenos Aires, Argentina

Prof. Dr. Angelus Eisinger
HafenCity Universität Hamburg
Averhoffstrasse 38, 2085 Hamburg

Axel Föhl
Amt für Denkmalpflege im Rheinland
Birkenstrasse 21, 40233 Düsseldorf

Prof. Hartmut Frank
Hafen City Universität Hamburg
Hebebrandstraße 1, 22297 Hamburg

Dr. Robert Habel
Freie Universität Berlin – Weiterbildungszentrum
Naumannstraße 60, 10829 Berlin

Prof. Dr. Carola Hein
Bryn Mawr College
101 N. Merion – Bryn Mawr PA 19010-2899 USA

Frank Pieter Hesse
Kulturbehörde Hamburg, Denkmalschutzamt
Große Bleichen 30, 20354 Hamburg

John Hinchliffe
Liverpool City Council
Municipal Building, Dale Street – Liverpool England

Senatorin Prof. Barbara Kisseler
Kulturbehörde Hamburg
Hohe Bleichen 22, 20354 Hamburg

Prof. Carol Krinsky
NEW YORK UNIVERSITY
370 First Avenue, Apt MF – 10010-4945 New York

Dr. Ralf Lange
Speicherstadtmuseum Hamburg
Am Sandtorkai 36, 20457 Hamburg

Prof. Dr. Robert Lee,
University of Liverpool
5 Cavendish Rd, Birkenhead, Wirral CH41 8 UK England

Jan Lubitz
Universität Stuttgart, Institut für Architekturgeschichte, Keplerstrasse 11, 70174 Stuttgart

Giulio Marano
ICOMOS, German National Committee
Postfach 100517, 80079 München

Prof. Dr. Paul Meurs
TU Delft/SteenhuisMeurs bv
c/o Lange Haven 9, 3111 CA Schiedam

Prof. Dr. Wolfgang Pehnt
Danziger Strasse 2a, 50858 Köln

Präsident Dr. Walter Pelka
HafenCity Universität Hamburg
Großer Grasbrook 9, 20457 Hamburg

Präsident Prof. Dr. Michael Petzet
Deutsches Nationalkomitee von ICOMOS
Postfach 100517, 80079 München

Prof. Dr. Axel Priebs
Geographisches Institut
Christian Albrechts Universität, 24098 Kiel

Dr. Kristen Schaffer
School of Architecture – North Carolina State
University, Brooks Hall Campus Box 7701 –
50 Pullen Road, Raleigh, NC 27695-7701

Dirk C. Schoch
Sutor-Stiftung Hermannstraße 46, 20095 Hamburg

Prof. Dr. Dirk Schubert
HafenCity Universität Hamburg
Winterhuder Weg 29, 22085 Hamburg

Dr. Agnes Seemann
Kulturbehörde Hamburg, Denkmalschutzamt
Große Bleichen 30, 20354 Hamburg

Prof. Dr. Georg Skalecki
Landesamt für Denkmalpflege, Bremen
Sandstrasse 3, 28195 Bremen

Prof. Dr. Vladimir Slapeta
University of Technology VUT Brno/ Bruenn,
Czech TU/CVUT/Prague
Slovinska 23, Prag 10 – CZ 10100 Czech Republic

Dr. Herman van Bergeijk
Institute of History of Art, Architecture
and Urbanism (IHAAU), Faculty of Architecture (TU Delft)
BG.Oost. 430, Julianalaan 134, NL-2628BL Delft

Dr.-Ing. habil. Wolfgang Voigt
Deutsches Architekturmuseum (DAM)
Hedderichstraße 108–110, 60594 Frankfurt

Sara E. Wermiel,
Massachusetts Institute of Technology
70A South Street – Jamaica Plain, Massachusetts USA

Christopher Woodward
80 Albert Street, London NW1 7 NR England

Architektenregister

ABRAHAM, Robert S. 206
ADLER & SULLIVAN S. 143, 149, 150, 152 ff.
ADLER, Dankmar S. 143, 149
AMEIS, Otto S. 211
BACH & WISCHER S. 218
BACH, Franz S. 212
BACH, Max S. 218
BAHRE, Ricardo S. 208
BALLIN, Albert S. 57, 225
BEHRENS, Peter S. 178 ff., 184, 187
BENEVOLO, Leonardo S. 222
BENŠ, Adolf S. 172, 174
BENSEL, Carl Gustav S. 212
BERG, Max S. 182
BONATZ, Paul S. 166, 188
BRESLAUER, Alfred S. 197
BRÖCKER, Paul S. 36, 229 f.
BROWN, Denise Scott S. 30
BRÜDER LUCKHARDT S. 181
BULFINCH, Charles S. 127
BURNHAM, Daniel H. S. 149
BUNSHAFT, Gordon S. 146
BURNHAM & ROOT S. 149 ff.
BURNHAM, D. H. & Co. S. 152, 154
CARDÉNAS PASTOR, Ignacio de S. 190
CARÖE, W. D. S. 37
ČERNÝ, Antonín S. 173 f.
ČERNÝ, František Maria S. 172
CHOCHOL, Josef S. 170 f., 173
CONDER, Josiah S. 29
CREMER, Wilhelm S. 200
DAEM, Hilde S. 105
DAHLERUP, Vilhelm S. 114, 116, 120
DE WITT, Paul S. 104
DIELTIENS, Ernest S. 104
DIESTEL, Arnold S. 217,
DISTEL & GRUBITZ S. 217 f.
DRYÁK, Alois S. 172
ELVERS, Carl S. 77
ENGEL, Antonín S. 171 f.
ERBE, Albert S. 209 f., 230 f.
FAHRENKAMP, Emil S. 188
FANTA, Josef S. 171
FERRISS, Hugh S. 145
FISCHER, Lothar S. 226
FISCHER, Theodor S. 170, 187, 230
FLAGG, Ernest S. 144
FRAGNER, Jaroslav S. 174
FRANZIUS, Ludwig S. 82
FREJTAG, Leon S. 209, 210
FUCHS, Josef S. 172 f.
GERSON, Hans und Oskar S. 218, 220 ff., 226 f., 234
GIBBS, James S. 35
GILBERT, Bradford Lee S. 142, 143
GILBERT, Cass S. 144
GILMAN & KENDALL S. 142
GOČÁR, Josef S. 173
GRAHAM, Burnham & Co. S. 144
GRELL, Henry S. 210 f.
GROSSHEIM, Karl von S. 195
GROTJAN, Johannes S. 67, 70, 78

GRUNDMANN, Günther S. 77
GUTSCHOW, Konstanty S. 190
HAGN, Heinrich S. 67
HAHN, Willy S. 187 f.
HALLER, Martin S. 207, 228, 234
HANSSEN & MEERWEIN S. 64, 67, 70 f., 76 ff.
HÄRING, Hugo S. 181, 234
HASE, Conrad Wilhelm S. 67, 228
HAVLÍČEK, Josef S. 173 ff.
HAY, W & J S. 38
HEGEMANN, Werner S. 181
HEIDTMANN, Albert S. 207
HENNEBIQUE, François S. 35
HENNING, Paul Rudolf S. 200
HERTZ, Paul S. 76
HITCHCOCK, Henry-Russel S. 222
HOENACKER, Jan van S. 190
HOFMAN, Vlastislav S. 171
HÖGER, Fritz S. 7 f., 10, 20, 22, 165, 184, 191, 194, 211 f., 214, 218 ff., 226 f., 229 ff.
HOLABIRD & ROCHE S. 153
HOLLAND, HANNEN & CUBITTS S. 40
HOLLEIN, Hans S. 181
HOLME, Thomas S. 25, 27
HONZÍK, Karel S. 173 f.
HOOD, Raymond S. 146
HÜBSCHMANN, Bohumil S. 171
HUUS, Ove S. 115, 119
IVES, Douglas S. 147
JACOB, Alfred S. 211
JACOBSEN, Arne S. 72
JANDORF, Adolf S. 199
JENNEY, William LeBaron S. 142 f., 148 f.
JOHNSON, Philip S. 147
JOLLASSE, Wilhelm S. 209, 211
KAHN, Albert S. 189
KALLMORGEN, Georg S. 210, 211
KALLMORGEN, Werner S. 22, 67, 71 ff., 77
KAUFMANN, Karl S. 225
KAYSER, Heinrich S. 195
KLOPHAUS, Rudolf S. 218, 225
KLOPHAUS, SCHOCH, zu PUTLITZ S. 218, 221, 223, 227 f., 234
KOERFER, Jacob S. 182, 184, 222
KOLLHOFF, Hans S. 103, 106
KOPPMANN, Georg S. 76
KOTĚRA, Jan S. 171 f.
KOZÁK, Bohumír S. 174
KREIS, Wilhelm S. 182, 191, 231
KREJCAR, Jaromír S. 172
KŘÍŽ, Josef S. 172, 174
KUNSTMANN, Ludwig S. 220 f.
KUÖHL, Richard S. 215, 220
LACHMANN & ZAUBER S. 198
LE CORBUSIER S. 135, 172 ff., 188 f., 194
LEBRUN, Pierre S 144
LEVY Frederik L. S. 114 ff., 118 f.
LINDHORST, Albert S. 209

LISKA, Oldřich S. 172
LÖWENGARD, Alfred S. 214
LUNDT, Werner S. 210 f.
MANZEL, Ludwig S. 197
MARTENS, Walter S. 209
MAY, Ernst S. 190
MEBES, Paul S. 195
MEIER, Richard S. 106
MENDELSOHN, Erich S. 178, 188 ff., 194, 200 ff.
MESSEL, Alfred S. 195 ff., 201 f., 210
MEWÉS & DAVIS S. 40
MEYER, Franz Andreas S. 22, 56, 61, 67, 69, 74, 76 f.
MIES VAN DER ROHE, Ludwig S. 146 f., 181, 188, 199, 202
MÖHRING, Bruno S. 181
MøLLER, Erik S. 72
MUTHESIUS, Hermann S. 187, 199
NEUFERT, Ernst S. 187, 191 f.
NEUPERT, Emil S. 218
NEUTELINGS, Willem Jan S. 106
NEUTRA, Richard S. 200
OSTENDORF, Friedrich S. 187
PAUWELS, Felix S. 105
PEVSNER, Nikolaus S. 158, 161, 214, 222
PFAU, Bernhard S. 192, 194
PFEIFFER, Antonín S. 171
POELZIG, Hans S. 178 f., 181 f., 184 f., 188, 190
POST, George B. S. 142
PRESCOTT, Howard B S. 131
PUGIN, A. W. N S. 35
PUTLITZ, Erich zu S. 187
PUTTFARCKEN & JANDA S. 77
QUERFELD, Carl S. 208
RADEL, George S. 208
RAMBATZ, Gottlieb S. 209, 211
RANCK, Christoph S. 214
RAYWOOD S. 67, 77
REILLY, Charles Herbert S. 36, 51
RICHARDSON, Henry Hobson S. 149 f., 210
RIEDIJK, Michiel S. 106
ROBBRECHT, Paul S. 105
ROCHE, Martin S. 156
ROITH, František S. 171, 173
ROOSENBURG, Dirk S. 189, 194
ROOT, John W. S. 149
ROŠKOT, Kamil S. 171 f.
RÖSSLER, Jaroslav S. 172
ROUSE and ASSOCIATES S. 30
SAARINEN, Eliel S. 145 f.
SAFFORD, Morton S. 131
SAGEBIEL, Ernst S. 191, 194
SÄUME und HAFEMANN S. 84
SCHAEFER, Philipp S. 201 f.
SCHAROUN, Hans S. 181 f.
SCHAUDT, Emil S. 199, 202
SCHIØDTE Erik S. 114
SCHMITTHENNER, Paul S. 188
SCHMITZ, Bruno S. 181, 231
SCHMOHL, Eugen S. 181, 201, 203
SCHOCH & PUTLITZ S. 187

SCHRADER, Gustav S. 67, 77
SCHRAMM & ELINGIUS S. 72
SCHRÖDER, Rudolf S. 188
SCHULZ, Josef S. 170
SCHUMACHER, Fritz S. 182 f., 211, 214, 216, 218, 227, 230 ff.
SCOTT, Walter S. 42
SECCHI, Bernardo S. 106
SÉDILLE, Paul S. 196
SEHRING, Bernhard S. 198, 202
SKIDMORE Owings & Merrill S. 146 f.
SLOAN & ROBERTSON S. 147
SLOMAN, Henry Brarens S. 24, 165, 217, 219
SOLÁ MORALES, Manuel de S. 105 f.
SPEER, Albert S. 191
SPERBER, Friedrich S. 67, 231 f.
STAMMANN & ZINNOW S. 64, 67, 70 f., 77
STARÝ, Oldřich S. 173, 175
STORTZ, Wilhelm S. 188
STRESEMANN, Gustav S. 197
STRUMPER, Friedrich S. 76
STÜBBEN, Josef S. 181
SULLIVAN, Louis S. 143, 149 f., 152 ff., 210, 214
SUMNERS, Henry S. 38
TAUT, Max S. 179, 189 f.
THIELEN, Georg S. 67, 68 ff., 74
THIEME, Martin S. 218
THOMAS, Aubrey S. 35
TROOST, Paul Ludwig S. 191
TROWBRIDGE & LIVINGSTON S. 144
TSUMAKI, Yorinaka S. 28
TYL, Oldřich S. 172 ff.
UTZON, Jørn S. 117, 121
VAN ALEN, William S. 145
VAN AVERBEEKE, E S. 107
VELDE, Henry van de S. 197 f.
VENTURI, Robert S. 30
VERMEHREN, Eduard S. 67, 77
VIGANÒ, Paola S. 106
VON GERKAN, MARG and Partners S. 30
WATERHOUSE, Alfred S. 41, 157
WENCK, Heinrich S. 115
WERTHEIM, Georg S. 196, 198 f., 201
WESTPHALEN, Adolph Libert S. 70, 77
WHITTICK, Arnold S. 222, 226
WILLINCK and THICKNESSE S. 40
WOLFFENSTEIN, Richard S. 200
WRIGHT, Frank Lloyd S. 150, 156, 166, 189, 227, 234
WURZBACH, Hermann S. 209 ff.
WYATT, T. M. S. 39
ZASCHE, Josef S. 170 ff.
ZAULECK & HORMANN S. 218
ZÍTEK, Josef S. 170
ZSCHIMMER, W. W. S. 191

ICOMOS · HEFTE DES DEUTSCHEN NATIONALKOMITEES

I ICOMOS PRO ROMANIA
Exposition/Exhibition/Ausstellung Paris, London, München, Budapest, Kopenhagen, Stockholm 1989/1990, München 1989, ISBN 3-87490-620-5

II GUTSANLAGEN DES 16. BIS 19. JAHRHUNDERTS IM OSTSEERAUM – GESCHICHTE UND GEGENWART
Tagung des Deutschen Nationalkomitees von ICOMOS in der Akademie Sandelmark, 11.–14. 9. 1989, München 1990, ISBN 3-87490-310-9

III WELTKULTURDENKMÄLER IN DEUTSCHLAND
Deutsche Denkmäler in der Liste des Kultur- und Naturerbes der Welt, eine Ausstellung des Deutschen Nationalkomitees von ICOMOS in Zusammenarbeit mit der Dresdner Bank, München 1991, 2., erweiterte Auflage von 1994, ISBN 3-87490-311-7

IV EISENBAHN UND DENKMALPFLEGE I
Erstes Symposium. Eine Tagung des Deutschen Nationalkomitees von ICOMOS, Frankfurt am Main. 2.–4. 4. 1990, München 1992, ISBN 3-87490-619-1

V DIE WIES – GESCHICHTE UND RESTAURIERUNG/ HISTORY AND RESTORATION, München 1992, ISBN 3-87490-618-3

VI MODELL BRANDENBURG
Eine Tagung des Deutschen Nationalkomitees von ICOMOS und der GWS – Gesellschaft für Stadterneuerung mbH Berlin/Brandenburg zum Thema Stadterneuerung und Denkmalschutz in den fünf neuen Bundesländern, München 1992, ISBN 3-87490-624-8

VII FERTÖRÁKOS
Denkmalpflegerische Überlegungen zur Instandsetzung eines ungarischen Dorfes/Müemlékvédelmi megfontaolások egy magyar falu megújitásához, hrsg. vom Deutschen Nationalkomitee von ICOMOS mit der Arbeitsgemeinschaft Alpen-Adria, München 1992, ISBN 3-87490-616-7

VIII REVERSIBILITÄT – DAS FEIGENBLATT IN DER DENKMALPFLEGE? Eine Tagung des Deutschen Nationalkomitees von ICOMOS und des Sonderforschungsbereichs 315 der Universität Karlsruhe, 24.–26. 10. 1991, München 1992, ISBN 3-87490-617-5

IX EISENBAHN UND DENKMALPFLEGE II
Eine Tagung des Deutschen Nationalkomitees von ICOMOS, Frankfurt am Main, 2.–4. 4. 1992, München 1993, ISBN 3-87490-614-0

X GRUNDSÄTZE DER DENKMALPFLEGE/PRINCIPLES OF MONUMENT CONSERVATION/PRINCIPES DE LA CONSERVATION DES MONUMENTS HISTORIQUES München 1992, ISBN 3-87490-615-9 (vergriffen)

XI HISTORISCHE KULTURLANDSCHAFTEN
Eine Tagung des Deutschen Nationalkomitees von ICOMOS mit dem Europarat und dem Landschaftsverband Rheinland, Abtei Brauweiler, 10.–17. 5. 1992, München 1993, ISBN 3-87490-612-4

XII ARCHITEKTEN UND DENKMALPFLEGE
Eine Tagung des Deutschen Nationalkomitees von ICOMOS, des Instituts für Auslandsbeziehungen in Zusammenarbeit mit der Deutschen UNESCO Kommission und der Architektenkammer Baden-Württemberg, 18.–20. 6. 1992, München 1993, ISBN 3-87490-613-2

XIII BILDERSTURM IN OSTEUROPA
Eine Tagung des Deutschen Nationalkomitees von ICOMOS, des Instituts für Auslandsbeziehungen und der Senatsverwaltung Berlin, 18.–20. 2. 1993, München 1994, ISBN 3-87490-611-6

XIV CHRISTOPH MACHAT (Hrsg.)
DENKMÄLER IN RUMÄNIEN/MONUMENTS EN ROUMANIE
Vorschläge des Rumänischen Nationalkomitees von ICOMOS zur Ergänzung der Liste des Weltkulturerbes/Propositions du Comité National Roumain de l'ICOMOS pour la Liste du Patrimoine Mondial, München 1995, ISBN 3-87490-627-2

XV MICHAEL PETZET UND WOLF KOENIGS (Hrsg.) SANA'A
Die Restaurierung der Samsarat al-Mansurah/The Restoration of the Samsarat al-Mansurah, München 1995, ISBN 3-87490-626-4

XVI DAS SCHLOSS UND SEINE AUSSTATTUNG ALS DENKMALPFLEGERISCHE AUFGABE
Eine Tagung des Deutschen Nationalkomitees von ICOMOS und des Facharbeitskreises Schlösser und Gärten in Deutschland, 5.–8. 10. 1994, München 1995, ISBN 3-87490-628-0

XVII DER GROSSE BUDDHA VON DAFOSI/THE GREAT BUDDHA OF DAFOSI München 1996, ISBN 3-87490-610-8

XVIII DIE TONFIGURENARMEE DES KAISERS QIN SHIHUANG
Monuments and Sites, Bd. II, München 2001, ISBN 3-87490-674-4

XIX MATTHIAS EXNER (Hrsg.)
STUCK DES FRÜHEN UND HOHEN MITTELALTERS
Geschichte, Technologie, Konservierung. Eine Tagung des Deutschen Nationalkomitees von ICOMOS und des Dom- und Diözesanmuseums Hildesheim, 15.–18. 6. 1995, München 1996, ISBN 3-87490-660-4

XX STALINISTISCHE ARCHITEKTUR UNTER DENKMALSCHUTZ?
Eine Tagung des Deutschen Nationalkomitees von ICOMOS und der Senatsverwaltung für Stadtentwicklung und Umweltschutz in Berlin, 6.–9. 9. 1995, München 1996, ISBN 3-87490-609-4

XXI DAS DENKMAL ALS ALTLAST?
Auf dem Weg in die Reparaturgesellschaft. Eine Tagung des Deutschen Nationalkomitees von ICOMOS und des Lehrstuhls für Denkmalpflege und Bauforschung der

Universität Dortmund, 11.–13.10.1995, München 1996,
ISBN 3-87490-629-9

XXII Die Bischofsburg zu Pécs. Archäologie
und Bauforschung Eine Publikation des Deutschen und
des Ungarischen Nationalkomitees von ICOMOS mit dem
Ungarischen Denkmalamt, Budapest 1999.

XXIII Matthias Exner (Hrsg.) Wandmalerei
des frühen Mittelalters. Bestand, Maltechnik,
Konservierung Eine Tagung des Deutschen
Nationalkomitees von ICOMOS mit der Verwaltung der
Staatlichen Schlösser und Gärten in Hessen, Lorsch, 10.–
12.10.1996, München 1998, ISBN 3-87490-663-9

XXIV Konservierung der Moderne
Über den Umgang mit den Zeugnissen der
Architekturgeschichte des 20. Jahrhunderts. Eine Tagung
des Deutschen Nationalkomitees von ICOMOS mit der
„denkmal '96", der Europäischen Messe für Denkmalpflege
und Stadterneuerung, Leipzig, 31.10.–2.11.1996,
München 1998, ISBN 3-87490-662-0

XXV Dom zu Brandenburg
Eine Tagung des Deutschen Nationalkomitees von
ICOMOS und des Brandenburgischen Landesamtes
für Denkmalpflege, mit Unterstützung des Domstifts
Brandenburg und des Fördervereins „Dom zu
Brandenburg", Brandenburg, 2.–3.12.1996;
München 1998, ISBN 3-87490-661-2

XXVI Legal Structures of Private Sponsorship
International Seminar organized by the German National
Committee of ICOMOS with the University of Katowice,
Weimar, 17th–19th of April 1997, München 1997,
ISBN 3-87490-664-7

XXVII Eisenbahn und Denkmalpflege III
Drittes internationales Eisenbahnsymposium des Deutschen
Nationalkomitees von ICOMOS, Frankfurt am Main,
14.–16.4.1997, München 1998, ISBN 3-87490-667-3

XXVIII Die Gartenkunst des Barock
Internationale Tagung des Deutschen Nationalkomitees
von ICOMOS in Zusammenarbeit mit dem Bayerischen
Landesamt für Denkmalpflege und dem Arbeitskreis Historische Gärten der Deutschen Gesellschaft für Gartenkunst
und Land-schaftskultur e. V., Schloß Seehof bei Bamberg,
23.–26.9.1997, München 1998, ISBN 3-87490-666-3

XXIX Martin Mach (Hrsg.)
Metallrestaurierung / Metal Restoration
Internationale Tagung zur Metallrestaurierung, veranstaltet
vom Bayerischen Landesamt für Denkmalpflege und vom
Deutschen Nationalkomitee von ICOMOS, München,
23.–25.10.1997, München 1998, ISBN 3-87490-665-5

XXX Michael Petzet
Principles of Conservation / Principes de le
Conservation des Monuments Historiques
München 1999, ISBN 3-87490-668-X

XXXI Opernbauten des Barock
München 1999, ISBN 3-87490-669-8

XXXII Das Konzept „Reparatur". Ideal und
Wirklichkeit München 2000, ISBN 3-87490-671-X

XXXIII Third International Conference
on Archaeological Prospection,
München 1999, ISBN 3-87490-670-1

XXXIV Michael Kühlenthal / Helge Fischer
Petra. Die Restaurierung der Grabfassaden /
The Restoration of the Rockcut Tomb Façades
München 2000, ISBN 3-87490-672-8

XXXV Michael Kühlenthal (Hrsg. / Ed.)
Ostasiatische und Europäische Lacktechniken /
East Asian and European Lacquer Techniques
Internationale Tagung des Bayerischen Landesamtes für
Denkmalpflege und des Deutschen Nationalkomitees von
ICOMOS in Zusammenarbeit mit dem Tokyo National
Research Institute of Cultural Properties, München,
11.–13.3.1999, München 2000, ISBN 3-87490-673-6

XXXVI Heritage at Risk / Patrimoine en Péril /
Patrimonio en Peligro
ICOMOS World Report 2000 on Monuments and Sites
in Danger, München 2000, ISBN 3-598-24240-9

XXXVII Matthias Exner / Ursula-Schädler-Saub
(Hrsg.) Die Restaurierung der Restaurierung? /
The Restoration of the Restoration?
Eine Tagung des Deutschen Nationalkomitees von
ICOMOS in Zusammenarbeit mit dem Hornemann Institut
und dem Fachbereich Konservierung und Restaurierung
der Fachhochschule Hildesheim / Holzminden / Göttingen,
Hildesheim, 9.–12.5.2001, München 2002,
ISBN 3-87490-681-7

XXXVIII Sport – Stätten – Kultur,
Historische Sportanlagen und
Denkmalpflege / Sports – Sites – Culture,
Historic Sports Grounds and Conservation
Internationale Fachtagung des Deutschen Nationalkomitees
von ICOMOS und des Landesamts Berlin im Deutschen
Sportforum auf dem Olympia-Gelände in Berlin,
15.–17.11.2001, München 2002, ISBN 3-87490-680-9

XXXIX Jürgen Pursche (Hrsg.)
Historische Architekturoberflächen
Internationale Fachtagung des Deutschen Nationalkomitees
von ICOMOS und des Bayerischen Landesamtes für
Denkmalpflege in München, 20.–22.11.2002, München
2003, ISBN 3-87490-682-5

XL Ursula Schädler-Saub (Hrsg.)
Die Kunst der Restaurierung / The Art of Restoration
Internationale Fachtagung des Deutschen Nationalkomitees
von ICOMOS u. des Bayerischen Nationalmuseums,
München, 14.–17.5.2003, München 2005,
ISBN 3-935643-28-4

XLI Cesare Brandi Theorie der Restaurierung
Herausgegeben, übersetzt und kommentiert von Ursula
Schädler-Saub und Dörthe Jakobs, München 2006,
ISBN 10-stellig: 3-935643-32-2;
ISBN 13-stellig: 978-3-935643-32-0

XLII Matthias Exner/Dörthe Jakobs (Hrsg.)
Klimastabilisierung und bauphysikalische Konzepte.
Wege zur Nachhaltigkeit bei der Pflege des
Weltkulturerbes
Eine Tagung des Deutschen Nationalkomitees von
ICOMOS in Zusammenarbeit mit dem Landesdenkmalamt
Baden-Württemberg, Insel Reichenau, 25.–27. November
2004, München und Berlin 2005, ISBN 3-422-06401-X

XLIII Orangerien in Europa – Von fürstlichem
Vermögen und gärtnerischer Kunst
Ergebnisse der Internationalen Tagung des Deutschen
Nationalkomitees von ICOMOS in Zusammenarbeit
mit dem Arbeitskreis Orangerien e.V., der Bayerischen
Verwaltung der staatlichen Schlösser, Gärten und Seen und
dem Arbeitskreis Historische Gärten der DGGL, Schloss
Seehof bei Bamberg 29.9.–1.10.2005, München 2007,
ISBN 978-3-87490-683-8

XLIV Claudia Denk/John Ziesemer (Hrsg.)
Der Bürgerliche Tod. Städtische Bestattungskultur
von der Aufklärung bis zum frühen 20. Jahrhundert
Internationale Fachtagung des Deutschen Nationalkomitees
von ICOMOS in Zusammenarbeit mit dem Bayerischen
Nationalmuseum, München, 11.–13.11.2005, München
2007, ISBN 978-3-7954-1946-2

XLV Ursula Schädler-Saub (Hrsg.) Weltkulturerbe
Deutschland –Präventive Konservierung und
Erhaltungs-perspektiven Internationale Fachtagung
des Deutschen Nationalkomitees von ICOMOS, der
Hochschule für angewandte Wissenschaft und Kunst
Hildesheim/Holzminden/Göttingen und der Diözese
Hildesheim in Zusammenarbeit mit der Evangelisch-
lutherischen Landeskirche Hannovers, Hildesheim,
23.–25. November 2006, ISBN 978-3-7954-2136-6

XLVI Jörg Haspel/Michael Petzet/Christiane
Schmückle-Mollard (Hrsg.) Welterbestätten des
20. Jahrhunderts
Defizitte und Risiken aus europäischer Sicht
Internationale Fachtagung des Deutschen Nationalkomitees
von ICOMOS in Zusammenarbeit mit dem
Landesdenkmalamt Berlin und dem ICOMOS International
Scientific Committee on 20th Century Heritage, Berlin,
9.–12.9.2007, Petersberg 2008, ISBN 978-3-86568-393-9

XLVII Erwin Emmerling (Hrsg.)
Toccare – Non Toccare
Eine internationale Konferenz des Deutschen
Nationalkomitees von ICOMOS in Zusammenarbeit
mit dem Architekturmuseum und dem Lehrstuhl
für Restaurierung, Kunsttechnologie und Kon-
servierungswissenschaft der Fakultät für Architektur,
TUM München, 7.–8. Dezember 2007; München 2009,
ISBN 978-3-935643-46-7

XLVIII Jörg Haspel (Hrsg.)
Das architektonische Erbe der Avantgarde
Berlin, 2010, ISBN 978-3-930388-58-5

XLIX Jörg Haspel (Hrsg.)
Welterbe weiterbauen – St. Petersburg und
Berlin-Potsdam, Berlin, 2010, ISBN 978-3-930388-57-8

L Jürgen Pursche (Hrsg.)
Stuck des 17. und 18. Jahrhunderts.
Geschichte – Technik – Erhaltung
Internationale Tagung des Deutschen Nationalkomitees
von ICOMOS in Zusammenarbeit mit der Bayerischen
Verwaltung der staatlichen Schlösser, Gärten und Seen,
Würzburg, 4.–6. Dezember 2008, Berlin 2010,
ISBN 978-3-930388-30-1

LI Sigrid Brandt/Jörg Haspel/Michael Petzet
(Hrsg.)
Weltkulturerbe und Europäisches Kulturerbe-Siegel
in Deutschland – Potentiale und Nominierungs-
vorschläge
in Zusammenarbeit mit TICCIH Deutschland, Berlin 2011,
ISBN 978-3-930388-26-4

LII Volkmar Eidloth (Hrsg.), Europäische
Kurstädte und Modebäder des 19. Jahrhunderts/
European Health Resorts and Fashionable Spas
of the 19th Century/ Stations thermales et villes
d'eaux européennes à la mode au 19ème siècle
Internationale Fachtagung des Deutschen Nationalkomitees
von ICOMOS, des Landesamtes für Denkmalpflege Baden-
Württemberg im Regie-rungspräsidium Stuttgart und der
Stadt Baden-Baden,
Baden-Baden, 25.–27. November 2010, Stuttgart 2011,
ISBN 978-3-942227-07-0

LIII Jüdische Friedhöfe und Bestattungskultur
in Europa/
Jewish Cemeteries and Burial Culture in Europe
Ergebnisse einer internationalen Fachtagung, Berlin-
Weißensee, 3.–6. April 2011
ICOMOS Deutschland und Landesdenkmalamt Berlin in
Zusammenarbeit mit der Jüdischen Gemeinde zu Berlin,
der Stiftung Neue Synagoge Berlin - Centrum Judaicum
und der Arbeitsgemeinschaft Friedhof und Denkmal e.V.
– Stiftung Zentralinstitut und Museum für Sepulkralkultur,
Kassel, Berlin 2011, ISBN 978-3-930388-25-7

LIV Stadtentwicklung zur Moderne: Entstehung
grossstädtischer Hafen- und Bürohausquartiere/
Urban Development towards Modernism:
The birth of the Metropolitan Harbour and
Commercial Districts
Internationale Fachtagung, veranstaltet von ICOMOS
Deutschland und der Kulturbehörde Hamburg/
Denkmalschutzamt in Zusammenarbeit mit der HafenCity
Universität Hamburg und der Sutor-Stiftung, Hamburg,
13.–14. Oktober 2011, Berlin 2012,
ISBN 978-3-930388-17-2

LV Weltkulturerbe Konstantinbasilika Trier –
Wandmalereien in freier Bewitterung als
konservatorische Herausforderung
Internationale Tagung des Deutschen Nationalkomitees von
ICOMOS in Zusammenarbeit mit der HAWK Hochschule
für angewandte Wissenschaft und Kunst Hildesheim/
Holzminden/Göttingen, der Generaldirektion Kulturelles
Erbe Rheinland-Pfalz und dem Landesbetrieb Liegen-
schafts- und Baubetreuung LBB Trier, Kurfürstliches
Palais, 7.–9. April 2011, Berlin 2012,
ISBN 978-3-930388-24-0